Organisational Behaviour

Organisational Behaviour

An Interactive Learning Approach

Text and Cases

Includes CD with Case Studies

Sarma V.S. Veluri

JAICO PUBLISHING HOUSE

Ahmedabad Bangalore Bhopal Bhubaneswar Chennai
Delhi Hyderabad Kolkata Lucknow Mumbai

Published by Jaico Publishing House
A-2 Jash Chambers, 7-A Sir Phirozshah Mehta Road
Fort, Mumbai - 400 001
jaicopub@jaicobooks.com
www.jaicobooks.com

ORGANISATIONAL BEHAVIOUR
With CD
ISBN 978-81-7992-996-4

First Jaico Impression: 2009
Fourth Jaico Impression: 2010

Printed by
Pashupati Printers
1/429/16, Gali No. 1, Friends Colony
Industrial Area, G. T. Road, Shahdara, Delhi - 95

To

My Mentor

GADEPALLI MADHAVA RAO

My Mother

SMT. KAMALAMMA

My Wife

VANI

Acknowledgements

An endeavour like this is impossible without guidance, cooperation, encouragement and sacrifice on the part of mentors, teachers, friends, well-wishers and family. I am not an exception to this. At the very outset I owe a depth of gratitude to my Uncle Madhava Rao G, to whom I dedicate this book.

My teacher and career builder Dr. A Shankaraiah, (Professor Retd.) is an invisible force behind me to write this book. I know that a galaxy of gentle friends, directly or indirectly, has helped me to complete this task – whose names run scores list. I sincerely acknowledge their help and encouragement. Well-wishers are always the backbone to any such activity. I thank them whole-heartedly.

I cannot resist expressing my emotion towards my family, my mother Kamalamma, the legend woman of sacrifice, my wife Vani, a never-say-no to any kind of work even pertaining to the book, my brothers, sisters, in-laws, and other family relatives I take pleasure in acknowledging.

Last but not the least I would like to make a mention of a few names of faculty and friends who helped me, as an expression of acknowledgement, though I know I cannot acknowledge every one by name in the limited space.

Professor V Bala Mohan Das, vice-chancellor, Nagarjuna University

Professor G Narasimha Murthy, Professor Ravi Prakash Singaravelu, Professor M Subrahamanya Sarma and Professor N Kusuma, Kakatiya University

Professor G Satyanarayan, Andhra University

Professor D Himachalam, Professor B Sudheer, Sri Venkateswara University

Professor Murali Krishna, Sri Krishna Deveraya University

Professor A Vidyadhara Reddy, Professor S V Satyanarayana, Professor Krishna Kumar, Professor Prashanta Atma, Osmania University

Professor K Eresi, Professor Sanjeevaiah, Professor M Ramachandra Gowda, Professor Muniraj, Bangalore University

Professor Raghu Rama Sarma Hari, Kakatiya Institute of Technology and Science

Professor Ravi K Jain and Professor K B S Kumar, ICFAI

D Muralidhar, Motivational Speaker and Personality Development Trainer

S Radhakrishnan, Chennai

On the other side of the coin, there is a highly dedicated team of editors, designers, technical personnel, marketing executives and executive directors at Jaico Publishing House whose contribution is embedded in the book to make readers more interested. I have a special mention of gratitude to them.

Wherever references are drawn from legendary books on organisational behaviour, mention has been made at various places acknowledging the sources. Yet I am aware that some of them could have missed my attention. I sincerely acknowledge all those sources from which information has been used in the book.

Contents

Preface

There are scores of books on organisational behaviour written by great personalities such as Stephen P Robbins, Fred Luthans and K Aswathappa to name a few. I regard those as great men who contributed to the academic literature, and consider myself too small to identify limitations in those great books. But there has been a void in the absence of a book on organisational behaviour suited to the Indian context. This book aims to fill that void, and is a culmination of my interest and my teaching experience of over two decades in the area of organisational behaviour.

Selection and retention of employees in the era of competition are the major challenges of human resource management. While selection is only looking at the person from an outer perspective, retention requires understanding deep insights of the employee. This requires knowledge about one's personality, his interaction in the group and organisation. Personality development is aimed at making the employee commit to the organisation. Mentoring and counselling require understanding one's psychological process. This book provides a wide coverage of these aspects that enable students and practising managers to know these concepts.

Unique features of the book

Pedagogy: Any text full of description is uninteresting to readers. Thus the book adopts diagrams, charts, pictures, tables, small practical examples and real time case descriptions at suitable places. In addition, short answer questions and long answer questions enable the students to exercise for learning.

Examples: A student is a student always and everywhere. He resists remembering the text matter except only at the time of examination, but grasps the examples and small live stories explaining the concepts. He tries to net the text around these examples at the time of presentation in the examination or at the viva-voce. Most of the matter is presented with suitable examples and incidents either from colleges or from students' lives. Students find these examples more convincing.

Testing tools: An individual's short-term memory limits his capability to remember. The span of attention is also limited due to a number of distractions. Requisite attention not shown on learnt matter fails to store it in the long-term memory. So at the end of every sub theme/part of the chapter a knowledge quest is provided to test one's understanding by providing easy to solve questions of various types. The book has about 1600 self-learning exercises. This makes the students to know their understanding immediately. In addition, at the end of each chapter, knowledge management exercises are provided with alternative answers. About 1000 questions with alternative answers make the student a thorough learner in the subject.

Writing style: The writing style is lucid and student friendly and not just a simple reproduction of material from various standard books and journals. As the students read the book they will find the presentation of the material the same as a face to face exchange of academic material, a lecture on organisational behaviour. Except for the technical jargon, the remaining text is presented to encapsulate in the minds of students.

Chapterisation: It is found that students become disinterested when chapters are too lengthy. Most of the students read the books with a view to gain a cutting edge of marks over other competitors in examinations. But to develop an in-depth knowledge over the subject, one has to refer to a number of journals and reference books. Keeping this in mind, the chapterisation is done to avoid too lengthy description of the subject matter. Wherever necessary, it is divided into two or three chapters. For example, description of leadership is divided into five chapters, that is usually found as a single chapter in most of the books. Moreover, the book can be used as a reference book.

Cross functional utility: The subject matter in the book does not only address the needs of students studying courses like MBA, DBA, M.Com., CA, ICWA, ACS, MCA, MA/M.Sc. (Psychology) and other graduate courses like BBA, BBM, BA/B.Sc. (Psychology), but also the needs of managers dealing with human resources in organisations. Human Resource Managers and executives will find the book more interesting to learn and sharpen their skills to develop various practices and strategies to manage their human resources in the most effective manner. In short, every person dealing with other persons and groups may find the book interesting with its extensive coverage of text and cases.

Contents: The book focuses on organisational behaviour and organisational development with all relevant sub themes.

- Organisational Behaviour: introduction to organisations, factors influencing organisational behaviour, emergence and challenges of organisational behaviour and understanding human behaviour
- Individual Behaviour: personality, theories, perception, attitudes, learning, learning behaviour, managerial values and status behaviour
- Group Behaviour: groups, group dynamics, group behaviour, group decisions, team development, conflicts and small group behaviour
- Leadership: communication behaviour, leadership theories, leadership behaviour, situational behaviour, emerging leadership behaviour and leadership effectiveness
- Motivation: motivation and motivators, motivation theories, job satisfaction, stress behaviour and stress management

- Organisational Development: organisational change, organisational culture and organisational effectivness.

Special focus: Apart from the above major themes, the book specially focuses on:

- Organisational behaviour models
- Personality development
- Emotional intelligence
- Team behaviour
- Leadership for the millennium organisations
- Job design
- Job redesign

I have made the book as interesting as possible, with the matter written in my own style as far as possible. I am also aware that there are always certain deficiencies in the presentations, drawings and errors in proof reading and printing. I request valuable readers to ignore tiny aspects in the book and feel free to mail any suggestions/ideas/modifications that can be taken care of in the subsequent editions. I can be reached at drsharvani@yahoo.co.in

Sarma V.S. Veluri

1. ORGANISATION

This chapter enables you:

- *To understand the meaning of an organisation*
- *To define the term organisation*
- *To appraise the characteristics of an organisation*
- *To understand the functions of an organisation*
- *To classify organisations*
- *To distinguish between formal and informal organisations*
- *To identify the principles of an organisation*

The structure of the chapter is as follows:

- Introduction
- Definition of an Organisation
- Characteristics of an Organisation
- Functions of an Organisation
- Classification of Organisations
- Principles of an Organisation
- Summary
- Key words

CHAPTER 1

Organisation

INTRODUCTION

'We are born in organisations, educated by organisations and most of us spend much of our lives working in organisations,' says Amitai Etizioni. The family, where we spend most of our time, is also an organisation. Hence, an organisation is a group of individuals who agree to share their effort in the realisation of common goals. The goals of an organisation are derived from individual goals, and hence, individuals in order to realise their goals join an organisation. Thus, the nature, size and purpose of organisations influence individuals and their behaviour. Organisations may be small, large, formal, informal, political, social, economical, cultural or religious. Interaction of individuals in organisations is within the scope of the structure and the structure itself defines the authority, responsibility and communication relationship among the people.

Man is a social being. Our family, which is a basic unit of our existence, consists of father, mother, sisters and brothers. Thus, family is a social organisation. When we go to school, we spend time with other children and teachers, and hence school is also an organisation. Even as employees, we spend time in organisations. In fact, most of us spend much of our lives associated with one or another organisation.

Mr. Raja sells goods in a small locality. He started a stationery shop in a small way and expanded the business as the demand grew. He employed two workers to assist him and also had to put in more capital. Therefore, he took Mr. Vihari as a partner, and the organisation grew from a sole proprietor to a partnership organisation. Since he now had two workers he defined duties of the workers, thus creating a structure of authority. The workers identified themselves with the shop, since their goal of earning a livelihood was satisfied by the organisation. This is how the goals of the organisation were derived from the goals of the individual workers.

DEFINITION OF AN ORGANISATION

An organisation is a group of individuals, who come together to realise their goals. Do you call a herd of buffalo an organisation? Do you call a group of trees and mountains, an organisation of trees and mountains! Clearly they are not identified as organisations. Therefore, persons having a relationship amongst themselves, determine an organisation. For example, a group of people found at a railway station or a village fair is not called an organisation. This is due to the fact that although there are people, they have no common purpose. Their relationships are not defined. Thus, an organisation requires people, goals and relationships. An organisation can be defined in two ways, either by structural definitions or process definitions.

Structural definition emphasise the fact that relationships among the people are the important determinants, while defining an organisation. They consider an organisation as a framework of identifiable relationships among people, deliberately created for the realisation of goals. We can understand the concept of an organisation by examining the following definitions.

- **Talcott Parsons** defined an organisation as '*a social unit deliberately constructed and reconstructed to seek specific goals*'.
- **McFarland** defined it as '*an identifiable group of people contributing their efforts towards the attainment of goals*'.
- **R.C. Davis** identified an organisation as '*any group of individuals, large or small, that are co-operating under the direction of executive leadership in the accomplishment of certain common objectives*'.
- **Mooney** and **Reily** considered '*Organisation is the form of every human association for the attainment of common purpose*'. They felt that the purpose of the organisation would determine the form and structure of an organisation.
- In the words of **Pfiffner** and **Sherwood** an organisation is '*the pattern of ways in which a large number of people, too many to have face to face contact with all others are engaged in a complexity of tasks, relate themselves to each other in conscious, systematic establishment and accomplishment of mutually agreed purposes*'.
- An organisation is a process of conducting several activities. Process definitions consider it is a process of determining the activities, and establishing authority and responsibility in relationships. According to **Haiman** '*an organisation is the process of defining and grouping the activities of the enterprise and establishing the authority relationship among them in performing the organizing function*'.
- An organisation can also be defined as process involving differentiation and integration of activities. According to **Oliver Sheldon,** '*the process of combining the work which individuals and groups have to perform*' is an organisation.

- **Louis Allen** defined an organisation as '*the process of identifying and grouping the work to be performed, defining and delegating the responsibility and authority and establishing relationships for the purpose of enabling people to work most effectively together in accomplishing objectives*'.
- **Jones** viewed '*an organisation as a tool used by people to co-ordinate their actions to obtain something they desire or value to achieve their goals*'. Modern organisational thinkers view organisations as value creation systems, which take inputs from the environment and use skills and knowledge to convert inputs into outputs. It is a system or roles integrated to achieve common goals.

Though the definitions stressed various aspects of an organisation, we can understand the concept by identifying the characteristics of organisations.

CHARACTERISTICS OF AN ORGANISATION

From the preceding section it can be clearly understood that organisations are created and maintained by people. Since different people join an organisation, they naturally have different goals, and the inherent selfish nature of man makes them compete in order to realise their individual goals, thus overlooking or even undermining the goals of others. In order to overcome this problem, organisations develop common goals that reflect the individual interests of its members. Despite this, some members try to meet their selfish ends. Therefore, an organisation is required to develop a sound structure, which defines the relationships and co-ordinates the efforts of the members of the organisation. This ensures that members' potential is directed towards the realisation of common goals. This complete exercise can be called 'organising and managing'. To properly organise and manage it is necessary to understand the nature and characteristics of an organisation. This enables one to design its structure effectively, so that its goals are realised. In the following section we learn more about the characteristics of an organisation.

1. **Social unit:** An organisation consists of people. According to **Etizioni,** an organisation comes into existence in the circumstances described below:

   a. When there are persons who are able to communicate with each other.
   b. When there are people who are willing to contribute collectively and individually.
   c. When there are people who are desirous of satisfying personal and social needs.

   From the above it is clear that the mere existence of a group of people is not enough to be called an organisation. Communication is needed. This is the reason why a group of people found in a cinema hall is not an organisation. Moreover, the people involved should be willing to co-operate and co-ordinate with each other. Their efforts should be co-ordinated for the sake of everybody concerned, and selfish motives need to be sacrificed. Another important aspect of an organisation is that it consists of people with a desire to achieve needs, which can be either personal or social. Hence even a group of people assembled to mourn the death of a person, or a group of devotees, could be called an organisation. Some examples of organisations thus include churches, temples, Waqf board, religious groups, political parties, government, military, hospitals, schools and educational institutions, corporate bodies etc.

2. **Goals:** Goals are the desired state of affairs, ultimate purpose and performance of an organisation. Goals of an organisation are derived from the needs, desires, purpose and goals of people. They are known as individual goals. For instance, earning a livelihood is an individual goal. Mutually agreed goals become organisational goals. Thus, organisational goals are derived from individual goals. Members of an organisation contribute their potential towards realisation of common goals. Notwithstanding, their individual goals are also fulfilled. Hence, the basis for human interaction in an organisation is the existence of goals. Other resources are also channelled to the realisation of goals. Thus, existence of goals is a vital feature of an organisation. Individual goals and organisational goals are not always similar, and this leads to conflict within an organisation and non-compliance with organisational goals. Dissimilarity is called incongruence. Congruence between individual and organisational goals leads to cohesion and provides motivation for achievement. This also rectifies behavioural disorders. Hence, organisations must try to bring congruence in goals.

3. **Substitution of personnel:** An organisation is an independent entity having a long-term existence. People in organisations are continuously replaced because of promotions, transfers, retirement etc. This implies that no member is permanent in an organisation. Everyone spends a limited time in the organisation and contributes to its development. People may come and go but the organisation exists forever, just as in the poem 'The Brooke' by Lord Tennyson. The brooke describes itself by saying 'men may come, men may go, but I go on forever'. Therefore an organisation continues and exists on a relatively permanent basis, irrespective of the changes in structure and membership.

4. **Structure:** A structure is an orderly arrangement of activities. The structure of an organisation is developed to identify the roles and tasks of members and establish relationships amongst them. It describes the authority, responsibility and accountability of each position. The structure also defines the scope and limits of authority, the span of management and line and staff relationships in an organisation. The positions created in the organisational structure are co-ordinated to ensure effective performance.

5. **Division of labour:** Division of labour is the sub-division of tasks. At the first instance, organisational goals are broken down into sub goals. Tasks necessary to attain the goals are identified. Each task is divided into the smallest manageable component, and each small task is assigned to a position. Thus the tasks required to realise the goals are performed by a number of individuals. Division of labour enables repeated performance of the tasks. When an individual performs a task repeatedly over a long period, he will learn to perform it in a more effective manner. Therefore over a period it leads to specialisation. Specialisation increases production. Increase in production leads to an increase in profit. Since profits are in turn shared by the employees of the organisation, both management and employees benefit from the division of labour.

6. **Existence of power:** Performance of tasks requires planning and controlling the efforts of the people, by the senior staff. Organisations assign authority to persons occupying various positions. They are expected to use the authority for directing the organisational resources in the pursuit of organisational goals. Every department or division will be given authority. This creates a power centre in the organisation, so that the organisation is characterised by multiple power centres.

7. **Rules and regulations:** Rules and regulations relate to the written directions that should be followed without any deviation. In the absence of clearly defined rules and regulations, activities of the organisation become random and improperly directed. In addition, rules and regulations are required to direct and control the behaviour of members. Rules are the guidelines and they set the limits to both individual and group actions. The existence of rules leads to a bureaucratic organisational structure. If rules are broken, employees are liable to be penalised. Thus rules are required to direct the organisational activity.

8. **Co-operation and communication:** Co-operation implies sharing of efforts. Generally, most organisational tasks are complementary. Hence, in order to perform these tasks successfully, there must be co-operation among the people. Co-operation increases harmony and develops a positive attitude, leading to co-ordinated effort. However, co-operation depends entirely on the individuals and cannot be enforced by the authorities. Co-operation is a characteristic of a good organisation.

   Communication is sharing of feelings. Organisational communication is transmission of directions of the top management to the lower levels and reporting the operational performance to the higher levels. This is formal communication. It is defined as a chain of command and passes through pre-defined levels of authority. **Henri Fayol** describes this as "*Principle of Scalar Chain*". In order to improve understanding among people there must be good communication. Effective communication leads to better performance and effective realisation of goals. Communication is the attitude of an individual to share information with colleagues in the organisation.

9. **System:** Modern organisations are a system of interrelated and inter dependent sub-systems. The elements are input, process and output. The system concept of organisation implies that organisations process inputs to produce a certain output. The inputs of the organisation are physical, material, financial and human resources. While physical resources are instrumental in a technical process, material resources are used in the production of the output. However, human resources are subject to the management processes of planning, organising, staffing, directing and controlling. These functions, also called management functions, are intended to facilitate human interaction and extraction of human energy in the realisation of organisational goals. The output of the organisation constitutes physical output in the form of products, financial output in the form of sales, revenue and profit and human output in the form of motivation, job satisfaction and psychological commitment. System concepts emphasise that a part of the output should be used as inputs to the organisation. For instance, motivation and satisfaction of employees becomes an input for qualitative productivity, reducing absenteeism and increasing

turnover. For this reason, organisations are known as systems.

10. **Openness:** Organisations as systems receive external inputs and export their output. A number of factors, both internal and external, influence the functioning of an organisation. Internal factors, such as goals, resources, policies and managerial behaviour, are within managerial control. External factors, which comprise political, economical, technological, legal, ecological, governmental, social, and ethical factors, are outside managerial control. Therefore, organisations must interact with the external environment and adapt to it in order to survive. Therefore organisations are considered as open, dynamic systems.

An examination of the above characteristics reveals that organisations are complex, dynamic, volatile and interactive systems. Individuals in organisations interact, share resources and channel their energy in the realisation of organisational goals. The achievement of organisational goals leads to the attainment of individual goals.

Corporate Goals of Andhra Bank

The changes introduced by the Government of India in the financial sector in general and the banking sector in particular call for increased dedication of the bank towards providing a variety of financial services. Apart from customer satisfaction, the bank has to maximize profits. To achieve this the following corporate goals have been established.

1. To increase the customer base by disbursing retail credit and mobilizing low cost deposits.
2. To create niche markets by introducing new products and improving services of the bank and to change the delivery system to match the ever-changing customer needs and expectations.
3. To improve technology and increase employee productivity by continuous training.
4. To strengthen the risk management systems and practices.

FUNCTIONS OF AN ORGANISATION

i. **To facilitate management:** A well-designed organisation facilitates the management, so that it can carry out its activities effectively. A poorly designed organisation adversely affects the performance of an enterprise. Properly defining, identifying and allocating objectives and activities in a systematic manner, helps in avoiding delays, duplication and confusion, and eliminates friction among personnel.

ii. **To optimise the utilisation of resources:** Change in technology is the order of the day. Organisations should make optimum use of both technical and human resources. The structure of an organisation is suitably adjusted from time to time to adopt technological improvements. It develops people by providing appropriate training and promotional opportunities. Thus, organisations by taking account of economies of scale and scope become efficient.

iii. **To encourage growth and diversification:** A good organisation will have division of work, proper delegation of work and decentralisation, which permits growth and diversification. Allen has rightly pointed out that an organisation facilitates growth and diversification of activities and goals.

iv. **To manage the environment:** Today environments in which organisations function are ever changing. A complex environment requires better understanding and management, which is only possible in a properly designed organisation.

v. **To economise on costs:** Costs are associated with realisation of goals. Individuals, by joining organisations, can share these costs and still realise their goals. An organisation is efficient if it exercises control over the costs yet increases its productivity and maintains its quality. A sound organisational structure by itself does not guarantee success. As stated by Drucker, "*Good organisation structure does not by itself produce good performance just as a good constitution does not guarantee great presidents or good laws or a moral society. But a poor organisation structure makes good performance impossible, no matter how good the individuals may be*".

vi. **To stimulate creativity:** Specialisation stimulates creativity. Well-defined areas of work with provision for development of new and improved ways of working, should be laid out.

CLASSIFICATION OF AN ORGANISATION

To most people the word 'organisation' means 'a business'. However, this is not necessarily true. The study of organisations is applicable to various types of institutions. Therefore, it is relevant to know the nature and characteristics of various organisations, as shown in Figure 1.1.

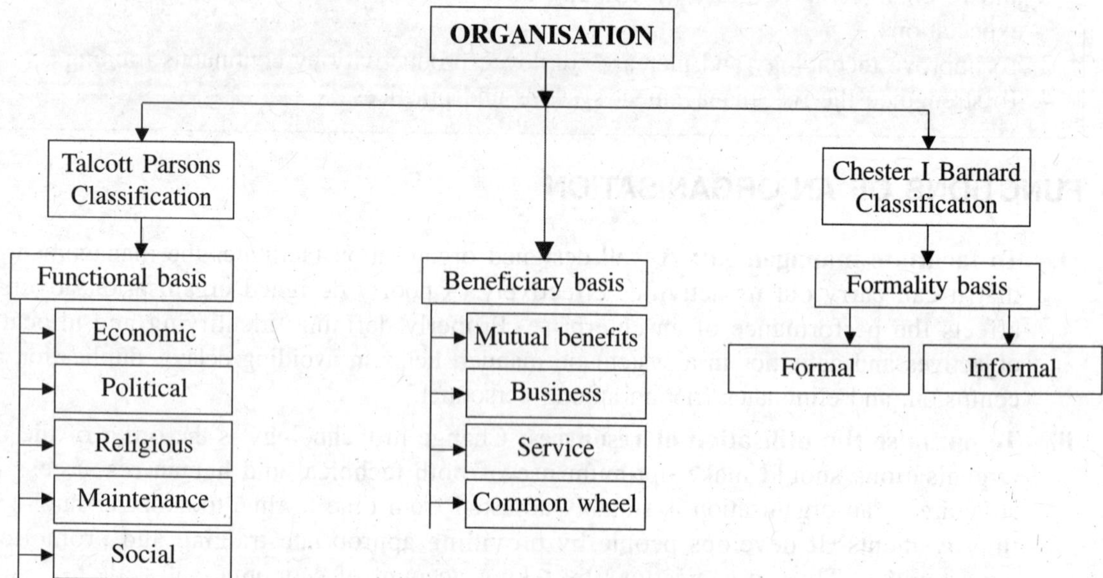

Figure 1.1: Classification of organisations

Examples of various organisations, along with their nature and goals are shown in Chart-1.1.

Chart 1.1: Classification of organisations at a glance

Sl. No.	Classification of the organisation	Nature	Objectives	Examples
1.	Economic or business	Providing value to society	Profit maximisation, wealth maximisation, creation of economic value	Industrial, Commercial Business Organisation
2.	Political	Providing direction to the growth of the economy and the country. Judicious distribution of societal wealth	Capture power to make legislation and administer public offices	Parliament, Legislative Body, Political Parties, Associations, Groups
3.	Religious	Developing religious faith and fulfilling spiritual needs	Spread religious philosophy and provide a good social order and establish a specific pattern of society	Temples, Trusts, Churches, Mosques, Wakf Boards
4.	Maintenance	Maintaining social order, protecting the minority social groups	Maintain peace and justice in the society. Punishing culprits and protecting the victims	Police, Judicial
5.	Social	Promoting social relationships	Developing social groups for creating a value and culture driven society	Clubs, Associations, Gatherings
6.	Mutual benefits	Securing benefits to a particular group	Regulate trade and professions, upkeep dignity of a profession and protect the interest of members	Trade Unions, Professional Association, Bodies

Sl. No.	Classification of the organisation	Nature	Objectives	Examples
7.	Service	Providing a service which is integral to society	Identifying the beneficiaries and providing expert, professional services to benefit them	Schools, Universities, Educational institutions, Hospitals, Welfare Societies, Charitable Associations
8.	Formal	Realising common objectives by providing structural interaction	Designing and maintaining stable, predictable and rational organisational goals, structure and exercising controls	Registered Companies, Bodies
9.	Informal	Providing Social satisfaction	Creating mutual spontaneous network of relationships to satisfy personal needs, aspirations and emotions	Groups found in formal organisations

PRINCIPLES OF AN ORGANISATION

The principles of an organisation are guidelines to managers to effectively design an organisational structure. **F.W. Taylor, Henri Fayol, Lyndall Urwick, Mooney** and **Reiley** have enunciated certain principles, which are summarised below:

i. **Principle of objectives:** Objectives are the statement of purpose of existence. So, an organisation and its internal divisions should indicate the objectives, otherwise they lose direction.

ii. **Principle of specialisation:** Specialisation is uniqueness in performing a task effectively, as compared to other tasks. Specialisation is the result of the principle of division of labour. Division of labour suggests dividing the total task into smaller manageable components and assigning them to individuals. When one is allowed to perform a task continuously, he will attain specialisation.

iii. **Principle of co-ordination:** Co-ordination is uniformity and consensus in thinking and action. People performing various activities at various levels should co-ordinate well, otherwise, an organisation can collapse.

iv. **Principle of authority and responsibility:** Authority is the right to take decisions for the commitment of organisational resources. Responsibility is the obligation to perform tasks.

Accountability is answerability to superiors. A sound organisation requires authority to flow in an uninterrupted manner from the top management to the lower levels. Fayol referred it as 'Scalar Chain'. A proper flow of authority promotes rapid decision-making. Similarly responsibility is absolute and it cannot be delegated. The superiors are ultimately responsible for the performance of their subordinates.

v. **Principles of definition and correspondence:** Authority and responsibility should be defined clearly, unambiguously in a manner which each person can understand. Similarly, there must be a balance between authority delegated and responsibility entrusted to a position. Otherwise, organisation relationships can be ambiguous.

vi. **Principle of span:** Span refers to 'span of control', 'span of supervision' or 'span of management'. It refers to the number of subordinates who are required to work under the supervision of a superior. Too many subordinates will over-burden a superior and too few subordinates means poor utilisation of the superior's capacity. Hence it is important to determine the number of subordinates a superior is capable of managing.

vii. **Principle of continuity:** Organisations are ongoing concerns. They are open, dynamic systems and should be allowed to change and survive over a long period.

viii. **Principle of balance:** Various organisational units are required to maintain a balance in relation to activities, importance, contribution to objectives etc.

ix. **Principle of exception:** Exception refers to concentration of those activities, which have an impact on performance. Therefore, each and every minor activity is not worth consideration by the management.

SUMMARY

Organisations are social entities; we have defined an organisation as a framework of structural relationships among people. Talcott Parsons, McFarland, Davis, Mooney, Reiley, Pfiffner, and Sherwood have used the concept of structure. Haiman, Oliver Sheldon and Allen defined an organisation as a process of activities performed. Hence, an organisation is a mechanism that provides for interaction among human beings and financial, physical and material resources for the realisation of common goals. Modern organisations are identified on the basis of several characteristics such as social units, goals, substitution of personnel, structure, division of labour existence of power centres, rules and regulations and open systems.

Organisations perform several functions. They facilitate management, optimise utilisation of resources, encourage growth and diversification, manage the environment, economise on costs and stimulate creativity.

In this chapter, you have learnt that the word 'organisation' need not refer to business organisations alone. Organisation can be economic, political, religious, social, mutually beneficial, service, formal and informal. Different organisations exhibit different characteristics and have different objectives. We have also discussed certain guidelines, which help managers to design the organisation structure. The main ones are: Principles of organisation, principles of objectives, specialisation, co-ordination, authority and responsibility, span, continuity, balance and the principle of exception.

Key words:

- **Bureaucracy:** Organisations should strictly adhere to the rules and regulations and make decisions impersonally.
- **Cohesiveness:** The extent to which the members of the group respect each other's feelings and adapt themselves.
- **Economies of scale:** Benefits derived by an enterprise from large-scale operations.
- **Grapevine:** Informal channel of communication existing among members of the group.
- **Law of individual differences:** Individuals are unique and possess differences, both physiological and psychological.
- **Open system:** System, which interacts with the external environment and adapts itself to changes in the environment.

Case study 1.1: Description of organisation structure and roles and responsibilities of executives of Sirpur Paper Mills Limited

Executive Director heads the company. President assists him in the administrative functions. Under the President, a Vice-President functions. The General Manager reports to the Vice-President. The General Manager supervises Deputy General Managers (DGMs). Senior Managers work under the directions of a DGM. The administrative structure in the line of reporting are managers, joint managers, deputy managers, assistant managers, senior officers, officers, assistant officers, clerks and workers in that order.

The company has four Vice-Presidents. They are in charge of Projects and Development, Finance and Commercials, Systems and Control respectively. There are four General Managers looking after the functions of Material, Personnel and Administration, Finance and Marketing. Four Deputy General Managers are responsible for Management Information Systems, Personnel and Administration, Legalities and Health and Safety. The company has 11 Managers who look after functions like Projects, Drawing Office, Accounts, Costs, Taxation, Marketing, Excise, Internal Audit, Purchase, Stores and Supply.

On the technical side the Vice-President (Mills Management) manages two Deputy General Managers. They are in charge of Production and Quality Control. Ten Managers are responsible for the effective functioning of the technical aspects of the company. They are responsible for such activities as the pulp mill, paper machine, boiler house, electrical, instrumentation, civil, finishing house, soda recovery, research and development and central laboratory and quality control.

The Vice-President heads the finance department. The General Manager (Finance) reports to him. The order of reporting is from the Joint Manager, Deputy Manager and Assistant Manager. The Assistant Manager supervises five Senior Accountants. They are responsible for the activities of general accounts, cost accounts, sales accounts, purchase accounts and treasury finance. Under the Senior Accountants, there are a number of accountants.

The company follows line and staff structure for the entire organisation. The finance department is the staff function in the organisation. The finance department has again line authority within it.

2. ORGANISATIONAL BEHAVIOUR

This chapter enables you:

- *To define the word organisational behaviour*
- *To appraise its nature and characteristics*
- *To understand the scope of the subject matter*
- *To know the factors which influence organisational behaviour*
- *To appreciate the managerial implications of learning organisational behaviour*
- *To understand the limitations of the study*

The structure of the chapter is:

- Introduction
- Definitions of organisational behaviour
- Nature of organisational behaviour
- Scope of organisational behaviour
- Factors influencing organisational behaviour
- Managerial implications of learning organisational behaviour
- Summary
- Key words

CHAPTER 2

Organisational Behaviour

> *Individuals are different in their motivational propensities, interaction with others, possession of tolerance and stress etc. Porter and Lawler state that 'individual differences determine the way in which people respond to various aspects of organisation and to the practice of organisation'. So understanding individuals and successfully managing them to improve organisational effectiveness become vital.*
>
> ***– The Law of Individual Differences***

INTRODUCTION

Organisational behaviour provides an in-depth understanding of employee behaviour in an organisational setting. It deals with individual behaviour and group behaviour and the effect it has on the organisation as a whole. It also examines the cause and effect relationship of behaviour and organisational effectiveness. For example the aggressive behaviour of an employee in an organisational set up influences both outsiders and the employees within the organisation. However, proper understanding of the reasons for aggression could avert ill effects on the organisation.

Scientific knowledge and experimentation are the basis of development of concepts of organisational behaviour. A number of environmental factors influence the behaviour of individuals and groups in organisations. The internal factors are technology, structure and human beings themselves. The external factors that influence behaviour are political, economical, technological, legal, ecological, governmental, ethical and social. Individual differences determine the way in which people respond to various aspects of an organisation and to the practice of organisation. So understanding individuals and successfully managing them to improve organisational effectiveness become vital. Individual behaviour is determined by culture and values, and motivated by desires. Taking this into account an individual's personality should be viewed holistically rather than in parts.

Organisational structure is the entire design of organisational hierarchy, the span of control, line and staff relationships and division into various sub units. Interestingly all these determine the behaviour of the individual in the organisation. One has to appreciate the influence of technology on behaviour. Consider the simple example of a mineworker and an information technology worker. One finds that the mineworker is more aggressive due to the environment in which he works, whereas an IT worker is comfortable even after working long hours.

Why is it necessary to study organisational behaviour? Obviously, the reasons are many. Managers are required to understand normal and abnormal behaviour in order to implement rules. Understanding the behavioural predisposition that motivates people is important in order to inspire them to fulfill the organisation's goals. Today, organisations are increasingly facing the problem of introducing change. Knowledge of employee behaviour enables managers to design suitable strategies of change management. At the same time, one can argue that understanding behaviour is a colossal task and it is not easy to derive a meaningful interpretation of behaviour. This is true to a certain extent. Another argument is that by understanding behaviour managers are able to extract more work from their employees. This is obviously true, and may cause one to wonder whether this leads to exploitation.

One should remember that organisational behaviour is not a prescription for all organisational ills. It can only be used as a guide. Using techniques of organisational behaviour is subject to the discretion of the manager and the organisation. It should be used for creative and innovative ideas and to promote human welfare.

DEFINITIONS OF ORGANISATIONAL BEHAVIOUR

The term organisational behaviour consists of two terms, 'organisation' and 'behaviour'. We have understood that organisation is a group of people, who have come together for the realisation of goals. **Talcot Parson** stated that organisations are social entities consisting of physical, financial and human resources. Behaviour is the actions and reactions of an individual in a situation. For instance, if you meet a friend, the smile on your face reflects emotional feelings. If you are angry or irritated with a person or situation you may vent your emotions by banging the furniture or shouting at your near and dear ones. Therefore, outward expressions provide an understanding of behaviour. In organisations, human resources are precious and their behaviour is unique. As such an understanding of their interaction in organisations is necessary, to integrate human effort towards realisation of goals. Organisational Behaviour (OB) is a specialised field of knowledge developed to understand human behaviour.

The following definitions help to understand the nature and scope of organisational behaviour.

- According to **Keith Davis,** "*Organisational behaviour is an academic discipline concerned with understanding and describing human behaviour in an organisational environment. It seeks to shed light on the whole complex of the human factor in organisations by identifying causes and effects of that behaviour.*"

- **Cummings** states that, "*Organisational behaviour is the study and application of knowledge about how people act within organisations. It is a human tool for human benefit. It applies broadly to the behaviour of people in all types of organisations, such as business, government, schools and service organisations.*"
- **Robbins** defined organisational behaviour as a "*Field of study that investigates the impact that individuals, groups and structure have on behaviour within organisations, for the purpose of applying such knowledge toward improving an organisations' effectiveness.*"
- According to **Szilagyi** and **Wallace**, organisational behaviour is concerned with "*the study of the behaviour, attitudes and performance of workers in an organisational setting: the organisation's and group's effects in the workers' perceptions, feelings, and actions, the environments' effect in the organisation and its human resources and goals, and the effect of the workers on the organisation and its effectiveness.*"

NATURE OF ORGANISATIONAL BEHAVIOUR

The nature of organisational behaviour is described below.

i. Organisational behaviour analyses the cause and effect relationship between behaviour and performance.
ii. Organisational behaviour deals with three variables. It studies individuals, groups, and organisation.
iii. It is an integrated science. The knowledge of organisational behaviour is drawn from both social and natural sciences.
iv. It is an emerging discipline of study though its foundations are deep rooted.
v. Organisational behaviour has contingency orientation, as behaviour is unique and unpredictable. It changes from situation to situation.
vi. It is both a science and an art. It is scientific as certain principles are applicable in all situations. However it is an art due to the use of creativity and personal skills in its applications.
vii. The knowledge of organisational behaviour is based on experimental knowledge drawn from other sciences. Thus certain universal principles can be formulated.
viii. Knowledge and application of organisational behaviour is applicable to all organisations.

Social entities: Groups of people combining to pool their energy for realisation of some purpose.

Cause and effect relationship: Helps in understanding the reasons for a particular type of behaviour. For instance, a worker becomes a poor producer. The cause could be a poor working environment. Thus the cause is the work environment and the effect is low production.

Integrated science: Various branches of science, like Psychology, Sociology, Anthropology and other natural and social sciences have contributed to the development of knowledge of organisational behaviour.

Contingency orientation: The behaviour of an individual is not constant. It changes from situation to situation. The same person may behave differently in different situations.

SCOPE OF ORGANISATIONAL BEHAVIOUR

Organisational behaviour deals with three variables viz., individuals, groups and the organisation itself. The individuals are the employees and the groups are both formal and informal sub sets of employees. Groups may take the form of committees, trade unions and workers' teams. Organisation is characterised by the structure and environmental factors that influence it. Figure 2.1 shows the scope of OB.

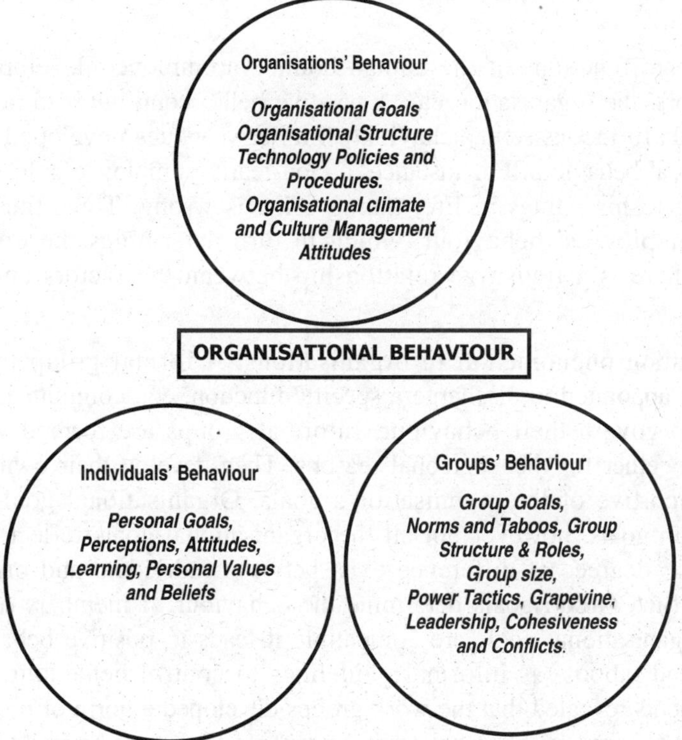

Figure 2.1: Scope of Organisational Behaviour

Personal goals represent an individual's desire or need to achieve something. Each employee in the organisation tries to prioritise his goals over those of others. Human nature tends to be selfish, and individuals attempt to accomplish their goals ignoring the convenience or inconvenience of others. The self is the concept of behaviour. The process of understanding other individuals and the organisation is perception. Perception is a mental process, which can only be understood through an individual's actions and expressions. Similarly, attitudes represent the permanent impressions developed by the employees of an organisation over a period of time. Behavioural expressions of employees reveal their attitude. The perceptions and attitudes influence the behaviour and the working of the organisation. For example, an employee who realises that the work environment is favourable, healthy and friendly develops a positive impression about it. The positive impression will facilitate a higher productivity.

Learning is the ability to understand and implement certain changes in work or behaviour. Not all employees possess the same learning ability. The degree of an employee's learning ability influences the manager's opinion of him. For example, a fast learner will understand instructions at once, and the manager does not have to communicate much with him. On the other hand, if an employee possesses a poor learning aptitude, the manager needs to repeat instructions, and hence has to communicate more with him. The manager develops a positive attitude towards a fast learner and a negative attitude towards a poor learner, which influences his judgement of the employee in future.

Values and beliefs are functions of the human brain. An employee develops a belief in God, religion, his superiors, the organisation etc. A positive belief contributes to normal behaviour. A negative belief leads to inconsistent behaviour. Similarly, values developed by the employees determine their ethical behaviour. For instance, a God-fearing employee is less likely to accept a bribe, as according to his values in life, taking bribe is wrong. Thus, these factors have an influence on the employees' behaviour, which in turn determines the effectiveness of the enterprise. Thus, there is a transitive relationship between the factors and effectiveness of organisations.

Groups are a common phenomenon in organisations. A formal group may be number of employees formally appointed to discharge a specific function, e.g. committees. Formal rules and regulations exist to govern their behaviour. Informal groups are formed when a number of employees gather together for their personal reasons. They develop their own goals, which may or may not be supportive of the organisation's goals. Organisational goals are the result of individual and group goals, however not all the organisational goals reflect the individual and group goals. Certain degrees of difference exist between individual and organisational goals, which leads to conflict. Group goals determine the behaviour of members of the group. If the group goals and organisational goals are compatible it leads to positive behaviour. Groups also formulate norms and taboos, as informal guidelines to control behaviour. For example, the Hawthorne experiments revealed that the work groups developed a norm of production below that of the management's norm and compelled its members to adhere to it. Non-conformity was viewed as a serious lapse on the part of the worker and the term 'rate buster' was coined to criticise employees who produced output over and above the group norm. Therefore, it is important to note that the group norms control the behaviour of employees. The group structure is based on the roles assigned to the members and the relationship between them. Clearly defined role assignments lead to positive behaviour, whereas unequal distribution of power among the members of the group results in conflicting behaviour. The group size is based on the number of members in the group. A group with too many members becomes uncontrollable, as the behaviour of the members is inconsistent. Experiments have also shown that small groups show more positive behavioural reactions to change, than larger groups.

A grapevine is an informal communication channel developed by a group. It is very fast, but often spreads gossip, half-truths and rumours. The communication process regulates the members' behaviour. Rapid transmission of information about involvement of a member in anti group activities takes place through this channel. For example, a group developed a norm that no employee should reveal the official secrets of the group to the supervisor. However, one employee met the superior after working hours. By the time the employee came to work the next day, other members of the group had put up posters defaming him. The employee was astonished as to how other members came to know about the meeting, and immediately stopped meeting the superior after the official hours. In this way the group regulated the member's behaviour. In the entire process, communication played an important role. The behaviour of the group leader determines the other members' behaviour and their contribution to the organisation. For example if the group has a democratic or positive leader, the members' attitude also becomes positive and contributing.

Cohesiveness is the degree of conformity of the members of the group. Members of a cohesive group respect one another's feelings. Therefore, a person's actions and reactions depend upon the behaviour of the group. Conflict among the group members leads to unconfirmed behaviour. It should be emphasised that group behaviour determines individual behaviour, which in turn determines the effectiveness of the organisation. Thus, it is imperative to understand group behaviour, so as to benefit the organisation.

As we have seen, the integration of individual and group goals leads to the development of organisational goals. The reflection of organisational goals in the individual and group goals is known as goal congruence. In the words of **McGregor**, *a true integration of goals results from the greater degree of sharing of organisational goals by the employees.* Greater compatibility of individual and organisational goals leads to motivated behaviour. Morale and performance will be low or negligible with incongruent goals. For instance, if employees find that their own goals conflict with the organisation's goals, they may engage in disrespectful behaviour.

The organisational structure establishes relationships among the employees by describing the authority, responsibility, span, delegation and line and staff relationships. All these elements have a significant impact on the behaviour of the employees. The status relationships created by the authorities for instance, discriminate between the employees, resulting in some employees developing grudge against their superiors, (see case example). The physical working conditions and psychological support systems constitute the climate and culture of the organisation. A favourable perception of the climate and culture leads to sound behaviour. For example, in India public enterprises are bureaucratic in their culture, employees work strictly according to rules, and may even use them to avoid work. The point to emphasise is that the organisations' behaviour influences the individuals' and group behaviour.

Case study 2.1:

A friend of mine, working in a private bank took voluntary retirement from the bank at the relatively early age of fifty. He was a hard worker and loyal to the organisation. His superiors used to appreciate his outstanding contributions to the organisation. He was responsible for expanding the network of branches of the bank in the city in which he worked. He did excellent work in developing the customer base of the bank. For his outstanding work, the bank even honoured him by inviting him to open a branch office in the same city. Unfortunately, while he was returning from the head office, after attending an interview and hearing the unofficial confirmation of his promotion, he met with an accident. He sustained multiple fractures and to add to his woes, he did not receive proper medical attention in spite of his treatment in a good private hospital, the cost of which was borne by the bank. As a result he was permanently crippled. He had to walk with a stick and was unable to sit for a long time. The bank removed his name from the promotion list, and all his appeals fell on deaf ears. Finally he was offered voluntary retirement with 60 months salary without any deductions. His retirement decision puzzled me and I asked him about it. Finally he revealed that the reason for his retirement decision was not his incapacity, but the fact that his colleague received a promotion and became his boss, and he was unwilling to work under him. His behaviour towards his erstwhile colleague turned hostile, as he could not digest the fact that his colleague, who was an average performer, was promoted over him.

This is a classic example of influence of authority and status bringing behavioural discrepancy.

FACTORS INFLUENCING ORGANISATIONAL BEHAVIOUR

Organisational behaviour provides scope for understanding human behaviour in organisations, and directing this behaviour to realise the employees' potential. It deals with the behaviour of individuals, groups and the organisation itself. However, one should understand that it is not restricted to the internal aspects of the organisation alone. The three elements of organisational behaviour are interdependent as explained earlier. For example, individual behaviour influences group behaviour and both of them influence organisational behaviour. Therefore, it has a system orientation. Inputs to an individual's behaviour are needs and desires; the process is the organisation process conditioned by the structure; and the output is the human behaviour and group behaviour. Not only that it is a system, but also the behaviour is dynamic. Thus, it has an open dynamic orientation.

Organisational behaviour is influenced by a number of factors, as shown in Figure 2.2.

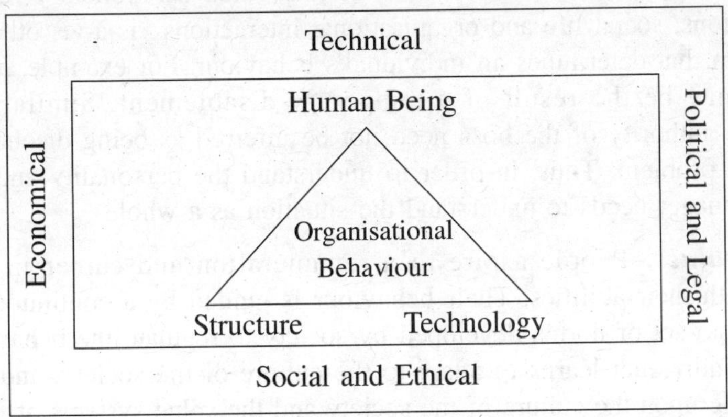

Figure. 2.2: Factors influencing organisational behaviour

(I) Human beings

Organisations are human systems. Human beings are core, but unique resources. It is necessary to co-ordinate efforts among individuals in order to achieve the goals of the organisation. This requires understanding of the behaviour of the people in the organisation. Certain unique characteristics of people in organisations are given below.

(a) ***Individual differences:*** Human beings have certain common physical attributes. Yet, certain distinctions are evident in certain geographical regions. For example, the colour of the pupil of the eyes, colour of the hair and skin colour differ according to climatic conditions. Other common factors in human beings are their zest for social relations, family structure, intelligence, self-reflexive, linguistic abilities and ability to work to earn a livelihood.

   The law of individual differences states that every individual is different from the other. Individuals are different in their motivational propensities, interaction with others, possession of tolerance and stress etc. Porter and Lawler state that 'individual differences determine the way in which people respond to various aspects of organisation and to the practice of organisation'. So understanding individuals and successfully managing them to improve organisational effectiveness become vital.

(b) ***Motivated behaviour:*** An individuals behaviour is caused by the importance they attach to the things that fulfil their needs. Individual needs motivate them to behave in a particular manner. Maslow has propounded a hierarchy of needs to show motivation behaviour of individuals. Accordingly, basic needs act as motivators. After they are satisfied, safety needs emerge as motivators. If these needs are reasonably satisfied it results in the emergence of esteem, affection and self-actualisation needs. Therefore, it can be stated that need fulfilment is a motivator or a need results in behaviour. For example, a hungry man is more aggressive, than a satisfied man. His aggressiveness is the result of hunger and may not be his normal behaviour.

(c) ***Holistic personality:*** Scientific management studies only the skills and capacities of a person and concludes that a person's productivity is motivated by monetary rewards. However, physical conditions, social life and organisational interactions vis-à-vis other persons form a complete system that determines an individual's behaviour. For example an employee's low productivity may be the result of a temporary disablement. Similarly, an employee questioning the authority of the boss need not be inferred as being disobedient, as he may have a genuine problem. Thus, in order to understand the personality and behaviour of an employee, a manager needs to understand the situation as a whole.

(d) ***Culture and values:*** People aspire to a remuneration and career in an organisation concomitant with their abilities. Their behaviour is guided by a continuous effort to attain them. Culture is a set of norms developed by society to regulate the behaviour of people in society. Every individual learns to adapt to the culture of the society, and develops certain values depending upon the culture of the society and the value systems of the family. Values are certain predispositions about the actions of individuals, which depend on the beliefs of the people. For example, accepting or rejecting a bribe, sincerity in work, and adhering to time are values of the individual. On the other hand the degree to which subordinates participate in the decision making process, depends on their culture. Treating the subordinates equally is an example of organisational culture. Culture, philosophy, values and ethics determine people's actions, and in turn influence organisational behaviour. There is both an internal and external influence in these elements. For instance, culture is an external element, whereas values are internal. Individual differences are mostly determined by the internal factors in individuals. Both internal and external factors influence motivation propensity of the individuals.

(II) Structure

Organisations are social systems. Therefore, people in organisations have mutual interests. However, organisational goals are super-ordinate goals and similarity of individual goals facilitates their achievement. Realisation of goals requires structured interaction. It is provided by clear definition of authority, responsibility and accountability, division of labour, span of control, and line and staff relations. Each of these aspects determines communication, motivation and commitment, which regulate individual behaviour. As such management cannot isolate the influence of structure on the behaviour in directing the subordinate's efforts. For example, ambiguous identification of the line and staff division creates a number of behavioural problems. In many organisations, personnel in finance often behave as if they are themselves providing finance to the other functionaries, which can lead to resentment among the staff, particularly those engaged in production, which is a line organisation. This results in behavioural discrepancy among the functionaries, and can cause personal problems that result in stress and emotional behaviour.

(III) Technology

In recent years technology has revolutionised the patterns of organisational relationships.

Mechanical devices like computers and robots have been used to replace human labour. This continuous improvement in the technology is a challenge to organisations as humans have a tendency to resist change. Technology has not only changed the design and structure of organisations, it has strongly influenced individuals' behaviour. Thus the technology used by the organisation should be taken into consideration while analysing behaviour in an organisation. For example a worker in a coal mine deprived of a casual leave by his superior is likely to become angry with his superior, whereas a computer operator working in an air-conditioned room is more able to deal with the situation calmly. This is due to the fact that in the former case the work environment and technology cause physical strain. Thus, technology determines the behaviour of the individuals.

(IV) Environment

The three factors viz., human beings, organisation structure and technology discussed above are inter-dependent on each other and dependent on the environment of the organisation. The level of technology used by the organisation determines the organisational structure, which influences the behaviour of the individuals. How these factors influence the effectiveness of the organisation is determined by the environmental dynamics. The external environmental factors are Political, Economical, Technical, Legal, Ecological, Government and Social cultural and ethical (PETLEGS). These factors are not static, but change with time and environmental dynamics. Thus, individual behaviour is also influenced by environment factors, which a manager should understand, when analysing acceptable and unacceptable behaviour of his subordinates.

To illustrate the influence of political factors, consider the time when elections are due in India. People spend time debating the political situation rather than attending to their duties. In addition, organisations also find their files are kept pending by government as the caretaker government can not take decisions on policy matters.

Ecology is concerned with the natural environment. For example, workers living in a colony near a thermal power plant experience the fall of coal ash at the end of the day. The sticky ash causes physical irritation, which can result in the workers getting irritated for even small things. Employees living in a healthy environment are happier and calmer. Thus, ecological factors affect a person's behaviour.

Organisational behaviour is widely accepted as a technique of increasing organisational effectiveness. It has taken the place of organisational psychology, management and organisation theory, and personnel and human resource management. Organisational psychology is limited to the psychological aspects of human behaviour; organisational theory is concerned with organisation at the micro level, it is not concerned with interactive elements of people; personnel and human resource management is application oriented and uses certain behavioural variables in the process. Organisational behaviour forms the basis for understanding human behaviour in organisations. It is an interactive science having a number of techniques, which can be applied.

MANAGERIAL IMPLICATIONS OF LEARNING ORGANISATIONAL BEHAVIOUR

The effectiveness or otherwise of any organisation is a function of human effort. Thus understanding human behaviour is of particular significance in directing human effort towards attaining the goals of an organisation. Organisational behaviour is significant due to following reasons:

(i) **Conditioned behaviour:** People behave differently in different situations. You might have observed that you feel free to express your opinion amongst friends, but feel restricted with your teachers. This is because your teacher is regarded as formal authority. In the same way, organisations function within rules and regulations, and compel employees to adhere to these rules. The rules have psychological implications in their application. A subordinate can criticise the manager in front of his colleagues, but not in front of his superiors, as the latter possess authority, which he can exercise. So a person's behaviour is conditioned by the rules, and a manager has to understand normal and abnormal behaviour in order to implement rules.

(ii) **Motivating individuals:** The behaviour of people in an organisation is caused by certain predispositions, which determine peoples' motivation. Understanding the motivation requires an understanding of the employees' predisposition.

(iii) **Application of human relations:** In today's organisations, the needs and aspirations of people have changed. Employees want recognition, equal treatment and esteem. So the traditional assumptions regarding human behaviour are no longer useful to managers. A study of organisational behaviour helps to formulate assumptions, which are oriented more towards human relations, and a favourable work environment. Thus, managers can direct personnel more effectively so as to increase organisational effectiveness.

(iv) **Psychological commitment:** The mere physical presence of employees in the work place does not ensure efficiency. They should show commitment to their work. Commitment is a function of psychological preparedness of an individual. Understanding organisational behaviour enables one to make a distinction between individual and group behaviour. It also enables one to understand the determinants of commitment. Hence, managers frame policies relating to psychological commitment to direct subordinates' efforts.

(v) **Change management:** Organisations function in a dynamic environment. Some environmental factors are more prone to change than others. Organisations have to adapt to changes in the environment to prevent negative entropy. Employees often resist change and a knowledge of organisational behaviour helps to reduce this resistance. Managers use various methods, like counselling employees etc., to overcome resistance.

(vi) **Knowledge management:** Since modern organisations are knowledge-based, knowledge management has become crucial in the work place. Companies employ techniques such as team building and learning about the organisation to build and share knowledge among employees. Knowledge has become essential for organisations and employees.

Organisational behaviour helps to determine the learning potential of employees and develop them as knowledge capital.

Organisational behaviour has the potential to provide an environment conducive to enhancing organisational effectiveness. However organisational behaviour is not a solution to all organisational problems. The following limitations are applicable to organisational behaviour:

(i) **Structural limitations:** Organisational behaviour is not a method of weeding out inept organisational structure, deficiency of organisation structure and deficiency of organisational systems. The authority, responsibility, accountability of employees makes them behave in a superfluous manner. Organisational behaviour enables one to understand human environment.

(ii) **Human exploitation:** Organisational behaviour is viewed as a technique to manipulate human labour without regard to the welfare of the workers. This is because organisational behaviour suggests understanding human behaviour in order to increase utilisation of their skills. However it is not correct to understand organisational behaviour as a tool to exploit people, as it also makes one aware of human happiness.

(iii) **Closed outlook:** Organisational behaviour over-emphasises the role of people in an organisation. In fact, people in organisations are influenced by a host of internal and external factors, and interact with a variety of groups in society. Organisational behaviour does not throw light on these interactions.

(iv) **Over-emphasising OB:** Over emphasising organisational behaviour practice does not free the authorities from responsibilities. Managers should use diligence and care in the application of organisational behaviour practices. They should not be applied ruthlessly.

Knowledge and application of organisational behaviour is useful to create a productive, physical and psychological environment in organisations in which people are committed to realise goals. In addition organisational behaviour also contributes towards the welfare of society by emphasising such aspects as energy conservation, health improvement etc.

Case study 2.1: Emotional disturbance and efficiency

One day I entered my regular bank, in the middle of banking hours. Heated discussions were taking place and some employees and customers seemed very agitated. The manager of the bank seemed to be angry and disturbed. I silently observed the proceedings. I gathered that a client wanted to encash a cheque. The bank clerk rejected the cheque, because it was not attested. The bank requires attestation of the signature of the presenter of the cheque if the cheque is an order cheque and the presenter does not have an account with the bank. Since the person presenting the cheque was neither an account holder, nor possessed the required identification, the banker was justified in refusing payment. However the presenter of the cheque argued that other cheques had been allowed, while his cheque was dishonoured. He refused to see that the other people had fulfilled the necessary requirements to encash their cheques, and took the refusal as a personal insult. As the person raised his voice other staff members intervened, supporting their colleague. This caused the customer to get even angrier and start using abusive language. The whole situation escalated, and got out of hand. The cashier stopped disbursing cash. The officer stopped authorising other customers' cheques. Obviously the customers objected to the delay and joined in the fray, venting their irritation on the hapless bank clerk. Finally to end the matter one of the customers intervened and shouldered the responsibility of attesting the cheque, as the amount was not very significant, although he had never seen the presenter of the cheque before. To everybody's relief the commotion ended.

However, I observed that the unpleasant situation affected the mood of the employees, and disturbed the efficiency, not only of the concerned cashier, but also other staff members. The cashier could not disburse the cash as efficiently as he was doing before the incident. There was delay in counting and often he had to check and recheck the counting of notes, and even requested the customers to count the money they had withdrawn. The bank clerk was unable to process the cheques of other waiting customers. He made a mistake in entering my balance and when I pointed out the error he requested me to come the next day to rectify it. He said that he was disturbed because the person and his supporters had made personal comments about him, saying that he was not suitable for the job, and did not care about the customers. They even went to the extent of bringing his family life into the argument. All this caused him a great deal of mental agony.

Questions:

1. Why did the bank clerk reject the cheque of the person?
2. What was the result of the customer losing his emotional balance?
3. What was the result of the disturbed mood and sentiments?
4. Desribe the emotional communication in the case?

SUMMARY

Organisational behaviour consists of two terms, organisation and behaviour. This chapter explained the meaning and nature of organisational behaviour, a discipline that helps in understanding the behaviour of employees in organisations. It deals with individual behaviour, group behaviour and the organisation's behaviour. It is an integrated science. It analyses cause and effect relationships. It is scientific in its principles, but it requires art to apply it. Nowadays organisational behaviour has also developed into a profession. Personal goals, perceptions, attitudes, learning, values, and beliefs influence employee behaviour. The goals, norms, structure and roles, power tactics, grapevine communication, leadership and cohesiveness determine group behaviour. Organisational goals, structure, technology, organisational culture and climate determine the organisational behaviour. All these elements are inter related and inter dependent. The characteristics of human beings, structure and technology, which are an integral part of the organisation, influence the behaviour of employees in organisations. Certain external environmental factors, be they political, economical, technical, legal, ecological, governmental, social, and ethical also influence the behaviour of individuals and groups in organisations. Individual behaviour is always motivated. The different culture and value systems of individuals also cause them to behave differently. Thus, individual behaviour is holistic.

Organisational behaviour is an emerging discipline. It is multi-disciplinary in nature. Knowledge of organisational behaviour is of great significance in understanding conditioned behaviour, motivating individuals, bringing about psychological commitment and change management. In recent years, organisational behaviour has become a technique of developing employees as knowledge capital. However, organisational behaviour is not a solution to all organisational problems. It has certain limitations such as structural limitations and a closed outlook. Its critics claim that organisational behaviour is used to exploit workers. However, this is not true, knowledge of behaviour helps in solving problems and leads to happier workers. Despite its limitations, managers benefit greatly if they apply organisational behaviour with skill and diligence. This is why organisational behaviour is considered both a science and an art.

Key words

- **Attitudes:** Permanent impressions developed by individuals.
- **Bureaucracy:** Organisations should strictly adhere to the rules and regulations and make decisions impersonally.
- **Cohesiveness:** The extent to which the members of a group respect one another's feelings and adapt themselves.
- **Economies of scale:** Benefits derived by an enterprise from large-scale operations.
- **Goal congruency:** When individual and organisational goals are the same.
- **Grapevine:** Informal channel of communication existing among members of a group.
- **Law of individual differences:** Individuals are unique and possess both physiological and psychological differences.
- **Open system:** A system, which interacts with the external environment and adapts itself to changes in the environment.
- **Perception:** The process of understanding and giving a meaning to the observed stimuli.

3. EMERGENCE OF ORGANISATIONAL BEHAVIOUR

This chapter enables you:

- *To highlight the contributions of organisation theories to the study of organisational behaviour*
- *To examine the challenges posed by globalisation vis-à-vis organisational behaviour*
- *To appraise the disciplines contributing to organisational behaviour*
- *To understand the contribution of Anthropology*
- *To analyse the contribution of Sociology*
- *To examine the contribution of Psychology*
- *To understand the contribution of other sciences*

The structure of the chapter is as follows:

- Introduction
- Contributions of organisation theories to organisational behaviour
- Global challenges of organisational behaviour
- Contributions to the study of organisational behaviour
- Anthropology
- Sociology
- Psychology
- Contributions of other sciences
- Summary
- Key words

CHAPTER 3

Emergence of Organisational Behaviour

In India, the recent economic reforms have changed the entire market economy as the new market economy has replaced the regulated economy. International corporations from Japan, the USA, Germany, France and other nations have established their markets in product areas such as processed foods, readymade garments, personal computers, steel etc. The products of top global brands like Coca Cola, Sony, McDonalds, Kellogs, Marlboro etc. have flooded the consumer markets. Multinationals have even invaded core sectors of the economy. For instance, in the steel sector there is US Steels and in the petroleum sector there is Shell Oil. This trend has created formidable challenges and competition to Indian companies, many of which had no option but to form strategic alliances with the global players in order to survive in the new world order. Some examples of such alliances are Trideon Limited with AT & T, Godrej with GEC. Other multinationals who have alliances with Indian companies are P & G, General Motors, Ford, Maruti, Coca Cola, Max Factor, Cosmat and Motorola. Certain other organisations have redesigned their manufacturing processes and restructured organisational designs in order to be able to compete with their competitors' strategies.

INTRODUCTION

Organisation theories have proposed a number of theories regarding the structure and process of organisations. The classical theory of organisation emphasised structure as an important element of organisational effectiveness. Later, neo classical theories have laid emphasis on the behaviour of human resources in organisations. In particular, the theory on human relations provided literature and research evidence to infer that human emotions, perceptions, attitudes, social relationships, leadership behaviour, communication etc., influence the organisation process and effectiveness. Similarly, the systems and contingency theories also stated that the behaviour of elements outside the control of managerial authority influence the functioning of an organisation. Thus, it is appropriate to say that these theories emphasised that behaviour processes in the organisation are relevant in understanding the organisation and achieving effectiveness, even with limited resources.

Organisations as social systems act according to the behaviour of the individuals i.e., the employees. The latter in turn is a function of personality and environment. Different stimuli cause different behaviour. Despite the fact that people are similar in certain respects, a number of physiological and psychological dimensions make each individual unique. Thus, human behaviour is not always rational. As Herbert Simon has stated, '*behaviour is subjectively rational.*' He therefore advocated the concept of bounded rationality, whereby behaviour can never be completely rational or irrational. Behaviour should be judged taking into account the situation, environment and person himself. The discipline used to understand the behaviour of individuals and groups within structural and environmental constraints is called organisational behaviour. Organisational behaviour is an emerging multi-disciplinary science, which has developed due to contributions from other sciences such as Anthropology, Sociology, Psychology, History, Geology, Physics, Chemistry, Botany, Zoology and Medicine.

CONTRIBUTIONS OF ORGANISATION THEORIES TO ORGANISATIONAL BEHAVIOUR

The great depression, which occurred in Europe, in 1929 was the catalyst that triggered the emergence of organisational behaviour. Figure 3.1 shows the historical development of organisational behaviour.

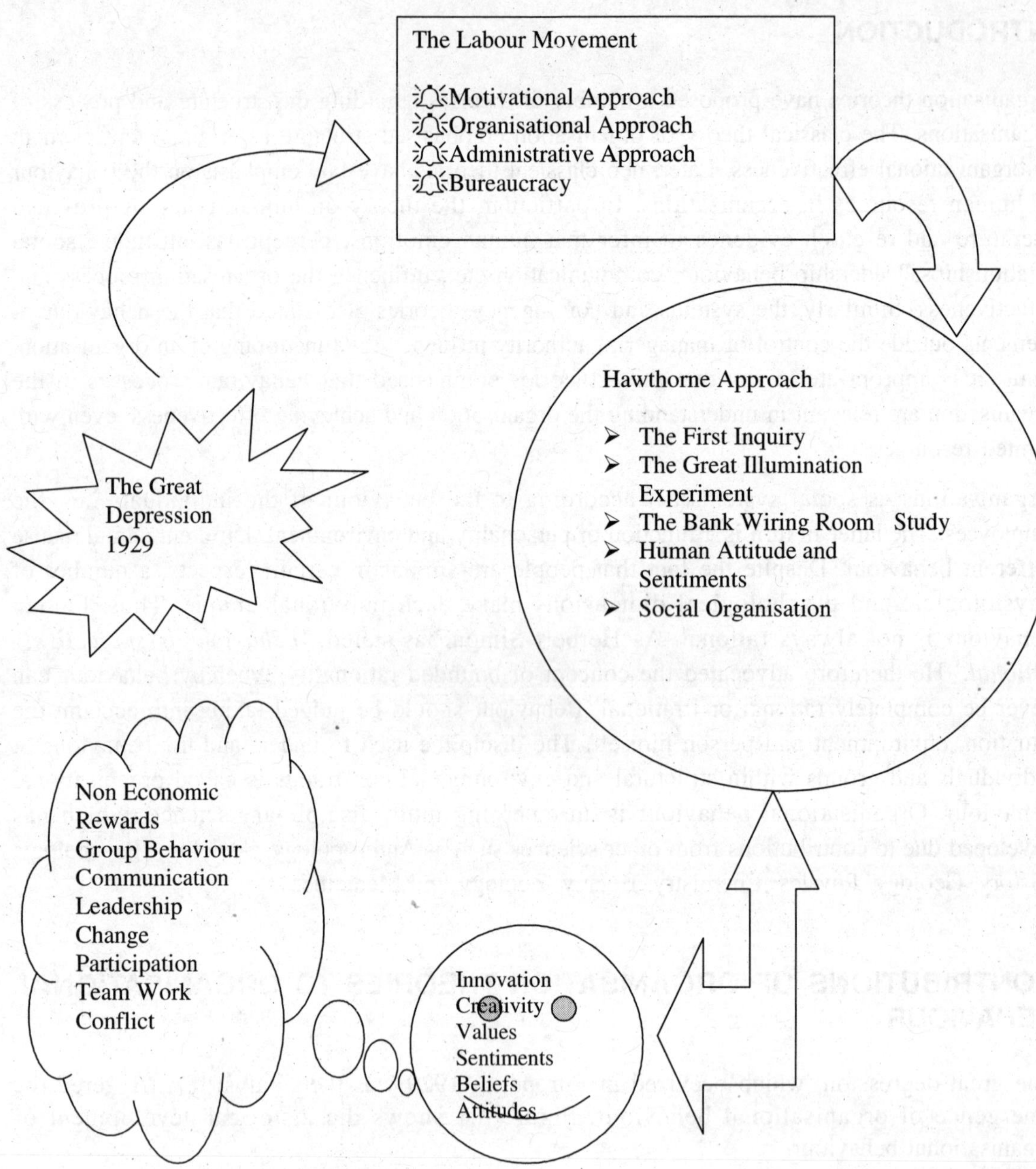

Figure. 3.1: Development of OB

Classical theories namely the Classical Organisational Theory, the Classical Motivational Theory, the Administrative Theory and Bureaucracy have emphasised that the organisational structure is important in achieving effectiveness. The theories have assumed that man pursues economic goals and economic motivation directs his behaviour towards realisation of goals. This is important in understanding motivation and resulting behaviour even in the modern organisations. Frederic Winslow Taylor, Gilbreth and Gilbreth, Henry Gantt, Harrington Emerson, Henry Fayol, Lyndall Urwick, Max Webber, Chester I Barnard are some of the pioneers of classical management thought. Others such as, Elton Mayo, Mary Parker Follet, Roethilisberger, and Douglas McGregor, disagree that man is motivated only by economic goals, and along with their associates have propounded theories on human relation. Their human relation and behavioural theories were popularised as neo-classical theories and have provided new insights into the understanding of human behaviour in organisations. In the middle of the nineteenth century, Blackett, Robert E. Markland, Arthur D. Little, Bertalanffy, Hames E. Rosenzweig, George P. Huber popularised quantitative and system thinking in organisations. These theories, which have been recognised as modern theories, established the importance of environment in influencing the behaviour of people. All the theories have made significant contributions to the understanding of people working in organisations and the dynamics of their behavioural interactions. The following table provides an explanation of the relationship between the theories and organisational behaviour.

Assumptions:

Classical theories	**Human relations theories**	**Modern theories**
1. Work is inherently distasteful to most people.	1. People want to feel useful and important.	1. Work is not inherently distasteful.
2. What workers do is less important than what they earn for doing it.	2. People desire to belong and to be recognised as individuals.	2. People want to contribute to meaningful goals, which they have helped to establish.
3. Only a few people want to, or are able to, handle work that requires creativity, self-direction, or self-control.	3. These needs are more important than money in motivating people to work.	3. Most people can exercise more creativity, responsibility, self-direction and self-control than their present job demands.

Policies:

Classical theories	Human relations theories	Modern theories
1. The manager's basic task is to closely supervise and control his subordinates.	1. He should keep his subordinates informed and listen to their objections to his plans.	1. The manager's task is to make use of his "untapped" human resources.
2. He must break the tasks into simple, repetitive and easily learned operations.	2. The manager should allow his subordinates to exercise some self-judgement in routine matters.	2. He must create an environment in which all members can contribute to the limits of their ability.
3. He must establish detailed work routines and procedures and enforce these firmly but fairly	3. The manager's task is to make each worker feel useful and important.	3. He must encourage full participation in important matters, continually broadening subordinate self-direction and control.

Expectations:

Classical theories	Human relations theories	Modern theories
1. People can tolerate work if their pay is decent and the boss is fair.	1. Sharing information with subordinates and involving them in routine decisions will sastisfy their basic needs of belonging and feeling important.	1. Expanding subordinate influence, self-direction, and self-control will lead to direct improvements in operating efficiency.
2. If tasks are simple enough and people are closely controlled, their production will meet the required standards.	2. Satisfying these needs will improve morale and reduce resistance to formal authority, subordinates will "willingly co-operate."	2. Work satisfaction may improve as a "by-product" of subordinates making full use of their resources.

Dimensions of organisations and behaviour:

Classical theories	Human relations theories	Modern theories
A. Organisation design and organisation models		
1. ***Variation of bureaucracy:*** Functional or divided foremanship. Hierarchy is still essential. Organisational structure is more important than attitudes.	1. ***Variation of bureaucracy:*** Participative Management hierarchy is still essential. Attitudes are more important than organisational structure.	1. ***Variation of bureaucracy:*** Both bureaucratic and non-bureaucratic models are important. Importance of the hierarchy is not emphasized much. Both attitudes and organizational structure are equally important.
2. ***Major influences on design:*** Technology and environmental uncertainty is of minor importance.	2. ***Major influences on design:*** Technology and environmental uncertainty is of minor importance	2. ***Major influences on design:*** Technology and environmental uncertainty are of major importance.
B. Planning and control		
3. ***Planning:*** Primarily at the operative or worker level. Short range and specific.	3. ***Planning:*** Planning is of minor importance.	3. ***Planning:*** It is done throughout the organization. Both short range and long range.
4. ***Control:*** Primarily at the operative level. Short range and specific.	4. ***Control:*** Control is of minor importance.	4. ***Control:*** Concerned about the entire organization. Both short range and long range
C. Behavioural processes		
5. ***Learning:*** Individuals learn to produce effectively only if their wages are regularly increased.	5. ***Learning:*** Individuals learn how to behave in organizations through group pressures and norms.	5. ***Learning:*** Individuals learn to produce effectively if they trust the organisational climate and an equitable reward system exists within organisation.

Classical theories	Human relations theories	Modern theories
6. ***Perception and interpersonal communication:*** Workers and management do not trust one another. Management must create a climate of trust and co-operation.	6. ***Perception and interpersonal communication:*** Individuals communicate with one another based on perceptions formed through interactions within and among groups.	6. ***Perception and interpersoanl communication:*** Many factors influence namely the design of the organisation, culture, group norms, etc.,
7. ***Motivation:*** Economic man motivated by money.	7. ***Motivation:*** Social man is motivated by attitudes formed through interactions in the informal group.	7. ***Motivation:*** Complex individual motivated by a variety of factors.
8. ***Leadership:*** It is of minor importance.	8. ***Leadership:*** Favours considerate supervisors and participative management.	8. ***Leadership:*** Emphasises traits of a leader, nature of the task, and other situational factors.
9. ***Interpersonal and group behaviour:*** Focuses primarily on the individual employee. However, the work group can undercut management by setting low setting low production standards.	9. ***Interpersonal and group behaviour:*** Focuses on interaction between employees in a single work group, and between the supervisor and the work group.	9. ***Interpersonal and group behaviour:*** Focuses on interaction between: (a) employees in a single work group, the supervisor and the work group. (b) two or more adjacent work groups. (c) Organisational levels (operative, middle, and upper levels.)

Classical theories	Human relations theories	Modern theories
D. Decision making:		
10. ***The nature of decision making:*** The best way is time and motion study.	10. ***The nature of decision making:*** The best way is to use human relations techniques.	10. ***The nature of decision making:*** There is no "best way".
11. ***Decision making techniques:*** Time and motion studies are major variables of decision-making	11. ***Decision making techniques:*** Testing hypotheses is the major approach.	11. ***Decision making techniques:*** Statistics, operations, research, and other quantitative techniques are used.

Source: Gannon J. Martin, Organisational Behaviour, Little, Brown & Co. Boston.

The above table shows that all the organisational theories unanimously emphasise various aspects of behaviour process. As can be observed scientific management stresses the importance of using logical and systematic techniques to improve work processes. It also lays emphasis on time and motion studies as a means of increasing productivity. According to this approach, supervisors should closely monitor the work of employees. The human relations theory identified the significance of behaviour processes in organisations. It found that attitudes of employees influence their behaviour and their productivity levels. Informal work groups determine the attitude of employees. These theories have popularised a number of aspects such as personality, perception, values, motivation, beliefs, culture, satisfaction, relationship orientation, mutual confidence and trust, leadership and communication. On the other hand, modern theories emphasise conservation of human energy by allowing individuals to assume greater responsibility in their work. They should be motivated towards achievement. Thus all the theories have contributed to understanding organisational behaviour. In the context of globalisation and the significant improvement in the internationalisation of economies, new paradigms such as excellence, process reengineering, total quality management, counselling, mentoring, organisational learning, team building, transformational leadership and interpersonal understanding have also been seen to have a significant influence on the behaviour of employees in organisations.

GLOBAL CHALLENGES OF ORGANISATIONAL BEHAVIOUR

We have understood that organisational behaviour is an emerging discipline used to understand the behaviour of employees in organisations. It is growing as an independent faculty of knowledge. During the last decade, a number of changes have occurred all over the world. In the name of liberalisation, privatisation and globalisation many countries have linked their trade and commerce with other countries. Organisational activity in general, and business and corporate activity in particular, has grown enormously. This has brought new challenges in managing organisations. Competition has become global. Corporate downsizing, changing attitudes of people, new cultures brought in by multinational corporate activity, business process reengineering, total quality management, information technology, and the changing structure of the occupational distribution of the working population are some of the emerging issues that have changed the corporate activity in a significant manner. All these have brought new challenges in understanding the behaviour of people in organisations. Some of the emerging challenges to organisational behaviour are given in the following sections.

1. Globalisation

Globalisation is the process of connecting world economies. It brings about multinational corporate activities. Managers must understand the language, laws and regulations, cultural aspects, needs, aspirations, attitudes, ethics and managerial styles of people of all the participating countries. This calls for professionalism in understanding people in organisations. Privatisation gave a new thrust to corporate activity, by creating new employment opportunities. This led to people migrating from rural to urban areas to seek employment. With privatisation, people believe that their skills and merit will be recognised, which are otherwise overlooked in the public sector enterprises. All these factors have made the task of understanding people complex. In order to develop a proper understanding of employees, their motivational propensities and direct the potential for growth and development of an organisation one should understand the subject of organisational behaviour.

2. Diversified workforce

Previously, people felt that they should work and live in the same city, or at least close to it. People thought in terms of family dislocation and responsibility to aged parents. Organisations were often compelled to follow the 'sons of the soil theory'. Slowly, changes in the thinking of the people, brought about increased mobility. Thus, with today's trends of liberalisation, privatisation and globalisation, which have brought about multinational activity, organisations have employed people from all over the world. Organisations have become heterogeneous in terms of race, culture, gender etc., which is termed workforce diversity. Thomas realised that organisations have to accommodate diverse groups of people by addressing their different lifestyles, family needs and working styles. As pointed out by Kossel, Lobel and Segal, diversity, if managed positively can increase creativity and innovation in organisations as well as improve decision making by providing different perspectives on problems. On the other hand diversity leads to problems of higher turnover, hurdles in communications and increased inter personal conflicts. In order to mitigate the ill effects of workforce diversity managers should learn to understand the behaviour, and various elements that make up the behaviour, of employees. This calls for understanding the culture, language, social practices, value systems, thinking and understanding etc. For instance, time management has different connotations in different countries. It is said that if one asks people of different countries to come at 10 o'clock, the Japanese will be present at the exact time, the Americans will come 5 minutes earlier and the Indians will ask whether they should come at 10 o'clock in the morning or evening. Indians are considered very poor in punctuality, but if they go to a country, where punctuality is a condition for work, they keep the timing perfectly.

3. Women in employment

Today it is recognised that women are an important part of the workforce and contribute to the prosperity of a nation. Many state governments in India have enacted legislation to provide reservations for women. Women themselves have also forgone their traditional thinking and are actively pursuing higher education and becoming career oriented. Many of them become entrepreneurs, starting their own ventures. They play an active role in all spheres of life, be it politics, education, or employment and often occupy senior positions. They are fighting for equal rights and many are prefering late marriages in life. Their feelings of insecurity and dependence have given way to confidence, both at home and in the workplace.

At the same time, one has to recognise that women have both skills and problems that are specific to them. For instance, women possess more patience and are more adaptable to change. Women hesitate to pick quarrels in the workplace, do not become easily emotional and are less likely to use and accept abusive language. The increased participation of women in employment has given rise to the concept of dual career couples, where both of them pursue an active career. This can pose problems of relocating them. Understanding the behaviour of the female workforce has become a challenge to managers. Sexual harassment, working late hours, easy mingling of the sexes, are just some of the issues that have engaged attention in recent times. These issues have a significant bearing on the behaviour of men and women. To cite few examples, in India, stretching hand for handshake as mark of greeting is interpreted as intentional act of sexual harassment. In most of the western countries, it is part of their culture. Similarly, men employees working under women managers regard it as degrading the respect of men in India. However, the same is a respect in other countries. A changing trend is observed even in India also in the recent past.

4. The younger generation

The latter part of the 19th century witnessed a change in the population distribution, with an increase in the percentage of youth and adolescents. Increased urbanisation created an awareness of education, and the literacy rate has increased significantly due to government policies. Recently, for instance, the central government introduced a scheme called '*sarva siksha abhayan*', which means education for all. Moreover, the younger generation has greater levels of persistence, potential to achieve their goals and a desire to excel. With the introduction of the voluntary retirement scheme, a number of older employees have taken super-annuation. In their place, organisations are looking to employ younger people. Young, fresh graduates are ambitious, enthusiastic, innovative, creative, possess interpersonal skills, and are more aggressive in pursuing goals. They also have a certain image of the organisations and certain expectations from it. Managing younger employees requires perfect understanding of their motivational potential, ambitions, expectations, skills and professionalism.

The tendency of changing jobs has increased in the private sector even in India. Jennings described people who change jobs even for small economic gains as mobicentric men. All these tendencies pose different challenges to managers. They need to understand the behavioural dimensions of the younger generation in order to retain them in the organisation and direct their effort towards the goals of the organisation. Knowledge of organisational behaviour helps a manager in this.

5. Quality management and productivity

Deming, Crosby and Juran initiated a new quality revolution in Japan. Many Japanese organisations adapted to this benchmark and became a model for other countries. Today organisations have recognised the importance of customers. As they say the customer is king, and in order to give increased customer satisfaction and ensure that customers remain loyal to their brand, corporations need to continually upgrade all organisational processes. In order to do this a manager can make use of a number of techniques, such as Total Quality Management (TQM), Kaizen, Business Process Reengineering (BPR) and Customer Relations Management (CRM).

In TQM the focus is on the customer, it is concerned with continuous improvement, and uses mathematical and statistical techniques to maintain quality and empower employees. TQM requires self-directed teams of employees. Managers continuously face the challenge of increasing productivity and quality and organisations use the concept of process re-engineering to increase productivity.

Business Process Reengineering redesigns the manufacturing, technical and human processes so that customers get value for their money.

Imai popularised the Kaizen concept, which means change for good. It advocates changing work place and management attitudes to bring about greater integration of management and employees. Another approach that is becoming popular is CRM. This involves devoting more attention to customers in order to gain their loyalty by serving them effectively.

All these techniques require extensive changes in human attitudes and their ways of thinking and learning. This requires employee involvement. Today managers are using counselling to change employee attitudes. Learning organisations also use the concept of team learning and shared vision for developing employees. These concepts have created a formidable challenge to organisational behaviour.

6. Contract employment

A new dimension in corporate employment is contract employment, as opposed to term and secured employment. Corporate downsizing and subcontracting have forced organisations to employ workers on contract basis. These workers are taken for their particular skills and for a particular job. Business Process Outsourcing (BPO) has created opportunities in the developing nations. India has the potential to capture outsourced jobs. In BPO, temporary jobs are provided to the extent the organisation needs them. The motivation, commitment and use of skills of temporary employees are different from those of permanent employees. As identified by Maslow, job security is also close to the basic needs of people.' Thus understanding the behaviour of contract employees is really a challenge to managers.

7. Empowerment

Delegation of authority has led to empowerment of employees. Over the last few years there has been a phenomenal growth in the number of educational institutions in India. They offer technical and management courses as well as a large number of other courses in various fields. These opportunities for learning and personality development have enabled many employees to manage knowledge. There is increasing pressure to allow employees to have full control over their work and teams of employees, who work independently are encouraged. As has been pointed out by Dumaine the difference between managers and workers is becoming blurred, with employees often being called associates. Empowerment requires the employees to be psychological mature and at the same time the superiors must have confidence in their subordinates. Empowering employees requires a change in the mindset of the superiors, so that they are ready to share their authority. They need to understand the perception and learning attitude of employees. For instance, an employee having a poor understanding of the organisation does not show adequate interest to learn, which prevents his or her empowerment. Therefore empowering requires a thorough understanding of employee behaviour. This is a challenge to managers who need to understand organisational behaviour.

8. Corporate ethics

Corporate ethics have reached new dimensions during the last decade. There is an increasing demand for productivity and quality. This has led some organisations to use questionable practices to survive in the market. A number of corporate frauds have come to light during the last decade. Managers are facing situations, where they have to define what is right and what is wrong. There is no clear-cut definition regarding ethical behaviour, and managers often have to take hard decisions. This is a challenge to managers, as ensuring ethical behaviour requires understanding individuals. For example Alacrity Group, a construction company involved in the construction of residential flats in Chennai has adopted a number of ethical practices. They do not charge the customer any extra costs once the contract has been signed and pay them interest at commercial rates for delays in completing the construction work. All transactions are registered and have total legal transparency. These ethical practices have enabled the company to realise about 50% of the market. Creating an ethical organisation is not an easy task. It requires developing sound managerial and organisational practices that are not always easily appreciated by employees within the organisation and others outside the organisation. However, a manager can achieve this by understanding the behaviour of employees and directing their behaviour towards sound organisational practices.

The variables described above are not exhaustive. A number of challenges relating to environmental changes affect individual behaviour in organisations. Organisational behaviour has become a dynamic faculty that changes and improves its knowledge base continuously.

Case 3.1: German time management

I observed the way Germans manage time when I visited the 130 Megawatt power plant constructed and operated by ABB India Limited. The entire plant has been constructed by ABB Limited with the help of German technology. Their German counterparts executed the plans, and supervised and exercised control over the operations. The plans and drawings, as well as the messages and mails were in German. The German engineers working in the plant used to adhere strictly to time. They would report for work at 8 a.m., and would work until late at night. They demanded that all the engineers, whether Indian or German should be present at the appointed time. Instructions for the day, however, were given only after checking the mail received from the German office. If any problem arose, they used to consult all the concerned engineers and take decisions on the spot. They respected the talented Indian engineers and used to consult them before taking any decision.

CONTRIBUTIONS TO THE STUDY OF ORGANISATIONAL BEHAVIOUR

Organisational behaviour is an interactive discipline, dealing with individuals, groups and organisational processes. A number of disciplines such as social sciences, natural sciences and behavioural sciences have contributed to the development of the principles and practices of organisational behaviour. The following discussion shows the important contributions from related disciplines:

Anthropology

Anthropology is the scientific study of man. It deals with the biological features of man, the development of civilisation, and the culture and value systems in society. Anthropology has five disciplines:

(i) Cultural Anthropology, which investigates the origin and development of culture in societies.

(ii) Physical Anthropology, which studies the development of the physical features of man.

(iii) Ethnology, which examines the economic, political and religious affiliations of men.

(iv) Linguistic Anthropology, which deals with the language and development of civilisation and culture in society.

(v) Archaeology, which studies the religious beliefs of people and the development of men. All these disciplines have contributed to understanding the culture of individuals, groups and organisation and its implications on behaviour.

The relationship between the various sub disciplines of Anthropology and organisational behaviour are presented in Chart 3.1

Chart 3.1: Contribution of Anthropology

Anthropology and allied fields	Concepts of organisational behaviour
Anthropology is the scientific study of man.	Man is the primary unit of study.
Cultural anthropology studies the origin and development of human culture.	Human culture influences the behavioural predisposition of individuals.
Physical anthropology deals with the development of the features of man.	Biological features such as speech, language etc., influence the behavioural patterns of communication.
Ethnology examines the economic, political and religious affiliations of man.	Economic factors influence the motivation of people in organisations and religious beliefs influence the attitude of people in organisations.

Sociology

Comte defined Sociology as a science that deals with the investigation of the laws of action and reaction of different parts of social systems. It studies the interaction of men with other individuals in society, social groups, institutions and social classes. It also studies the social culture, social status and social esteem of individuals. Sociology uses scientific methodology to suggest solutions to social problems. Sociology is sub-divided into three disciplines:

(i) Family Sociology, which deals with the relationship between family members and the relationships between various families in society.

(ii) Political Sociology, which examines the political affiliations and patterns of political interactions.

(iii) Industrial Sociology, which studies the social problems of workers living in industrial colonies. Chart 3.2 presents the relationship between sociology and organisational behaviour.

Chart 3.2: Contribution of Sociology

Sociology and allied fields	Concepts of organisational behaviour
Sociology deals with the roles of people in society	Development of formal organisational theory.
Sociology studies social group behaviour.	Group dynamic process, group norms and behaviour and power conflicts.
Sociology deals with social culture and beliefs.	Organisational culture.
Political Sociology studies political affiliations.	Theory of bureaucracy.
Family Sociology deals with the relationships of family members in relation to other families in society.	Social systems theory.
Industrial Sociology examines relationship between social group in industrial societies.	Organisational technology and behaviour

Psychology

Psychology is the science of human behaviour. It uses scientific principles and methodology to gather facts about human behaviour in order to measure, analyse and explain it. The following concepts of psychology have contributed to the development of organisational behaviour.

Concepts	Contributors	Behavioural concepts
Behavioralism	Ivan Pavlov, John Waston, B.F. Skinner, Albert Bandura.	Stimulus response connection Learned behaviour Conditioned behaviour Observable behaviour Cognitive element
Functionalism	William James, John Deway.	Study of total behaviour and experience Interest in adaptive functions Learning, forgetting, motivation and adaptation.

Concepts	Contributors	Behavioural concepts
Gestalt Psychology	Max Wertheimer, Muller, Layer, Kurt Lewin.	It is important to understand the whole and not just the part Configuration Illusions
Psychoanalysis	Sigmund Freud, Alfred Adler, Carl Jung.	Unconscious elements Mental process Id-ego-super ego
Social Psychology	William Mc Dougall, Edward Ross	Individual behaviour in groups: Affiliation Cohesion Attitudes Communication Problem solving Leadership Cognitive dissonance
Structuralism	Wilhelm Wundt	Mental states Sensation Memory Imagination Feelings Introspection

Psychology has been developed into two disciplines:

(i) Social Psychology, which analyses the interaction of individuals and group affiliation and cohesion.

(ii) Industrial Psychology, which deals with the problems associated with fatigue, boredom, work conditions etc. Psychology has contributed to organisational behaviour more than any other science. Many concepts of organisational behaviour were developed and understood with the help of psychological models and processes. Chart 3.3, given below shows the contribution of psychology to organisational behaviour.

Chart 3.3: Contribution of Psychology

Psychology and allied fields	Concepts of organisational behaviour
Perception, attitudes, learning	Decision making behaviour, Communication behaviour, Leadership effectivness, Motivation, Job satisfaction
Psychological attributions	Values and status
Structuralism and industrial psychology	Fatigue, boredom, stress and behaviour
Functionalism	Learning, motivation, adaptation
Behaviourism	Learning and decision making
Social Psychology	Group behaviour, affiliations, Cohesiveness and social influence.

Psychology contributes to the solutions of all human relations within organisations. Hence, it is often described as the cornerstone of organisational behaviour.

CONTRIBUTIONS OF OTHER SCIENCES

Apart from various behavioural sciences, other disciplines have also contributed to the development of organisational behaviour. They are:

a. ***Economics:*** This is used to study the motivation and satisfaction of people in an organisation. It also enables one to understand the rationality of human actions. For instance, money is a basic motivator for any individual. The value of money is a function of economic variables.

b. ***History:*** This helps in analysing the culture and development of values and beliefs that affect human behaviour. It enables one to understand the behaviour and development of people in a country.

c. ***Political Science:*** This is used to examine power, inter-organisational politics, and conflict and cohesion among individuals and groups. Obviously, politics plays a greater role in dictating the behaviour of people in society.

d. ***Medicine:*** This is used to understand impact of work stress on the biological functioning of human beings and its impact on performance and organisational effectiveness.

e. ***Natural Sciences like Physics, Chemistry, Botany, Zoology, Geology:*** These are useful in the design of a suitable work environment to reduce fatigue, stress and monotony in order to ensure psychological commitment and satisfaction in an organisation. Chemistry helps in understanding the chemical changes that occur in the human body and the consequent behaviour. Certain levels of chemical compounds cause a disturbance in the biological system, which results in stress. Similarly certain colours are pleasing and will have a positive impact on people, for example, the colour green gives rise to feelings of peace and pleasure, whereas red creates irritation. Thus providing vegetation and plants in an office produces a pleasant ambience and has a positive impact on the thinking of employees. Many organisations put green plants in their offices, which not only help to create a pleasant working environment, but also because it has been proved that the oxygen ejected by them, helps to keep employees fit.

SUMMARY

This chapter dealt with the relationship between organisational theories and organisational behaviour. Some of the concepts of classical theory provided an impetus to the development of behavioural concepts. Human relations theory has contributed a number of concepts that are used to understand the behavioural process in an organisation. Today organisational behaviour is an emerging discipline. Corporate activity has seen a sea change because of liberalisation, globalisation and privatisation. A number of factors such as globalisation, diversified workforce, participation of women in the workforce, managing the younger generation, the continuous need to improve quality and productivity, contractual employment, empowerment and need to practice ethical dimensions pose a formidable challenge to organisational behaviour.

Organisational behaviour is multi disciplinary in nature. Anthropology, Sociology, and Psychology are the major contributing disciplines. A number of concepts in these subjects have given rise to the development of certain vital concepts of organisational behaviour such as formal organisation theory, personality, perception, attitudes, culture, motivation, leadership, communication and group behaviour. Knowledge of organisational behaviour is of great significance in understanding conditioned behaviour, motivating individuals, bringing about psychological commitment and change management. However, organisational behaviour is not a solution to all organisational problems. It has certain limitations such as structural limitations, critiques of human exploitation and a closed outlook. In spite of these limitations, the skilled application of organisational behaviour greatly benefits managers of modern organisations.

Key words

- **Attitudes:** Permanent impressions developed by individuals.
- **Bureaucracy:** Organisations should strictly adhere to the rules and regulations and make decisions impersonally.
- **Business process outsourcing:** Contracting out jobs of an organisation in order to reduce costs.

- **Business process reengineering:** Redesigning the technical, functional and human processes of an organisation.
- **Cohesiveness:** The extent to which the members of the group respect one another's feelings and adapt themselves.
- **Customer relations management:** Giving more attention to serving customers in order to retain them.
- **Economies of scale:** Benefits derived by an enterprise out of large-scale operations.
- **Empowerment:** Allowing employees full control over their work.
- **Globalisation:** The process of liberalising economic and other policies of a country to adapt to other nations.
- **Grapevine:** Informal channel of communication existing among members of the group.
- **Job-hopping:** Tendency to change jobs frequently even for small economic gains.
- **Kaizen:** Japanese philosophy of continuous improvement of all organisation processes to integrate the management and work place.
- **Labour mobility:** Willingness of people to move to other geographical areas to earn a livelihood.
- **Law of individual differences:** Individuals are unique and possess differences both physiological and psychological.
- **Mentoring:** Attempting to modify behavioural attitudes of employees.
- **Mobicentric man:** A person who is mobile and does not work in one organisation for a long time.
- **Open system:** A system that interacts with the external environment and adapts itself to changes in the environment.
- **Perception:** The process of understanding and giving a meaning to the observed stimuli.
- **Rationality:** Selection of alternative suitable to goals.
- **Stimulus:** Information received by the sensory organs.
- **Total quality management:** A process of continuous improvement in quality in all organisational processes to give customer satisfaction.

4. UNDERSTANDING HUMAN BEHAVIOUR

This chapter enables you:

- *To make assumptions about human behaviour*
- *To understand the similarities and differences in human behaviour*
- *To appraise the differences in the ability of people*
- *To understand the differences in individual and situational variables*
- *To analyse the behaviour process with the help of the SOB process*
- *To understand the concept of rationality*
- *To appraise the limitations of human rationality*

The structure of the chapter is as follows:

- Introduction
- Assumptions of human behaviour
- Similarities and dissimilarities continuum
- Behaviour process: Stimulus – Organism – Behavior (SOB)
- Rationality in human behaviour
- Summary
- Key words

CHAPTER 4

Understanding Human Behaviour

INTRODUCTION

We learnt that organisational behaviour is an emerging discipline. It has recently emerged as a discipline, due to the pressures created by Liberalisation, Privatisation and Globalisation (LPG). When you meet a person for the first time, it is normal to make certain assumptions about the person from his or her external appearance. These assumptions affect your interaction with the person. After some interaction, your assumptions about the person are likely to change. In the same manner, in an organisational set up, assumptions about employee behaviour enable a manager to direct his subordinates in an appropriate manner, so that they do not become misfits. Two propositions are important to understand behaviour: (i) behaviour is shaped by the environment and (ii) it is caused by certain stimuli. The basic understanding of behaviour arises from understanding the similarities and dissimilarities between individuals. Individual differences arise out of a number of factors relating to abilities, motives, individual and situational variables. A proper understanding of these variables is necessary to direct a person's energies in the right channels. As has been mentioned in the previous chapter, behaviour is the result of a cause. A stimulus causes a person to function in a manner that ultimately produces a certain response. The Stimulus Organism Behaviour (SOB) model describes this phenomenon. Herbert Simon introduced the concept of rationality. However, individual behaviour is not always rational. This is because behaviour is a cognitive process. Knowledge of perfect information is not possible at all times and human satisfaction is not measurable. We will learn more about the human behaviour from the following discussions.

Case study 4.1: Human behaviour

One day Mr. Rao aged about 72 years, a professional Financial and Insurance Advisor entered our premises of the office. He intended meeting one of our colleagues, Mr. Rajan, who was about half his age. As he entered the premises, he observed Mr. Rajan is at a moderate communicating distance. Thus he slightly raised his voice and showed a hand signal to call him. He uttered "O! Mr. Rajan…O! Mr. Rajan". The latter noticed the verbal and sign cues and approached Mr. Rao, and the following conversation took place.

Rao: Hello sir, I have come to deliver your insurance policy.

Rajan: (with a slightly emotional tone) O! That is later, first you should learn manners of calling attention of a person.

Rao: (slightly astonished by the words) What is the matter?

Rajan: (with an elevated level of emotion) You have called me as Rajan by taking singular form. You should know that I am an educated person and in a respectable profession. As I belong to a lower caste, you are trying to exploit me by calling in a singular form.

Rao: Sorry sir, you might have not properly heard me. I have called you by the word 'Mr.' which is a respectable word in English language.

Rajan: (with emotion and anguish) We too know English, you need not teach me English. That means you only know English and we are all illiterates. You are again trying to belittle me of my poor English language.

(The situation slowly led to aggression and emotion based on caste discrimination. People started gathering and are trying to assess what the argument is about.)

Noticing the change in the situation Mr. Rao recovered first and immediately said in a little serious tone "Sorry Sir, kindly pardon me if I have said so. My intention is only to provide a service and not to quarrel with my clients." Having said this he withdrew from the situation.

The fact is that even if the elderly man called Rajan in a singular form (in fact he has not done) Mr. Rajan could have convinced himself respecting the old age and elderliness. Instead, he started displaying his emotion and ego for nothing. He himself belittled him by styling himself as belonging to a lower caste. It is a case of poor communication and consequent behaviour of human being. Such cases are very common in most of the organisations.

ASSUMPTIONS OF HUMAN BEHAVIOUR

Human beings are an important resource in any organisation. The effectiveness of any organisation depends on the efficient use of these resources. Knowledge of human behaviour leads to effective utilisation of a person's energies. However, human behaviour is complex and often cannot be predicted and controlled. Hence, understanding an individual's behaviour is necessary for managers to design strategies to direct their employees and benefit from their full potential.

There are two propositions for understanding human behaviour. They are:

1. Human behaviour is a function of the individual and the environment. Individual factors like biographical factors, skills, efficiency, experience, health, attitude, perceptions, learning, etc., influence the willingness to do the work. Similarly, micro and macro level environmental factors influence behaviour. At the micro level working conditions, reward systems, organisational policies, communication, control system, leadership and motivation, and interaction with peers, superiors, subordinates and groups influence behaviour. At the macro level technology, economy, society, ecology and ethical factors of organisational environment affect behaviour.

2. An individual's behaviour has a cause and effect relationship. Therefore to understand behaviour one has to understand the causes. According to this proposition, a stimulus is responsible for causing individual behaviour. While environmental factors influence behaviour, individual behaviour is spontaneous and cultural values influence it.

Both the propositions emphasise the person and the environment. Understanding individual behaviour requires certain assumptions about behaviour. They are:

(i) Behaviour is a function of enduring qualities of personality.

(ii) Behaviour is the result of psychological concepts like beliefs, attitudes and expectations.

(iii) Behaviour occurs as a result of certain outcomes driven by stimuli.

Apart from these assumptions, people develop assumptions about behaviour based on their own experience. Assumptions differ from one individual to another, but they allow one to understand, predict and control human behaviour. In the next section we learn more about behaviour with the help of a model known as the 'Similarities and Dissimilarities Continuum.'

SIMILARITIES AND DISSIMILARITIES CONTINUUM

The process of stimulus-organism-behaviour tells us that individuals respond differently to different stimuli. Therefore, a person's behaviour varies according to his personality. Performance is a function of individual differences and the influence of situational or environmental variables. The process of understanding individual behaviour is complex, because not all individuals are the same. Individual differences can also cause variations in abilities and motivation. Hence, knowledge of similarities and dissimilarities enable a manager to understand acceptable and unacceptable behaviour. Differences in individuals reflect over time and with other individuals. Individual differences are described below:

(A) Differences in ability

Ability is the power to carry out an act. It determines the ultimate performance of a person. The following factors lead to individual differences.

(i) ***Physiological, intellectual and personality factors:*** Individuals are different in physiological characteristics such as height, weight, stamina, color of skin and eyes, and muscle power. Intellectual factors like problem solving, understanding, determination, academic merit and thinking give rise to individual differences. Personality factors viz., perception, learning, attitudes, values, analysis of information, cognition, beliefs etc. also determine individual differences.

(ii) ***Skills and aptitudes:*** Individual differences in skill determine the ability to perform. It is a function of knowledge and experience. Similarly, aptitude determines the rate of learning. Differences in aptitude affect the ability to learn skills and apply them in jobs.

(iii) ***Knowledge:*** Academic processes and experience lead to accumulation of knowledge. Not all individuals possess the same amount of knowledge, even though they may be exposed to the same academic situation.

(iv) ***Experience:*** Experience is one's tendency to perform a particular job on the basis of learnt or observed traits. Individual differences in experience can cause variations in performance. However more experience does not necessarily ensure a better performance.

(B) Differences in motives

Motives of reward, achievement, esteem etc., influence performance. The need for achievement is the main determinant of performance. Motives can emerge from physiological needs, safety, social, esteem or self-actualization needs. People have diverse needs at different times and even at the same time different people have different needs.

(C) Differences in individual variables

Dissimilarities in individuals are due to the nervous system, glands, age, sex, educational levels, value systems, cultural background etc.

(D) Differences in situational variables

Situational variables leading to individual differences comprise the nature and type of the organisation, type of supervision, training provided, rewards, work groups, methods and techniques of work, work design, physical conditions of work environment and tools, maintenance etc.

Understanding individual differences is important as they affect organisational activities, managerial skills, strategies, leadership styles and motivational strategies.

BEHAVIOUR PROCESS – STIMULUS-ORGANISM-BEHAVIOUR (SOB)

We have seen that behaviour is caused by stimuli. A stimulus is an agent that directly influences the activity of any organism. It may be due to the environment or a situation that provides information (cognition) to a person, who reacts to the stimulus based on the interaction of a number of elements. Hence, behaviour is understood as an open dynamic system process. Figure 4.1 shows the SOB process.

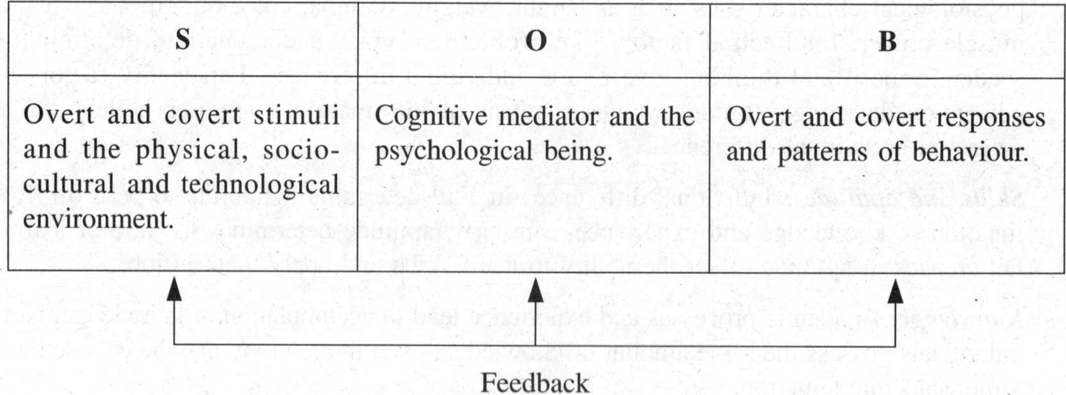

S	O	B
Overt and covert stimuli and the physical, socio-cultural and technological environment.	Cognitive mediator and the psychological being.	Overt and covert responses and patterns of behaviour.

Figure 4.1: SOB process

The behaviour process shown in the above figure reveals that a person receives a stimuli or information (S) through their sensory organs. It is considered as input for processing. Not all information is processed. The organism (O) i.e., the person processing the information is dynamic, and thus interacts with the socio-cultural environment. Hence, the stimuli is organised and understood through a perceptual process. Then it is evaluated in relation to established beliefs, values and attitudes of the human mind. The attitudes, beliefs and values are formed through the cognitive process. This process can take three functions. While understanding is known as perception, thinking, reasoning and problem solving are part of the core cognitive process. And selecting among alternatives is decision-making. Then the idea is transformed into action through a physical response, which is final output of stimulation. This is called behaviour. Sometimes, the action is examined by the individual to see whether it suits the external environment. If it does not the action is revised. This is called feedback.

Case study 4.2: Stimulus leading to change in behaviour

Mr. Shankar took charge as General Manager of Kaling Automotive Company Limited. He had earlier worked as a senior manager in a large company. He joined the company in the hope of a growth-oriented career. The administrative situation of the company at the time of his joining was not satisfactory. Employees were not adhering to the office timings. Customers were complaining about deliveries not being on time.

From the day he joined the company he worked tirelessly bringing about many administrative changes. He counseled employees so that they would strictly adhere to office timings and delivery schedules. He organised meetings of the heads of various sections wherein he emphasized the importance of time management. He introduced small rewards for employees who kept the best time, and arranged for their names to be displayed at the entrance of the office. On the other hand, names of latecomers were circulated among all the departments. It was extremely difficult for him to change the mindset of the employees. However, to his surprise the situation started to improve in a very short time, as the reward worked as a positive stimulus to change the behaviour of most of the employees.

RATIONALITY IN HUMAN BEHAVIOUR

Mr. Bhanu was in charge of disbursing the employees' salaries. He was good at his job, and did not need many instructions. He was able to follow his superior's orders very quickly. At times however, he could be arrogant. For example, once when the Head of Unit visited the Section, Mr. Bhanu did not even bother to greet him. Such behaviour amounts to insubordination and is taken as a serious aberration (not a preferred behaviour).

According to Herbert Simon, "rationality is the selection of preferred behavior alternatives in terms of values, whereby the consequences of behaviour can be evaluated". In other words, an individual action is said to be rational if the result of the action is very close to the realisation of objectives. According to Simon, a decision is considered organisationally rational, if it is oriented towards organisational goals. Rationality of a personal decision means that the consequences of behaviour enable a situation to give maximum satisfaction. Since an individual cannot be perfectly rational, Simon advocated the concept of bounded rationality or the theory of satisfying.

Understanding human behaviour and dealing with it presupposes predicting the degree of rationality of individual behaviour. Behaviour does not always match the demands of rationality. A number of factors, which limit rationality, are given below:

1. Behaviour is a function of the human mental process, which is difficult to visualise.
2. Individuals pursue conflicting objectives over a period of time.
3. The human mind has a limited capacity to understand and process information.
4. Environmental factors limit individual's actions.
5. Knowledge of perfect information is not possible.
6. Personal values, beliefs, perception, attitudes and learning differ from individual to individual.
7. Satisfaction is not measurable.

8. Individual goals are vague and dynamic over a period of time.
9. Commitment to behavioural actions is not universal.

Adopting appropriate strategies to deal with the behaviour depends on the degree of rationality one can expect in individual actions.

SUMMARY

This chapter enabled one to understand human behaviour. It is relevant to mention two assumptions about the human behaviour: (i) behaviour is a function of the environment and (ii) behaviour has a cause and effect relationship. Not all individuals are similar. Individuals are similar with respect to the physiological factors, race, religion, colour of the skin and eyes, food habits etc. Differences in physiological and intellectual ability, personality factors, skills and aptitudes, knowledge and experience, motives, individual variables and situational variables cause individuals to differ in their competency, performance, efficiency and the way they contribute to the effective functioning of an organisation. The SOB process shows that stimuli can be considered as anything that attracts the attention of the organism. Behaviour is a response to the stimuli. Rationality in behaviour is difficult, because behaviour is a mental process, and the human mind has limited ability to process information. The environment also exercises a profound influence on behaviour and satisfaction is not measurable.

Key words:

- **Behaviour:** Overt or covert response shown by an organism.
- **Rationality:** The selection of preferred behaviour alternatives in terms of values, whereby the consequences of behaviour are evaluated.
- **Stimuli:** Any information received from the sensory organs of the human body.

5. ORGANISATIONAL BEHAVIOUR MODELS

This chapter enables you:

- *To understand the importance of models in understanding behaviour*
- *To appraise the nature of models used in organisational behaviour*
- *To examine the various variables used in model building*
- *To understand the role of stimulus in behaviour*
- *To explain the significance of developing information in behaviour*
- *To analyse the role of environmental reinforcement in behaviour*
- *To understand the personality systems developed by Freud*

The structure of the chapter is as follows:

- Introduction
- Importance of models of organisational behaviour
- Nature of organisational behaviour models
- Model building in organisational behaviour
- SOBC model
- Cognitive model
- Reinforcement model
- Psychoanalytic model
- Summary
- Key words

CHAPTER 5

Organisational Behaviour Models

INTRODUCTION

To understand behaviour we have to develop a model of behaviour, which represents reality. This is the same as building a model, or drawing a plan, when you want to construct a house.

Within an organisation, a manager has to understand that human behaviour is complex, and act accordingly. Developing models help him to do so. Models help in predicting the reactions of employees in different situations. It is necessary to prepare descriptive, predictive and prescriptive models. These models show that a number of dependent and independent variables influence the behaviour of a person. Various useful models of organisational behaviour are discussed in this chapter.

The SOBC model shows that behaviour is a consequence of stimuli. We know that the human mind continuously receives, stores and interprets information called 'Cognition'. This cognitive function of the brain is relevant to the process of decision-making. For example, you must have observed that you respond positively if the result of an action is favourable. Have you ever thought why you felt tension. Tension results from unconscious mental activity. Conscious behaviour results when we are aware of our actions and thought processes. The psychoanalytical model analyses the cause of human behaviour as an interaction of id, ego and super ego. So organisational behaviour models help to develop strategies to deal with behaviour problems in organisations.

IMPORTANCE OF MODELS OF ORGANISATIONAL BEHAVIOUR

Organisational Behaviour (OB) is an emerging discipline. The inexact nature of the subject can be understood by developing models and quantifying the variables that influence behaviour. Models of organisational behaviour are important for the following reasons:

(i) They help in understanding and evaluating complex human behaviour. Thus, human behaviour is vital in designing models.

(ii) Models of OB make assumptions about people and their behaviour. They also incorporate interpretations of events to understand behaviour of people in organisations.

(iii) Models showing cause and effect relationships are used by managers in predicting the effects on behaviour.

(iv) Models demonstrate the effects of certain variables on behaviour. Hence, they are useful in understanding and rectifying behaviour before it influences the organisational performance in a negative manner.

(v) Models of organisational behaviour include all variables that influence the performance. Therefore, they determine the climate of organisations within which managers are required to operate for increasing efficiency.

In spite of their usefulness, models should not be applied indiscriminately. Models of OB should be used as a guide by managers in understanding organisations and interaction processes. However, they do not provide absolute solutions. Every situation needs careful analysis and understanding before a model is developed and applied.

NATURE OF ORGANISATIONAL BEHAVIOUR MODELS

Organisational behaviour models can be classified as:

i. Descriptive
ii. Predictive
iii. Prescriptive

Descriptive models help to describe the behaviour of variables. They do not provide conclusions regarding the cause and effect in relationships. Hence, the utility of the model is limited.

Predictive models show the cause and effect in relationships with the help of mathematical and statistical concepts. Continuous observation and laboratory experiment enable the development of predictive models. However, predictive models are few because of the difficulty in measuring the variables that cause behaviour.

The descriptive and predictive models become the basis for the development of prescriptive models. They assume an accurate knowledge of the situation and the cause effect relationship. Hence, these models suggest a right course of action in a given situation. As organisational behaviour is not an exact science, prescriptive models are rare.

In spite of certain limitations in the nature of OB models, managers can use these models to solve many organisational problems, however they must be used with caution.

MODEL BUILDING IN ORGANISATIONAL BEHAVIOUR

A model is an abstraction of reality, a simplified representation of some real world phenomenon. It consists of a set of variables influencing another set of variables in a given environment. The sets of variables that influence other variables are independent variables. Dependent variables are influenced by independent variables. The impact within a given environment is shown with the help of OB models that are developed using these variables.

Independent Variables

Three independent variables are responsible for influencing dependent variables. They are:

(i) **Individual level variables:** Individual variables like sex, educational levels, marital status, age etc., and personality variables like values, attitudes, and abilities influence the behaviour of employees at work. Other variables like perception, decision-making ability, learning process and motivation also affect the behaviour and performance. These variables are less amenable for change in a short period.

(ii) **Group level variables:** Group characteristics like norms, communication, decision making, leadership attitudes, power and politics, cohesiveness and conflict shape individual behaviour. They significantly influence the work performance and organisational performance.

(iii) **Organisational variables:** Organisational variables comprise structure of organisation, rules, regulations, policies, strategies, practices, planning and control systems, decision-making, organisational climate and organisational culture. All these variables are included in model building to show their impact on dependent variables.

Dependent Variables

Dependent variables are output variables. The impact of independent variables produces a particular outcome. The following variables are widely accepted as dependent variables.

(i) **Productivity:** Productivity is obtaining the highest value at the lowest cost. It reflects efficiency and effectiveness. Measures of efficiency like ROI, profit, output and realisation of goals are dependent variables. A host of factors influence the productivity of an organisation. However, human contribution has the most significant influence on productivity.

(ii) **Absenteeism and employee turnover:** Absenteeism is not reporting for work when one is supposed to be present. The voluntary leaving of personnel from an organisation is referred to as employee or labour turnover. The positive aspect of absenteeism is that it helps to relieve the stress and strain of employees. However, frequent absenteeism leads to interruption of work, under-utilisation of production facilities, poor utilisation of the work force, reduced productivity, poor income and loss of goodwill of the company. These factors have considerable influence on the performance of the organisation. Individual, group and organisational level variables influence absenteeism.

Turnover gives an opportunity to replace employees with others having higher skills, but it impairs efficiency as the organisation loses experienced employees. This adversely affects decision-making and organisational performance. The climate and culture of an organisation influence turnover and absenteeism.

(iii) **Job satisfaction:** An employee has job satisfaction if his rewards, financial or otherwise, are commensurate to the effort put in. Job satisfaction results in increased productivity. It is a psychological variable, and develops an employee's attitude towards his or her work. Job dissatisfaction leads to poor productivity, frequent absenteeism, and loss of interest in the job, procrastination and even leaving the organisation.

An examination of the variables described above reveals that all the independent variables influence these variables.

S-O-B-C MODEL

The concept of social learning is the basis for the development of the Stimulus-Organism-Behaviour-Consequence (SOBC) model. The model uses the interactive nature of the environment, intra-personal cognition and other variables to explain human behaviour in organisations. Figure 5.1 shows the model.

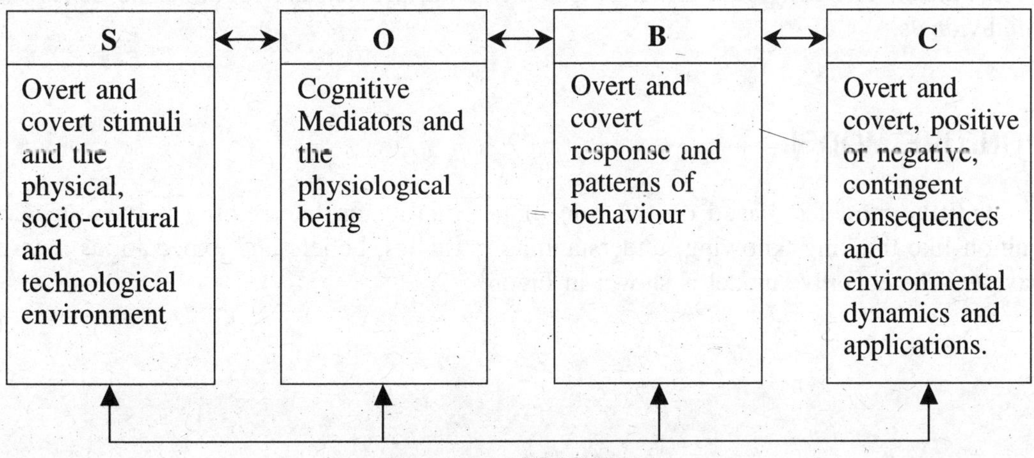

Figure 5.1: SOBC Model

Concepts of the SOBC Model

(i) **Stimulus:** Stimulus is information received by the sensory organs, which produces an action or reaction. It can also be understood as a physical or material, observable and measurable act influencing behaviour. It is made up of cues. Overt cues are external and observable. Covert cues are internal and non-observable. The internal and external environments of an organisation, which consist of technological and socio-cultural factors provide important stimuli causing behavioural response.

(ii) **Organism:** The organism is the physical being or individual. Stimuli influence physical factors. They alter psychological or cognitive structure. The response occurs as a result of interaction between the stimulus and the structure of cognition.

(iii) **Behaviour:** Behaviour is the way in which an individual reacts to a stimulus. Individuals show a pattern of behaviour in response to certain stimuli. Hence, these patterns help in understanding their behaviour. For example, a worker works overtime for the sake of monetary rewards. Hence, monetary rewards determine the pattern of his behaviour.

(iv) **Consequences:** Consequence is the result of behaviour. Structure and environmental stimuli lead to behaviour, which determine the consequence. While a positive consequence is associated with reinforcements, a negative consequence brings about a change in behaviour.

Utility of the Model

a. **Direction of human behaviour:** The SOBC model is a simple and useful model. It identifies the important variables and depicts the relationships that direct human behaviour in the accomplishment of goals.

b. **Regulation of behaviour:** It helps to understand, predict and regulate the behaviour of individuals.

COGNITIVE MODEL

The cognitive model is based on the role of personality in determining behaviour. Covert cognition like thinking, knowing, understanding, attitudes, beliefs and expectations determine behaviour. The cognitive model is shown in Figure 5.2.

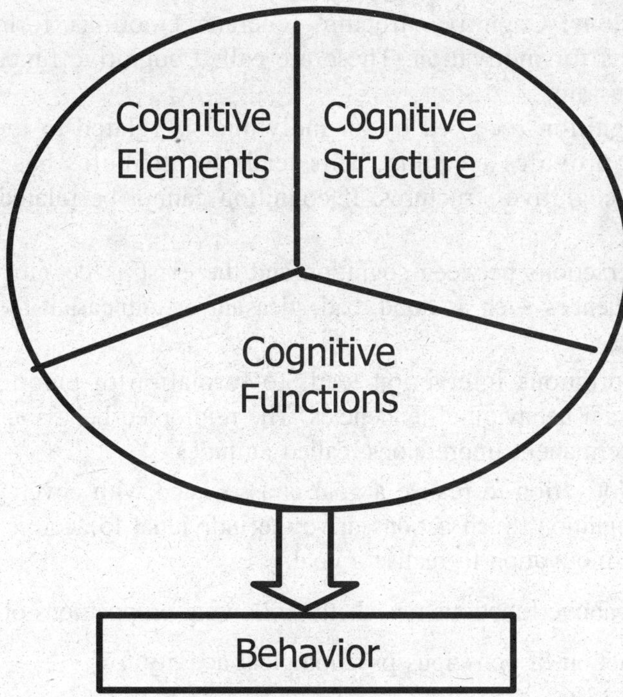

Figure 5.2: Cognitive Model

Concepts of the Cognitive Model

(i) **Cognitive elements:** Cognition is the process of obtaining knowledge through thought, experience, and the senses. An individual organises his behaviour and tries to internalise his experiences. Thus, the response of an individual to stimuli is a cognitive element. These elements when matched with the individual's cognitive structure, lead to a response.

(ii) **Cognitive structure:** A series of experiences lead to the development of cognitive structure. Reinforced cognition leads to the formation of impressions. Cognitive structure is developed based on the characteristics of stimuli and the experiences of individuals.

Cognitive structure has the following characteristics:

1. *Differentiation:* Cognitive structure is formed by a series of different experiences. This is known as differentiation.
2. *Consonance:* The degree of forming impressions is called consonance. If cognition is uniform, it leads to consonance and the formation of impressions.
3. *Interconnectedness:* If cognition is uniform, it is formed into a system. Therefore, this process forms a number of different cognitive systems. Cognitive systems are mostly interrelated. The more they are interrelated, the easier it is for a person to formulate an ideology. Otherwise, it forms compartmentalised systems, which are often conflicting.

(iii) **Cognitive functions:** Cognitive structure generates emotions, formulates attitudes and provides the basis for motivation. These are called cognitive functions. The important cognitive functions are:

1. *Meaning:* Cognition received by an individual is related to the existing cognitive structure and provides meaning. This leads to attributes based on the degree of interaction of cognitive structures. If cognition cannot be related, it is considered as meaningless.
2. *Emotions:* Interactions between cognition and the existing cognitive structure results in certain consequences such as good, bad, pleasant or unpleasant feelings etc., which are called emotions.
3. *Attitudes:* Continuous interaction leads to formation of emotions, which result in generating certain behavioural tendencies. The reinforced behavioural tendencies lead to formation of permanent impressions, called attitudes.
4. *Motivation:* Motivation to realise a goal is associated with covert actions generated by inconsistent cognition. Such actions drive the individual to acquire consistent cognition, thus providing motivation to realise a goal.

An examination of the above functions reveals the following propositions of the cognitive model:

- Behaviour is a function of conscious psychological activity.
- Behaviour is organised and it comprises physical, mental and emotional elements.
- An individual's response can be overt or covert behaviour.
- Cognition is organised and tries to be consistent with the existing cognitive structure.
- Cognition is reorganised with time.

Utility of the Model

a. **Individual behaviour:** Individual behaviour and performance are influenced by expectations, which are in turn developed by cognition.

b. **Decision making:** In the process of decision making, managers use additional information, if the original information does not match with his cognitive structure. Hence, how information is processed to take a correct decision depends on one's cognitive structure.

c. **Perception:** An individual's perception influences his behaviour and performance at work, which are results of cognitive consistency.

d. **Group formation:** Individuals are attracted and associated to form a cohesive group based on similarities. Such similarities are produced by cognition.

REINFORCEMENT MODEL

The Classical Conditioning concept advocated by Ivan Pavlov and the Law of Effect propounded by Edward Thorndike became the basis for this model. The model emphasises that the environment determines an individual's behaviour. Accordingly, a stimulus leads to a response and an outcome follows it. The outcome in turn may influence the response to the stimuli in other situations.

Concepts of the Reinforcement Model

(i) **Stimulus:** Stimulus is a physical or material, observable and measurable act that causes changes in the behaviour of an individual.

(ii) **Response:** An observable change in the behaviour of an individual, due to a stimulus is called a response.

(iii) **Reinforcer:** A reinforcer is the outcome of a response. While a positive reinforcer strengthens the relationship between the response and the stimulus, a negative reinforcer dilutes it. A positive reinforcer ensures a similar response to a particular stimulus; on the other hand negative reinforcer when removed causes the same behaviour associated with the stimulus. For example admiration, gratitude etc., are positive reinforcers. Distastefulness, unpleasantness are examples of negative reinforcement. A negative reinforcer leads to avoidance behaviour. For instance, if an individual is injured by going close to a working machine, then the injury is a negative reinforcer, which regulates the behaviour of all workers by inducing them to observe safety measures.

(iv) **Extinction:** When a response elicits no result, it is abandoned. It is believed that the response is ineffective in the realisation of the goal. For example, if high quality production goes unrecognised, the worker relinquishes the act of producing quality.

(v) **Punishment:** This is withholding a reward or applying corrective actions to generate a response. For example stopping payment punishes an absentee. He tries to be regular if he regards it as punishment.

The reinforcement model is shown in Figure 5.3.

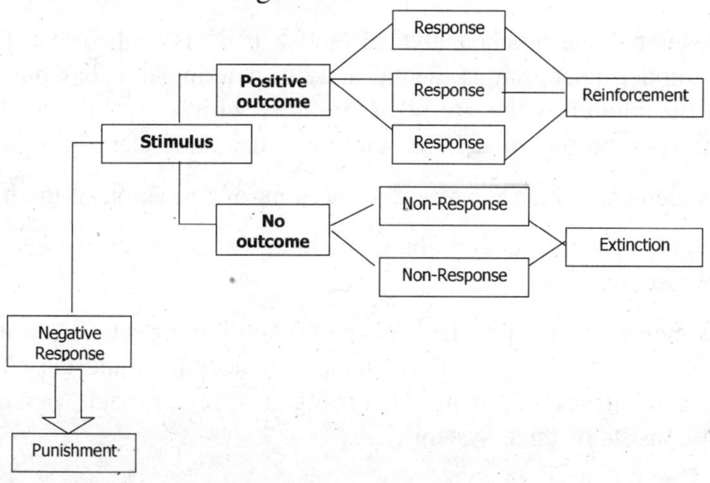

Figure 5.3: Reinforcement Model

An examination of the above concepts of the reinforcement model reveals the following:

a. Environment is the initial stimuli. It shapes behaviour.
b. Interaction with the environment leads to a response.
c. Stimulus produces a response which again leads to outcome i.e. behaviour.
d. Outcome influences the relationship between stimuli and responses, hence reinforces future behaviour.
e. Both positive and negative reinforcers produce a certain outcome.

Utility of the Model

i. **Productive behaviour:** As a reinforced response results in repetitive actions, managers can design the reward system to produce the desired output. This is possible only when a manager tries to understand the concept of reinforcement in the subordinates.

ii. **Learning:** It is a function of the reinforcement concept. Training and development programmes are designed to provide an opportunity to learn skills that produce rewards. The model helps a manager to understand the cognitive structure of the employees and design suitable training and development programmes to suit their requirements.

iii. **Conflict:** Reinforced experience leads to the development of norms in the groups. Groups compel members to adhere to group norms. In this process, conflicts arise, which are difficult to resolve. This is because group norms bring pressure to bear, and act as a punishment. Understanding the reinforcement model enables a manager to reinforce such experiences that do not lead to conflicts among subordinates.

PSYCHOANALYTICAL MODEL

Sigmund Freud developed the psychoanalytical model. It is also called the 'Theory of Tension'. According to this model, unconscious mental activity determines behaviour. The methodology used to develop the model is the study of dreams, which are observed through clinical investigations. According to this model, consciousness has three elements. They are:

i. Preconscious element, which is present at the time of formation of the human brain.

ii. Conscious element, which is composed of thoughts, beliefs, feelings and desires, learnt through introspection.

iii. Unconscious element, which is the dormant cognitive aspect. The principle of reasoned reality guides the consciousness. The principle of hedonism and the principle of pleasure rule the unconsciousness element. According to this approach, personality determines behaviour. It consists of three systems.

Concepts of the Psychoanalytic Model

Certain systems of human mental activity known as the id, the ego, the super ego and the libido are described below.

1. **The id:** Id is the totality of instincts oriented towards increasing pleasure, avoiding pain and striving for immediate satisfaction of desires. It is the foundation for development of personality characteristics. The characteristics of id are given below:
   i. Id is a basic and original psychological system. It is present even at the time of birth. It is inherited from the parents.
   ii. The principle of greed and pleasures governs the actions of id, which aims to reduce tensions. Id cannot bear stress caused by an uncomfortable atmosphere, so it releases tensions by primary forces or reflex actions.
   iii. It is the storehouse of all instincts, wishes and desires. It demands immediate gratification of desires.
   iv. Id is irrational, demanding, unsatisfied, destructive and childish.
   v. It is uninfluenced by reality, ethics, morals, reason or logic.
   vi. It supplies psychic energy for the operation of personality systems.

   Organisation of personality systems are shown in Figure 5.4.

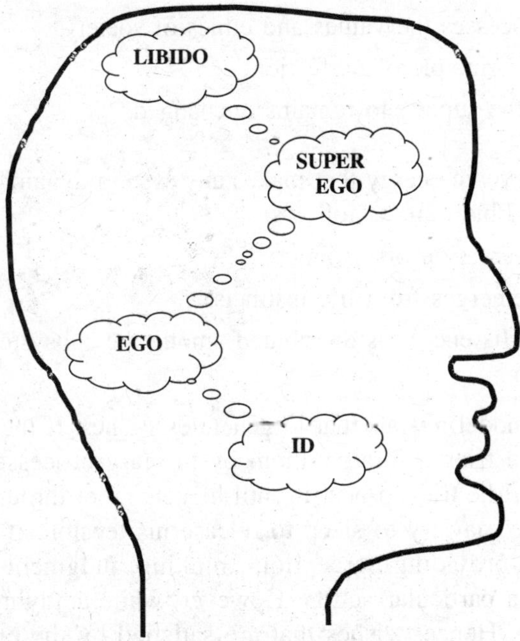

Figure 5.4: Psychoanalytic model

2. **The ego:** The ego is the executive part of the personality. It selects the features of the environment and stores them. It is rational and logical. It is the conscious mediator between realities of the world and the id's demands. The salient features of the ego are:
   i. Ego is a conscious, organised, executive subsystem.
   ii. Ego translates the wishes of the id into activity by matching them to the outside environment.
   iii. It is developed in individuals, when they learn to understand reality and unreality. It works on the reality principle. It is the rational master of the id.
   iv. It regulates and integrates inner motives and conflicting demands and thus facilitates judgment to learn.
   v. It helps to reduce tensions caused by the id.
   vi. The ego does not contain any energy but can turn the energy of the id against itself to keep it under control.
3. **The super ego:** The super ego is a moralistic segment of human personality consisting of the noblest thoughts, ideals and feelings, which are developed through absorption of cultural values and attitudes. The super ego has the following characteristics:
   i. Super ego is the moral arm of personality. It judges whether the actions of the ego are right or wrong.
   ii. It develops through the interaction of the ego and the functioning of society.
   iii. The super ego processes the values and ethics of society.
   iv. It operates on the principle of perfection.
   v. Once developed, the super ego remains unchanged.
4. **The libido:** This is psychic energy that makes any system dynamic and causes it to function. The characteristics of libido are as follows:
   i. Libido is self-preservation of instincts.
   ii. Energy of libido emerges from life instincts.
   iii. It is vital energy. Its energy is distributed among the subsystems of personality viz., id, ego and super ego.

An understanding of the model reveals that id generates wishes. If these wishes are not gratified it leads to tension. The id tries to gratify them by primary processes and reflex actions. For example, if a person is hurt he tries to bear it until he gets relief through some form or the other. If he fails to get relief, he may try to sleep to release his tension. If the primary process fails, energy flows to the ego, providing perception, thinking, judgment and memory, so that the individual can decide on a particular action. However, while applying a secondary process the super ego acts as a judge. Hence, wishes that are satisfied by the ego are consistent with the values established by the super ego. If the ego is able to integrate the actions of the id and the super ego an individual gets satisfaction. Otherwise, he becomes frustrated as the super ego tries to punish the ego.

Utility of the Model

i. **Creativity:** Creativity is an unconscious element. Creativity is developed under permissiveness. Defensiveness and fear kill creativity. In every organisation, creativity is required to solve problems in contingency situations. An understanding of the model helps a manager design strategies of developing convergent and divergent thinking in their subordinates. This develops creativity in them.

ii. **Job satisfaction:** Satisfaction results from balancing work values and individual goals. Dissatisfaction occurs when organisational culture and ethics are in opposition to the values of individuals. Dissatisfaction is expressed in the form of sickness, anxiety, conflict, absenteeism, tardiness, alcoholism, etc. Thus, the model suggests the development of congruent thinking that leads to job satisfaction.

iii. **Group development:** Groups are developed to form certain values and protect individual values. Group cohesiveness is developed when the values of the super ego are consistent with the norms of the group. Therefore, the psychoanalytic model is useful in developing certain value systems that enable development of productive work groups.

iv. **Leadership:** The actions of the id guide a manager in the process of how he uses authority and power. Superiors use authority to satisfy their emotional needs. Allowing participation of subordinates requires a manager to develop certain human related beliefs and values. The development of values is a function of the development of the ego. Hence, whether a leader uses authority or allows participation is reflected in the values developed by his ego and super ego.

Thus, this model provides a basis for understanding the energy and dynamics of individuals' interaction.

An examination of organisational behaviour models reveals that they are useful in depicting the dynamics of interaction among individuals, groups and structure. They show how organisational structure and relationships are to be integrated. They also guide practicing managers regarding strategies of leadership and work motivation that lead to a more committed behaviour towards realisation of goals. At the same time it is important to understand that although these models are not exact prescriptions to solve organisational behaviour problems, they help to develop and analyse strategies to deal with the situation. Hence, situation and contingent variables are more useful than a particular model.

SUMMARY

This chapter enables one to understand the importance of model building in OB. A model is an abstraction of reality. It consists of dependent and independent variables and the process of influence. Organisational behaviour models help in understanding the cause and effect relationship in the human behaviour. They also help us to predict individual behaviour in organisations. The models that describe behaviour are known as descriptive models. Predictive models show the cause and effect relationship, and thus help in predicting behaviour. Prescriptive models suggest certain course of action suitable for a given situation.

Independent variables used in the models are individual level, group level and organisational variables. Productivity, absenteeism, turnover, and job satisfaction are some of the dependent variables. The behaviour process influences these variables. We have also learnt about certain useful models of OB. They are SOBC model, cognitive model, reinforcement model and psychoanalytical model. The SOBC model shows that information received by the sensory organs produces reactions in individuals. These reactions are called behaviour. Behaviour leads to consequences. In the cognitive model, we have learnt that factors like thinking, knowing, and understanding determine behaviour. An individual receives cognition, (information) matches it with the already established cognitive structure and generates emotions, attitudes, motivation etc. The model is significant for decision making and motivating subordinates.

The classical conditioning concept became the basis for the development of the reinforcement model. Under this model, reinforced consequences direct the actions of individuals. If the consequences are reinforced, an individual is likely to behave in certain predicted ways. The model helps in determining learning behaviour and it is used in conflict resolution. Sigmund Freud developed the psychoanalytical model to understand personality and behaviour. Behaviour is the function of mental activity. Certain systems of human mental activity known as id, ego and superego are responsible for producing certain behavioral actions. The model is extensively used in understanding creativity, leadership and job satisfaction.

Key words

- **Behaviour:** The way individuals act or react to certain stimulus in different situations.
- **Classical conditioning:** A situation in which an individual shows an abnormal response to a stimulus.
- **Cognition:** Cognition is information helpful in organising behaviour.
- **Emotion:** A psychological feeling that emerges from contextual stimuli.
- **Law of effect:** If several stimuli are presented simultaneously, the stimulus leading to a positive reinforcement is likely to reoccur. This reoccurrence is called the law of effect.
- **Motivation:** An abstract force that drives individual actions and behaviour.
- **Perception:** To understand a situation and draw meaning from it.
- **Perfection principle:** Perfection occurs when behaviour conforms to the ego.
- **Principle of reasoned reality:** Behaviour based on external reality.
- **Stimulus:** Stimulus is any physical or material, observable and measurable act that causes behaviour.

6. PERSONALITY

This chapter enables you:

- *To define personality*
- *To understand the salient features of personality*
- *To appraise the determinants of personality*
- *To understand the biological impact on personality*
- *To examine the influence of family factors that determine personality*
- *To appraise the environmental factors of personality*
- *To identify situational factors of personality*
- *To examine the implications of personality on organisational behaviour*

The structure of the chapter is as follows:

- Introduction
- Definition of personality
- Characteristics of personality
- Determinants of personality
- Attributes of personality that influence organisational behaviour
- Summary
- Key words

CHAPTER 6

Personality

INTRODUCTION

An organisation is made up of material, physical, financial and human resources. Human resources are a vital factor, as all the resources have no utility without the human element. However, human beings are complex and difficult to understand, and the purpose of this chapter is to make you understand them better. We have learnt that although people are similar in certain respects, there are a number of dissimilarities observed in the individuals. The concepts of personality, such as perception, attitudes, learning etc., help us to understand human beings in organisations. This chapter explains the concepts of personality in detail. The personality of a person includes both their physical appearance and inner feelings, and the reactions associated with them. The former are characterised by facial features, skin colour, height, muscle composition etc. In organisations, understanding personality is important for managers. For example, even talking to an aggressive person is difficult and uncomfortable, whereas a cheerful and calm personality attracts us and makes us feel comfortable. Without understanding the nature of employees, it is difficult to know them. Personality is both a qualitative concept and dynamic. Therefore, it is a complex phenomenon. This is because a number of factors determine the personality of an individual. Certainly, biological factors determine personality, but one cannot overlook the influence of situational factors. Personality develops over a period, and in certain stages. There are a number of theories that explain personality. Allport and Cattel have developed the trait theories. These theories distinguish personality based on unique traits possessed by individuals. Sigmund Freud, Sheldon, and Carl Jung have developed psychoanalytical theories. They considered the physical characteristics of an individual. Self-theories and social learning theories emphasise the influence of social and environmental factors in determining and understanding personality.

Case Study 6.1: Positive Vs Obsessive

Signor Software Private Limited is a company that provides computer software solutions. The CEO of the company is experienced in software technology. He spent some time in USA with the parent company. The company got an excellent opportunity to take up work for the government. Since the CEO respected his staff's ideas, he called a meeting to gauge their opinion. The Technical Manager, Mr. Ram, felt very strongly that the company might not be in a position to take up the work, as there could be hurdles in the form of political and bureaucratic forces, and other inexplicable formalities. However, the CEO was of the opinion that they should try to obtain more information about the contract. If the Technical Manager's views were confirmed, they could abandon the effort, otherwise they would proceed with the project. From the above it is clear that the CEO has a positive opinion and looks at things optimistically, whereas the Technical Manager is pessimistic and discouraging of the effort. It seems he has preconceived notions. Obviously, he is less likely to succeed in a competitive environment that requires risk taking.

DEFINITION OF PERSONALITY

Human beings are the most important factor in an organisation as they provide life to other resources. It is with the human effort that other resources are used to accomplish goals and objectives. If properly directed, human energy makes all the difference in organisations. Personality determines human energy, and individual actions and reactions are the index to understand one's personality. Thus, it becomes imperative to study individual behaviour and personality. A study of personality and its determinants provides an opportunity to understand employee behaviour in organisations. This enables managers to direct their energy and motivation in a proper manner.

From earlier chapters, we have already learnt that understanding human personality is vital to the study and analysis of organisational behaviour. Individuals differ in their manner of responding to the organisational environment. This is because of differences in personality. Personality includes both the external appearance and the inner psychology of an individual, and hence is the study of the characteristic traits of an individual, their interrelationship and the way in which a person responds and adjusts to other people and situations.

The term personality is derived from the Latin word *'personnare'*, which means *'to speak through'*. It is used to know the internal and external aspects of an individual. Accordingly, personality is understood as an act of influencing others through external appearance. Very often you feel attracted to a person because of their good looks, this is because of the external traits of the person. Mere external appearance does not make the whole personality. One has to understand the invisible traits and observe behaviour over a period to know the real personality of an individual. It is not easy to give a single definition of personality. The following definitions help to clarify the understanding of the term.

Personality may be defined in terms of organised behaviour as a *'predisposition to react to a given situation in a particular manner'*.

According to **Gordon Allport,** personality is *'the dynamic organisation within the individual of those psychophysical systems that determine his unique adjustments to his environment'*.

Kolasa defined personality as a *'broad, amorphous designation relating to fundamental approaches of persons to others and themselves. It is the study of the characteristic traits of an individual, relationships between these traits, and the way in which a person adjusts to other people and situations'*.

Glueck has defined personality as *'a pattern of stable states and characteristics of a person that influences his or her behaviour toward goal achievement. Each person has unique ways of protecting these states'*.

Floyd Ruch has defined personality as *'how a person affects others, how he understands and views himself, and his pattern of inner and outer measurable traits'*.

Personality *'is the sum total of ways in which an individual reacts and interacts with others'* – **Stephen Robbins**.

Personality *'is the combination of psychological characteristics or variables one uses to classify someone'* – **Szilagyi and Wallace**.

CHARACTERISTICS OF PERSONALITY

The definitions above reveal that personality has the following characteristics.

1. Personality refers to the psychological qualities of an individual.
2. It is unique. So two individuals differ in terms of their personality.
3. Personality is the manner of adjustment of an individual to the members of the group.
4. It is a qualitative aspect, but there are certain techniques to quantify it indirectly.
5. Personality is dynamic. It changes with the time and situation.
6. It consists of both physical and psychological systems.
7. Personality is a system. It has input, processing and output mechanisms.
8. Personality influences goal achievement and performance of an individual.

After having understood the concept of personality, we will learn about the determinants of personality.

DETERMINANTS OF PERSONALITY

We have understood that human personality is an intangible concept and it is complex. It is related to the cognitive and psychological process. Understanding personality is difficult, but not impossible. Personality depends on a number of factors, and there are various views about these factors. It is believed that a person is born with certain physical and mental qualities and that the environment in which he is brought up in shapes his personality. However, there is no unanimous agreement on what determines personality, and the determinants of personality can be categorised in several ways. Scoot and Mitchell have based their classification on heredity, group and cultural factors. Both physiological and psychological factors play an important role in determining personality. These factors are interrelated and independent. The major determinants of the personality of an individual are described under four broad headings: biological factors, family factors, environmental factors and situational factors.

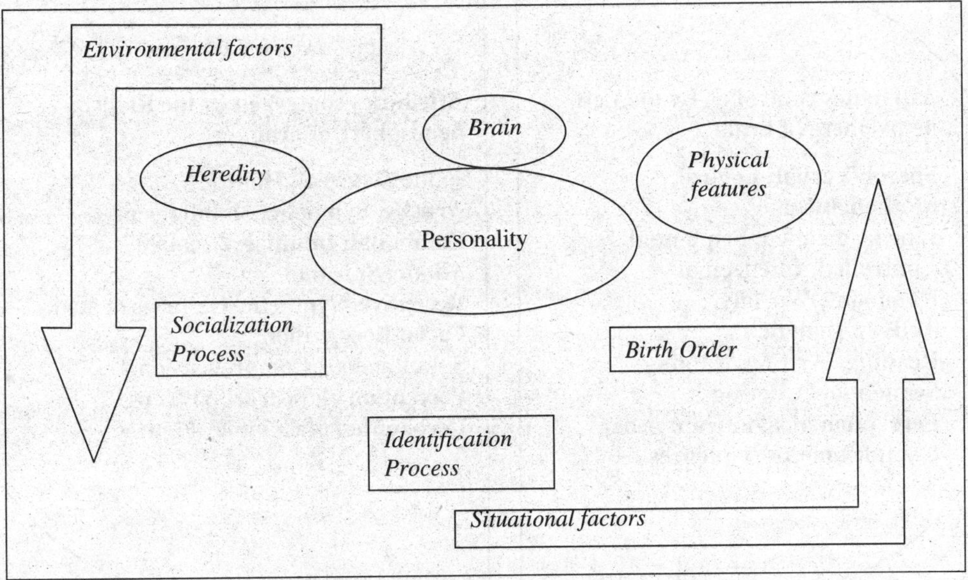

Figure 6.1: Factors influencing personality

Biological Factors

Biological factors are related to the physiological aspects of the human body. Three factors: heredity, brain and physical stature are considered as relevant. They are explained below:

(i) **Heredity:** Heredity refers to those factors that were determined at conception. It is a mechanism by which certain qualities are transmitted by parents to the next generation. Physical stature, facial attractiveness, gender, colour of skin, hair and eyes, temperament, muscle composition, sensitivity, skills and abilities, intelligence, energy level and biological rhythm are some of the features that are generally considered to be either completely or

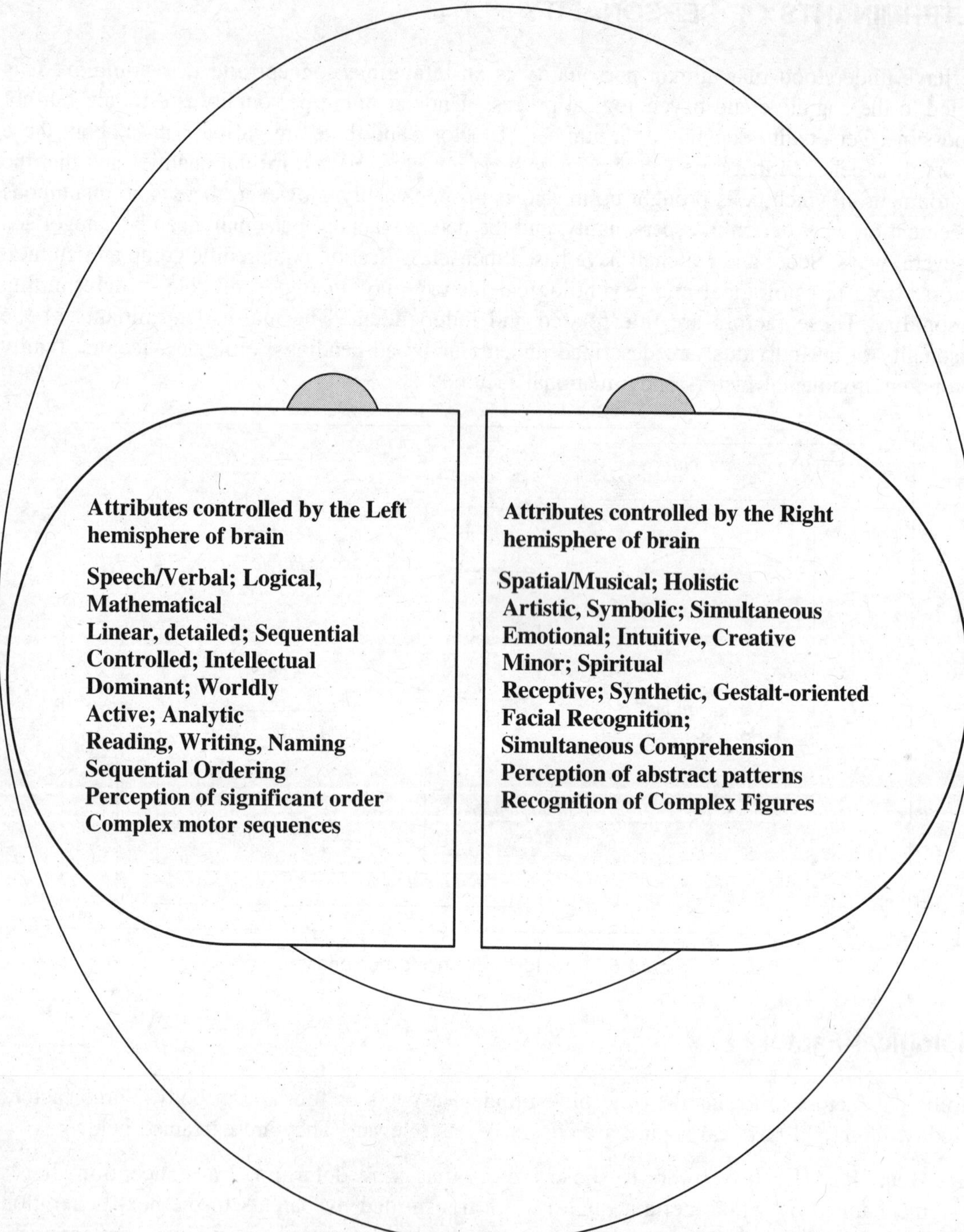

Figure 6.2: Split-Brain Psychology-personality traits controlled by left and right side of brain

substantially influenced by parents. There is no conclusive evidence to state the degree of influence of heredity. Genetic engineering experts are of the view that personality is largely affected by heredity. According to them, the basic genes are transmitted by the parents, leading the child to acquire certain physical and mental characteristics. Research in Genetic Engineering also suggests that heredity determines the emotional states and thus shapes personality. Nevertheless, there is no conclusive evidence that personality is completely determined by single factor 'heredity'.

(ii) Brain: Another biological factor, which plays an important role in shaping personality, is the structure and composition of the brain. There are few empirical findings to show that the brain influences personality. Certain techniques like Split Brain Psychology (SBP) (see Figure 6.2), Electrical Stimulation of Brain (ESB) and Bio Feedback Training (BFT) are used to understand the role of the brain in determining personality. For instance, Split Brain Psychology identified certain features associated with the brain. Though there is no conclusive proof relating to the findings, they help in understanding some aspects of personality.

(iii) Physical Features: Both physical features and the rate of maturation influence personality. The rate of maturity relates to a person's physical stature. The aspects of an individual's external appearance, like height, skin colour, facial features, and muscle strength have a tremendous effect on personality. For example, a person having powerful muscles is likely to be more dominant.

In the words of **Mussen,** *a child's physical characteristics may be related to his approach to the social environment, to the expectancies of others, and to their reactions to him.*

These, in turn may have an impact on personality development. Similarly, the rate of maturation also affects personality because persons of varying maturity react differently to different physical and social situations and activities.

Family Factors

Family factors are also important in determining the personality of an individual. Three factors: the socialisation process, identification process and birth order influence personality. They are presented below.

(i) Socialisation process: Socialisation is the process by which a child learns behaviour from the wide range of customary and acceptable behaviour patterns of his family and social groups. Members of the family compel the infant to conform to certain acceptable behaviour. Initially a child acquires knowledge of acceptable and unacceptable behaviour emulating from its parents. Thus, a person's socialisation starts from interaction with family members, and later on from socialisation with a number of social groups like school and college groups, peer groups and other groups of which the person becomes a member.

(ii) Identification process: Shaping of personality starts from the time the identification process commences. The identification process occurs when a person tries to identify himself with some person in the family, whom he feels is ideal. Normally a child tries to behave like his father or mother. The identification process can be looked at from three different perspectives. First, identification can be understood as the similarity of behaviour between a child and the model. Secondly, identification can be looked at as the child's motives or desire to be like the model. Thirdly, it can be viewed as the process through which the child actually emulates the characteristics of the model.

(iii) **Birth order:** Birth order is another significant variable influencing the personality of an individual. For instance first-born boys are likely to be more dependent, more rational, ambitious, hardworking, cooperative, more prone to guilt, anxiety and are less aggressive. Similarly, first-born girls are likely to be more responsible and sensitive to the family prestige. The last-born is likely to be more risk taking, aggressive, less fearful and more likely to break family norms.

Environmental Factors

Environment factors are those factors, which exist in and around the individual. They are society and cultural factors.

Thompson and **Houton** described culture as '*the complex of beliefs, values and techniques for dealing with the environment that are shared among contemporaries and transmitted by one generation to the next*'.

Culture determines human decision-making, attitudes, independence or dependence, sobriety, aggression, competition, co-operation and shyness. There are two vital aspects of culture. Firstly, conformity by the individual, and secondly, acceptance by the larger group. The culture in which a person has been brought up determines the personality of an individual to a significant extent. A person's learning is a function of culture. Culture establishes norms, values and attitudes, which are enforced by different social groups. Individuals are compelled to behave in conformity to the culture established by society. Thus, culture and society exert considerable influence in shaping the personality of an individual. In spite of the importance of the culture on personality, linear relationship between personality and culture has not yet been established.

Situational Factors

In recent times, the influence of situational factors on personality has been increasingly recognised. Generally, an individual's personality is stable and consistent; however, it changes in different situations. The SOB model considers the situation as a major determinant of behaviour.

A study conducted by **Milgram** suggested that *the actions of an individual are determined by the situation.* He stated that *the situation exerts an important influence on the individual.* It exercises constraint and may provide the necessary impetus. For example, in a situation of appraisal and motivation, subordinates develop a positive personality and perceive the organisation as promising and rewarding. However, under an authoritarian culture, they feel fear and discomfort. Understanding personality is very important for organisational behaviour.

It must be understood that no single factor determines personality. A host of factors exert an influence in shaping the personality of an individual. Therefore, one has to understand personality as a holistic system.

PERSONALITY ATTRIBUTES INFLUENCING ORGANISATIONAL BEHAVIOUR

> In the context of managerial personality, Robert L. Katz opines that a leader is one who makes "a sincere effort to understand himself, his motivations and his behaviour that will help him to understand and lead others. The chief executive who is aware of himself, his values, his prejudices, his loyalties, in fact, aware of how his personality screen interprets events is going to stop, look and listen before he reaches conclusions about human problems. Gaining insight into ourselves and how our past experiences influence the way we perceive events and judge their significance increases our wisdom as executives."

Personality attributes of employees are used in understanding the behaviour of employees and designing suitable strategies to deal with their behaviour. Some of the traits that influence behaviour in organisations are described below.

1. **Authoritarianism:** Authoritarianism is an attribute used to describe persons having certain negative beliefs about work and workers. Considering this concept, the behaviour of employees in an organisation is explained by using the following traits:
   - i. Believes in formal authority.
   - ii. Is obedient to the authority.
   - iii. Adheres to conventional values and resists new ideas.
   - iv. Conforms to the rules and regulations.
   - v. Believes in directing subordinates rather than listening to them.
   - vi. Is rigid and prefers a structured environment.

   Using these characteristic traits, an 'authoritarian' style of leadership was developed. Employees who prefer authoritarian attributes will command respect from their superiors. They will achieve production targets in the short run, but in the long run will not be able to maintain the level of motivation and satisfaction.

2. **Locus of control:** This relates to beliefs regarding the outcome of a person's actions. Certain people believe that their skills and abilities influence the outcome of their actions, while others believe that external factors like fate or chance influences their results. According to Robbins, individuals who believe that they control what happens to them are called

'internals' and individuals who believe that what happens to them is controlled by outside forces such as luck or chance are called 'externals'. Certain personality attributes of internals and externals are shown in Table 6.1.

Table 6.1: Personality Attributes of Internals & Externals

Attribute	Internals	Externals
Self control	Greater degree of self control and caution.	Control is left to external chance.
Risk taking	Lower degree of risk aking.	Higher degree of risk assumption.
Information processing	Acquisition and retention of more information.	Accepts information as it is received, makes no effort to acquire information.
Expectations	Positive expectations of results. Establishes a positive relationship between effort and performance.	Outcome is left to chance. Do not believe that effort rewards relationship.
Use of skills	Prefers to use skills to achieve results.	Looks for chance or fate to determine the result rather than the use of skills.
Direction and control	Prefers to participate and exercise self control.	Prefers directive leadership and subject to others control.

Certain implications of 'locus of control' behaviour of individuals in organisations are described below.

a. *Absenteeism:* People having internal locus of control possess a belief that health is under their control. They inculcate good health habits and take proper care of their health. Thus, they have a lower rate of sickness, and absenteeism is less.

b. *Turnover:* Internals tend to take action, and thus might be expected to quit their jobs more readily. However, they tend to be more successful on the job and more satisfied.

c. *Decision-making:* People having an 'external locus of control' are more oriented towards intuitive decision making. On the other hand, internals take more information into account, before taking decisions. They are motivated by their achievements and like to control the outcome of the decisions.

d. *Motivation:* Internals possess greater achievement motivation than externals, the latter are satisfied with the available rewards.

e. *Job satisfaction:* People having 'external locus of control' are more dissatisfied with their jobs. This is because they believe that the outcome is not under their control. In the case of internals, job satisfaction is greater due to the belief that the outcome is a result of their actions.

f. *Psychological commitment:* Externals are less involved in the jobs. Internals possess greater psychological commitment.

g. *Social interactions:* People having 'internal locus of control' are more sociable and depend on social relationships for identification and esteem.

The locus of control also influences job selection. Professional and managerial jobs require the ability to process complex information, quick learning, initiative and independence of actions. People having internal locus of control are successful in such jobs. On the other hand, people having external locus of control are suited to well-structured and routine jobs. They are also successful in those jobs that require following the instructions.

3. **Machiavellianism:** Niccolo Machiavelli introduced this concept, and hence its name. The term refers to the degree of individual effort to gain control over organisational tasks. According to Robbins, Machiavellianism is the degree to which an individual is pragmatic, maintains emotional distance, and believes that ends can justify means. The characteristics of Machiavellianism personality are:

   i. They are active to participate in organisational politics.

   ii. They are manipulative, win more and persuade less.

   iii. They are adept at playing interpersonal games; power tactics and identifying the influence systems in organisations.

   iv. They consider ethics.

   The success of Machiavellian people depends on the situation. They perform better in the following situations:

   a. Face to face interactions

   b. Minimum number of rules and greater scope of framing the rules of the game

   c. There is low emotional involvement

   Thus, it can be stated that the Machiavellianism has an influence on organisational behaviour.

4. **Self-esteem:** Self-esteem is the feeling of liking or disliking of one's self. It is related to the individual's desire for success. A person having a greater desire for success is rated to have a high self-esteem. They believe that they possess the required abilities to succeed in their jobs. People with high self-esteem are risk takers, and tend to choose risky and challenging jobs. They have internal locus of control. They give preference to pride, recognition, flair, success, independence, and are satisfied with higher order needs rather than simple monetary rewards. On the other hand, people having a low self-esteem are influenced by the external factors. They give more respect and importance to other peoples' opinions. They do not want to face unpleasant situations and hence try to please others.

5. **Self-monitoring:** Self-monitoring is the ability to adapt to the demands of the situation. Individuals possessing high self-monitoring abilities, observe the behaviour of others closely, in order to adjust their own behaviour. People with this characteristic like mobility in their career. They are more successful in discharging conflicting roles as they simply wear a mask suitable to the situation. Thus, there is a high degree of behavioural inconsistency in self-monitoring people. The self-monitoring attribute helps managers to understand the personality and behaviour of their subordinates in order to direct, communicate, motivate and regulate them in their jobs.
6. **Risk-taking attitude:** Persons differ in their attitudes towards taking risk. The propensity to take risks influences decision-making. High-risk takers are likely to take rapid decisions. Risk-taking is also related to job demands. Caste, religion, nationality and gender, can also influence an individual's attitude towards taking risks. In organisations, risk-taking behaviour is seen to be more common in those employees who are willing to take up challenging tasks and are highly motivated.

From the above, we can see that a number of personality attributes influence the behaviour of a person in an organisation.

SUMMARY

In this chapter, we have understood the concept of personality. Understanding personality helps managers to direct the energy and motivation of employees appropriately, so as to achieve goals. Personality refers to both the physical and psychological attributes of an individual. The term is derived from the Latin word that means to 'speak through'. Personality is complex. It determines the way an individual behaves in different situations. The major determinants of personality are biological, family, environmental and situational factors. Biological factors relate to heredity, the brain, and physical stature. While heredity is genetically transformed traits, techniques such as SBP, ESB and BFT help to understand the influence of brain on personality. Physical features like height, facial features, muscle strength etc., also play a part in determining the personality of an individual. The socialisation process, identification process, and birth order are other factors that influence personality, along with cultural environment and a number of situational factors. It is relevant to mention that personality characteristics influence organisational behaviour. Authoritarianism enables one to understand the beliefs of managers regarding their subordinates. Locus of control explains beliefs regarding the outcome of individual actions. This helps to direct the behaviour of employees. An important attribute known as Machiavellianism helps to explain the pragmatic attitude of individuals. The other characteristics of personality that influence organisational behaviour are self-esteem, self-monitoring, and risk-taking attitude.

Key words

- **Absenteeism:** Intentional or unintentional absence from work.
- **Bio-feedback training:** Analysing electronic signal feedback to understand the internal rhythms of the body.
- **Electrical stimulation of the brain:** Analysing the stimulation of brain cells by implanting electrodes in the brain.
- **Genetic engineering:** Analysing the influence of genes on personality characteristics.
- **Heredity:** Inherited attributes acquired at the time of conception and transmitted to the next generation.
- **Locus of control:** The belief possessed by an individual that the outcome of an action is influenced by certain factors.
- **Machiavellianism:** The degree of individual effort to gain control over organisational tasks.
- **Split brain psychology:** Compartmentalising the structure of the brain into left and right hemispheres that have different functions.
- **Socialisation:** The process of acquiring a wide range of behavioural reactions from society.
- **Turnover:** Changing of jobs.

7. MODELS OF HUMAN PERSONALITY

This chapter enables you:

- *To understand the nature of individuals*
- *To know the nature of a rational economic man*
- *To appraise the characteristics of an organisation man*
- *To comprehend the features of a social man*
- *To identify the nature of a self-actualising man*
- *To explain the nature of a complex man*
- *To know the characteristics of a mobi-centric man*
- *To examine the characteristics of an administrative man*
- *To distinguish between different models of man*

The structure of the chapter is as follows:

- Introduction
- Models of man
- Rational economic man
- Organisation man
- Social man
- Self-actualising man
- Complex man
- Mobi-centric man
- Administrative man
- Key words

CHAPTER 7

Models of Human Personality

> *Human resources consist of totality of knowledge, skills, creative abilities, talent and aptitude of an organisation's workforce, as well as the values, attitudes and beliefs of the individuals involved in it. They are the sum total of inherent abilities, acquired knowledge and skills represented by the talents and aptitudes of the employees.*
>
> ***– Leon C. Megginson***

INTRODUCTION

Personality does not mean only the external appearance. Inner personality is more important in understanding behaviour. Human nature is unique and interesting, and personality is a complex phenomenon. Some people give more importance to monetary rewards, whereas others give importance to love and affection, recognition and esteem. Schein has classified human nature into four categories. They are: (i) economic man, (ii) social man, (iii) self-actualising man, and (iv) complex man. William White advocated the concept of organisation man. Herbert Simon described man as an administrative man and Jennings used the concept of mobi-centric man. Without understanding the nature of employees it will be difficult to know them. This chapter describes certain models of man that enable to understand human behaviour.

MODELS OF MAN

Individuals are the centre of activity in an organisation. Therefore, their behaviour considerably influences the functioning of an organisation. Assumptions made about people help the practicing manager to understand, predict and control their behaviour. The four models of man, identified by Edward Schein are described below.

RATIONAL ECONOMIC MAN

This is the oldest model, and it has been used by classical theorists. F.W. Taylor, Henri Fayol, Adam Smith, McGregor, March and Simon have used this model. The basis for the model is the principle of maximisation of self-interest. According to this model, an individual strikes a balance between costs and benefits of his actions. He is more concerned with calculating the value for his effort in terms of economic rewards and maximising it. Economic rewards regulate individual behaviour. The salient features of this model are given below.

(i) An individual is able to evaluate alternative courses of action. While evaluating them, he is concerned with economic benefits.

(ii) The actions of individuals operate on the principle of hedonism rather than social values.

(iii) Man is always passive and self-centred.

(iv) High degree of rationality measured in terms of monetary rewards guides individual decisions.

(v) Man is irrational with respect to money.

(vi) Higher doses of economic incentives provide higher inducements.

The rational economic man model assumes that economic rewards motivate a man and that variation in economic rewards controls his behaviour. Thus, it is relevant in designing appropriate strategies of motivation and control. It is helpful in determining reward systems. It suggests that provision of monetary rewards leads to the best use of human energy. As increased economic rewards induce production, there is no conflict between management and workers. This leads to the creation of a good industrial relations system. This model is a realistic description of human behaviour. Even today, this model is relevant for understanding man.

In spite of its relevance, the rational economic man model was criticised for overlooking the human aspect. It also ignored environmental factors of human actions. Moreover, it laid emphasis on economic rewards. Economic rewards lead to more autocratic controls, which in turn finally lead to negative consequences. Hence, the model is an insufficient model in understanding and predicting human behaviour.

SOCIAL MAN

This model is an outgrowth of empirical behavioural research and the development of human relations. Elton Mayo, Kurt Lewin, and McGregor have popularised and used this model. The basis for development of this model is the concept of social relationships. According to this model, group pressure, norms and sanctions direct individual actions. Social rewards motivate an individual, and the individual's status in the group is a measure of one's satisfaction. Therefore, employees accept management orders as long as they are congruent with group norms. The characteristics of this model are given below.

(i) Industrialisation, division of labour and specialisation has led to autonomy, frustration and conflicts. These create psychological pressure, tension and stress.

(ii) Employees try to establish interpersonal relationships in order to get relief from psychological pressure.

(iii) Man has an inherent desire for affiliation, recognition and socialisation with others. Hence, satisfaction of social needs motivates him.

(iv) An individual desires to become a member of a group. The group is a part of society.

(v) An individual is subject to group pressures, norms and group sanctions. Hence, he gives more value to social relationships than economic motives.

(vi) Individuals obey the orders of the management as long as these conform to group goals.

The social man model is helpful in designing the structure of the organisation, communication techniques, motivation systems, and rewards. It suggested an organisational structure based on concern for employees and oriented towards freedom, rather than one based on the strict division of labour, as suggested by the rational economic man model. The leader should be facilitator, supporter and creator. His attitude should be democratic in order to motivate people and his employees should be able to consult him about problems. It should be a two-way communication. The behaviour is analysed with reference to groups. Hence, according to this model, greater output results when more attention is paid to the employee's welfare, rather than the structure of the organisation.

The model was criticised on the grounds that it over-emphasised the human aspect and undermined the importance of economic rewards. However, it is true that even though an individual has an inherent desire to socialise, economic rewards are equally important to him. Critics of the model also felt that the model overlooked the influence of environmental factors on the behaviour of an individual.

SELF-ACTUALISING MAN

This model resulted from the concepts developed in the models of organisational man and social man. Abraham Maslow used self-actualisation to explain his need hierarchy. Self-actualising is making full use of an individual's capability. Therefore, it suggested that man should be innovative, creative and dynamic. An individual releases his full potential energy to achieve his final goal. The characteristics of a man according to this model are as follows:

(i) Self-actualisation is the ultimate need of an individual. He tries to seek self-actualising goals after reasonably satisfying his other basic needs, like safety and security, belonging and respect from other people.

(ii) Man is dynamic. He develops maturity over time.

(iii) Man is self-motivated and self-controlled.

(iv) An individual gives his best performance in an organisation in which there is freedom.

(v) Conflict between man and a formal organisation is an inevitable phenomenon, which makes him think and create.

(vi) People use energy in the pursuit of organisational goals.

The self-actualising man model suggested that autonomy is the essential element in designing the structure of the organisation. Intrinsic factors rather than physical energy, determines the rewards and incentive systems applicable to individuals. The leadership style practiced is democratic and employees are encouraged to participate in order to use their creativity to the greatest extent.

The self-actualising man model was criticised for its excessive emphasis on higher order needs. In fact, individuals try to pursue higher order needs only after satisfying the lower order needs to a reasonable extent. Critics also feel that self-actualisation is an ultimate need. It motivates the individual at the close of his tenure in organisation.

COMPLEX MAN

This is a recent model. It assumes that an individual is unpredictable in his behaviour. According to this model, a human being is a complex mixture of needs, goals, aspirations, perceptions, attitudes, learning, values and beliefs, all of which influence his behaviour. A man is complex because of lack of cause and effect relationship in his behaviour and due to individual differences. The following characteristics describe the complex man.

(i) Behaviour of human beings is complex and unpredictable, hence simply understanding a person's needs is inadequate.

(ii) A diverse and complex set of variables motivate a man.

(iii) Satisfaction of needs differs from individual to individual and from time to time.

(iv) There are overlapping needs.

(v) Since individuals are unique, individual differences are bound to exist which determine behaviour.

(vi) There is no direct cause and effect relationship between need and behaviour at all times.

(vii) Individual behaves differently in different situations.

The complex man model is relevant in the present day context as it suggests that there is no universal way of understanding behaviour and managing the individuals. Management is required to adopt a contingency organisational design and situational management approach. A manager should be capable of distinguishing between individuals and diagnosing their behaviour in order to adopt an appropriate style of leadership, motivation pattern, communication techniques and control strategy. Hence, a continuous change is required in organisational design and management philosophy to suit situational demands.

This model was criticised on the ground that it lacks an empirical base, as no cause and effect relationship exists between behaviour and situations.

Apart from the models of man advocated by Schein, there are certain other models, which are used to understand behaviour. They are given below.

ORGANISATION MAN

William Whyte advocated the concept of organisation man. An organisation man will sacrifice his own interests for the sake of the organisation. Individuals, who believe that social satisfaction, rather than competition, is a powerful tool to achieve objectives, fall in this category. Henri Fayol also suggested the sacrifice in his principles of management as *'subordination of individual interest to general interest'*. The basic propositions of the model are given below.

(i) Group is a source of creativity for individuals.

(ii) An isolated individual does not contribute to production, unless he coordinates with others.

(iii) Individuals are capable of producing a synergistic effect.

(iv) Belonging is the ultimate need of man.

(v) Needs of individuals and society are one and the same.

(vi) Proper application of scientific methods brings about consensus between individuals and society.

This model suggested that individual behaviour is oriented towards loyalty, belongingness, conformity and sacrifice of individual interests in the realisation of organisational goals. Therefore, an individual develops an attitude of resolving conflicts.

The organisation man model is helpful in creating an organisational structure that provides satisfaction to individuals, by taking adequate care of their interests. Leadership is highly democratic, and communication is open. Self-control and objective control are applicable rather than fact controls. Motivation is positive and ensures commitment.

In the real world, it is very difficult to find individuals who totally sacrifice their individual interests for the sake of the organisation. Therefore, this model is hypothetical. The model was also criticised on the ground that it overlooks environmental influences.

MOBI-CENTRIC MAN

This model was put forward by Jennings. He developed it from an empirical study of 230 individuals. According to this model, a mobi-centric man has the following characteristics:

(i) Individuals have a high degree of mobility and action.

(ii) They are self-confident, but do not keep faith in an organisation.

(iii) They measure their efficiency by dynamic movement and growth and not by the worth of organisational effort.

(iv) They are always ready to move from one job to another.

(v) They show a lot of enthusiasm in the beginning but do not complete the job properly.

The model suggests that a manager needs skill, intuition and patience to make such individuals work.

ADMINISTRATIVE MAN

This model was advanced by Herbert Simon. According to him, an individual is more interested in obtaining satisfaction from his work, rather than maximising his output. The latter is not always possible due to constraints of time, cost, environmental dynamics etc., and therefore, the individual is happy if he gets satisfaction. This model is descriptive of realistic individual behaviour.

Key words:

- **Administrative man:** An individual who is interested in satisfaction, rather than maximising his work.
- **Complex man:** A person having a complex mixture of needs, goals, aspirations, perceptions, attitudes, learning, values and beliefs.
- **Mobi-centric man:** An individual having a high degree of mobility and action.
- **Organisation man:** A person who sacrifices his individual interests for the organisation.
- **Principle of maximisation of self-interest:** The attitude of a person who only cares about his own interests and ignores others' interests.
- **Rational economic man:** A person who calculates the value of his effort in terms of economic rewards and maximizes it.
- **Self-actualisation:** Using one's capacity to the optimum capability.
- **Social man:** A person who values social rewards than economic rewards.

8. PERSONALITY THEORIES

This chapter enables you:

- *To understand the propositions of trait theories*
- *To understand the meaning of common traits and personal dispositions*
- *To distinguish between surface and source traits*
- *To understand the psychoanalytic theory*
- *To distinguish between the concepts of id, ego and super ego*
- *To identify the principles of personality*
- *To identify personality traits according body structures*
- *To distinguish between extroverts and introverts*
- *To understand the four types of personality*
- *To examine the elements of self concept*
- *To appraise the social learning process and development of personality*

The structure of the chapter is as follows:

- Introduction
- Trait theories
- Allport's trait theory
- Cattell's trait theory
- Psychoanalytic theory
- Physiognomy theory
- Extrovert-introvert theory
- Self-theory
- Summary
- Key words

CHAPTER 8

Personality Theories

INTRODUCTION

Understanding personality and directing human beings towards certain objectives has been a challenge to many people, especially to the organisational thinkers, who have suggested strategies of motivating employees. In the middle of the 19th century, George Elton Mayo and his associates realised that employees have social binding rather than structural binding. They stated that increased productivity and effectiveness of human beings depends on factors such as attitude, sentiments, creativity, innovation, communication etc. This has brought about a new dimension in the thinking of the management in understanding the personality of employees within the organisation. The aim of this chapter is to provide an in-depth understanding of the theories developed to explain personality. Allport and Cattell have developed the trait theories, which state that personality is a combination of distinct traits. Traits are used develop two personality characteristics known as extrovert and introvert. Sigmund Freud, Sheldon and Carl Jung have developed psychoanalytic theories, which state that psychological characteristics determine the personality of an individual. Self-theories and social learning theories also contributed to the understanding of personality.

THEORIES OF PERSONALITY

A number of theories exist to understand personality, namely the trait theories, psychoanalytic theories, self-theory and social learning theories. They are discussed in detail below.

Trait Theories

Trait theories put forward the proposition that personality is holistic, it is a combination of the actions and reactions of an individual. A trait is defined as *"an enduring attribute of a person that appears constantly in a variety of situations"*. It can be understood as a distinguishable characteristic that describes behaviour. The propositions of the trait theories are given below.

i. A trait is a common characteristic found in an individual.

ii. It varies absolutely from one person to another hence, it can be used to distinguish personality.

iii. It is a qualitative attribute, but can be quantified and measured.

iv. Trait is individualistic. Hence, it can only be inferred from behaviour.

v. Traits possessed by an individual are relatively stable and universally understood.

vi. Personality and behaviour differ due to traits.

The theories of Gordon Allport and Raymond Cattell are popular amongst the trait theories. A number of traits have been identified. Allport has identified 17,953 traits, while Cattel has described 171.

Personality traits provide an understanding of the personality types.

The Myers-Briggs Type Indicator:

The MBTI framework identified sixteen personality types. The identification was possible with the help of answers to 100 questions provided in the test. Some of them are Extroverted vs. Introverted, Sensing vs. Intuitive, Thinking vs. Feeling, Perceiving vs. Judging etc.

Qualities of a personality type 'Introverted, Intuitive, Thinking and Judging' (INTJ) possess certain qualities. They:

i. Possess Vision

ii. Think with original mind

iii. Have original ideas

iv. Have great drive

v. Are Skeptical, critical, independent, determined and stubborn

Allport's Trait Theory

Gordon Allport has identified a number of traits to describe the complex behaviour of human personality. He classified traits into two categories.

a. Common traits, and

b. Personal disposition

While common traits are comparable attributes used to compare people, personal disposition is unique. Six distinguishing traits namely, social, political, economical, aesthetic, religious and theoretical, are used to provide comparisons. For instance social traits emphasise love and affection, care, interest in others and expression of sympathy. Political traits are related to power consciousness, and emphasise leadership for self-gain. Economic traits place emphasis on practicality and cost and benefits of a situation, aesthetic traits are concerned with creative and artistic aspects, and religious traits relate to unity and integrity. Finally, a person possessing theoretical traits is rational and has an empirical approach.

The Big Five Personality Types

Personality dimensions are identified in terms of the Big Five Factors. The types of personality are given below:

Personality Type	**High Dimension**	**Low Dimension**
Extrovert	Gregarious, assertive and sociable.	Reserved, timid and quiet.
Agreeable	Cooperative, warm and trusting.	Cold, disagreeable and antagonistic.
Conscientious	Responsible, organised, dependable and persistent.	Distracted, disorganised and unreliable.
Emotionally stable	Calm, self-confident and secure.	Nervous, anxious, depressed and insecure.
Open to experience	Creative, curious and artistically sensitive.	Conventional, comfortable with known persons.

- Extrovert: Giving importance to relationships.
- Agreeable: Thinking in a different manner.
- Conscientious: Possessing reliability.
- Emotional stability: Ability to withstand stress.
- Open to experience: Interested and fascinated by novelty.

Type A and Type B Personality

Type A personality is defined as *"aggressively involved in a chronic, incessant struggle to achieve more and more in less and less time, and, if required to do so, against the opposing efforts of other things or other persons"* – **(Friedman and Rosenman)**. They have defined Type B personality as *"rarely harried by the desire to obtain a wildly increasing number of things or participate in an endless growing series of events in an ever-decreasing amount of time"*. The characteristics of these personalities are shown below:

Type A Personality	Type B Personality
1. Always moving, walking, and eating rapidly. 2. Feels impatient with the rate at which most events take place. 3. Cannot cope with leisure time. 4. Strives to think or do two or more things at once. 5. Obsessed with numbers, measuring their success in terms of how many or how much of everything they acquire.	1. Never suffers from a sense of urgency with its accompanying impatience 2. Feels no need to display or discuss either their achievements or accomplishments unless such exposure is demanded by the situation 3. Plays for fun and relaxation rather than to exhibit their superiority at any cost 4. Can relax without guilt

Cattell's Trait Theory

Cattell's theory has developed a new approach. By eliminating overlapping meanings, the theory identified 171 traits. They are identified as:

a. Surface traits, and

b. Source traits.

Surface traits are visible, and are determined largely by underlying source traits. While the source trait is a cause, the surface trait is an effect. Using factor analysis technique, 35 surface traits and 12 source traits were identified. Some of the traits are shown here under.

Surface Traits	Source Traits
Wise – Foolish Affectionate – Cold Sociable – Seclusive Honest – Dishonest	Reserved – Outgoing Submissive – Dominant Timid – Adventurous Trusting – Suspicious Practical – Imaginative Self-assured – Apprehensive Conservative – Experimenting Uncontrolled – Controlled Relaxed – Tense

The source traits are constant. They are used to predict behaviour by taking specific situations into account.

With the help of trait theories four types of personalities were developed, as shown below.

Trait Characteristics	High Anxiety	Low Anxiety
Extrovert	Tense, excitable, unstable, warm, sociable and dependent.	Composed, confident, trusting, adaptable, warm, sociable and dependent.
Introvert	Tense, excitable unstable, cold and shy.	Composed, confident, trustful, adaptable, calm, cold, and shy.

The traits leading to different personalities are given below.

1. High anxiety and extroversion lead to tense, excitable, unstable, warm, sociable, and dependent personality traits.
2. High anxiety and introversion lead to tense, excitable, unstable, cold, and shy personality traits.
3. Composed, confident, trusting, adaptable, warm, sociable, and dependent personalities are associated with extroversion and low anxiety.
4. Introversion and low anxiety lead to composed, confident, trusting, adaptable, calm, cold and shy personality traits.

The trait theories recognise the continuity of personality. The theories have shown the utility of quantitative applications in behavioural sciences. They have a great deal of intuitive appeal.

Psychoanalytic Theories

The psychoanalytic approach was put forward, amongst others, by **Sigmund Freud,** who carried out extensive work on dream analysis. He found that dreams are the result of unconscious mental activity. They reflect wish gratification of individuals. Dreams may be of certain childhood experiences, or things, or a person one has never seen. Often one does not remember one's dreams. Why do these things happen? They are due to the fact that, the brain continuously establishes relationships, analogies, congruencies and divergence. Freud calls this as inaccessible mental activity. The central tenet of the approach is that *'inaccessible unconscious mental activity strongly influences human behavior'*. Freud became known as the father of psychology for his outstanding contributions in the field.

The central theme of the psychoanalytic approach is a transitive relationship that can be stated in the following way:

- Personality determines behaviour; and
- Behaviour is a result of unconscious mental activity; and, therefore
- Personality is influenced by unconscious mental activity.

The superiority of the Freudian approach lay in the methodology of mapping unconscious mental activity for analysing dreams. He used clinical investigations and collected data relating to normal and abnormal behaviour. In the words of **Hall** and **Lindzey,** *'Freud's concept of the nature and importance of unconscious levels of mental activity, together with his methodologies for studying that activity and his analyses of abnormal behaviour form the bases for the psychoanalytic approach'*. The structure of the brain and functioning of the personality systems are vital in understanding the behaviour of individuals. According to this approach, structure of brain consists of three elements: the unconscious, the conscious and the preconscious elements. Figure 8.1 describes this.

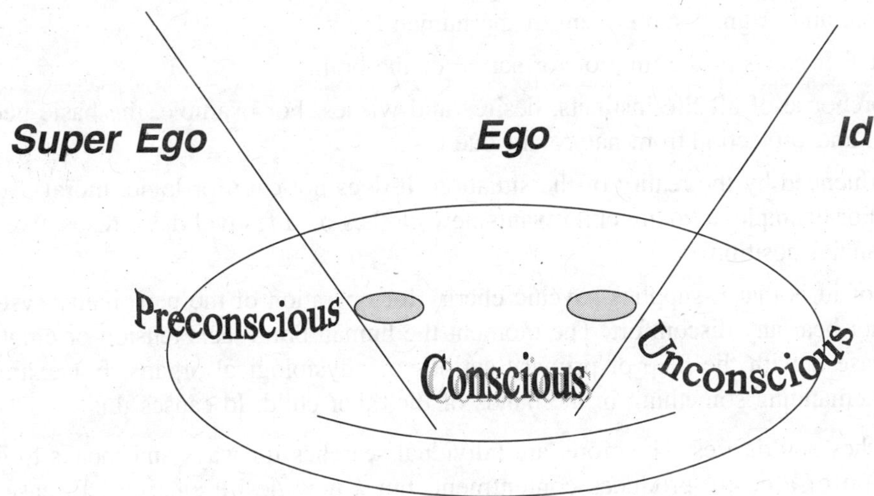

Figure 8.1: Elements of the brain

The preconscious element is present at the time when the mind is formed. It is believed that the preconscious is transmitted through the genes of one's parents. This is compared to *'poorva gyana'*, the self-revelation. The conscious part consists of thoughts, beliefs, feelings and desires learnt through introspection. This is known as *'loka gyana'* or worldly knowledge. For instance, we learn many things from our experiences. For example, the way we respond to people who are older than us is different from the way we respond to people who are younger than us. This kind of discriminatory behaviour is an example of our consciousness, and is based on the principle of reasoned reality. The unconscious is the dormant cognitive aspect. It is based on the hedonistic principle or principle of pleasure. When we feel happy we try to express it unmindful of the presence of others. The inability to withstand emotions is due to the influence of the unconscious element. The structure of human brain is responsible for certain behaviour, but how do we understand the structure of brain? Obviously it is not possible to see what lies inside the brain, and hence it is often described as a black box. To try and see what is in the brain is like trying to find a black cat in a dark room. Freud conceptualized three elements of the structure of the brain.

The Id

The id is defined as the totality of instincts oriented towards increasing pleasure, avoiding pain and striving for immediate satisfaction of desires. For example, you may have made unreasonable demands on your parents, which were turned down or fought with a figure of authority, like your teacher, because you felt that they were not justified in reprimanding you. In both the examples, you may be aware that your behaviour is childish, but the *id* compels you to behave like this. Thus, the psychological system is irrational, demanding, unsatisfied and destructive. It wants immediate gratification of its needs, otherwise, it releases the tension through primary forces of destruction. Some of the characteristic features of *id* are described below:

- Id is the basic and original sub system of the human brain
- It is inherited. It exists at the time of formation of the brain.
- It is the storehouse of all life instincts, desires and wishes. For example, the basic needs of hunger, sex, and protection from nature are due to id.
- Id is not influenced by the reality of the situation. It does not care for logic, morals, reasons and ethics. For example, a young child wants new clothes on a festival day irrespective of his father's financial position.
- The nature of id is that it supplies psychic energy for operation of the personality system.
- The id cannot bear any discomfort. The moment the human brain feels tension or emotion, it tries to release it with the help of primary actions of physiological organs. For example, a child cries demanding something in the hands of the other child. Id causes this.

Id generates wishes and desires. Therefore, an individual searches for ways and means to gratify them. Satisfaction of a desire produces contentment, but a new desire emerges. In case these wishes and desires are not satisfied, tension is developed in individuals. Either primary force or hallucination releases the tension.

The Ego

As you grow to understand the worldly environment, you think before carrying out an action, rather than simply doing something because you derive pleasure or reduce pain. This is because you learn to understand the world around you and act accordingly. As a child, you might have refused to share your chocolate with others, but when you grow older you yourself distribute chocolates on your birthday. This is due to the fact, that, you learnt that sharing brings happiness. *Ego* regulates the understanding of the outside world and the individual acts accordingly. Therefore, the ego is the rational master of the human brain and regulates behaviour according to reality. Hall and Lindzey put the ego as the executive part of the personality, that selects features of environment, stores them, responds and decides which instincts have to be satisfied. It is rational and logical, in essence, it is the conscious mediator between realities of the world and the demands of the *id*. The basic features of the *ego* are given below:

- Ego translates the demands of the id by matching them with the outside environment.

- It works on principle of reality as against principle of pleasure.
- Ego is developed in the individual when one learns to understand and distinguish between reality and unreality.
- Ego is the rational master of personality. It balances the impulsive demands of the id and the restrictive guidance of the super ego. Thus, it regulates inner motives and conflicting demands of the individuals.
- It facilitates judgement and learning in individuals.
- Ego helps in reducing the tensions caused by the actions of the id. It contains psychic energy. This energy, if necessary, turns the energy of id on to it.

Therefore, individual actions are rationalised relating them to reality. For instance, employees learn to respect their superiors even if they are younger in age. Similarly, managers are more diligent and cautious while taking organisational decisions, as compared to personal decisions, as the former impact the entire organisation. Interestingly the force of the *ego* sometimes becomes ineffective due to the psychic force of the *id*. In such circumstances, the psychoanalytic model believes that another element known as the *super ego* provides guidance to the individual's energy.

The Super Ego

Freud considers that human personality has a moral part. Individuals develop moral values, norms, and standards of behaviour and ideals, which help in judging what is right or wrong. This is the *super ego*. It is the moralistic segment of personality consisting of one's noblest thoughts, ideas and feelings developed through absorption of cultural values. Thus, the *super ego* directs the actions of individuals based on the culture in which they are brought up. For instance, the average American is far more independent than the average Indian. The *super ego* has the following features.

- Interaction of the ego and functioning of society develop the super ego.
- It operates on the principles of perfection.
- It processes the values and ethics of society from one generation to the next.
- Super ego is the moral arm of personality. It judges the actions of the ego to establish whether they are right or wrong.
- The development of super ego is almost permanent. Once developed, it remains unchanged until a strong force changes it.

Super ego is instrumental in the development of our attitudes. Attitudes are permanent impressions developed by the individuals. They are not developed in a single interaction. For example, you may develop an impression about an individual at first sight. However, it may not be permanent. If the same impression is reinforced a number of times, you develop a certain permanent impression, which is part of the *super ego*.

The characteristics of personality sub systems are shown in the following table.

Characteristics	Id	Ego	Super ego
Basis	Biological	Psychological	Social
Acquisition	Inheritance	Experience	Socialisation
Goal	Pleasure	Reality	Perfection
Function	Wish generation	Self-preservation	Wish inhibition
Quality of mental life	Unconscious	Conscious	Preconscious
Outcome process	Reflex actions, hallucinations	Perception, memory thinking, judgement	Surveillance, evaluation, sanction

Source: Approaches to Understanding Behavior in Organizations, in Reitz, H. Joseph, Behavior in Organizations, Richard D. Irwin, Inc. Homewood, Illinois, 1977, p.67.

The psychoanalytic theory is referred to as the theory of tension. The essence of the theory is that *'inner tensions initiated by the wishes of the id cause the system to function. The ego is under pressure to gratify these wishes both quickly and at low cost, while it is under the tension of close scrutiny by the super ego'*. The theory stated that understanding individuals means understanding their personality systems. Personality is comprehended only when one knows the personality systems viz., *id, ego* and *super ego.*

Principles of Personality

The psychoanalytic theory developed certain principles that shape the personality of individuals. They are:

1. *The principle of pleasure:* This principle states that individuals simply gratify their needs, to get pleasure, without judging the implications of their actions. The behaviour is regarded as immature and childish, and may be irrational.
2. *The principle of tension:* An individual develops tension when his wishes are not satisfied with the available choices. In this case, he searches for alternatives. The non-availability of viable alternatives results in showing the tension through primary forces or reflex actions.
3. *The principle of reality:* An individual tries to learn reality from interactions with the worldly environment. Accordingly, actions depend upon inner instincts and outside reality.
4. *The principle of heredity:* This principle states that individuals acquire certain characteristics from their parents. These are present at the time of birth.
5. *The principle of reasoned reality:* The learning of thoughts, beliefs, feelings and desires through introspection is the basis for conscious actions of the individual.
6. *The principle of greed:* When other people have something that he desires, an individual

becomes envious. This is known as greed, which makes a person behave irrationally.

7. *The principle of perfection:* This states that an individual's behaviour conforms to certain ideals established by society. Actions violating the cultural ethos are judged as wrong and are punishable.

It is interesting to note that the psychoanalytic approach is of great relevance to practicing managers. It has a number of applications in an organisation, some of which are mentioned below:

1. Creativity and innovation are requirements in organisational learning. It is believed that every individual is a creative being. Creativity is the functioning of the id. Emotions caused by the id lead to tensions and defensive behaviour. Tension makes individuals think divergently to satisfy their wishes. This results in innovative thinking. If the wishes are gratified in the normal course, an individual feels satisfied, which may prevent him from thinking in a divergent manner.

2. Satisfaction is a psychological function. Satisfied employees are assets to the organisation. They can positively influence the functioning of the organisation and can contribute to its positive corporate image. Dissatisfied employees develop anxiety and frustration, which results in conflicting behaviour. The psychoanalytic model states that certain behavioural reactions are associated with dissatisfaction, e.g., daydreaming, forgetfulness, apathy, rationalisation, sickness, disability and pain. Similarly, absenteeism, tardiness, aggression and alcoholism are some effects caused by interaction of the id.

3. Groups and teams are common forms of informal associations among employees. If properly used they can be instrumental in organisational building. Otherwise, they distract the organisational performance. Then the question is how groups are developed. Obviously, development of groups is a function of consensus mindset among the employees. Interestingly ego plays a crucial role in developing identity of minds by association of thoughts, beliefs, feelings, and emotions.

4. Managers need to understand the model to interpret the process of psychoanalysis in order to create organisational influence, attitude development, learning and competency building, motivation, leadership building and to ensure that the employees are psychologically committed to effectively channel their energies to organisational goals.

Case study 8.1: *Id* – the irrational factor

I am an executive in the placement and training division of an organisation, having a number of plans. The structure in our division was as follows: Executive, assistant executive, assistant and office boy. However, liberalisation, privatisation, globalisation and government policy have affected our office structure, leading to downsizing. This compelled me to work with the HRD Director, whose office had an assistant executive and an assistant.

I had to elicit work from people over whom I had no control, as the structure of the organisation placed them for my service too. The difficulty started with the assistant, who was known for his poor discipline. He expected immediate financial benefits for every job he carried out for my division. This was obviously not possible. I tried to explain to him that I was working on a budget, and could not fulfill his demands, but he was not willing to understand, and even called me on my mobile phone and started to abuse me. Finally, I was forced to bring the matter to the attention of the Director. An inquiry was initiated and he revealed that since I had not allowed him to submit bills as he wanted to, he spread the rumour that I was manipulating the budget.

The point, I am trying to emphasise, is that the role of *id*, became disproportionate in him. His only objective was to make money and he did not understand the ethics in an organisation. He behaved like this because the *id* rather than the *ego* guided his actions.

Physiognomy Theory

William Sheldon propounded a theory that related human anatomical or physical structure and psychological characteristics. According to the theory, human behaviour and temperaments are influenced by the physical size of the body. The theory identified three different body types, which are described below:

a. Endomorph
b. Mesomorph
c. Ectomorph

(a) Endomorph

An endomorph body is fat and thick. The size of the body is proportional to the height of the body. The personality and behaviour of persons with this type of body are as follows. They are friendly, concerned about others, helpful, very slow to react to stimuli, comfort seeking, and are fond of food. Due to these personality characteristics, they are likeable people.

(b) Mesomorph

Persons having moderate physical characteristics are known as Mesomorph. Their body is strong and tough and they often wish to develop muscle power. The personality and behaviour of persons with this type of body are as follows. They seek physical adventure, enjoy body building, feel restless, show high aggression and self assertiveness, like to take risks and develop a competitive spirit. The person is liked due to his physique.

(c) Ectomorph

The ectomorph body type is characterised by a thin and flat chest. The body is delicate due to light muscles. However, the person is intelligent, shy and avoids social contact. Typically, he is anxious, ambitious and dedicated to his work. He is quick to react and hypersensitive to pain and pleasure.

Based on the above classification of body types and concomitant physical and personality characteristics, Sheldon has developed a seven-point scale to quantify personality. The theory allows one to draw generalisations, but it is criticised on the grounds that it is not possible to place a person strictly into one category as suggested by Sheldon.

Extrovert-Introvert Theory

Carl Jung is the proponent of this theory, which uses an analytical psychology approach. According to the theory, personality is developed as a process of creativity. It consists of four phases: Thinking, feeling, sensation and intuition. Individual personality is a mixture of these factors. The theory proposes two opposing personality characteristics, namely extrovert and introvert personalities. While extroverts are more sociable, introverts are more self-confident and are guided by their own individual thinking. The following table describes the characteristics of the extrovert and introvert types of personality.

Extroverts	**Introverts**
Optimistic	Pessimistic
Willing to move in groups	More aloof
Objective oriented	Subjective oriented
Aggressive	Withdrawn
Flexible and absorbs social feelings	Rigid and absorbs inner feelings
Friendly and cordial	Avoids social contacts and is less cordial
Interactive oriented	Quiet and calm
Enterprising	Retiring

Extroverts are sociable and reality oriented individuals. They are performers. On the other hand, introverts take less risk and require strong motivation and specific directions. While extroverts think in terms of objective and interactive relationships, the thinking of introverts is guided by their own philosophy and ideology.

The four types of personality based on the creative process are shown in Figure 8.2.

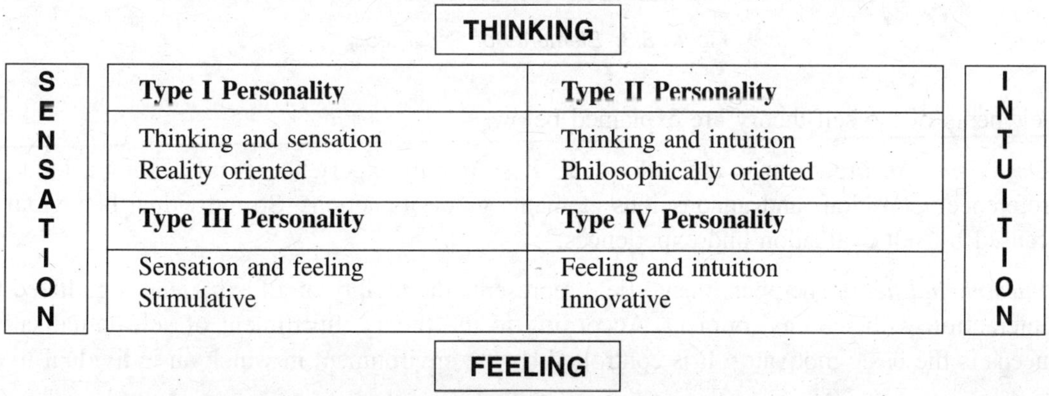

THINKING

SENSATION

Type I Personality	**Type II Personality**
Thinking and sensation Reality oriented	Thinking and intuition Philosophically oriented
Type III Personality	**Type IV Personality**
Sensation and feeling Stimulative	Feeling and intuition Innovative

INTUITION

FEELING

Figure 8.2: Types of personality based on the creative process

These four types of personality have specific implications in the organisational process. For instance, Type I personality is associated with an individual who is reality oriented and is more pragmatic in the application of techniques of management, whereas an individual having a Type IV personality is innovative and more successful in adapting to changes.

The extrovert and introvert theory is very useful in the management of organisational behaviour. Job design, motivation, leadership styles, career development, training, organisational changes, organisational development, and organisational effectiveness are some of the organisational features based on personality characteristics. An introvert is likely to perform better in repetitive jobs, whereas an extrovert performs better in dynamic and environmental jobs. An extrovert needs a democratic style of leadership, whilst an introvert needs more direction. Thus, the theory is used in developing organisational strategies to deal with individual employees to increase organisational effectiveness.

Self-Theory

Carl Rogers put forward the self-theory, also known as organism theory or field theory. The theory emphasises that the individual is creative and initiates and influences behaviour within the environmental framework. Figure 8.3 presents the elements of the self-theory.

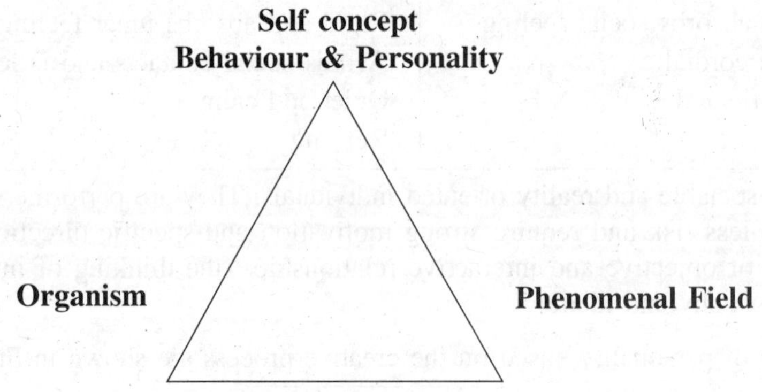

Figure 8.3: Elements of Self Theory

The elements of the self-theory are explained below.

(a) *Organism:* An organism is the individual. It stores all experiences, and is thus a locus of reference. Conscious and unconscious elements guide its actions. So individual behaviour is caused by self-evaluation and experiences.

(b) *Phenomenal field:* The phenomenal field represents the totality of all experiences gathered by interaction with the environment. According to the theory, fulfillment of self-actualisation needs is the basic motivator. It is controlled by the environment in which an individual lives.

(c) *Self-concept:* Self-concept is an outcome, which forms the basis for individual behaviour and personality. Self is a combination of perceptions, attitudes, beliefs, values and traits. It characterises the concept of *'I'* and *'me.'* In this context, *'I'* indicates one's own psychological process, hence, it is called the personal self. *'Me'* is related to how a person thinks he appears to others, therefore, it is called social self. Both the personal self and social self determine individual behaviour.

Self-theory is a valuable guide in understanding behaviour. The theory is organised around the individual and not around the environment, which is uncontrollable.

SOCIAL LEARNING THEORY

Albert Bandura has propounded the social learning theory to explain human behaviour. The theory states that a person's personality is determined by the situation in which he finds himself. The theory makes the following assumptions.

i. Behaviour is a unit of analysis.
ii. People behave in ways that produce reinforcement.
iii. An individual chooses certain actions in expectation of certain specific results.
iv. Learning influences behaviour and personality.

According to the theory, a person's behaviour is determined by, and modeled on observational learning from the environment. It is shown in the Figure 8.4.

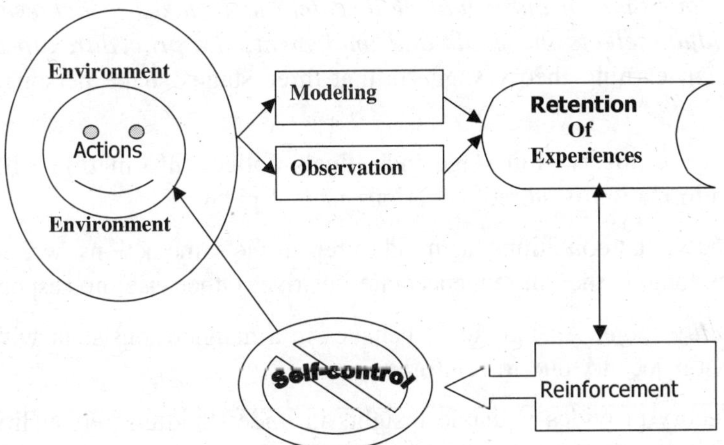

Figure 8.4: Social Learning Theory

A person interacts with the environment. He imitates and observes the stimuli in the environment. He is aware of certain experiences, which are retained. When the same conditions are reinforced, he acts. These actions are called behaviour. Bandura stated that '*It is largely through their actions that people produce the environmental conditions that affect their behaviour in a reciprocal fashion. The experiences generated by behaviour also partly determine what a person becomes, and what he can do. Which in turn affects subsequent behaviour'*

The two important factors that determine the behaviour are modeling and self control. They are discussed below.

Modeling Process

Modeling is the process of imitating and building a concept of a reality. It involves four interrelated sub processes. They are:

i. *Attention:* This is the process by which attractive, important, reinforced and contrast characteristics of a situation are identified.

ii. *Retention:* An individual converts features of the attention process into codes and remembers them for future actions.

iii. *Mortoric reproduction:* By this process an individual converts model features into actions by the process of imitation.

iv. *Reinforcement:* An individual is likely to repeat imitation based behaviour as long as a positive reward is associated with the actions.

Self-control Process

Self-control is a process of exercising control over one's actions. A person tries to adopt appropriate behaviour after observing different kinds of behaviour. **Henry Sims** defined self-control as *'the behaviour that an individual deliberately undertakes to achieve self-selected outcomes. The individual selects the goals and implements the procedures to achieve these goals'*. Thus, the social learning theory suggests that three stages shape personality. They are described below.

Observation stage: In the observation stage individuals collect information with the help of sensory organs. The information is stored as various mental pictures.

Learning stage: An individual conditions his mind to repeat the same actions, which are stored in the mental pictures, as long as the consequences are positive. Otherwise, no response is shown.

Behaviour or personality stage: An individual behaves in a manner consistent with the positive response. Thus, behaviour occurs due to reinforcement.

The social learning theory provides valuable insights in understanding personality. The theory considers the environment, rather than an unconscious element, as the determinant of behaviour. Thus, it suggests that by controlling the environment, behaviour can be suitably modified to suit the organisation.

The theory has been criticised on the following grounds.

i. The theory neglects individual differences caused by physical and psychological factors.

ii. It gives more emphasis to situational factors, which are contingent in nature.

iii. The methodology is sensitive to the influence of situational factors.

However, interaction between a person and the situation he is in, is the most powerful aspect in understanding behaviour and personality.

Case study 8.2: Technology and personality characteristics

Today organisations are facing the challenges of technological adaptation. Since it is capital intensive it appears simple, but in fact, the problem is complicated due to the human element. Four important personality characteristics are prevalent from the point of view of technological adaptation. They are:

- Synergy
- Allergy
- Emplacement
- Adaptation

An important implication is that the new technology affects the psychology of the employees, as they fear that their job profiles will be altered and their skills will become redundant. Their fears include being replaced, layoffs, retrenchments, time pressures, new accountability, electronic monitoring, strict surveillance, learning of new conceptual, perceptual and communication skills etc. Some behavioural reactions to the technology are polarisation, stress, job hopping, slowdown of work, pleading innocence, loss of productivity etc. Two personality types are found in technological adaptation. They are based on positive and negative thinking. Positive thinking persons are '*promoters*' and negative thinkers are '*inhibitors*'. Each of these personaltiy traits results into several possible personalities. Promoters are:

- **Participants:** Are aware of the responsibility of technological adaptation for the success and profitability of the enterprise.
- **Movers:** Remove barriers in the adaptation of technology and moving ahead.
- **Shakers:** Recognise the opportunity and have the determination to adapt.

Inhibitors are of the following types.

- **Spectators:** Feel satisfied with the conventional systems and hence do not think of new technology.
- **Protectors:** They want to protect the present structure and feel it will be lost if new technology is implemented.
- **Doubters:** Unable to estimate the results of adapting to new technology.
- **Worriers:** Afraid of the hardware aspects of technology.
- **Switchers:** Will shift the responsibility to others in an attempt to avoid carrying out the work.

SUMMARY

Personaltiy is the central focus in the study of organisational behaviour. It is complex and unique. Various theories exist to explain the propositions relating to personality. Traditionally, an enduring attribute of a person that appeared constantly in a variety of situations was used to identify personality. These are known as traits. The theory of Allport identified common traits and personal dispositions. Cattell identified surface and source traits. This led to the emergence of four different personalities based on high and low anxiety and extrovert and introvert traits. Sigmund Freud propounded the psychoanalytic theory that identified three states of mind viz., preconscious, conscious, and unconscious. To explain personality Freud conceptualised three elements of the structure of the brain, namely the *id, ego* and *super ego.* While the id operates on the principle of pleasure or the hedonist principle, the ego functions on the principle of reasoned reality. It acts as the executive component of the personality. It tries to balance the irrational demands of the id with the situations of the outside world. Freud considers human personality to have a moral arm, called the super ego. This directs the actions of individuals according to the culture in which they are brought up. The theory is of special significance in understanding and directing the creativity and innovative skills of employees, understanding team development and satisfaction of the employees. William Sheldon has propounded a theory, which relates the anatomical or physical structure and psychological characteristics of a person. According to this theory, human behaviour and temperaments are influenced by the physical size of the body. The theory identified three different body types viz., *endomorph, mesomorph* and *ectomorph.* He developed a seven-point scale for quantifying personality. Another significant theory developed by Carl Jung is the extrovert and introvert theory. While extrovert persons are more sociable, introvert persons are more self-confident and are guided by their own individual thinking. The two personality characteristics identified four personality types. The traits embedded in these personality types are thinking, feeling, sensation and intuition. Carl Rogers contributed the self-theory, which states that personality is influenced by the concept of selfish perceptions, attitudes, beliefs, values and traits. Albert Bandura has propounded the social learning theory to explain human behaviour. This theory states that a person's personality depends on the situation in which he finds himself. Two situational factors are the modelling and self control processes. All these theories of personality are of great relevance to understanding personality.

Key words:

- **Common traits:** Attributes used to compare people.
- **Ego:** Rational master of the human brain that regulates behaviour according to the conditions of reality.
- **Extroversion:** Establishing objectives and interactive relationships.
- **Id:** Totality of instincts oriented towards increasing pleasure, avoiding pain and striving for immediate satisfaction of desires.
- **Introversion:** Being guided by one's philosophy and ideology.

- **Motoric reproduction:** Conversion of model features into actions by the process of imitation.
- **Personal dispositions:** Unique and the most pervasive attributes that describe the complexity of human personality.
- **Phenomenal field:** Totality of all experiences gathered by interaction with the environment.
- **Principle of heredity:** Acquiring certain characteristics from one's parents.
- **Principle of perfection:** Conforming behaviour to certain ideals established by society.
- **Principle of pleasure:** Individuals gratify the needs simply to provide pleasure at that time without judging the implications of the action.
- **Principle of reality:** Learning reality from interactions with the worldly environment.
- **Principle of reasoned reality:** Learning thoughts, beliefs, feelings and desires through introspection.
- **Reinforcement:** Repetition of behaviour based on imitation as long as a positive reward is associated with the actions.
- **Self concept:** A combination of perceptions, attitudes, beliefs, values and traits possessed by an individual.
- **Self-control:** Deliberately behaving in a certain way to achieve self-selected outcomes.
- **Surface traits:** Visible and conspicuous attributes that appear on the surface of personality.
- **Super ego:** A moralistic segment of personality consisting of the noblest thoughts, ideas and feelings developed through absorption of cultural values.
- **Trait:** An enduring attribute of a person that appears constantly in a variety of situations.

9. PERSONALITY DEVELOPMENT

This chapter enables you:

- *To appraise the stages in the development of personality*
- *To distinguish development of personality at various stages*
- *To examine the social adaptation approach of personality development*
- *To distinguish between immaturity and maturity characteristics*

The structure of the chapter is as follows:

- Introduction
- Freud's physiological approach
- Erikson's social adaptation approach
- Levinson's adult life stages approach
- Hall's career stage approach
- Argyris' maturity and immaturity continuum approach
- Summary
- Key words

CHAPTER 9

Personality Development

> *"Socialization is not a haphazard accumulation of bits of behaviour but entails, instead, some orderly development."*
>
> **– Mitchell**

INTRODUCTION

Personality development is a process and it is time-oriented. Freud was the first to put forward the theory that personality develops in stages. Personality development has an influence on productivity, motivation, satisfaction and career development of employees in organisations. Our life is divided into a number of stages, and in each stage our behaviour is different. Freud considered the stages of personality development as a biological process. Erikson also supported the idea of stages in personality development. His emphasis was on social interaction. Argyris stated that personality development progresses along a continuum from immaturity to maturity. Levinson considered that personality development consists of two periods. Douglas Hall supported the stage approach. However, he considered that a person's needs determined his or her personality development. This approach is widely used in career development of employees. This chapter explains personality development, and after reading it you should be able to understand and shape your personality using the theoretical background provided here.

DEVELOPMENT OF PERSONALITY

> *Development of personality is concerned with "the process by which children gradually acquire patterns of overt behaviour, thinking, problem solving, and above all, the motives, emotions, conflicts, and ways of coping with conflicts that will make up their adult personalities."*
>
> **– Jerome Kagan and Ernest Hareman**

Personality development influences an individual's behaviour towards productivity, goal realisation, motivation and satisfaction, and career development. Hence understanding personality development is of special significance to managers. A number of factors, such as heredity, environment, maturity and learning contribute to the development of personality. It also depends on the different situations a person finds himself in.

> In this regard, **Mitchell** stated that, "*Socialization is not a haphazard accumulation of bits of behaviour but entails, instead, some orderly development*". He further states that "*accumulation of behaviour is true atleast to the degree that some complex social behaviour patterns occur sequentially.*"

A number of approaches, which are described below, exist to explain personality development. Some consider the physiological and psychological stages, while others consider the determinants of personality as contributing factors.

(i) Freud's Physiological Approach
(ii) Erikson's Social Adaptation Approach
(iii) Argyris' Maturity and Immaturity Continuum Approach
(iv) Levinson's Adult Life Stages Approach
(v) Hall's Career Stage Approach

FREUD'S PHYSIOLOGICAL APPROACH

Freud was the first to put forward the theory that personality develops in stages. According to him, personality develops along with physical development. Hence, his approach is called the physiological approach. It states that an individual's personality develops in four stages: Oral, anal, phallic and genital. Personality characteristics develop according to the treatment given to a child at different stages. It is not out of context to mention here that even in the Bhagavad Gita, Lord Krishna said "*Dehinosmin yada dehai, koumaram yavvanam jara, thadha dehantara prapthihi, dheerestatra na muhyathi*", which means that there are different stages in the life of a man, namely childhood (*koumara*), youth (*yavvana*) and adult (*jara*). Individuals acquire a variety of psychological characteristics at different stages of their personality development. Figure 9.1 shows the number of stages involved in the physiological development. These are described below.

Oral Stage

The oral stage is the basic stage in the development of personality. It lasts for about a year. In this stage the oral organs of the body are completely developed. The child begins to observe others, and learns from them. At this stage, the child cannot learn from his own experiences, and the personality orientation associated with this stage is dependent orientation. Some of the personality characteristics associated with this stage are: optimism, trust, gullibility, passivity, immaturity, argumentation, cynicism, pessimism, exploitation and domination. Certain personality dispositions associated with the stage are gum chewing, nail biting, smoking, kissing and overeating.

Anal Stage

The anal stage is the stage during which a person's behaviour develops due to his experiences. This stage normally extends to the second and third year of a child's life. This is a stage of compulsive orientation, because he leads his life due to compulsions. Freud identified two personality types associated with the way a child is reared during this stage. Anal retentive personality, which is characterised by obstinacy, stinginess, orderliness, punctuality and over responsive to cleanliness. The second type is the anal aggressive personality with traits like cruelty, destructive attitude, disorderly behaviour and hostility.

Phallic Stage

The phallic stage normally occurs at the age of four years. A person slowly develops maturity in this stage. The characteristic feature of this stage is association with his family members, who influence the characteristics he develops. Some of the personality characteristics associated with this age are anxiety, guilt and frigidity. In males characteristics such as brashness, vanity, conceit, ambition, assertiveness and virility are associated with the stage and in females characteristics such as flirtatiousness, seductiveness and promiscuity.

Genital Stage

The genital stage is a mature one. It occurs during the period from adolescence to adulthood. At this stage, a person accumulates knowledge and experience and transfers them to younger generations. At this stage, one develops characteristics to fulfill one's life achievements. The personality characteristics associated with the stage are concern, love, affection and altruism.

The Freudian approach has made a significant contribution to understand personality development and the associated attributes that are relevant to understand organisational behaviour. It has however, been criticised for the choice of language and reliance on sex-related concepts.

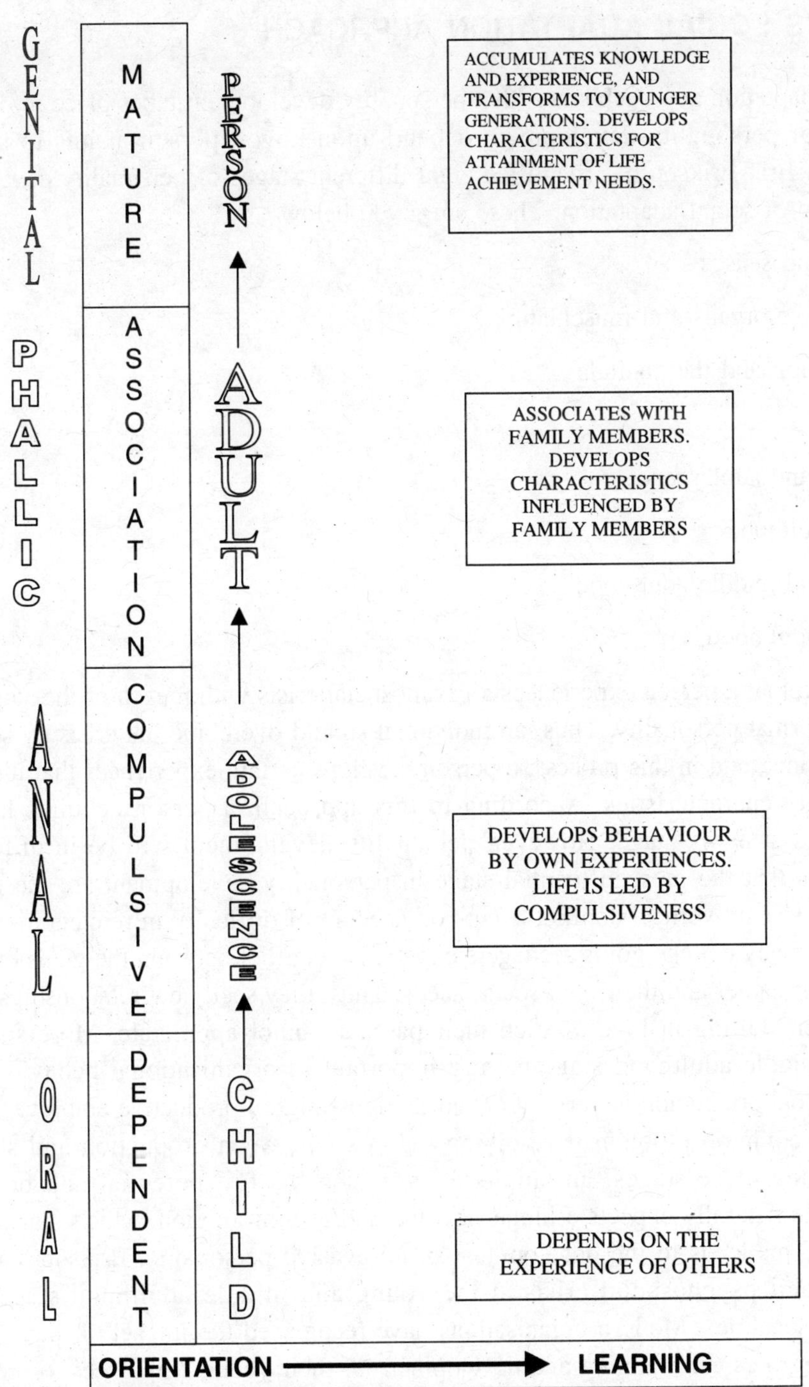

Figure 9.1: Stages in the development of personality

ERIKSON'S SOCIAL ADAPTATION APPROACH

The social adaptation approach states that personality development takes place in different stages. The stages of personality development depend upon how a person adapts to society and its environment. Erik Erikson has identified eight different stages of personality development based on the degree of social adaptation. These are given below.

1. Mouth and senses
2. Eliminative organs and musculature
3. Locomotion and the genitals
4. Latency
5. Puberty and adolescence
6. Early adulthood
7. Young and middle adulthood
8. Mature adulthood

Erikson stated that a person experiences a psychosocial crisis within each of the stages before one develops a normal personality. Thus, an individual should overcome the crisis by solving it in an optimum manner, and in this process, a person develops certain experiences that ultimately shape his personality characteristics. According to this approach, a person acquires his personality characteristics at every stage. However, personality development will be in different degrees. Erikson states that the most influential stage in personality development are the teenage years. During these years a vertical conflict occurs on account of difficulty in reintegration of the goals. For instance, many college going teenagers experience conflict between the goals of their parents, regarding their career and their own social needs. Thus, they seek new relationships to share their feelings, often 'falling in love', which their parents cannot appreciate. More specifically, the young and middle adulthood stage is very important in organisational behaviour because an individual's goal orientation is very high, and the most highly productive employees are found in this stage. A common problem is resolving the crisis between production and stagnation. For example during these stages, an employee works to his full potential and becomes highly productive. He naturally expects a higher income and/or a promotion, which many organisations do not give. This leads to the development of an evasive personality. Erikson states that those who solve their psychosocial crisis at the young and middle adulthood stage develop the healthiest personalities. Modern organisations have recognised the impact of this, and are paying more attention to career planning and development of their young employees to prevent burnout.

Table 9.1 Personality characteristics related to the Erikson psychosocial stages

Erikson psychosocial stages	Age	Personality Attributes
Mouth and senses	0-1	Observation
Eliminative organs and musculature	1-2	Risk taking
Locomotion and the genitals	3-5	Learning from others
Latency	6-12	Seeking pleasure
Puberty and adolescence	12-18	Conflict resolution
Early adulthood	18-25	Association
Young and middle adulthood	25-40	Goal achievement
Mature adulthood	40 and above	Counseling

LEVINSON'S ADULT LIFE STAGES APPROACH

Daniel Levinson developed the adult life stages approach to describe personality development. The approach makes three assumptions, namely:

(i) The life structure of a person evolves through a relatively orderly sequence throughout the adult years.

(ii) Personality development is not event-oriented, rather it is age-based.

(iii) There is a little variability in the development of personality in different stages.

The approach identified two periods attributed to personality development, which are shown in Table 9.2.

Table 9.2 Development of Personality Periods

Stable Periods		Transitional Periods	
Entering the world	22-28	Age: Thirty	28-33
Settling down	33-40	Midlife	40-45
Entering middle adulthood	45-50	Age: Fifty	50-55
Culmination of middle adulthood	55-60	Late adult	60-65

According to this approach personality development takes place in transitional periods and behaviour is constant during stable periods.

HALL'S CAREER STAGE APPROACH

Douglas Hall propounded a career stage model to explain personality development. The model identifies four stages, which are given in Table 9.3.

Table 9.3 Stages of Personality Development

Stage	Need	Personality Development	Approach
Exploration	Identity	Self examination and role tryouts	Child ego
Establishment	Intimacy and love and affection	Adoptive and adjustment	Adolescence
Maintenance	Generatively	Ideal and emulated by the younger generation	Paternalistic
Decline	Integrity and self-actualisation	Living a peaceful and purposeful life	Full maturity

According to this model, personality development is a function of the needs of a person. In the exploration stage as an individual wishes to establish his identity, he develops his personality by self-examination and trying out roles. However, in the establishment stage, an individual tries to develop intimate relationships with others, thus, gratification of love and affection is a priority. He therefore, becomes adaptive and adjusting to develop intimate relationships. The maintenance stage is characterised by the need to transfer his personality to the next generation. Therefore, an individual assumes a paternalistic approach, and tries to develop a personality that the younger generation can emulate. In this process of personality development an individual may grow further or start declining. Finally, in the decline stage a person ardently wishes to behave with the highest degree of integrity. As such, his personality development is oriented towards leading a peaceful and purposeful life.

This model is of great relevance to industrial settings. It is used as a guide to career development and provides valuable insights into personality development.

> *"Man knows only a part of his being, his surface mentality. We are sometimes completely overcome by emotions, instinctive and involuntary reactions that upset the role of conscious reason.... Under the stress of strong emotions we say or do things, which we regret afterwards. Unless the individual has complete self-awareness, he cannot become master of his life, by developing purity of intentions, man marches to success."*
>
> ***– Dr. Sarvepally Radhakrishnan***

ARGYRIS' MATURITY AND IMMATURITY CONTINUUM APPROACH

Chris Argyris developed a continuum model to explain development of personality. The model makes two assumptions, which are stated below.

i. Human personality is not developed in strict stages, rather it progresses along a continuum.
ii. Personality is developed from immaturity characteristics to maturity characteristics.

Argyris developed the immaturity and maturity continuum with seven dimensions, which is shown in Table 9.4.

Table 9.4 Immaturity and Maturity Dimensions

Immaturity Characteristics	Maturity Characteristics
Passivity	Activity
Dependence	Independence
Behaves in a similar way in most situations	Diverse ways of behaving
Shallow interests	Deep interests
Short-term perspective	Long time perspective
Subordinate position	Super-ordinate position
Lack of self-awareness	Self-awareness and control

According to Argyris, the seven dimensions in the continuum represent only one aspect of the total personality. The human personality starts with immature characteristics acquired through the process of pleasure and self-satisfaction. It develops into a mature personality, as one develops an understanding of the world and society. According to Argyris, personality development is complete when one displays maturity characteristics, which then become permanent attitudes that direct the remaining part of a person's life. Therefore, it is suggested that an organisation should develop maturity dimensions in order to develop their employees. However, the difficulty arises when the organisation fails to meet the expectations of the employees, so their goals conflict with those of the organisation. This leads to frustration, stress, and poor development of employees' personalities. Perception, self-concept, adaptation and adjustment also determine personality. There is a close relationship between individual maturity levels and an organisation and its structure. Figure 9.2 shows the relationship between life stages and personality development.

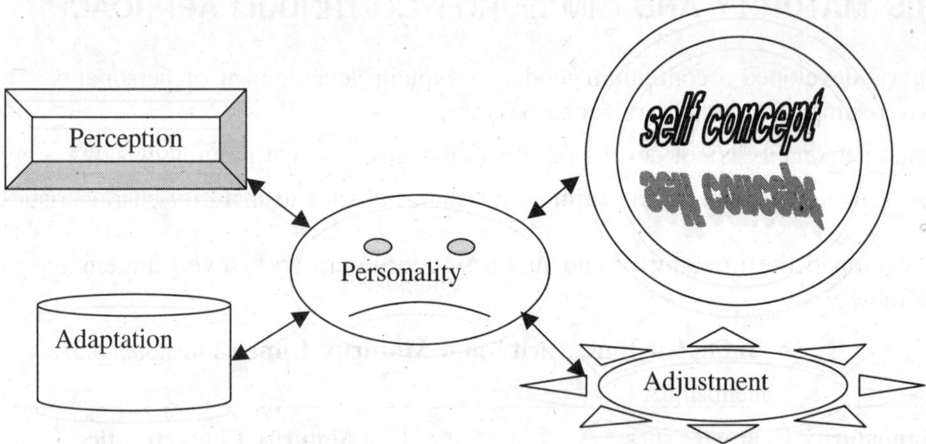

Figure 9.2: Adult life stages and personality development

Perception is the process of understanding the worldly environment. In this process individuals receive stimuli and process them with the help of the cognitive structure of the brain. The personality of the individual depends on the cognitive structure, therefore development of personality takes place through perception. Adaptation is the ability of the individual to change his behaviour to situational demands. Personality development occurs with adaptation. Interestingly adjustment also determines the development of personality of individuals. At the same time, it is necessary to briefly understand the concept of the self to appraise the theory. A description of the various self concepts is undertaken in the following section.

(i) Self Image

Every person develops certain beliefs about himself. Some of them are developed unconsciously over a period. A person looks at himself from the point of view of beliefs. This is called self image or self identity. According to Erikson, *self-identity is a life long development, largely unconscious, of the individual to society. Its roots go all the way back to the first recognition.* For instance, even when children first smile at others, there is something of self-realisation along with mutual recognition. Everyone wishes to protect his self-image and behaves in a way that establishes his identity.

(ii) Ideal Self

An individual develops certain standards of behaviour consistent with the environment. They are perceived as ideals for controlling behaviour. Hence, the ideal self is the way in which an individual wants to behave.

(iii) Looking Glass Self

People in society develop an understanding of other persons. Thus, the looking glass self is the perception of a person about how others perceive him. The perception of others is developed by the nature of the society and the degree of face-to-face interaction developed at the early stages of life. Therefore, self-concept is a function of the looking glass self.

(iv) Real Self

It is the reality of one's personality. A person's beliefs are evaluated and adjusted to the perceptions of others. This is because the self-concept of a person should conform to the general standards of behaviour. Thus the real self validates one's self-image.

Individual behaviour is determined by one's self-concept. The closer the association between the ideal self and the real self, the greater is the contentment, happiness and satisfaction. This results in normal behaviour. If the ideal self is far from the real self, an individual becomes frustrated and unhappy. The result is abnormal behaviour.

According to Gellerman, "*the average individual is not well acquainted with himself, but remains faithful to it*".

In organisational behaviour self-concept is related to the application of reinforcement motivation, the leadership styles adopted by the superiors, job satisfaction and psychological commitment of employees, and the effectiveness attained by the organisation.

However, the approach has the following limitations:

i. The model cannot predict specific behaviour.
ii. The dimensions of the model reflect latent personality characteristics. Hence, observable behaviour may differ according to the situation.

In spite of the limitations, the model is of great help in understanding how personality develops.

SUMMARY

This chapter provided the background of the theoretical foundations of personality development. It is a process of acquiring certain personality characteristics throughout one's life. Mitchell is of the opinion that socialisation determines personality development. In his words, 'it is not a haphazard accumulation of bits of behaviour but entails, instead, some orderly development'. He further stated that the accumulation of behaviour is true at least to the degree that some complex social behaviour patterns occur sequentially. Freud, Erikson, Levinson and Hall propounded the stage theories. Argyris put forward the continuum approach. Freud's physiological approach considered oral, anal, phallic and genital stages in the development of personality. While the oral stage leads to dependent orientation, the anal stage develops compulsive orientation. The phallic and genital stages are associated with maturity orientation. In these stages, the personality is transformed from adult to complete person. On the same lines as those of Freud, Erikson identified eight stages in personality development in his approach known as social adaptation. The stages are mouth and senses, eliminative organs and musculature, locomotion and the genitals, latency, puberty and adolescence, early adulthood, young and middle adulthood, and mature adulthood. In each of these stages, one experiences psychological crises. An attempt to overcome a crisis leads to the development of personality. Levinson described the adult life stage approach. According to this approach, personality development takes place in two phases. He terms them as stable and transitional periods. The stable stages comprise entering the world, settling down, entering middle adulthood and culmination of middle adulthood. The transitional stages are age thirty, midlife, age fifty and late adult. According to this approach, personality development takes place in transitional periods. Hall developed the career approach. His career development stages are exploration, establishment, maintenance and decline. The model stated that personality development is a function of needs. At each stage, personality development occurs. As against the stage proposition, Chris Argyris stated that personality development takes place on a continuous basis. He developed a continuum consisting of immaturity and maturity. According to this theory personality development starts with the immaturity characteristics and it is said to be complete with the disposition of maturity characteristics. There are four interrelated processes responsible for personality development. They are perception, adaptation, adjustment and self-concept. Self-concept again consists of self-image, the ideal self, the looking-glass self and the real self. Personality development is greatly influenced by self-concept. Personality development theories are necessary to understand an employee's behaviour and plans for career development over a period of time.

Key words

- **Adaptation:** The process of changing to adapt to new behaviour.
- **Adjustment:** Behavioural disposition to adjust to new environmental stimuli.
- **Anal stage:** Stimulation of anal organs produce pleasure and determine the personality.
- **Genital stage:** Stage of achievement orientation that determines personality.
- **Oral stage:** The stage in which stimulation of the oral organs produces pleasure, and thus determines personality.
- **Perception:** Understanding of worldly environment.
- **Phallic stage:** Stage of association and identification with family members.
- **Self concept:** Strong inclination to satisfy one's own needs ignoring those of others.
- **Socialisation:** An orderly accumulation and development of behaviour.
- **Stable periods:** The periods in which behaviour does not change.
- **Transitional periods:** The periods of personality development.

10. PERCEPTION

This chapter enables you:

- *To define perception*
- *To be aware of the principles of perception*
- *To understand the difference between perception and sensation*
- *To appraise the perceptual process*
- *To understand the factors that determine perception*
- *To comprehend distortions in right judgement*

The structure of the chapter is as follows:

- Introduction
- Definition of perception
- Characteristics of perception
- Principles of perception
- Perceptual process
- Factors influencing perception
- Perceptual distortions
- Summary
- Key words

CHAPTER 10

Perception

INTRODUCTION

By now, it is clear that a number of factors shape the personality of an individual, and that learning is a process by which a person's behaviour is changed. Perception, learning and attitudes are the elements of personality, and in this chapter we will learn more about perception. Perception, attitude and values are all psychological processes. Perception is the process of understanding the information received from the environment. It is a psychological system. Perception is not the same as sensation. Sensation is due to stimuli from the sensory organs. An individual's perception is not formed spontaneously, but is developed by interaction with a number of elements. It often happens that we misunderstand others. This is called perceptual distortion, and leads to misunderstandings. Therefore, it is relevant to remove distortions.

DEFINITION OF PERCEPTION

When we look at some one or something, we select, organise and interpret the sensory stimulation into meaningful information. This is called perception. Perception is the main mechanism by which people learn about their surroundings. A successful manager correctly assesses the perception of his employees and uses different ways to make them work. Understanding the various aspects of perception helps one to understand human behaviour.

> *"Perception is the intellectual process by which a person acquires information from the environment, organises it and obtains the meaning from it"*. **Kolasa**
>
> **Robbins** defines perception *"as a process by which individuals organise, and interpret their sensory impressions in order to give meaning to their environments"*.

According to **Joseph Reitz**, perception includes *"all those processes by which an individual receives information about his environment – seeing, hearing, feeling, tasting, and smelling. The study of these perceptional processes shows that their functioning is affected by three classes of variables – the objects or events being perceived, the environment in which perception occurs, and the individual doing the perceiving"*.

CHARACTERISTICS OF PERCEPTION

Perception is the basic cognitive or psychological process. The definitions given above reveal the following characteristics of perception.

i. Perception is a psychological process.
ii. It is a cognitive and intellectual function of the human brain.
iii. It forms and develops out of experiences.
iv. Perception satisfies needs.
v. Perception is through the sensory organs, but interpretations are made by a psychological process.
vi. It is related more to the environment than personality.

PRINCIPLES OF PERCEPTION

The basic principles of perception are given below.

1. Selectivity:

Selectivity refers to the process, by which certain information is selected by the brain. Individuals cannot sense all the information surrounding them due to biological and psychological limitations. They consider only the more interesting and relevant information. Individuals select that information which is consistent with their experiences, interests, needs, desires, wishes and goals. For example, a student reading the newspaper will be interested in information on employment, movies and sports.

2. Closure:

Closure is a tendency to complete information with the help of imagination in the absence of the required information. Often, individuals have to make a judgment using the available information, which is often incomplete. In the process, they have a tendency to make their own assumptions about missing information and close the gap. This tendency is called closure. It is interesting to note that people behave as if they have complete knowledge. Look at the following figure. Most people will immediately understand it as two parallel lines, ignoring the fact that there is a slight break in the lines.

This is due to closure. Because of this tendency, people ignore slightly disturbing stimuli and try to judge the entire situation. This is referred to as Gestalt psychology.

3. Context:

Context is the environment or situation in which individual understanding occurs. It is made up of physical factors such as light, heat, colour, size of the object etc., and emotional and social factors. Perceptual context is an important characteristic of perception. For example, the figure shows a circle inside the square. Can you say which is bigger?

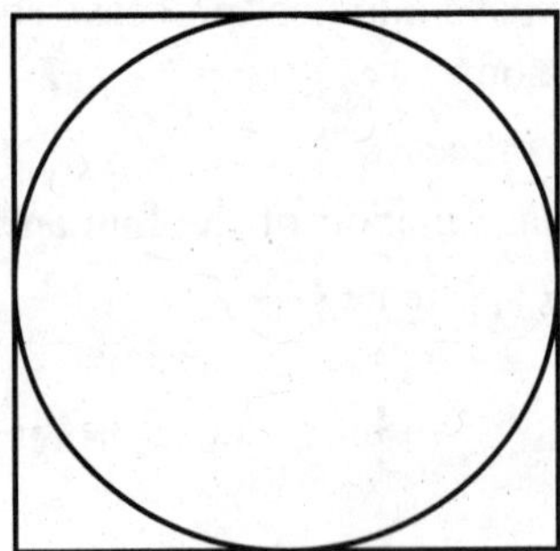

You are likely to infer that the square bigger than the circle. This is because the circle embedded inside the square is perceived as smaller. The fact is that both are the same size. The reason for misperception is that the circle shown inside the square is perceived in the context of square.

Perception vs. Sensation

Sensation, which is often equated with perception, is the act of recognising stimuli with the help of sensory organs. The human body has five sensory organs, the eyes, ears, nose, tongue and skin, called the *panchendriya.* The sensory organs receive the stimulus and the brain interprets it. Differences exist between perception and sensation that are shown in table 10.1.

In an organisational context, understanding the perceptions of employees is very important for managers to perform their functions effectively. Managers must be in a position to understand the perception of their subordinates and the actual situations they are in. Sometimes, a manager may act with the best of intentions, but his actions are misunderstood by the employees. For instance, a manager, who is strict about discipline, as he feels it is necessary for the optimum functioning of the organisation, may be considered authoritarian. Therefore, a manager should also be concerned about how his actions are interpreted by others. A manager can improve the perceptual accuracy if he becomes aware of how perceptions are formed and distorted. In the following section, we will learn more about the formation of perceptions.

Table 10.1 Perception vs. Sensation

Variables	Sensation	Perception
1. Meaning	Sensation is information received through physical organs: namely the skin, eyes, ears, nose and tongue, leading to the sensations of touch, vision, hearing, smell and taste respectively.	Perception is a cognitive and psychological process of sensing, filtering, modifying and interpreting the data received from the sensory organs.
2. Scope	Sensation is elementary to behaviour. It is largely determined by physiological functioning.	Perception is much more complex and broader than sensation.
3. Response	It is bodily response. For example, when the temperature is hot the body sweats.	It is a psychological response. For instance heat produces discomfort, which leads to poor work performance.
4. Orientation	It is external orientation of the body. It is immediately visible by the physical actions of human beings. For instance, tears appear when we are unhappy.	It is internal cognitive orientation. It is slow. It is inferred from the behaviour of individuals.
5. Impact	Sensation plays an important role in the private life of individuals.	Perception is crucial in organisational life. For example, if a worker perceives that his salary is not adequate to lead a comfortable life he is likely to show a poor response to work.

PERCEPTUAL PROCESS

Perception is a psychological activity. It is not a one-time activity, but is developed by a process. It is an input and output system that occurs in the human brain. The perceptual process is shown in Figure 10.1.

Figure 10.1 consists of four variables – input, process, output and behaviour. They are explained below:

Input

Input is the information received by the sensory organs. It is the basis of perception. Objects, events, people, information etc. are generally understood as inputs. Sensory organs receive a variety of stimuli such as smell, taste, touch, sight, sound etc. The brain gives meaning to them after processing the stimuli. For example, if a circular is sent to an erring employee, he understands that it is disciplinary action even before reading it.

Process

Process involves analysing the inputs with the help of the cognitive structure of the human brain. The mechanisms of processing perceptual inputs are – selection, organisation and interpretation, which take place in the brain. This results in the interpretation of the information provided by the sensory organs.

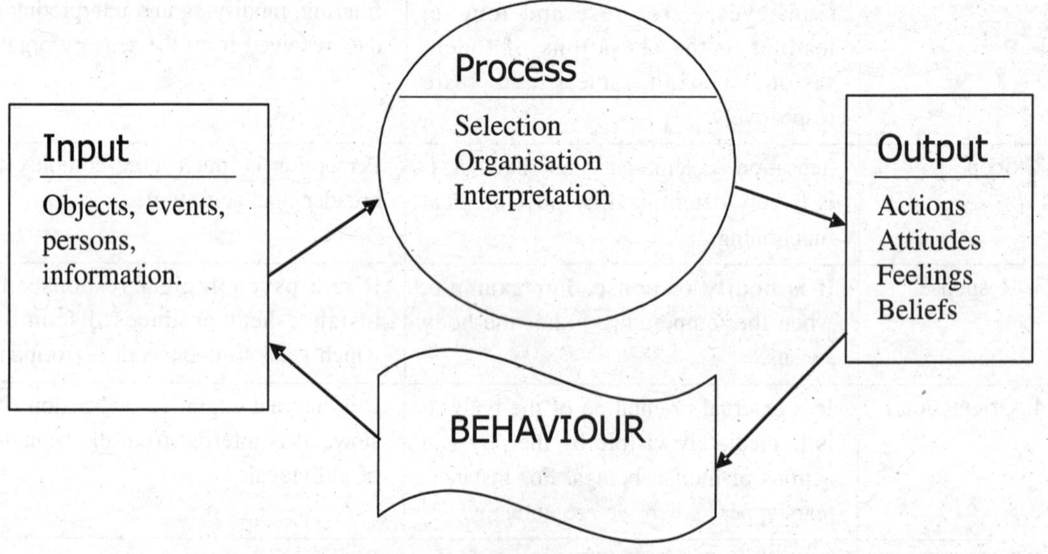

Figure 10.1: Perception Process

i. Selection: Selection is the process of choosing stimuli for further processing. Individuals cannot assimilate all the stimuli that they receive. They select only the stimuli, which are relevant to them, depending on their interests, experiences and attitudes.

The studies conducted by Dearborn and Simon revealed that *out of twenty-three business executives, from different functional areas like sales, finance and production, every executive tended to identify the most important problem as the one which belonged to their own field of specialisation.*

ii. Organisation: Organising is an orderly arrangement of the information that is sensed by the organs. This process is also called the 'Gestalt Process'. Gestalt psychology states that an individual understands things as a whole and not by parts. Organisation helps to give a meaningful picture to the perceiver from the perceived inputs. There are three ways of organising the perceived inputs, objects and events. They are grouping, closure and simplification.

(a) Grouping**:** People or things can be grouped based on similarity or proximity. Objects that are in close proximity are grouped under one head though they are unrelated. For instance, three or four students waiting in the library may be understood as a group, and they are perceived as intelligent. In fact, one of them may be waiting for his friend. This is called grouping.

(b) Closure: People have a tendency to fill in the gaps in information. This tendency to organise perceptual stimuli through which they try to complete the message is known as closure. In organisations, managers who have to make a decision, but do not have the complete information, are likely to fill in the missing information.

(c) Simplification: People having more information face the problem of understanding what is relevant and what is irrelevant. Therefore, they try to simplify it and make it more meaningful and understandable to them. Individuals overlook less important information and concentrate on what they consider is important. Simplification is an essential step in organisation because in the absence of this, things may look complicated. For example when you are reading this book, you will try to ignore the words that are difficult to understand.

iii. Interpretation: Another element in the process of perception is interpretation. It is a process of drawing meaning from the inputs and is a subjective and judgmental process. Interpretation is influenced by factors such as the halo effect, stereotyping, attribution, impression and inference. These factors are discussed subsequently. For example, a pat given to a friend is understood as friendship. A teacher giving a pat to the student is understood as punishment.

Outputs

Output is the result of processing the input. A person tries to judge or draw a meaningful inference based on his mental process. This output ultimately results in actions and reactions.

Behaviour

Behaviour is the result of perception. People try to elicit a response based on their interpretation. If they understand something positively, they show a positive response and vice versa. For instance, an employee having a positive understanding of the work is likely to show more interest in the work.

FACTORS INFLUENCING PERCEPTION

The understanding of an individual is influenced by a number of factors. These factors are explained below.

1. Physiology:

Physiological factors are related to the biological arrangement of organs. Perception of an individual is influenced by his or her physiological conditions. For example, a worker having hearing problem cannot hear the instructions of the superior and understand them.

2. Needs and Desires:

Needs and desires play a vital role in perception. For example, a frustrated individual understands everything in a negative manner. Power seekers are more likely to notice power related stimuli, whereas socially oriented people give attention to inter-personal stimuli.

3. *Personality:*

Personality has a profound influence on perceived behaviour. Research findings revealed the following.

(i) Secure individuals tend to perceive others as warm and not cold.

(ii) Thoughtful individuals do not express extreme opinions of others.

(iii) Persons who have faith in themselves perceive things favourably.

(iv) Individuals, who have self-acceptance perceive themselves as liked, wanted and accepted by others.

4. *Experience:*

Successful experiences enhance positive understanding and self-confidence whereas failure decreases self-confidence.

5. *Family:*

Family has a major influence on perception. People develop attitudes and value systems, which are generally prevalent in the family.

6. *Culture:*

The society and culture in which a person lives have a major impact on one's attitudes, values and way of perceiving the world. For example – a cow may be sacred for a Hindu, but Europeans consider it as an animal useful for its milk and meat.

7. *Stress:*

Stress is a situation created by the pressure of job responsibilities. Sometimes, stress helps in perceiving things in the proper perspective, but more often it leads to less accurate impressions.

8. *Group Pressure*:

Individuals are members of groups. The perception of an individual changes due to pressure from the group. Often, an individual's perception changes when one finds that one's beliefs or attitudes are not shared by others.

9. *Interaction:*

Interaction is the process of sharing information among group members. It helps in improving perception about a person or situation. It provides an opportunity for sharpening perception.

10. *Role:*

Role and perception are related. A person may play multiple roles – father, husband, student, brother etc. Therefore, while perceiving the behaviour of a person, his role should be taken into account. Otherwise, the perception may be wrong.

11. Reference Groups:

Many people use groups to clarify or change their perception. For example, if an employee wants to be identified as a member of a productive work group, he will observe the qualities of the members of such group and try to follow them.

12. Organisational position:

The position and status held by an individual in an organisation influences his perception. For example, a finance manager views every problem, taking into consideration budgetary constraints.

13. Reward System:

A reward system has an impact on an individual's perception process. If an employee observes that hard work, devotion and productivity are recognised and rewarded in the organisation, he develops a positive understanding about the reward system.

14. Size:

A larger object is likely to attract attention and it influences perceptual selectivity of an individual. For example, a full-page notice is perceived as more important than a notice of a few lines.

15. Intensity:

Intensity is the impact of things. It influences selection. For example, bold lettered words are understood to be more important than words in ordinary letters.

16. Frequency:

Frequency is repetition of the same stimuli. Frequency of occurrence is likely to attract more attention and develop a positive understanding. For example, a frequently sent circular is understood by the employees to be a serious matter.

Factors influencing the perception of employees are of specific significance to a manager in an organisation. Managerial strategies of communication, motivation and eliciting a positive response from employees are designed based on these factors. For instance, financial motivation is used for an employee who has a positive perception about monetary rewards; otherwise, a manager may use non-monetary rewards, such as praise, recognition and esteem to motivate the employee. In another case a manager may give detailed instructions and personal counseling to an employee who has a poor understanding, whereas, he gives one time instructions to those who can grasp the matter quickly.

PERCEPTUAL DISTORTIONS

Distortions in perceptions are those elements that come in the way of proper understanding.

Frequently, individuals misunderstand situations due to a number of reasons. Distortions in perception, which arise because different individuals understand things in a different manner, are very common. They are due to a number of factors, such as physical conditions, personality of the perceiver, the environment, and are presented below:

(i) Halo Effect: The halo effect uses a single personality trait in an individual to draw a general meaning about him. The single trait influences the judgement of the other characteristics of the individual. The halo effect has important implications for evaluation of employees in an organisation. It may have a positive or negative effect. For instance, a good looking employee may be considered to be smart, whereas in actual fact, he may be the opposite. Here, his facial features influence the understanding of him in a positive manner.

(ii) Stereotyping: Stereotyping is judging a person based on the characteristics of the group to which they belong. In the process of stereotyping, individual characteristics are overlooked. This causes an error in the understanding, as certain important traits are not considered. For example, the Japanese are perceived as industrious, Americans are perceived as materialistic, Indians are perceived as democratic etc. Similarly, if an employee is frequently seen in a group of productive workers, he is likely to be judged as a productive worker, whereas he may in fact be spoiling the productive group. On the other hand, an employee found in a group of agitating persons, is likely to be judged as an agitator or an insincere worker, whereas he may be calm and sincere. The advantage of stereotyping is that it helps the perceiver to simplify a complex situation, but the disadvantage is that people are perceived as members of a group, rather than individuals.

(iii) Attribution: Attribution is explaining behaviour by a cause and effect relationship. It is an important factor in perception, because it creates a tendency to look at identical behaviour differently. For example, if two students arrive late for class, they may give different explanations. While one uses the excuse that train was late, the other uses the excuse of ill health. In this case, a teacher is likely to show more concern for the second student. To take another example, suppose two workers do not perform a given task. One worker cites ill health as the reason, while the other worker says the poor quality of the raw materials prevented him from doing the job. The supervisor is likely to show sympathy for the first person and look on the second as a 'work evader', even if the raw materials are really of poor quality. Here the supervisor is unable to accept that the fault was his, as he supplied poor quality materials.

(iv) Impression: Formulating certain ideas about others even before knowing their personality traits is known as impression. It leads to perceptual distortions. The first impression lasts longer unless it is contradicted by the information received later. For example, if a worker is seen to be very serious in his work, when he first joins the organization, his superior has a favourable impression about him. Later, even if the worker slackens off, the superior may not believe it unless he experiences it for himself.

(v) Inference: Inference refers to drawing judgements based on information. The right inference requires complete information; otherwise, an inference based on limited information can lead to a wrong inference or judgement. This leads to a perceptual error. For example, a finance manager making an investment decision without obtaining complete information about the available investment opportunities is likely to make a wrong choice, and the result would be a loss. Therefore, inference is an important perceptual error.

(vi) Projection: In projection, the perceiver assumes that others have the same characteristics as himself. Therefore, a person is likely to be judged based on the traits of the person making the judgement. Moreover, people like to anticipate future events. In this case, the projections are based on expectations, which are sometimes far from the reality. Thus, an error is caused if the anticipated events do not materialise. For instance, an honest person is likely to assume that others are also honest, and deals with them in that way. However, in reality, all people do not have the same degree of honesty. In another instance, a production manager who was promoted due to his hard work and sincerity, will expect his workers to be as hardworking as he is and is likely to develop an authoritarian style of supervision. This makes it difficult for him to deal with them. However, he does not realise that all workers are not as devoted as he is.

Case study 10.1: The First Impression the Best – Yet Distorts Perceptions

Mr. Ravinder is a postgraduate in Human Resource Management, and Mr. Rao is a postgraduate in Management with a specialisation in human resources. Both of them have been short-listed for the final interview in a reputed company. They have been called for a final discussion at the corporate office. The discussion will be held with the Head of the Human Resource Department, along with a few others. The two candidates presented themselves at the corporate office. The first round of discussions was held with Mr. Rao, whom the Head did not find suitable for the position. He requested Mr. Rao to leave without disturbing the other candidates, as he did not want the discussions concerning pay and perquisites revealed to the other candidates waiting for the interview. However, after he came out of the room, his friend anxiously enquired about the interview and Mr. Rao talked to him. This was perceived as a very serious mistake by the Head, who requested him to leave in no uncertain terms. Such a serious warning was not really necessary, but he issued it due to perceptual distortion. Finally Mr. Ravinder was selected for the position and was instructed to report for duty after three days at exactly 10 a.m. On the appointed day, Mr. Ravinder called the Head at about 9.30 a.m. to request him to give him about a half an hour more he had to purchase a bus pass for travel. Unfortunately due to inordinate delays, it took him more than two hours to obtain the bus pass, and he finally reported to the office at about 1.30 p.m. His late coming was taken very seriously by the Head, who immediately prepared a termination order withdrawing the offer given to him. Mr. Ravinder pleaded that as he was given to understand that no leave would be granted for the first month and therefore he wanted to secure the bus pass on the same day. However, the contention of the Head was that his act amounted to act of disobedience and showed lack of interest in the company. This is an example of forming an impression judging an individual, based on one experience. This is perceptual distortion.

SUMMARY

Perception is a process of selecting, organising and interpreting the stimuli received from the environment. Individuals understand things, persons and organisations based on perception. It is a psychological process, which is developed from experience. Perception depends on the environment. It is based on selectivity, closure and context. Perception and sensation are different. Although perception is developed through the sensory organs, sensation is only a bodily response, whereas perception is a psychological response. Sensation plays an important role in private life and perception is crucial in organisational life. The process of perception consists of input, process and output. The process involves selection, organisation and interpretation of the input and an output is produced in the form of actions, attitudes, feelings and beliefs. A number of factors such as, physiology, needs and desires, personality, experience, family, culture, stress, group pressure, interaction, role, reference groups, status in an organisation, reward system, size of the object, intensity and frequency, influence the perception of individuals. Understanding perception is important in organisational behaviour. However, a number of factors distort the perception of individuals. Some of these factors are attribution, halo effect, impression, inference, projection and stereotyping. These distortions come in the way of proper understanding. Thus, managers should eliminate the distortions to improve their understanding of employees.

Key words:

- **Attribution:** Attaching a cause and effect relationship to behaviour.
- **Closure:** The tendency to organise perceptual stimuli so as to complete the message.
- **Context:** An environment or situation in which individual understanding occurs.
- **Grouping:** Combining all the related information to understand it.
- **Halo Effect:** Using the information about a single personality trait to understand an individual.
- **Perception:** It is a process of selecting, organising and interpreting the stimuli from the environment.
- **Projection:** Assuming the characteristics of the perceiver in the perceived.
- **Role:** Expected behaviour of an individual.
- **Selectivity:** The process of selecting stimuli based on one's interests.
- **Sensation:** It is bodily response elicited by the response of sensory organs.
- **Simplification:** It is ignoring information considered as irrelevant in understanding.
- **Stereotyping:** The process of judging people based on traits of the group to which they belong.

11. ATTITUDES

This chapter enables you:

- *To understand the meaning of attitudes*
- *To evaluate the characteristic features of attitudes*
- *To appraise the importance of employees' attitudes towards managers*
- *To appraise how attitudes are formed in organisations*
- *To understand various components of attitude formation*
- *To comprehend the role of cognitive dissonance in attitude formation*
- *To know the strategies adopted by managers in attitude formation*
- *To identify the motives of forming attitudes*
- *To see how social judgement influences the formation of attitudes*
- *To appraise the factors of attitude change management*
- *To examine the techniques followed in attitude change management*

The structure of the chapter is as follows:

- Introduction
- Definition of attitudes
- Characteristics of attitudes
- Attitude formation
- Factors influencing formation of attitudes
- Cognitive dissonance theory
- Functional theory
- Social judgement theory
- Attitude change management
- Summary
- Key words

CHAPTER 11

Attitudes

INTRODUCTION

Attitude is a psychological phenomenon. The evaluative statements made by individuals express the attitudes possessed by him. Attitudes relate to an individual's job, superiors, satisfaction, security, and the organisation to which he belongs. Attitudes are not in-born. They are learnt and developed by worldly interaction. Attitude structure is responsible for the development of attitudes. Attitudes are permanent impressions and are developed by repeated experiences. A single experience does not develop attitudes. Individuals develop an attitude by associating the information received from a stimulus with information in the brain. Consistency of information enables one to develop an attitude. Inconsistency leads to rejection of information, and no attitude is developed. Festinger has developed the cognitive dissonance theory to explain the formation of attitudes. According to this theory, individuals attempt to reduce dissonance, which leads to attitude development. The functional theory and social judgement theory have also been put forward to explain the formation of attitude. Attitude change is inevitable to any organisation. Employees possess certain attitudes, which may be congruent or incongruent with those of the organisation. Therefore, they should try to change their attitudes so that they are suited to the organisation. Although attitudes are learnt as permanent impressions, consistent efforts can change attitudes. Managers use a number of strategies to change attitudes. In this chapter we will understand the implication of attitude on organisational behaviour.

Case study 11.1: Benchmarking: An organisational attitude or a physical process

Organisational attitudes are very important and useful for organisations that are operating in a climate of uncertainty and complexity. It is a challenge for companies to survive in the midst of competition, and continuous improvements in products and processes, quality of customer service and monitoring the market are essential. Benchmarking is a useful tool for most organisations, to target the weak areas and identify the strengths for better customer service quality. Benchmarking is a process of identifying standard practices to meet the expectations of internal and external constituencies. It is essential both internally and externally at all levels of management viz., strategic, tactical and operational. It uses knowledge to design strategies to attain superior performance. Benchmarking is carried out for products, services, organisational and business processes, organisational procedures and human resources. Obviously, this brings about customer satisfaction, a competitive edge, and overall effectiveness of organisations. Benchmarking is not only a skill, but also an attitude of the people involved in the application. McKinsey & Co adopted benchmarking to achieve excellence. The company believed that it should be developed as an attitude and not merely a change. The company developed an approach called the 5Ps. They are (1) Partners, (2) People, (3) Procedures, and systems, (4) Product and (5) Process design and physical configuration. A similar procedure, which compared mail services in the UK, Germany, France, Netherlands, Italy and Spain, revealed that Royal Mail, UK, provides the best service. It claims it as an attitude of their delivery personnel. The benchmarking for British Airways is the quality of service that is again related to the attitude of the airhostesses, pilots and terminal staff. Some other examples of organisations that changed the organisational attitudes of their human resource department with respect to benchmarking are Ford, General Electric, IBM, Canon and NEC.

DEFINITION OF ATTITUDES

Attitude is an evaluation of an object or a person in a specific way. It is the formation of certain permanent impressions. It is a psychological phenomenon and forms a basis for human behaviour. A human being behaves in a particular way based on impressions formulated by him. These impressions are predispositions. Certain definitions of attitude are:

> *"Attitude is a persistent tendency to feel and behave in a particular way toward some object."* **Joseph Reitz**
>
> According to **Allport,** *"Attitude is a mental state of readiness, organised through experience, exerting a specific influence upon a person's response to people, objects and situation with which it is related."*

According to **Krech** and **Crutchfield,** *"Attitude is an enduring organisation of motivational, emotional, perceptual and cognitive processes with respect to some aspect of the individuals world".*

Katz and **Scotland** defined attitude as, *"a tendency or predisposition to evaluate an object or symbol of that object in a certain way".*

CHARACTERISTICS OF ATTITUDES

The characteristics of attitudes are given below:

(i) Attitude is a psychological concept.

(ii) Attitudes do not exist at the time of birth. They are learnt through experience.

(iii) It is a permanent impression and remains unchanged unless there is a force to change it.

(iv) Attitude exists in every person. Because every person possesses attitudes on innumerable things or objects or persons.

(v) Attitudes have a cause and effect relationship.

(vi) It is both a physical and behavioural reaction to an external stimulus.

(vii) Attitudes have emotional and motivational aspects.

(viii) Attitudes are almost permanent. A strong force is required to change an existing attitude.

(ix) Attitudes and opinions differ on a conceptual basis. Opinion is an expression of personal judgement after an evaluation of circumstances and evidence gathered by the sensory organs.

(x) Attitudes and beliefs also differ. A belief is an understanding evaluated through internal feelings. It is one's expectations about the nature and characteristics of an object or situation.

(xi) Attitudes and values are different concepts. Values are ideals related to the conduct of one's own behaviour. Not all values relate to a specific object or situation.

Employees working in organisations develop certain attitudes and express their feelings about the organisation. An individual's enthusiasm, satisfaction, energy, motivation, apathy, antagonism and dissatisfaction are expressions of his attitudes. Individual feelings regarding wages, working conditions, supervision, co-workers, responsibility, job security, prestige etc., reflect in one's attitudes. They influence a person's work and communication, vis-à-vis productivity of the organisation. Above all, attitudes influence behaviour. Therefore, managers need to understand attitudes.

ATTITUDE FORMATION

Formation of an attitude is the psychological process of developing impressions and using them in the process of judgment. We are not born with attitudes but form them due to worldly experiences. Attitude development requires an understanding of its structure. Several aspects comprise the totality of attitude. The various elements of attitude structure are:

(i) **Affective component:** The affective component of human brain is the part that leads to an emotional expression towards an object. It is developed by a conditional response by association with stimuli that lead to either a reward or punishment. Therefore, expressions of good or bad, likes or dislikes, pleasure or displeasure, beauty or ugliness are part of attitudes. Similarly, tendencies of love, hate, warmth, friendship, affinity etc. are expressions of attitudes.

(ii) **Cognitive component:** Cognitive component is the information gathered and stored in the human brain. Experience and perception are responsible for its development. This leads to development of an opinion or belief. A person uses beliefs based on his cognition to show certain behavioural reactions, and thus, formulates a certain attitude. For instance, an employee seen out of the work place, may lead the superior to develop an opinion of the employee as being 'uninterested in the work.' This may influence all his future evaluations, unless contradictory information about the sincerity of the employee disproves his earlier belief.

(iii) **Behavioural component:** The behavioural component shows an action or reaction towards an object or person. The intensity of the action shows the strength of attitude. For example, a supervisor having a negative attitude about a worker always finds fault with the worker. Similarly, a finance manager, who feels that a particular accountant cannot prepare a trial balance correctly always looks to find fault, even if the trial balance is correct.

(iv) **Valence:** Valence is the degree of strength or weakness of attitude. Indifference is a low valence in one's attitude towards the situation.

(v) **Multiplicity:** A variety of factors influence attitudes of an individual. Therefore, in the study of formation of attitudes, a manager should understand more than one factor.

(vi) **Need orientation:** Needs and desires of individuals influence attitudes. Greater needs have a stronger influence on the formation of attitudes.

(vii) **Stimuli:** Stimuli are the central concept of attitudes. A stimulus is any item of information received by the sensory organs and interpreted by the brain. Change in attitudes is a function of the strength or weakness of the stimuli. Attitudes formed due to strong stimuli are less open to change.

The discussions on formation of attitude show that attitudes are not formed due to a single experience in any situation. A continuous reinforcement of the same experience develops beliefs and consequently attitudes are developed. Attitudes, once developed, are less vulnerable to change unless a strong stimulus changes the earlier belief.

FACTORS INFLUENCING FORMATION OF ATTITUDES

Attitude structure is responsible for formation of human attitudes. A number of factors influence formation of attitudes. Factors influencing the formation of attitudes are described below.

(a) **Experience:** Continued interaction with a person or object leads to the development of an experience in an individual. A person retains information about whether an experience is rewarding or punishing, and uses this information in all future interactions with the person or object. For example, a hard nut is given to a child, and he fails to crack it in the first attempt. This may not lead him to believe that all nuts are hard and cannot be cracked, but if he experiences the same thing again and again, he formulates an attitude that certain nuts are hard to crack. Rewarding experience leads to the development of a positive attitude, whereas a punishing experience leads to a negative attitude. In organisations, employees develop impressions about salary, perquisites, working conditions, performance, superiors' behaviour, group interaction etc. Continued experience with these factors leads to the formation of attitudes. For example, if the working conditions are safe and superior's behaviour is encouraging a person develops a positive attitude towards work.

(b) **Association:** Association is correlating two objects or situations. A close relationship or association with two objects or persons leads to the development of opinions. A reinforced opinion leads to the formation of an attitude. For instance, a teacher finds that a few students in a group are sincere, punctual and interested in studies. When he evaluates the group, he remembers those students and evaluates the entire group of students as positive. Therefore, the teacher formulates a positive attitude of the group.

(c) **Interaction:** Interaction is the sharing of opinions and expression of views. Primarily, individuals develop opinions from their experience and observation of family members. The characteristics of family members, such as parents, brothers and sisters exert an influence on formation of right or wrong attitudes. For example, children belonging to hardworking and sincere parents are likely to develop a positive attitude towards work. Similarly, group interaction, characteristics, norms, styles, communication, etc., influence a member's attitudes. Group members form and develop opinions that conform to the characteristics, norms and values of the group. Therefore, work groups, reference groups and friendship groups influence attitude formation. However, all these groups do not exert the same degree of influence on attitude formation. A work group having strong positive values towards increasing productivity is likely to influence all its members to develop a positive attitude towards work.

(d) **Society:** Society is a large group of individuals, it defines an individual's actions according to the expectations of the society. It helps in transmitting culture from one generation to the other, and stipulates restrictions about unacceptable behaviour. A society develops its own culture, religion, language, and value systems. An individual's affiliation to social groups, culture, language, and religion is responsible for formation of attitudes.

For example, the Japanese have a positive attitude towards innovation and productive work culture, Americans have a positive attitude towards capitalism, the Chinese have a positive attitude towards communism, and the Indians have a positive attitude towards socialism and democracy.

(e) **Personality factors:** Personality leads to the formation of attitudes, which in turn determine the personality of individuals. Hence, both are inter-related. Personality factors like authoritarianism and democracy, pride, prejudice, conservation, liberalisation, optimism, pessimism etc. lead to formation of attitudes. For example, *authoritarian personality has a more positive attitude towards work and a negative attitude towards peoples' welfare.*

The above discussion shows that permanent impressions and beliefs held by individuals are responsible for formation of attitudes. Therefore, they are less susceptible to change. Attitudes do not exist at the time of birth; they are learnt from environmental interaction. Therefore, developing a strong argument against an attitude can change it.

Case study 11.2: Attitudes are formed by the influence of society

The Japanese have different attitudes from those held by people of other countries. They are very proud of their nationality, to the extent that there is a tendency to look down upon non-Japanese. This is a clear-cut example of the influence of society on the formation of the attitudes. Their national pride is so strong that they always prefer to buy goods manufactured in Japan. Despite the fact that globalisation has led the Japanese to import rice, sign boards such as 'pure Japanese rice available' and 'eat Japanese rice and live like a Japanese', are often seen. The Japanese retain their mannerisms, for example a Japanese manager working in an Indian establishment bows his head as mark of greeting rather than saying good morning, which the Indians have copied from the western world, in place of their 'namaskar'.

Theories of Attitude Formation

Attitude formation and change are not one time activities. It takes a long time for attitudes to form and change. A number of theories have been advanced to explain the process of attitude formation. Three classes of theories exist to explain the process. They are cognitive consistency theories, the functional theory, and the social judgement theory. Cognitive consistency theories have been further classified into balance theory, congruity theory, affective-cognitive consistency theory and cognitive dissonance theory. Of all these theories, cognitive dissonance theory is the most popular. The framework of these theories is given below.

COGNITIVE DISSONANCE THEORY

Festinger propounded the theory of cognitive dissonance. The theory explained the relationship between attitudes and behaviour. The theory states that individuals try to reconcile between divergent attitudes and balance their attitude to rationalise their behaviour. The following are the propositions of the theory.

(i) Cognition is information received, processed, and stored in the human mind.

(ii) Consonance of cognition exists when individuals are able to establish a relationship between life events based on logic or experience. Consonance leads to formation of attitudes. Individual behaviour is normal in the case of consonance.

(iii) Processing of unrelated information between current events and already existing information leads to the irrelevance of cognition. Irrelevant cognition leads to formation of unrelated attitudes. Therefore, a person displays a reserved pattern of behaviour.

(iv) Dissonance arises when the relationship of events is opposite to that of the existing experience.

(v) The degree of dissonance varies in its magnitude from one situation to another.

The theory thus states that dissonance gives rise to discomfort and stress. Individuals try to reduce it to the greatest extent possible. In any situation, proportion of number of inconsistent elements constitutes total dissonance. The greater the dissonance, the greater the effort to reduce it, so that attitudes are more consistent. Festinger suggests that attitude formation is closely associated with the strategies of reducing dissonance. He has suggested the following three strategies.

Managerial Strategies of Attitude formation

1. **Discount the importance:** Dissonance arises when individuals relate a piece of information with the information possessed by the human brain. The more the value attached to it, the more severe is the discomfort he experiences. Thus, overlooking information that causes discomfort reduces dissonance. For example, dissonance arises when a manager expects higher productivity from an employee whose productivity is poor. The more he attaches importance to the productivity of the employee, the more he will worry, causing dissonance. By overlooking productivity, the manager may be able to reduce his dissonance.

2. **Enhance consonance:** We know that dissonance arises due to mismatch of information with the existing cognitive structure of the human mind. This is due to lack of adequate information relating to the event. Therefore, compatibility increases if more information is given to the existing cognitive structure of individuals, leading to consonance. Consider the example of a student experiencing discomfort while reading this text for the first time. The reason is lack of information about the subject in the mind; he feels that the subject is difficult. However, as he reads more literature on the subject of organisational behaviour, he is likely to feel more comfortable with the subject, and find it easy.

3. **Attempt change:** Another strategy to reduce dissonance is attempting to change the cognitive structure of the brain. The cognitive structure having incompatible information is replaced with new information or certain inconsistent information is dropped. This reduces dissonance. Taking the earlier example a manager can reduce his dissonance about the unproductive employee by reducing the production targets. If the manager evaluates the

employee from the point of view of lower production targets, the employee may also be productive. This reduces his dissonance about the employee.

Application of Cognitive Dissonance Theory

The cognitive dissonance theory suggested by Festinger has a specific application in organisational behaviour. The following discussion relates to this:

(i) **Disconfirmed expectancy:** The theory states that inconsistency of information leads to increased anxiety or discomfort in individuals. Disconfirmed expectancy is a situation in which expectations are not realised. In such a situation people try to develop attitudes to substantiate disconfirmed expectancy. In the process, more mistakes are committed in their evaluations. For example, an employee who does not get the promotion he is expecting is likely to develop a negative attitude towards the promotion system and policy. He is likely to argue that he was denied the promotion due to favouritism of the superior, despite the fact that he has no evidence for this. He will not accept that his performance is not as good as the performance of the person who was promoted.

(ii) **Post decision dissonance:** Decision-making is a continuous job for any manager. Decisions aim at attaining certain objectives. Moreover, decisions are reflected in future actions. Since the future is risk-oriented, the results of the decisions may not conform to the objectives every time. If the decisions do not yield the intended benefits, dissonance develops in the decision-makers. In order to project the fact that the decision is sound one tries to support only positive aspects of the decision and develop a negative attitude towards the other alternative courses of action. For example a finance manager made a decision to invest in shares. After an analysis of the various alternatives, he finally decided to buy certain shares, expecting that there would be rise in the price of the shares. However, the share price did not increase as per his expectations, and furthermore, the price of the shares of other companies increased. This naturally leads to dissonance. In this case, in order to protect his interests he is likely to argue that the increase in the share price of the other companies is only a temporary phenomenon. In the long run, the share price of the company chosen by him will increase beyond expectations. In this way, he tries to substantiate his decision and satisfy himself, thereby reducing his dissonance.

FUNCTIONAL THEORY

Katz and Kelman pioneered the functional theory. The theory considered the relationship between attitudes and effort, and motivational structure. It suggested that attitudes are formed and changed in accordance with the motivational propensity of individuals. Kelman has identified three processes in the formation of attitudes, namely compliance, identification, and internalisation.

Compliance: A person tries to acquire an attitude in order to comply with a certain person or thing. People form attitudes that are consistent to a group in order to be recognised in the group.

For instance, a worker who is willing to join a group of high achievers is likely to acquire the attitudes of the group. Otherwise, he will not be admitted or recognised in the group.

Identification: Formation of attitudes also takes place for the purpose of identification with an agent of change. If an individual feels adopting new attitude enables him to establish a positive self-defining relationship, he is likely to develop such attitude. For instance, an employee may try to adopt the attitudes of his superior, in order to identify with him.

Internalisation: Internalisation of an attitude occurs when certain attitudes are congruent to the internal value system of an individual. Thus, people of different cultures are likely to formulate different attitudes. For example, Americans believe in being independent from an early age. This attitude may not be prevalent in other cultures. An employee, who believes in punctuality, will develop a favourable attitude towards those who arrive at the office on time and a negative attitude towards latecomers.

The functional theory is of great relevance in understanding formation and change of attitudes. Managers attempting to change the attitude of their employees should understand the motivational structure of the employee.

SOCIAL JUDGEMENT THEORY

Sherif and Hoveland formulated the social judgement theory of formation and change of attitude. The theory explained two dimensions of attitudes: (i) Existing attitudes are likely to produce distortions and (ii) judgements made in this respect mediate the change in attitudes. The theory explains that individuals develop attitudes based on social judgements. The propositions of the theory are given below.

(i) Every person develops certain initial attitudes by interaction with the family.

(ii) Individuals use initial attitudes to judge the stimuli received from social interactions.

(iii) Initial attitudes become the basis and serve as a point of reference to evaluate the opinion of others.

(iv) Formation and strengthening of attitudes takes place when stimuli received from society are similar to the initial attitude. Otherwise, an individual rejects the social stimuli.

The social judgement theory states that formation of attitudes follows a continuum, which comprises latitudes. The latitudes are acceptance, rejection and non-commitment. Consonance of opinions from an individual's standpoint falls in the region of acceptance. Opinions, that are most objectionable, fall in the rejection latitude. Opinions that may be either acceptable or unacceptable fall in the region of non-commitment. The social judgement theory is especially relevant to organisational behaviour. Managers try to understand formation and change of attitudes based on the group interaction. Groups in an organisation can be regarded as the society in which employees spend most of their time. Thus, understanding the ways and means of social judgement enables a manager to design strategies of attitude change.

CHANGE IN ATTITUDE

Though attitudes are permanent impressions, organisations are required to change them to suit the organisation. Change in attitude may be congruent or incongruent. Congruent change means changing a slightly favourable attitude to a strongly favourable attitude. Incongruent change means changing a negative attitude to positive attitude or *vice-versa*. For example, if a worker has a somewhat positive attitude towards work, it is possible to develop a strong positive in him. This is a congruent change. On the other hand, if a worker's negative attitude towards his work is changed to a positive attitude, it is an incongruent change.

Changing a person's attitude is not a simple task, at the same time however, it is not impossible. It is difficult because a host of factors influence it. Changing a person's attitude requires consideration of the following factors:

(i) Characteristics of attitude.
(ii) Personality characteristics.
(iii) Traits of the agent, which brings about the change.
(iv) Communication techniques.
(v) Group affiliation.
(vi) Situational factors.

Techniques used for changing attitudes are:

(a) *Persuasion*: Persuasion involves continuously telling the person to change the attitude.

(b) *Additional communication*: This is providing more communication about the attitude and its positive and negative effects.

(c) *Behaviour discrepancy*: This is engaging in different behaviour towards a person whose attitude requires changing.

(d) *Disapproval of incongruent attitudes*: Disapproval is shown towards attitudes that are not consistent with those of the organisation, so that person will not practice the same, in future.

(e) *Group pressure*: This involves applying pressures on the individual through members of the group.

(f) *Discriminating leadership styles*: The superior practices a different leadership style to discriminate between persons having different attitudes.

(g) *Positive or negative motivation*: This involves providing incentives to positive attitudes and threats and punishments to negative attitudes.

In organisations, the management may use one or more than one technique to change the attitude of a person, depending upon what is most appropriate.

Case study 11.3: Should we respond to personal woes?

Tundra Fiber Systems Limited is a well-established company, which produces and sells plastic and fiber items. The company has a wide market network and its products enjoy a brand loyalty of the customers. The company has an efficient production section, and sound managerial practices. It successfully uses TQM, MBE, and MBO to mention a few. The case in point is related to one of the employees, Ravi, in the production department. Ravi was an efficient worker, and had been with the company for the last 20 years. He was obedient, hardworking, well behaved and above all productive. His teamwork and commitment was appreciated by the General Manager of the company who gave him a special award for his outstanding contribution. Although, his emoluments were sufficient to meet the basic needs of his family, he was unable to save much. Further, although the company had a policy of reimbursing medical expenses it never introduced any scheme of giving a lump sum on special occasions. Thus, when Mr. Ravi's only daughter was to be married, he approached the Head of the Department requesting him to provide a lump sum to meet the expenditure of the wedding. However, his request was refused.

About a week afterwards, the section supervisor complained to the Head about Ravi's behaviour. The Head did not take the complaint seriously, but told the supervisor to observe him for some more time. Meanwhile, Ravi was frequently absent from work and became habituated to chewing tobacco and drinking alcohol. The result was that his individual productivity dropped significantly and the team productivity and motivation also suffered a setback. At this point of time, the matter was brought to the notice of the General Manager, with a recommendation of severe action against Ravi. Looking at the previous positive contribution of the employee the General Manager entrusted the HR Manager, Mr. Ghosh, with the job of enquiring into Ravi's conduct. Mr. Ghosh made first hand enquiries with the colleagues of the employee, who said that there had been a sudden change in Ravi's attitude. Mr. Ghosh was astute enough to realise that this was not a change in attitude, but a transitional period. Nevertheless, it was a sign, and if ignored could result in a change of attitude.

He decided to pay a visit to the house of the employee. Ravi's wife and daughter were very happy to see him, and during the conversation stated their observation about the change in Ravi's behaviour. Ravi's wife also confided that they were in financial difficulty due to the impending wedding of their only daughter and that despite the fact that Ravi had been with the company for a long time and was a good and conscientious worker, the company was not forthcoming with any help. She informed Mr. Ghosh that Ravi was looking for another job. Since Ravi was a good worker the company did not want to lose him, and Mr. Ghosh assured them of help.

He apprised the General Manager of the situation, who personally knew the history of Ravi. He expressed concern for him, but was not sure that he could convince the management to help him financially. However, he determined to talk to the management. Consistent with his belief, the management was not prepared to give an advance or loan to the employee. Although the management felt that Ravi was a deserving employee, they were apprehensive of setting a precedent. However, they also felt that deserving employees needed encouragement and support even in family matters. They finally decided to sanction a certain sum on such occasions as a gift or special recoverable loan. The decision was conveyed to Ravi's wife. This was good news for them and the amount was sufficient to cover their expenses. The next day, Ravi was back at his work, well dressed and cheerful as he used to be. The production report showed that his team production was at an all time high and that Ravi had given up his bad habits.

1. Analyse the attitudes of Ravi and the management.
2. If you were in Ravi's position, how would you have behaved?
3. Did a change of attitude take place in this case?

SUMMARY

Attitudes are permanent impressions, which are formulated based on experience. All of us develop attitudes on a variety of objects, situations and persons. Attitude formation is a psychological process of developing impressions and using them in the process of judgement. Certain important elements in attitude formation are: Affective component, cognitive component, behavioural component, valence, multiplicity, need orientation and stimuli. Attitudes are not based on a single experience, but are influenced by a number of factors, such as experience, association, interaction, society and personality. Theories of attitude formation explain the process and methodology of attitude formation. They are divided into three classes, cognitive consistency theories, functional theory and social judgement theory. Cognitive consistency theories are further classified into the balance theory, congruity theory, affective-cognitive consistency theory and cognitive dissonance theory. Festinger propounded the theory of cognitive dissonance. The theory puts forward the viewpoint that individuals rationalise their behaviour by reconciling divergent attitudes. Managers use three important strategies. They are ignorance, enhancement, and change management. The organisational implications of the cognitive dissonance theory are seen in overcoming disconfirmed expectancy and post decisional dissonance. Katz and Kelman pioneered the functional theory. The theory suggests that an individual formulates an attitude or changes his attitude for compliance, identification or internalisation. Sheriff and Hoveland formulated the social judgement theory of attitude formation and change. It stated that individuals develop attitudes based on social judgements. Attitudes developed by employees are of great relevance to managers since employees' attitudes influence organisational effectiveness. Thus, managers should make an effort to change the attitudes to direct an employees' energy in the proper direction. This is not an easy job. Strategies that deal with a change in attitudes differ with respect to the organisation, managers and situations involved. Some of the prominent strategies are persuasion, using additional communication, showing behavioural discrepancy, disapproval of incongruent attitudes, applying group pressure, using discriminating leadership styles and inducing positive and negative motivation.

Key words:

- **Affective component:** An emotional expression towards an object, a conditioned response by association of stimuli with a reward or punishment.
- **Association:** Correlating two objects, persons or situations.
- **Attitudes:** Permanent impressions formed by individuals based on their experience.
- **Behavioural discrepancy:** Using different behaviour towards a person whose attitude requires change.
- **Cognition:** An item of information gathered, processed and stored in the human brain.
- **Disconfirmed expectancy:** A situation represented by non realisation of expectations.
- **Internalisation:** Establishing congruence of internal value system and attitudes.
- **Persuasion:** Continuous effort of telling a person to change his impression.
- **Stimuli:** An item of information received by the sensory organs and interpreted by the brain.
- **Valence:** The degree of strength or weakness of an attitude.

Role Play Game

In the chambers of the Managing Director, the Managing Director (MD), the Director of Finance (DF), Production Director (PD) and Quality Controller (QC), are seated.

MD : Well friends, a very good morning to all of you. I am very happy to note that our company has been making very good progress over the past few years. You are aware that our Marketing Director could not be present today on account of the delay in his flights. He was touring one of the regions. He spoke to me expressing his regrets, and during the conversation, mentioned that some of our market share has been captured by our competitors. The reason is that they are selling their goods at a cheaper price, which is quite astonishing.

QC : I believe they do not bother about the quality and unfortunately, our customers are more price conscious than quality conscious. They do not realise that their health will be affected with poor quality. Oh…

MD : Well I partly agree with you, but this could not be the only reason. Perhaps we should think in another direction … cutting costs! (Laughs, driving the point straight home).

DF : Sir, I agree with you. If you will permit, I would like to put forward our cost figures for the past few years. Our overheads are increasing slightly every year, even taking inflation into account. If we do not think of some controls, we may land in trouble.

PD : (Slightly perturbed) Do you mean to say that our production costs are high?

DF : No, I never mentioned about production costs. There is no need to be perturbed.

PD : (Still rather agitated) I know production is a major cost, but sir sorry to mention that our finance friend is always envious of mine and feels he is Karna ...donor... and we all donee.

MD : There is no need to get agitated! Let us come back to the point I was mentioning, and that is we should examine cause of increased costs. Will the DF let us know the areas of cost escalation... frankly?

FD : Sir, with due respects to my friend the PD, the production department is one important area where our costs are definitely higher compared to our competitors and others in the industry. Then other is R&D. The remaining areas are not so important, and need not be considered at this moment.

QC : I understand our quality is almost comparable to international standards. I feel the PD is making a commendable effort to maintain the quality by effectively managing technical resources. I am afraid that without his active support I could not be assured of the present quality.

MD : Let me elaborate a bit here. We are second to none in terms of quality. I know that. As you are aware the competition has intensified due to the present tendencies of the market policies of the Government. I think we need to look at all the functional areas not only the areas of production and R&D. Travel is another major expense, most of our executives travel Business Class. The point I want to make is that we have to look at costs involved in training, waste control, quality maintenance, computerising accounting operations and marketing costs, at the same time. I believe we should think in terms of changing our attitude and that of the employees, to accomplish this.

DF : I agree with you sir, we need to look at this point with all the other functional heads also. I don't think we should make this an emotional issue. Looking at the PD.... there is nothing to misunderstand. I propose to meet all the other functional heads to apprise them of the cost cutting measures that might be possible in their respective areas.

QC : Not at the cost of quality please!

The students can play the roles and elaborate the discussions to come to a conclusion of how attitudes matter in cost cutting, and arrive at strategies to be adopted.

12. LEARNING

This chapter enables you:

- *To understand the meaning of learning*
- *To define the term learning*
- *To understand the importance of various elements in the learning process*
- *To understand the characteristics of learning organisations*
- *To know the significance of learning organisations*
- *To understand why people prefer learning in organisations*
- *To explain a four level model of learning*
- *To describe the various types of learning organisations*
- *To examine the strategies necessary to implement learning organisations*

The structure of the chapter is as follows:

- Introduction
- Definition of learning
- Characteristics of learning
- Learning process
- Learning organisations
- Summary
- Key words

CHAPTER 12

Learning

> *"Without learning, the wise become foolish; by learning, the foolish become wise. Learn as if you could never have enough of learning, as if you might miss something."*
>
> **– Confucius**

INTRODUCTION

Learning is a continuous process of change in the behaviour and personality of a person. An important variable that influences behaviour is learning. Learning is a general phenomenon. Learning takes place from the moment a child is born. We learn to eat, learn to stand and walk and learn to respond. Learning occurs by observation and imitation and is a continuous, lifelong process. The environment also plays a significant role in individual learning. The degree of learning differs from person to person. Learning has specific managerial applications. The rate of learning, learning aptitude, learning habits and learning curve of subordinates determine managerial strategies to be used to make subordinates committed to their jobs. For instance, reinforcement is required for those subordinates who are very slow in learning and a manager should use redundancy in communicating with them. A subordinate with an aptitude for learning needs little direction and communication from the superior, and a manager can use a participative approach with these subordinates. Thus, a manager needs to understand the learning patterns of his subordinates to know their behaviour and shape his own behaviour suitable to them. However, individual learning alone does not contribute to the effective building of an organisation in the new millennium. Today, learning organisations have become a philosophy for companies. They encourage learning by every one, irrespective of position and role in the organisation. Peter Senge, a pioneer in learning organisations, views it as a group of people who expand their capacity to create the results they truly desire. A number of reasons compelled organisations to convert to learning organisation. The notable ones are: thrust on quality, innovation, adapting to continuous change and emphasis on community development. Even at an individual level, people prefer to create learning organisations as they promote creativity, promote system thinking and enable them to accept changes with less resistance. Learning involves detection and correction of errors. By continuous learning, an organisation transforms into an adaptive, caring and innovative organisation. For this purpose, organisations should adopt a number of strategies such as the accidental strategy, subversive strategy and declared strategy. In this chapter we will learn more about learning and learning organisations.

DEFINITION OF LEARNING

Learning is the basis of the human development process. It is a continuous process of changing oneself. Learning is a cognitive function of the human brain. Thus, learning is a psychological process of understanding, acquiring information, processing, storing and using the same in the future. It is a natural human activity commencing from the birth of an individual, which determines and influences behaviour. In the context of an organisation, learning involves acquisition of skills and manners, formulating attitudes etc., which will influence the work behaviour and performance of employees.

A permanent change in the behaviour of an individual is an indication of learning. Learning is defined in many ways. Some definitions of learning are presented below:

Learning can be defined as relatively permanent change in the behaviour that occurs as a result of experience or reinforced practice. ***Fred Luthans***

According to ***Hillgard and Bower,*** *"Learning is the process by which an activity originates or is changed through reacting to an encountered situation, provided that the characteristics of the change activity cannot be explained on the basis of native response tendencies, maturation, or temporary states of the organism".*

Learning is "a process of acquiring the ability to respond adequately to a situation, which may or may not have been previously encountered, the favourable modification of response tendencies consequent upon previous experience, particularly the building of a new series of complex and coordinated motor responses, the fixation of items in memory so that they can be recalled or organised: the process of acquiring insight into a situation." ***Howard C. Warren.***

According to ***Schiffman and Kanuk,*** *"Learning is a process by which individuals acquire knowledge and experience which they apply to future related behaviour."*

Mitchell *defines learning as "a change process of acquisition of new knowledge and skills by repeat or practice which acts as a feedback to cause fairly permanent change in the behaviour of an individual."*

Another definition that deserves attention is that, 'Learning is the process of having one's behaviour modified, more or less permanently, by what he does and the consequences of his action, or by what he observes." ***Steers and Porter.***

CHARACTERISTICS OF LEARNING

(1) Learning is a psychological process and a behavioural reaction.

(2) It is the cognitive function of the human brain.

(3) Learning involves a permanent change. Temporary change in the behaviour does not reflect learning.

(4) Change in behaviour is brought about by the practice of experimentation and not by physical maturity alone.

(5) Learning occurs through repetitions or reinforced practices or experience.

(6) It involves responses from the outside environment.

(7) Learning disappears with inadequate opportunities to display skills.

(8) It is related to the future, based on past actions.

LEARNING PROCESS

Having understood the concept of learning we will now learn more about the learning process. It is not a one time activity, but occurs for as long as a person lives, albeit at different rates, with a change in behaviour. A stimulus that drives individual response is responsible for learning. Some times, learning is possible with a single observation, and need not follow the process. Although there are differing views about the learning process, it can be described as in Figure 12.1.

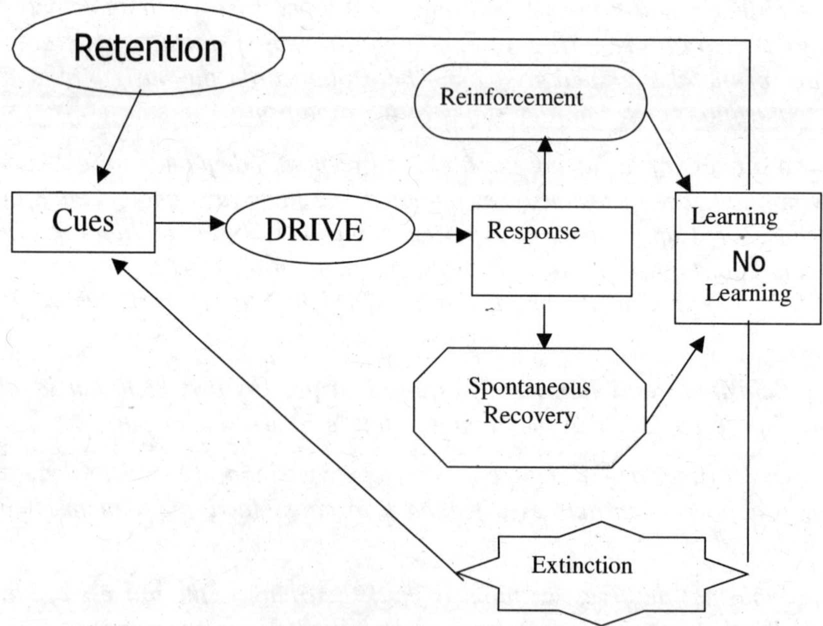

Figure 12.1: Learning Process

Cues give direction to a drive to produce a response. If a response is reinforced, the experience is retained and behaviour is learnt, otherwise, it produces spontaneous recovery, which results in no learning. This leads to loss of memory called extinction. The result is that an individual seeks different cues. A retained learnt behaviour may produce new cues, which may lead to creativity. Elements of the learning process are explained below.

(a) **Cues:** A cue is an object or information, also called a stimulus that draws the attention of an individual. Sensory organs receive cues from the environment. Strong cues provide direction to human motives. Weak cues are ignored by the brain. Cues are of two types, generalized and discriminative. Generalization occurs when the same cue or stimulus is present but in a new way. The more cues are related to each other, the more they are likely to generalize the characteristics for retention. Discrimination is eliciting a positive response to a certain stimulus and ignoring the other stimuli, which are unimportant. In both cases, there is a possibility of driving human motivation.

(b) **Drives:** Drive is an action produced by a strong stimulus or cue. It is the basis for human motivation. Drives can be physiological or psychological. Physiological drives are related to the human body, and psychological drives are related to the human brain. They are interdependent and both may respond to a given stimulus. However, the response may vary with the intensity of the cue.

(c) **Response:** Response is any action or reaction shown by an individual to stimuli. The response may be overt, that is physically observable or can be covert that is only an expression of behaviour.

(d) **Reinforcement:** Reinforcement is bringing strength of association between a cue and response. A single response is less likely to bring about a change in behaviour. Repetition of response is known as reinforcement. Individual learning occurs when the same response is observed for a similar cue. If the response is positive, there is a greater probability of learning, whereas if the response is negative, the probability for learning is less. This is because individuals like to avoid discomfort, which results from a negative response.

(e) **Retention:** Retention is storing of information in the brain. Behaviour is learnt in response to reinforced stimuli. A reinforced stimulus becomes stable and consistent over a period. The stability is known as retention. The more the strength of the response, the greater is the retention. Retained response directs future behaviour. Sometimes, it may lead to formation of new cues because of the creativity of people.

(f) **Spontaneous recovery:** A non-reinforced response is known as spontaneous recovery. It is a one-time response. It does not lead to change in behaviour.

(g) **Extinction:** Extinction is loss of memory. If a response is not reinforced, individuals are likely to forget the response, which slowly disappears from the mind. Therefore, behaviour is extinguished under conditions of non-reinforcement. When behaviour is extinguished individual searches for new cues.

Therefore, managers reinforce stimuli to bring about change in behaviour. Having learnt about the learning process, we will now learn about learning organisations.

Case study 12.1: Technology Learning

In almost all organisations, computers have replaced human energy. Although people resisted the implementation, they slowly adapted to them, and learnt computer-related skills. Mr. Venkat, an employee of Albearing Company Limited, was working in the typing pool. Like many others, he also had inhibitions about the use of computers in the office, and resisted typing office correspondence on a computer. However, one day the manager compelled him to use the computer. He used the computer keyboard in the way he used a mechanical typewriter. This led to a couple of keyboards being spoilt, and he realised he was damaging the keyboard. This became the basic cue for him. He realised that he should not show the same kind of response i.e., 'harsh use of key board' in future. Thus, reinforcement occurred in the process. He was able to establish an association between the response and outcome, namely 'spoiling the key board'. Mr. Venkat slowly started learning to use the computer in a gentler way. In the process, he found it was a 'magic box'. He learnt to create animated texts on the computer for presentations in meetings. Now Mr. Venkat is a personal assistant to the manager, and the latter feels incapacitated if he is absent, even for a single day.

Signals of badly performing organizations

- Employees seem unmotivated or uninterested in their work
- Workforce lacks the skill and knowledge to adjust to new jobs
- Workforce simply follows orders
- Teams argue constantly and lack real productivity
- Lack of communication between personnel

LEARNING ORGANISATIONS

The concept of learning organisations is becoming increasingly widespread in modern companies. From the largest multinationals to the smallest ventures, companies are trying to become learning organisations. The results achieved by this philosophy depend considerably on interpretation and commitment to it. An organisation has a responsibility to its fund providers, employees, customers, prospects, the society and the government; it has responsibility as a corporate citizen and as a global corporate citizen. According to the changes that are occurring in the expectations of these stakeholders organisational objectives must undergo change. This indicates that an organisation must have adequate and timely knowledge of all such internal and external factors and it should be able to update its knowledge from time to time. This is the reason why an organisation and its employees must go on learning. An organisation's capability, capacity, and competitive edge depend on its ability to learn faster than its competitors. A learning organisation represents an organisation of people who keep on learning, irrespective of their position or level. Such an organisation is bound to show a good performance under normal conditions.

History of learning organisations

Major research into 'the art of learning' did not actually start until the 1900's. In the 1950's, the concept of systems thinking was introduced. However, interestingly it was never implemented. According to Gould-Kreutzer Associates Inc., system thinking is "*A framework for seeing interrelationships rather than things; to see the forest and miss the trees.*"

Organisations need to be aware of both the company as a whole as well as the individuals within the company. Until the introduction of this concept, companies concentrated on their own needs, and not the needs of their workers. Systems thinking tries to change the managerial view so that it includes the ambitions of individual workers, not just the business goals.

Decision Support Systems (DSS) are required by corporate executives to help them make decisions for the future. It involves building models, which define systems that benefit the management rather than the system's operation. This is because the model focused on examining the present situation of the business and the alternatives available for the future. One benefit of DSS was that it made implicit knowledge, explicit. This makes extra knowledge available to the organisation and tends to allow the organisation to learn better because explicit knowledge will spread through an organisation faster. In this respect, DSS becomes an additional method of communication in organisations. This systems tool is necessary for every executive's desktop. However, this did not happen.

In the 1970's, the same idea was renamed as organisational learning. One of the early researchers in this field was Chris Argyris from Harvard. He published a book on the subject in 1978. Even with this published information the concept was still not taken up by any company. In the 1980s, companies discovered time as a new source of competitive advantage. This led to 'capabilities-based competition,' which included the capability of learning. Many other people have continued with this line of research, such as Peter Senge – one of the modern day 'gurus'. Information on the topic has been passed to various companies. These companies are now trying to become learning organisations. If the changeover to a learning organisation happens overnight, the workers' environment will be complex and dynamic. There will be agitation and confusion, which means learning may not take place because of the chaos caused. Thus, the concept can only be introduced into a company that is prepared to reach a balance between change and stability, i.e. a balance between the old and the new. Since organisations must interact with the environment around them, the environment must be suitable for such interaction to take place.

Becoming a learning organisation seems a logical step for all companies to follow. The 'learning organisation' has its origins in companies like Shell, where Arie de Geus described learning as the only sustainable competitive advantage. The learning organisation is seen as a response to an increasingly unpredictable and dynamic business environment. Peter Senge stated that, "*Organisations must develop a capacity for fast-paced innovation. Learn to love change.*" Hamel and Prahlad are of the opinion that, "*As the competitive environment becomes more complex and variegate, the need for greater genetic variety – a broader range of managerial beliefs, and a greater repertoire of managerial actions – grows apace.*" "*Top companies seem to organise around people honoring these needs – feeling of control, something to believe in, challenge, lifelong learning, recognition,*" says Waterman. With the pace of change ever quickening, the need to develop mechanisms for continuous learning and innovation is greater than ever.

DEFINITION OF A LEARNING ORGANISATION

The following are some of the definitions of learning organisations.

A learning organisation is one in which people at all levels, individually and collectively are continually increasing their capacity to produce results, they really care. It is an organisation that learns and encourages learning among its people. It promotes exchange of information between employees, creating a more knowledgeable workforce. This produces a very flexible organisation where people accept and adapt to new ideas and changes through a shared vision.

"The essence of organisational learning is the organisation's ability to use the amazing mental capacity of all its members to create the kind of processes that will improve its own." ***Nancy Dixon.***

According to ***Pedler, Burgoyne and Tom Boydell,*** *"A learning company is an organisation that facilitates the learning of all its members and continually transforms itself."*

Peter Senge *defines learning organisations as "places where people continually expand their capacity to create the results they truly desire, where new and expansive patterns of thinking are nurtured, where collective aspiration is set free, and where people are continually learning to learn together."*

Learning organisations are those that have in place systems, mechanisms and processes, that are used to continually enhance their capabilities and those who work with it or for it, to achieve sustainable objectives – for themselves and the communities in which they participate.

An examination of the definitions reveals certain important points to note about learning organisations.

1. Learning organisations are adaptive to their external environment.
2. They continually enhance their capability to change/adapt.
3. Learning organisations develop collective as well as individual learning.
4. These organisations use the results of learning to achieve better results.

A learning organisation combines the essential elements of strategy development and personal development. It creates a space for people to achieve remarkable business and personal results. It values the scientific method of hypothesis development, testing and validation, as well as the personal development pathway found in the concepts of "personal mastery." Connecting humans to organisations in a vital, mutually beneficial way is why learning organisations are worth creating.

Significance of Learning Organisations

The importance of learning was first put forward by a Chinese philosopher, Confucius (551 - 479 BC). He believed that everyone should benefit from learning. Several large corporations have been attracted to this concept in recent times and they are investing considerable sums of money to support organisational learning. The underlying cause for the recent emphasis on organisational learning is due to the increased pace of change. Classically, work has been thought of as being conservative and difficult to change. Learning was something divorced from work and innovation, and was seen as a necessary but disruptive way to change. A corporation, which is able to quickly learn and adopt new practices in their work, will be able to change their work practices to perform better in the constantly changing environment. Change is now measured in terms of months not years, as it was in the past. Learning organisations are emerging fast and successfully because of a number of reasons, which are given below.

- Desire for superior performance and competitive advantage
- To improve customer relations
- To avoid decline
- To improve the quality of the product and organisational processes
- To have a better understanding of risks and diversity
- To encourage innovation
- For the personal and spiritual well being of the employees
- To increase the ability to manage change
- To improve interpersonal understanding
- To develop an energised and committed work force
- To expand organisational boundaries
- To engage in community development
- To gain independence and liberty
- To create awareness of the critical nature of interdependence
- To meet the demands of the time

Organisations need a different way of viewing the process of conducting an activity in a business environment and achieving change within the environment. The existing views and ways of understanding are not in keeping with the realities of the environment or with the beliefs about the environment. In this context, a learning organisation embodies new capabilities beyond those of traditional organisations. Learning organisations are built by communities of servant leaders. Obviously learning arises through performance and practice.

Why Do People Prefer a Learning Organization?

Learning organisations provide an environment, which is essential to the continued growth and development of employees and the organisation. This makes work a pleasure and not an obligation. Without learning organisations, there will not be progress. Learning organisations are the only way to live and work, as they provide a healthy environment for employees, and make for effective organisations. The maximum effectiveness is achieved through continuous learning resulting in continuous improvement. This enables the organisation to achieve a competitive advantage. Learning requires transmission of information and knowledge throughout the organisation. However, competitive advantage at the individual level is based on "know-how", that is "knowledge is power". People prefer a learning organisation due to the following reasons.

- Learning organisations give people hope that things can be better
- Learning organisations provide a playground for creative ideas
- Learning organisations provide a safe place to take risks with new ideas and behavior and the challenge needed to stretch beyond perceived limits
- In learning organisations everyone's opinions are valued and the amount that people can contribute is not determined by their position in the organisation

The approach of a learning organisation promises to tap energy. Any approach that makes work a pleasure, and encourages an employee to take pride in the quality of products and services raises the overall quality of life. The following points enable us to know more about the significance of learning organisations.

1. Learning organisations allow people to live more satisfying and interesting lives, making them happier.
2. They promote systems thinking and offer theory-based avenues that contribute to reducing fragmentation in the world.
3. The learning organisation approach flows out of and speaks to the deepest human values that everyone attempts to embody into their life, values such as wholeness, the interconnectedness of all beings and things, collective endeavor and intelligence.
4. A learning organisation channels, supports and enhances the basic human passion to learn.
5. It provides a rational explanation of the necessity for caring about others.
6. It offers a way to cut through some of the dead ends that have arisen in a more "technical" approach to organisation development. It is a way that calls upon inherent qualities to support, inspire and illuminate the movement.
7. A learning organisation provides an invitation and a rationale for building communities.
8. A learning organisation empowers people to effect change with less resistance. It enables a change to take place in attitudinal and institutional barriers of learning.

It is not out of context here, to mention that learning is living, and living is being open. The basic philosophy of a learning organisation is "thriving" rather than "surviving" and achieving extraordinary results.

Types of Learning

A learning organisation is not about 'more training'. While training does help develop certain types of skills, a learning organisation involves the development of higher levels of knowledge and skill. A 4-level model describes the learning types:

Level 1 – Learning facts, knowledge, processes and procedures. This level of learning applies to known situations where changes are minor.

Level 2 – Learning new job skills that are transferable to other situations. This level is applicable to new situations where existing responses need to be changed. Bringing in outside expertise is a useful tool in implementing the level.

Level 3 – Learning to adapt. This level is applicable to dynamic situations where the solutions need developing. The mode of learning in this level is experimentation and deriving lessons from success and failure.

Level 4 – Learning to learn. This level is about innovation and creativity and designing the future rather than merely adapting to it. This is where assumptions are challenged and knowledge is reformed.

Furthermore, this model can be applied at three levels – to the learning of individuals, teams and organisations. Hamel and Prahalad are of the opinion that organisations that achieve learning to Level 4 will "reinvent not just their organisation but their industry".

Models of Learning

Chris Argyris has made a significant contribution to the development of organisational learning. Donald Schön developed two models of learning. They are single-loop and double-loop learning. They are discussed here.

Single-loop and Double-loop Learning

Learning involves the detection and correction of errors. When something goes wrong, it is suggested that we should look for another strategy that will address and work within the situational parameters. In other words, the given goal, values, plans and rules are followed rather than questioned. According to Argyris and Schön this is single-loop learning. They described double loop learning as an alternative response that questions the situational parameters themselves and makes a critical scrutiny. It leads to an alteration in the situational parameters.

Obviously, this enables a shift in the way in which strategies and consequences are framed. Argyris and Schön described the process of organisational learning in the following manner.

When the error is detected and corrected, if it permits the organisation to carry out its present policies or achieve its present objectives, then that error and correction process is single-loop learning. It is like a thermostat that senses when it is too hot or too cold and adjusts the heating system accordingly. The thermostat performs corrective action as it receives information (the temperature of the room). Single-loop learning exists when goals, values, frameworks and strategies are taken for granted to a significant extent. The emphasis is on 'techniques and making techniques more efficient'. Therefore, reflection is directed toward making the strategy more effective. In single-loop learning routines and plans that are both less risky for the individual and the organisation are followed. Obviously, this provides greater affordability to exercise appropriate controls.

Double-loop learning occurs when an error is detected and corrected in such a way that it involves modification of an organisation's underlying norms, policies and objectives. It involves questioning the role of the framing and learning systems, which underlie actual goals and strategies. It is more creative and reflexive, and involves consideration of notions of the good. Reflection here is more fundamental: the basic assumptions behind ideas or policies are confronted, hypotheses are publicly tested and the processes are evaluated to examine whether they conform to the standard, and at the same time the system is not self-seeking. Double-loop learning is necessary to meet the rapidly changing and often uncertain contexts of the environment and to communicate managerial decisions. As Edmondson and Moingeon observed:

'The underlying theory, supported by years of empirical research, is that the reasoning processes employed by individuals in organisations inhibit the exchange of relevant information in ways that make double-loop learning difficult – and all but impossible in situations in which much is at stake. This creates a dilemma, in the very organisational situations in which double-loop learning is most needed.'

In order to provide a more detailed explanation of these concepts Argyris and Schön have set up two models that describe the features of the theories-in-use that either inhibit or enhance double-loop learning. The assumption that all people use a common theory-in-use in problematic situations is referred as Model I. It describes – and it can be said to inhibit double-loop learning. The philosophy of Model II assumes that the situational parameters associated with theories-in-use enhance double-loop learning.

According to Argyris, Model I involves 'making inferences about another person's behaviour without checking whether they are valid and advocating one's own views abstractly without explaining or illustrating one's reasoning'. Theories-in-use are shaped by an implicit disposition to winning (and to avoiding embarrassment). The primary action strategy is to exercise unilateral control of the environment and the task is to secure unilateral protection of oneself and others. As such, Model I leads to deeply entrenched defensive routines and these operate at individual, group and organisational levels. Exposing actions, thoughts and feelings makes a person vulnerable to the reactions of others. However, the assertion that Model I is predominantly defensive has a further consequence. Anderson stated that *'Acting defensively can be viewed as moving away from something, usually some truth about ourselves. If our actions are driven by moving away from something then our actions are controlled and defined by whatever it is we are moving away from, not by us and what we would like to be moving towards. Therefore, our potential for growth and learning is seriously impaired. If my behaviour is driven by my not wanting to be seen as incompetent, this may lead me to hide things from others and myself in order to avoid feelings of incompetence. For example, if my behaviour is driven by wanting to be competent, honest evaluation of my behaviour by myself and others would be welcome and useful'.*

TYPES OF LEARNING ORGANISATIONS

The primary responsibility of any business is to enable economic performance. It is also responsible to its customers and society at large. The list of corporate responsibilities is exhaustive. Corporate business is responsible to the state, the community, society and also to global corporate citizens. In order to fulfil the responsibilities, all organisations must convert themselves to learning organisations. An organisation converts into a learning organisation in any of the following ways.

Adaptive organisation: An adaptive organisation seeks to adjust its human structure to the ever-changing environmental dynamics. This immediately makes the organisation stable even in the case of changes. Encouraging continuous learning in the organisation accomplishes this. According to Harwood, adaptive organisations have the following characteristics, which enable them to convert to learning organisations.

(1) They encourage risk and innovation.

(2) There is a visible acknowledgement of good performance

(3) Rewards are fair.

(4) Employee assignments change frequently.

(5) There is a shared inner core of values.

(6) Versatility is encouraged.

(7) Change is managed.

(8) Adaptive organisations are transparent – they make things visible and open to discussion.

(9) People are busy and they feel a sense of urgency.

(10) Sufficient resources exist, they are not allocated according to power or authority.

Caring organisation: A "caring organisation is one that provides exceptional opportunities to its people." The characteristics of caring organisations are given below.

(i) Knowledgeable employees have greater motivation to make a contribution to organisational goals and objectives.

(ii) The organisation takes care of the needs and aspirations of both its skilled and unskilled workers.

(iii) It provides an opportunity for self-development to personnel.

(iv) It encourages proper use of talent, knowledge and ability.

Thus a caring organisation is bound to be an effective organisation.

Team building organisation: A team building organisation is different from other organisations, in that equal importance is given to each position, rather than stressing a superior subordinate relationship that emphasises the inherent superiority or inferiority attached to certain people. Peter F. Drucker has identified three types of teams: Tennis doubles, European football and American baseball. At any point of time, an organisation can play only one kind of game and only one kind of team can be used for any given task. Team building managers and organisations may succeed in developing effective organisations. In countries like India, in particular, a team building organisation has special significance.

Innovative organisation: An innovative organisation is a dynamic organisation. It emphasises achievement of results. According to Charles F. Kiefer and Peter M. Singe, such organisations have five characteristics. They are:

(1) Purposefulness and vision

(2) Alignment of individual energies

(3) Personal ability and mastery

(4) Attention to organisational design

(5) Intuitive ability to extemporise

All organisations are capable of becoming innovative organisations, which is often necessary in the context of a dynamic environment. Otherwise, survival is a great problem. In becoming a learning organisation, the attitude of every employee is important. The top management cannot simply impose its views.

Learning Organisations: Implementation Strategies

Any organisation that wishes to implement the philosophy of a learning organisation, requires an overall strategy with clear and well-defined goals. Once these have been established, the tools needed to facilitate the strategy must be identified. It is clear that everyone has his or her own interpretation of the idea of a "learning organisation." Such varied interpretations make it difficult to design an action plan that will transform groups into learning organisations. However, it is possible to identify three generic strategies that highlight possible routes to developing learning organisations. The specific tools required depend on the strategy adopted, but the initiatives are generic throughout. The three strategies are:

1. Accidental strategy

An accidental strategy is adopted by those companies that believe that adopting a learning organisation philosophy is the second step. These companies unconsciously take steps to achieve their business goals that fit into the framework of implementing a learning organisation. Hence, it is called an accidental approach, as it was not initiated through awareness of the concept of a learning organisation.

2. Subversive strategy

Once an organisation has discovered the philosophy of a learning organisation, it must make a decision as to how it wants to proceed. Thus, the company tries to explore the possibilities of implementing the learning organisation. This is called subversive strategy. However, the company has to make a choice between a subversive and a declared strategy. A subversive strategy differs from an accidental strategy in the level of awareness, as the former is not accidental, but is secretive. Under this strategy, the company may not openly endorse the learning organisation ideal, but will exploit its ideas and techniques.

3. Declared strategy

According to this strategy, the principles of a learning organisation are adopted as part of the company ethos and they manifest openly in all company initiatives. Thus, all the sub-systems of the organisation are geared to implement the steps required to convert the organisation into a learning organisation.

However, these strategies are not exhaustive. Interrogating and changing the governing values produce new action strategies that can address changing circumstances.

SUMMARY

Learning is a continuous process, which influences behaviour to a great extent. Learning is said to occur when there is a permanent change in behaviour. It is not a one-time activity, but a process. Cues give direction to a drive, which produces a response. If a response is reinforced, learning occurs. Otherwise, no learning takes place. An individual is likely to forget the response and search for new cues. When learning occurs, the learnt characteristics are retained in a person's memory and will be used in future behaviour. The new global order has generated a need for continuous learning in organisations. This has led to the emergence of learning organisations. Moreover, learning organisations provide a number of benefits to the organisations, employees, and other stakeholders. Learning organisations are developed using a 4-level model that comprises learning facts, knowledge, processes and procedures, learning new job skills that are transferable to other situations, learning to adapt and learning to learn. Donald Schön developed two models of learning viz., single-loop, and double-loop learning. Single loop learning lays emphasis on detecting an error and correcting it. Double loop learning occurs as a response to the situation. It also involves modification of organisational norms, policies, and objectives. Learning organisations exhibit different characteristics. Based on the attributes they are classified into adaptive organisations, caring organisations, team building organisations and innovative organisations. An adaptive organisation adjusts its human structure to the changing environmental demands. A caring organisation provides opportunities for development of the human element. In a team-building organisation, people are encouraged to form teams that ignore superior subordinate relationships. Similarly, a dynamic organisation that emphasises the attainment of results becomes an innovative organisation. Learning organisations are not accidental. They are purposefully built by committed and dedicated people who are prepared to learn continuously for the long term survival of the organisation. Some of the strategies adopted to develop learning organisations are: accidental, subversive and declared. In the case of accidental strategy, an organisation transforms into learning organisation automatically in the process of realisation of its goals. The subversive strategy is one by which the organisation makes a conscious effort to develop into a learning organisation. In the declared strategy, the concepts of learning are adopted as part of the organisation's vision and mission.

Key words:

- **Accidental strategy:** A strategy followed unconsciously to achieve goals that fit into the framework of a learning organisation.
- **Adaptive organisation:** An adaptive organisation is one that seeks to adjust its human structure to the ever changing environmental dynamics.
- **Caring Organisation:** An organisation that provides exceptional opportunities to its people.
- **Cue:** A cue is an object or information also called a stimulus that draws the attention of an individual.
- **Declared strategy:** The strategy in which the principles of learning organisations are adopted as part of the company ethos and which are openly manifested in all company initiatives.
- **Double loop learning:** An alternative response that questions the situational parameters themselves and makes a critical scrutiny.
- **Drive:** A drive is an action produced by a strong stimulus or cue.
- **Extinction:** Extinction is loss of memory. If a response is not reinforced, an individual is likely to forget the response, which slowly disappears from the mind.
- **Innovative organisation:** An innovative organisation is a dynamic organisation that innovates continuously.
- **Learning to adapt:** The mode of learning by experimentation and deriving lessons from success and failure.
- **Reinforcement:** Reinforcement is bringing strength of association between a cue and a response.
- **Single-loop learning:** A learning situation in which the given or chosen goals, values, plan and rules are followed rather than questioned.

- **Spontaneous recovery:** A non-reinforced response that is a one-time response. It does not lead to change in behaviour.
- **Subversive strategy:** A strategy in which the company tries to explore the possibilities of implementing a learning organisation.
- **Team building organisation:** An organisation that gives equal importance to each position, instead of stressing upon a superior subordinate relationship.

- **Spontaneous recovery**: A [illegible] conditioned response that [illegible] one-time learning. It does not lead to change in behaviour.
- **Subversive strategy**: A strategy in which the company tries to exploit the possibilities of [illegible] learning organisation.
- **Team building organisations**: An organisation that gives equal importance to each position instead of [illegible] superior-subordinate relationship.

13. LEARNING BEHAVIOUR

This chapter enables you:

- *To understand the importance of learning theories*
- *To know how perception is instrumental in learning*
- *To understand learning by totality of components*
- *To grasp the connection between stimuli and response*
- *To examine the significance of environment in learning*
- *To distinguish between classical conditioning and operant conditioning*
- *To appraise the concept of observational learning*
- *To understand the relationship between cues and response*
- *To derive the principles of learning*

The structure of the chapter is as follows:

- Introduction
- Gestalt psychology theory
- Field theory
- Classical conditioning theory
- Operant conditioning theory
- Social learning theory
- Cognitive learning theory
- Principles of learning
- Summary
- Key words

CHAPTER 13

Learning Behaviour

INTRODUCTION

Gestalt psychology is the basis of understanding learning behaviour. Interestingly Pavlov, Skinner, Albert Bandura etc., have provided valuable contributions to understanding the learning process. Classical conditioning theory, Operant conditioning theory, Social learning theory, and Reinforcement learning theory have advanced a number of learning strategies. Learning is a powerful tool for modifying the behaviour of employees to change their attitude in order to ensure commitment to the organisation's goals. In this chapter we will learn more about the theories of learning.

LEARNING THEORIES

Learning is a continuous process, which takes place in various degrees. Learning theories explain how and why learning takes place. They have a universal application in predicting and controlling learning situations, and provide valuable insight into the basic aspects of learning. There are two categories of learning theories.

One classification is cognitive learning theories, which assume that interval information storage and usage mechanisms of the human mind are responsible for learning. Two theories are popular among cognitive learning. They are:

(a) Gestalt Psychology Theory

(b) Field Theory

Another classification is stimuli-response theories. They emphasised that learning is a conditioning process. Popular theories are:

(a) Classical Conditioning Theory

(b) Operant Conditioning Theory

(c) Social Learning Theory

Gestalt Psychology Theory

The Gestalt psychology theory is a classical theory. It assumes that learning is a function of perception. According to the theory, an individual understands an object by the total content of configuration which the embedded object contains. Thus, individuals learn similar activities more easily than dissimilar activities. An object having greater similar physical characteristics provides a close relationship at other times also. If a greater number of similar features occur repeatedly, it provides a permanent impression, which leads to learning. In the same way, more disassociation exists with dissimilar objects, which minimises the chances of understanding. So learning is not likely to take place.

The theory provides general guidelines as to how individuals perceive and learn in different situations. It is very logical and a majority of psychologists accepted it, and hence, the theory became the basis for explaining learning behaviour.

Field Theory

Field theory is an outgrowth of the Gestalt psychology theory. The theory stated that an individual understands an object by its total components. Therefore, characteristics of individual components do not determine understanding. This is because individuals try to understand the situation as a whole and differentiate the component parts. Hence, a relationship among the component parts in the perceptual field determines perception. Thus according to this theory learning occurs when an individual differentiates and understands the components of the total field.

The proponent of the theory, Kurt Lewin related learning behaviour to understanding of life space. According to him, life space consists of one's personal and psychological environment. He stated the relationship in a mathematical fashion.

Learning = f (Person + Environment)

Therefore, learning occurs when there is a change in conditions of a person's life space.

In the context of an organisation, a production bonus is a financial incentive. In actual fact, the bonus is related to the productivity and the profits. However, employees are likely to understand it as one of the financial incentives, and demand a bonus irrespective of the productivity and profitability of the organisation. They consider that profitability is only a manipulation of figures. This is by application of phenomenal field.

Both the cognitive theories of learning provided the basic framework for understanding the human learning process.

Classical Conditioning Theory

Ivan Pavlov, a Russian psychologist has introduced the concept of "conditioning" to explain the learning process. A "condition" is a situation. Conditioning means eliciting a known response through repeated exposure to a condition. Conditioned behaviour means ensuring an automatic response to a situation. According to the theory, in the initial stage conditioned learning occurs when a stimulus that elicits a known response, is paired with another stimulus, which at a later stage produces the same response by itself, even if the initial stimulus is withdrawn. Pavlov called the initial stimulus an unconditioned stimulus and response elicited is an unconditioned response. The second stimulus is a conditioned stimulus, which leads to a conditioned response.

In order to prove his concepts, Pavlov experimented with a dog to explain conditioned response.

> *A surgical operation was performed to accurately measure the saliva secreted by a dog, when it was presented with a piece of meat. Naturally, Pavlov noticed an increase in salivation. He termed the piece of meat as an 'unconditioned stimuli' and salivation as an 'unconditioned response'.*
>
> *After some days, Pavlov used the ring of a bell as a stimulus. The dog did not show any response. Then, before presenting the meat to the dog, Pavlov rang a bell, thus associating the bell with the presentation of a piece of meat. This process was repeated for several days.*
>
> *He then observed that when the bell was rung even without presenting the meat, the dog would salivate. So ringing a bell is a 'conditioned stimuli' because the bell has conditioned dog to respond, and in this case, salivation is a 'conditioned response'. Thus, the theory suggested that a conditioned stimulus brings about a conditioned response, when it is associated with an unconditioned stimulus. This happens even if the unconditioned stimulus is not reinforced.*

Certain basic concepts of the classical conditioning theory are repetition, stimulus generalisation, and stimulus discrimination. They are explained below.

- **Repetition:** Repetition is presentation of similar stimulus over a sufficiently long time. Repetition attracts attention. It increases the strength of association, and thus helps in more retention. However, if repetition occurs beyond a certain point attention becomes saturated, and consequently, retention power is reduced. This is the same as the principle of diminishing returns.
- **Stimulus generalisation:** This is understanding and associating the stimulus and the consequent response. Generalisation and understanding of stimuli leads to learning. For example, if dog did not learn that the bell was a precondition to presentation of the meat, its

ringing would not have elicited the same response. Therefore, association of a stimulus and its response leads to learning.

- **Stimulus discrimination:** A particular response occurs for a particular stimulus, due to discrimination of various stimuli. What happens when a different stimulus is presented? A slightly different stimulus elicits no response because it is understood as a totally new stimulus and there is no association with it. Thus, discrimination has taken place. For instance, if music was played instead of a bell being rung, the dog did not salivate. Hence, learning occurs when each stimulus is discriminated and associated with a specific response.

For instance, in school, a teacher tries to bring about an analogy between the subject and facts that are known to the pupil to make him understand the concept. As an example, consider the following. A teacher in a village school asked his pupils whether they knew about the Taj Mahal. The answer was negative. He then asked whether they knew about cows. The answer was in the affirmative. So, he decided to bring about an analogy between a cow and the famous monument. This seems rather far-fetched, so let us see how he went about it. He asked about the colour of cows. The pupils gave the various colours of cows they had seen, amongst them being white. The teacher then said that the Taj Mahal is also white, and is built from a white stone called marble. This analogy made it clear to the pupils that the Taj Mahal was built from white marble stones. The teacher continued. A cow has four legs and there are four pillars on the four sides of the monument. As a cow has a head with horns, the monument has a tomb inside it with a semi circle on the top, with the same shape as the horns of a cow. The lesson went on like this and the teacher explained the history and other features of the monument. The students developed a comprehensive understanding of the subject. In future when they saw a cow, the pupils will recollect the monument. Here the cow is classical conditioning and thus learning occurs.

The classical conditioning theory was considered logical. The theory provided an explanation of behaviour. However, the theory was criticised as it does not explain how certain behaviour is unique. Hence, the theory has limited utility in organisational learning.

Case 13.1: Learning to Produce

Alloy Engineering Company is a moderately sized company with about 250 employees. Until Mr. Kirpal Singh took over as General Manager, the company had an average productivity level. A few days after taking charge, Mr. Singh studied the problem. He found that the company had a policy of giving a bonus to the workers in the month of August. He also noticed that in August the productivity of the company was higher than in other months. He found that there was a relationship between productivity and the bonus, as the employees considered the bonus a motivation. Thus, he established that the bonus was an unconditional stimulus, and the month (in which the bonus was given) acted as a conditioned stimulus. So, he designed a new policy for giving the bonus. On a particular day in each month, he announced that a bonus would be given. Thus, the employees have learnt that in certain months they would get an additional incentive in the form of a bonus. So they started producing more every month. This happened without their being told that a bonus would be paid in a particular month. After some time Mr. Singh discontinued the scheme temporarily and found that the productivity did not drop. He found that employees have learnt that every month is a stimulus.

Operant Conditioning Theory

B.F. Skinner, an American psychologist used the concept of 'operant conditioning', sometimes also called 'instrumental conditioning' as an instrument in the learning process. According to this theory, learning takes place when an individual makes an effort to gain control over the environment. This is a process of trial and error. If a certain type of behaviour results in more favourable outcomes than other behaviour, the favourable outcomes reinforce the behaviour. Therefore, individual responds to learn the behaviour that is rewarded and does not respond to the behaviour that is punished or not rewarded.

The following are the propositions of the theory:

(i) Behaviour is determined by environment.
(ii) Change in environment produces learning.
(iii) Individuals explore and obtain control over environment.
(iv) Behaviour is instrumental in determining consequences faced by the individuals.
(v) Consequences determine the chance of reoccurrence of an operant conditioning in future.
(vi) Change in behaviour requires change in consequences of behaviour.

Operant conditioning theory emphasizes the concept of reinforcement. Reinforcement is increasing the strength of association between the stimuli and response because of repetitive favourable responses. The theory has an extensive application in clinical and educational research. Some important applications of operant conditioning are controlling absenteeism, quality control, managing deviant behaviour and controlling alcohol, chewing tobacco and sexual harassment.

In the context of organisation, an employee can be motivated to work overtime for overtime pay. This is a normal conditioning. However, this will continue as long as the worker has pressing financial need. So continuing motivation for a long period is difficult. But if the manager promises him that he would be considered favourably in the next promotion, the worker will respond positively. This is done in an expectation of promotion. Here promotion is an operant conditioning. But at the time of promotion, the manager has changed the stand. The employee was ignored. Surely, the promotion must have acted as an operant conditioning. Positive belief would motivate to do overtime; ignoring at the time of promotion is a negative conditioning that forces him not to accept any overtime work in future. Even it may lead to development of disbelief over the management.

Operant conditioning theory is a comprehensive approach because of the following reasons:

(i) The theory makes a series of assumptions about behaviour and environment.

(ii) A set of definitions used in the theory can be used in an objective and scientific description of behaviour and its environment.

(iii) A number of facts and principles have been demonstrated by experimentation.

(iv) A group of techniques and procedures are available for the experimental study of behaviour.

Distinctions between Classical Conditioning theory and Operant Conditioning theory:

Difference	Classical Conditioning theory	Operant Conditioning theory
Cause of Response	Association of a conditioned stimulus with unconditioned stimulus causes response.	Association of a reward with specific response leads to learning.
Type of Response	The response is automatic and involuntary.	The response is deliberate to obtain reward.
Type of Learning	Simple behaviour, attitudes, and feelings are learnt.	Learning is relatively complex and goal directed behaviour.

Social Learning Theory

Social learning is observational learning. Learning takes place by watching, observing, and understanding the experiences of others. Social Learning theory was propounded by Albert Bandura. Generally, most of the behaviour is learnt by observing parents, teachers, peers, pictures etc. A child learns to produce certain response by imitating the parents. You must have observed that your youngsters imitate your behaviour. If you are kind towards animals, they too develop a positive attitude towards animals. This is based on the observation, though you never told them to be kind towards animals. Similarly an employee performing extremely well enjoys the confidence of the manager. He is given equal importance in the process of decision making. Other employees keenly observe this. They learn to perform well if they feel they also should be recognised by the manager. Learning also takes place when one tries to formulate certain models of behaviour by observing the family members and society. He learns to show certain response by following the model. This is called as role models in the context of organisation. Nowadays in order to motivate the employees organisations are introducing the concept of role models. For example in APSRTC, the names of employees who have achieved highest km per litre are displayed and other drivers are counseled to take him as their role model to achieve economy in fuel consumption. The following are the assumptions of the theory.

Assumptions:

(i) People learn to behave in response to reinforcement.

(ii) Individual chooses certain action in expectation of specific result.

(iii) Learning influences personality.

According to social learning theory, modelling, and self-control process, determine the learning. They are explained below:

Modelling

Modelling is instrumental in learning. Modelling is the process of imitating and learning from others. Modelling involves two stages in learning process.

Stage-I:

Observation: Sensory organs of individuals collect information about actions of others. This is called as observation. The actions or behaviour and consequences are stored in human brain with the help of various mental pictures. For instance, the leader of employees union may observe the voice modulation of the manager or other union leaders. He stores the modulation in his brain for imitation in his speech.

Stage-II:

Learning: Individuals act or behave based on mental pictures. If consequences are positive, they repeat the same acts. Otherwise, no response is shown. Hence, when positive consequences are felt learning occurs. Take the instance of union leader who used executive accent of voice modulation in a meeting with the workers, they may not applaud it. So he tries to quit that modulation.

Modelling involves four sub-processes. They are explained below:

(i) **Attention Process:** Individual pays attention and recognises critical features of a model. Therefore only attractive, important, reinforced and contrast characteristics receive attention. For instance, the dressing style of a successful sales person may be closely observed by the co-sales persons in order to imitate the style. This is a critical feature for the success that receives attention of the employees.

(ii) **Retention Process:** Model's actions are likely to be remembered if the actions are conforming to the individuals requirements. They are used in their future actions.

(iii) **Motor Reproduction Process:** Individuals convert observed models into actions. It is imitating the behaviour. Therefore, the process of imitation produces certain actions.

(iv) **Reinforcement Process:** Individuals are likely to act according to the model as long as positive rewards are associated with the actions. Such repetitions result in learning the model.

Self-control process

Self-control process is another instrument of learning. In this process individuals observe and watch variety of behaviour. They try to adopt it as long as it is applicable to them. This is decided by self-control. Carl Thoresen and Michel Mahoney defines self control as *'a person displays self control when in the relative absence of immediate external constraints, he engages in behaviour whose previous probability has been less than that of alternatively available behaviour'*. For instance, a subordinate observed that his superior is authoritarian in dealing with the subordinates. This is because the superior holds authority. But the same may not be applied in dealing with his subordinates, as he does not hold necessary authority. Self-control process involves stimulus management and consequence management. Stimulus management is selective exposure to stimuli that evokes specific learning. Consequence management is the application of new reinforcers to increase the frequency of similar behaviour. For example a worker observes that the superior scolds a subordinate for late-coming. He observed the same on a number of occasions. Then, he tries to exercise self-control to improve his attendance on time.

Cognitive Learning Theory

Edward Tolman propounded the cognitive learning theory. The methodology adopted in the theory was controlled experimentation using white rats as the subjects. Cognitive learning is the relationship between cognitive environmental cues and expectation. The theory stated that learning occurs when the association between cues and expectancy is strengthened. Obviously weak relationship does not lead to learning. The theory established a relationship between one stimulus and another stimulus. Thus, the theory was also known as stimulus-stimulus theory.

Laboratory experimentation is the basis for formulation of the theory. Tolman selected white rats as the experimental subjects. Food was kept at the end in a maze. A maze is a specially designed area in which the paths are separated by small walls that makes it difficult to find the path. It can be understood as 'Padmavyuha'. It is like a puzzle to find the path. As one moves in a path, one observes two directions. Each direction is a choice point. Tolman established expectations at each choice point in the maze. He observed that the experimental subjects learned to expect that certain cognitive cues associated with the choice point lead them to the area where food is kept. As the rat ran through the maze, finds the expectations at a point led to the area of food, it started associating the food (cue) and the expectancy. Finding food with certain expectancy strengthened the association. Thus, he found that white rats could learn to run through the complicated paths with purpose and direction towards the goal (food). Tolman observed that learning occurred.

The theory proposed the following.

1. An organism receives, remembers, retrieves and interprets the stimulus and shows action in future to the repeated stimulus. Thus, organism learns the meaning of various objects and events.

2. One stimulus leads to other stimulus.
3. Learned response is the result of meaning assigned to stimulus.
4. Cognitive structure is formed in every human being that stores the information.
5. Cognitive learning occurs by the expected relationship between events, goals, and expectations.

In the context of organisations, cognitive learning theory is important in designing training programs. The proposition is that an employee likes to learn more in the job to increase his productivity when he establishes association between the effort and reward. Thus, the theory made important contribution to understand human motivation. Moreover, the theory is useful in understanding expectations, attributions, goal setting, and locus of control in the context of organisational behaviour.

Musuro Tushi corporation is wedded to the total quality management concept. The processes are highly controlled. The technology is of world class. The state of art management is the Japanese culture. The corporation has made all efforts to make the employees learn the concept of quality in all aspects of the work. The financial incentives, fringe benefits and even the promotions are wielded to the quality standards. All these cues provided the employees the ideology of the management. They identified a strong relationship between the quality standardisation and employees benefits. All employees received promotions based on their commitment to the quality. This has become the belief and culture of the organisation. Even the new employees are also learning the concept of TQM. Obviously this is because of the cognitive learning.

PRINCIPLES OF LEARNING

Reinforcement is the single most important principle of learning. Reinforcement refers to the repetition of response to the stimulus. It also refers to the consequence of behaviour. Reinforcement is anything that increases the strength of the response and tends to induce repetitions of the behaviour that preceded the reinforcement. The concept of reinforcement is dependent on the law of effect propounded by Thorndike. It states that 'of several responses made to the same situation, those which are accompanied or closely followed by satisfaction will be more likely to reoccur. Those, which are accompanied or closely followed by discomfort or punishment, will be less likely to occur'. In the process of learning there are various types of reinforcements. They are presented below:

1. **Positive Reinforcement:** Positive reinforcement is stimulus presented in a situation which strengthens association between stimulus and response. Hence, it encourages displaying similar kind of behaviour. Showing appreciation for good work done, increase in monetary reward for higher production, recognition of the effort are some of the positive reinforcers,
2. **Negative Reinforcement:** A negative reinforcement is averting a consequence or removing a positive consequence contingent upon a response. It is also called avoidance. Negative

reinforcement is more complex. It should not be understood as punishment. It strengthens and increases behaviour by the termination or withdrawal of an undesirable consequence. Punishment is one of the forms of negative reinforcement.

3. **Intrinsic Reinforcement:** The person himself mediates intrinsic reinforcement. It is directly related to the actual performance of the job. It represents internal feelings of an individual. Feeling of responsibility, drive of skill acquisition, inner fires for increased performance are some of the examples of intrinsic reinforcement. For instance developing a sense of commitment to the job acts as an intrinsic reinforcement.

4. **Extrinsic Reinforcement:** It consists of factors in the environment in which the job is performed. It is related to external situations and others mediate it. Hence, extrinsic reinforcement is less directly related to behaviour as it is arbitrary and artificial. For example, supervisor observing the work of the subordinate and giving appraisals for the good work becomes extrinsic reinforcement.

5. **Primary Reinforcement:** A primary reinforcement is innately satisfying to people and directly reduces their primary motivational drives. This is independent of past experience. It is used in most of the simple learning situations.

6. **Secondary Reinforcement:** Secondary reinforcement is a response conditioned by past experience. Sometimes, it may also work as a learning device. For example a worker, who out performed his job, received appreciation amongst his co-workers. Such situations reinforce his experience of positive attitude towards production. He tries to learn to produce more because of his positive past experience.

In practice, managers are more concerned about the reinforcement of the behaviour that is positive and shows favourable consequence in organisational effectiveness. Administering reinforcements depends on the schedules and personality of both people reinforcers and reinforced.

SUMMARY

A number of theories exist for explaining the learning process. Notably Gestalt Psychology theory, Field theory, the Classical Conditioning theory, the Operant Conditioning theory and Social Learning theory are important. Ivan Pavlov propounded the concept of classical conditioning. Learning occurs when a conditional stimulus is associated with the unconditional stimuli. Repetition, stimulus Generalisation and stimulus Discrimination are the basic concepts of the theory. Similarly, operant conditioning theory proposed that learning is a function of rewarded behaviour. The concept of observational learning is the base of social learning theory. An individual learns in two stages: Observation and Learning stages. Accordingly, imitation, model assumption and self-control process are responsible for learning to occur. Modelling involves four sub processes: Attention, Retention, Motor Reproduction, and Reinforcement. Self-control involves stimulus management and consequence management.

Key words

- **Conditioning:** A process of eliciting a known response through repeated exposure to a condition.
- **Cues:** Cue is any object or information that attracts the attention.
- **Drives:** Action produced by a strong stimulus or cue.
- **Extinction:** A situation of loss of memory.
- **Learning:** A process of bringing permanent change in the behaviour.
- **Modelling:** Modelling is imitating and learning the behaviour.
- **Operant Conditioning:** It is learning the behaviour based on reinforcement.
- **Reinforcement:** Repetition of similar response to a similar stimulus.
- **Spontaneous Recovery:** Non-reinforced response that does not lead to a change.
- **Stimulus Discrimination:** A new stimulus that is unrecognized by the brain.
- **Stimulus Generalisation:** Understanding the association between stimulus and response.

14. MANAGERIAL VALUES

This chapter enables you:

- *To define values*
- *To comprehend the meaning of managerial values*
- *To understand different types of values*
- *To distinguish between terminal and instrumental values*
- *To know the dimensions of values across countries*
- *To examine the value orientation of Indian managers*

The structure of the chapter is as follows:

- Introduction
- Definition of values
- Types of values
- Values across cultures
- Value orientation of Indian managers
- Summary

CHAPTER 14

Managerial Values

INTRODUCTION

Values are the result of one's abstract individual philosophy. They are developed over time, and once developed, remain permanent and stable. At the same time they contain system orientation and are susceptible to change. A number of values have been identified, which may be theoretical, economic, aesthetic, social etc. Milton Rokeach has made a survey of values with the help of an instrument called the Rokeach Value Survey (RVS), which identified terminal and instrumental values. Values differ across the cultures, with respect to the country, religion, occupation, caste, gender etc. Managerial values of Indian managers are deep-rooted.

DEFINITION OF VALUES

Values reflect one's personal philosophy in responding to a given situation. Values slowly but consistently affect an individual's way of life. A society has values that represent its cultural heritage. Values emerge and change over generations. Personal values emerge out of societal values. The term value is abstract. However some definitions help clarify the concept of values.

> ***White and Bednar*** *defined values 'as the desirable, internalized criterion or standard of evaluation a person possesses. Such concepts and standards are relatively few and determine or guide an individual's evaluations of the many objects encountered in everyday life'.*

According to ***Rokeach,*** *'values are a specific mode of conduct or end state of existence, which is personally or socially preferable to an opposite or converse mode of conduct or end state of existence'.*

The characteristics of values are as follows:

(i) Values are abstract terms.
(ii) They determine the mode of individual behaviour.
(iii) Values emerge out of a societal value system.
(iv) They are normally permanent and stable.
(v) Values represent the general conduct of individuals rather than a particular individual.
(vi) Values differ from individual to individual.
(vii) They also vary from society to society. A host of factors influence the adoption and adherence to values by individuals.
(viii) Values contain system orientation. They are susceptible to change due to external and internal influences.

Values determine an individual's behaviour in an organisation. An individual may enter an organisation with certain vague values. Organisations are required to impart values regarding code of conduct, work culture, commitment etc.

Certain values based on karma

Sakam karma (Greed driven work)	**Nishkam karma (Selfless work)**
Psychological burnout	Psychological energy conservation
Total reaction	No reaction
Erratic action	Steady action
Aim is success	Perfection is the aim
Dependence on praise	Inner autonomy freedom
Socio-economically questionable	Socio-economically appropriate
Reward based commitment	Work commitment
Competitive rivalry for excellence	Work as worship for excellence
Job enrichment	Mind enrichment
Alienation	

Source: Chakraborty, Ethics in Management

TYPES OF VALUES

Values are abstract. They represent the psychological state of an individual. Allport, Ernon, Lindzey, Rokeach, Fredrick etc. have made an extensive survey of values and attempted to classify them. The following section describes various types of values.

(i) **Theoretical Values:** Theoretical values emerge out of an attempt to discover truth by using a critical and rational approach.

(ii) **Economic Values:** Economic values emerge out of a natural human interest in satisfaction with material rewards. They emphasise seeking practical and immediate benefits along with monetary benefits.

(iii) **Aesthetic Values:** Aesthetic values emerge out of psychological contentment. The expression of these values takes place by applauding creative and innovative aspects.

(iv) **Social Values:** These values represent love and affection, belonging and a need for recognition by people at large. Social values relate to welfare, convenience, and sympathy of the society.

(v) **Political Values:** Political values emerge when individuals believe that power and control in society causes people to respect them. Hence, they relate to a section of people who constantly make efforts to control societal power.

(vi) **Religious Values:** Religious values emphasise unity, integrity, and non-material aspects as being important to lead a peaceful life. These values are omni-present, irrespective of society.

(vii) **Reactive Values:** Reactive values are basic to any individual. They relate to the satisfaction of biological desires.

(viii) **Tribalistic Values:** These values arise out of the traditions and customs of society. As these values emerge from time-tested customs and traditions, they are deep-rooted.

(ix) **Egocentric Values:** Aggression, selfishness and an individualistic approach represent egocentric values. They relate to satisfaction of one's esteem, recognition and power.

(x) **Conforming Values:** Conforming values are related to egocentric values. They are related to low tolerance for ambiguity, difficulty in accepting people with different values, and a desire that others should accept the values of the particular society they live in.

(xi) **Manipulative Values:** Manipulative values pertain to the selfish nature of individuals. These values arise when individuals believe that the means justify the end. Thus, they are manipulative even at the cost of others, for their own benefit.

(xii) **Existential Values:** Existential values represent high tolerance for ambiguity, empathy and criticism, which become part of the general context.

Milton Rokeach in his Rokeach Value Survey (RVS) has identified two sets of values, namely terminal values and instrumental values. Terminal values are those values, which one wishes to achieve during one's lifetime. They relate to self-actualisation needs of individuals. Instrumental values refer to the means of achieving terminal values. Table 14.1 gives the terminal and instrumental values as found in the RVS.

Table 14.1: Values according to Rokeach Survey

Terminal values	**Instrumental values**
A comfortable life (prosperous life)	Ambitious (hardworking)
An exciting life (active life)	Broad-minded (openness)
A sense of accomplishment (lasting contribution)	Capable (competent)
A world of peace (free from fear of war)	Cheerful (light-hearted)
A world of beauty (beauty of nature)	Clean (neat)
Equality (equal opportunity to all)	Courageous (standing for one's beliefs)
Family security (taking care of loved persons)	Forgiving (willing to pardon others)
Freedom (free choice)	Helpful (standing by the needy)
Happiness (contentment)	Honest (truthful)
Inner harmony (freedom from inner conflict)	Imaginative (creative)
Mature love (intimacy of family)	Independent (self-sufficient)
National security (protection from attack by other countries)	Intellectual (intelligent)
Pleasure (leisurely life)	Logical (rational)
Salvation (eternal life)	Loving (affectionate)
Self-respect (self-esteem)	Obedient (dutiful)
Social recognition (respect)	Polite (well-mannered)
True friendship (close and intimate relationship with friends)	Responsible (reliable)
Wisdom (a matured understanding of life)	Self-controlled (self-disciplined)

Source: Robbins P. Stephen, Organisational Behaviour

Case Study 14.1

Mr. Kedia, the owner of a small enterprise, has entrepreneurial skills, despite the fact that he has only passed the 12th standard. He has an intimate friendship with one of his childhood classmates, which he values highly. This friend approached his father who is a bank officer and knowledge disseminator, with the idea of starting an enterprise. Understanding the friendship between his son and Kedia, the bank officer encouraged him to come out with the project proposal, which involved printing on the polythene bags. The project was approved for its financial and operational feasibility, and he was given financial assistance.

After a period of five years, Kedia got married. His wife, who was a graduate, showed a lot of interest in the business and supported her husband in all his endeavors. Kedia does not believe in concealing profits for tax evasion. In a meeting with his friend who had started the enterprise to print on polythene bags, he expressed his unhappiness over his mounted sales tax dues. His friend stated that he had gone to court to dispute the levy of sales tax to cause delay. However Kedia was not convinced on the point, he believed that his friend, on the advice of his tax consultant had initiated the legal process to delay payment of taxes. The friend confessed this was the case and even advised Kedia to do the same, however the latter flatly refused.

One morning, Kedia received a telephone call from his friend's wife who requested him to come to their house immediately. As he stepped into the corridor of his friend's house, he saw the mortal remains of his friend who had committed suicide for being caught by the tax authorities. He immediately cleared all the tax dues of his friend and took over the management of his business.

VALUES ACROSS CULTURES

The relationship between the managerial values and success is the same in the USA, Japan, Australia, and India. Japanese workers are the most highly motivated in the world. They are workaholics. They believe in the maxim 'No work, no food'. They carry their work problems home. This is because of their strong affiliation with their organisation. Such work values lead to both personal and organisational success.

Values emerge over time and differ from one individual to another. They also differ with respect to country, religion, occupation, family structure, caste, gender, time etc. Development of values is a continuous process and results from the reinforced experience of individuals. They are not rigid, but change slowly and consistently. Globalisation has brought many challenges to managers throughout the world. Thus, there is an increasing need to understand the value dimensions across different countries. Values differ with culture. In order to understand values across cultures, the findings of Hofstede are relevant. Based on the survey, value dimensions vary across cultures with respect to five dimensions, as follows.

1. **Power distance:** It is the acceptance of power in organisations by people in society.
2. **Individualism vs. collectivism:** Individualism is the preference to lead an independent life and be less likely to be influenced by the group.
3. **Quantity vs. quality of life:** Quantity of life is giving preference to material rewards. Quality of life is relationship-oriented life, giving importance to the welfare of people.
4. **Uncertainty avoidance:** It is the preference to lead a structured and normal life.
5. **Long term vs. short term orientation:** Long term orientation lays emphasis on the future and accumulation of wealth for future needs. Short-term orientation emphasises regard for traditions and fulfillment of social obligations in the present rather than caring for future.

Table 14.2 shows that values differ from society to society. Culture, climate, beliefs, history of the society, composition etc., determine the values of an individual. For instance, in China there is a high power distance, low individualism, high collectivism, moderate quantity and quality of life, moderate uncertainty avoidance, high long term orientation and low short term orientation. Table 14.2 depicts the values across cultures as understood with reference to the above dimensions.

Table 14.2: Values across countries having different cultures

Country	1	2	3	4	5	6	7	8
China	High	Low	High	Mod	Mod	Mod	High	Low
France	High	High	Low	Mod	Mod	High	Low	High
Germany	Low	High	Low	High	Low	Mod	Mod	Mod
Hong Kong	High	Low	High	High	Low	Low	High	Low
Indonesia	High	Low	High	Mod	Mod	Low	Low	High
Japan	Mod	Mod	Mod	High	Low	Mod	Mod	Mod
Netherlands	Low	High	Low	Low	High	Mod	Mod	Mod
Russia	High	Mod	Mod	Low	High	High	Low	High
USA	Low	High	Low	High	Low	Low	Low	High
West Africa	High	Low	High	Mod	Mod	Mod	Low	High

1. Power distance 2. Individualism 3. Collectivism 4. Quantity of life 5. Quality of life 6. Uncertainty avoidance 7. Long term orientation 8. Short term orientation.

Mod = Moderate

Source: Hofstede, G., *Cultural Constraints in Management Theories*, Academy of Management Executive, February, 1993, p. 91.

VALUE ORIENTATION OF INDIAN MANAGERS

In this section we study the value orientation of Indian managers.*

Some values of top level managers in India

Absence of hatred, aggressiveness, benevolence, caste, cosmic causation, compassion, code of life, dependence, equanimity, forgiveness, gratitude, love, liberation, loyalty, modesty, non-violence, power, purity of mind, personal relationship, purity of motive, reverence, rest, status, self actualisation, truth, and wealth.

Certain generalizations of the managerial value system in India are:

1. Managerial value system is uniform irrespective of organisational affiliations, i.e., private or public.
2. Value system of Indian managers is deep-rooted.
3. Value system is different according to the age group of the managers.
4. Younger managers have more economic and political value orientation than their counterparts.
5. Indian managers have a greater belief in super natural powers, while adopting values.
6. Indian managers have developed different values according to their educational status.

Value system of Indian managers is more diversified and similar across various groups.

Table 14.3: The values of Indian managers

Studies	Values
Ganesh and Malhotra	Existential, conformist, manipulative, sociocentric, tribal, egocentric.
Thiagarajan	Performance, futuristic change, work culture, achievement, competition and religion.
Rai and others	Recognition, status, job satisfaction, career prospects, security, money and power.
England and Lee	High production, profit maximisation, customer service, satisfaction, sub-ordination, aggressiveness, prejudice, achievement, autonomy, individuality, power, creativity, success, change, competition, conflict, propriety.
Singh	Autonomy, subordination, adventures, challenging, special ability, status, talent, creativity, originality, prestige, opportunity to work with people, exercising lordship, earning money, stability, security.
Monappa	Unethical values such as: Nepotism, bribes, gifts, personal favour, unfair competitive practices, dishonesty, personal benefits.
Hussain	Progressive values: Truth, purity of mind, self-actualisation, love, compassion, code of life, purity of motive, ahimsa, gratitude, modesty, benevolence, absence of hatred and liberation. Regressive values: Personal hatred and liberation.

* Based on the study by A.K. Sing, Suneel Maheswari and Krishan Kumar Goel.

SUMMARY

Personal philosophy consists of impressions developed over a period of time. A reinforced philosophy results into a value. Values guide the general conduct of individuals. Exhaustive research conducted by Allport, Ernon, Lindzey, Rokeach, Fredrick etc. unearthed a number of values, such as: theoretical, economic and aesthetic, social, political, religious, reactive, tribal, egocentric, conformist, manipulative and existential values. Rokeach has classified values as terminal and instrumental values. Values differ across cultures, time, nations and persons. Hofstede identified eight value dimensions to determine the values across cultures. They are: power distance, individualism, collectivism, quantity of life, quality of life, uncertainty avoidance, long term orientation and short term orientation. They may be high, low or moderate according to the culture of different nations. In India, Ganesh, Malhotra, Thiagarajan, Rai, England, Lee, Singh etc. have conducted a number of studies. These studies confirmed that even Indian managers differ in terms of value orientation. Certain positive value dimensions of Indian managers are work culture, status, high production, security, profit maximisation, aggressiveness, autonomy and competition. Nepotism, bribes, gifts, personal favours, unfair competition and dishonesty are some of the unethical values.

Case Study 14.2: Material and non material values

Today western culture dominates Indian ethos and traditions. The basis for management of western businesses is profitability, growth and survival. They attach great significance to material attainments. Increased rates of divorce, child abuse, poor trust and exploitation are some of the menaces of the western materialistic concept.

Indian values are deep-rooted and emerged out of social culture. The *Bhagvad Gita* is an embodiment of *Karma Yoga, Sathsamskara, Triguna* etc., which aims at promoting quality of life, ethical behaviour and motivates self-actualisation. Following this dichotomy, Malhotra started his business. He follows the values that are believed to have led to the success of personalities like Rossi Mody, Ratan Tata, Vijay Mallaya, Kumar Mangalam Birla, Bill Gates, Anil Ambani, Narayana Murty, H.D. Parekh, Ramesh Gelli, among others. These values include preparing a list of things to be performed each day, prioritising activities, contingency planning, time management and work itself. These personalities inspired him. He became successful in business due to sheer hard work. His friends praise him by saying that he is a prototype for sincerity. He maintains a personal relationship with all his subordinates. This is evidenced by the way he extended personal invitations to all his colleagues and subordinates to attend the marriage of his daughter. He always respects his elder staff and treats them with reverence. He aims at becoming an ideal businessman, who in his view, is one who believes in being grateful to the employees who work for him. He stands for some of the values identified such as purity of mind, self-transcendence, collective life, truth, love, ahimsa, modesty, benevolence and idealism.

Vision, mission values of BHEL

Vision

A world class engineering enterprise committed to enhancing stakeholder value.

Mission

To be an Indian multinational engineering enterprise providing total business solutions through quality, product, system, and services in the fields of energy, infrastructure, industries, transportation and other potential areas.

Values

- Zeal to excel and zest for change.
- Integrity and fairness in all matters.
- Respect for dignity and potential of the individual.
- Strict adherence to commitment.
- Ensure speed of response.
- Foster learning, creativity and team-work
- Loyalty and pride in the company.

Objectives

1. **Growth:** To ensure a steady growth by enhancing the competitive edge of BHEL in existing businesses, new areas and international operations, so as to fulfill national expectations from BHEL.
2. **Profitability:** To provide a responsible and adequate return on capital employed, primarily through improvements in operational efficiency, capacity utilisation and productivity, and to generate adequate internal resources to finance the company's growth.
3. **Customer focus:** To build a high degree of customer confidence by providing increased value for money through product quality of international standards, quality, performance, and superior customer service.
4. **People orientation:** To enable each employee to achieve his maximum potential, improve his capabilities, perceive his role and responsibilities, and participate and contribute positively to the growth and success of the company. To invest in human resources continuously and be alive to their needs.
5. **Image:** To build up a high degree of customer confidence by sustaining international standards of excellence in product quality, performance and service, particularly in regard to supply of spares and after sales service. To fulfill the expectations that stakeholders, like the

government as owners, employees, customers, and the country at large have from BHEL.

6. **Technology:** To achieve technological excellence in operations by development of indigenous technologies and efficient absorption and adoption of imported technologies to suit business needs and priorities and provide a competitive advantage to the company.
7. **Continuity:** To invest in human resources development, sustained R&D, to strive for excellence in management and other long-range activities to ensure a leadership status for BHEL.

15. STATUS BEHAVIOUR

This chapter enables you:

- *To define and understand the meaning of organisational status*
- *To distinguish between organisational and social status*
- *To understand various classifications of status*
- *To examine the determinants of organisational status*
- *To recognise status*
- *To examine the behaviour associated with assumption of status*

The structure of the chapter is as follows:

- Introduction
- Definition of organisational status
- Classification of status
- Distinctions between organisational and personal status
- Sources of organisational status
- Behavioural functions and dysfunction of status
- Summary

CHAPTER 15

Status Behaviour

INTRODUCTION

Status is a relative ranking given to individuals. An individual's status provides esteem and motivates to perform better. Status provides satisfaction of esteem, social and self-actualisation needs. In society, status also leads to recognition of one's position. Possession of skills, competence of individuals and certain personality traits provide social status. People like the ex-President of India, Abdul Kalam have status because they possess knowledge. In organisations, the employees' functions, hierarchy and position give them their status. Sometimes certain persons acquire status due to their association with persons of high status in organisations. In a district, the wife of the District Collector enjoys a special status although she may not hold any position. What is the status of Anil and Mukesh Ambani? Their association with the family identifies them. Of course, after the demise of their father, they became more important in the organisations. Similarly, Ratan Tata has created wealth that is distinctly recognised in the world of Indian business. This status is attained by wealth and acumen as a businessman. The late Yasser Arafat, who was a leader of Palestine, had status in political circles as he represented a race. Similarly, most chief ministers of Tamilnadu were cine actors who enjoyed the confidence of the public and later they enjoyed their status in politics. In organisations, managers having the authority to give a bonus are given a higher status by the employees. Union leaders also enjoy relative status and they will be allowed to sit with the highest officials in the organisation. It is true that organisations create a number of unique markings to denote the status of employees. Organisational status is both an advantage and disadvantage to the organisations. However, the functional consequences outweigh the dysfunctional ones. In this chapter we learn about the implications of status.

DEFINITION OF ORGANISATIONAL STATUS

A definition of status states that it is a 'Statement of an individual's rights, privileges, immunities, duties and obligations in the organisation and obviously the statement of restrictions, limitations and prohibitions conditioning and governing the behavior'.

– Chester I. Barnard

***Dubin** defined status as a 'set of visible external markings that systematically rank individuals and groups in relation to each other, and that includes all the members of the organization some place in the scheme of rankings'.*

A close examination of the above definitions reveals the following characteristics of status:

a. Status is relative ranking and comparison.
b. It is a position and provides esteem.
c. It is an intangible and qualitative phenomenon, but a fundamental reality.
d. Status is judged and determined by certain criteria set by society or a group.
e. It is multi-dimensional. Status is measured by aggregate of worth conferred on a person.
f. Status can be limited to micro level or macro level i.e., it is universal.
g. Expenditure of individual effort leads to acquisition of status. It can be attained in many ways.
h. Status differs from one society to the other. It is also different in different groups even for an individual.

CLASSIFICATION OF STATUS

Status is broadly classified into social status and organisational status. Social status is determined by the society. It is influenced by a number of factors, like age, wisdom, wealth, family relationship, occupation, and personality, which determine the status of a person. On the other hand, organisational status is determined by the formality of structure, qualification, and reward systems of organisation. It is the differentiation that occurs within an organisation.

Social status is classified as follows:

(a) Achieved status: Status conferred in recognition of certain specific skills and competence is achieved status. For example, doctors have status due to the importance of their skills in society. Status is also achieved through work, as in the case of Russi Mody, Ratan Tata, Vijay Mallaya, Kumar Mangalam Birla, Bill Gates, Anil Ambani, Narayana Murty, H.D. Parekh and Ramesh Gelli. These successful personalities have achieved high status.

(b) Personal status: Personal status is achieved purely by personality characteristics, such as personal charm, kindness, decisiveness etc. It is unique because personality determines status.

Organisational status is of the following types:

(a) **Ascribed status**: Status attached to an individual due to his association with another person who has a status, is ascribed status. For example, the wife of the Managing Director acquires status due to the status of her husband.

(b) **Functional status:** In organisations, the importance of functions performed by different individuals determines the status of employees. People having certain functions are viewed as having greater status. For example, in a public enterprise, employees working in the finance department are viewed as important persons. Thus, they feel they have greater status.

(c) **Scalar status:** Status attained by occupying a position in the formal hierarchy of an organisation is scalar status. Hence, as a person moves in the organisational hierarchy his status also changes.

(d) **Positional status:** Positions in organisations have their own status, irrespective of the person occupying the position. For instance, the position of Managing Director has its own status, irrespective of who the person may be. The authority and other reward systems are often due to positional status.

DISTINCTIONS BETWEEN ORGANISATIONAL AND PERSONAL STATUS

Organisational status is attained by the formality of structure. It is given by the organisation. The position denotes the status. It is represented by the functions of the organisation. Personal status comes from power rather than authority, responsibility and accountability of the organisation. Sometimes certain persons attain status due to their association with persons having a certain status in the organisation. In this case, it is only personal status. Some factors that determine personal status are age, sex, wisdom, intelligence, charm, qualification, possession of skills etc. Similarly, organisational status is influenced by the structure, communication, position, accountability, reward systems etc.

Other types of status an individual enjoys are as follows:

(i) **Active status:** A person may perform a variety of roles in society. In each role he is given some recognition and status. Status enjoyed in a particular organisational context is called active status.

(ii) **Latent status:** Latent status refers to recognition enjoyed in general. It is viewed relatively. For instance in a bank an individual is an ordinary clerk, but he is captain of a sports team representing the country in world sports. This is his latent status, as it influences his status in the bank.

(iii) **Occupational status:** In society status is attached to individuals according to their occupations. Certain occupations, irrespective of organisational attachments are valued more than others by people in society. For example, lawyers and doctors have independent practices, but they have a high status in society.

The type of status influences an individual's behavior and performance, both within and outside an organisation. Therefore, people strive to achieve status in general.

SOURCES OF ORGANISATIONAL STATUS

A number of factors determine the source of status in organisations. These are explained below:

(i) **Family:** Traditionally, certain families have acquired high status due to their position in society. Individuals born in those families automatically acquire the status of the family.

(ii) **Material possession:** Possession of wealth is another determinant of status. Persons with more wealth are accorded high status in society. For instance, the chairmen of the Tata group of industries and the Reliance group of industries have high status due to the assets possessed by the groups.

(iii) **Personal qualities:** Physical, racial, personality and religious qualities also confer status. Age, sex, charisma, religion etc., determine relative status. For example the original inhabitants of a country are highly regarded than immigrants.

(iv) **Reward power:** Persons having power to sanction financial or non-financial rewards are viewed as having a higher status, especially when there is a scarcity. Similarly, in a organisation, financial authority and power, also determine an individual's status.

(v) **Achievements and rewards:** Educational and professional achievements and rewards determine one's status. For example, a professional is accorded high status, especially amongst people who are not professionally qualified. An employee, who earned a gold medal in the MBA examination will have a higher status than his colleagues.

(vi) **Personal sacrifice:** Individuals willing to sacrifice or expend their personal capacity are recognised as having a higher status. For instance, people view a person who performs a difficult task, even at the risk of his life, as a hero. A union leader is viewed as having status since he sacrifices his personal life for the sake of union activities.

STATUS SYMBOLS

Status may be identified by certain symbols that are externally visible. For instance, the '*Param Vir Chakra*' is given to mark the bravery of armed personnel with a gold plated star. Such status symbols enable us to understand status by observation. Another example, very different from this is a well decorated, air conditioned office room, which reflects the high status of the occupant. Certain status symbols are explained below:

(i) **Official designations:** A designation is a title indicating one's position in the organisational hierarchy. Impressive titles indicate status, for example, Controller of Finance and Production Director, or instead of being called a sales person, a person could be called a sales executive, giving a sense of official status.

(ii) **Symbols:** Status is displayed by certain symbols unique to that position. These symbols carry the prestige of the position. For instance, the office of the head of an institution bears a national flag. The name board in front of the office of the director is a status symbol, whereas an assistant's office does not have a name board.

(iii) **Monetary rewards:** Salary, perquisites and allowances are given commensurate to a person's qualifications. But monetary rewards can be given to distinguish high status. For example, an officer who has allowance for a peon is regarded as having higher status.

(iv) **Physical facilities of work environment:** Good working conditions, layout of office, decorative design of the work place indicate the status of people.

The above enumerates only a few status symbols, in practice there are an innumerable number.

BEHAVIOURAL FUNCTIONS AND DYSFUNCTIONS OF STATUS

Status satisfies an individual's need for recognition. Acquiring status is a constant social process. Status enables establishing relationships and behaving in apt manner congruent to the relationships to do the things using the relationships.

It provides many functional benefits to an organisation. Status denotes the prestige, integrity and motivation of persons. The functional benefits of status in organisations are given below.

(a) **Communication function:** In organisations, the communication system is designed along with status. Communication requires both functional and scalar authority to enforce orders and directions in the realisation of objectives. Authenticity and intelligibility of communication is achieved by status, as communication from persons of low status is not valued and followed. In certain emergency situations quick actions are possible only by authoritative communication. For example, if there is a fire in the office, the manager's directions will take precedence over those of a clerk.

(b) **Responsibility function:** Status is recognised by the responsibility and accountability. Persons occupying a particular status accept to discharge responsibility and undertake accountability. This is because occupying a status is an achievement. People try to retain status, as they cannot live with lower status. Hence, once a status is occupied people undertake responsibility.

(c) **Motivating function:** Status is a non-monetary. It provides psychological appeal, pride and recognition among individuals. Therefore, people with high status feel more motivated. This apart, status satisfies egoistic and self-actualisation needs. Thus, individual motivation is enhanced by assigning a higher status.

(d) **Integrity function:** Personal integrity and commitment to one's job are provided by status. Persons with certain status are expected to protect the integrity of office. Similarly, persons commit themselves to perform jobs in order to retain their status. For example, a member of the managing committee does not disclose the discussions unless orders are issued. He maintains secrecy due to the status he enjoys. A person not having this status may not maintain this secrecy as he has no responsibility to do so.

(e) **Behaviour modification function:** Status differentials in organisations require a certain behaviour. Individuals are required to modify their behaviour in accordance with their status. For example, a supervisor who usually goes to a worker to solve the worker's problems, stops doing so if he is promoted to production manager, and will require the worker to come to his office. Hence, status brings about behaviour modification.

Status leads to functional benefits, but it may also lead to conflicts and dissatisfaction in organisations. Dysfunctional aspects of the status system are explained below:

(i) **Creation of distance:** Status creates a feeling of pride in an individual, and causes him to develop an ego. Hence, people with higher status tend to keep others at a distance in order to protect their pride and ego. This creates problems of communication, interaction and coordination, which adversely affect organisational functioning.

(ii) **Maintenance of status**: Status requires maintenance of facilities, symbols and creation of a work environment, all of which involve costs. For example, a manager, who has an air-conditioned room, requires other facilities, like carpets and interior design that involve costs to the organisation. If they are withdrawn in order to save costs, it may create serious motivation and morale problems.

(iii) **Inconsistent status:** Status inconsistency arises when status and skills are imbalanced. If persons with inadequate skills and competence are given status, it leads to inefficiency.

(iv) **Status competition:** Every member of an organisation tries to attain higher status. Thus competition increases. Healthy competition increases organisational effectiveness. However, unhealthy competition to attain status leads to serious personal differences, envy and anxiety, which retard organisational effectiveness.

(v) **Status incongruence:** Organisations are expected to provide equity in status. This follows the principle of distributive justice, which states that rewards should commensurate to the effort. A feeling that a person's status is commensurate to his characteristics and effort gives satisfaction. On the other hand, if it is generally felt that the characteristics of the person are unsuitable to his status, it leads to status incongruence. This leads to feeling of frustration and dissatisfaction.

(vi) **Status discrepancy:** It is the difference between expected and actual behavior of status holders. For example, a maintenance manager is not supposed to ask a foreman about the working of a machine. This status discrepancy leads to workers feeling that their superior is incompetent. As a result, they may under estimate the manager's potential, and not obey orders or they may behave casually with him. This severely affects the work performance.

SUMMARY

Status is an intangible rank determined amongst a group of people. It is a multidimensional phenomenon. It has an impact on the performance of tasks. Status can be either organisational or social. Social status can be classified into achieved and personal status. Organisational status can be classified into ascribed status, functional status, scalar status and positional status. It can also be classified as active status, latent status. Some of the factors that influence status are family, material possessions, personal qualities, reward power, achievement, rewards, and personal sacrifice. Certain symbols identify status. They are official designations, symbols, monetary rewards, and physical facilities of the work environment. Status has both functional and dysfunctional consequences. The functional consequences are communication function, responsibility function, motivating function, integrity function and behaviour modification function. Similarly creation of distance, maintenance of status, inconsistent status, status competition, incongruent status and status discrepancy are some of the dysfunctional consequences of status.

Case study 15.1: Does status really matter?

The Minerals and Metal Research and Development Corporation is a medium sized company that employs about 726 employees in different cadres. The head of the organisation is known as the Chief Executive Officer (CEO) and looks after the total management of the organisation. The decision-making authority of the enterprise rests in his hands. However, implementation is carried out by the Chief Administrative Officer and Vice President of the organisation. The official orders and communication are given in the name of the Executive Vice President. The employees work in departments, some of which are interconnected and some of which are independent. The categorisation of the departments into line and staff is not made. However, at the same time the functions of the departments are on the same lines. There are 16 departments identified as line departments that have about half the employee workforce. The rest of the employees are working in 8 layers in the administration of the organisation. Their designation structure is that of Joint Administrative Officer, Deputy Administrative Officer, Assistant Administrative Officer, Senior Administrative Officer, Administrative Officer and Administrative Ministerial staff. The line departments have a three-tier structure. The designations are Executive R&D Officers, Regional Executive R&D Officers and Lower Level Executive R&D Officers.

The basic research and development personnel are responsible for implementing the projects and undertaking schemes of knowledge development. The completed research projects undergo rigours testing, and are sent to client organisations for implementation. The funding is through the budgetary allocation of MMRDC and most of the scheme-based research is funded by the beneficiary organisations. The line personnel thus totally concentrate on the research activities. Even a small snag would be a costly affair. Usually they will never divert their attention to administrative activities and are often totally ignorant of how things move in the administration, and how decisions are taken. Of late, the organisation has recruited additional personnel in the category of Lower Level Executive R&D Officers. The department maintains a seniority list of the R&D personnel. Organisational communications are addressed in order of seniority. Positions are also given in order of seniority. The schemes are processed for financial assistance based on seniority.

The research departments where the Executive R&D Officers, Regional Executive R&D Officers and Lower Level Executive R&D Officers function has a section for assisting them in their functions. This section is mostly staff activity. In some strategic departments, the designations of the staff are Assistant Administrative Officer, Senior Administrative Officer, Administrative Officers and Administrative Ministerial staff. In some other departments, the designations of the staff are Senior Administrative Officer, Administrative Officers and Administrative Ministerial staff.

One day a few of the newly recruited Executive R&D Officers went to the Joint Administrative Officer in the audit and accounting department. They complained that the names of the department staff on the salary claim forms, were not in order of seniority, which according to them was a serious mistake of the administrative staff posted in the department. They even argued that this had been done deliberately. This led to other senior R&D personnel, who had until then, never even noticed this, to support them. All this was nonsense according to the Joint Administrative Officer. He stated that the R&D personnel were supposed to concentrate on research and development matters, and should not be concerned about such matters. Dissatisfied by this argument, the R&D personnel represented this matter as gross violation of status in the organisation. They threatened that if the anomaly was not rectified, it would lead to serious consequences.

The organisation maintains a central pay-processing department. The salary and wage claims of the research and development personnel and other administrative staff working in the department are prepared at the individual department level. For operational convenience, the claims are written in the same form that is provided for the purpose. However, the organisation provided two separate forms, one for the R&D staff and another for the administrative staff. The prepared claims are sent to the central audit section. The section passes the claims for payment. Then the claims are sent to the accounting section where the salary and wage claims are recorded in the individual accounts of the employees. A consolidated cheque is prepared for all the staff working in a department under intimation to the head, the cheque will be sent to the bank for payment through credit to the individual savings bank accounts. This practice had been in vogue for a long time, but the R&D personnel never observed this operational process. They only checked the salary credited into their bank accounts. Even the audit and accounting sections seemed not to have paid serious attention to it.

Questions:

1. What status problems have been identified in the case, which led to the conflicting situation?
2. Distinguish between organisational and social status. Do you think that social status has a cascading effect on organisational status?
3. What do you think are the behavioural implications of the personnel representing the incongruent status?
4. If you were in the position of the CEO how would you react to the argument of the R&D personnel and convince them to ignore this trivial matter?

16. EMOTIONAL BEHAVIOUR

This chapter enables you:

- *To define the term emotion*
- *To understand the components of emotions*
- *To distinguish between emotions and moods*
- *To appraise as to why different individuals express different emotions*
- *To examine the determinants of emotions*
- *To identify the area of application of emotions in organisations*

The structure of the chapter is as follows:

- Introduction
- Definition of emotions
- Distinctions between emotions and moods
- Dimensions of emotions
- Factors determining emotions
- Application of emotions in organisational behaviour
- Summary
- Key words

CHAPTER 16

Emotional Behaviour

INTRODUCTION

Emotions and sentiments are strong elements of the mental make up of an individual. They are psychological in nature. No organisation can function without emotions. Feelings are known only when they are expressed, but emotions are not always expressed. This leads to stress in individuals. If emotions are not expressed for a long time, it leads to moody behaviour, which is dangerous. You must have experienced a pensive mood when you heard bad news and a happy mood when you found out that you had secured a gold medal in the graduation course. Your moods will affect your behaviour throughout the day. If you are happy you will be calm and cool, whereas if you are in a sad or bad mood every small thing disturbs you. In an organisation, personal emotions play a major role in determining interaction between individuals. Interpersonal communication, conflict resolution and interpersonal understanding are guided by one's emotions. For example, employees will speak to the boss about an increment or promotion when they feel the boss is in a good mood. When an individual is in a good mood, he is more likely to be a good listener. On the other hand, if a person is in a bad mood it will not create a good interpersonal communication network. Thus, every manager should understand how to deal with the emotions and moods of subordinates, superiors and peers. In this chapter, we will learn about emotions in organisational behaviour.

DEFINITION OF EMOTIONS

Emotions relate to the psychology of an individual and the inner feelings expressed in a situation. When a person experiences stimuli, he is likely to develop inner feelings. Facial expressions, verbal sounds and body actions are used to express inner feelings.

An emotion can be defined as an expression of fear, anger, joy, love, hate, grief, frustration, satisfaction etc. Emotions are important in understanding employees' behaviour in an organisational setting.

> ***Stephen P. Robbins*** *defined emotions 'as intense feelings that are directed at someone or something. Understanding emotions requires understanding of two components. One is affect: it is a broad range of feelings that people experience. Second are moods: they are feelings that tend to be less intense than emotions and that lack a contextual stimulus.* Emotions contain four elements. They are stimuli, organism, feelings and expressions. Figure 16.1 shows the components of emotions.

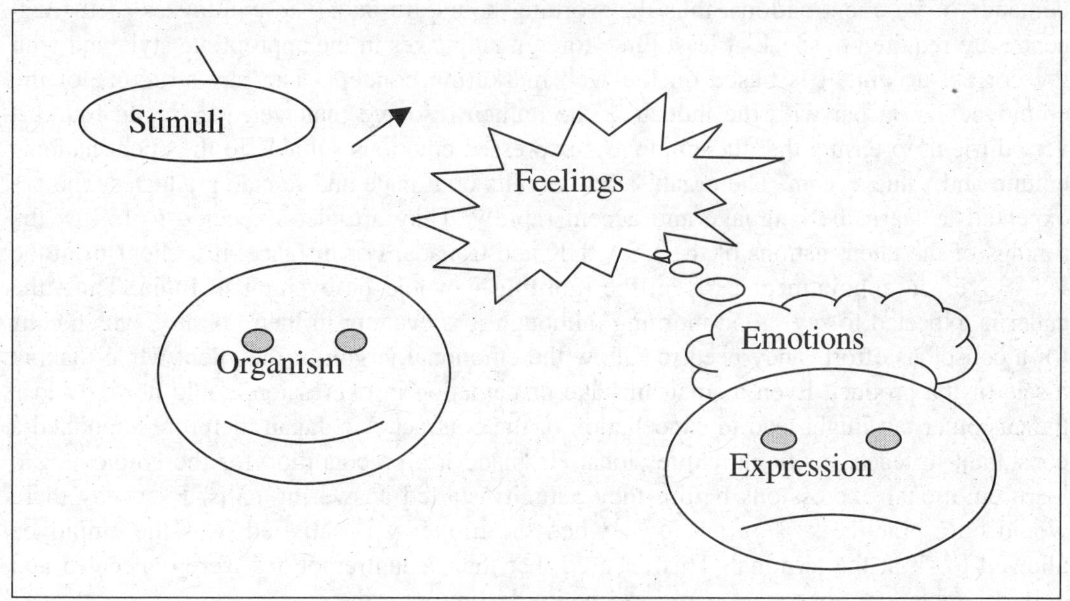

Figure 16.1: Components of emotions

An organisation is a group of human beings. The Hawthorne experiments conducted by Elton Mayo showed that human beings have feelings, sentiments and emotions. No organisation can be designed to keep emotions away. Classical theories have assumed that an organisation is a rational instrument of production. Organisation structure is designed to incorporate rationality in actions, but they have ignored the human element. As such, emotions are considered as disruptive to an organisation. The human relations approach identified the human element as being important in organisations. This approach considers that human beings are composed of various psychological attributes. Thus, organisation structure, process, systems, and procedures are designed taking into account human emotions.

Emotions are known only when they are expressed. When an individual does not express a feeling, it is known as a felt emotion. It is the actual emotion of a person. However, when a person expresses a feeling, it is called a displayed emotion. In organisations employees display certain emotions, which are considered appropriate to carry out their work. These displayed emotions need not be their actual feelings. For instance, a salesman is required to be cheerful with a customer even if he is facing a sad situation in his personal life. Therefore, felt emotions and displayed emotions are different. Employees exhibit appropriate emotional behaviour concealing their actual emotions.

Case study 16.1: Felt vs. displayed emotions

SK Technologies is an 18 x 6 call centre, with 120 call booths. It works according to the demands of its client nations, thus the working hours are odd. The employees of the call centre are required to speak at least three foreign languages in the appropriate style and with the correct accent. It is based on the web marketing concept. The pay structure of the employees is on par with the industry. The human resource manager, Mr. Jagan found it very difficult to ensure that the employees expressed emotions suitable to the client nation's culture and value system. The organisation recruits both male and female graduates who are expected to learn the language and accent rapidly. They are also expected to follow the timings of the client nations of the USA, UK and Canada. For instance, if a client from the USA gives an appointment early in the morning it would be evening in India. Thus, the caller is expected to say 'good morning' although it is evening in their country, which calls for a conscious effort. They need to follow the emotional jargon of the client while making a sale of the product. Even a small mistake or deviation in expression, could not only lose the customer but might lead to cancellation of the contract. Mr. Jagan therefore appointed a consultant to teach emotional expressions. He made it a precondition for the employees to learn emotional expressions before they actually started answering calls. Everyday there would be a practice session and only when the trainer was satisfied, was the employee allowed to sit at the terminal. This ensured that their actual emotions were concealed and only desirable emotions were expressed while dealing with the customers.

DISTINCTIONS BETWEEN EMOTIONS AND MOODS

Often, emotions and moods are treated as synonymous. Emotions are always associated with an object, person or situation. For instance, the feeling of joy when you meet a close relative after a considerable time. This feeling is associated with a smiling face. On the other hand, the feeling of sadness, when you hear of the demise of a near and dear person, is associated with tears and perhaps an unconscious utterance of 'I still cannot believe it.' Thus, a situation causes an emotion. Emotions are often expressed with the help of words or facial expressions. Moods are outgrowth of emotions. They may not have any particular association. Persons usually display moods by silence, rather than noise. For instance, if you have not performed well in the examinations, you will silently keep away from your friends and family. The following table shows the distinctions between emotions and moods.

Emotions	Moods
Emotions are a reaction to an object, not a trait.	Moods are not directed at an object.
Emotions can turn into moods.	Moods arise out of emotions.
Emotions are often displayed.	Moods need not be displayed.
Emotions are more intense in nature.	Moods are less intense than emotions.
Emotions are associated with contextual stimuli.	Moods lack contextual stimuli.
Emotions are part of moods.	Moods encompass emotions.
Emotions are displayed through facial expressions, verbal sounds and body actions.	Moods are displayed through silence and behavioural reactions.

Dr. Sarvepally Radhakrishnan said that "Man knows only a part of his being, his surface mentality. We are sometimes completely overcome by emotions, instinctive and involuntary reactions that upset the role of conscious reason. Under the stress of strong emotions, we say or do things, which we regret afterwards. Unless the individual has complete self awareness, man marches to success."

DIMENSIONS OF EMOTIONS

Every person does not display emotions in the same manner. As there are differences in individuals there are differences in expression of emotions. There are three dimensions of emotions. They are presented below.

1. **Emotions are different types:** Emotions are different and numerous. Six types of emotions are identified as universally acceptable. They are: anger, disgust, fear, happiness, sadness and surprise. However, there is a possibility of confusing emotions because of the similarity of facial expressions. For instance, happiness is confused with surprise. It should be noted that interpretations of emotions is influenced by the situation, environment, personality, and social and cultural factors. In any organisation, all these different types of emotions are often displayed in one or another situation every day. For instance, an irregular worker, who receives a suspension order, shows the emotion of anger. In another case, an insurance agent met a client and tried to convince him that he was under insured. However, after repeated attempts by the agent, the client became impatient and no sale took place. After some time however, the customer himself walked into the insurance office and took out an insurance policy, specifying the agent's name. The insurance agent got credit for the policy and was paid commission for it. On learning about this, the agent expressed the emotion of surprise.

2. **Emotions vary in their intensity:** Response to stimuli causing emotions is not identical hence, persons do not display emotions in the same manner. It differs from person to person and situation to situation. For instance, an employee may be angry when his superior reproaches him, but does not show it on his face. After he comes out of the office however, his anger will be clear from his facial expression. Persons also differ in their ability to show emotions. Some people show their emotions clearly, whilst others have more control over their feelings. The latter are capable of concealing their feelings when necessary and expressing them when the situation demands. In organisations jobs demand expression of emotions in different situations with varying intensity. An individual's effectiveness depends on his ability to control his emotions. This is known as emotional balance.
3. **Emotions differ in their frequency and duration:** Emotions are not expressed with the same frequency all the time. In addition, the duration of expressions varies with the job and personality. Certain jobs require the expression of emotions very frequently. Other jobs require the expression of emotions for a long time. For instance, a teacher has to express the emotions as long as he is in the classroom, whereas an accountant, who mostly works at his books, expresses his emotions only when he has to interact with others. In these cases, the felt emotions are displayed, but emotions can also cause conflict. Thus, a person's efficiency is a function of his expression of emotions. The higher the frequency and duration individual can express displayed emotions, the more he is considered efficient.

FACTORS DETERMINING EMOTIONS

Emotions play a vital role in the discharge of one's job. Organisations define the boundaries in which emotions are accepted or rejected. For example, an employee working in a public relations department cannot show an emotion of disgust. It is not acceptable work behaviour. A doctor cannot show disinterest in the result of a prescription given to patient. An advocate is not expected to become excited whilst citing his case before a judge, as the judge may infer that his argument is weak. A sales person attending a customer late in the evening should be as cheerful as he was with the first customer of the morning. Cheerfulness is an acceptable emotion for an efficient sales person. Factors that determine or exert influence on human emotions are presented below.

1. **Organisational factors:** The nature and type of organisation, the demands of the job, climate of work place, the degree of interpersonal interactions required on the job, leadership styles of superiors, and organisational culture influence the dimensions of emotions. If the boss is an authoritarian, his subordinates will always resent him. Certain jobs require showing emotions such as sincerity, enthusiasm, confidence and a sense of humor. Emotions also differ from person to person. A higher authority expressing impatience with a lower level subordinate is not considered objectionable. A subordinate expressing disinterest is objectionable. Negative emotions and intense emotions are usually unacceptable, however at times negative emotions need to be expressed. For instance, a common problem in modern organisations is sexual harassment, which needs to be dealt with by expressing a negative emotion. Otherwise, the harassment may continue, even with others. This may even lead to a

poor impression of the organisational culture.

2. **Cultural factors:** The culture, climate, traditions, norms and taboos of a country influence emotions. Emotions also differ between genders. Women are more prone to immediate expression of emotions than men. The interpretation of emotions is related to the culture of the country. For instance, in Islamic countries, a smile may be inferred as a sign of sexual attraction, whereas in the USA it is taken as an act of friendliness. Certain countries do not have equivalent words to express some emotions. For instance, anxiety, depression and guilt do not find expression in many countries.

Thus, emotions are influenced by the factors beyond one's personality.

APPLICATION OF EMOTIONS IN ORGANISATIONAL BEHAVIOUR

Emotions are important determinants of employee behaviour in organisations. Managers use their knowledge of emotions to direct their subordinates in an effective manner and achieve organisational objectives. Some applications of emotions in organisations are given below.

1. **Employee selection:** Organisations generally look for persons who can interact with others and work within a group. The ability to adjust to job demands, environmental pressures and go along with other persons is an absolute requirement for success in any job. Emotional stability implies controlling aggression. Employees are often required to conceal their real emotions and display emotions suitable to the situation. Organisations select employees who possess this quality. It is also known as emotional intelligence. According to Robbins, emotional intelligence is "*an assortment of non cognitive skills, capabilities, and competencies that influence a person's ability to succeed in coping with environment demands and pressures.*" It is composed of five elements: Self-awareness, self-management, self-motivation, empathy, and social skills.

2. **Decision-making:** Decision-making is an integral quality of every employee in an organisation. Decision-making must be rational if it has to yield the intended results. However, while taking decisions emotions such as fear, anxiety, frustration, doubt, excitement, anger and stress, can dominate rational thinking. Managers overlooking the importance of negative emotions in the decision making process are likely to overlook a number of alternatives also. They also overlook information processing and are more intuitive in making decisions. Similarly, positive emotions increase the ability to solve complex problems and deal with the complex persons. In the process of collective decision-making, emotional stability is required to ensure that employees feel that their suggestions are considered, whilst arriving at a final decision. A manager who can balance rationality, intuition and emotions is likely to make sound decisions, which are acceptable to his subordinates. Employees are more likely to feel psychologically committed to those decisions, which are arrived at by taking their opinions into consideration.

3. **Leadership:** Communication of directions, motivation of subordinates, and resolving inter

personal conflicts are an integral part of leadership. Emotions play a vital role in all these aspects, which are described below.

i. ***Communication:*** Communication is the process of making others understand a message in the manner in which it is intended. Use of words, medium, language, technology, and environment alone do not convey a message. Appropriate facial expressions, body language and tone of communication convey the meaning as it is intended. All these relate to the emotions of the sender. The emotions of the receiver are also very important. For instance, to motivate a productive worker, simply saying 'very good' or 'keep it up' may not be sufficient, whereas 'you are doing an excellent job,' with the appropriate facial expression, will really motivate the worker to produce more.

ii. ***Motivation:*** Motivation is the feeling of an inner drive and enthusiasm to act in a predetermined way in expectation of certain desired outcomes. Emotions influence the desired outcomes. Rational economic man always desires to maximize his monetary satisfaction. Thus, emotions related to money enthuse them. Nevertheless, can we say that he always does this? No. He considers certain situations in which he satisfies with a lesser reward. This is because of the emotions. Even the achievement motivation comes from an emotional attachment of employees to the jobs. Thus, managers use emotional content to motivate their subordinates in a proper direction. For example if an achiever is appraised before the group of colleagues he will become emotional with excitement and then he tries to keep his achievement up.

iii. ***Inter personal conflicts*:** Misunderstanding communication in an emotional situation can lead to conflict. It is often said that communication should be withheld when either the sender or receiver are angry, as it leads to interpersonal conflict. This is because of emotions, which leads us to understand that emotions are interwoven in conflicts. However, these emotions may not necessarily be visible in a conflicting situation. A manager has to address the emotional component in order to resolve the conflict and increase harmony among the subordinates. On the other hand addressing the task and structural aspects of the conflict alone do not redress the conflict. A successful manager learns to consider the emotions in the resolution of inter personal conflicts.

4. **Management of change:** Change is a common phenomenon as is resistance to it. Employees resist change if the goals are vague. Thus, emotional attachment to goals elicits a positive attitude towards change. Managers can elicit a positive response to change by the suggestion, framing and mobilisation of emotions. Thus, proper linking of emotions with change is necessary to overcome resistance to change.

5. **Deviant behaviour in the workplace:** Emotions influence moods and consequently employees involuntarily deviate from norms and rules, defy authority and cause damage to property of an organisation. Certain observed deviations are 'going slow,' sabotage, politicking, recriminations, harassment, aggression etc. Another negative emotion that causes stress and anxiety in individual behaviour is envy, which leads to aggressive and moody behaviour. Promotion of positive emotions controls envy. If an employee is denied the

promotion he has been expecting, he is likely to become impatient, and may show his resentment by not working properly or by disinterest in his work.

SUMMARY

This chapter discussed the emotional behaviour of individuals. Emotions result from interaction with stimuli. An individual feels emotions, but others only come to know about them if they are expressed by facial expressions or body language. Emotions relate to fear, anger, love, hate, joy, frustration, satisfaction, motivation etc. There is a conceptual and structural difference between emotions and moods. In fact, emotions are broader in scope and moods are a part of emotion. Moods are often displayed through silence, while emotions may be displayed through acts of aggression. Emotions differ in different situations. They also differ in frequency, duration and intensity. Though emotions relate to an individual's psychology, they are also determined by a host of organisational factors. Social and cultural factors also play a major role in determining the emotions of individuals. Emotions have a number of implications in organisational behaviour, such as, employee selection, decision-making, leadership, communication, motivation, conflict resolution, change management and deviant work place behaviour.

Key words:

- **Emotion:** An inner feeling expressed by an individual in a situation
- **Emotional balance:** An individual's ability to control emotions
- **Emotional intelligence:** Skills and capabilities in coping with the demands and pressures of the environment
- **Felt emotion:** Feeling not specifically expressed
- **Mood:** An act of silence that expresses the emotion of an individual

Case study cum business game 16.2: How emotions are taken

Shriram Chit Fund Private Limited is a non-banking financial institution, with a wide area of operations. Originally from Chennai it has spread to the entire south India. It is a reputed organisation in matters of chit and financial operations. This case study deals with an employee's emotions whilst dealing with a customer.

Mr. Rangarajan, an employee of a public sector organisation, joined a chit group in one of the branches. As he is an employee having fixed commitments, he thought of the chit as a means of saving rather than lifting it in the initial stages. He paid the monthly subscriptions regularly by cheque, in order to have a record for income tax purposes. However, it so happened that a few months before the chit was to close there was a delay in payment of the monthly installments due to the fact that the collection agent of the company, did not turn up at Mr. Rangarajan's house, despite repeatedly promising to do so. Thus, Mr. Rajan used to make the payment at the office counter according to his convenience. Every time when he visited the office, the staff raised the issue of the collection agent and every time Mr. Rangarajan complained that the agent does not show up for collection.

Five months before the closure of the chit, Mr. Rajan decided to take the amount at minimum commission. On the day of auction, the following incident took place.

Rangarajan: (R) (Addressing one of the office bearers.) "Sir, I have come to the auction of the chit with a reference number."

Office Staff: (O) (Questioningly) "What is the number?"

R: "lk23"

O: (Looking into a file, and without any change in emotion.) "It is at 11.50. Wait outside."

R: "Sir, I will go out and come back. Meanwhile I would like to give the offer for a minimum amount. If I miss by chance, I will lose the opportunity of being a prized subscriber. I want an application form for that."

O: "Collect it from the madam."

R: "What is the letter known as?"

O: (Impatiently) "It is a bid offer letter."

Mr. Ranagarajan approached the lady officer and inquired about the bid offer letter. He was directed to another lady officer who gave him a red coloured form on which he completed the details and tried to hand it over to her.

O: "No, not to me. Please hand it over in the auction room." (She gazed at the auction room and noticed that the door was closed for auction in progress.) "All right, I will hand over to them."

Rangarajan left the office and returned at the appointed time.
In the auction room.

O: "Sir, what is your number?"

Mr. Rangarajan showed the passbook. It was verified and found that the current month subscription was not paid.

O: "Sir, you have to pay the current month's subscription."

R: "I have not received the intimation letter for payment. Otherwise I was a regular payee."

O: (Impatiently) "I do not deny it. Please pay and then come to the auction room."

As Rangarajan took out his cheque book and started writing, the office staff looked at him impatiently and said, "We do not accept cheques, you have to pay cash."

R: (Smiling) "Sir, I have always paid the monthly subscription by cheque, suddenly what is the objection?"

O: (Looking slightly disgusted) "I do not know about all this; you can even bring cash in about fifteen minutes and make payment. We will allow you to participate in the auction, as there are no competing bidders."

R: "Exactly, as there are no competing bidders, the auction will have to go in my favour, so accept my cheque, as today is a Sunday I cannot bring cash."

Another person, who was not supposed to be present in the auction room, suggested to the office staff that in the situation there was no point in insisting on cash payment, as the chit will have to go in favour of Rangarajan, and they should accept the cheque. The office staff appeared angry at the suggestion and stated that it was not possible, however they told Mr. Rangarajan to make the payment, and they would ask the manager whether it was possible to accept the cheque. Mr. Rangarajan presented the cheque at the counter and obtained the receipt. The receipt was shown to the office staff who took the necessary signatures and told him to meet another officer to complete the formalities. When Rangarajan approached the lady officer, she was processing another application and requested him to wait for some time. Rangarajan said he would come back in half an hour, to which she agreed. When he came back to the office, she was having lunch, so he waited till she had finished and the following discussion took place.

O: (Smiling) "Sir please sign these papers."

R: "Yes madam, I have completed the signatures on the papers. When will I receive the cheque? What formalities do I need to complete?"

O: (Continuing to smile) "You have to give a surety of two parties and after completing the formalities you will receive payment after one month."

R: (Rather impatiently) "As the chit gets over in 5 months I am prepared to pay the subscription amount in full. You can deduct the amount in the payment and pay me the balance. Thus, no question of giving sureties arises. One month is too much time to wait for payment, as there are no other formalities.

O: (Still smiling) "Sir why don't you join in another chit as the current chit has come to an end?"

R: "Oh no! I am not interested in joining a chit with your company, as I have experienced poor response throughout."

O: "Such as?"

R: "I will tell you later, now why don't you give me an account copy to be submitted in my income tax assessment?"

O: "You can collect it after completing the chit."

R: "Why do I have to visit the office again? Is it not possible now?"

O: (Cheerfully) "It is possible, I will get it, but why don't you join in our insurance scheme? It is beneficial and necessary."

R: "No! I have sufficient insurance, I do not need any more."

The officer became impatient as Rangarajan rejected all her proposals, angrily she turned to the other computer operator and asked him to give her a copy of the account, which she gave to Rangarajan.

R: (Looking at the account copy given to him) "It does not specify the total amount of the bid and the amount I am going to receive, it is incomplete and does not specify that I am a prized bidder, so it is not useful to me."

O: "That is what I told you sir, you will receive the full account copy after completion."

R: "After completion means, I will receive it after the completion of the chit, that is of no use as I have to submit the income tax return in a month's time."

O: (Rather rudely) "After preparing your cheque we will enter the details into the computer and the final copy of the account will come to you.

R: "Oh! I see, I understood it as completion of the chit! I am very sorry, it must have been a communication fault."

O: (Still more rudely) "It is not a communication fault at all, I have understood you perfectly, you got confused and are trying to confuse me."

R: "I am sorry! Will you please send the cheque and copy of the account to my residential address?"

O: "No, you have to collect the cheque personally."

R: "How will I know that the cheque is ready? Could you please call me at my residence."

O: "It is not possible but we will see, you will have to enquire often and the account copy will not be sent by post either."

R: (Angrily) "Why can't you do this service for customers? It will only cost about five rupees."

O: (Loudly and frustratedly) "It is not possible, we have thousands of customers."

R: "Madam, now do you realise why I was not interested in joining another scheme. It is due to this kind of attitude of your firm. Anyhow thank you very much."

As Rangarajan was leaving the office, he heard the office staff murmuring as to what kind of customer he was? Unfortunately, they did not seem to realise that one customer lost could have a geometric effect. With a little control over their emotions they could have changed the attitude of the customer to a positive mood.

17. GROUPS IN ORGANISATIONS

This chapter enables you:

- *To define groups in an organisation*
- *To examine the characteristic features of the groups*
- *To identify the group development process*
- *To understand why individuals are interested in joining the groups*
- *To appraise different types of groups found in organisations*
- *To distinguish between formal and informal groups*
- *To understand the meaning and types of cliques*
- *To distinguish between open and closed groups*

The structure of the chapter is as follows:

- Introduction
- Definition and characteristics of groups
- Model of group development process
- Reasons for formation of groups
- Types of groups
- Functional and dysfunctional consequences of groups in an organisation
- Summary
- Key words

CHAPTER 17

Groups in Organisations

INTRODUCTION

An organisation is a formal group. It is composed of people, material and financial resources. People in an organisation form groups for various reasons. For example, in college you are likely to associate more with selected friends, rather than all your classmates. Thus, you have formed a friendship group of your own. Similarly, the members of the college cricket team form a group. In this case, some members of this group may also be part of a group of common friends. In the same way, a number of groups exist in an organisation, of which a person may or may not be a member. The formation of a group is not always spontaneous. It may be formed by a process and with a specific purpose. Thus, there is always a reason for the formation of groups in organisations. These groups need not have a defined structure. Groups having a defined structure are formal groups, and they provide structured interaction. For instance, a college or cricket team is a formal group. Some groups, known as informal groups, are formed out of mutual attraction, and provide social satisfaction. They serve to realise short-term goals, like a friendship group. As long as you continue to make friends the group will exist. In the same way, a number of groups are continuously formed in an organisation for various reasons. For example, a finance committee may be formed to frame a budget for the current year. A disciplinary committee may be formed to tackle a serious disciplinary problem on the shop floor. Therefore, groups serve the purpose for which they are formed. However, groups can also cause certain dysfunctional consequences. If groups are used effectively, they will be an asset to the organisation, and contribute to its effectiveness. Otherwise, they will be a liability to the organisation. The purpose of this chapter is to give you a clear idea of the process of formation of groups and their functional and dysfunctional effects.

DEFINITION OF A GROUP

Organisations are social units composed of individuals interacting to realise goals. Formation of groups within an organisation is natural. While an organisation is a formal group, members of the organisation form various informal groups. If properly used groups contribute to organisational performance. At the same time, groups can negatively affect an organisation's effectiveness. It is in this context, that understanding the reasons for formation of groups and the interaction that occurs within the group is relevant for managers. Some definitions of a group are given below.

> ***Marwin E. Shaw*** *defined a group as 'a collection of two or more people who interact with and influence each other towards a common purpose'.*
>
> *According to* ***David Horton Smith,*** *a group is 'the largest set of two or more individuals characterised by a network of relevant communications, a shared sense of collective identity and one or more shared dispositions with associated normative strength'.*
>
> *'A group is two or more individuals interacting and interdependent, who have come together to achieve particular objectives'.* ***Robbins***
>
> ***Wallace and Szilagyi*** *defined a group as 'a collection of two or more individuals who are interdependent and interact with one another for the purpose of performing to achieve a common goal.'*
>
> ***Cartwright and Zander*** *have given a comprehensive definition of a group. 'A group is a collection of individuals who have relations to one another that make them interdependent to some significant degree. The group refers to class entities having in common, the property of interdependence among three constituent members.'*

An examination of the above definitions reveals the following characteristics of groups:

(i) A group is a collection of people.
(ii) It provides an interaction through communication.
(iii) Group facilitates members realise their goals.
(iv) Members of the group are interdependent and interacting.
(v) A group has common goals.

MODEL OF GROUP DEVELOPMENT PROCESS

Development of a group is not always spontaneous. Groups are formed out of a conscious effort of the members to come together and share common goals. Groups are developed due to interaction among members. It follows a model or a process. Ralph Stogdill identified five stages in the development of groups.

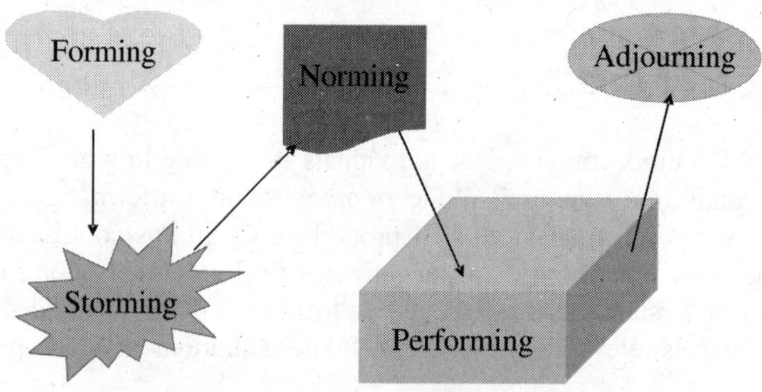

Figure 17.1: Model of Group Development

1. **Forming:** The first stage is forming the group. In this stage, members of heterogeneous characteristics are assembled. The purpose, structure, membership, norms, and leadership are vague. Members make an effort to recognise the importance of belonging to a group, which enables the group to become homogeneous by sacrificing some of their individual goals. Common goals slowly emerge at this stage. Interaction among members takes place based on common interests. Norms and structure are developed slowly but consistently.
2. **Storming:** The second stage is storming. Having come together members become aware of group existence, they also try to protect their own individuality. This leads to intra group conflict. Members storm their mental process and thinking leads to clear establishment of common objectives and norms. Only clearly understood and generally agreed objectives are put forward for achievement. The realisation of goals requires coordination and cooperation of the members, so clarity of authority, communication, definition of responsibility, role clarity and leadership are required. Hence, the group develops a formal structure characterised by clear definition, guidance and motivation in order to reinforce the achievement of goals.
3. **Norming:** This is the third stage. Norming is establishing norms or commonly agreed behaviour. Appropriate leadership and effective communication developed at the second stage strengthen the structure of the group. Members develop and strengthen group norms by assimilation of common expectations and defining members' behaviour. This develops a sense of identity of members with the group. Members become cohesive and try to protect themselves by the process of identification. In the norming stage conflicts are resolved and the group realises its objectives.

4. **Performing:** This is the fourth stage. Structure, group norms, and group leadership developed at the norming stage enable the group to perform its tasks in a coordinated manner. The group becomes fully functional at this stage. Members respect the value of the group, grapevine communication is developed and members aim for results. Intermediate disagreements and conflicts are overlooked and the work group becomes effective.
5. **Adjourning:** This is the last stage. Temporary groups like committees and task forces, which are formed for a specific purpose, are disbanded, as their work is complete. Group members evaluate the performance and success is rewarded. Members prepare to wrap up activities. If new tasks emerge, then they regroup to carry out the work. Sometimes members feel depressed due to loss of social contact caused by adjourning the group.

Group development is a dynamic process so all groups may not exactly follow the five-stage model. Some stages occur simultaneously. The distinctions between various stage of group development are shown in Table 17.1.

Table 17.1: Distinct characteristics among various stages of group development

Distinctions	Forming	Storming	Norming	Performing	Adjourning
Nature	Assembly of member	Awareness of existence	Strengthen the structure	Performance and coordination	Disbanding
Structure	Vague purpose and structure	Development of formal structure	Strengthening of structure	Functional and facilitated structure	Wrapping up
Member behaviour	Belonging-ness and sacrifice	Intra group conflict	Commonly agreed behaviour	Respect values	Motivated and energetic
Goals	Emergence of common goals	Clarity of goals and norms	Realisation of goals	Aim at final results	Completion of goals
Member interaction	Common interest based interaction	Coordination and cooperation	Cohesive and protection of identity	Conflict resolution	Evaluative

REASONS FOR FORMATION OF GROUPS

There are a number of theories regarding formation of groups, which provide reasons for formation of groups in organisations. Some of the reasons for formation of groups are given below. They are shown in Fig. 17.2.

(i) **Goal realisation:** Groups assist members in the realisation of goals. Groups pool resources and provide support for members. They provide knowledge, strength, experience, and power for the realisation of goals. Groups also help members in problem solving.

(ii) **Authority and power:** Groups provide an opportunity to use authority and power. An individual's strength is enhanced in a group, as one can put forth demands and force the management to accept them. Hence, groups are regarded as power centres in organisations. Groups use authority and power against management oppression.

Figure 17.2: Reasons for formation of groups in organisations

(iii) **Satisfaction of social and security needs:** A group is a source for understanding, companionship, interaction and creating social relationships. Groups create an environment in which members are free to discuss their problems and find solutions. Friendship and warm relationships are promoted. Groups fulfill an individual's inherent desire for socialising, affiliation and relationships with others, and acceptance by others.

(iv) **Satisfaction of ego, self-esteem, and self-actualisation needs:** Members are happy and their ego is boosted when other members of the group recognise their capacities, skills, intelligence and personality. Apart from this, groups allow members to become 'what they are capable of becoming.' Thus, individuals satisfy their self-actualisation needs. Therefore, groups satisfy the higher order needs of self-ego, esteem and actualisation. Abraham Maslow identified these concepts as part of his hierarchy of needs.

(v) **Identity:** One of the most essential desires of an individual is recognition and identity as human being. A group recognises the individuals as members. It also helps individuals to identify themselves with the group. This identity gives them security and esteem.

(vi) **Esprit de corps:** As the saying goes 'United we stand and divided we fall.' Groups help individuals to unite in order to solve many organisational problems. They help in protecting individual interests in the work place. Even Henry Fayol used this concept in his 14 principles of management.

(vii) **Safety valve:** Groups act as a safety valve to release daily tensions, worries and stress. For instance, if an employee has problems with his superior, he can share his experience with other members of the group, and release any tension he may be feeling.

Groups satisfy a variety of other needs. Thus, these needs can also promote formation of groups. They are:

(a) Groups assist members in meeting objectives.

(b) They work as a source of information.

(c) They facilitate increasing economic benefits.

(d) Groups provide relief from psychological fatigue.

(e) They help in forming the right perceptions and attitudes.

(f) Groups provide an opportunity for influence and creativity of members.

(g) They help in perpetuation of cultural values.

(h) Groups facilitate learning.

Groups provide individuals with an opportunity for exchange of ideas, thoughts, experiences and knowledge.

Case study 17.1: Induction into a club is prestigious

I used to often wonder why a number of social groups function. Recently I happened to attend a function of the Lions Club, where new members were inducted. I observed the entire function very closely, and got the answer. The club was started with a modest 35 members in 1985 in the city. The basis for membership as described by one of the dignitaries was the 'triple T', namely Time, Talent and Treasure. One may have one or all of these, and the club members share them with others for the betterment of society. As one of the newly inducted members rightly stated, 'giving is life, possession has no value unless it is shared with others'.

There are now about 1,50,000 members, in numerous clubs, spread all over the country. The club, whose function I attended, had two major onerous programs, with respect to village development and youth development. In villages, there is a need for the development of human resources. They live in pathetic conditions. They suffer from ill health, are illiterate and bound by superstition. The programs proposed to conduct awareness camps on superstition, carry out literacy programs, conduct health camps and bring about a change in the attitude of the rural masses. For the purpose of youth development, they proposed camps in colleges to deal with drug addiction, incorporation of values and ethics, developing nationalism, and promotion of positive thinking.

I observed that most of the members are from business and professional circles. Although one of the objectives is social service, the hidden purpose is social and business contacts. It seems this particular club has largest membership among 140 clubs functioning in the district. The average age group of members is more than fifty, however some young members were also seen. The District Governor complemented the club on becoming a centurion club, as with the induction of the new members the strength rose to 103. Half the members are labeled as '*kuru vrudha Bishmacharyulu*'. This shows that members have joined the club with a clear intention of recognition and esteem.

Before the start of the ceremony, they installed the national flag and took a pledge to respect the flag. They called it 'invocation of the national flag of the country.' A testimony of nationalism. The invocation is a protocol. The orderliness in which the meeting was conducted and organised showed strict discipline.

The induction ceremony started with the Master of Induction commanding the new members and the inductors to stand. He then explained the objectives, purpose, norms, and conditions and expected behaviour to the new members. Then the new members had to take a pledge, and the prestigious Lions Pin (a brass piece with the logo of two lions) was pinned on them. This was a testimony of membership. The new members were garlanded and presented with a shield of membership. All the new members were business people and joining the club would help them further their business interests. At the same time however, their happiness of becoming members of an elite club, was evident from their faces.

One of the Governors present at the function was asked to give a message after release of a souvenir. The Master of Ceremonies introduced him with the words, 'Mr. Venu Murthy the

PDG is an embodiment of knowledge, achievement, and service. Coming from a small village Mr. Murthy grew to own a large business worth crores of rupees. He has been a source of inspiration for all the activities of the club. He has devoted all three Ts to the illumination of the club and helping the society. Without his commitment, we could not have made progress in all spheres, and reached where we are today'. Then a brief introduction of his family was given in equally glowing terms. Mr. Murthy's face glowed, due to the esteem given to him. He expressed that he had attained all his dreams and goals, including the highest goal of self-actualisation.

A lavish dinner, sponsored by one of the members, followed the meeting. One of the purposes of the meeting is to spend time informally and allow members to share their opinions.

TYPES OF GROUPS

An organisation is itself a large formal group. It has a defined purpose and structure of activities. Within an organisation there are several small formal and informal groups. While formal groups are in the form of committees and other work groups, informal groups exist among the employees. These groups serve different purposes. Various types of groups found in an organisation are presented below.

Formal Groups

A formal group is a combination of two or more people, interdependent and interacting for a shared purpose. There is continuous interaction among the members. The characteristics of a formal group are:

(i) Goals, roles, and responsibilities are clearly defined. It has a well-defined structure of activities, formal communication and controls.

(ii) They are usually larger than informal groups.

(iii) The focus is on functions to be performed rather than informal interaction. Committees, plural executives, work groups etc., are examples of formal groups.

(iv) They are relatively permanent and provide continuous interaction. They regulate behaviour by a well-defined set of rules and regulations.

Two types of formal groups are found in organisations:

(a) **Command groups:** A command group consists of subordinates, who report to a given superior.

(b) **Task Groups:** Task groups are formed to achieve specific tasks. The members of a task group report to every level of management with whom the work is required to be coordinated.

Informal Groups

Informal work groups are groups of two or more employees, formed by mutual attraction. They are formed to achieve short-term goals, and provide social satisfaction. They are also called cliques. The characteristics of informal groups are as follows:

(i) Informal groups are formed voluntarily and spontaneously. They provide social satisfaction.

(ii) The goals are not well defined. The structure is not defined clearly and the nature of the group is dynamic.

(iii) Informal groups are usually smaller than formal groups.

(iv) Group norms, values and beliefs regulate the behaviour of members.

(v) Leadership is informal. The leader's authority is given by members and is not due to the position.

(vi) Rewards are non-financial. They are in terms of recognition, praise and esteem.

(vii) Communication is unstructured, does not follow any particular direction and is mostly in the form of gossip. It is referred as a 'grapevine'.

(viii) Controls are based on group goals.

Informal groups support organisational goals, provide social satisfaction, relieve psychological tension, and facilitate communication. However, if the groups are not properly managed they will work counter to organisational objectives by spreading rumours, resisting changes, and compelling conformity to the group's values. This involves social costs. These are dysfunctional effects of informal groups.

Informal groups exist for a longer time and are called 'cliques'. They are classified into three types.

(a) Horizontal cliques: Employees of the same rank and status in an organisation form horizontal cliques. Horizontal cliques can be either defensive or aggressive. Horizontal defensive cliques have the following characteristics.

1. It is formed to fight against a crisis or threat.
2. This clique functions for a short time, until the adjustment takes place.
3. It is a stronger clique in the situation and remains dormant until another crisis is faced.

Horizontal aggressive cliques have different directions and goals. They mostly carry out cross-departmental drives to effect changes rather than to resist them. They promote inter departmental harmony and act as a mutual aid block in the organisation. Thus, these cliques are positive for the management. Management encourages the formation of these cliques.

Symbiotic cliques (defined below) often influence horizontal cliques by causing vertical breaks. Thus, these cliques should be cautious in their working.

(b) Vertical cliques: Employees belonging to different hierarchical levels working in the same functional department form vertical cliques. It is a tie between superiors and subordinates.

Vertical cliques are developed to satisfy a need for security, accomplishment and affiliation. Vertical cliques are classified as symbiotic and parasitic cliques. A vertical symbiotic clique has the following features.

1. The manager in a symbiotic clique tries to protect the subordinates and help them to realise their goals.
2. The superior ignores mistakes and even tries to conceal them. He allows the group to learn from their mistakes.
3. He creates a human relationship oriented situation but still makes the subordinates to adhere to their tasks.
4. Subordinates are given freedom to advise their superiors in matters of dealing with the outsiders and troublemakers.
5. Members of the clique may assume authority in times of emergency, or in the absence of the superior. However, they make decisions keeping the welfare of the organisation in mind.

Vertical symbiotic cliques are found in large organisations. These cliques are effective if the subordinates are mature and not too concerned with promotions.

A vertical parasitic clique has the following features:

1. In a parasitic clique, lower level members are more dependent on the superiors.
2. The exchange of service between lower and higher ranks is unequal.
3. The subordinates normally receive more advice than they give to their superiors.
4. The higher ranked persons get more diffraction because the members advise.

Vertical parasitic cliques are considered harmful to the organisation as they frequently interfere with the functioning of the vertical symbiotic clique, leading to conflicts in the organisation. Thus, managers must be careful about these cliques.

(c) **Random clique:** Employees of all ranks and status, working in different departments, form random cliques. They are formed to share power and authority in order to neutralise management oppression. Random cliques have the following features.

1. Random cliques are formed to develop intimate association among members.
2. They have no conscious formal goal.
3. The basic purpose is mutual attraction. Development of friendship and social satisfaction are the other goals.
4. Both managers and subordinates are members of random cliques.
5. These cliques rarely interact with other cliques in the organisation.

Random cliques are used to intensify informal activities in the organisation.

There are two other types of informal groups found in an organisation. They are described below.

a. **Interest groups:** A group, spontaneously formed by employees, to attain a specific common objective is called an interest group. It supports peers and oppressed members and provides security.

b. Friendship groups: Friendship groups are formed purely by social interactions. They exist outside the work environment, and usually consist of persons of the same age, with similar habits and attitudes and a common work environment.

The distinctions between formal and informal groups are presented in Table 17.2.

Table 17.2: Distinctions between formal & informal groups

Distinctions	Formal Group	Informal Group
1. Nature	It is deliberately created and consciously planned.	It is natural and arises spontaneously.
2. Authority	The authority, responsibility, and accountability are clearly defined.	The members give authority. It is not clearly defined.
3. Rules	Rules are defined by the structure. They are clearly defined and strictly observed.	Rules in informal groups are related to expected behaviour of members. They are called norms.
4. Description	Formal groups are shown in the organisational charts.	Informal groups are not depicted in the chart.
5. Permanency	It is relatively permanent and stable.	It is temporary and wrapped up after the purpose is achieved.
6. Goals	Goals of a formal group are well defined by the formal organisation.	Goals of informal groups are defined by the members' desires and needs.
7. Size	They are usually larger than informal groups.	Normally smaller than formal groups.
8. Leadership	The leadership is formal and appointed by the organisation. The leader's role is clearly defined.	The leadership is situational. The members of the group support the leaders.
9. Communication	Communication in these groups is formal and follows the chain of command.	Communication is unstructured and is called a grapevine.
10. Motivation	The rewards are monetary. They are provided by the formal organisation.	The rewards are non-monetary. Praise, recognition and appraisal are the rewards in informal groups.

Leonard Sayles' Classification of Groups

Apart from formal and informal groups, a number of other groups are found in organisations. Leonard Sayles' classification of groups is described below:

Apathetic Groups

Apathetic groups are developed at the operational level of an organisation. It is a group of employees possessing lower level skills and receiving low monetary rewards. People belonging to these groups lack unity and power. They are discontented with their position.

Erratic Groups

An erratic group is formed by employees possessing relatively higher skills, who work together in closely related jobs. Hence, members of these groups display a relatively high degree of unity among themselves. As such, behaviour of the members with the management is often found to be erratic or unpredictable.

Strategic Groups

Employees possessing high levels of skills are formed into strategic groups. They have a high degree of unity. The jobs of strategic group members are highly interdependent and occupy a vital place in the functioning of an organisation.

Conservative Groups

A conservative group consists of top management. For example, the Board of Directors. They are highly skilled, self confident and independent and hold vital jobs such as policymaking, decision-making etc. Such groups are formed to bring about changes in the environment. They take vital decisions for the organisation's growth and development.

Some other groups found in an organisation are described below.

Open and Closed Groups

An open group is a dynamic group formed at a particular time to achieve specific objectives, whereas, a closed group consists of employees who are working on a more permanent basis. The distinction between open and closed groups is given in Table 17.3.

Table 17.3: Distinction between open & closed groups

Group Characteristics	Open Group	Closed Group
Dynamic group membership	Membership, authority, power and status is subject to constant change.	Stability of membership, constant power and status relationships.
Extended activities	Activities are dynamic, creative and challenging. This makes the group innovative.	Stability and narrow frame of activities in a closed group result in hesitation to take up challenges.
Time perspective	Ever changing membership in an open group permits the group to take an interest in current perspectives to satisfy their objectives. The welfare of the group is overlooked in the long run.	Stability enables the group to have long-term plans, which leads to development of the group in the future.
Equilibrium	Open groups are frequently disrupted due to heterogeneous membership. This causes imbalance resulting in poor group performance	Closed groups are less erratic and more stable. They reach a state of equilibrium as quickly as possible. This results in favourable group performance due to fast adaption to changes.

Both open and closed groups exist in organisations. Managers need to evaluate them effectively, based on the goals pursued by them, to enhance organisational performance.

Reference Groups

A reference group enables an individual to take it as a standard for self-evaluation and a source of development of personal values and attitudes. Reference groups are formed to satisfy those members who often try to identify themselves with certain groups and become active members of that group.

A reference group provides its members social comparison, in which members evaluate their behaviour by comparing it to the behaviour of other members of the group. It also serves as social validation, in which members' attitudes, beliefs and values are evaluated, according to those of other members to verify their validity in a reference group. Reference groups exert a great deal of influence over a member's capacity to produce. They can be counter productive if prejudiced members engage in work restriction, rate busting and mutiny.

Primary Group and Secondary Group

A primary group is a small group developed by face-to-face interaction and cooperation of members. Members develop a close interaction, hence they satisfy the social and affiliation needs of individuals.

FUNCTIONAL AND DYSFUNCTIONAL CONSEQUENCES OF GROUPS IN AN ORGANISATION

Groups benefit an organisation in a variety of ways. Organisations encourage group formation as groups offer the following advantages:

1. **Help the socialisation process:** Socialisation is the process of educating and counseling new recruits about the rules, regulations, organisational values, behaviour and all other aspects of the organisation. Groups educate new recruits by teaching them the work norms, standards of behaviour, values, organisational culture, etc., to enable them to be aware of their role and responsibilities. They help adapt behaviour to suit demands.
2. **Training on the job:** Groups teach the new incumbents the ways and means of coping with the job. This facilitates 'on the job training'.
3. **Assist in decision-making:** Groups help in accumulating greater knowledge, by using varied approaches to a problem, analysing more information and better judgement. This leads to effective, qualitative and acceptable decisions.

From the above it is clear that existence of groups is inevitable and necessary. Groups serve a number of functions, both to individual members and the organisation. Hence, effective managers learn to use groups positively for their survival. However, groups have a number of dysfunctional consequences, as explained below.

(a) **Independence:** Groups compel members to conform to norms. Serious consequences may result if any member deviates from the norms. Therefore, individual members lose their independence, resulting in greater interdependence and loss of creativity and innovative spirit.

(b) **Inefficiency:** A group can support complacent members and managers. However, more the group wants them to improve their performance, members may become inefficient and lazy under the umbrella of a group.

(c) **Obstruction to organisational goals:** Powerful groups in organisations can set and enforce norms against those of the organisation. They may behave in this way to solve certain problems of the group. However, more powerful groups may threaten the organisation by working against its goals for the selfish interest of a few members.

(d) **Waste of time:** As managers have little control over a group, the members often engage in gossip and unproductive discussions. This not only hinders their own work, but also affects others in the organisation.

Managers can effectively manage these dysfunctional aspects.

SUMMARY

Organisations are social entities and are designed to provide rationality and orderliness. An organisation is a large, formal group. Members in an organisation form a group. A group is a collection of people interacting to realise common goals. Groups are not always developed out of spontaneous interaction. Ralph Stogdill showed that group development takes place in five stages – forming, storming, norming, performing and adjourning. Each stage is characterised by features of group development. Groups are formed for a variety of reasons such as goal realisation, authority and power, satisfaction of social and security needs, satisfaction of ego, self-esteem and self-actualisation needs, identity and esprit de corps. Organisations encourage formation of a variety of groups within the organisation, which help in realisation of goals. These are called formal groups. In these groups, the interaction of members is totally structured. At the same time, a number of informal groups are formed by employees, to satisfy their social and self-esteem needs. These are formed spontaneously. Certain informal groups are permanent in the organisation structure. They are called 'cliques'. Cliques are of various kinds, horizontal, horizontal defensive, horizontal offensive, vertical, symbiotic vertical, parasitic, random, interest groups and friendship groups. Leonard Sayles classified groups into apathetic, erratic, strategic and conservative. Some other groups found in organisations are open and closed groups, reference groups, primary and secondary groups. Groups are the source of many functions. Groups benefit the organisation in a variety of ways, such as socialising amongst employees, training, assistance in decision making. Some dysfunctions are independence, inefficiency, obstruction to organisational goals and wastage of time. The dysfunctional consequences are manageable and hence they do not influence the group dynamic process.

Key words:

- **Apathetic group:** A group formed by employees with lower level skills, who receive low monetary rewards.
- **Cliques:** Informal groups which exist for a long time.
- **Cohesiveness:** The degree of attraction or repulsion of members to share the effort in the realisation of goals.
- **Esprit de corps:** A management principle, which states that unity is strength.
- **Horizontal cliques:** A group of employees of similar rank and status in an organisation.
- **Norming:** Establishing a code of conduct for regulating the behaviour of members in a group.
- **Random clique:** A group formed by employees working in different areas, department, ranks and status to develop intimate association among members.
- **Reference group:** A group, which is taken as a standard for self-evaluation and a source of development of personal values and attitudes by individual members.

- **Safety valve:** A device that is used to release pressure built inside a pressure cooker.
- **Vertical parasitic clique:** Groups in which lower level members are more dependent on the superiors.
- **Vertical symbiotic cliques:** Groups that are found in large organisations with mature subordinates, for whom promotion is not the only priority.

18. GROUP DYNAMICS

This chapter enables you:

- *To understand the meaning of group dynamics*
- *To appreciate the implication of group membership on group dynamics*
- *To understand the role of interpersonal attraction and factors determining interpersonal attraction*
- *To understand the relationship between environment and group dynamics*
- *To explain the factors of group structure that determine the group dynamics*
- *To analyse impact of status relationships on the dynamics*
- *To identify the influence of the group process on the process of group dynamics*
- *To understand the influence of task behaviour on the process group dynamics*

The structure of the chapter is as follows:

- Introduction
- Meaning of group dynamics
- Factors influencing group dynamics
- Group dynamics and interpersonal attraction
- Environment and group dynamics
- Group structure and group dynamics
- Group status and group dynamics
- Group process and group dynamics
- Group tasks and group dynamics
- Summary
- Key words

CHAPTER 18

Group Dynamics

INTRODUCTION

Group dynamics refers to two important concepts relating to groups. In organisations a number of factors influences group dynamics. These factors can lead to changes in the membership and they also influence the dynamics of interaction between group members. Since group dynamics influence the behaviour of members of groups, its understanding is relevant to managers. Kurt Lewin has carried out extensive research on group dynamic processes, and hence has been rightly given the status of 'father of the group dynamic movement'.

MEANING OF GROUP DYNAMICS

Group dynamics is the study of groups and the changes that occur in the group in order to understand the behaviour of members of the group. The concept of a group has come from the Hawthorne movement. A group is an assembly of people for a common purpose. A very large group is known as an organisation. Thus only associations having a limited number of people can be considered as a group. For example an employee working in an organisation can be also considered as a member of a group. However, the group is known as an organisation as it is large and permanent. After office hours he will either join his family or spend some time associating with people outside the organisation, e.g., friends, a club, a religious association etc. All these are considered as groups. If he has any grievances regarding his work, he may want to share them with other friends in the organisation who have the same problems. All of them may form a group to represent the matter to the higher level management. This is obviously a group formed with a short-lived purpose of presenting the demands to the management. Once the representation is made and the management deals with their problems, the group is likely to be disbanded. This is an example of a group in an organisation. Suppose now, that the demands were presented to the management by the leader of the group, who was the dynamic force behind the group, but who eventually left the organisation. After he left the demands of the other members were not met. If there is no other member to take the place of the one who left, they may simply reconcile themselves to their fate. This means that there is a change in the composition of the group, which led to a change in the behaviour of the other members. This is called 'dynamics'. In this example the change in understanding the behaviour of the group members can be attributed to the change in the composition of the group. Thus, group dynamics is concerned with studying change in the behaviour of members with a change in the size, composition, membership, leadership, communication, and norms of a group.

The word dynamics is derived from the Greek word for 'force'. Elton Mayo and Kurt Lewin have carried out extensive experimentation on group processes in organisations. An important contribution of group dynamics is the effect of 'synergy'. The group contribution is always greater than the sum of the individuals' contribution. This is expressed as one plus one is equal to three. This may be illogical in mathematical terms. But it is logical in the group effort.

There are two conceptualisations of group dynamics. One uses the organisation and conduction of the group. This is known as the normative point of view. The other one gives importance to the techniques of the group process. This is known as the dynamics set of techniques. Some definitions of group dynamics, which make the understanding of the concept easier, are presented below.

According to **Keith Davis** group dynamics is *'the social process by which people interact face to face in small groups. It is the study of forces operating within a group'.*

Kelly Joe defined group dynamics as *'the study of group formation, structure and process of groups and their influence on members and other groups and the organisation as a whole.'*

Another meaningful definition of group dynamics is *'the study of the interaction of the members of a group and assessing the impact of changes in the group on the behaviour of members and organisational effectiveness'.*

The characteristics of group dynamics are as follows:

1. Group dynamics studies the formation of a group and the changes that take place in group size, structure and process.
2. It is the study of the interaction between group members in order to understand the changes in their behaviour.
3. In the process of understanding the changes in the group, the environment of the group is studied.
4. It examines the effect of changes in the group and the behaviour of members on the effectiveness of the organisation.

5. Group dynamics have a synergetic effect on the performance of the group.
6. It is the study relating to small groups.
7. It is concerned with time orientation.
8. Group dynamics determines the effectiveness of managers.

Managers have to understand the significance of group dynamics. Group dynamics influence the behaviour of the members, positively or negatively. For instance in the earlier example the presence of the aggressive member made others also seriously talk about their grievances. The moment the aggressive member left the organisation, the remaining persons became submissive. Thus managers have to understand the dynamics of the behaviour of members in the groups. A manager can effectively manage the members of a group based on their knowledge of the group dynamic process.

FACTORS INFLUENCING GROUP DYNAMICS

Group dynamics are influenced by a host of factors, which may or may not be within managerial control or actions. It is necessary to understand that the factors are desirable. The following factors influence the process of group dynamics in any organisation.

- **Nature and types of groups in organisations:** The nature and types of groups found in organisations have been discussed in the earlier chapters. The reasons for joining a group influence its dynamic process. There are a number of reasons that motivate members to join various groups in an organisation. Depending on their needs, they behave in a particular manner. For instance a person, who joined a group to fight management oppression, influences members to become aggressive and demanding, while another member, who joined the group for their own self esteem may be more co-operative with the management. Another member, who may have joined the group for self-actualisation, will try to influence members to achieve his desire.

  Various types of groups are found in an organisation. They are classified based on the formality of structure, degree of interaction, purpose of formation, nature of membership etc. The type of group also has an impact on the process of group dynamics. A member of a finance committee is likely to be dominating as he feels that resources for allocation are at his command. A member of the shop disciplinary committee is likely to view every thing cautiously, whereas a member of the board of directors is likely to behave in an authoritarian manner, as he holds decision-making power. The dynamics of group and member behaviour in an informal group is different. An informal group formed to welcome a new manager and bid farewell to the outgoing manager exists only for a short period and for a particular purpose. Here the members will praise the outgoing and incoming manager, despite the fact that the outgoing manager may have a number of shortfalls.

  A 'horizontal defensive clique' is formed to fight against a crisis or threat. Thus members of this clique are aggressive and decision-makers. 'Vertical cliques' exist to support certain needs like security, accomplishment and affiliation, so the dynamics of behaviour of this group is calm and predictable. Employees possessing relatively higher skills, who work together on closely related jobs, form an 'erratic group'. Hence, members of these groups display a relatively high degree of unity among themselves. As such behaviour of members with the management is often found to be erratic or unpredictable. 'Strategic group members' are highly interdependent and occupy a vital place in the functioning of an organisation, so they try to behave respectably. 'Reference groups' provide standards of identity to the members, so the members behave as role models.

Process of formation and development stages of groups: Formation of a group in an organisation is not always spontaneous. Most groups are formed in the following stages: Forming, storming, norming, performing and adjourning. At each stage, the group displays certain unique characteristics, which influence the dynamics of group interaction and the behaviour of members. In the first stage of group development, the characteristics of the members change from heterogeneous to homogeneous. Ambiguity of purpose, structure, membership, norms, and leadership cause them to behave as a cohesive group, sacrificing their heterogeneous goals and giving importance to common goals. Interactive behaviour is seen in the members at this stage. There are more changes in the membership at this stage. The dynamics in the storming stage is conflict oriented, as every member tries to protect his or her own individuality. In spite of conflict orientation members behave rationally to establish common objectives and norms. Members show work oriented behaviour in order to develop a formal structure characterised by clear definition of purpose, clarity of authority, communication, definition of responsibility, role clarity, motivation methods and leadership. In the third stage of group formation, norms influence group dynamics. Leadership and effective communication regulate members. Members become cohesive and try to protect their identity. Obviously, the members' behaviour is predictable. At the performing stage, the structure, group norms, and group leadership develop coordination oriented behaviour. Members respect the other members and the values of the group. The 'office grapevine' provides the opportunity to interact, which strengthens their relationship. So relationship oriented behaviour is seen at this stage. Members display result oriented behaviour, overlooking disagreements and conflicts. In the last stage group members try to evaluate the performance and success of the group. Some members may also feel depressed due to the sudden loss of social contact.

Nature of membership, behavioural implications and group dynamics: Group dynamics is influenced by the nature of membership and the resultant behavioural implications. Some factors that influence group dynamics are given below:

1. *Similarity of membership:* As the famous saying goes 'birds of a feather flock together'. Members coming from similar geographical places, caste, gender, education, and religion are likely to develop a greater interaction. This influences the changes in the group. They are more likely to continue their membership of the group. Thus, changes in membership are less and the group becomes stronger and less volatile.
2. *Degree of co-ordination:* The degree of co-ordination influences the dynamics of the group. If members develop a greater co-ordination, they are likely to sacrifice their personal

purpose for the sake of other members in the group. Moreover, there will be greater communication, understanding and co-operation. This makes the group unite, so that change in membership is less likely to occur, leading to less dynamics in the group.

3. *Competition:* Competition in the group has two dimensions. Intra group competition results in frequent outflow of members in the group, so change in membership is more likely to occur. This requires the group to formulate structure and norms. Leadership also changes with the admission of new members, leading to dynamics of group interaction. On the other hand, intra group competition leads to strengthening of the group. This is because of protection of identity of the group. Hence, members become more cohesive and group dynamics are less likely to be observed.
4. *Aggression:* Aggression is a personality characteristic. Groups consisting of more aggressive members have greater disagreements. This causes a lot of inconvenience to other members, so there is a likelihood of members leaving the group, resulting in greater dynamics in the group due to changes in the membership of group. Sometimes this may lead to formation of sub groups within the group. Thus, the group experience more dynamics of interaction.
5. *Sharing of goals:* Sharing of goals is a function of the identity of the goals of the group members. Close individual and group goals will allow members to share group goals, otherwise, greater disagreement will exist regarding the goals, this leads to frequent changes in membership, and more dynamics. On the other hand if the members find the group goals to be almost the same as their individual interests, the group becomes stronger and tries to protect the members. This makes the group to be more consistent.

Group dynamics is related to a number of organisational and human processes. Some of the important processes that have a bearing on group dynamics are discussed below.

Group Dynamics and Interpersonal Attraction

The degree of interpersonal attraction influences the process of group dynamics in organisations. Interpersonal attraction is an emotional element. The rationality behind interpersonal attraction cannot always be explained. Members' behaviour is influenced by the degree of interpersonal attraction of the group members. A greater degree of interpersonal attraction leads to more cohesive and supportive behaviour, whereas poor interpersonal attraction leads to disagreements and conflict oriented behaviour. The relationship between the degree of interpersonal attraction and group dynamics is shown below.

Factors	High	Low
Attraction effectiveness	Cohesion, favourable to organisational . and goal displacement.	Conflicts, retarding organisational
Repulsion	Dissonance, poor relations and non co-operation.	Congruence, integrity and consonance.

The degree of interpersonal attraction is dependent on a number of factors, described below.

1. **Opportunity to interact:** One of the reasons for development of groups in organisations is the opportunity for people to communicate more frequently with others. People who do not have an opportunity to communicate are less likely to be attracted to each other. Therefore, the opportunity to interact provides more dynamics among the members. Some of the prominent reasons that develop the opportunity to interact are:
   (a) *Proximity of working*: Proximity of working and interpersonal attraction is directly related. In organisations, employees working together closely are likely to have greater opportunities to interact. Thus they have more interpersonal attraction. For example, people working in the same branch office will have a greater chance to develop interpersonal attraction than those who are working in different geographical locations.
   (b) *Structure of office and layout*: The interaction between employees depends on the physical structure of the office. In many older offices, people sit in big, open rooms, which gives them greater opportunities of face to face interaction. On the other hand, most modern offices have a cabin system, leading to less interaction, and a secluded working environment.
   (c) *Waiting space and time*: In some organisations specific places are provided to employees for their lunch hour, instruction time, rest time etc. This gives them an opportunity to spend time together, which naturally enhances their interaction.
   (d) *Time spent together: Another important variable is the time spent together*. The degree of time spent and interpersonal attraction is directly related. The more the time people spend together, the more the scope of interaction. Marketing executives, who only meet in various review meetings, albeit frequently, have little time to spend together, whilst employees working in the finance department are likely to have more time to spend together.
2. **Status:** Status is an important determinant of interpersonal attraction, which influences the group dynamic process. Groups having members with a high status have less dynamics than groups with members of a lower status. Very often, people of a higher status are attracted to each other, or in a meeting, people assemble near the chief executive, to attract his or her attention. This provides more opportunity to interact. Some of the salient aspects of status are:
   (a) *Equality of status in the organisation*: In organisations people of equal status have a greater degree of interpersonal attraction. All members of the board of directors, and functional managers' committee have equal status.
   (b) *Low status and high status*: There is also interpersonal interaction between persons having a different status in the organisation, e.g., the managing director might develop an interaction with the union president even though the latter is lower in the organisational hierarchy.
   (c) *Incongruent status*: When the status of members of a group is not the same, it is known as incongruent status. This leads to more heterogeneity. People with heterogeneous status have more inhibitions, doubts and reservations about interacting, which does not promote

interpersonal attraction.

(d) *Status dissonance*: Dissonance in status does not promote interpersonal attraction due to differences among people with different status.

3. **Similarity of background:** Similarity of background and interpersonal attraction is positively related. Demographic, economic, and psycho-graphic similarities produce more interpersonal attraction. There is less attraction between people with different backgrounds and status, such as between younger and older people, illiterate and literate, persons having different levels of education, nationality, or economic backgrounds. For example, even in your own case you are more likely to establish a strong association with your classmates than younger persons. Similarly, people of same religion and nationality will readily form a group. People tend to exhibit greater interpersonal attraction based on factors such as age, religion, education, and nationality and socio economic status. Interestingly all these factors influence group dynamics.

4. **Personality:** Personality characteristics are an important determinant of interpersonal attraction. They also determine the group dynamic process. The personality characteristics that determine the interpersonal attraction are:

   (a) *Similar physical characteristics*: Persons with similar physical characteristics like body structure, skin colour, colour of the eyes and hair are likely to develop greater interpersonal attraction.

   (b) *Perception, attitudes, and values*: People try to become closer to others based on their similarity of perception, attitudes and value systems. This is because similarity of perception and attitudes reinforce the relationship. In the same way similarity of values produce ego defensiveness. Attitudes of college students, married couples, skilled employees and neighbourhood households influence the degree of interpersonal attraction.

   (c) *Beliefs, learning, aggression*: Interpersonal attraction is observed to be greater among the people with similar beliefs, learning habits and other personality characteristics, such as aggression, dominance, locus of control, optimism, submission, dogmatism, selfishness, authoritarianism etc.

5. **Degree of success:** Success is a common thread that binds many people together. Associations are formed based on the history of past success. It is unlikely that a hardworking, diligent student will associate with a group of students who consistently fail in their examinations. In one study on entrepreneurship, people have expressed a willingness to associate with successful entrepreneurs in order to emulate their characteristics of success.

   The relationship between success and group dynamics is as follows:

Factors	High	Low
Success	Attraction	Repulsion
History of failures	Disbanding	Togetherness

ENVIRONMENT AND GROUP DYNAMICS

Environment has a major influence on the dynamics of groups. Here we consider only internal environmental factors. These factors have an impact on the dynamics of members' behaviour. Moreover, these factors are within the managerial control. The following environmental factors influence the group dynamics process.

1. **Organisational strategies:** Organisational strategies have a vital impact on the dynamics of group behaviour. In fact, the primary driver of the group in an organisation is the policy of the organisation. If the policies are restrictive, they give rise to group activity. For example, strikes that often occur in organisations are due to the organisational policies that counter employee interest. Some of the important factors that have a bearing on group dynamics are:
   (a) *Plans, goals and missions:* These provide direction to the organisation. Often however, conflict arises due to divergence between individual goals and organisational goals. This leads to the formation of more groups and the dynamics that occur within them. Organisations that follow ambitious plans and missions, but are unable to co-ordinate them with the competencies of the employees, drive the formation of groups, and the member activity within them.
   (b) *Decision making strategy:* Decision-making strategy determines the degree of authority that lies with the higher level staff. If this power lies only with the managerial staff, subordinates will feel left out, as they also want to participate in decision making. Lack of such an environment, will lead them to form groups to pressurise the management for such authority. Thus group dynamic activity becomes more prevalent.
   (c) *Resources:* Every member requires a share in the resources of the organisation. If resources are scarce, the management may be unable to allocate the resources in a rational manner, which gives rise to the formation of groups. The dynamics that occur within the group demand more resources.
2. **Authority and responsibility:** An organisation allocates authority, responsibility and accountability to each and every position. Authority enables managers to influence a subordinate's actions. Some of the variables of authority and responsibility that influence group dynamics are:
   (a) *Degree of centralisation:* According to Louis Allen consistent reservation of authority at the central points is centralisation, and dispersal of authority to the lower levels is decentralisation. Centralisation and decentralisation are functions of the structure of the organisation. The greater the degree of centralisation of authority, the greater will be the degree of group dynamics.
   (b) *Power and influence:* While authority enables to influence because of position, power is purely personal influence. Influence through power also leads to greater dynamics of group interaction.
   (c) *Accountability:* This refers to the answerability of a person to a higher authority. A greater degree of accountability than the resources at a person's command and authority

leads to greater group dynamics. People resist such accountability. Thus accountability should be commensurate with authority and the resources available.

3. **Bureaucracy:** Bureaucracy is following rules and regulations rigidly. It determines the kind of structure in an organisation. A greater degree of bureaucracy in an organisation leads to more group activity. Public enterprises are the best examples of bureaucracy and the resultant group dynamics. The following bureaucratic structural variables influence the group dynamics.
   (a) *Rules and regulations:* They are related to every operation of the enterprise. They are a written code of conduct, which members have to follow rigidly. However, they are flouted at times. The seriousness of punishment associated with these leads to dynamics of group interaction.
   (b) *Policies and procedures:* Policies are laid down for rationalising human actions in organisations. Procedure is in bureaucracy.
   (c) *Precedents and practices:* These are unwritten sanctions for various activities based on past experience. They have little place in bureaucracy. Thus bureaucracy leads to more group action.
4. **Work environment and climate:** Members of organisations demand a well, non-hazardous and friendly work environment, along with a sound organisational climate. The provision of a friendly work environment and climate are related to the cost, and may also be impossible due to the nature of the work itself. Consider the example of The Singereni Collieries Company Limited. The work environment in an underground mine will be uncongenial, dangerous and unhealthy. But it is very difficult to provide a congenial work environment. Thus group dynamics is very strong and effective in collieries. On the other hand in the case of software development companies the environment will be neat, cool, and clean. It may not force a group action, but the overall climate of the organisation may lead to group dynamics.
5. **Organisational culture:** Organisational culture is indoctrination of various standards of behaviour, and norms of actions inherited from previous generations. They are qualitative in nature. Organisational culture is said to be good in organisations following sound practices of human resources. Poor organisational culture leads to group dynamics for the demand of good practices. Some aspects of organisational culture that influence group dynamic activity are: *Code of conduct, standards of behaviour, past practices, values and ethics and beliefs.* All these factors lead to a greater degree of dynamic interaction among groups in organisations. Organisations characterised by authoritarian culture, poor interpersonal relationships, lack of opportunities to learn, unhealthy organisational practices etc., face greater dynamics among group members.
6. **Human resources management systems:** In modern organisations human resource management is concerned more with behavioural management, rather than the traditional functions of recruitment and selection. Some of the human resources management practices that have a bearing on group dynamics are:
   (a) *Recruitment and selection:* Employees trying to induct persons known to them and ideas

put forward by politicians, like 'sons of the soil', regionalism and caste are some of the variables related to recruitment that influence dynamics. Counter organisational practices cause members to swiftly form and operate groups to protect their interests.

(b) *Reward and evaluation:* Perception of unequal monetary and non-monetary rewards and sanctions lead to more group activity. Negative evaluations of superiors also lead to greater dynamics of group interaction.

(c) *Performance appraisal:* Performance appraisal and potential appraisal systems that are in vogue are of vital concern for organisational members. They feel their career is linked to these systems. So any understanding of an inappropriate appraisal system and linking their promotions, increments and other perquisites to performance appraisals lead to greater resistance by the members of a group, increasing group dynamics.

(d) *Legal administration:* A number of legislative provisions are adopted in the interests of employees. The application of these provisions has both a positive and negative influence. For example in a colliery, miners often resist wearing protective, safety devices, but if any untoward incident occurs they blame the management for not providing a safe environment.

(e) *Collective bargaining:* At the time of redressing industrial disputes, group dynamics influence the collective bargaining process. Inter and intra group politics play a vital role in the framing and signing of a collective bargaining agreement. In some organisations, group dynamics determine whether the members participate in the collective bargaining process.

(f) *Trade unions:* In the public sector, trade unions have emerged as a strong force to protect the employees' interests. Intra and inter union politics lead to a greater degree of dynamics in groups and consequently influence the functioning of the organisation.

Group Structure and Group Dynamics

The nature and type of structure in a group has a profound influence on the dynamics of group interaction. The following factors of group structure influence group dynamics.

1. **Power, communication, leadership, status relationships:** Groups develop power centres, communication through the grapevine, leadership and status relationship among members to realise their goals. However, there will be frequent changes in a group on account of some new members joining and old ones leaving. For example, if a member capable of fighting management oppression leaves the organisation, the leadership of the group is lost. Very often, a leader emerges spontaneously from among the other members of the group. Thus the dynamics will change. Similarly, grapevine communication leads to political behaviour. Changes in membership of the group change the dynamics of group interaction.

2. **Group leadership:** This can be explained by an example. In a certain organisation, the managers are fighting for a share of power. The general manager, who had been resisting their moves for some time, suddenly changed his stand and joined the group to fight against

the top management. This entirely changed the group structure, as due to his higher status, he assumed the role of leader. This resulted in resentment of the existing leader, resulting in the group being vertically split.

3. **Role relationships:** Group members develop a common understanding of role relationships among themselves. All the group members have to clearly understand these relationships. Any misunderstanding will lead to more group dynamics. Some of the factors of role relationships are: *Role perception, role expectation, role identity, role conflict and psychological contact.* For example, suppose that all the employees in an organisation have shared power on some previously agreed terms for a decade. Suddenly, there was a move to share the power based on caste criteria. The role conflict began and members belonging to specific caste have formed a group to demand the management a proportionate share in the administrative power. This has become handy to the management to revise the administrative power.

4. **Group norms:** Group norms are a very strong binding force on members of the group, and thus regulate the dynamics of the group. At times a strong force against existing norms leads to changes in group behaviour. The result may be the formation of new norms or formation of a new group that believes the existing norms are useless. Two aspects of group norms regulate group dynamics.
   (a) *Deviates*: Deviates are members who flout the group norms. They have a strong resistance to the existing norms and change the dynamics.
   (b) *Isolates*: Isolates also influence norms, not by flouting them but by keeping silent.

5. **Size and composition:** The number and quality of members have a profound influence on the dynamics of group interaction. Kurt Lewin found that smaller groups are more effective in completing the tasks assigned to them than larger groups. Larger groups face the problem of lack of face-to-face interaction within members. There are frequent conflicts and disagreements among members of large groups, causing members to quit the group. Thus dynamics of membership occurs. In the case of small groups there is a possibility of interpersonal attraction that causes the group members to develop cohesion. The interaction between group members is more in the case of small groups. Thus the size and dynamics of a group are inversely related to each other. Another important factor that determines the dynamics of a group is the composition of the group. Composition refers to the nature and quality of members in the group. The greater the similarity of members, the greater is the dynamics of interaction and less is the change in the membership. Marwin E. Shaw found that diversity of group composition in terms of personality, gender, age, education, functional specialisation, and experience increases the probability of assimilation of the characteristics needed to complete the tasks effectively. Diversity of a group may have a negative impact on the dynamics of interaction. Group demography is another variable that influences the dynamics of group interaction. According to Robbins, group demography is the degree to which members of a group share a common demographic attribute, such as age, sex, race, level of education, or length of service in the organisation, and the impact of this attribute on turnover. Similarity of group demography leads to fewer resignations from a group, which

thus becomes more constant in terms of interaction. Cohorts in a group are group members who hold common attributes. These attributes may relate to date of birth, date of entry into the organisation, graduating from the same educational institution, similarity of marital status, or similar ideas or problems. The degree of dynamics of group interactions among cohorts is greater. Thus the size and composition of a group has a profound influence on the dynamics of group interaction.

Group Status and Group Dynamics

Group status and group dynamics are very closely related to each other. Group status refers to the relative ranking given to the groups in the organisation. Some groups have a higher status than others. These status differentials are common for both formal and informal groups. For example, a finance committee possesses high status in the organisation due to the authority to sanction the financial budgets. The board of directors has a high status in the organisation by virtue of its decision-making authority. In the case of unions, a recognised union will possess a higher status than an unrecognised union. A group of high status makes efforts to protect its status. So the dynamics of change in membership is less likely in spite of the fact that members enjoy a relatively greater degree of freedom to deviate from the norms. In the case of groups having a lower status, dialectical behaviour, i.e., argumentative behaviour exists. This implies that people with a lower status may challenge the way of doing the things. They may either show a greater degree of group dynamics by a greater turnover of members, or a greater degree of member interaction, so that the group develops a good status. Status equity is the perception of equity and just status enjoyed by the group. If the members of a group believe that the group enjoys the status that it deserves, they feel status equity. This leads to a smaller turnover of group members. It is relevant to note that culture has an impact on the group status. It differs from country to country. For example the French are more status conscious, so managers have to understand the cultural differences to understand the group dynamics.

Group Process and Group Dynamics

Group process refers to the internal working of a group. It relates to the various systems designed in the group such as communication, conflict resolution, decision making, leadership, power sharing and member support. These processes determine the degree of changes in membership and member interaction. A clearly laid down process leads to greater synergy in the group. Group synergy is the outcome of the group, it is usually greater than the outcome of individual members in the group. However, this may not always be true. Ringleman found a phenomenon known as social loafing, where the group contribution tends to be less than the individual contribution. All this happens due to dynamics of interactions. Often it is found that group process results in the effect of social facilitation. According to Robbins the social facilitation effect is the tendency to improve or worsen performance in response to the presence of other group members. Due to this effect members of group gain support and confidence to carry out tasks. Social facilitation can also be negative. In the case of complex tasks it is found that the presence of other members may have a negative effect on the performance of the members carrying out the task. Thus group processes determine group dynamics.

Group Tasks and Group Dynamics

The nature of group tasks determines the degree of group dynamics. A group performing tasks that require more information sharing, interdependence, decision making, and control have a greater degree of interactive dynamics. Members not only interact among themselves, but they also interact with the others in the organisation. On the other hand, groups performing standardised and routine tasks do not display dynamics of group interaction. For example, a budget committee in an organisation compiles the budget for various departments, so they have to interact with other departments. Thus dynamics of interactions among the budget committee are greater. Groups performing complex tasks and tasks of high uncertainty, have a greater degree of interaction amongst group members.

SUMMARY

Group dynamics refers to the changes in group membership and interaction of group members. It is the study of the dynamics of groups in organisations. The study of group dynamics is important because it influences the behaviour of employees in organisations. Kurt Lewin is known as the father of the group dynamics movement. A numbers of factors influence group dynamics in organisations, namely, the nature and types of groups in organisations, the process of formation and development stages of groups, and nature of membership and behavioural implications and group dynamics. Some factors in the nature of membership and behavioural implications and group dynamics are similarity of members, degree of co-ordination, competition, aggression, and sharing of goals. In the study of group dynamics some of the important factors are interpersonal attraction, the environment, group structure, group status, group process, and group tasks. Group dynamics and interpersonal attraction are positively related. Factors that influence interpersonal attraction are the opportunity to interact, status and similarity of background, personality and degree of success. Environmental factors such as, organisational strategies, authority and responsibility, bureaucracy, work environment and climate, organisational culture, and human resource management systems, have a major influence on the dynamics of groups. Group structure determines group dynamics. The various factors of group structures are power, communication, leadership, status relationship, group leadership, role relationships, group norms, and size and composition. Group status is closely related to group dynamics. Groups with a higher status in organisations are likely to have a greater degree of group interaction. Group process and group dynamics are inter-related. Groups create social facilitation for members to perform tasks. Group tasks determine the dynamics of group interaction. The nature of group tasks that have a bearing on group dynamics are information sharing, interdependence, routine, standardised, complex and tasks with greater degree of uncertainty.

Key words:

- **Cohorts:** Group members who hold common attributes.
- **Deviates:** Members who flout group norms
- **Group demography:** The degree to which members of a group share a common demographic attribute and the impact of this attribute on turnover.
- **Group dynamics:** The study of groups and the changes that occur therein
- **Group synergy:** The contribution of the group is always greater than the sum of individual contributions
- **Isolates:** Members who do not flout the norms but remain silent
- **Social facilitation:** The tendency for performance to improve or decline in response to the presence of other members. Due to this effect, members of a group gain confidence to carry out the tasks
- **Status equity:** The perception of equity and status of the group

19. GROUP BEHAVIOUR

This chapter enables you:

- *To define group cohesion*
- *To understand the factors that indicate cohesive group behaviour*
- *To appraise the factors that determine group cohesion*
- *To examine the development of group dissonance*
- *To comprehend the functions of group norms*
- *To identify how groups are dysfunctional to creativity*
- *To understand Ringleman's effect*
- *To understand the relationship between group size and performance*
- *To identify the principles of group behaviour*

The structure of the chapter is as follows:

- Introduction
- Group cohesion and group dissonance
- Group norms
- Group think
- Social loafing: Ringleman's effect
- Summary
- Key words

CHAPTER 19

Group Behaviour

INTRODUCTION

Individual and group behaviour influences organisational behaviour. Formation of groups in an organisation is common. Every employee in an organisation is a member of some group or the other within the organisation. Thus, his behaviour is regulated by the group. You, yourself may have followed your group of friends, irrespective of your circumstances or feelings. This is because of your relationship with the other members of the group and the unity between all of you. However, there may be some members of the group, who always differ and are in conflict with each other. This is because of the force of repulsion amongst group members, called dissonance. For instance, one person in a group of friends may not agree to evading class work and going to movies. This leads the others to feel that the person is indifferent to the group, and not following the expectations of the group. These expectations are known as group norms. If a person repeatedly deviates from these norms, the group will not tolerate it and will try to force the person out of the group. Thus, sometimes one may feel compelled to accept group norms, even though the person does not agree with them. This situation is called 'group think.' There is a saying in Indian context that '*ek niranjan, dho sukhi, theen gadabid, char chatpat and panache patpat*'. This means that as the number of members of a group increase, the performance of the group becomes negative. In fact, a group should display synergy. The members of a group expend less energy than they would have spent individually. This phenomenon is known as Ringleman's effect or social loafing. This chapter gives a clear explanation of these concepts of group behaviour.

GROUP BEHAVIOUR

All the different groups in organisations perform different functions. Members of these groups come from different functional and managerial categories of organisation. Therefore, they have different attitudes, perceptions, learning and personality, which makes them behave in a different manner. The behaviour of members of groups found in organisations is discussed below under four categories: Group cohesion, group norms, group think and social loafing.

GROUP COHESION AND GROUP DISSONANCE

Group Cohesion

Cohesion is the extent to which group members attract each other and share their efforts towards realisation of common goals. The degree of attraction or repulsion of members determines the extent of group cohesion.

> *Group cohesion can be defined as 'the degree to which group members are attracted to each other and share common goals. The more members are attracted to each other, the more the group goals align with individual goals and the greater the group cohesion.*
>
> ***– Robbins.***
>
> ***Lott and Lott*** *defined group cohesion as 'the sum of the forces acting on the members to remain in the group. And it is the number and strength of positive attitudes shared by the members. Cohesion grows out of the attraction of the members for one another and for the group as a whole'.*

The characteristics of group cohesion are as follows:

1. Cohesion is a force of attraction or repulsion between group members.
2. Membership in a cohesive group is relatively small.
3. Cohesion develops out of similarity of interests, attitudes and understanding.
4. Cohesive groups enjoy a higher status.
5. Intra-group communication is highly developed.
6. The leader plays an important role and rewards cooperative behaviour to bring cohesion.
7. A cohesive group always has a history of past success.
8. Cohesion is qualitative. The degree of interaction is a measure of its expression.
9. Social relationship analysis is useful in identifying cohesive groups.

Having seen the characteristics of group cohesion, we will learn more about the factors that indicate cohesion, which are given below.

(a) Greater status congruence of the group members indicates greater group cohesion.

(b) Very infrequent changes in membership means higher cohesion.

(c) Fast and informal communication indicates greater cohesion.

(d) Greater intra group influence indicates greater cohesion.

(e) Greater cohesion exists when there is higher dependence of members on the group.

(f) Minimal intra-group conflict indicates high group cohesion.

Figure 19.1 shows the relationship between cohesion and indicators.

	HIGH....................COHESION....................LOW	
H I G H	STATUS CONGRUENCE GRAPEVINE INTRA GROUP INFLUENCE HIGHER DEPENDENCE DEGREE OF DYNAMIC MEMBERSHIP INTRA GROUP CONFLICT	L O W
	HIGH..................COHESION..................LOW	

Figure 19.1: Relationship between cohesion and indicators

Factors Influencing Group Cohesion

Group cohesion influences the behaviour of members of the group. A number of factors influence the cohesion of the group. These factors may be internal to the group, organisational factors or factors outside the organisation. The following factors influence group cohesion.

(i) Group size: Size of the group and cohesion are inversely related. In a larger group, there is a greater likelihood of the members having different attitudes and backgrounds. Therefore, as the size increases, agreement on common goals and mutual interaction decreases. Similarly, increased size restricts inter-group and intra-group communication and encourages the formation of sub groups. Thus, smaller groups are more amenable for cohesion than large groups.

(ii) Degree of dependency: Degree of dependency and cohesion are positively related. Degree of dependency is the extent to which a member of the group expects help in case of need. It exists when a group is able to communicate with all the individual members. Dependency requires greater attractiveness. Therefore greater the degree of dependency, the greater the attraction and consequently higher group cohesion.

(iii) Physical distance: Cohesion and physical distance are inversely related. People who work together physically will have a greater opportunity for interaction. This enables free exchange of ideas, and sharing of problems and prospects. Hence, closeness develops among members leading to greater cohesion. With greater physical distance, interaction is restricted. This minimises the possibility of cohesion.

(iv) **Time spent together:** Cohesion is proportional to the time group members spend together. People who meet frequently and spend time together are likely to develop mutual interaction and interpersonal attraction. They also develop friendships and communication among themselves. On the other hand, people who rarely meet do not have an opportunity to interact. Therefore, there is little chance of developing cohesion.

(v) **Severity of initiation:** There is a positive correlation between severity of initiation and cohesion. Strict admission procedures for entry into a group, makes the group unique and elite in the eyes of others. Prescribing strict admission procedures arises out of a natural human tendency to share the benefits secured by one's efforts. This is because members have to sacrifice their interest with admission of new members. Therefore, severity of initiation leads to fewer members in the group and consequently greater cohesion is developed.

(vi) **Cooperation:** Cohesion and cooperation are positively related. A cooperative spirit among members exists when each member values the opinions of the other members. Group tasks, reward systems, clear goals and a well-designed structure promote greater cooperation. Therefore, it enhances cohesion in the group.

(vii) **Status:** Status and cohesion are positively related. Status is the relative worth attached to a group. A group with strong and effective leaders and a history of past success creates a favourable opinion. Thus, the group is highly ranked. High status is also characterised by effective achievement of group goals. All these make people associate more and develop cohesion to protect the status of the group.

(viii) **Threats:** Threats and cohesion are positively related. An external and tangible threat makes members of the group protect the identity of the group. They feel that the group is a source of protection. Therefore, the group becomes strong and united to face threats effectively. Cohesion increases when the threat is from an external source, or when internal cooperation is necessary to overcome the threat. If fighting against a threat, such as managerial pressures, becomes inevitable, the group becomes more cohesive. However, external threats do not ensure cohesion. If a group believes that its strength is inadequate to meet the threat effectively, it will not respond.

(ix) **History of past success:** Cohesion and history of past success are positively related. Achieving its objectives, leads to the group being evaluated favourably and considered successful as compared to other groups in the organisation. This evaluation and recognition of past success elevates the pride of the group, and association with it is prestigious. Therefore, past rewards and success cause members to develop strong cohesion and continue with the same group in the future.

(x) **Leadership:** Leadership is an important element promoting group cohesion. Employees feel good when they work under a democratic leadership, which promotes interpersonal communication, warm relationships, interpersonal attraction and confidence in members. These factors enable members to interact and share their feelings freely, and the group becomes more cohesive. On the other hand, an authoritarian leader does not allow subordinates to interact. Hence, cohesion is not developed.

Further, a positive relationship exists between cohesion and productivity, group performance, communication, conformity and influence, and positive evaluation. Thus, managers should try to develop cohesive groups in order to manage them more effectively.

Group Dissonance

Dissonance is the opposite of cohesion. It is the degree of aversion amongst group members lead to dissonance. While cohesion increases the strength of the group, dissonance adversely influences the coordination and cooperative strength of the group. The following factors contribute to the development of dissonance in groups.

(a) **Divergent goals:** The existence of divergent and conflicting personal goals of members lead to dissonance. Though it is a fact that members' goals differ, cohesive groups pursue common goals. However, dissonant groups encourage disagreement, which results in misunderstandings and rigid personal relationships. Thus, members repel each other affecting the combined strength of the group.

(b) **Unmanageable size:** More members leads to more divergent personal goals. Members compete to accomplish personal goals and use the resources of the group. This increases disagreement and results in splitting the group. In addition, more members means less interaction amongst the members. More divergent thinking within a group increases dissonance amongst the group members.

(c) **Domination:** Groups develop informal leadership. The leader changes with the situation. However, a few members may dominate the group and take control of it. This leads to a split in the group. Therefore, domination increases dissonance amongst the group members.

(d) **Intra-group competition:** This arises when there is scarcity of resources and weak leadership. Members of the group competing amongst themselves develop more misperceptions. Such a situation leads to disagreement and disbanding the group structure. Thus, intra-group conflicts promote group dissonance.

(e) **Loss of mutual confidence:** A group will experience adversity due to loss of mutual belief, trust and confidence. This creates a distance between members and severely limits frequency of interaction. Thus, coordination potential decreases. These adversities lead to dissonance.

A dissonant group is more dangerous than a group without cohesion. Therefore, managers should deal with dissonance with greater caution and care. They have to use their skill and intelligence to prevent dissonance and promote teamwork, leading to cohesion.

Commandments of Group Cohesion

1. Small groups have a greater probability of being cohesive than large ones, other things being equal.
2. The more individual members of a group depend on the group, the more cohesive it will be perceived as.
3. The greater the congruence of the status attributes of the group's members, the greater the cohesion of the group.
4. Higher status congruence in a group leads to better social relationships and improved personal emotional states.
5. Cohesion of a group is greater if the members change infrequently or not at all.
6. The more cohesive the group, the greater the communication addressed to deviates.
7. Cohesive groups have a higher level of inter-member communication than non-cohesive groups.
8. The influence the group exerts upon its members is greater if the group is more cohesive.
9. Competition between groups increases the cohesion within the competing groups.
10. Competition within a group has a negative influence on group cohesiveness.

Cohesion and Organisational Effectiveness

Cohesion influences the effectiveness of an organisation in a number of ways. Some indicators of the effectiveness of an organisation are productivity, group performance, communication, hostility and aggression, conformity and influence, and positive evaluation. They are explained below.

1. **Cohesion and productivity:** Cohesion in an organisation is positively related to productivity. High productivity is observed with cohesive groups. The reasons are obvious.

	HIGH..................COHESION..................LOW	
HIGH PERFORMANCE	HIGH PRODUCTIVITY	MODERATE PRODUCTIVITY
LOW	MODERATE TO LOW PRODUCTIVITY	LOW PRODUCTIVITY

Figure 19.2: Relationship between productivity and cohesion

Cohesive work groups have less work tension. A democratic environment is created among members, which leads to lower absenteeism and higher turnover. Members of cohesive work groups show greater psychological commitment to the goals of the organisation. Figure 19.2 shows the relationship between cohesion and productivity in an organisation.

2. **Group performance and cohesion:** Group cohesion brings about congruence between organisational goals and group norms. The goals of members of the organisation become clear. Role clarity develops amongst the members. The structure and purpose of the organisation and the group become clear. Cohesion removes any ambiguous structure and makes everyone clear about the performance.
3. **Cohesion and communication networks:** Mutual sharing of information is the essence of cohesion. Members of a cohesive group share a common purpose, ideas and goals. The group develops an informal communication network known as a grapevine, which allows members to communicate without any kind of apprehension. This leads to greater understanding of oneself and others in the group, resulting in better performance.
4. **Hostility and aggression and cohesion:** Group cohesion develops hostility among members and aggression towards non-members. Hostile approach to members is developed on account of the feeling of oneness. Sense of belonging is developed among the members. This leads to satisfaction of social needs of group members. The group then becomes more cohesive. Similarly members try to protect the group interest. Thus they develop aggressive behaviour towards others. So other members cannot create any distortions in the relationships among members of cohesive groups.
5. **Cohesion and conformity and influence:** Members of a cohesive group display greater similarity in characteristics. They develop group norms. All members of a cohesive group are compelled to conform to the group norms, which are strictly enforced. This brings solidarity to the group. Thus, cohesive groups will have more influence on the management than other groups in the organisation.
6. **Positive evaluation and cohesion:** Group cohesion reinforces strength among the members. The self-esteem and self-respect of the members is upheld. The personal ego of the members is sacrificed to accommodate the feeling of group members. There will be greater perceptual congruence. Thus greater understanding is developed. This reduces interpersonal conflicts, leading to greater harmony, which in turn leads to greater cohesion.

GROUP NORMS

Group norms are unwritten rules. They are the agreed code of conduct of group members, and clarify how members should behave. Members follow them strictly. Any deviation becomes a serious issue. Group norms become the basis for rewards and punishments. Norms come from traditions, culture and values of group members. Thus, not all groups have the same norms. Norms differ in formality, performance, appearance and resource allocation.

Performance related norms are also called work norms. These norms are related to the quantum of output, procedure of performance of jobs, extent of energy spent on the job, methods of communication etc. These norms affect the motivation and behaviour of employees with respect to production. The ability and capability of employees is influenced by the norms.

Another category of norms relates to the manner in which employees should present themselves in the organisation. Dress codes, pleasant manners, cheerful demeanor, being well groomed and showing respect are some norms enforced by groups. These norms are called 'appearance norms.' Employees are expected to behave in accordance with the norms. These norms are formalised by the organisation. For example, drivers and conductors in road transport companies wear a uniform. Schools usually have a uniform, and students are taught to greet the teacher.

There are also norms relating to allocation of resources. They include systems of payment of wages, salaries, perquisites, allowances and reimbursement of expenses, assignment of duties and allocation of work resources like tools and equipment. Some of these norms will be recognised formally by the organisation. These norms significantly influence the performance and behaviour of employees.

According to **Fieldman,** norms are important both for the group and the organisation. Norms facilitate the group's survival, they increase the predictability of group behaviour, regulate embarrassing interpersonal problems and allow members to express the central values of the group, and clarify the distinctiveness of the group. Therefore, members are forced to conform to the norms of the group. Conformity refers to the adjustment of behaviour and alignment of activities according to the dictated norms.

In organisations, the management accepts certain norms prescribed by groups and applies them uniformly to all employees. These norms will be circulated in written form. Organisation manuals, employees' code of conduct and formal rules and regulations are some examples of organisational norms. Therefore, they are known as 'formal norms'. The customs and traditions of group behaviour stipulate certain norms, which may not always be in written form. They are called 'informal norms'.

Informal groups control the behaviour of their group members with the help of social arrangement norms. These norms relate to encouraging and restricting friendships, greeting others, socialising with members and other groups and participating in informal events.

Thus, norms exert a powerful influence on the behaviour of group members, and are therefore important for an organisation.

Some norms adopted by Lions' Club members are:

1. Strict adherence to time.
2. Compulsory attendance of all meetings.
3. To initiate new members.
4. Pay the yearly subscription regularly.

5. Respect other members' feelings.
6. To be patient in dealing with others.
7. Help in fund raising.
8. Spare time for the activities of the club.
9. Participate in social service activities.
10. Abide by the norms.

GROUP THINK

Group think is a negative norm. It is the tendency of a member not to express what he really feels, due to pressure to conform to the ideas of a majority of the members. This phenomenon significantly affects the intelligence, creativity and new ideas of members, so that even good ideas are overlooked in the process of group decision-making. Thus, decisions are made according to the direction and judgement of the majority. Hence decisions are likely to be lopsided. According to Robbins, the symptoms of 'group think,' are as follows:

(a) Group members rationalise any resistance to the assumptions they have made. No matter how strongly the evidence may contradict their basic assumptions, members continually reinforce their assumptions.
(b) Members apply direct pressure on those who momentarily express doubts about any of the groups' shared views or who question the validity of arguments supporting the alternatives favored by the majority.
(c) Those members, who have doubts or hold differing points of view, seek to avoid deviating from what appears to be the group consensus by keeping silent about misgivings and even minimizing the importance of their doubts to themselves.
(d) There is an illusion of unanimity. If someone does not speak, it is assumed that he or she is in full accord.

SOCIAL LOAFING: RINGLEMAN'S EFFECT

Kurt Lewin, Homans, Bales etc. have conducted a number of experiments on the effect of the size of the group on the behaviour of its members. These experiments revealed that in terms of both productivity and strength, the size of the group has a positive relationship. A group provides a synergistic effect. Synergy means the total effort of all the group members will be greater than their individual efforts. However, Ringleman came up with the interesting observation, that the effort a member contributes as part of a group, is less than the effort he would contribute as an individual. Members of a group were found to expend less energy than they would have spent as individuals. This is called social loafing or the Ringleman effect. Due to this tendency the output of the group does not follow the logic of synergy. In support of the concept of social loafing, Ringleman found that *"increase in group size is inversely related to individual performance"*.

There are a number of reasons for social loafing.

(i) Members of the group are likely to develop a false notion that the contribution of other members of the group is not equal to their contribution.

(ii) Social loafing also arises because of the dispersal of responsibility.

(iii) Absence of appropriate techniques to measure the performance of the individual members.

(iv) A feeling that a member's contribution is not properly recognised and rewarded.

(v) Fear or shyness to oppose elder or experienced members may lead to a careless attitude.

Social loafing influences the behaviour of members of the group in a negative manner. This tendency leads members to behave in an indifferent manner at the time of both decision-making and execution. It can be managed by inviting ideas and opinions from all members, if any decision is to be taken. Adequate motivation must be provided, and members must be encouraged to participate in the objectives of the group.

SUMMARY

Groups are an inevitable phenomenon in an organisation. They exist for organisational and personal reasons. While an organisation deliberately sets up groups to assist in the organisation process, social needs compel formation of many groups in an organisation. Groups influence employees' behaviour. Some important behavioural consequences of groups are group cohesion, group norms, group think and social loafing. Cohesion is the extent of attraction among members of a group, and dissonance is the degree of repulsion. Group size, degree of dependency, physical distance, time spent together, severity of initiation, status, threats, history of past success, and leadership influences group cohesion. Certain factors influencing dissonance are divergence of goals, large size, domination, intra group competition and loss of mutual confidence. Managers need to understand the effects of cohesion and dissonance on the effectiveness of an organisation. It is said that dissonance is more dangerous than having poor cohesion. Some of the effects of cohesive group behaviour are elevation in organisational productivity, changes in the performance of group, formation and use of communication networks, displaying hostility and aggression, conformity and the degree of influence, and positive evaluation of the group. Yet another behavioural disposition is group norms. They are standards of behaviour that are developed for members of the group, and are enforced ruthlessly. Norms relate to performance, appearance, and allocation of resources. Members who conform to group norms are allowed to continue in the group. Members who violate the norms are known as deviates, and are expelled from the group. Thus, group norms regulate a member's behaviour. Groups also enforce certain negative norms. In the process, members tend to not express what they really feel, due to pressure to conform to the ideas of a majority of the members. This is group think behaviour. Kurt Lewin, Homans, Bales etc. have conducted a number of experiments on the effect of the size of the group on the behaviour of its members. Two opposing effects were seen, namely synergy and loafing. Synergy means that the sum of the effort of all the group members will be greater than their individual efforts. However this may not be always true, as shown by Ringleman, who found that the effort a member contributes as part of a group, is less than the effort he would contribute as an individual. Thus managers need to understand all these influences on an individual's behaviour and develop strategies to deal with groups in organisations.

Key words:

- **Cohesion:** The degree of attraction of group members.
- **Deviates:** Members violating group norms.
- **Dissonance:** The degree of discord among members of a group.
- **Group think:** A tendency not to present what one really feels due to pressure to conform to a course of action suggested by a majority of members.
- **Norms:** Generally agreed conduct of behaviour.
- **Severity of initiation:** Strict procedure for admission into membership of group.
- **Social loafing:** Increase in the size of the group is inversely related to individual performance.
- **Synergy:** Contribution of group is greater than contribution of individuals.

20. GROUP DECISION BEHAVIOUR

This chapter enables you:

- *To understand the concept of group decision making*
- *To appraise the steps in the group decision making process*
- *To examine the significance of group decision making*
- *To understand the problems in the group decision making*
- *To comprehend the strategies of making effective group decisions*
- *To distinguish between individual and group decision making*

The structure of the chapter is as follows:

- Introduction
- Group decision making
- Group decision making process
- Assets of group decision making
- Liabilities of group decision making
- Effective group decision making
- Summary
- Key words

CHAPTER 20

Group Decision Behaviour

INTRODUCTION

Decision making is omnipresent in every function of management. In organisations rationality of decisions is very vital. The use of groups in decision making is common. You must have observed that whenever a problem arises in the government, a committee is formed to look into the problem and suggest a suitable solution. This is one way of using groups in the process of problem solving. Committees can be described as formal groups. Group decision making is commonly used in most modern organisations. It is believed that group action has a synergistic effect.

The process of group decision making is similar to that of individual decision making. The only difference is the formation and the winding up of the group after making the decision. This is unique to the process of group decision making. Group decision making is more rational than individual decision making, because interaction between group members results in the generation of a greater number of ideas and solutions. This brings in more rationality and commitment of the members to execute decisions without much resistance. However, the result of group decision making is not always rational, it is only more rational than individual decisions. Rational decisions are more likely to be made when the group meeting is conducted effectively. It is necessary for the chairperson and members to follow certain guidelines. Over a period of time a number of techniques of group decision making have been developed. They help the manager in more rational and effective decision making.

GROUP DECISION MAKING

Modern organisations are characterised by large-scale activities. They exist in a complex environment. Managers have the responsibility of making decisions on a continuous basis. Managers in modern organisations seldom take individual decisions. Individual decisions have a number of limitations mainly because the human mind has a limited capacity to come up with new ideas or analyse the alternatives. Moreover, individual decisions can be less rational. Managers prefer to use groups for taking decisions, thereby increasing the popularity of group decision making.

In its simplest meaning group decision making is the use of skills of two or more persons in the process of decision making. In making a group decision all the members of the group discuss the problem in detail and come up with various alternative solutions. An acceptable solution is arrived at by consensus. Group decision making involves thinking, understanding and judging through coordinated actions to arrive at the best possible result.

The characteristics of group decision making are as follows:

1. A group of persons are involved in the decision making process.
2. Coordination is the essence of group decision making.
3. Group members are selected to represent various interests.
4. Group decisions enhance motivation due to participation in decision making.
5. Group decision making is employed both in line and staff functions.
6. It is used at all levels of managerial hierarchy.

GROUP DECISION MAKING PROCESS

Decision making is not a single step activity. It is a process. The following are the steps in the decision making process.

1. Forming groups by official designation
2. Planning agenda and date of meeting
3. Identifying and diagnosing the problem
4. Searching for alternative solutions
5. Analysing alternative courses of action
6. Seeking suggestions of the members of the group
7. Selecting the best alternative course of action
8. Announcing the decision and wrapping up the group

In group decisions, the first step is to form a group. In organisations, a formal group is often called a committee. When a problem arises that requires a group decision, a group is constituted. Sometimes groups exist as part of the formal structure of the organisation. An agenda is a list of the topics that will be discussed by the group. It enables the members to arrive for the meeting prepared on the subject matter. Group decision making requires the members of the group to come together at one place. Therefore, a date and time are fixed for the group members to meet. It also involves specifying the venue of the meeting.

On the day of the meeting the problem is presented to the group. The group is expected to discuss the problem in order to bring clarity of thought. In this process, the members discuss and list out alternatives and the problem is viewed from different angles. However, not all alternatives are viable in the context of the problem. Decision making requires selection of one of the alternatives. Sometimes alternatives are mutually exclusive. Therefore, the alternatives need to be analysed using certain accepted criteria. The criteria could be related to the quantitative or qualitative aspects of the problem. It may be related to the financial aspect. Thus, members try to discuss the alternatives in the light of the criteria. In group decision making it is important that the members' suggestions are sought before the final solution is selected. This is called participation in the decision making, which enhances the acceptability of the decision. Members are psychologically committed to implement the decision irrespective of personal differences. This is because the final solution is arrived at after the suggestions of the members are taken into account. The alternative which most of the members believe to be the best is selected. This becomes the group decision. Even at this stage, there could be disagreement. However, when the majority of members accept the alternative, it has to be announced so that all the members come to know about the decision. When the group completes the decision making process the meeting is concluded on a positive note, appreciating the members' active participation and assistance in the decision making.

ASSETS OF GROUP DECISION MAKING

Group decision making is superior to individual decision making. There is a general saying that '*Two heads are better than one*'. More people involved in the process of decision making bring in more rationality. Group decision making enables democratic functioning and increases commitment in the end. The benefits of group decision making are described below:

(i) **Group discussion and judgement:** A group is a source of integrated knowledge. It is collection of a wide range of experience. A close interaction among members of the group permits probing of facts, generation of a wide range of ideas, alternatives and approaches, free exchange of views and ideas, evaluation of more alternative courses of action and understanding of problems. It leads to better discussion and evaluation of the problem. Thus, more balanced and rational decisions are made. The process reduces the chance of personal bias.

(ii) **Greater acceptance:** Group decision making provides an opportunity of eliciting opinions of members. It also enables interested members of the group to participate in decisions. This develops a sense of loyalty, commitment and moral responsibility to execute the decision. Hence, increased acceptance is possible in this process.

(iii) Coordination: For the purpose of group decision making, employees working in different departments are made members of the group. This enhances the scope for understanding mutual problems and prospects. Members exchange their feelings in a healthy, cordial and harmonious environment. This reduces conflicts among them and facilitates inter and intra-departmental coordination. It also promotes inter personal relationships.

(iv) Balanced use of authority: In group decision making, all members are given equal authority and responsibility. It creates a fearless environment coupled with trust and mutual respect. It also prevents concentration of power in the hands of few, which can result in unbalanced decisions, favouritism, bias etc.

(v) Training: In group decision making the group often consists of executives from top, middle and lower levels. They are engaged in setting objectives, goals and policies and making decisions on complex problems. Participation is encouraged in all activities of the group. This facilitates individual thinking on important issues. Such knowledge and experience can be used in identical situations in the future. In this process, personnel try to improve their skills. Therefore, group decision making permits group members to learn through experience and develop skills and abilities to become potential managers of tomorrow.

(vi) Motivation and satisfaction: A prerequisite in group decision making is the effective participation of members of the group. Participation inculcates a feeling that their ideas are considered. Hence, members' motivation is enhanced. Similarly, a member feels satisfied as he is allowed to participate in the decision and the decision reflects his ideas and thoughts.

LIABILITIES OF GROUP DECISION MAKING

In spite of the benefits, group decision making is not without flaws. It is often said that managers thinking to avoid making decisions conveniently assign the task to groups. Groups are considered as protective devices for managerial deficiencies. We often observe that whenever decisions are to be delayed, the government appoints committees. The limitations of group decision making are presented below.

(a) Cost of group decision making: For the purpose of group decision making, groups are formed by drawing executives from all departments or divisions of an organisation. They are required to meet frequently to take decisions on various issues. If the members are spread over a large geographical area, payment of travel costs, daily allowances etc., are made to attend the meetings. Apart from this direct cost, prolonged discussions are time consuming. This leads to wastage of executive time that could have been used for productive purposes. Therefore, critics feel that the cost of a group decision outweighs the benefit accrued by it.

(b) Indecision and avoidance of decisions: Indecisiveness is a common problem with the group decision making process. Groups allow discussion of the problem as every member has freedom to express his feelings and attitudes. This can result in dilution of the best solution in an attempt to satisfy and compromise with the views of a majority of members. The meeting may end up adjourned because of lack of consensus among the members and the result is indecision. Group decision making is often considered as an effective technique to avoid decisions on complex problems. Groups require more time for elaborate discussion and to arrive at a consensus. Thus, disproportionate time is consumed to arrive at a final decision. By the time they make the decision, the purpose may be lost. Sometimes avoidance of a decision is worse than no decision at all.

(c) **Domination:** Domination is a serious problem that limits the usefulness of group decision making. Domination results because of a variety of reasons. The chairperson of the group is normally the senior executive of the organisation. He enjoys formal authority in the organisational hierarchy. Therefore, members out of fear may accept whatever he says. This tendency results from a wish to project themselves as sincere and loyal subordinates and to be in the good looks of the superior. Often members do not want to oppose the ideas of the superior in order to secure the favourable opinion of the chairperson. It results in domination by the chairperson. In this way members compromise and the result is suppression of real creativity. The second case in which domination results is when strong members come together to dominate weak members. Generally, members having control over the resources form themselves into a small group, called a 'ring'. They try to compel the other members to accept their ideas, sometimes even using threats. This kind of domination leads to partial decisions. Continued suppression due to domination leads to serious psychological problems of withdrawing, becoming callous and disinterested. All this may be a result of a hidden agenda to cover the real problems.

(d) **Avoidance of responsibility:** When group decisions are successfully implemented, every member comes forward to claim credit and appreciation. In the case of failure of decisions, members seldom accept the responsibility. They either make the chairperson responsible or blame the other members to safeguard their interests. Hence, they shift the risk. This leads to recrimination, disagreements, conflicts and emergence of competing groups.

EFFECTIVE GROUP DECISION MAKING

Despite certain limitations, group decision making is considered as an effective and rational approach for solving many complex organisational problems. Use of group decision making promotes a climate of democracy and participation. There are certain guidelines for making group decisions effective. These guidelines concern the formality of procedure, chairperson of the group and members of the group. They are described below.

1. **Formality of procedure:** Formality of the procedure is related to the manner in which the group meeting is conducted in order to make an effective decision. In the process of group decision making, formality of procedure has a special significance. This is because the effectiveness of group decision making depends on the orderliness and consistency of the deliberations and the procedure followed in the process of discussions. As group decision

requires the voluntary participation of members, it is important that members participate in the discussions. Otherwise, the concept of group decision making itself becomes useless. Moreover, conflicts and disagreements arise among members. There are some procedures to be followed to help in the process of decision making.

(i) The objectives, goals and matters for decisions should be stated in very clear terms to the members.

(ii) Authority and responsibility of all the members should be stated in an unambiguous and precise manner. This avoids confusion and delay in decisions.

(iii) The size of the group should be reasonable. Normally 5 to 15 members are considered as optimum to secure full benefits from group decision making.

(iv) A careful selection of chairperson and members ensures the utility of the decision making.

(v) Group members should be directly concerned with the problem and its solution. Otherwise, unconnected members are likely to engage in gossip and wasteful discussion. This leads to no decisions.

(vi) A proper procedure for conducting the meeting should be designed. It should include the format of the notice, the time limit for sending the notice and agenda, time for commencing and closing the meeting, providing notes and clarifications, distributing approved minutes and follow up action.

2. **Chairperson of the group:** The chairperson is an important person in the group decision making process. He or she should be capable of inspiring the members, securing confidence and eliciting participation. An efficient chairperson can avoid conflicts, recriminations, aggressions, wasteful discussions and side tracking by using tact and skill. The following points should be considered by the chairperson while conducting the meeting.

(i) Ensure that the meeting commences and ends exactly at predetermined times.

(ii) Introduce the problem gently, clearly and unambiguously by clarifying all the technical aspects. The chairperson should initiate discussions and start the meeting with his introductory remarks.

(iii) Ensure participation of all members by creating an open and trustworthy environment. He should gently provoke the silent members to participate in the discussions.

(iv) Exercise control over aggressive behaviour and handle conflicts smoothly but firmly. The chairperson should be impartial in dealing with all the members

(v) He should be tactful with impulsive members.

(vi) Empathy and attentiveness towards all the members instills confidence in the members that their opinions are being taken into consideration in making the decisions.

(vii) Exercise self control and regulate the meeting even if it does not please some members.

(viii) Sum up discussions at the end of the meeting and announce the final decisions. He should express appreciation for participation and involvement of the members. At the same time, he should address inattentive members to make them aware of their attitude and let them know that their participation is needed.

3. **Members of the group:** The effectiveness of group decision making depends on cooperation and harmonious interaction among the members. Certain inherent characteristics should be the basis for selecting members to form a group. Their intelligence, inquisitive spirit, sharpness, decisiveness, willingness to accept authority, assumption of responsibility and accountability are crucial to success. Some guidelines that help the members in the process of group decision making are given below.
   (i) Members should study the agenda carefully before going to the meeting and prepare brief but comprehensive notes or points for discussion.
   (ii) Every member should assert his position, but also listen carefully to all the other members.
   (iii) A member should develop careful, logical, rational and objective thinking and present his ideas and opinions openly and clearly without fear.
   (iv) Members should avoid hurting the feelings of co-members, but they need not be submissive.
   (v) Members should maintain psychological balance by avoiding impatience and loss of temper.
   (vi) They should allow other members to express their views freely and frankly. Dominance and unnecessary interruptions may bog down the discussion.
   (vii) At the end of the meeting written copies of minutes and approved decisions should be given.
   (viii) Once the meeting is over, tensions should be left behind, and members should relax and interact with each other in a friendly manner.

TECHNIQUES OF GROUP DECISION MAKING

Modern organisations find group decision making a useful technique for decision making. It requires creativity, thinking, judgement and coordinated action. Use of various techniques can enhance the quality of the group decision making process.

Brainstorming

Brainstorming is a process of encouraging members to use their thinking and judgement in the development and analysis of alternative courses of action. It specifically encourages development of alternatives while withholding criticism on the alternatives suggested by other members. It was developed by A.F. Osborn. In brainstorming, a group of persons is presented with a problem. They are encouraged to develop a number of solutions according to their ability. The characteristic features of brainstorming are as follows.

(i) A brainstorming group consists of about 6 to 12 persons.

(ii) The leader of the group presents the problem in a clear manner to ensure that every member understands it.

(iii) A free and frank discussion is encouraged.

(iv) Criticism on ideas presented by the other members of the group is prohibited. However, suggestions are elicited for improving other members' ideas.

(v) The leader ensures a supportive and encouraging climate for the group.

(vi) Brainstorming is a process of generating ideas and not obtaining final solutions.

Two other techniques which are little different from brainstorming are also used. They are story boarding and lotus blossom techniques. Story boarding is used to comprehend the entire problem. In this technique, the members are asked to identify the major issues. The brainstorming takes place on these issues. This method is used in solving complex and ambiguous decision situations.

Lotus blossom is a Japanese technique. The technique is used to unleash the creative potential of the members of the group. At the first instance, a core idea is identified. This is called 'the petal base' in the lotus. About eight ideas are developed in the second instance. Each of these ideas is taken as a core idea; again, eight ideas are developed. This process of developing ideas will continue until all the members are convinced that the problem is fully understood and creative alternatives are developed.

The utility of the brainstorming technique is that members are given adequate opportunity to use their mental energy. Hence a greater number of alternatives are developed. In addition, the problem is analysed in depth. Therefore, it gives rise to the appropriate solution to the problem. However, the limitation of this technique is that it is only a technique of developing alternative courses of action. The solutions leading to the decision are not developed. The effectiveness of this technique depends on the qualities of the members.

Nominal Group Technique (NGT)

Nominal Group Technique is a method in which individuals meet and pool their ideas in a systematic and independent manner. However, there is a restriction on discussions and interpersonal communication during the course of the decision making process. Hence, it is called a 'nominal' group. It is also known as a 'paper group'. This technique was developed by Andre Debecq and Andrew Van de Ven. The characteristics of this technique are as follows:

a. The problem is presented to group members.

b. All the members meet formally and write their ideas on the problems before the discussion takes place.

c. Each member presents his idea to the group. Discussions are not allowed until all members present their ideas.

d. After all the members complete the presentation of their ideas, group members discuss them clearly and evaluate them.

e. Members silently and independently rank the ideas. The idea with the highest rank is selected as the solution.

NGT is a highly structured process of group discussion. The main advantage is that it permits independent thinking. It also promotes inter personal interaction. This technique is logical because the idea that ranks the highest is selected.

Delphi Technique

Delphi technique is a process of pooling the ideas by a group of people acting independently without any face-to-face interaction. It is similar to the NGT technique. It was developed by Norman Dalkey and Olaf Helmer. The characteristics of Delphi technique are presented below.

(i) The problem is presented to members and members are asked to provide all possible solutions.

(ii) Members are often asked to answer a questionnaire independently and anonymously.

(iii) The results of the questionnaire are processed and sent to all members. After looking at the results, members may again suggest solutions, which are again processed. This process is continued until the best solution is developed.

The advantage of this technique is that it allows independent thinking and it does not require face-to-face meetings. The limitation of this technique is that it is time-consuming and therefore cannot be used for urgent decisions.

E–Meeting

In the age of computers, a new technique has been developed – electronic meeting. It is use of information technology for the purpose of decision making. The characteristic features of e-meetings are as follows:

1. A large group of people is involved in the process of decision making.
2. All the group members can assemble at one place and take seats in a semi-circle. Otherwise, they may be at different places.
3. Each of the members is provided with a computer. All the computers are networked.
4. A large electronic screen is placed in the room if the meeting is conducted in a closed room.
5. The problem is presented to all the participants via computer terminals.
6. Participants after careful thinking and judgement provide suggestions via the computer terminals.
7. Individual suggestions and comments are displayed on the screen, so all members know the

other members' views. However, the identity of the other members is kept secret to avoid misunderstandings.

8. Finally, a decision is arrived at after considering all the suggestions.

The advantage of this technique is that it elicits frank opinions, as the members' identity is kept confidential. This also enables them to be more honest. The meeting is conducted with greater speed. No personal contact is needed. Members can sit at different locations and conduct the meeting. There is no disruption to the normal duties of the members. The decision is logical as large numbers of persons are involved. However, it is costly, as all the persons require computer terminals and necessary software. Moreover, it is difficult to achieve consensus with a large group. Therefore, this is not suitable when immediate decisions are needed.

Summary

Group decision making is involving many persons to think, judge and arrive at a decision. Nowadays it has become quite common in organisations. It is similar to individual decision making in many respects except for forming and wrapping up the group. A number of benefits such as group discussions and judgement, greater acceptance, coordination, training, motivation and satisfaction are derived from the group decision making process. At the same time it not without limitations. Financial and time related costs associated with group decision making are a major limitation. Indecision and avoidance of decisions, domination of strong members and avoidance of responsibility are some other limitations. Limitations of group decision making do not belittle its utility. Group decision making is used in all modern organisations for a number of reasons. There is a need to make it more effective and rational. A number of guidelines are prescribed with respect to the formality of procedure, the chairperson and members of the group. Creativity, thinking, judgement and coordinated action are the four pillars that make the group decision making process effective. A number of techniques were developed to make group decision making more effective. Brainstorming, story boarding, lotus blossom, nominal group technique, Delphi technique and E-meeting are some of the popular techniques.

Key words:

- **Brainstorming:** The technique of using mental processes of thinking and judgement to develop alternatives.
- **Delphi technique:** A technique of pooling of ideas by a group of people who are acting independently without any face-to-face interaction.
- **E-meeting:** Use of computer technology for group decision making.
- **Lotus blossom:** Identifying the core idea and developing a number of ideas around the core idea.

- **Nominal group technique:** Arranging face-to-face interaction to collect ideas in an independent manner.
- **Petal base:** A core idea is identified to unleash the creative potential of the members of the group.
- **Ring:** A process of forming a small group with the members having control over the resources in a group decision making situation.
- **Story-boarding:** Process of identifying the major issues to comprehend the problem in its totality.

21. TEAM DEVELOPMENT

This chapter enables you:

- *To understand the teams in organisations*
- *To distinguish between groups and teams*
- *To understand the various types of teams managers use for effective working*
- *To examine the significance of teams over groups*
- *To understand the development of team spirit*
- *To suggest measures for using teams to build organisations*

The structure of the chapter is as follows:

- Introduction
- Meaning of teams in organisations
- Distinctions between groups and teams
- Classification of teams
- The cutting edge of teams
- Team development
- Teams for building an organisation
- Summary
- Key words

CHAPTER 21

Team Development

INTRODUCTION

The Hawthorne movement popularised the concept of groups. However, today teams have replaced groups and are increasingly being used in modern organisations. Groups only have members, who work under the directions of focussed leaders, to achieve goals. The leader is accountable for the group's performance. On the other hand, teams function effectively even without directions from a formal leader. Every member of the team takes responsibility according to the demands of the situation. The team is jointly accountable to achieve results. For example, sales teams are intended to achieve a higher level of performance. This lesson deals with teams and team building in organisations.

THE MEANING OF TEAMS IN AN ORGANISATION

An organisation is a collection of individuals who are willing to work collectively to attain certain goals, both individual and of the organisation. An individual tends to give preference to his own goals. This may lead to sacrificing the goals of the organisation. It used to be believed that an individual's contribution was most important, and therefore, efforts were made to increase productivity of individuals. The differential piece wage system introduced by F W Taylor may have been an effort to motivate individual workers to increase their level of production. Most classical works on organisations have suggested that focus should be on the individual, when designing the structure of the organisation and motivational strategies. Then the Human Relations

Movement recognised the importance of groups and their contribution. The famous works of Kurt Lewin relating to group dynamics highlighted the fact that an individual can achieve certain goals through group action, which may be difficult or even impossible to accomplish individually. For about fifty years, organisations followed this philosophy in organisational structure, work design, motivational strategies, performance appraisal and organisational development. Nowadays however, the concept of groups has become obsolete. The team has become popular for managers who want to improve performance, by guiding employees in a specific direction, and increase their proficiency and capabilities. The concept of teams is accredited to the Japanese. As early as the 1950s, Joseph Juran used the team approach to solve problems related to quality. It is often said that for the Japanese, teams are as natural as breathing. Managing teams effectively assumes considerable significance in today's context of organisations. Most successful companies have been using self-managed and high performance teams. Other organisations followed suit and revamped their organisational structure and other strategies around teams rather than individuals or groups. Another country, which uses teams effectively for achieving higher productivity and results, is the USA. Some examples of international companies using teams include Videocon International, the New United Motor Manufacturing, Motorola, Toyoto, General Motors, US Navy, Hewlett-Packard, Massachusetts General Hospital. In India, a few examples are Modi Xerox, TISCO, SAIL, Philips India, Cadbury India etc. How often, in a cricket or football match, have we heard the phrase 'playing for the team.' Team effort is needed to win the match. This analogy is applicable to organisations also. The definitions of 'team' given below will help you to understand the concept more clearly.

Based on the work of **Eric Sandstorm** and others, work teams are defined as, *'any formal groups made up of interdependent individuals, responsible for attaining a goal'*.

According to **Dorwin Cartwright** and **Ronald Lippitt** a team is, *'two or more people who interact and influence each other toward a common purpose'*.

John Katzenbach and **Douglas Smith** defined team as, *'a small number of people with complementary skills who are committed to a common purpose, set of performance goals and approach for which they hold themselves mutually accountable'*.

A team can be defined as *a collection of two or more, but not necessarily a large number of individuals possessing unique skills, who are willing to be interdependent and interactive by contributing their skills, capacities and knowledge for the realisation of common, mutually agreed goals. The members assume joint accountability and try to produce synergy.*

The characteristics of teams are as follows:

1. A team is a collection of people who are willing to sacrifice their individual goals for a common purpose.
2. The number of members in a team is usually small.
3. Team members each contribute their unique proficiency, skill, capability, and competency, to enhance the effectiveness of the team.
4. Teams have greater degree of interdependence and shared commitment.

5. A team possesses a high degree of interpersonal communication, trust, attraction between members and relationships.
6. A team generates synergy. The sum total of outcome of a team is always greater than the sum of the individual outcomes.
7. The members of a team are accountable individually, and the team also has a collective responsibility.
8. The leadership in a team is shared amongst the team members.

DISTINCTIONS BETWEEN GROUPS AND TEAMS

Teams and groups are basically a collection of individuals who are willing to collectively contribute to a common purpose under the direction of focussed leaders. However, teams have certain distinct characteristics, which are given in Table 21.1.

CLASSIFICATION OF TEAMS

Today, organisations are using a number of different teams to perform effectively. These teams help in solving problems, accomplish tasks and achieve organisational effectiveness. The various kinds of teams are given below.

- **Formal teams:** Formal teams are the most common teams found in many organisations. They are appointed for a specific purpose. Authority to take decisions is delegated by superiors. These teams sometimes form part of the organisational structure. Command teams are the most common forms of formal teams. A command team consists of a manager and all the subordinates who report to him in the formal hierarchy. The manager of command team is called a *coach* and the team members are known as *associates.* Another kind of formal team is a committee. A number of committees are appointed to accomplish specific tasks. For instance, a budget committee is responsible for preparing and implementing a budget. Some other kinds of formal teams are quality circles, task forces, project teams.
- **Informal teams:** Many organisations have informal teams, which provide social satisfaction and a sense of belonging among members of the organisation. They give employees a sense of self-esteem and an opportunity to share their feelings. Often, these teams do not have the approval of the management. Informal teams function, within their own norms and work under the direction of informal leaders. A reference team is a commonly found informal team whose activities are taken as a standard to compare the performance of other teams.
- **Self-managed teams:** A team in which members are capable of managing affairs effectively without the presence of a formal leader is called a self-managed team. Many organisations encourage such teams. Charles C. Manz and others have described the following characteristics of self-managed teams.

Table 21.1: Distinction between groups and teams

Characteristic	Groups	Teams
Accountability	The leader of the group assumes accountability for performance of the group.	The accountability of teams is both individual and collective. Each member assumes accountability for the performance.
Goals	Groups have common goals and group members share the work irrespective of their interest and capability to achieve the common goal.	Teams also pursue common goals, however the members collectively achieve the goals by contributing their unique skills and capabilities.
Leadership	Leadership of a group is focussed on one individual.	Teams members share leadership. Each member assumes the role of the leader, depending upon the demands of the situation.
Membership	A person becomes a member of a group through the formal structure of the organisation.	Members of a team are selected based on their skill and competency.
Nature	Productivity and performance of an individual are given importance.	A team gives importance to the collective productivity of its members rather than to individual productivity.
Performance	A group takes a joint decision as to who should perform a task. Members of a group are delegated to perform a job.	A team also takes decisions with participation of members, but members take on a task without waiting for it to be delegated to them.
Purpose	The purpose of groups is to accomplish a given task.	Teams ensure that they perform a task, and also work towards overall effectiveness of the organisation.
Skills	Group members develop skills to realise objectives.	Members of a team try to sharpen their skills and specialise in their area of competency rather than develop general skills.
Synergy	The performance of a group is the sum of the individual outputs.	The output of team is greater than the sum of individual performances.

1. They assume responsibility for the complete task.
2. All members have task-related skills.
3. Decisions are made taking into account work designs, methods and schedules, and assignments to members.
4. The overall performance of the group is taken as the basis for compensation and feedback.

Self-managed teams are found to be more effective in attaining greater productivity, developing a positive attitude, reducing absenteeism, and reducing employee turnover. Certain organisational obstacles that come in the way of good performance of these teams are compensation and reward systems. Some of the hurdles due to individual members are as follows.

- Unwillingness on the part of team members to give up past practices and set aside power and position.
- Uneven distribution of abilities, knowledge and skills cause some members to contribute more and shoulder more responsibilities than other members. This creates a feeling that the latter are taking advantage of those who are working more.
- Mismatch of personal beliefs and team challenges can give rise to conflicts, resulting in poor performance.

According to Hovemeyer, a team can slide down to a lower level of effectiveness at any point, if the members do not continuously work together as a team, listen and communicate effectively, deal with conflicts, recognise each other's unique contributions, provide honest feedback and demonstrate other characteristics of an effective team. Thus, certain key areas were identified for effective functioning of self-managed teams. They are team missions, goal achievement, empowerment, open, honest communication and positive roles and norms. Effective use of self-managed teams requires comprehensive training of members of an organisation. Table 21.2 provides a series of steps and guidelines, which the trainer should provide in order to develop effective self-managed teams in an organisation.

- **Problem solving teams:** This is the most common form of team. These teams are employed at all levels. Their basic purpose is to share information, discuss various solutions and suggest the one most suitable for the ultimate decision. Sometimes teams are appointed to solve a specific problem and once this problem is solved, they are disbanded. However often problem solving teams exist permanently in the form of committees, and act whenever required. For instance, the shop-floor disciplinary team is permanent. Whenever a disciplinary problem arises in the plant, the team swings into action to ensure discipline. However, a core member team, which is appointed to solve a specific industrial dispute, will cease to exist immediately after the dispute is resolved.

- **Cross functional teams:** As the name suggests this is a hybrid team. It consists of members of the same rank from various departments of an enterprise. For example, a team of managers from the production, marketing, engineering, human resources and research and development departments, can be formed temporarily to work on a specific project or can be permanent and work on various projects. Thus, the team will have the expertise of various departments.

Table 21.2: Training guidelines for developing effective self-managed teams

Guidelines	Intended action to be provided in the training program by the trainer to the trainees
Credibility	A series of interpersonal interactions to establish members' knowledge, skill and proficiency and develop confidence and belief of members in each other.
Ventilation	A climate of free and frank expression of feelings, emotions, anxieties, doubts and all other unresolved issues among members before starting team interaction.
Orientation	Clear communication of directions, expectations and models of team behaviour to all members.
Goals	Establish interaction among team members to identify problems, issues and concerns of team at the initial stage. Members agree to develop vision, a mission statement, goals, procedures, structural aspects and behaviour in order to achieve the goals.
Facilitate	Teach the techniques of developing and facilitating interaction among members of team. Some techniques are nominal group technique, lotus blossom, paired comparison etc.
Meeting procedure	Establish a procedure to be followed at the meetings, such as writing the minutes, making announcements, discussing problems and new assignments.
Inter-group process	Identify suitable members to take up the role of leaders to develop purposeful and meaningful interaction with other teams and authorities in the organisation. This is required as self-managed groups do not have formal leaders.
Passivity	Withdraw from active direction as soon as it is recognised that members are empowered.
Independence	Give independence to the team to function on its own and emerge as a self-managed team.

Source: Paul E. Brauchle and David W. Wright (1993), "Training Work Teams", Training and Development, March, pp 65-68.

Cross functional teams are very effective in improving productivity and organisational performance. The greatest difficulty with these teams is difficulty in co-ordination. Some of the steps needed for managing cross functional teams effectively are given below.

1. **Select members carefully.** Members of cross functional teams should have a high degree of integrity, motivation, patience, flexibility, be accommodating, willing to co-operate and sacrifice, and above all have a very positive attitude.

2. **Identify the purpose clearly.** Often conflict arises due to the fact that the purpose is ambiguous and not well defined. The purpose for which the team is set up depends on how the vision, mission, goals, procedure and behavioural norms are developed. Therefore, clear definition and communication of purpose is mandatory for success.
3. **Develop clear understanding among members.** A team functions on clear principles of structure, communication, control and performance appraisal. To avoid any perceptual errors, communication should be perfect. It should be ensured that all members think in the same way regarding the functioning of the team.
4. **Team building.** Before cross functional teams actually start to function, intensive team building should take place. A high degree of attraction, communication, trust, confidence and understanding should be developed between members, before the team becomes functional.
5. **Noticeable performance.** One of the reasons for poor performance of cross functional teams is loss of motivation and morale. This happens due to lack of careful identification of standards of evaluation, and lack of clarity on methods and techniques of evaluation. Thus, it is necessary to develop performance standards clearly. Objective appraisal and sincere feedback inculcates a high degree of motivation and commitment of members.

Apart from the above classification of teams, there are certain other types of teams used in organisation, such as product development teams, reengineering teams, quality circles, directed teams, permanent and temporary teams.

THE CUTTING EDGE OF TEAMS

In recent years, most organisations have replaced the concept of groups with the concept of teams. Teams offer a number of benefits that the groups also offer, such as increased productivity, rapid decision-making, diversity in thinking, enhanced employee motivation and morale, satisfaction of social, esteem and actualisation needs, training ground for members, loyalty and commitment towards goals. However, teams have a cutting edge over groups, as they have certain benefits unique to them. These are explained below.

1. **Unique skills:** Members of a team possess unique skills. In the case of a group, every member tries to acquire all the skills necessary to undertake a task. As against this, in a team, members only undertake that part of the task in which they are competent. For instance, in a sales group every member uses skills of attracting customers, explaining the product, making visits, attending customer queries, and finalising the deal. Thus, if a member does not possess a particular skill, such as analysing information, he may not achieve the goal, even though he possesses other skills. However, in a team, each member uses his particular skill to maximise sales, for example one member may be competent in communication, another proficient in analysis, and still another possesses the skill of closing the deal. Thus if a sale is to be made by the team, every member plays his own part.

Publishing a newspaper

It takes a lot of co-ordination and teamwork to publish a newspaper. The team consists of news contributors, reporters, sub-editors, news editors, and editorial board. At the operational level, are the news contributors who gather news from various walks of life. Reporters also gather information but in a more refined way. In this sense, contributors assist the reporters. The news so gathered is then passed to the sub-editors, who refine the content and pass it on to the news-editor for editing. The important matters are referred to the editorial board or the editor, as the case may be, for approval. Only after going through these stages, does the news go to press for publication. Thus, it is seen that in publishing a newspaper, the whole team plays a crucial role.

2. **Synergy:** Synergy means that the outcome of a combined activity is greater than the sum of individual sub-activities. In the case of a group, the outcome of group activity is simply the sum of the performance of the individual members. However, in the case of a team, the outcome of the team is greater than the sum of the contributions of the individual members. This is called team synergy. Team synergy arises due to positive motivation and co-ordinated efforts of the team members.
3. **Self-managed leadership**: Groups always have a focussed leader who directs the efforts of the group members. Thus, members always look for specific instructions from the leader in order to contribute towards a goal. In teams, there is no concept of a focussed leader. Every team member becomes a self-managed leader, and assumes leadership as the situation demands.
4. **Accountability:** In the case of a group every member is accountable to the leader and the leader assumes accountability for the performance of the group. As against this, in the case of teams all team members assume both individual and joint accountability. Thus, every member is answerable for his actions, and also the actions of other members. This makes a team more effective than a group.
5. **Self-evaluation:** Team members are given adequate freedom to evaluate their performance and contributions at regular intervals. A leader does not finally evaluate the performance of the team. Members of the team evaluate each others performance. This method of self-evaluation enables members to get feedback from others and take the necessary steps to achieve optimum performance levels. In the case of groups, the leader evaluates the performance of group members. In this case, the leader may not accept evaluations by members of the group, his own evaluation may be biased, or he may make a wrong judgement.

Therefore, teams have a cutting edge over groups in an organisation, that is why there is an increasing tendency of using teams in organisations.

TEAM DEVELOPMENT

Team development and group development are similar in many respects. A team is developed by defining the purpose and goals, determining the norms, structure and procedure of interaction, undertaking tasks, evaluation and feedback. Teamwork requires a congenial environment, interpersonal attraction, trust, confidence and good relations between team members. Both the management and team members should inculcate a supportive culture to develop effective teams.

Team building is a method of improving the effectiveness of an organisation by diagnosing barriers to team performance and improving inter-team relationships and accomplishment of tasks. In the context of team development, two types of team building activities exist, namely family team and special team. A family team is a team of managers and subordinates. A special team consists of members belonging to various levels of the organisation. Table 21.3 summarises the activities relating to team building.

Table 21.3: Team building activities

Activity	Family teams	Special teams
Diagnosis	Diagnostic meetings: How are we doing?	Diagnostic meetings: Where would we like to go?
Task accomplishment	Solving problems, making decisions, role clarification, setting goals, etc.	Clarification of special problems, role and goals, utilisation of resources, etc.
Building and maintaining relationships	Focus on effective interpersonal relationships, including superior-subordinate and peer relationships.	Focus on interpersonal or inter-unit conflict and under utilisation of other team members as a resource.
Management of group processes	Focus on understanding group processes and group culture.	Focus on communication, making decisions, and task allocations.
Role analysis and role negotiation	Techniques used for definition and clarification of roles.	Techniques used for clarification and definition of roles.

Source: Stoner A.F. James, Management, Sixth Edition, 2000, Prentice Hall, India Private Limited, New Delhi, p.423.

Team building requires a number of activities, from defining the purpose to providing feedback. The team building process in a large manufacturing organisation is described below.

Steps	Processes	Actions
Step 1	Team skill workshop	The production team first went through a two-day workshop that consisted mainly of a series of exercises based on experiences. The purpose of this first phase was essentially to unfreeze the various teams and help them readily accept change.
Step 2	Data collection	In a questionnaire survey, data were collected on organisational climate, supervisory behaviour, and job content from all first line supervisors in the programme.
Step 3	Data confrontation	The consultants presented the teams with the data gathered in step 2. The teams, with the consultant present, openly discussed problem areas, established priorities, and suggested some preliminary recommendations for change.
Step 4	Action planning	On the basis of what went on in step 3, the teams developed specific plans for the changes to be actually carried out on the job.
Step 5	Team building	The first four phases were preliminary to the actual team building. In this phase, each team met as a whole to identify barriers to effectiveness, developed ways of limiting barriers, and agreed upon plans to accomplish the desired changes.
Step 6	Inter group building	This is a final phase. Two-day meetings were held between various teams that were interdependent in accomplishing goals. The purpose of this phase was to establish collaboration on shared goals and problems and generalise the organisational development effort to the total organisation.

A few techniques of team building are presented below.

1. **Role analysis technique:** Team development requires clarification of the role of each team member, so that they understand the behaviour expected from them. Otherwise, there will be role ambiguity. Clarification of a role involves the following steps.
   - Analysis of the role
   - Analysis of expectations
   - Analysis of desired behaviour
   - Preparation of role profiles
   - Review of role profiles

Role analysis is an effective technique for team building, but it requires careful examination of the various aspects of the members' roles.

2. **Role negotiation technique:** This technique was developed by Roger Harrison. One of the reasons for lack of team effectiveness is resistance to change. This technique is useful in such situations. The basic assumption of this technique is that most people prefer a fair negotiation settlement to a state of unresolved conflict and they are willing to invest some time and make some concessions in order to achieve a solution. The basic methodology of this technique is that all the team members come to an understanding and mutually agree to change certain behaviour. For instance in a production team one member may agree to cut down wastage of material, if other members agree to maintain the quality of the product. Such agreement may be necessary because incentive is based on both quality and waste reduction. The following steps are involved in this technique.
   - Establishing a climate conducive to interpersonal communication, understanding and agreement, leading to a contract being signed.
   - Understanding how a change in one member's behaviour will lead to others' behaviour becoming more effective. For this purpose a diagnostic questionnaire is used. Every member fills it out to understand behaviour patterns.
   - Establishing a time frame for negotiations between team members. In this step, members understand the importance of a give and take approach. Thus an agreement is reached and a contract is signed.
   - Follow-up. A meeting is arranged between team members to evaluate whether the agreement is honoured or not. Members can also assess some possible effects of the contract.

TEAMS FOR BUILDING AN ORGANISATION

It is recognised beyond doubt that teams have a cutting edge over groups in increasing productivity, motivation, morale, satisfaction and overall effectiveness of an organisation. Many organisations have benefited by using teams in recent years. So managing the teams for effective organisational building is of paramount importance. Douglas McGregor, Rensis Likert, Glenn Parker, Katzenbach and Smith, amongst others, have developed various guidelines for teams to contribute to organisational building. Each of them has identified certain characteristics of effective teams. The list developed by Glenn Parker is shown in Table 21.4.

Table 21.4: Characteristics of effective teams

Features	Indicators for effective team performance
Clear purpose	Vision, mission, goal, task and action plan defined.
Informality	Informal, comfortable and relaxed climate.
Participation	Encouraging discussions and participation from every member.
Listening	Questioning, paraphrasing and summarising for effective listening.
Civilised disagreement	Civilised expression of disagreements and avoidance of conflicts to prevent unnecessary aggressions.
Consensus on decision making	Agreement on various aspects of the decision through straightforward discussions. Voting is to be avoided.
Open communication	No hidden agenda, free expression of feelings, emotions and attitudes. Maintaining emotional balance (embal) and personal integrity.
Clear roles and work assignments	Clear expectations and even division of work to avoid poor performance.
Shared leadership	All members of the team should share the leadership role.
External relations	Developing cordial relations with members who are not on the team and establishing credibility of the team.
Style diversity	Task skills and group process are different from those of other teams.
Self-assessment	Periodical self-evaluation of each member and of the team.

Some of the characteristics identified by McGregor are mentioned below.

- Relaxed, comfortable and informal atmosphere
- Well understood tasks and acceptance by members
- Discussions relevant to the task, participation of members and listening carefully to each member
- Free and frank expression of feelings, ideas and emotions
- Conflicts and disagreements should centre on ideas and methods, and not around personalities and people
- Self-conscious team operations
- Unanimous decisions and no oppression of members

Therefore, organisations can build themselves by developing, nurturing and managing various teams for improving effectiveness.

SUMMARY

An organisational team is a collection of members who are willing to sacrifice their personal goals to achieve organisational goals. Groups and teams are similar in certain respects. Both have common goals, norms, structured interactions, leadership, and performance appraisal. However, teams are distinct with respect to accountability, leadership, unique skills, synergy and self-evaluation. Organisations use a variety of teams based on the time frame of the task. These may be formal teams, informal teams, self-managed teams, problem solving teams and cross-functional teams. Teams are important because they have a cutting edge over groups. Teams are developed for a number of reasons, and the development is a process. Some techniques used in the team development process are role analysis and role negotiation. As teams are superior to groups, they are very effective for organisational performance. Some of the characteristics of effective teams are clarity of purpose, informality, participation, listening, civilised disagreement, consensus in making decisions, open communication, clarity of roles and work assignments, shared leadership, good external relations, style diversity and self-assessment.

Key words:

- **Associates:** Team members of a command team
- **Coach:** Manager of a command team
- **Cross functional team:** A team whose members are of the same rank, drawn from different departments of the organisation
- **Family team:** A team of managers and subordinates
- **Formal team:** A team appointed to accomplish a specific purpose
- **Self-managed teams:** Teams in which members are capable of managing the affairs effectively without the presence of a formal leader
- **Special team:** A team whose members are drawn from different levels of an organisation
- **Synergy:** The outcome of the combined activity is greater than the sum of individual sub-activities

22. BEHAVIOUR OF SMALL GROUPS

This chapter enables you:

- *To define and understand the meaning of small groups found in organisations*
- *To examine the importance of the study to managers*
- *To identify various functions performed by small groups*
- *To examine the process of influence that occurs in small groups*
- *To identify the findings of studies on the behaviour of small groups*
- *To derive the principles of behaviour of small groups*
- *To explain the environmental influences on the behaviour of small groups, with the help of a model*
- *To understand the interactive elements in small groups*
- *To develop a sociometric diagram for the small groups we observe*

The structure of the chapter is as follows:

- Introduction
- Definition of small groups
- Significance of studying the behaviour of small groups
- Functions of small groups
- The behaviour process in small groups
- Findings regarding the behaviour of small groups
- Principles of small group dynamics
- Models of behaviour of small groups: Homan's model
- Bales' laboratory technique
- Sociometric analysis
- Summary
- Key words

CHAPTER 22

Behaviour of Small Groups

INTRODUCTION

Small groups are omnipresent in all organisations. A small group consists of about four to twelve people, and because of the small number, it is easy for the members to interact. You must have noticed that employees move around in small groups in any organisation, whether it is during the coffee breaks, at the sports grounds or during formal discussions. Small groups provide invaluable guidance to managers in many ways. However at times, they may prevent efficient functioning. Therefore, care and caution are necessary in dealing with these groups. **Edgar Schien** identified two functions of small groups, namely task and maintenance functions. While task function is to accomplish the tasks assigned to a group, maintenance functions relate to sustaining the group for a long time. Groups influence the behaviour of members in an organisation in many ways. They shape attitudes, provide status, reinforce culture and provide interpersonal interaction. **Cartwright** studied the dynamics of small groups and propounded certain principles to understand and determine their effectiveness. The behaviour of small groups and the relationship between their members is complex. **Homan** developed a model to understand these complex relationships. According to his model, effective behaviour results when the required behaviour leads to emergent behaviour. **Robert Bales** developed Interaction Process Analysis. This model identified six problem areas. According to this model, a group with both tasks and human relations becomes an effective group. The model developed by **Moreno** uses sociometric diagrams to explain the likes and dislikes of group members.

DEFINITION OF A SMALL GROUP

A small group is "*two or more persons interacting to accomplish a common goal; the interaction is durable and displays at least a minimum degree of structure.*" **Marvin E. Shaw.**

Homan defined a small group as "*a number of persons who communicate with one another over a continuous span of time, and who are few enough, so that each person is able to communicate with all the others in a face to face interaction*".

A small group is "*any number of persons engaged in interaction with one another in a single face to face meeting or a series of such meetings, in which each member receives some impressions or perception of other members distinct enough so that he can, either at the time or in later questioning, give some reaction to each of the others as an individual person, even though it be only to recall that the other was present*". **Bales.**

A small group is a "*collection of individuals who usually have face to face relationships and who consider them as differentiated either explicitly or implicitly. The size of the group normally varies between 4 and 12*". **Kamala Chowdary.**

The above definitions reveal the following characteristics of a small group:

(i) It is a collection of individuals.

(ii) Members of the group possess homogeneous attributes.

(iii) The size of the group normally varies from four to twelve. However, the size is not mandatory.

(iv) A small group always tries to behave differently from other groups in the organisation.

SIGNIFICANCE OF THE STUDY OF THE BEHAVIOUR OF SMALL GROUPS

It is important for practicing managers to study and understand the behaviour of small groups for the following reasons:

a. Small groups are omnipresent and an inevitable part of an organisation.
b. People mostly work in small groups irrespective of their level in the managerial hierarchy.
c. Managers have more influence on the behaviour of members in small groups as compared to large groups.
d. Managers use small groups, such as committees, as tools for making decisions, accomplishing tasks and faster communication.
e. Motivating members in small groups is easier.

FUNCTIONS OF SMALL GROUPS

Small groups discharge certain specific functions, which Edgar Schien has identified as task functions and group maintenance functions. They are described below.

Task Functions

They relate to the accomplishment of specific tasks assigned to small groups. They include:

(i) **Creativity**: Small groups develop creativity. They search for new and improved methods of performing tasks in an organisation. This is possible due to improved sharing of information and thinking process in a small group that would not be possible in a large group.

(ii) **Information agents**: Small groups are effective in collecting facts, enquiring about feelings, and developing ideas and values. It is easy to share information among a few members. All the members of a small group share the information collected by other members of the small group. Such information is useful to accomplish the tasks on hand.

(iii) **Disseminating information:** Information can be effectively circulated in a small group. Every member is prepared to offer information to the others. The purpose of offering information is to seek suggestions, present facts and convey beliefs of the members. Members of the group use the shared information for development and growth of the group. The information disseminated by small groups is useful to an organisation in designing plans, policies, motivational programs, communication strategies, and training and development interventions.

(iv) **Summarising:** Small groups can quickly and effectively analyse a problem. They can easily review the information, reach a consensus and offer suggestions in a comprehensive manner. This is possible due to the size of the group. A large group would not be able to do this, as it is difficult for a large number of people to reach a consensus.

(v) **Controlling:** Small groups keep constant watch on the activities of group members, to ensure whether a member is ready to perform a task. If any members fall behind they can help them carry out the tasks. Groups support members in a variety of ways and ensure that the group attains its goals. Hence, it becomes an effective tool to control members.

Group Maintenance Functions

Group maintenance functions relate to sustaining the group for a long time. Some of the functions are setting up norms, beliefs, feeling and attitudes. These functions provide direction to the group effort. Group maintenance functions of small groups are given below.

(i) **Harmonising:** Small groups can effectively settle differences and reconcile disagreements due to harmonious relationships among members, thus facilitating compromise on important issues. This leads to greater understanding among members and creates a cordial atmosphere for group functioning.

(ii) **Participating:** Small groups encourage members to give suggestions on various important matters. The leader encourages all the members to participate. This creates an environment, where views can be exchanged freely and frankly, enabling members to interact continuously. Participation of members in group decisions ensures commitment and motivation. In addition, they develop their overall personality.

(iii) **Communicating:** Members of small group develop a friendly, warm and considerate environment by effectively sharing and understanding verbal and facial communications. Every member respects the feelings of other members. This leads to mutual agreement among all members.

(iv) **Understanding:** Members of small groups are trained to listen to others effectively. Thus, members understand information in a right spirit and share it among others in the right way. Poor listening leads to a person misunderstanding information, and in turn providing wrong information to others. Proper understanding allows members to expend their energy in attaining the goals. This avoids a number of behavioural problems such as aggression, negative emotions, suspicion and doubt.

(v) **Setting norms:** An important objective of any group is to protect the survival of the group. A group should not disband very frequently. To this end, a mutually agreed code of conduct is required. Small groups are much more effective in setting and enforcing values, ethics, standards, and norms, as compared to large groups.

The Behaviour Process of Small Groups

A member of a small group influences other members, relationships and the behaviour process. The study of factors influencing the behaviour of small groups is essential for effective utilisation of groups in supporting the organisation process. The following paragraphs discuss the mutual influence process in small groups.

Influence of Small Group

A group influences the behaviour of individual members in two ways.

(a) **Influence on group members:** In a small group, every member of the group follows the norms and values of the group. Members of a group always observe the deviators and compel them to follow group norms. Therefore, the expectations of the group exert a greater influence on a member, than his own expectations. For example, if the students' union in your college opposes a certain examination system, you are compelled to abide by its views, even though you may be in favour of the system. Similarly, a manager who is part of a project group is supposed to follow the norms of the group regarding the execution of a project rather than his own plan of action.

(b) **Influence of the leader:** Informal leaders emerge to direct the groups' effort. The style and attitude of the leaders has a major influence on the behaviour, unity and contentment of the members. Charismatic and democratic leaders influence the behaviour of group members more positively than other types of leaders. Hawthorne experiments found that the leaders try to control production by implementing production norms. They encourage members to criticise deviators, for instance, members who intentionally reduced production below the informal norm were criticised as 'chiselers'.

Individual Influences on Behaviour in Small Groups

Members possessing certain personality characteristics guide the activities and behaviour of the group. The major individual influences on small groups are dealt with below.

(a) **Attitudes:** Attitude is a tendency to respond to a person, situation or event in a particular way. It consists of awareness, emotions and behaviour. A member's awareness of others is affected by appraisals, emotions, personal treatment and interest. Attitudes can be changed by continued reinforcements. A change in a member's attitude is possible with the help of such techniques as role-playing and group discussions. Attitude Change Education (ACE) should be undertaken in organisations to change negative attitudes to positive ones.

(b) **Status:** A member's status in a small group has a profound influence on his behaviour. Status is evinced by job title, salary, facilities, authority etc. Members with high status behave in a manner suitable to their status. After attaining a certain status, an individual will consciously try to retain it and prevent others from occupying the position. In doing so, he is likely to limit his interaction with others. For example if a member of a sales team is promoted to team manager, he is likely to keep away the other team members, who were until recently his colleagues, at a distance in order to protect his own position. Sometimes a student, who tops an examination, may not share notes and books with other students. This is because he believes that by doing so, they will become his competitors, and his rank may be affected.

(c) **Culture:** The culture of the individual members influences the behaviour of the group. Members tend to enforce dominant characteristics of their culture on group members. If the other members are weaker, the dominant culture influences the culture of the group.

(d) **Personal space:** It is the physical distance between members of a small group. Members grant or withhold favours to keep other members close or at a distance. For example, in an organisation, a manager may favour a few members of a group by sanctioning leave, granting permission for them to come late or leave early. By doing so he hopes to keep these members close to him and get information about the working of the group.

FINDINGS ON THE BEHAVIOUR OF SMALL GROUPS

Rothelisberger and Kurt Lewin studied the behaviour of small groups extensively. They conducted a series of experiments as part of the Hawthorne studies. The important findings of these experiments are described below.

A. Productivity in small groups increased due to a permissive atmosphere. Friendly relations developed among people.

B. Faster production is achieved in a congenial group rather than in an oppressive group.

C. Group norms are developed and enforced by members of groups. Any member found deviating from the norms is criticised and expelled from the group. The member will not be eligible for the benefits the group enjoys.

D. Members view values and customs for the group as more important than monetary benefits.

E. Groups develop their own integrated social structure and code of conduct, irrespective of the formal organisation.

F. Only members who conform to group norms are allowed to become informal leaders.

G. Group discussions increased commitment.

H. The decisions of the group determine its performance.

I. Acceptance of change is a group function. The degree of acceptance of change depends on the controls and sanctions provided by the group.

PRINCIPLES OF THE DYNAMICS OF SMALL GROUPS

Cartwright propounded the following principles regarding the dynamics of small groups. These principles determine the effectiveness of the group.

(i) **The principle of belonging:** Belonging is the degree of relationships developed among members. The greater the feeling of belonging, the greater the influence members have on one another to accept or reject changes. Changes are introduced effectively when the persons bringing about the change and those adopting the change belong to the same group.

(ii) **The principle of attraction:** The influence of the group on its members depends on the values and norms of the group. Feasible, logical and rational attitudes, values and norms attract members of a group. Attraction leads to a strong influence as members wish to adhere to each other.

(iii) **The principle of prestige:** Recognition by other members in the group and the organisation determine prestige. The greater the prestige, the greater the member's influence on others. For example, a worker, who attains production targets with the least cost, becomes a role model for the group, and exerts a greater influence on other members.

(iv) **The principle of conformity:** Conformity to norms is an important characteristic of group behaviour. Members who do not conform are prevented from seeking benefits due to the group. Hence, strict conformity of members to norms, brings about changes successfully.

(v) **The principle of shared perception:** The greater communication and interaction among members of a small group leads to increased understanding.

(vi) **The principle of the grapevine:** The grapevine is an informal communication system developed in all groups. It is a fast, concise and effective way of sharing information among members of the group. Often the grapevine leads to half-truths, hunches, expectations and inaccurate information. In spite of its drawbacks however, it is a fast way of spreading important news. News carried by the grapevine influences the behaviour of members in a small group. For instance in the matter of change, it provides information on the need for change and consequences of bringing about change. At the same time, it has the capacity to provide information to resist change.

(vii) **The principle of readjustment:** Members of an organisation are required to adapt to various changed situations quickly, before the effectiveness of the organisation is affected. Adjustment and readjustment is a continuous process. Small groups quickly adjust to changes.

MODELS FOR THE BEHAVIOUR OF SMALL GROUPS

Models used in understanding the behaviour of small groups are discussed below:

Homan's Model

George Homan (1950) developed a model to understand complex relationships and behaviour in small groups. This model is also known as the AIS model.

The model assumes the following hypotheses:

a. Individual interaction and interpersonal sentiments are closely related. Favourable sentiments occur between members who like each other.
b. Unfavourable sentiments are developed against members who violate the norms of the group.
c. Unfavourable sentiments are used to punish violators of the norms.
d. Punishment may in turn lead to further defensive or aggressive activities of the violators.

Homan's model, which is explained below, is shown in Figure 22.1.

1. **Background factors:** Background factors are related to the environment of an organisation. These factors influence both the required and emergent behaviour of people. They also determine the level of productivity, satisfaction and personal growth of group members Background factors include the following aspects:
   (a) Physical aspects of work, i.e., technology, job design and working conditions.
   (b) Organisational policies and practices, which include values, assumptions and practices of top management, the behaviour of superiors, formality of procedures, rules, regulations, precedents and reward mechanism.
   (c) External environmental factors, such as economic, political, and cultural factors.
   (d) Personal background of the members of the group, such as previous history of success, status etc.
2. **Required behaviour:** Required behaviour consists of those activities and sentiments, which are an essential part of the group process. The elements of required behaviour include:
   (a) Required activities: Activities that group members must perform are required activities. They are determined by the style of leadership, nature of the job, degree of technology and external constraints.
   (b) Required interaction: This is the interpersonal interaction required to complete tasks

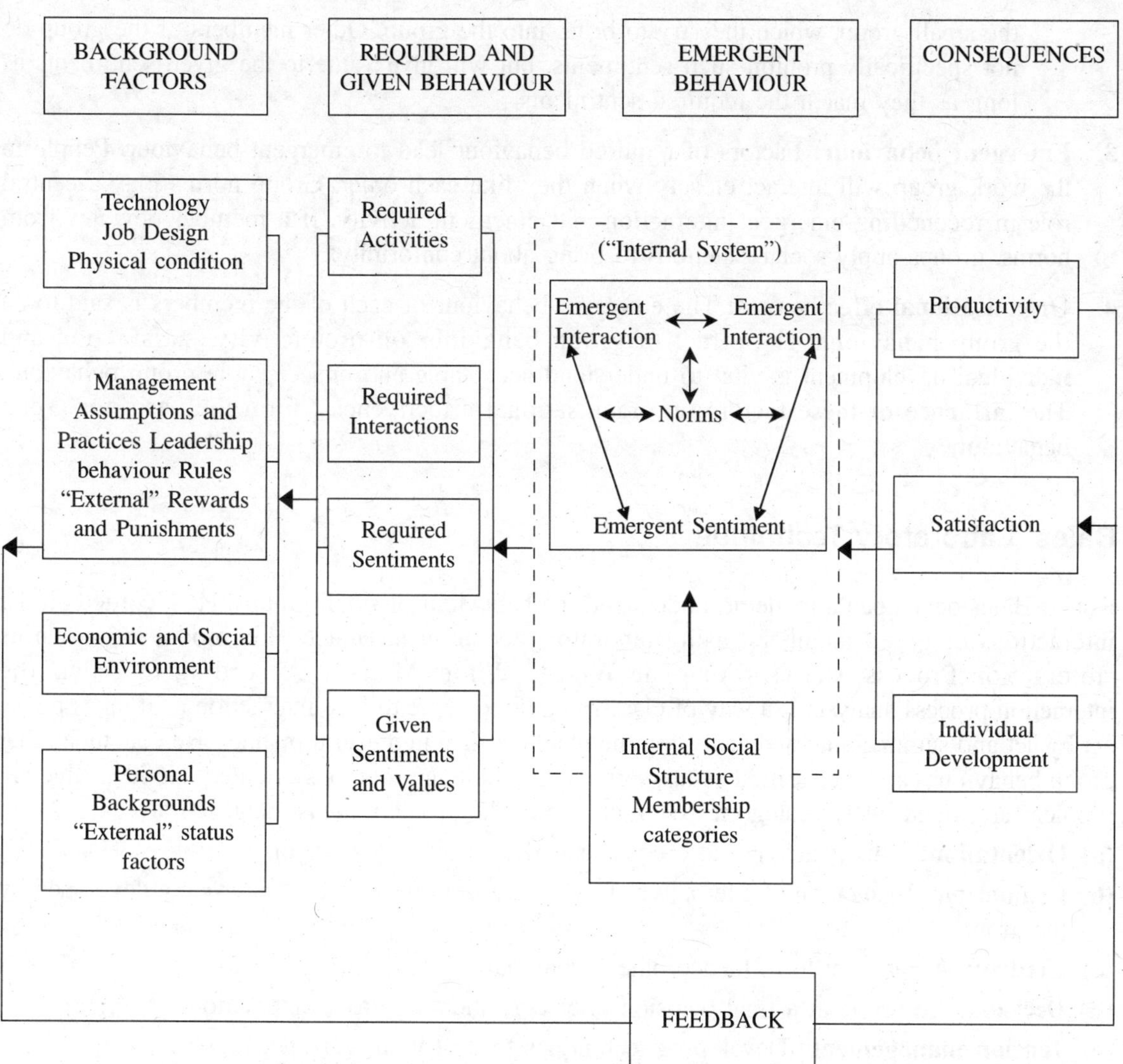

Figure 22.1: Homan's Model of Work Group Behaviour

Source: Gray L. Jerry and Starke A. Fredrick, Organizational Behavior: Concepts and Applications, Second Edition, Charles E. Merrill Publishing Company, Columbus, 1980, page, 244.

successfully. For example, the job description provides both technical and behavioural interaction expected on the job.

(c) *Required sentiments:* The individual feelings, attitudes, values, opinions and beliefs one must have to perform the job effectively. Different jobs require different sentiments, which are developed by the group.

(d) *Given sentiments:* Beliefs, values and attitudes possessed by the individual members of the small group, which they try to bring into the group. Other members of the group do not specifically prohibit such sentiments, but will give value to the given sentiments as long as they match the required sentiments.

3. **Emergent behaviour:** Factors of required behaviour lead to emergent behaviour. People in the work group will interact closely when they like each other. Group norms play a central role in reconciling emergent interaction and emergent activity. If a member deviates from norms, groups apply social sanctions to bring about conformity.

4. **Organisational effectiveness:** The emergent behaviour of each of the members is said to be the group behaviour. The effect of group behaviour on productivity, satisfaction and individual development is vital to understand acceptable and unacceptable group behaviour. The influence of these factors on organisational effectiveness, form the basis for group behaviour.

Bales' Laboratory Technique

Robert Bales developed a model to understand the behaviour of small groups. He recorded all the interactions of group members, using laboratory techniques. Hence, this model is known as 'Interaction Process Analysis' or 'The Who-to-Whom Matrix'. According to Bales, the interaction process analysis is a way of classifying direct, face to face interaction as it takes place, act by act and summarising and analysing the resultant data in a useful manner. He concluded that group behaviour can be classified as task-oriented and human relations oriented. He identified six problem areas and twelve categories of interaction. The problem areas identified are:

(a) **Orientation:** This is arriving at a consensus definition of a situation.

(b) **Evaluation:** Evaluation of alternatives takes place in terms of the value system developed by the group.

(c) **Control:** An attempt to influence other behaviour.

(d) **Decision:** To arrive at a final decision after consolidating group interaction.

(e) **Tension management:** Developing techniques to deal with work tensions.

(f) **Integration:** Maintaining cohesion.

Bales' group interaction process analysis model is shown in Figure 22.2.

The basis for developing the model is the two-dimensional theory of leadership. The behaviour of group members is divided into two behavioural areas: (i) task area and (ii) socio-emotional area. The model assumes that a group proceeds in a distinct direction in arriving at decisions, and that different individuals occupy different roles to facilitate this process. Hence, the model provides feedback to members on behavioural interaction. This helps to evaluate the behaviour and performance, and allows the group to take the necessary steps to improve performance.

Conclusions that emerged out of the Bales' interaction experiment are as follows:

i. Groups without formal leaders show tendency of participation.

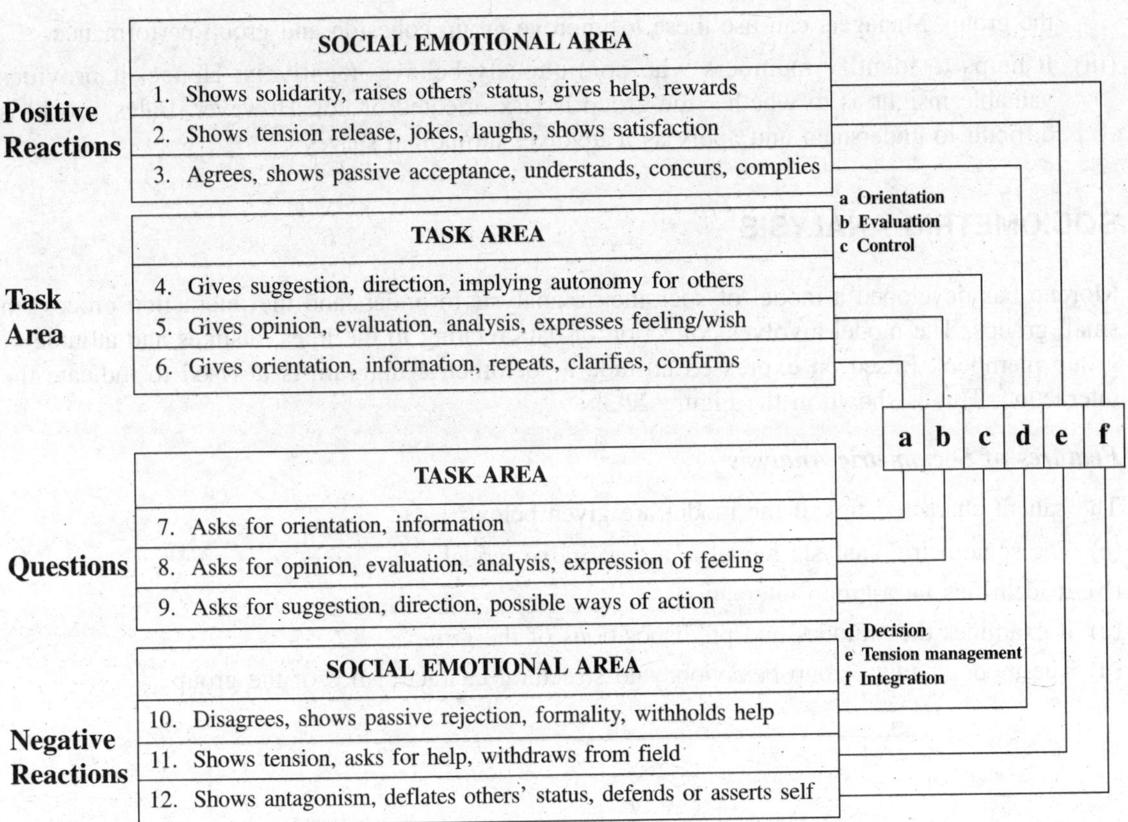

Figure 22.2: Bales' group interaction process analysis model

Source: Gray L. Jerry and Starke A. Fredrick, Organizational Behavior: Concepts and Applications, Second Edition, Charles E. Merrill Publishing Company, Columbus, 1980, page 246.

ii. The size of the group determines the limit of face to face communication.
iii. The person who provides continuous guidance to the group becomes a 'group task specialist' and 'ideal man'.
iv. A person who is liked by all the members emerges as a 'human relations specialist'.
v. Groups with a task specialist and a human relations specialist, are most effective.

Functions of Bales' Laboratory Technique

Bales techniques are mostly useful in analysing the behaviour of small groups in experimental settings. Some of the advantages of this model are given below.

(i) It is useful in analysing the behaviour of a committee in the process of making a decision.
(ii) It helps managers to study communication patterns, role relationships, and status systems of

the group. Managers can use these to improve group cohesion and group performance.

(iii) It helps to identify members who continuously behave negatively. Hence, it provides valuable insight as to whether the group is task-oriented or not. However, Bales' model is difficult to understand and apply as it involves attitudinal survey.

SOCIOMETRIC ANALYSIS

Moreno has developed a model of sociometric analysis to understand the interaction process in small groups. The model involves collection of data relating to the likes, dislikes and attitude of group members. Based on expressed attitude a sociometric diagram is devised to indicate the interaction. This is shown in the Figure 22.3.

Features of Sociometric Analysis

The salient characteristics of the model are given below:

(a) The sociometric analysis model is a descriptive model.

(b) It identifies intra-group interactions.

(c) It examines the attitudes and predispositions of the group.

(d) The model studies group behaviour and structural characteristics of the group.

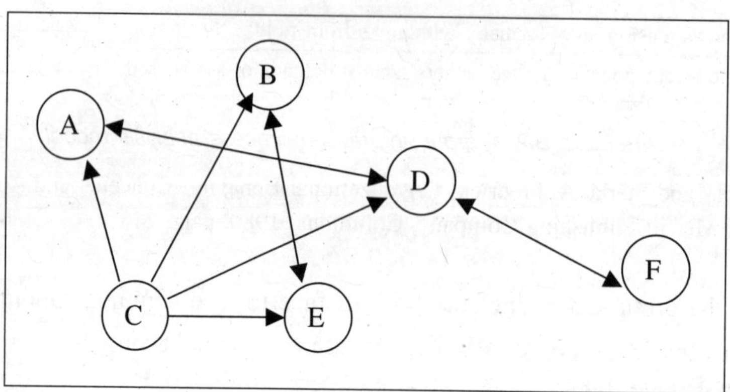

Figure 22.3: Model of sociometric analysis. Single-headed arrows denote one way interaction and double-headed arrows indicate mutual interaction. It can be seen that A and D, D and F, and B and E have mutual interaction, whereas, B does not have direct interaction. However, 'C' interacts with all the members. Hence, 'C' is liked by all.

Functions of Sociometric Analysis

(a) Sociometric analysis is useful in identifying an informal leader of the group.

(b) It helps in understanding informal channels of communication and potential intra-group conflict.

(c) It is specifically applied to examine the effectiveness of an organisation and the morale of group members.

However, this model is difficult to use and has very limited applications due to difficulties in collecting data on likes and dislikes, which are subject to change over time and in different situations.

SUMMARY

Small groups perform task functions and group maintenance functions in an organisation. In a small group, each individual exerts an influence on the group as well as on other members of the group. In turn, the group exerts an influence on the members through group norms, beliefs and psychological sanctions. Rothelisberger, Kurt Lewin, Homan and Bales are some of the important contributors to the study of dynamics of small groups. Some of the principles of small group dynamics are belonging, attraction, prestige, conformity, shared perception, grapevine and readjustment. Homan's model of small group dynamics provided background factors that determine the required behaviour of group members, which leads to emergent behaviour. Emergent behaviour influences the members' productivity, satisfaction and morale. Bales' laboratory technique identified orientation, evaluation, control, decision, tension management and integration as problem areas in behaviour of a group. It is useful in experimental settings. Sociometric analysis, developed by Moreno is a descriptive model. It analyses the likes and dislikes of members of group to form a socio-gram. This model helps in examining leadership and effectiveness of groups.

Key words:

- **Personal space:** It is the physical distance between members of small group.
- **Sociometric diagram:** A figure devised to indicate the interaction of members of a small group.
- **Task functions:** They are related to the accomplishment of specific tasks assigned to small groups.

23. COMMUNICATION BEHAVIOUR

This chapter enables you:

- *To define the term communication*
- *To appraise the characteristics of organisational communication*
- *To understand exchange of information*
- *To understand the relevance of communication in the functioning of organisations*
- *To classify organisational communication*
- *To distinguish between formal and informal communication*
- *To identify the reasons for misunderstandings in communication*
- *To learn strategies to improve understanding*

The structure of the chapter is as follows:

- Introduction
- Definition of communication
- The communication process
- Functions of communication
- Classification of communication
- Barriers of communication
- Improving understanding in communication
- Summary
- Key words

CHAPTER 23

Communication Behaviour

Common-sense in communication is most uncommon

Once Dr. Sarvepalli Radhakrishnan, the great scholar and teacher was asked to distinguish between a stationmaster and a schoolmaster. He instantaneously replied 'the former minds the train, the latter trains minds'. Yet, another classic incident describes the significance of environment in communication. In this example, simply common sense of the great archer, Arjuna in replying made him the great. Dronacharya led the disciples to a forest one day to test the proficiency in archery. He made his disciples to stand near a big tree and showed the target. He instructed all of them to aim at the target. By following the custom, he first asked Duryodhana to tell him what he could see. He replied that he is able to see the tree and the beautiful green leaves. The rest, all except Arjuna, gave similar reply. Later, the turn of Arjuna came. He said he is unable to see anything... Dronacharya was astonished. Arjuna slowly replied.... Except the target (eyeball of the bird). One can understand how commonsense plays a vital role than anything else.

INTRODUCTION

Communication is exchange of information between two or more people. It is the lifeblood of the organisation. Just as blood flows to every organ in the human body, communication flows to every unit and person in an organisation. It is the basis for human activity. Every person in an organisation has to communicate with his co-workers, superiors, subordinates and the general public. Managers are involved in passing on orders and directions of the higher level management, clarifying policies and strategies of the top management and giving detailed instructions to their subordinates. Moreover, they are involved in reporting the subordinates' performance to their superiors. Communicating with customers, dealers and the general public are integral functions of managers. In all these functions, they transmit messages, ideas, opinions, feelings etc. It is therefore vital that the message is understood properly, otherwise misunderstandings are possible. Therefore, communication occupies an important place in any organisation, and more so in the context of management functions. It is often described as the thread running through the garland. As the thread holds every flower, communication holds all the activities together. Without communication, no organisational activity can take place. Communication can be written or verbal. In the latter case, facial expressions play an important part in conveying the message. Since communication takes place between people, there is a possibility of misunderstanding due to certain barriers or gateways in the communication process. These barriers are due to language, which is the main barrier, organisational structure and the human environment are the others. However, it is not difficult to overcome them. Proper planning, use of appropriate semantics and understanding the human environment make communication effective. After studying this chapter you should be able to communicate effectively.

DEFINITION OF COMMUNICATION

Communication is the process of transmitting ideas, facts, opinions, feelings, behaviour and information. The person sending the information is the 'sender' and the person receiving it is the 'receiver.' Communication between them should promote understanding. Otherwise, it leads to problems of misunderstanding. Thus, one needs to understand the nature and process of communication. **Chester I. Barnard** stated that, "*Communication is the centre nerve of management, and an executive is in the centre of communication.*" Certain important definitions of communication are presented below:

> According to **Billy J. Hodge,** *'communication is an attempt to achieve as complete and as accurate an understanding as possible between two or more people. It is an act characterised by a desire in one or more individuals to exchange information, ideas or feelings. The desire is implemented by using symbols, signs, actions and pictures as well as other verbal and non-verbal elements in speaking and writing.'*
>
> **Herbert A. Simon** described communication as, *'any process whereby decisional premises are transmitted from one member of an organisation to another.'*
>
> **Koontz** and **O'Donnel** have described communication as *'the transfer of information from one person to another whether or not it effects confidence.'*

Louis A. Allen defined communication as, *'the sum of all the things one person does when he wants to create understanding in the mind of another. It is a bridge of meaning. It involves a systematic and continuous process of telling, listening and understanding.'*

Mc. Farland described communication as *'the process of meaningful interaction among human beings. More specifically, it is the process by which meanings are presented and understandings are reached among human beings.'*

Newman and **Summer** defined communication as *'an exchange of facts, ideas, opinions, or emotions by two or more persons.'*

Theo Haimann defined communication as *'the process of passing information and understanding from one person to another. It is the process of imparting ideas and making oneself understood by others.'*

The above definitions reveal the following characteristics of communication:

1. Communication is a social process. It is transmission of a message between two or more persons.
2. It is a natural instinct. Individuals have a natural desire to communicate.
3. It is intended to promote understanding.
4. Communication is a process. It involves persons, technology and environment.
5. Communication is a pervasive function. It runs as a thread in every managerial function.
6. It is a system consisting of input, process and output. It is influenced by the human environment.
7. Communication is continuous. Every person in the organisation spends most of his or her time in communicating.
8. Communication can be formal or informal.

THE COMMUNICATION PROCESS

Communication is a process in which a person sends information to other persons, by encoding his thoughts and feelings. In the process of sending the message, he uses a channel, which may be words, expressions, facial expression or technology. The process of communication is shown in Figure 23.1, which reveals the following elements of communication:

1. **Sender:** Sender is a person or group of persons who intends to transmit information.
2. **Ideas:** Communication takes place when the sender wants to convey an idea or ideas. Thus, ideas, thoughts and feelings constitute the subject matter of communication. These can be in the form of opinions, attitudes, views, orders or suggestions etc.

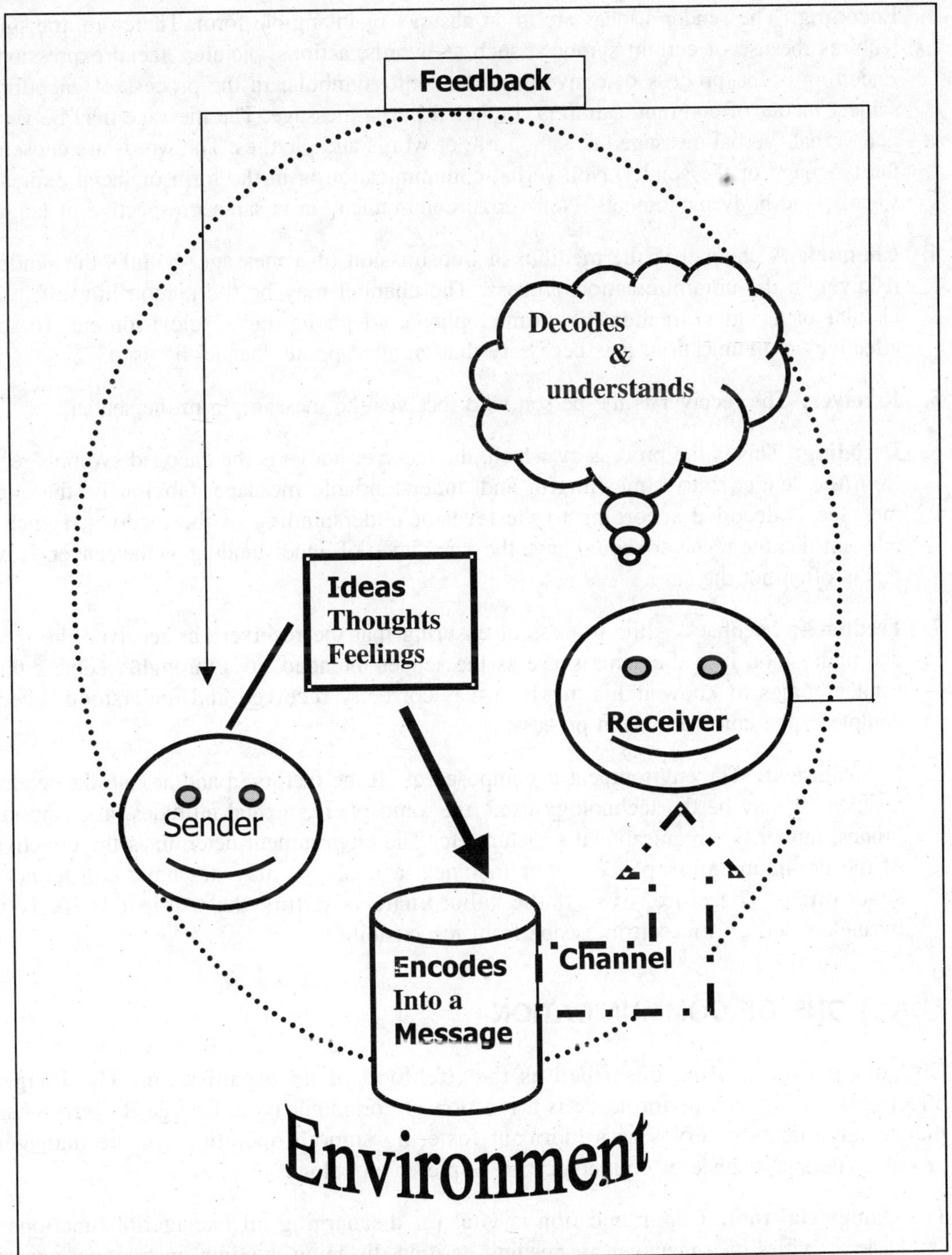

Figure 23.1: Communication Process

3. **Encoding:** The sender's ideas are in an abstract or intangible form. Therefore, transmission requires the use of certain symbols, such as, words, actions, pictures, facial expressions etc. Encoding is the process of converting ideas into symbols. In the process of encoding, the subject matter of communication is converted into a message. The message may be verbal or non-verbal. Verbal message takes the form of words and pictures. The words are chosen from the language of the sender. Non-verbal communication is in the form of facial expressions, signals, and body movements. Non-verbal communication is same irrespective of language.

4. **Channel:** A channel is the medium of transmission of a message. It links the sender and receiver in the communication process. The channel may be the person himself, a letter, circular or technical medium like a microphone, telephone, radio, television etc. To achieve effective communication, it is necessary that an appropriate channel be used.

5. **Receiver:** The receiver is the person who receives the message from the sender.

6. **Decoding:** This is the process by which, the receiver converts the encoded symbols received from the sender, into a meaningful and understandable message. Obviously, the encoded message is decoded according to the level of understanding of the receiver. Hence, it is relevant that the receiver should have the same level of understanding as the sender. However this is often not the case.

7. **Feedback:** Feedback is the process of ensuring that the receiver has received the message and understood it in the same sense as the sender intended. It is through feedback that the sender comes to know if his message was correctly received and understood. Feedback completes the communication process.

8. **Environment:** The environment is composed of all the factors in and around the sender and receiver. It may be the technology used, the atmosphere, mental attitudes, association with groups, authority, organisational structure etc. The environment determines the effectiveness of the communication process. For instance, a manager may not have confidence in a subordinate. Therefore, even if the subordinate is telling the truth, it is likely to be misunderstood as a reason to escape from responsibility.

FUNCTIONS OF COMMUNICATION

Communication is often described as the lifeblood of an organisation. The image and effectiveness of human performance is a function of communication. George R. Terry observed that, communication serves as a lubricant fostering smooth operations of the management process. The significance of communication is presented below:

1. **Managerial tool:** Communication is vital for discharging all managerial functions. The basic activities of a manager are reading, writing, listening, guiding, instructing, approving, reporting performance and reprimanding. Managers often spend about 90 percent of their time in communicating with subordinates, peers, superiors and persons outside the

organisation. The effectiveness of a manager depends significantly on his ability to communicate with these parties.

2. **Making decisions:** Communication is a primary requirement in making decisions. In this process, a manager is required to collect, analyse and understand a lot of information, in order to avoid making decisions intuitively. In the absence of effective communication in the organisation, it may be difficult to take any meaningful decision.

3. **Coordination:** Coordination is the essence of the management process. In large organisations, the work is executed by a number of persons. The larger the size of organisation the greater the degree of specialisation and division of work. Coordination requires mutual understanding of organisational goals, how they are to be achieved and the relationship between different jobs. This is possible through proper communication.

4. **Effective leadership:** This is the process of influencing subordinates to achieve the goals of the organisation. A leader directs subordinates by communicating with them. The attitude of communication determines the style of leadership. A leader having a positive attitude towards communication is democratic, and is more readily accepted. With good interpersonal communication, a leader becomes more effective.

5. **Motivation and morale:** Motivation is the process of driving subordinates towards goals. This may require changing their attitudes. Addressing and changing attitudes is possible through communication. Good communication leads to positive morale of the subordinates.

6. **Cooperation:** To conduct operations effectively, it is necessary that all persons cooperate. A prudent management will try to see that all persons cooperate, to achieve organisational goals. Cooperation is possible when employees are able to communicate freely and fairly.

7. **Industrial harmony:** In any organisation, the management and employees should work together harmoniously. They should be able to share their problems in an environment of trust and confidence. Otherwise, misunderstandings can occur, that disturbs the industrial peace. Two-way communication can promote mutual understanding between the employees and the management.

8. **Effective functioning:** Communication is the basis for all organisational interactions. A manager's basic function is to coordinate the physical, material, financial and human resources of an organisation into an efficient and active working unit that achieves common objectives. Human resources are crucial, and only proper communication can link them appropriately. Herbert G. Hicks pointed out that, communication is the basis for any organisation's existence from birth of the organisation throughout its continuing life. When communication stops, an organisation's activity ceases.

Thus, communication is the essence of human relations in an organisation.

CLASSIFICATION OF COMMUNICATION

In organisations, communication takes place in a variety of forms. Managers use various channels and forms suitable to the situation. The various forms of communication can be classified as follows:

Based on the formality:

1. Formal communication
2. Informal communication

Based on modes:

1. Verbal communication
2. Non-verbal communication

Based on direction

1. Upward communication
2. Downward communication
3. Horizontal communication
4. Circular communication

These are discussed below:

Formal or informal communication

Formal communication in an organisation takes place by following the rules and regulations. These are mostly in the form of written orders, circulars, notices, minutes and manuals. Formal communication is associated with levels of authority. For instance, the Managing Director of the company issues directions to the General Manager by virtue of his authority and position. This is known as formal communication.

Informal communication is in the form of unwritten rules, norms and taboos. It does not follow any formalities. It is based on informal relationships that exist among employees. The informal channel of communication is known as the grapevine. It spreads gossip, half-truths, opinions and preferences. The communication can be in the form of facial expressions, gestures, smiles or even silence. For example, a supervisor may nod his head and smile as an act of approval. If the management decides to declare a bonus, then it is likely that news of this will spread through the grapevine, long before it is formally communicated.

The grapevine has a number of positive functions in an organisation. It is fast and convenient; it fulfills the basic desire of human beings to communicate; it is used to communicate certain information that cannot be officially communicated.

Its limitations are: It is not an official channel, therefore, it is not reliable; no action can be taken based on informal communication. Communication through the grapevine may be erratic, hence, it is not dependable; there is a possibility that the information is distorted in the process of transmission from person to person; it is difficult to locate the origin of such communication, therefore responsibility cannot be placed on a specific person.

However, informal communication is inevitable in an organisation, and managers cannot escape it. The only solution is to minimise its negative effects.

Verbal or written, and non-verbal communication

Verbal communication is important in any organisation. Formal communication is mostly verbal or written. Orders, circulars, directions, office notes, interviews, personal discussions, counseling, public speeches, audio visual aids like slides and movies and plant broadcasts are examples of verbal communication. Some other examples of verbal or written communication are in-house journals, newspapers, bulletin boards, official letters, memos, reports and forms, manuals and handbooks, posters, payroll inserts, annual reports, written grievances, suggestions, attitude questionnaires, newspaper inserts etc.

Non-verbal communication is in the form of signals, facial expressions, behaviour attributes, gestures and body movements. Factory whistles, nodding the head, pointing with a finger, facial expressions of anger, happiness, anxiety and other emotions are examples of non-verbal communication.

In an organisation, there is combined use of verbal and non-verbal communication in all situations, so both forms are relevant.

Upward, downward, horizontal and circular communication

Communication can be upward, downward, horizontal or circular based on its direction. In an organisation, when directions are issued from superiors down to subordinates, it is said to be downward communication. Upward communication flows up from subordinates to their superiors, for example, assistant managers report subordinates' performance to the managers. Horizontal communication takes place between two persons of the same rank, for example, the Production and Finance Manager, discussing the allocation of the budget. Circular communication, also called wheel communication, is between employees of different ranks. An employee in the Finance department communicating with an employee of the Marketing department is called circular communication.

BARRIERS OF COMMUNICATION

Attentive listening: The greatest art

Communication involves both listening and talking. Listening is a great art. The communicator must pay attention to the listener. Similarly, the listener's acceptance of the other's communication is the essence of effective understanding. The cognitive message, hidden feelings and ideas have to be grasped properly. Dr. Robert McHenry, stated that, 'a good communicator knows how to listen and use probing questions'. Those skills can be picked up quite quickly. However, learning to listen takes time and patience. The speaker should encourage questions from the listener and reply patiently. Developing inter-personal communication with empathy reinforces confidence in a person. It is important to maintain balanced emotions. Is inter-personal communication possible without emotions? Can we find a person who listens without getting angry? Can everyone properly appreciate the language? How much personal ego should be sacrificed for effective listening?

Communication is an effort to make another person understand the intentions of the sender correctly. If a person clearly understands what another person is saying it can bring about a change in behaviour. For example, if your friend does not understand what you are saying, he or she tends to interrupt. This acts as a barrier in communication. In organisations, employees may also find it difficult to exactly communicate what they want to. This is again due to communication barriers, which can prevent or provoke a person's action. Barriers in communication are classified as below.

Organisational barriers

Organisational barriers are created by the management, and are common in an organisation. They arise due to the natural limitations of organisational structure, which changes with changes in the environment. Some common reasons for the breakdown or distortion in communication due to structural factors are as follows.

1. **Specialisation:** Specialisation obstructs communication, as a person tends to speak in technical jargon, when he talks about his work. The other person fails to understand, as he is ignorant of the jargon.
2. **Structure and procedures:** In every organisation a number of procedures are described for official communication. This is called the 'scalar chain'. Any deviation in the scalar chain is viewed seriously. Thus, it acts as an obstacle. For instance, the Managing Director should communicate through the General Manager to the functional managers. If the M.D. communicates directly to the functional managers, it leads to a misunderstanding by the General Manager.

3. **Relationship between power, authority and status:** Defining authority, responsibility and accountability of employees creates the structure of the organisation. These factors give status to an employee. For example, a General Manager speaks very politely to the Managing Director out of respect for his position. Very often, as persons rise in the hierarchy of the organisation, they develop a false ego and tend to become less communicative. Their subordinates will tell them only what they want to hear. Thus, they often deny valuable feedback, because they do not like to listen to hard truths.
4. **Physical distance:** Employees working in units or departments, which are physically far apart, find it difficult to communicate easily.
5. **Transmission through several links:** In a formal organisation, information passes through various levels. Ignoring any level is not permitted. Therefore, it takes a long time to send and receive a message. Thus, communication is delayed. This acts as a barrier in the process of communication.

Semantics

Semantics relates to the language and use of words. The language of the sender and receiver should be the same, otherwise, misunderstandings will arise. Semantics also relates to terminology of the language. In effective communication, conceptual clarity is essential. For instance, certain terms and concepts like democracy, labour, management, profit and efficiency have different meanings for different people. For effective communication the listener has to understand the message in the sense the sender intended. Often however, the message is interpreted according to the listener's experience and environment. This leads to barriers in communication. The importance of semantics can be better stated as follows, 'it is not only words but actions, implications and the entire situational context that produce understanding.' Semantic barriers arise due to the following reasons:

1. Poorly expressed message
2. Improper translation
3. Lack of clarified assumptions
4. Professional language

In a written message, the text is a very important aspect. The use of words in writing the message, the composition of the message, concepts and jargon can all pose a problem. Faulty translations can convey the wrong meaning. Lack of clarity and precision results in blunders, which may have far reaching consequences. Faulty interpretation results either from lack of understanding or because of undue emphasis given to the message communicated. It is essential for the sender to communicate the importance or urgency of the message in order to elicit the correct response from the receiver.

Behavioural Barriers

Behavioural barriers relate to the personality of employees. Perception, attitudes, mindset and motivation influence the communication process. The right attitude towards communication has a positive influence on people. Certain behavioural barriers are described below:

1. **Bypassing:** Bypassing is ignoring the semantics and persons. It occurs when the sender ignores the fact that the words can have similar meanings or sound the same, and that the receiver may understand them differently. For example, the words, align and alien, sound alike, but 'align' means to arrange in a line, and 'alien' means foreign. Bypassing also arises when a level of authority is dropped out of the communication chain.
2. **Allness:** Allness relates to the perception process of a person. Perception relates to understanding a person, thing or situation. It is a human mental process. Allness occurs due to special perceptions, and perception of situations and persons. For example, if an employee is known to be a liar, the manager will not try to listen to him even if he is telling the truth.
3. **Evaluation tendencies:** Tendency is the permanent behaviour of a person. It relates to the formation of attitudes. When certain permanent impressions are formed, evaluation takes place according to the impressions. Evaluation tendencies arise because of the following.
   i. Confusion of facts
   ii. 'Either or' thinking
   iii. Bias or prejudice
   iv. Frozen evaluation
4. **Blinkers:** Blinkers are small leather pieces that are used to prevent a horse from looking to the side. In communication, this term relates to the tendency to evaluate a person or situation without taking the environment and other factors into consideration. For example, a manager, who evaluates everything according to the rules, without taking the situation into account is said to be using blinkers. Another amusing example occurred when a criminal was sentenced to death by hanging. As the sentence was being carried out, the knot broke and the person fell and suffered injuries. The jailer considered that his work was done, and the verdict of the judge had been implemented. The culprit was released because he survived the punishment. This is an example of understanding communication with blinkers. Interestingly after this incident the death sentence was changed to 'hanged till death'.
5. **Thalamic reactions:** The hypothalamus in the brain is responsible for a person's actions and reactions. Thalamic reactions are instantaneous reactions shown by a person without listening to others.

Situational Barriers

Situational barriers are oriented towards unforeseen events. They arise due to the demands of the situation. The environment of the sender and receiver has important implications on the communication. Situational barriers relate to the following:

i. Poor listening and memory retention.
ii. Lack of proper communication planning.
iii. Vague or poorly clarified assumptions about the person and situation.
iv. Distrust, threats and fear.
v. Insufficient period of adjustment.

An examination of the reasons for misunderstandings reveals that most of them relate to the attitude of the person. Therefore, most organisations emphasise that it is necessary to understand personal relationships, for effective inter personal communication.

IMPROVING UNDERSTANDING IN COMMUNICATION

Communicating with emotion

Communication depends a lot on the attitude of the communicator rather than just the language. However, language cannot be overlooked. Proper use of language appropriate to the situation is necessary to achieve effective inter personal communication. Attitude is related to the intent of the individual. Certain persons possess a positive intention to communicate, whereas others withdraw from communication. Style and expression are important factors in communication. Style is related to the behavioural dimensions of the communicator. Personality, perception, values and ethics determine behaviour. A good impression encourages interaction, whereas a poor impression acts as a barrier. Developing a communication wheel and amenities to disseminate information, facilitates a sound communication process. Facial expressions communicate internal emotions effectively.

Emotions can make communication difficult. In the Bhagvat Gita, Lord Krishna says, "dhyâyato visayân pumsah, sangas tesû 'pajâyate, sangât samjâyate kâmah, kâmât krodho bhijâyate, krodhâd bhavati sammohah, smrtibhramsâd buddhinâso baddinâsât pranasyati' (Srimathbhagvat Gita, Chapter II, Verses 62 & 63). That is 'When a man thinks of objects, attachment for them arises; from attachment desire is born; from desire arises anger; from anger comes delusion; from delusion loss of memory; from loss of memory the destruction of discrimination from which he perishes.' Thus, for good communication both the communicator and listener should be emotionally balanced. A smile relieves tension, and encourages expression. No other living being can smile, it costs nothing, but can convey a lot.

Barriers in communication are human problems and most of them can be overcome. Certain managerial strategies to overcome the barriers of communication are presented below:

1. Communication planning

For effective communication it is necessary to understand the purpose of the message, and have clarity of thoughts and ideas. For example, if a manager is entrusted with the responsibility of inculcating good health habits in the workers, telling them about the organisation will not help the listeners. The purpose of the communication is not fulfilled. In good communication planning, the sender should be attuned to the listeners' needs. The message should be clear, concise and to the point.

2. Language

Difficulties arise in communication because of semantics. As already noted semantics relates to language and grammar. Today a manager has to work with people from different regions and different countries. Developing linguistic skills, requires hard work. For example in the English language, about 500 of the most frequently used words have on an average 28 separate meanings. This makes communication complex. Regional variations also make lot of difference in communication. Consider for example, the word '*kudu*,' which means to drink in Tamil or Kannada. However, the same word has an obnoxious meaning in Telugu. Phonetics is also important in communication. For example the Hindi spoken by the Railway Minister Laluprasad Yadav, while presenting the budget for 2005-06, caused much humour in Parliament. Managers should follow certain guidelines in communicating. The language must be direct, simple, meaningful and easily understood. They need to understand the grammar and phonetics, otherwise it can lead to misunderstandings.

3. Understanding the environment

Both the physical and human environment are important to achieve effective communication. The message should be adequate and appropriate to the situation. The sender should be aware of unintentional meanings, as intentions can also be communicated through expressions. Consider a situation that actually took place in an organisation. In one organisation, the meeting of the Board was fixed on a certain date. Preparation of the tentative minutes and other important information to be rendered in the board meeting was assigned to an officer. A woman assistant is required to do all this. As the woman assistant is not very regular and effective in her duties, the officer had a poor perception of her. However, at this moment he wanted to request her to spend some more time in the office to assist him to prepare necessary information. The communication went on like this: "See madam, I request you to spend your time in the office beyond sex o'clock (in fact six o'clock was mis-pronounced like this) and assist me to complete everything for tomorrow". The female employee immediately started weeping and lodged a complaint against the officer for sexual harassment. The officer had to face an enquiry over this matter. In the enquiry, it was revealed that the officer has a stammering problem that made him unintentionally and without recognizing, utter the work sex instead of six. A lot of evidence was to be submitted to the enquiry officer to plead his innocence. The fact is that the environment had created all the misunderstanding coupled with the attitude of the officer and woman employee.

4. *Effective listening*

Listening is an art. Many people are great orators. However, when it comes to listening they become impatient. Effective communication requires effective listening, only then will one be able to hold the interest of the receiver. Remember the words. 'Talk less. God wants us to speak less and listen more. Otherwise, he would not have bestowed us with only one mouth but two ears. The more one speaks, the more he is likely to expose himself and in the process, to hurt others and create aberrations'. Today organisations lay emphasis on the practice of CRM. This requires employees, to listen to workers, suppliers, peers and customers, patiently, effectively and without becoming emotional. Ford Motors has started a system wherein the Chief Executive Officer regularly meets supervisors and workers, and encourages them to give their views on the work environment and make suggestions. In the Elly and Lilly Company, sales persons are allowed to give their views on the company in a meeting organised once in six months. The top officials observe the interaction through CCTV and reward employees, who have given worthwhile suggestions and comments. This leads to the development of learning organisations. Developing learning organisations requires developing the habit of effective listening in employees. In the words of Peter Drucker, downward communication can work effectively only when the upward communication is established effectively. This underlines the importance of effective listening by managers. A good listener becomes a cogent communicator and a cogent communicator becomes a successful manager. In fact, encouraging communicating and listening attentively gives invaluable information for further communication. Unfortunately, many managers are not good listeners, and this eventually reflects in their performance.

5. *Redundancy*

Redundancy is repetition in communication. As a rule communication should be short, crisp and to the point. Repetitions lead to boredom and disinterest. However, the same thing may have to be repeated to different groups or individuals, so that the message reaches everybody. If there are concepts and words, which are difficult to understand, they should of course be repeated. If all the subordinates are prudent listeners and understand the message in one instance, it is not necessary for a manager to repeat the same instructions, as it will only cause boredom, but in other cases, if the subordinates are not fast learners, the manager has to repeat himself. To hold the interest of his listeners, a good manager will devise ways and means of making the message pleasing. Managers should recognise that some amount of redundancy is helpful. In fact, in our traditional '*gurukulas*,' learning took place by repetition. This is often the case today.

6. *Follow up*

Feedback is essential for effective communication. If the sender wants to elicit the intended response, he should confirm that his message is properly understood, by following up after communication has taken place. Regular interaction, review meetings, encouraging subordinates to talk to superiors, performance reviews, and appraisal reports are some of the techniques to obtain comments on communication.

Some other tips to achieve effective communication are:

1. Get up from your seat, when someone enters your room, irrespective of whether the person is your junior or senior. This shows respect for the person and creates a favourable impression.
2. Greet the other person; it prepares him to listen to you positively.
3. Welcome the person with a smile, and offer him or her a seat.
4. Show pleasant facial expressions.
5. Show your appreciation for meeting them. Tell them it was pleasant to spend some time in their company. This will motivate others to share their experiences with you.
6. Confidence in communication: Communication has to be mutually interesting.
7. Communication training: Rehearse what you want to say. Even great orators unconsciously rehearse their speeches.
8. Address reality: Do not speak on subjects in which you are ignorant.
9. Allow people to change their opinions.
10. If you are busy, always give an alternative time.
11. End the interaction with appreciation. Tell the person, you have learnt a lot by talking to him and look forward to meeting him again.
12. Thank the person profusely from the core of your heart.

Interpersonal communication is vital for developing understanding and harmony in an organisation. A manager acts as a link in the communication process, and his role is significant in transmitting strategies and policies to the operational staff, in a way in which they can understand them. Free flow of communication among various levels is of utmost importance for an effective organisation. Interpersonal communication provides a way to understand the potential of employees.

SUMMARY

Communication is a natural and intrinsic desire of people. It relates to the process of exchanging views, feelings and opinions between two or more persons in a situation. Thus, people and the environment are vital in the process of communication. The person sending the message is the sender and the person receiving it is the receiver. When the sender has certain thoughts, he encodes them to form a meaningful message, sends the message to the receiver through a channel and the receiver decodes the message and understands it. According to Chester I. Barnard, communication is the central nerve of an organisation, with the manager at the centre. Communication is a basic managerial tool. It helps in making decisions, coordination, motivation and cooperation. It enables the manager to be an effective leader. In organisations, various forms of communication are used. These are formal, informal, verbal and non-verbal. According to the direction of communication, it is classified as upward, downward, horizontal and circular. Informal communication is also known as a grapevine. It is the fastest mode of communication, but there is a danger of communicating gossip and half-truths.

There are a number of barriers to effective communication and understanding. Barriers in communication result from the structure and process of the organisation, language, behaviour and the situation. Specialisation, procedural aspects, power, authority and status relationships, physical distance, and existence of several levels of authority are some of the structural and process related barriers. Language or semantic barriers relate to poorly expressed messages, improper translation, lack of clarified assumptions and technical or professional language. Perception, sentiments, attitudes and personality are behaviour-related barriers. Bypassing, allness, blinkering, evaluation tendencies, and thalamic reaction cause instability in the behaviour resulting in misunderstanding the communication. Similarly, the situation determines the effectiveness of communication. Poor listening, lack of proper communication planning, vague assumptions, distrust, threat, fear, and insufficient time for adjustment, arise because of the situation. In spite of the obstacles managers need to achieve effective communication. Effective communication results when the receiver understands the message in the sense it was intended by the sender. Communication planning, use of appropriate language, understanding the environment, practicing effective listening, redundancy and follow up of the communication are some of the guidelines for achieving effective communication. Communication is a basic managerial task and it requires care and caution, otherwise it can lead to misunderstandings. This can have far reaching consequences even to the extent of breaking relationships.

Case study 23.1: Ethical communication

Communication depends on the attitude of the persons involved, rather than only on the language. In an organisation, communication reflects its culture, climate, values, traditions and the personal habits of employees. Formal and informal interaction, in an organization, takes place through exchange of verbal and non-verbal cues. Communicating goals, giving directions and orders, performance expectations on the one hand, and reporting performance, employee expectations of organisational motivation on the other are vital aspects that affect the effectiveness of the enterprise. A tendency witnessed in the value system of organisations is to recognise open sharing of communication. These are popularly known as learning organisations. Effective communication presupposes coherent thinking of both managers and employees. Ethical communication requires that both the manager and subordinate should exercise emotional control in the communication process otherwise, it can lead to a stressful experience. Obviously, managers need to be more careful than subordinates. Managers need to be conscious of every word uttered in communicating with subordinates. The process of encoding of communication reflects perceptive values and ethics. Faith in the listener is the core of ethics. Managers need to have clear thinking, intellectual sharpness combined with emotional purity, humility and self-control. They must take the moral responsibility for what they report. The don'ts of ethical communication include preventing angry outbursts, impulsiveness, inattentiveness, spreading gossip, poor listening, and unwarranted criticism. Managers need to answer the following questions to judge whether they are practicing ethical communication.

Is the message subjective?

Is the message free from bias?

Is the message true?

Is the effect of the message positive?

Is the message theoretical?

Is the message free from emotions?

Is the message pure and holistic?

Does the message synthesise both personalities?

Is the message tactful and at the same time not trouble making?

Does the message go against the customs and traditions of the listener?

You are required to:

1. Visit any organisation and study its communication, to see the extent of ethical communication among organisational members.
2. List the ethical values in communication referred to in the case.
3. Develop your own ethical code of communication assuming that you are a manager.

Key words

- **Allness:** Poor perception due to obstinacy of the listener.
- **Blinkers:** The tendency to evaluate a person or situation without taking the environment and other factors into consideration.
- **Bypassing:** Ignoring the fact that the same or similar sounding words can have different meaning. Ignoring a level in the chain of communication.
- **Communication:** The process of exchanging ideas, feelings and opinions between persons.
- **Encoding:** The process of symbolising ideas for transmission.
- **Grapevine:** An informal communication channel to express opinions, feelings and attitudes.
- **Redundancy:** Repetition of the same message in order to emphasise the matter.
- **Semantics:** The language, text, grammar and formation of words used in the communication process.
- **Thalamic reactions:** Reacting without completely hearing and understanding the message.

Case study 23.2: Communication in the Airport Authority of India

Air transport is a convenient and time saving means of travel. This mode of travel is usually the prerogative of well-to-do people in society. LPG has brought heavy competition in the service. Customer satisfaction is very important in air transport, because expectations of the commuters are very high. Both the pre-boarding procedures and the journey should be efficient, safe and comfortable for the passengers. This requires highly efficient communication both technical and human.

The Airport Authority of India (AAI) provides highly efficient services at the airport terminals. It has a dedicated team of professionals and aims to provide the best infrastructure and efficient human service. Terminal management is one of the core functions of the AAI. This function assumes greater significance as it involves direct interaction between commuters and the service providers. Communication establishes the link. The important roles and responsibilities of terminal management with respect to communication are liaison with various agencies and provision of passenger information. They have to coordinate with a number of agencies, like airlines and other regulatory agencies to provide the desired facilities to commuters. They also have to coordinate with the local traffic police, law enforcing agencies and other district authorities to ensure smooth flow of traffic both inside and outside the air terminal.

Functions of the AAI: To ensure that the directional and location signage are in working condition; to check the public address system; to ensure that the correct flight information is shown on the display system and CCTV; to maintain a complaint register for the public to enter complaints; to retrieve complaints and suggestions from the suggestion boxes and take the necessary action; to assist the public in redressing their grievances; to maintain records of lost and found property; to facilitate VVIP and VIP movement and to issue personal passes for terminal buildings as per the given procedures. In addition, the terminal management is also responsible for staff supervision within the terminal.

Grievance handling in the AAI: It is a fact that grievances are more common in a service industry than in other industries. Complaints and suggestion boxes are placed at strategic locations in the terminal buildings of airport. Complaint and suggestion forms are also provided. These boxes are serviced at regular intervals. The officer in charge sorts out the complaints, and submits a quarterly report on grievances that have arisen, and the action that has been taken. Other types of grievances such as articles and complaints published in local newspapers, complaints received by post are also reported. This quarterly report is submitter to the Regional Officer at Chennai. In a survey conducted at Hyderabad Airport, it was revealed that commuters are impressed by the way in which grievances are handled. In addition, information regarding baggage is satisfactory. Both technical and human communication, have been found satisfactory. Courteous behaviour, tone of communication, immediate response to requests, personal attention, convincing manners have all received a good score. Proper perception, positive attitude, learning attitude, psychological commitment of employees to organisational matters and in dealing with outsiders becomes imperative to attain a good image of the organisation through communication.

Questions:

1. Identify major elements of communication in the above case study.
2. How would you organise a training programme to improve the communication skills of airport staff? What factors would you consider in designing the training programme?
3. 'Communication is a bifocal lens. Attitude and language require equal focus.' Examine the statement with reference to the above case.

24. LEADERSHIP

This chapter enables you:

- *To define and understand the meaning of leadership*
- *To examine the significance of leadership in organisations*
- *To appraise the important skills required for effective leadership*
- *To trace the emergence of leadership phenomenon*
- *To appreciate the important traits of leadership*
- *To distinguish between production centred and employee centred leadership*
- *To have an overview of the various contingency approaches developed to understand leadership*

The structure of the chapter is as follows:

- Introduction
- Definition of leadership
- Functions of leadership
- Leadership skills
- Emergence of leadership
- Trait theories
  - Great man theory
  - Trait theory
- Behavioural theories
- Contingency theories
- Summary
- Key words

CHAPTER 24

Leadership

INTRODUCTION

Leadership has been a subject of interest to academicians, organisational thinkers and researchers for many centuries. Although F.W. Taylor recognised the importance of leadership in organisational settings, it was not until the Hawthorne studies that the subject of leadership saw the light of the day. Kurt Lewin was the first to identify leadership styles. In the early nineteenth century, Greeks and Romans believed that a king was born to lead. Later it was realised that just because a person was born in a great family, he would not necessarily be a good leader. This led to the emergence of concept of traits. A trait is a quality possessed by an individual, which identifies leadership qualities. A number of traits were defined to distinguish the characteristics of success and failure. Unfortunately, there were no universally accepted traits or definition of a trait. The studies conducted at Ohio State University and Michigan State University, identified behaviour as a predominant factor of leadership thus ruling out the inherited trait concept. In recent years, the systems concept of organisations has given importance to the situation or environment in every sphere. Leadership is no exception to this, and thus we have the situational or contingency approaches to leadership. This chapter enables you to understand the conceptual framework of leadership, styles of leadership and effectiveness of leadership in different situations.

DEFINITION OF LEADERSHIP

Leadership is the process of influencing subordinates to accomplish predetermined goals. Organisational leadership is concerned with integrating the needs of people with the overall goals of the organisation. The following important definitions clarify the concept of leadership.

Leadership is influencing people to follow in the achievement of a common goal.

– Koontz and O'Donnel

Leadership is the activity of influencing people to strive willingly for group objectives.

– George Terry

Leadership is a set of interpersonal behaviors designed to influence employees to cooperate in the achievement of objectives.

– Glueck

Leadership is the imitation and maintenance of structure in expectation and interaction

– Stogdill

Leadership is the process of influencing the activities of an individual or a group in effort towards goal attainment in a given situation.

– Hersey and Blanchard

Leadership is an "interpersonal influence exercised in a situation and directed through communication process, towards the attainment of a specialized goal or goals".

– Tannenbaum, Weschler, Massarik

Leadership is 'a form of social influence, an inter-personal relationship in which power and influence are unevenly distributed so that one person is able to direct and control the actions and behaviors of others to a greater extent than they direct and control his'.

– Mc Gregor

Leadership is 'the influential increment over and above mechanical compliance with the routine directives of the organisation'.

– Katz and Khan

Leadership is 'the ability to persuade others to seek defined objectives enthusiastically. The human factor binds a group together and motivates it towards goals'.

– Keith Davis

Hodge and Johnson defined Leadership as 'a fundamental ability to form and mould the attitude and behaviour of other individuals, whether informal or formal situation and that management relate to the formal task of decision and command'.

The above definitions bring out the following characteristics of leadership:

(a) Leadership is a process of influencing the people.

(b) It requires followers and specific goals.

(c) Leadership directs the energy of followers towards goals using the process of communication.

(d) Leadership exercises inter-personal influence. This signifies that the leader and followers have a mutual relationship.

(e) It motivates the followers, and initiates them to action.

(f) It attempts to bring about a permanent change in behaviour. A leader achieves this by moulding the personality and attitude of subordinates.

(g) Leadership makes use of situations to accomplish goals effectively.

FUNCTIONS OF LEADERSHIP

Leadership is an essential element in the successful attainment of organisational objectives. A leader is a good planner, decision-maker, innovator, controller, effective communicator and a skilled trainer. He maintains good interpersonal relationships with his subordinates or followers. An effective combination of these qualities brings success to both the leader and the organisation. The important functions of leadership in an organisation are given below:

(i) **Planning:** A leader determines the course of action, and communicates it to his subordinates, for execution. He makes decisions and organises various aspects of work in an organisation.

(ii) **Developing teamwork:** A leader clarifies the roles of each individual subordinate and links the multifarious activities into a unified whole. Thus, he develops teamwork to successfully attain the goals.

(iii) **Motivation:** A leader motivates people, guides and directs their potential energy to elicit the desired contribution towards accomplishment of goals.

(iv) **Managing conflict:** Conflicts are omnipresent in the day to day process of an organisation. A leader tries to understand the reasons for conflict, mediate between the conflicting parties, and solve the problem in order to achieve coordination.

(v) **Counselling:** A leader plays the role of advisor and a counselor in organisational tasks when subordinates find it difficult to resolve them. He may also give advice in personal problems if he is requested to do so.

(vi) **Maintaining interpersonal relationships:** An effective leader creates a two-way exchange of ideas. He establishes a mutual relationship of trust and confidence.

(vii) **Managing change:** A leader initiates all the necessary changes in an organisation and implements them by effectively overcoming any resistance to change.

(viii) Training and development: A leader trains and develops employees into future managers. He uses his experience to teach subordinates the various techniques of management, and helps in their career development. He visualises future human potential requirements and develops subordinates to fill the gap.

Leadership is thus a critical factor in the effectiveness of an organisation.

The American Management Association has identified the following functions of a leader:

a. Taking decisions in the pursuit of goals.

b. Rendering service to the organisation and persons who interact with the organisation.

c. Eliciting a response by creating good understanding.

d. Creating a good example by enforcing self-discipline and a high standard of performance.

e. Achieving results by providing specific direction and influence.

LEADERSHIP SKILLS

Leadership is the personal ability of an individual. Ability is a function of personal skills in handling a variety of tasks. Leadership requires the following skills.

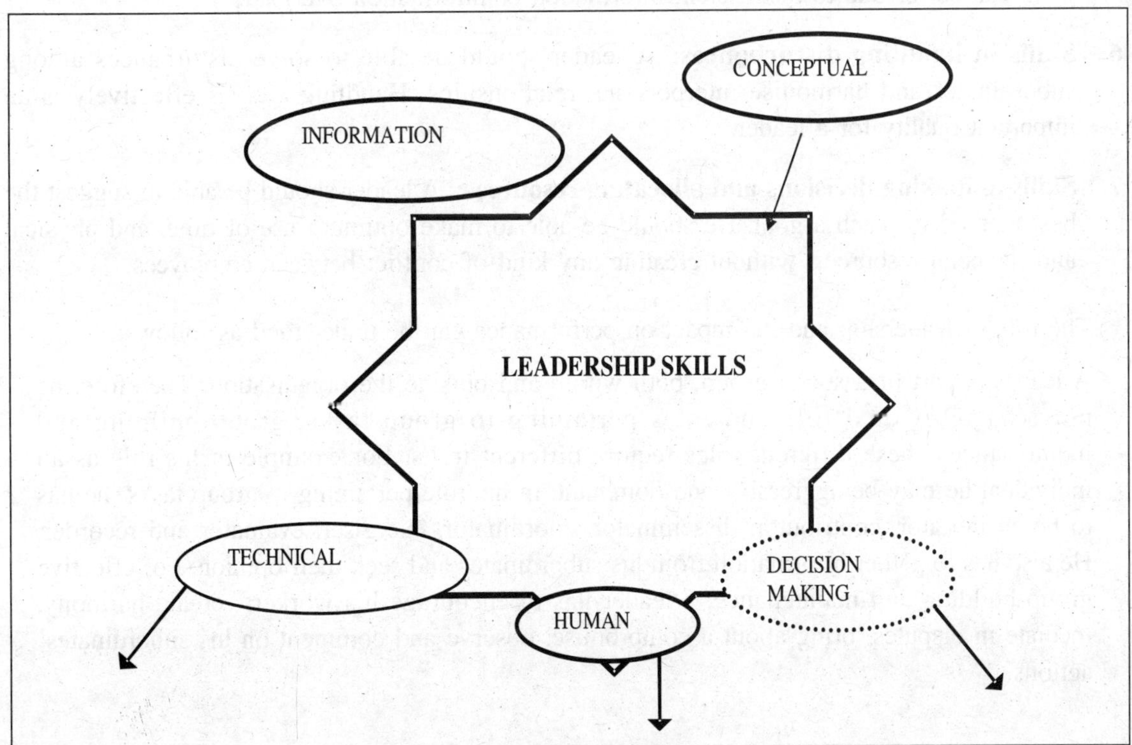

1. **Technical skills:** Knowledge and comprehension of the technical aspects of the manufacturing process are essential for leaders. Although a leader need not be a technician, he should understand the operational aspects otherwise, he will have to rely on others. This may cause him to be unaware of certain critical aspects of operations and in addition, he will not be able to influence the personnel in the production department.

2. **Human skills:** A leader works with human beings. Hence, a leader needs tact to understand the needs and aspirations of subordinates, in order to develop a feeling of teamwork in them.

3. **Conceptual skills:** A leader has to plan missions and objectives, in order to develop a framework and model for survival of the organisation. He can only do this if he has an understanding of the organisation as a whole.

4. **Communication skills:** Leadership involves establishing interpersonal interaction. This requires effective communication, however a number of distortions can take place in communication. Hence, a leader needs to be skilled in both verbal and non-verbal communication. (See Chapter 23).

5. **Information skills:** This involves collecting, editing, processing and disseminating the necessary information to subordinates. Consistent, Accurate, Reliable and Timely (CART) information enable followers to carry out appropriate and rational actions. Otherwise, the work can suffer due to insufficient information or information overload.

6. **Skills in handling disturbances:** A leader should be able to solve disturbances among subordinates and harmonise interpersonal relationships. Handling a crisis effectively is an important quality for a leader.

7. **Skills in making decisions and allocating resources:** A leader should be able to suggest the best method to reach a goal. He should be able to make optimum use of time, and physical and financial resources, without creating any kind of conflict between employees.

The role of leadership and its impact on performance can be understood as follows:

A leader is part of a social group, both within and outside the organisation. Therefore, he plays an individual role and roles pertaining to group tasks, group building and maintenance. These different roles require different traits. For example in his role as an individual he may be aggressive and dominant, in his role pertaining to group tasks, he has to be an initiator, contributor, disseminator, coordinator, energiser, evaluator and recorder. He also has to gather information from his subordinates and seek their opinion. For effective group building and maintenance, a leader has to encourage his workers, create harmony, mediate in disputes, bring about a compromise, observe and comment on his subordinates' actions.

A leader has to solve a number of day-to-day problems in an organisation. The following problems are dealt with by a leader:

1. **Integration:** This requires developing and rewarding the human system to integrate individual needs and goals with those of the organisation.
2. **Social influence:** To develop executive constellations to solve the problems concerning distribution of authority and power.
3. **Collaboration:** Encouraging collaborative efforts to solve conflicts among individuals and groups.
4. **Adaptation:** Identification with the adaptive process to respond to a turbulent and volatile environment is required.
5. **Identification:** Developing organisational goals and clarifying them to ensure commitment and consensus among the workers.
6. **Revitalisation:** This relates to growth and vitality of the organisation.

EMERGENCE OF LEADERSHIP

Leadership received considerable attention, and became a research topic for many scientists after the breakthrough achieved by the Hawthorne studies. A number of theories have been propounded to study leadership, some noteworthy ones are given below.

a. Trait theories
b. Behavioural theories
c. Contingency theories

THEORIES OF LEADERSHIP BEHAVIOUR

Trait Theories

Trait theories were the first attempt to understand leadership. Early contributors understood leadership in terms of certain innate capabilities possessed by individuals. There are two popular theories. They are:

Early genetic theory
Traits theory

Early Genetic Theory/Great Man Theory

The early genetic theory also known as the 'Great Man' theory was popular before 1920. Thomas Earlyle, Frances Galton and William Jances supported this theory. They adhered to the belief that

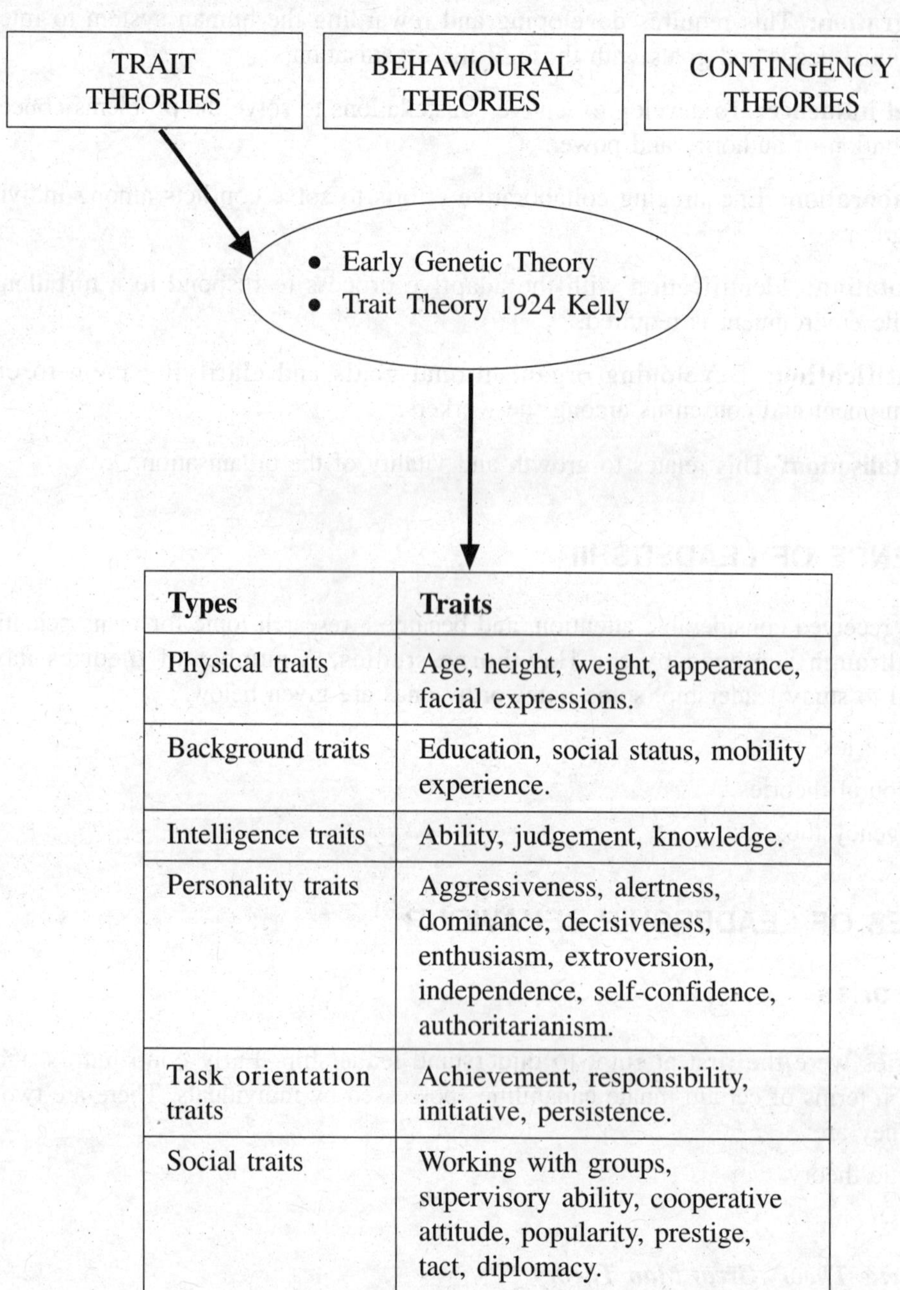

Types	Traits
Physical traits	Age, height, weight, appearance, facial expressions.
Background traits	Education, social status, mobility experience.
Intelligence traits	Ability, judgement, knowledge.
Personality traits	Aggressiveness, alertness, dominance, decisiveness, enthusiasm, extroversion, independence, self-confidence, authoritarianism.
Task orientation traits	Achievement, responsibility, initiative, persistence.
Social traits	Working with groups, supervisory ability, cooperative attitude, popularity, prestige, tact, diplomacy.

prevailed in ancient Greece and Rome, namely that leaders are born. Leadership was associated with special powers gifted by God, and inherited by birth or established in early childhood. Some of the powers are abundant energy, intuition, the ability to take fast decisions etc. This theory also held the view that great men are geniuses, and their greatness was due to genetic factors. For example, they considered Napoleon, Caesar and Churchill as 'Great Men', who were born to become leaders and rule the people. However, with more research in leadership, this theory lost its acceptability.

Trait Theory

The Trait theory is the most common study of leadership. This theory was popular from 1920 to 1950. According to this approach, a person must possess certain qualities or traits to become a successful leader. Therefore, this theory assumes that leaders are distinct from others due to the fact, that they possess certain unique traits. Researchers, identified about eighteen thousand traits in all, a few of them are listed below.

Leadership traits

Intelligence,	Emotional stability
Initiative,	Skill
Supervisory ability,	Ambition
Verbal fluency,	Achievement
Organising ability	Creativity
Social insight	Loyalty
Responsibility	Trust
Task completion	Honour
Vigour and persistence	Tolerance
Problem solving	Dignity
Self-assurance	Rationality
Decisiveness	Personality
Maturity	Appearance
Affinity	Energy
Dominance	Self-actualisation, Self-confidence, Sensitivity

Successful leaders possess the following traits.

(a) **Physical traits:** Physical traits are externally visible. They include age, height, weight, pleasant facial expressions and attractive appearance.

(b) **Personality traits:** Personality traits are internal rather than external. They relate to behaviour of the leader. Personality traits are shaped by perception, attitudes, learning and motivation, self-confidence, control, integrity, dominance, assurance, alertness, maturity, affinity, etc.

(c) **Intelligence traits:** Intelligence is a major factor in determining whether a person is a leader. Traits such as, superior decision making, judgement, knowledge, communication etc. relate to intelligence and to the skills developed in the learning process.

(d) Task traits: Certain characteristics, like achievement, responsibility, intuition, task orientation and technical understanding are necessary for a successful leader.

(e) Social traits: Social traits relate to the society in which a person interacts. Traits like education, social status, harmony, trust, cohesion etc., help in the successful integration of people in social situations.

Utility of the Trait Theory

The Trait theory has led to greater understanding of leadership. Traits identified by these theories allowed psychological tests to be developed to establish existence of traits. The theory has been valuable in distinguishing leaders from non-leaders. The utility of this approach can be stated as follows:

(i) Studying traits serves as a practical guide in selection, placement, transfer and promotion of managers in organisations.

(ii) This theory is useful in predicting the effectiveness of various managerial levels.

(iii) Knowledge regarding the traits possessed by employees is very useful in identifying training needs. It facilitates planning the training and development programs to improve leadership.

(iv) This approach helps in planning the work force in organisations.

(v) Assessment of traits and skills help executives in planning their careers. Young executives who would like to reach higher positions can make suitable plans.

Criticism

Although this theory is useful in practice, a number of criticisms, which are listed below, have been levelled against it.

(a) The long list of traits identified by various research studies did not produce universally acceptable traits. The list is exhaustive but inconclusive.

(b) The definition of a trait has been the subject of controversy. There is no valid definition of a trait.

(c) There was considerable disagreement over whether to consider traits as essential to identify leaders.

(d) Quantification and measurement of a trait is not possible.

(e) Leadership skills do not vary only according to qualities possessed, but also according to the work environment. For example, the nature of the work, nature of subordinates, nature of organisation etc.

(f) Effectiveness of leader is not a function of a single trait. A number of traits determine effectiveness.

(g) The trait approach fails to consider the external environment of the leader.

Due to severe criticism leveled against the trait theory, behavioural theories emerged.

Behavioural Theories

Behavioural theories considered the behaviour of the leader to understand the leadership process. The theories stated that the behaviour and attitude of leaders towards production and employees, determine their effectiveness. Studies conducted by researchers at the University of Michigan and Ohio State University researchers fall under this category.

Leadership theories developed by researchers at the University of Michigan and the Ohio State University

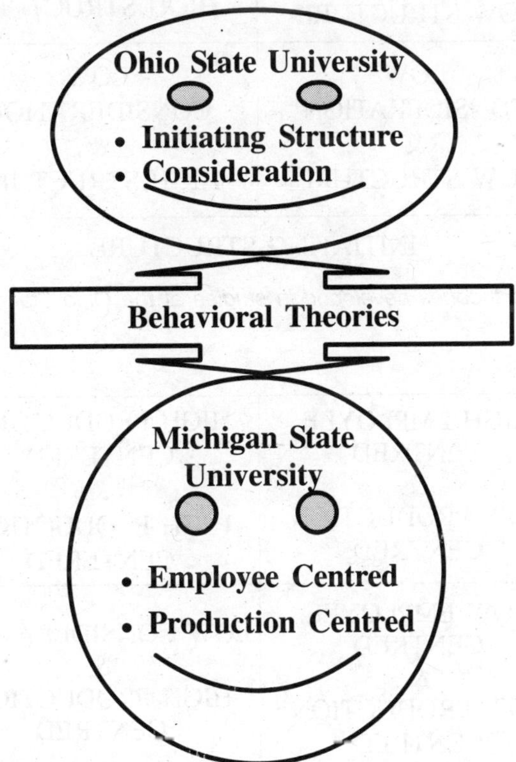

The studies conducted at Michigan State University identified two kinds of behaviour of leaders, viz., employee centred and production centred. While the former shows concern for the welfare of employees, the latter emphasises the technical aspects and advocates close supervision to achieve production goals.

The researchers at Ohio University developed the Leader Behaviour Description Questionnaire (LBDQ), to describe the behaviour of a leader. It used two dimensions of leadership behaviour known as initiating structure and consideration. Initiating structure refers to structuring work and work relationships. The leader lays emphasis on maintenance of performance standards and meeting work schedules. On the other hand, consideration describes emphasis on mutual trust, respect, friendship, warmth, accessibility and above all helping subordinates to solve personal problems.

Four quadrants were developed to show the combination of leadership attitudes.

CONSIDERATION (High ↑ / Low)	Low — INITIATING STRUCTURE	High
High	HIGH CONSIDERATION & LOW STRUCTURE	HIGH CONSIDERATION & HIGH STRUCTURE
Low	LOW CONSIDERATION & LOW STRUCTURE	LOW CONSIDERATION & HIGH STRUCTURE

Leadership theories developed in studies at the Ohio State University

EMPLOYEE CENTRED (High ↑ / Low)	Low — PRODUCTION CENTERED	High
High	HIGH EMPLOYEE CENTRED & LOW PRODUCTION CENTRED	HIGH PRODUCTION CENTERED & HIGH PRODUCTION CENTERED
Low	LOW EMPLOYEE CENTRED & LOW PRODUCTION CENTRED	LOW CONSIDERATION & HIGH PRODUCTION CENTRED

Leadership theories developed by studies at the Michigan State University

The following presentation relates to the behavioural characteristics of production centred/ initiating structure and employee centred/consideration.

Behavioural characteristics of production centred/initiating structure leadership are:

(1) Leaders design objectives, goals for subordinates, plans, and policies. They assign tasks and

jobs to subordinates and give detailed instructions.

(2) The leader designs job structures, schedules, production requirements etc. Emphasis is laid on meeting production targets irrespective of situational constraints. He closely checks the performance of subordinates.

(3) The leader refuses to compromise and explain his actions. He insists that every task is performed strictly according to his expectations.

(4) Organisational structure, communication methods, procedures, controls etc., are clearly defined. Moreover, members are compelled to follow them scrupulously.

(5) Threat and punishments are used to control non-compliance of instructions.

Due to these behavioural characteristics, subordinates carry out the work mechanically. Productivity and quality of work are high due to excessive pressure on subordinates, but it is difficult for them to maintain due to poor motivation and morale. Lack of initiative on the part of subordinates makes them ill-equipped to take up managerial positions in the future.

Behavioural characteristics of consideration/employee oriented leadership are:

(1) Emphasis is laid on relationships. The leader shows more consideration towards employees, treating them as equal.

(2) Leaders take a personal interest in subordinates, care about their personal problems, and listen to them patiently and attentively. In addition, the leader suggests possible solutions to their problems at work.

(3) Leaders are friendly and easy to approach. This builds an effective work group with high performance goals.

(4) New ideas, suggestions and alternative solutions from subordinates are invited. Any changes are communicated to the concerned persons in advance.

(5) Appreciation is shown to subordinates for their work. Subordinates are allowed to work in the manner that they think best, but should learn through suitable guidelines.

(6) Free flow of communication, both vertically and horizontally, is maintained. The leader creates a supportive and warm work environment.

Due to the above behaviour, subordinates are highly motivated. This results in maximum productivity. Creativity of subordinates equips them to develop into potential leaders.

The two leadership styles described above are independent. It is not possible for an individual to exhibit both styles of leadership.

Behavioural theories have made a significant contribution to understanding the attitudes and predispositions of leaders. Identification of behaviour that influence productivity, is a landmark in these theories. These theories are based on reasoning, hence practicing managers praised their utility. The theories have enabled organisations to develop their employees through behaviour modification training programs. Therefore, these theories facilitated further research in the area of leadership.

However, these studies were criticised for failing to identify the relationship between a leader's behaviour and performance. The questionnaire approach was subject to criticism. These theories did not consider environmental and situational aspects such as a subordinate's personal characteristics, group characteristics, tasks, etc. Hence, they failed to identify contingency factors of leader behaviour.

Contingency Theories

Neither trait nor behavioural theories of leadership emphasised situational factors. Although behavioural theories recognised personality, attitudes and motivation of leaders in understanding their leadership styles, they did not assess their importance on the effectiveness. Contingency theories were developed after 1960.

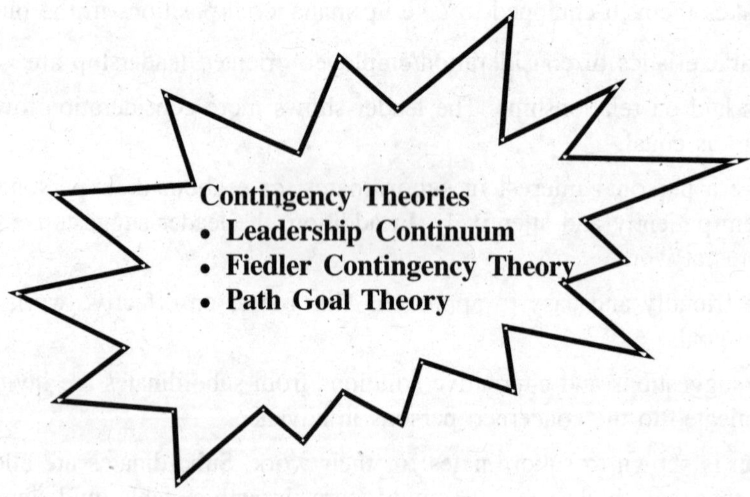

Contingency theories are based on the assumption that a successful leader in one situation need not be always successful in other situations. These theories integrated both leadership styles and effectiveness. The theories stated that effectiveness is a function of contingency or situational factors of the environment. The theories include:

- Tannenbaum and Schmidt's 'Leadership Continuum',
- Fielder's 'Contingency Theory',
- Hersey and Blanchard's 'Situational Theory',
- Robert House's 'Path Goal Theory' and
- Victor Vroom and Yetton's 'Leader Participation Theory'.

Contingency factors identified by the theories are:

(a) Degree of structure of the task

(b) Leader-member relations

(c) Positional power

(d) Maturity and immaturity of subordinates

(e) Formal authority

(f) Work group and its norms

(g) Locus of control, experience and perceived ability

(h) Role clarity

These factors determine the attitude of the leader and the degree of influence they exercise on the effectiveness of the leader. A detailed explanation of contingency theories is given in the next chapter. However, a brief discussion regarding a few important contingency theories is presented here.

Fiedler's Contingency Model used a questionnaire known as the Least Preferred Co-worker (LPC), to determine whether a leader is task or relationship oriented. According to this model, the situation is the essential factor. Situation factors identified are: leader-member relations, structured tasks and positional power. Fiedler stated that better leader-member relations, a highly structured task and strong positional power make a leader effective and *vice versa*.

Robert House developed the **Path Goal Theory.** According to this model effective leaders clarify the path or direction to the subordinates in the achievement of goals. The leader also removes difficulties in the path, enabling followers to easily achieve the objectives. Behaviour of the leader is acceptable and is considered effective when subordinates view it as a source of satisfaction.

Another **Situational Leadership Theory** was propounded by **Hersey and Blanchard.** This theory stated that successful leadership depends on the selection of the leadership style appropriate to the maturity level of subordinates. According to this model, if the subordinates are capable and willing to take responsibility, a leader can delegate responsibility otherwise, a leader should give clear instructions (telling style). Four leadership styles are propounded by this model, namely telling, selling, participating and delegating styles.

Contingency theories have become popular due to the fact, that they recognise the importance of the situation. They are logical and fill the gap between theory and practice. Moreover, these theories are based on empirical observations conducted through structured questionnaires. The theories have made a significant contribution by identifying important situational variables and the corresponding styles of leadership in complex organisational settings. For instance, the **Vroom and Yetton model** prescribes participation as an essential variable in the style of leadership that is a precise answer for effective decision making.

However, situational theories are not beyond criticism. Critics pointed out the lack of theoretical support in these theories. Although a number of situational elements are identified, the theories have failed to explain the influence of situational factors on styles of leadership. Another criticism is that the theories have adapted complex methodology unsuitable for empirical testing.

SUMMARY

Leadership has been defined in terms of influencing people towards attaining goals. This requires structure, communication, socialisation, control and favourable situation. Leadership is the fulcrum that makes an organisation effective. A leader controls all organisational activities. He is involved in planning, development of teamwork, motivating employees, managing conflicts, counselling, maintaining interpersonal relationships, managing change, and training of subordinates. Leadership depends on the personal capability of an individual. It requires technical skills, human relation skills, conceptual skills, communication skills, skill in handling information and disturbances, making decisions and allocation of resources. Three streams of thought became popular in understanding leadership, *viz.*, trait, behavioural and situational. Trait theories identified a number of traits, such as physical, background, intelligence, personality, task orientation and social traits. Trait theories are valuable, because they were the first to give an insight into leadership. However, lack of definitions and conceptual limitations led to the development of behavioural theories. Ohio University and Michigan University have made noteworthy contributions to behavioural theories. Studies in these two places, classified leadership based on the behaviour of leader. Initiating structure, production centred, consideration and employee centred, were the behavioural attitudes identified. As behavioural theories overlooked situational elements in determining the effectiveness of leaders, situational theories were developed. Tannenbaum and Schmidt's 'Leadership Continuum', Fielder's 'Contingency Theory', Hersey and Blanchard's 'Situational Theory', Robert House's 'Path Goal Theory' and Victor Vroom and Yetton's 'Leader Participation Theory' are popular contingency theories. Some of the contingency factors identified are degree of structure of task, leader-member relationship, positional power, maturity and immaturity of subordinates, formal authority, work group and its norms, locus of control, experience and perceived ability, and role clarity.

Case study 24.1: The star of the information business

'It is better to under-promise and over-deliver' says Narayana Murthy, the head of Infosys, the globally recognised Indian software major. The company has shown an impressive performance over less than two decades. The industry is based on knowledge resources and its leader, a transparent human being, is willing to share his knowledge. The philosophy stated above lays emphasis on the value he places on relationships. He believes that a person should do something in which he has confidence. This belief has led him from a village, Siddalghata, in Karnataka across the globe. Despite his busy schedule, Murthy finds the time to talk to children about determination, discipline, good values and a systematic timetable for carrying out one's work. These are his secrets of success. According to him, there are four things that he learnt, which distinguish him from others. The first is that the only way one can make people better is by creating opportunities, and new wealth. The second, is that there are only a few people who are capable of creating wealth. The third is that gifted people require incentives to create wealth, as they are human beings. The incentive should be in the form of money, power and freedom. The last one is that it is not the job of the government to create wealth, it should facilitate environment for people to generate wealth. Thus, his philosophy states the significance of a facilitating agent. From being a believer in communism, Murthy now developed a firm belief in capitalism and liberalisation. J.R.D. Tata, Mahatma Gandhi and Lee Kwan Yew created indelible impressions on him, changing his mindset. Despite the fact that he is deeply entrenched in the system of Hindu values, western thinking has largely influenced him. His logic is that western people are largely self-sufficient. They do most of the work on their own rather than being dependent on others. This led to his belief that 'one should live within one's means'.

Simple living and high thinking aptly describe Murthy. He believes that man's needs are simple. That is why his life style is remarkably modest. After he returned from France, he wanted to help society. To this end, he teamed up with his mentor, Prof. Krishnayya. Then he decided to gain experience in the private sector before he started his own business. He strongly believed in work ethics. He visualised a business opportunity in offshore development as Indians are highly skilled in software development. Unlike in the US and Japan, in India the best and the brightest enter the field of software development. He conceived the idea of 'Infosys'. The advantage of this industry is that it produces quality jobs, disposable incomes and provides a challenging work environment and good opportunities. It is one industry where India sustains a competitive advantage, and the government should do all it can to encourage this industry. Initially his business was not spectacular, but with excellent management of human resources, Infosys carved a niche for itself in later years. Raghavan, the HR Director, insists that any one who joins must be able to use the latest technology. Rather than a specific set of skills, they look for attitude and evidence that a person can learn. The human management in Infosys has created an ambience, which nurtures human dignity. Their middle class value based system, and informal, unpretentious and industrious style of leadership has a significant impact in producing a transaction-based result oriented culture.

Questions:

1. Identify the leadership traits of an industrious leader with the help of the trait theory of leadership.
2. Comment on the dictum, 'it is better to under-promise and over-deliver.'
3. What are human values created and nurtured relationship orientations for Narayana Murthy?

Key words:

- **Behaviour modification:** The process of changing the behaviour of a person.
- **Leadership**: The process of influencing people to achieve common goals.
- **Motivation:** Transforming the potential energy of individuals into real energy.
- **Trait:** The characteristic features of an individual.

25. LEADERSHIP BEHAVIOUR

This chapter enables you:

- *To comprehend the meaning of styles of leadership*
- *To trace out the historical development of leadership behaviour*
- *To distinguish between authoritarian and democratic styles of leadership*
- *To examine the behaviour of decision making by leaders*
- *To use the grid approach to understand styles of leadership*
- *To distinguish between styles of leadership identified in the managerial grid*
- *To understand the Likert approach of identifying leadership behaviour*
- *To understand the dimension in leadership behaviour*
- *To distinguish between effective and ineffective leaders*

The structure of the chapter is as follows:

- Introduction
- Definition of styles of leadership
- Authoritarian, democratic and laissez faire styles of leadership
- Decision continuum
- Managerial grid
- Likert's Four systems of managerial leadership
- Reddins' Three dimensional leadership
- Summary
- Key words

CHAPTER 25

Leadership Behaviour

INTRODUCTION

You may have often heard comments from your peers or seniors about the behaviour of their superiors. While one person may complain that his superior is very strict and does not allow him to leave the office without completing the day's work, another may comment that their senior is always kind enough to give permission to leave the officer early, if you have a valid reason. These descriptions relate to styles of leadership. Sometimes the leader may not realise the effect of his behaviour on his subordinates. In an organisation a leader makes decisions, which his subordinates are expected to execute. There are two basic styles of leadership, authoritarian and democratic. A number of variations in these basic styles have been developed over the years. Robert Blake and Jane S Mouton, Rensis Likert, William J Reddin and Robert Tannenbaum popularised various styles of leadership. In their studies they all took the effects of task orientation, people orientation, and decision making into consideration, however none of them considered the effect of the situation. This chapter is intended to explain the various styles of leadership developed over the last century.

DEFINITION OF STYLE OF LEADERSHIP

Style of leadership refers to the behaviour of the leader when dealing with his followers. A leader's behaviour depends on his assumptions regarding his subordinates and his mode of interaction with them.

Mc Gregor defined style of leadership as 'the method of coping with organizational reality, which evolves out of trail and error and is not deliberately, adopted or eventually recognized by the leader. The predictable ways of coping with the reality of the work environment is managerial style'.

Style of leadership is understood as the behavior of an executive in making decisions to enhance the effectiveness of an organisation.

Historical development of styles of leadership is given in the following chart.

Leadership styles – Historical development

Year	Studies	Leadership Dimensions
1911	Scientific management, F.W. Taylor	None
1924-1932	Hawthorne studies, Elton Mayo	None
1939	University of Iowa Kurt Lewin, Lippit and White	Authoritarian, democratic and laissez-faire
1957	Ohio State University, Ralph Stogdill	Initiating structure & consideration
1960	Douglas McGregor	Theory X and Theory Y
1961	Michigan State University, Rensis Likert	Employee orientation & production orientation

Leadership style varies with the behavioural predisposition of leaders. There are as many styles as there are leaders. However, certain characteristics allowed them to be classified into specific categories. The important styles of leadership are given below.

(i) Authoritarian, democratic and laissez faire

(ii) Decision continuum

(iii) Managerial grid

(iv) Likert's: Four systems of managerial leadership

(v) Reddin's: Three dimensional leadership styles

AUTHORITARIAN, DEMOCRATIC, LAISSEZ FAIRE LEADERSHIP STYLES

Authoritarian, democratic and laissez faire styles of leadership have been scientifically identified by Lewin, Lippit and White. These styles depend upon whether the leader takes complete responsibility for making decisions, or allows subordinates to make decisions within certain clearly defined limits. The characteristics of these styles are described below.

Authoritarian Style of Leadership

An authoritarian leader has the following characteristics:

1. The leader assumes full authority for deciding goals. Activities relating to work flow and division of work are decided by the leader, who assigns them to subordinates.
2. Policies and strategies to achieve objectives and goals are decided solely by the leader.
3. The leader makes all the important decisions and plans relating to every aspect of the subordinate's work. These have to be carried out by the subordinates.
4. The leader does not take his subordinates into confidence.
5. The leader uses his power and prestige to ensure that the subordinates carry out his orders. He exercises strict, close and detailed supervision over their work. Subordinates have to strictly act in accordance with his dictates.
6. The leader does not believe in sharing information and communication with his subordinates. Neither does he provide them any feedback, nor listen to them.
7. The leader insists on loyalty from his subordinates. He will not tolerate any interference by subordinates.
8. Leader tries to evaluate performance of subordinates through appreciation for good jobs and criticism without objective reasoning for all mistakes.

Due to the above characteristics, subordinates working under authoritarian leaders become highly dependent and submissive, and avoid all responsibility. They work hard only when the leader is present and tend to relax in his absence. The quantity and quality of their output will be good in the short run, but suffers adversely in the long run. The subordinates' motivation and morale are adversely affected. They tend to become aggressive and in turn follow the same style of leadership.

Democratic Style of Leadership

The characteristics of this style are given below:

(i) The leader allows subordinates to participate in all decisions. Activities, techniques and division of work are suggested to them.

(ii) Joint discussions are held to decide objectives, goals and policies, in which a majority of the subordinates participate. The leader only reserves the authority to give final approval.

(iii) There is delegation of authority. The leader allows his subordinates to take decisions, even on certain important matters, within certain limits.

(iv) Total freedom is given to subordinates to choose the persons they want to work with. Communication between subordinates is promoted and nurtured.

(v) The leader shows his appreciation for his subordinates. He will overlook trivial mistakes. His criticism is objective and factual. He evaluates performance based on clearly established and predetermined objective standards.

(vi) Any proposed changes are disclosed to subordinates, who are free to discuss them and suggest any modifications they feel necessary. Only then are the changes implemented.

(vii) The leader treats all subordinates as his equals. He listens to their personal problems and suggests suitable solutions. He is easily approachable, friendly, and cheerful.

(viii) The leader supports his subordinates in all aspects by taking them into confidence. He creates an environment of mutual trust, confidence and loyalty.

Subordinates working under a democratic leader learn through participation. They readily assume responsibility. Since they participate in decisions, they take moral responsibility for their work, and are more committed. Due to the freedom given to them, productivity and quality may initially be low. However due to positive motivation, friendship, trust, confidence and better listening, a greater understanding will be developed between the leader and his subordinates, ultimately leading to higher productivity, enhanced morale, and greater job satisfaction. The work group is highly contended.

The dimensions used to distinguish between authoritarian and democratic styles of leadership are shown in Figure 25.1.

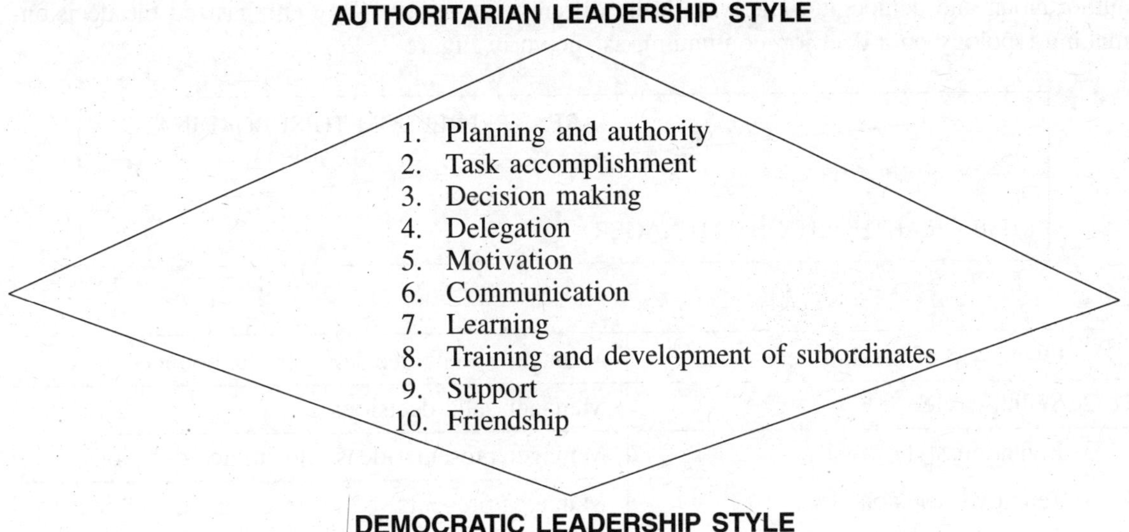

Figure 25.1: Characteristics of authoritarian and democratic leaders

Laissez Faire Style of Leadership

In this style the leader neither assumes responsibility to determine the objectives, goals, policies, nor takes decisions. Subordinates are given complete freedom to do things in a manner convenient to them. The leader is uninvolved in the affairs of his subordinates, and does not offer appreciation, support, or criticism. The worker's performance is evaluated by co-workers. No controls are exercised by the leader. Subordinates working under such a leader make little contribution to the organisation. They work or do not work as they wish, irrespective of the presence or absence of leader. Once they realise that, due to non-involvement of the leader, their efforts are waste and the group stops working. This ultimately leads to de-motivation.

Authoritarian, democratic and laissez faire are the basic styles of leadership. They provided an understanding of styles of leadership and are the basis for further development of leadership styles. Although the two dimensions are mutually exclusive, critics have pointed out that a leader will never be completely authoritarian or democratic. There will always be an overlap in a leader's behaviour. This has led to the development of a behaviour continuum.

DECISION CONTINUUM

Robert Tannenbaum and Warren H. Schmidt have identified leadership styles on a continuum showing seven types of styles from complete authoritarian or task oriented to democratic or employee oriented. According to them, there are a number of styles rather than just authoritarian, democratic, and laissez faire as suggested by Lewin, Lippit and White. Between the extremes of authoritarian and democratic, there could be different situations. They emphasized the decision-making typology on a decision continuum, as shown in Figure 25.2.

AREA OF FREEDOM TO SUBORDINATES

USE OF AUTHORITY BY MANAGER

1 2 3 4 5 6 7

1 Own style of making decisions	Manager makes decisions and announces them
2 Selling style	Manager sells decisions
3 Invitation style	Manager presents ideas and invites questions
4 Tentative decision style	Manager presents tentative decisions subject to change
5 Suggestive style	Manager presents problems, elicits suggestions and makes decisions
6 Group decision style	Manager defines limits, asks group to make decisions
7 Delegative style of making decisions	Manager permits subordinates to function within limits defined by the superior

Figure 25.2: Decision Continuum

1. **Own style of making decisions**: This is the first situation. In this situation, the leader makes all decisions relating to his workgroup and announces them. Subordinates are expected to follow them strictly. Any deviation is viewed seriously. Leader will not allow any subordinate to criticise the decisions. Strict compliance is required. It can be observed from Figure 25.2 the area representing use of authority by manager is greater than the area represented by area of freedom to subordinates.

2. **Selling style:** In the second situation, the leader continues to make decisions unilaterally. However, he uses skill, intelligence and tactics to convince subordinates to accept the decisions. This is similar to a sales representative convincing a customer to purchase his product. Subordinates accept the decision as consumers accept the product. The leader is talkative, empathetic and tactful. Subordinates accept the decision depending upon persuasive capacity of the superior to sell his decision. The leader appears to have considered subordinates, whereas in fact he has convinced them to accept his decisions. The area of use of authority is still greater.

3. **Invitation style:** The third situation is akin to a teacher, taught relationship, whereby teachers explain the lesson and ask questions, which the students are expected to answer. Here the leader presents all problems relating to a decision. He invites questions from subordinates and answers them but ultimately makes the final decision. Subordinates can represent their problems and difficulties, which may or may not be dealt with in the final decision taken by the superior. In this situation subordinates feel happy as the leader is prepared to answer their questions. They enjoy some amount of freedom, unlike in earlier styles. The area of freedom to subordinates slightly increases.

4. **Tentative decision style:** In the fourth situation, the leader suggests various alternative decisions to a problem. All these alternatives are communicated to subordinates. They are asked to discuss them thoroughly amongst themselves and suggest any changes. All workable or feasible changes are incorporated before a final decision is taken. Thus in this style subordinates apply their minds to think the problem through. This behaviour leads to a sense of satisfaction. In this style the area representing use of authority and freedom to subordinates is equal.

5. **Suggestive style:** In the fifth situation, the leader still continues to make decisions, but shows tact in presenting problems to his subordinates. He provides all information necessary to make a decision by incorporating feasible suggestions. In this situation, the freedom of subordinates is increased to the extent of offering suggestions. Subordinates are motivated to offer suggestions as the leader is prepared to listen to their ideas and accept them if they are feasible.

6. **Group decision style:** In the sixth situation, the leader delegates authority to his subordinates to make decisions. He reserves the right to set and define limits within which decisions are to be taken by subordinates. However, the superior can suggest any changes in decisions. The group of subordinates takes decisions that are beneficial to the group. As the participation level has increased, they are even capable of suggesting changes in the basic premise of the decision. The overall commitment to implementation of the decision will be greater.

7. **Delegative style of making decisions:** The seventh situation is at the extreme end of the continuum. The leader defines only a broad framework of policies, procedures and limits, within which subordinates are given total freedom to operate. Interference of the leader is minimal. Delegation suggests a belief in the subordinates, which leads them to be highly motivated in this situation. As can be observed from Figure 25.2 the area of freedom given to subordinates considerably increases, but observe that the area representing use of authority by manager still remains. Thus leader reserves atleast certain authority to take decision.

The topology of the decision continuum suggests various possibilities for interaction between a leader and his subordinates in the decision making process. The characteristics of a leader may fall at any point on the continuum, and may change depending upon the situation. However, a leader cannot exhibit all the different styles depicted in the continuum, at the same time.

The decision continuum to understand leadership behavior is of great value in designing organisational patterns, structure and managerial motivation, and it is used as a practical guide to managers in shaping their own behavior. However, certain difficulties arise in locating the leader's style exactly on the continuum, thus it is difficult to predict his behavior with precision. A criticism leveled against it is that since managers may move along the continuum it is very difficult to understand their managerial style.

MANAGERIAL GRID

Robert Blake and J.S. Mouton have developed a more exact portrayal of leadership on a two dimensional graph. It is well known as a managerial grid. The managerial grid popularised five styles of leadership, on the basis of concern for production and concern for people, which were identified by studies on leadership carried out at Ohio State University. They are presented in Figure 25.3.

Concern for production is shown on the 'X' axis and concern for people on the 'Y' axis. Each axis of the graph is divided into nine divisions. The various styles depicted in the grid are explained below.

Style–1.1. Impoverished manager: This style is characterised by the least concern for both production and people. The leader does not exert much effort to guide, direct and motivate subordinates to accomplish the tasks. He takes hardly any interest in the personal welfare of subordinates. This type of leader is unpopular with both the management and subordinates. They are not successful in any situation.

Style–9.1. Task manager: A leader exhibiting this style shows high concern for production and low concern for people. He believes that working conditions should be conducive to extracting the maximum amount of work, with the fewest number of people. He structures all tasks clearly, defines patterns of work, and motivates subordinates to meet production targets irrespective of personal conveniences and inconveniences. A leader exhibiting this style is liked by the management, but disliked by subordinates. These leaders are successful in situations, which demand that tasks be completed quickly and efficiently.

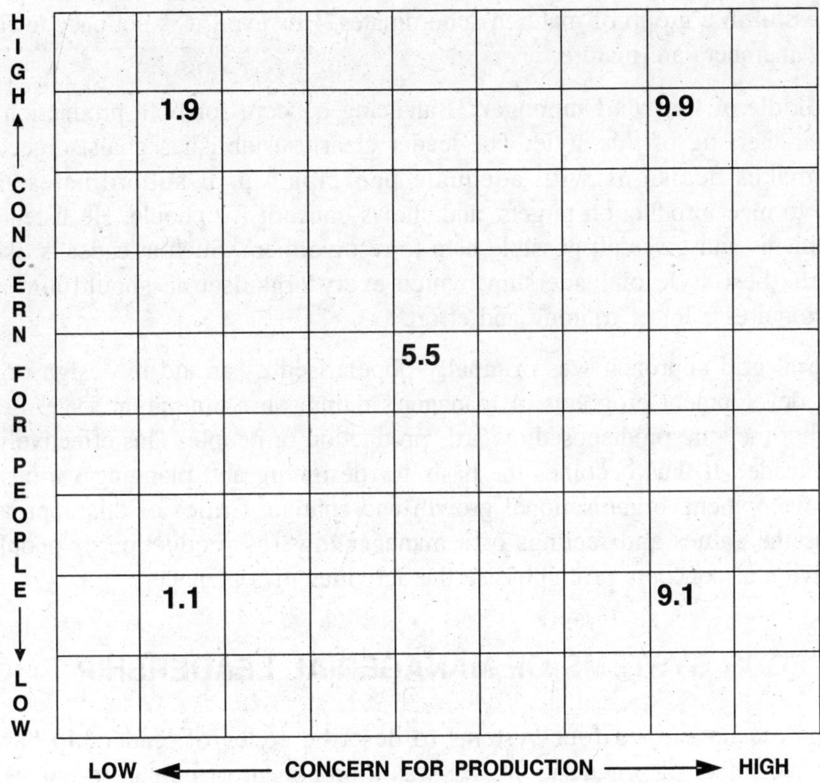

1.1 IMPOVERISHED MANAGER
9.1 TASK MANAGER
9.9 TEAM MANAGER
1.9 COUNTRY CLUB MANAGER
5.5 MIDDLE OF THE ROAD

Figure 25.3: Managerial Grid

Style–9.9. Team manager: In this style a team leader shows high concern for both production and people. He pays attention to the personal needs and welfare of employees. By establishing an environment of warmth, friendship and trust, he ensures commitment towards organisational goals. Subordinates are highly motivated, and will do their best to meet common goals. Such a leader is liked equally by both management and subordinates. It is difficult to find such leaders.

Style–1.9. Country club manager: A leader exhibiting this style is considered to be a human relations expert. He has the maximum concern for people but cares little for production. He takes great care of the personal welfare of group members by effectively establishing a relationship of mutual trust, love, affection, friendship, personal warmth and personal communication. He does not enforce production targets strictly; performance of subordinates will be low initially, but will ultimately increase. Such a leader is liked by subordinates but disliked by the management. He will be successful in a group of matured subordinates. However, it is not easy to find a group, in which all the members are mature.

Style–5.5. Middle of the road manager: Balancing concern for both production and people is the chief characteristic of this style. The leader clearly establishes goals, objectives, policies, plans, and makes decisions with adequate participation of subordinates. He motivates subordinates to meet production targets, and shows concern for people. He listens attentively to personal problems and gives all possible help to resolve them. Such a leader is liked by one and all. This is the best style of leadership, which every organisation should aim at developing. However, it requires a lot of training and effort.

The managerial grid approach was originally popularised as an aid to design organisation and management development programs. A manager's rating, on a nine-point scale used by the grid, reveals whether they are predisposed towards production or people. This effectively measures the attitude of a leader. It thus becomes the basis for designing and planning various programs for leadership development, organisational growth and change. Critics of this approach feel that it only portrays the values and feelings of a manager towards production or people. It does not include behavioural concepts or emphasise the activities of a manager.

LIKERT'S FOUR SYSTEMS OF MANAGERIAL LEADERSHIP

Rensis Likert has developed four systems to describe styles of leadership based on studies conducted in a number of organisations. He was a proponent of human resources, and believed that effectiveness and employee satisfaction in organisations is maximum when leaders involve subordinates in making decisions. The styles of leadership designated by him are explained below.

System 1: Exploitative authoritative: In this style, all decisions are taken by the management. The management does not have confidence in its subordinates, and they are not involved in the decision making process. Therefore, subordinates are compelled to accept the decisions made by their superiors. This can lead to their feeling of being exploited by the management, or that the management is setting standards, which are too high for them to achieve.

The characteristics of the style are as follows:

a. The leader does not have trust and confidence in the subordinates. They are not involved in making decisions.
b. The leader treats subordinates as instruments of production. Thus, his emphasis is on production.
c. Communication is formal and only downward.
d. The leader believes in surveillance, threat, coercion and chastisement to motivate subordinates.
e. Positive rewards are used only occasionally.
f. The top management level has complete control.

Due to these characteristics, the beliefs of leaders using this style are very close to the philosophy of theory 'X'. The leader uses positional authority to direct subordinates. He is highly committed towards production, and uses his own skill, intuition and mental abilities to make decisions. There is not much interaction with subordinates, leading to disharmony and lack of interest in work.

System 2: Benevolent autocrat: Under this style, the top person in the organisation makes most decisions relating to organisational matters. The management has confidence in subordinates. Subordinates are motivated by rewards.

Characteristics of a benevolent autocrat are as follows:

i. The leader possesses certain degree of confidence and trust in his subordinates.
ii. He is concerned about his subordinates but more so about production.
iii. The leader delegates authority to his subordinates to take minor or routine decisions within carefully prescribed limits. However, the leader reserves the authority to finalise decisions.
iv. Although policies and major decisions are made by the leader, subordinates are given an opportunity to comment on them.
v. Communication is formal.
vi. Motivation is through a combination of rewards and punishments.

Due to these characteristics, the beliefs of the benevolent autocrat are still close to those of theory 'X', but he shows more consideration towards his subordinates. The leader uses positional authority and personal power to make subordinates work. Subordinates are fairly satisfied with such a leader. However, very little teamwork exists among subordinates.

System 3: Consultative: This style of leadership is characterised by the leader reposing substantial confidence in subordinates. Consequently, they delegate authority to subordinates to take specific decisions.

Characteristics of the style of consultative leadership are as follows:

i. The leader expresses substantial confidence and trust in subordinates.
ii. The leader makes major decisions, however subordinates take most other decisions, within specific limits.
iii. There is two-way communication.
iv. Motivation is through rewards but coercion is also significantly used.
v. The leader uses his personal power to gain acceptance from subordinates.
vi. Controls are delegated to subordinates, with the leader reserving the right to take final decisions and corrective action.

A consultative leader's beliefs are close to those of theory 'Y'. Though the leader is committed to production, he tries to achieve a balance by showing equal consideration for subordinates. Both higher and lower levels of management feel responsible to achieve goals. There is moderate interaction between superiors and subordinates.

System 4: Participative: A participative leader has complete confidence in his subordinates. The authority to make decisions is widely distributed throughout the organisation. Lower level subordinates are allowed to participate in almost all decisions. The style has the following characteristics:

i. The leader has absolute confidence in his subordinates.
ii. Communication is mostly informal and open, in all directions.
iii. The leader believes in his subordinates' capacity to accomplish production targets.
iv. Participation is widely invited from subordinates. Moreover, it is used as a motivating technique.
v. Controls are not emphasised. Nevertheless, the leader encourages subordinates to assume responsibility.
vi. The leader grooms subordinates to undertake future managerial tasks.

Due to these characteristics, the leader respects his subordinates as an essential part of the organisation. He builds a cohesive, highly motivated and participative group of subordinates. Coordination is perfect due to mutual confidence, and accurate and open communication. Subordinates working under such a leader are highly satisfied, and respect him.

Likert argued that leaders, who put high pressures on subordinates, regarding production tend to have increased production, but this is achieved at the cost of subordinates' motivation and satisfaction, in the long run. General supervision, greater reliance on punishments and control over the work situation are likely to help increase productivity. He believed that System 4 - Participative management, is the ideal one. It promises lower absenteeism and turnover of labour, a low grievance rate, and a consistent increase in production, morale and satisfaction. He also emphasised that human resources take a long time to develop into an efficient and committed work force. Thus, a participative leader should aim at developing human resources to reap benefits in the long run.

Styles of leadership developed by Likert, have been criticised for not emphasizing the situational aspects of leadership. Likert's conclusion, that supportive and participative relationship invariably lead to a desirable outcome, is considered as over-simplistic.

REDDIN'S THREE-DIMENSIONAL LEADERSHIP STYLES

Reddin has developed two category styles of leadership famously known as 3-D leadership styles, based on Blake and Mouton's managerial grid. He used the dimensions of effectiveness to task orientation and relationship orientation to formulate a three-dimensional theory. He suggested certain styles that can be effective or ineffective depending upon the situation. The styles of leadership prescribed by Reddin are enumerated below.

Effective Leadership Styles

(i) Executive style: A leader following this style shows significant concern for both production and people. He sets high standards, but uses teamwork. Therefore, he is highly successful in accomplishing goals. Above all, he is a good motivator.

(ii) **Developer style:** In this style a leader has a great concern for people, and minimal regard for production. He has implicit trust and confidence in his subordinates, and always tries to train them to have a positive attitude and be good human beings.

(iii) **Benevolent autocrat style:** A leader who follows this style shows great concern for accomplishment of tasks, and little to workers. As he plans and executes tasks carefully, he attains goals without subordinates resenting him.

(iv) **Bureaucrat style:** A bureaucrat leader shows great concern for work by clear structuring of tasks. He develops, maintains and lays great emphasis on rules and regulations. He controls his subordinates' actions, by strict vigilance and formal controls. Hence, most subordinates dislike him. However, he achieves goals successfully.

Ineffective Leadership Styles

(i) **Compromiser style:** A leader who follows such a style is weak in making decisions. He is often undecided as to whether to give priority to tasks or people, and due to this may become ineffective.

(ii) **Missionary style:** Such a leader lays emphasis on concern for people even in a situation that demands more emphasis on the task at hand. Thus, he is unable to get the task accomplished. He is good for the workers, but bad for the organisation.

(iii) **Autocrat style:** An autocrat leader lays great emphasis on accomplishment of the task, even when the situation demands consideration of the employees' welfare. He does not have confidence in his subordinates, and hence, creates unpleasant situations.

(iv) **Deserter style:** Such a leader is passive, pessimistic and escapist. He is not much concerned about either production or the employees' welfare. Therefore, he is not liked by anybody.

Certain other styles of leadership have also been propounded by other researchers. Some of them are: Tough autocrat, manipulative leadership, expert leadership, consultative leadership. Interestingly all styles of leadership, whatever they may be called, fall between 'authoritarian' and 'democratic'.

SUMMARY

Style is the manner in which a person acts or reacts in a situation. Leadership style is the way a leader behaves with his subordinates. Evidence shows that the concept of leadership style emerged from scientific studies of management, although definite dimensions were not developed. Studies conducted in 1939 at the University of Iowa led to three mutually exclusive styles of leadership called authoritarian, democratic and laissez faire, based on the way in which a leader makes decisions. Thus, decision making became a major dimension in understanding styles of leadership. Robert Tannenbaum and others rejected the hypothesis that leaders may be exclusively authoritarian or democratic. They developed a continuum depicting seven dimensions of behaviour regarding making decisions. The studies conducted at Michigan State University and Ohio State University, later became the basis for Robert Blake and Jane S. Mouton to develop the managerial grid, which has five styles *viz.*, impoverished, task, team, country club and middle of the road. The managerial grid considered concern for production and concern for people as the basis for developing styles of leadership. Extending the same philosophy but adding a third dimension called effectiveness, Reddin identified two styles of leadership, namely, effective and ineffective. Effective leadership styles are executive, developer, benevolent autocrat, and bureaucrat. Compromiser, missionary, autocrat and deserter are ineffective styles. Rensis Likert conducted extensive studies on management systems and propounded four systems of management, akin to styles of leadership *viz.*, System 1: Exploitative authoritative, System 2: Benevolent autocrat, System 3: Consultative, System 4: Participative. All these styles of leadership served as a guide to understand the phenomenon. However, all styles depict two phenomenon i.e., authoritarian and democratic.

Key words:

- **Authoritarian:** A leader who expects strict compliance from his subordinates
- **Authority:** The right to command obedience from subordinates
- **Benevolent autocrat:** Expressing moderate concern towards subordinates and significant consideration towards production.
- **Compromiser:** A leader who is weak in making decisions.
- **Country club:** A human relations expert. He shows great concern towards employees.
- **Democratic:** A leader who shows appreciation and allows participation.
- **Deserter:** A passive, pessimistic and escapist leader.
- **Developer:** A leader who shows great concern for the welfare of people.
- **Exploitative authoritative:** A leader who treats subordinates as instruments of production and does not involve them in making decisions, due to lack of trust and confidence in them.
- **Impoverished:** The belief that minimum effort is sufficient to organise tasks.
- **Laissez faire:** A leader who does not take any responsibility for production or people
- **Middle of the road:** A leader who expresses equal concern for both production and people.
- **Missionary:** A leader who shows more concern for people, even when accomplishment of the task is a priority.
- **Power:** Personal capability to command obedience.

Case study 25.1: The selection paradigm

Mr. Atreya is the Managing Director of Vani Engineering Company. In order to increase sales, the company decided to start a full-fledged marketing department. The M.D. was entrusted with the task of finding a suitable candidate to lead the proposed marketing department.

Mr. Atreya preferred internal recruitment rather than external recruitment. After careful screening, he selected two candidates, Mr. Koundinya and Mr. Vishwamitra.

Mr. Koundinya has been with the company for fifteen years. He is liked by all his colleagues due to his high-quality workmanship and pleasing manners. He believes that employees should participate in taking decisions, unlike Mr.Vishwamitra. He encourages his subordinates to come out with innovative ideas and useful suggestions. Before arriving at a decision, he always makes it a point to consult his subordinates. Not surprisingly, all his subordinates are very pleased to work under him and praise his leadership qualities. They readily admit that the environment he has created encourages them to use their talents fully in the service of the organisation. Company records also show that there was an increase in production soon after Mr. Koundinaya became the head of the department.

Mr. Vishwamitra, who has been with the company for ten years, has an excellent record of accomplishment. He is always enthusiastic and innovative in his work. He is still young (35 years) dynamic and aggressive. He is result oriented and is, naturally, more interested in the end rather than the means. One of the workers, testifying to his leadership qualities remarked that although he is harsh at times, you will know where you stand when you work with him. When you have done a good job, he lets you know it. Mr.Vishwamitra is willing to shoulder additional responsibilities. He decides things quickly and when action is required, he is always on his toes.

Questions:

1. Analyse the leadership styles of the prospective candidates.
2. What is the leadership style required to manage the marketing department?
3. If you were in the position of Mr. Atreya, whom would you select for the proposed department? Why?

26. SITUATIONAL LEADERSHIP BEHAVIOUR

This chapter enables you:

- *To understand the meaning of leadership effectiveness*
- *To appreciate situational variables used in the Fiedler model*
- *To examine the path goal approach of leadership effectiveness*
- *To examine the role of participation in effective leadership*

The structure of the chapter is as follows:

- Introduction
- Definition of leadership effectiveness
- Fiedler's contingency model of leadership effectiveness
- Path goal theory of leadership effectiveness
- Normative model
- Summary
- Key words

CHAPTER 26

Situational Leadership Behaviour

INTRODUCTION

Managers adopt a variety of styles of leadership, depending on the situation. For example, in an emergency, say a fire, the manager has to take an immediate decision. Whereas, if a decision has to be taken on a policy matter it would be best to take an opinion from subordinates. A number of theories were developed to explain the effectiveness of leadership styles. Some popular theories are the Fiedler Contingency Theory, the Path Goal Theory and the Normative Model. This chapter explains these theories in detail.

DEFINITION OF LEADERSHIP EFFECTIVENESS

Leadership effectiveness is the degree to which a leader is effective in making subordinates work towards the attainment of goals. It can be understood by dividing it into less effective and more effective behaviour. The role a leader plays, according to the demands of the situation, determines how effective he is. Thus, the situation determines the effectiveness or otherwise of a style of leadership.

While describing effectiveness, Reddin stated that, 'Leadership effectiveness is the extent to which the leader influences his followers to achieve group objectives'.

Managerial effectiveness is the extent to which a manager achieves the output requirements of his position.

'Managerial effectiveness is defined as any set of managerial actions believed to be optimal for identifying, assimilating and utilising both internal and external resources toward sustaining, over the long term, the functioning of the organisational unit for which a manager has some degree of responsibility'.

– Campbell

The above definitions reveal the following:

1. An effective leader influences his group positively.
2. Effective managers meet the output requirements.
3. Optimum use of internal and external resources is the job of an effective manager.
4. Managerial effectiveness is a long run concept.
5. Managerial effectiveness depends on the situation, and varies from situation to situation.
6. Managerial effectiveness is a multi-dimensional phenomenon. It is influenced by a host of factors. Hence, it is judged by multiple variables.

Leadership effectiveness largely depends on an effective match between personality, attitude, task, power of the leader and the environment in which the leader is working. Therefore, most of the situational theories have integrated the dimension of effectiveness in leadership behaviour.

The following models have been developed to study leadership effectiveness:

i. Fiedler Contingency Model
ii. Robert House Path Goal Model
iii. Vroom and Yetton Normative Model

FIEDLER'S CONTINGENCY MODEL OF LEADERSHIP EFFECTIVENESS

Fiedler propounded the contingency model of leadership. He concluded that people become effective leaders because of various situational factors and their interactions with them. He has used task-oriented and relationship-oriented styles of leadership to examine the model. The model has the following assumptions.

Assumptions and Methodology:

- Leadership is fixed
- Situation determines effectiveness of leadership style
- Style of leadership is measurable

The model uses the following methodology.

The model was developed after conducting studies in about 1200 groups of people. For this purpose, two variables were used: Assumed Similarity Control (ASM) and Least Preferred Coworker (LPC). A high score suggests that the leader is oriented towards human relationships and a low score indicates task orientation.

Description of the Model

'Effective performance of a group depends upon a proper match between leadership style and degree of situational control and leadership influence.' Leadership style is fixed. If a leader's style does not match the situation, either the situation or the leader should be changed. The score of LPC can be understood from Figure 26.1.

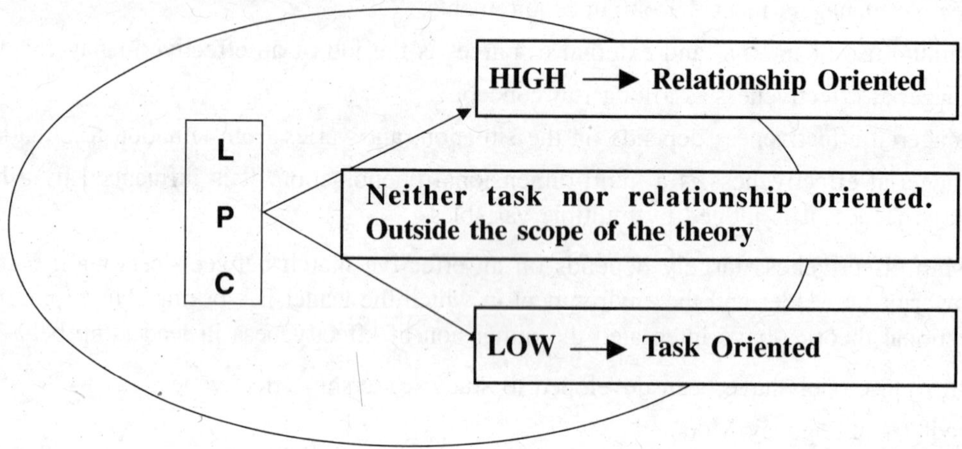

Figure 26.1: Understanding LPC

According to the model, three variables determine effectiveness of the style of leadership. They are discussed below.

Structure of tasks: According to Fiedler the structure of a task is the extent to which the various jobs or tasks, a person is expected to perform, are defined along with Standardised Operating Procedures (SOP). Highly structured tasks enable a leader to evaluate the task, monitor and influence subordinates and control the quality of performance. Thus, he can take complete responsibility for the subordinates' behaviour. On the other hand, if tasks are unstructured and vague, it becomes difficult for the leader, as he has to give detailed directions to subordinates. In addition, he cannot evaluate their performance easily. This can lead to considerable disagreement, on various factors, with his subordinates.

Power: Power is the capacity to influence a person. It can be positional power or personal power. In organisations, managers have power due to the position they occupy in the hierarchy of organisation. According to Fiedler, a leader with high positional power, who can take decisions to hire or fire employees, enforce discipline, give promotions and salary increments and award incentives, is most effective. Leaders without power have to rely on their subordinates and various other factors.

Leader-member relations: The degree to which subordinates repose confidence and trust in their superior and respect him determines their willingness to follow him and accept him as their leader.

Fielder's contingency model is shown in Figure 26.2. According to Fiedler, leader-member relations are the most important factor in determining the style of leadership and its effectiveness. He classifies situations as favourable and unfavourable. According to the theory, a highly structured task, strong positional power and good leader-member relations are favourable to the leader, as they enable him to exert influence over the group. In contrast, an unfavourable situation arises, when the task is ill-structured, the leader has weak positional power and strained leader-member relations. This limits his influence over subordinates. A leader is said to have situational control when the situation is favourable to him and *vice-versa*.

On the other hand, in intermediate situations leaders with high LPC scores are more effective. Fiedler's contingency model is an extension of trait and behavioural theories of leadership effectiveness. This theory is valuable in understanding leadership effectiveness, and the causal effect of leadership on performance. Thus, it enables managers to review their own behaviour and assess motivation of their subordinates.

Very favourable situation	LEADER MEMBER RELATIONS	TASK STRUCTURE	POSITIONAL POWER OF LEADER	SUCCESSFUL LEADERSHIP STYLE
↑	GOOD	Structured	Strong	Task orientation
			Weak	Task orientation
		Unstructured	Strong	Task orientation
			Weak	Consideration
	POOR	Structured	Strong	Consideration
			Weak	Consideration
↓		Unstructured	Strong	Task orientation
Very unfavourable situation			Weak	Task orientation

Figure 26.2: Fiedler's Contingency Model

However, the model is subject to the following criticism:

(a) The theory relies more on the situation rather than the behaviour of the leader.
(b) The interpretation of LPC scores is not uniform in all studies conducted by Fiedler. It has been subject to arbitrary change.
(c) This theory failed to explain the causal effect of LPC scores on subordinates' performance.
(d) Contingency variables used in this theory are difficult to assess through quantitative terms.
(e) The theory does not take the characteristics and capacities of the leader and the led, into consideration.
(f) The correlation and the supporting data are not statistically significant.
(g) Leader-member relations are more an intervening variable rather than a situational variable.

PATH-GOAL THEORY OF LEADERSHIP EFFECTIVENESS

The contingency theory of leadership proposed by Robert J. House is known as the Path-Goal Theory. This theory is based on both leadership and motivational theories. It assumes that the primary functions of a leader are to motivate subordinates, set goals and show them the path that leads to effective achievement of predetermined goals. Thus, the leader is expected to provide direction, guidance and incentives to his subordinates, which are not provided by the organisation. He should devise methods to satisfy the needs of subordinates, reduce stress and avoid pitfalls. Hence, according to this theory certain leadership styles are effective in situations, which facilitate effective matching of paths and goals of work. The various dimensions of leadership used in this theory are explained below.

Directive leadership: It is also known as instrumental leadership. It includes providing clear and specific directions and guidance. The leader ensures that subordinates follow standard rules and regulations.

Participative leadership: This style lays stress on the importance of subordinates participation in making decisions.

Supportive leadership: In this style the behaviour of the leader is characterised by consideration and affection towards his subordinates. The leader creates an effective, friendly and warm work environment.

Achievement oriented leadership: This seeks to set challenging and high performance goals. The leader has great confidence in his subordinates, and believes that they are capable of achieving high performance.

The path goal theory is shown in Figure 26.3. As can be seen from the figure, the leader influences the valence and expectations of subordinates. However, both of these are influenced by the characteristics of the work environment and subordinates' characteristics. These are known as situational factors. These situational factors determine the degree of subordinates' motivation and satisfaction. The propositions of this theory are summarised below.

(i) In the situation of role ambiguity, directive leadership is effective. This increases a subordinate's efforts and satisfaction.

(ii) If a task is difficult, causing anxiety and stress, supportive leadership is effective in increasing the subordinate's self-confidence to achieve the task.

(iii) Participative leadership is effective when tasks are unstructured. It is also effective when roles are clearly defined.

(iv) If subordinates like to be independent and are achievement oriented, then the participative style is effective.

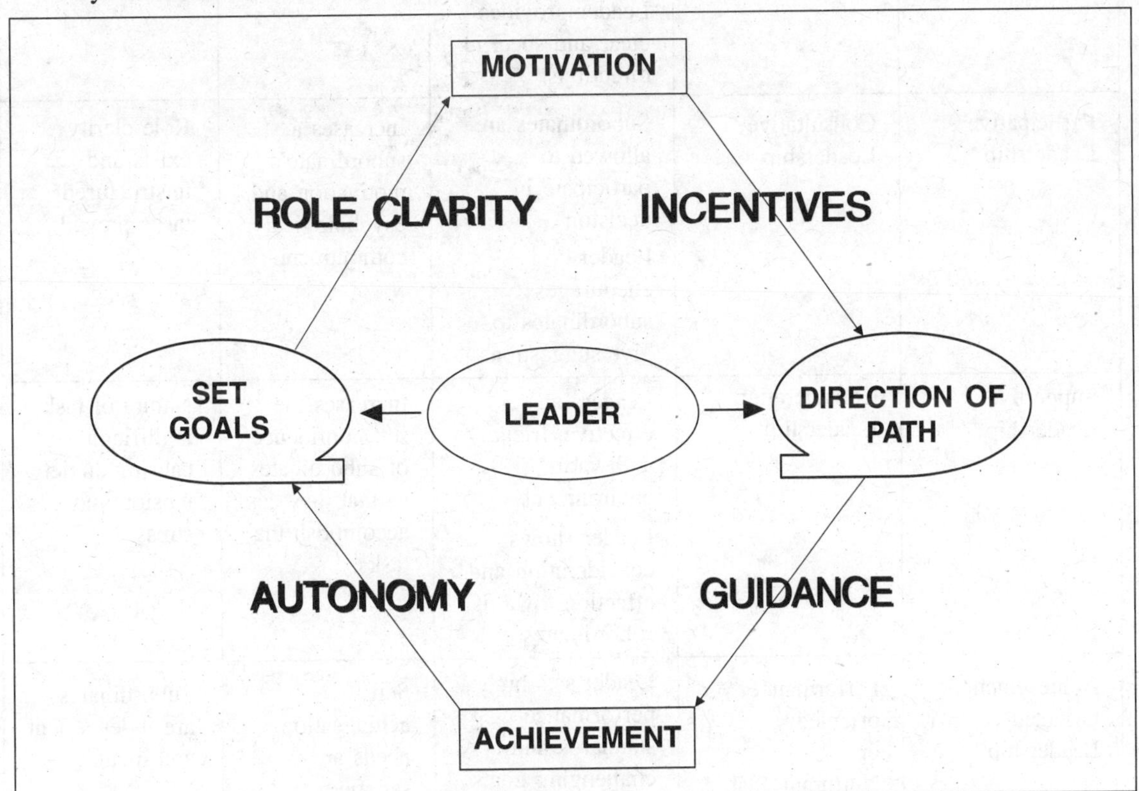

Figure 26.3: Robort House's Path Goal Theory

Table 26.1 shows leadership effectiveness of the path goal theory. The Directive leadership style used in the path goal model provides clear and specific directions and guidance. The leader ensures that subordinates follow standard rules and regulations. The moderating situation characterised by increase in subordinates' effort results from this style. The effectiveness is role ambiguity. This indicates that directive leadership style does not provide a right path to the effectiveness. In the case of achievement oriented style of leadership, the leader has confidence in his subordinates, resulting in satisfaction of self-actualisation needs. Thus, subordinates develop independence and maturity.

Table 26.1 Leadership Effectiveness of Path Goal Theory

PATH GOAL LEADERSHIP	ALTERNATIVE STYLE	LEADER'S BEHAVIOUR	MODERATING SITUATION	EFFECTIVE-NESS
Directive Leadership	Instrumental Leadership	Leader ensures that subordinates folow standard rules and regulations. Leader provides clear and specific directions.	Increases a subordinate's efforts and satisfaction.	Role ambiguity prevails.
Participative Leadership	Consultative Leadership	Subordinates are allowed to participate in decisions. Leader encourages subordinates to give suggestions	Increases a subordinate's motivation and psychological commitment.	Role clarity exists and unstructured tasks prevail.
Supportive Leadership	Consideration Leadership	Leaders an effective, friendly and warm environment Leader shows consideration and affection towards subordinates.	Increases the self-confidence of subordinates so that they can accomplish the tasks.	Nature of task is difficult causing anxiety, tension and stress.
Achievement Oriented Leadership	Performance oriented or Nurturant Task (J B P Sinha)	Leader sets high performance standards and challenging goals Has high confidence in his subordinates and believes they are capable of attaining a high standard of performance and achievinggoals, and lays emphasis on these.	Self - actualisation needs are satisfied.	Subordinates are independent and mature.

This theory is increasingly useful to practicing managers. Apart from explaining leadership factors, it tries to explain motivation of subordinates. However, the theory has certain deficiencies, which are explained below.

(i) Lack of clear definition of variables and casual relationship in the theory results in conceptual ambiguity.

(ii) This theory only partially explains leadership effectiveness. Leaders use motivational techniques coupled with other methods to guide the performance of subordinates.

(iii) This theory specifies that situational factors influence a leader's behaviour, however it does not explain how this takes place.

(iv) There is not much evidence that the primary input of the theory 'valence and expectancy,' affects employees' effort and satisfaction.

NORMATIVE MODEL

Victor Vroom and Philip Yetton developed a normative model of leadership effectiveness. This model relies on the fact that participation is an essential variable of effectiveness. According to this model, the style of leadership is effective or ineffective depending on the degree of participation related to the work situation. On the other hand, a leader uses a combination of five styles depending upon the situational requirements of the work.

Vroom and Yetton provided a list of questions to make a decision, favourable to the situation.

1. What are the quality requirements? Are they high or low?
2. How much information is there to make a qualitative decision?
3. How structured is the problem?
4. To what degree will the decision be accepted by the subordinates?
5. What is the possibility of acceptance of unilateral decisions?
6. What is the degree of sharing of organisational goals and the level of motivation?
7. To what degree will subordinates disagree with the decision?

The model uses five styles of leadership, which are explained below.

A. **Autocratic I:** An autocratic leader solves all problems and takes decisions based on information available with him.

B. **Autocratic II:** This leader makes decisions after obtaining information from subordinates. Subordinates are not involved in making decisions at all.

C. **Consultative I:** A consultative leader shares problems and discusses them with subordinates one at a time. After obtaining the required information, he makes decisions.

D. **Consultative II:** Under this style, a leader discusses problem with subordinates in a group. The decision is made based upon suggestions and opinions of subordinates.

E. **Group II:** A Group II leader shares problems with a group of subordinates. A feasible solution is generated by the group, which is converted into decision.

According to this model, a leader first diagnoses the situation and adopts a particular style of leadership suitable to the situation, so that the final decision will be the best one and it will be accepted by all. The model prescribes certain styles of leadership to meet the demands of different situations.

Table 26.2 gives the feasible set of leadership styles appropriate to different situations.

Table 26.2: Leadership styles appropriate to different situations

Situational demands	Feasible set of leadership styles
Subordinates reasonably accept an autocratic decision. An accepted solution gives rise to conflict among subordinates. Subordinates have sufficient information to make good decisions.	Autocratic I Consultative I Consultative II Group II
Subordinates are ready to share organisational goals.	Autocratic II Consultative I Consultative II

From Table 26.2 it will be seen that:

(i) More than one leadership style is effective in a particular situation. Obviously, no single style of making decisions is appropriate in all situations.

(ii) Development of subordinates is possible with a participative style of leadership.

(iii) Leader uses an autocratic style in a situation if there is a time constraint.

(iv) In terms of cost, the leader selects that style which results in least expenditure.

(v) When the quality of the decision is important, and the subordinates will not accept the decision without participation, the leader functions in the participative style, if the subordinates are trustworthy and mature, and vice-versa.

A feasible set of leadership styles consists of a range of styles, varying from autocratic to group. Therefore, a leader tries to adopt the style of leadership most appropriate to the demands of the situation.

Factors affecting Leadership Style in Normative Model

According to Vroom and Yetton, the effectiveness of the style of leadership depends upon quality, rationality, commitment to acceptance of the decision and the time factor. These are discussed below:

Quality of the decision: It refers to the degree of effectiveness of the decision and its impact on the performance of subordinates. A decision is said to be qualitative when the subordinate's performance increases due to implementation of the decision. In this case, if the subordinates possess information, the leader uses the participative style of making decisions.

Rationality: Rationality in making decisions is the extent to which a preferred solution allows the decision-maker to realise his goals. Since making a decision is a human, mental process complete rationality is not possible. As such, a leader attempts to be as rational as possible with the given information. Greater rationality will necessitate consulting subordinates to obtain comprehensive information.

Acceptance: Subordinates accept decisions when they are convinced that the decisions allow realisation of goals. Once subordinates are convinced about the decision, they will commit themselves to implement it. According to the normative model acceptance is achieved by absolute participation.

Time constraints: Time is a crucial factor in determining participation. Urgent decisions have to be made without participation. Therefore, a leader assumes the autocratic style. On the other hand, less important decisions and decisions that can be taken leisurely enable the leader to elicit complete participation of subordinates and he assumes a group decision making style.

The normative model is a theory, which is practically effective. It prescribes styles of leadership acceptable to the demands of the situation. The theory recognises participation as a vital tool for effectiveness. In addition, the model was developed after considerable experimentation with other similar models. However, the model is subject to following criticism:

- The model suggests that an effective leader chooses an appropriate style that helps to conserve time. However, these propositions do not hold in all cases.
- The model has been developed recently. As such little empirical evidence exists for it.
- The methodology of the model is considered incomprehensive for operational application.
- The model does not consider the subordinates' predisposition to participation.

In spite of its limitations, the model is very relevant to practicing managers in selecting the appropriate style of making a decision. The utility of the theory is summarised by Luthans. He stated that, 'Overall, the Vroom and Yetton model has much surface logic and it does give precise answers to practicing managers. However, as in the case of other approaches, more research is needed on the positive side. Its attempt to bridge the gap from theory to practice may be a step in right direction, and it can serve as a prototype for the actual practice of contingency management'.

SUMMARY

Leadership effectiveness is the extent to which a leader makes subordinates realise the goals of the organisation. Fiedler propounded a contingency model by considering styles of leadership oriented towards relationships and tasks. The model used ASM and LPC. According to the model, the structure of a task, power and leader-member relations determine the effectiveness of leadership. Robert House's path goal theory identified four styles of leadership *viz.*, directive, participative, supportive and achievement oriented. The model argued that an effective leader should match paths and goals. Four factors that influence path-goal collaboration are autonomy, guidance, role clarity and incentives. The model developed by Vroom and Yetton described five styles of leadership, namely: Autocratic I, Autocratic II, Consultative I, Consultative II and Group II. According to this model effectiveness of the style of leadership is a function of quality, rationality, commitment to accept the decision and time constraints of a situation.

Key words:

- **ASM:** Assumed Similarity Control
- **Leadership effectiveness:** The extent to which a leader influences his followers to achieve objectives of the group.
- **LPC:** Least Preferred Co-worker
- **Managerial effectiveness:** The extent to which a manager achieves the required output, according to his position.
- **Power:** The capacity to influence a person.
- **Rationality:** The extent to which a preferred solution allows the decision-maker to realise his goals.
- **SOP:** Standardised Operating Procedures

Case Study 26.1: A leader will not be successful without facing certain hardships

The Oracle Corporation is one of the world's most successful database software companies. Its CEO and Director Mr. Larry Ellison has faced ups and downs over the last 25 years, which provided ample scope for growth of his leadership qualities. He is among the world's richest people. He has been described as the 'ultimate narcissist,' and he has been a most intriguing and influential leader. Today his company has more than 43,000 employees. However everything has not always been a bed of roses, there have been some very hard and difficult times.

Ellison has always been a very logical person, even as a child. However due to his poor interest in academics, he was unsuccessful in his University examinations. He said, 'I never had the discipline to do the things that I did not like'. Since his interest was physics and programming, he joined a firm called Amdahl, but was retrenched. This acted as a challenge to him to start his own firm known as Relational Software, Inc. The firm concentrated on software development, but experienced a severe cash crunch. The crisis was so critical that the firm could not pay employees' salaries and the CEO could not claim his. There had been a setback in his personal life with the breakdown of his second marriage. On the business front, there was intense competition to his software, Oracle, from a company called Sybase that announced its unique 'referential integrity and two phases commit'. To combat this, the company took a hasty decision to release a new version of Oracle. Unfortunately, it was not very good and only worsened the situation, as it did not do well on the market. However, Ellison took it up as a challenge. He targeted a packaged application to computerise business operations, known as Enterprise Resource Planning (ERP). During the 1980s his company showed a continuous downward trend in sales figures and a poor performance on the stock market. Even in this disastrous situation, he was confident of rejuvenating the company.

Ellison was a great visionary and optimist. He studied Japan's economy closely and his negotiations with Japanese companies for purchase of his software slowly started giving positive results. The company brought about significant changes in hiring policies and introduced cost control measures that led to great improvement. Ellison introduced Parallel Processing, otherwise known as Cluster Technology, which brought computer networking into the limelight. Some of these measures did bring brand recognition to Oracle, but it still faced competition from SAP, IBM and Microsoft. Ellison felt that the only real threat was IBM, as IBM had a number of innovative products like a disk drive, core memory, scanning etc. By 2001 Oracle had more than 40 percent of the market share, almost double that of IBM. Today, Oracle is one of four main pillars of the internet infrastructure, along with Sun Microsystems, EMC and Cisco Systems.

Although Ellison's style of leadership created a vast business enterprise, it had its faults. His autocratic management style caused the Executive Vice President and the Chief Operating Officer (COO) to leave the company. It is relevant to note that Lane, EVP, stated that, Ellison had pushed him out, diminishing his duties and assuming them himself. In the opinion of Bloom, COO 'there was no room left to grow at Oracle since the leader is not going to accept the top spot anytime soon. This despite the fact that the COO position was never filled and no one holds the title of president at the company'. Ellison's industry predictions were legendary. There is no doubt that he is a great entrepreneur. His vision that the relational database would be commercially feasible made Oracle very successful. This remarkable achievement came from his profound technical expertise and skill in acknowledging people's talent.

Questions:

1. Analyse the situational dimensions of Ellison's leadership.
2. What were the qualities of leadership Ellison possessed and which enabled him to make the company a success?
3. If you were in his position, how would you have managed to raise the company from the deep trouble it was in?

27. EMERGING LEADERSHIP BEHAVIOUR

This chapter enables you:

- *To distinguish between charismatic and non-charismatic leaders*
- *To distinguish between transactional and transformational behaviour of leaders*
- *To comprehend the articulation of vision to build an organisation*
- *To appreciate the need of adapting leadership behaviour to manage millennium organisations*
- *To understand certain trends in the styles of leadership in Indian organisations*

The structure of the chapter is as follows:

- Introduction
- Charismatic leadership behaviour
- Transactional leadership behaviour
- Transformational leadership behaviour
- Visionary leadership behaviour
- Leadership for millennium organisations
- Leadership for Indian organisations
- Summary
- Key words

CHAPTER 27

Emerging Leadership Behaviour

INTRODUCTION

Leadership is a catalyst in the process of organisational development. Traditional conceptualisation of leadership is slowly becoming obsolete in millennium organisations. The changing face of organisations is demanding new vistas in leadership for managing in turbulent times. Global dynamics require organisations to be more competitive, effective, oriented towards development and adaptive. The adaptation is not a structural one, but psychological one. Even if structural changes are made to suit the demands of the environment, a change in the employees' attitudes can only make organisations more effective. Thus leadership plays a significant role in shaping the human element to the dynamics of the organisation. In the organisations of today, i.e., in the 21st century, a successful leader has to have charisma, morality, vision, and emotional balance. This chapter provides an understanding of the emerging dimensions of leadership that are necessary in organisations of the future.

CHARISMATIC LEADERSHIP BEHAVIOUR

A good leader influences his subordinates so that they direct their energy towards realisation of goals. The influence is not physical but psychological. Psychological influence depends on the kind of behaviour a leader establishes with his subordinates. There are a number of propositions relating to how a leader should behave with his subordinates so as to influence them. Leadership behaviour is identified by the style of leadership. Initially, identification of styles of leadership were based on the transactions needed in the realisation of goals. Thus the styles were identified in terms of authoritarian-democratic (Lewin), theory X and theory Y (McGregor), impoverished, task, team, country club, middle of the road (Blake and Mouton) and decision continuum (Tannenbaum), which laid stress on the task or relationship for smooth processing of organisational transactions. Fiedler's model, the Vroom and Yetton Model, the Path Goal Model and the Tri-dimensional Grid, considered the dimensions of the situation and provided some prescriptions for effective leadership. The latter models have become more popular and are used more often to assess the effectiveness of leaders.

There have also been some extremists who asked the question, "Is really leadership required?" All our previous discussions have been based on the precept that leadership is necessary. Arguments that counter the idea of leadership are known as 'irrelevance approaches'. Their proponents believe that individual elements like experience, professionalism, and self-actualisation; job related variable such as highly structured tasks and organisational characteristics *viz.*, goal clarity, and rules on the one hand and personality variables on the other hand lead to performance, irrespective of leaders' presence. But it should be remembered that the unique nature of individuals require the fulcrum in driving the energy, that is 'Leadership'.

There are many instances that show how the presence of a leader provided the right direction. For example Mahatma Gandhi, Jawaharlal Nehru, Abraham Lincoln, John F. Kennedy, Roosevelt, Nelson Mandela are great political and social leaders who have provided a unique direction. J.R. D. Tata of Tata Limited, G.D. Birla of Birla Group, R.P. Goenka, Dhirubhai Ambani of Reliance, Narayana Murthy of Infosys, Ramalinga Raju of Satyam, Azim Premji, Bill Gates, Jack Welch, Andrew Grove have provided visionary leadership to business organisations. J.C. Bose, Vikram Sarabhai, Amartya Sen are great personalities in the realm of research and development. If one looks at the life and success of these personalities, it can be seen that their mantra for success is work up from the bottom. They have not become leaders by virtue of authority but due to their personal power to influence, because of their charisma. For instance, N.T. Rama Rao emerged as a national leader in a very short period due to his popularity as a film star, Chiranjeevi has a great following and is therefore successful in influencing people to donate their eyes after death. It is not necessary that great leaders follow the theoretical models and principles mentioned above. An average person can emerge as a charismatic leader, for example, Dhirubhai Ambhani who established Reliance Industries, worth crores of rupees, once upon a time worked in a petrol pump.

In recent times, a set of theoretical propositions known as Neo-Charismatic leadership theories, have been put forward. These theories emphasise symbolism, emotional appeal and extraordinary commitment of followers. House defined charismatic leaders as those 'who by force of their personal abilities are capable of having profound and extraordinary effects on followers'.

The features of charismatic leadership are mentioned below:

1. **Vision:** This is the ability to foresee the trends of the future. Not every one has this attribute, but persons who have this ability, will be able to direct their energy towards attaining it. Unfortunately, most individuals by nature seek immediate gratification of needs and are too impatient to wait for future benefits. A good leader will always link the present with his future vision in order to elicit greater commitment of followers. Such leaders impress their followers with their communication skills, and show a high degree of confidence in their followers' abilities, which motivates them to direct their energy to achieving the goals. These leaders, do not lead only by words, but also by their actions. An example is Ramoji Rao, an industrialist, who is known as a man of insight and vision. He established a film city in Hyderabad that even made Hollywood stars and film producers to look at our country.
2. **Risk orientation:** Charismatic leaders will always look beyond conventional ways and means, and will even be willing to take personal risks in directing their subordinates. This requires sacrifice on the part of a leader. He will be willing to incur personal costs, to elicit the commitment of his subordinates.
3. **Sensitivity:** Sensitivity refers to the perception of strengths, weaknesses, opportunities and threats. Charismatic leaders possess sensitivity towards both the environment and their followers. They make an effort to understand threats to the environment realistically. They follow strategies to adapt to the dynamics of the environment, and will not be satisfied with a *status quo*. At the same time, charismatic leaders develop an understanding of the abilities and skills of subordinates. They are responsive to their needs, feelings, emotions and attitudes. This kind of sensitivity makes a leader more popular, respected and revered.
4. **Different behaviour:** The actions and reactions of a charismatic leader, in different situations, may go against the conventional norms of behaviour followed in an organisation or group. Such a leader establishes novel norms of behaviour, which the subordinates emulate, as they see the leader as a role model. A charismatic leader has a strong personality, and usually good oratory power, clear thinking and an invincible mind. In dealing with followers he will maintain direct eye to eye contact, and be relaxed yet expressive, both vocally and through his body language. A charismatic leader often establishes new value systems for the group. His subordinates develop a sense of loyalty, confidence and belonging, and identify the leader with his behaviour and values rather than the person as such.

Nadler and Tushman identified three types of charismatic leadership styles based on behaviour. They are shown in Table 27.1.

Charismatic leaders are found in all fields, be it politics, military, religious activities, films, social associations, philanthropic activities, marketing and human resource, mentoring activities.

Distinctions between charismatic and non-charismatic leadership are shown in Table 27.2.

Table 27.1: Three types of charismatic leadership styles

Leadership styles	Characteristics
Envisioning leadership	Creating a picture of the future – or a desired future state – with which people can identify and which can generate excitement.
Energizing leadership	Directing energy and the motivation to act, among members of the organisation.
Enabling leadership	Psychologically helping people to act or perform in the face of challenging goals.

Source: Luthans, Organizational Behavior, p.413.

Table 27.2 Distinctions between charismatic and non-charismatic leadership behaviour

Characteristics	Charismatic leaders	Non-charismatic leaders
1. Vision	Possess vision that may be very different from that of others.	Goals and vision are not dynamic. Static vision.
2. Power	Attraction is based on personal power that comes from expertise, emotional association and respect.	Compliance is based on positional authority. Rewards, expertise and value of friendship determine personal power.
3. Leader follower base	Elitist, entrepreneurial and exemplary. Transforms followers to adopt radical changes.	Egalitarian, seeking consensus, or directive.
4. Behaviour	Unconventional behaviour. Behaviour is well within the existing norms.	Conventional behaviour. Actions are within the existing norms.
5. Risk	Takes personal risks and incur costs.	Not interested in taking risks. Attempts to elicit subordinates' commitment through persuasion.
6. Emulation	Leader's visualisation and ideal behaviour makes subordinates consider him as a role model and identify with him. Subordinates imitate the leader's behaviour.	Shared perception of the leader motivates subordinates to like the leader.
7. Articulation	Future goals are clearly articulated. There is motivation to lead.	Goals are not clearly articulated and there is poor motivation to lead.
8. Sensitivity	Sensitive to the environment with a view to change himself and his subordinates.	Insensitive to environmental changes. Desire to maintain status quo.
9. Expertise	Uses expertise to transcend the existing order.	Uses expertise in availing of the available means with the existing work order. Not very innovative.

Source: Based on Hodgetts M. Richard, 'Organizational Behavior'

Evidence from research shows that charismatic leaders are effective in motivating followers and ensuring that they are satisfied. Charismatic leaders elicit a positive commitment from their followers, who show high performance when working with them.

Are charismatic leaders born or made? There are arguments for both points of view. One school of thought believes that charisma is a purely personal and inherited trait, while another believes that charisma can be acquired. A charismatic leader is optimistic in viewing things, people and situations. He is enthusiastic and action-oriented. He develops a personal bond with his followers through his inspiration. He develops skills to tap the innate energy of followers.

Charismatic leadership is not always effective. It will only be effective if there is an ideological bondage between the leader and followers. It will not succeed if the leader is authoritarian. A charismatic leader can change an uncertain situation into a successful one. However, such a leader may also have an unethical side. The pessimistic side of charismatic leadership is associated with certain unethical elements also. For example, after the assassination of former Prime Minister Rajiv Gandhi, P.V. Narasimha Rao was made as prime minister. He gave a new direction to come out of turbulence of leadership in Congress at the moment. At the same moment, he faced charges of bribing the members for winning the confidence motion, which later was proved to be wrong. Some of the distinctive features of ethical and unethical charismatic leaders are given in Table 27.3.

Table 27.3: Distinctive features of ethical and unethical charismatic leaders

Distinctive features	Unethical charismatic leaders	Ethical charismatic leaders
1. Communication	One way communication	Open, two-way communication.
2. Followers' needs	Insensitive to followers' needs	Coaches, develops, and supports followers, shares recognition with others.
3. Learning	Censures critical or opposing views of followers.	Considers and learns from criticism.
4. Moral values	Relies on convenient, external moral standards to satisfy self interests.	Relies on internal moral standards to satisfy organisational and societal interests.
5. Power	Uses power for personal gain.	Uses power to serve others.
6. Stimulation of thinking	Demands that his own decisions be accepted without question.	Stimulates followers to think independently and to question the leader's views.
7. Vision	Promotes one's own personal vision.	Aligns his vision with followers' needs and aspirations.

Source: Jane M. Howel and Bruce J. Avoilo, (1992) 'The Ethics of Charismatic Leadership: Submission or Liberation?' Academy of Management Executive, May, p. 45, in Luthans, Organizational Behavior, (8th Ed.) p. 396.

TRANSACTIONAL LEADERSHIP BEHAVIOUR

Transactional leadership behaviour is associated with attainment of goals by identifying the transactions, providing resources, rewards and directing the followers' efforts to the objectives. The characteristics of transactional leadership behaviour are:

1. Providing direction to followers by establishing goals.
2. Motivating followers.
3. Designing the order of work and task relationships.
4. Developing a relationship with followers or subordinates.
5. Laying emphasis on the performance and effort of followers.

Most of the earlier leadership theories and models laid the emphasis on transactional leadership behaviour. The authoritarian theory, democratic theory, Fiedler's contingency model, and House's path goal model, are amongst the earlier theories. Transformational leaders have an impact on the followers' performance. They lay emphasis on convergence between organisational and individual goals. However, if individual goals and those of the organisation are not analogous, human nature is such that people will usually look to their self-interest. A leader should be able to inspire behaviour in his subordinates, that transcends self-interest.

TRANSFORMATIONAL LEADERSHIP BEHAVIOUR

Transformational leadership is the answer to the above situation. It is believed to be the leadership behaviour, most relevant to the 21st century. Transformational leadership behaviour lays emphasis on inspirational and developmental needs of followers. Such leaders create an indelible impression on their followers. They motivate and inspire followers to make additional efforts to achieve group goals. Tichy and Devanna identified the following characteristic features of transformational leaders.

1. Bring about change
2. Courage
3. Belief in people
4. Value driven
5. Life long learners
6. Ability to deal with complexity, ambiguity and uncertainty
7. Visionary

Bass identified the salient features of transactional and transformational leadership behaviour. They are shown in Table 27.4.

Transformational leadership has improved productivity and job satisfaction and has helped to reduce employee turnover.

Table 27.4: Salient features of transactional and transformational leadership behaviour

Characteristics	Transactional leaders
1. Contingent reward	Contracts exchange of rewards for effort, promises rewards for good performance, recognises accomplishments.
2. MBE (active)	Watches and searches for deviations from rules and standards, takes corrective action.
3. MBE (passive)	Intervenes only if standards are not met.
4. Laissez-faire	Abdicates responsibilities, and avoids making decisions.

Characteristics	Transformational Leaders
1. Charisma	Provides vision and a sense of mission, instils pride, gains respect and trust.
2. Inspiration	Communicates high expectations, uses symbols to focus efforts, expresses important purposes in simple ways.
3. Intellectual stimulation	Promotes intelligence, rationality and care in solving problems.
4. Individual consideration	Gives personal attention, treats each employee individually, coaches, advises.

Source: Bass M. Bernard (1990) 'From Transactional to Transformational Leadership: Learning to share the vision', Organisational Dynamics, Winter, p. 22 in Luthans, Organisational Behaviour, (8th ed.) p. 397.

VISIONARY LEADERSHIP BEHAVIOUR

Visionary leadership behaviour is an outgrowth of charismatic and transformational leadership behaviour. In modern organisations strategic vision has become popular. An organisation that visualises the future in a realistic manner can gear its human resources to meet future challenges with the required skills, capabilities and competencies. This enables the organisation to have planned growth and development. Thus persons who occupy positions of leadership and who provide a purposeful direction to the organisation should have future vision, i.e, they should have visionary leadership. Examples on the political front are the former chief minister of Andhra Pradesh, N. Chandra Babu Naidu, who declared a vision document 'vision 2020', and the former President of India, Dr. A.P.J. Abdul Kalam, who had a vision for the new millennium. On the business front we can cite Deepak Parekh, who gave a vision to HDFC Bank. His ability to anticipate emerging living patterns, spot business opportunities and prepare his corporation well in advance to launch new initiatives is proof of his vision.

Table 27.5: Behaviour and approaches of outstanding leaders

1. Vision	Outstanding leaders articulate an ideological vision that is congruent with the deeply held values of followers, a vision that describes a better future to which the followers have a moral right.
2. Confidence, determination and persistence	Outstanding leaders display a high degree of faith in themselves and in the attainment of the vision they articulate. Theoretically, such leaders need to have a very high degree of self-confidence and moral conviction because their mission usually challenges the status quo and, therefore, is likely to offend those who have a stake in preserving the established order.
3. Expectation of and confidence in followers	Outstanding leaders expect a high performance from their followers and they have confidence in their followers' ability to meet such expectations.
4. External representation	Outstanding leaders act as the spokesperson for their organisation and symbolically represent the organisation to external constituencies.
5. Frame alignment	To persuade followers to accept and implement change, outstanding leaders engage in frame alignment. This refers to the linkage of individual and leader interpretative orientation such that some set of the followers' interests, values, and beliefs, as well as the leader's activities, goals, and ideology, becomes congruent and complementary.
6. Image building	Outstanding leaders are self-conscious about their own image. They recognise that they must be perceived by followers as competent, credible, and trustworthy.
7. Inspirational communication	Outstanding leaders often, but not always, communicate their messages in an inspirational manner using vivid stories, slogans, symbols, and ceremonies.
8. Passion and self-sacrifice	Leaders display a passion for, and have a strong conviction of, the moral correctness of their vision. They engage in outstanding or extraordinary behaviour and make extraordinary self-sacrifices in the interest of their vision and the mission.
9. Role modelling	Leader image building sets the stage for effective role modelling because followers identify with the values of role models that are perceived positively.
10. Selective motive arousal	Outstanding leaders selectively arouse those motives of their followers that are of special relevance to the successful accomplishment of the vision and mission.

Source: Luthans, Organizational Behavior, p.421.

According to Nutt and Backoff, 'Vision has a clear and compelling imagery that offers an innovative way to improve, which recognises and draws on traditions, and connects to actions that people can take to realise change.' Vision taps people's emotions and energy. Properly articulated, a vision creates the enthusiasm that people have for sporting events and other leisure time activities, bringing this energy and commitment to the workplace'. Imagination, inspiration and value centred vision of leaders can bring a totally new organisational order that is distinct from that of other organisations. Simple articulation of vision is not the parameter for success. These leaders create an impression in the minds of followers that their vision is not a simple articulation, but it is attainable, with challenging commitment.

The unique skills of a visionary leader are given below.

1. The ability to visualise the future taking into account past and present trends. The vision should be rational and realistic.
2. Having a strong belief that the future they have envisaged can be attained.
3. Clarifying and aligning the vision with intended actions.
4. Communicating their vision through a written document, called a 'vision statement'.
5. The ability to instil a feeling in their followers that the vision of the future, will be put into action.
6. The way they behave is how they feel they should behave.
7. They reinforce their ideas about the future from time to time to encourage their followers.
8. They have the same vision in different situations.

A visionary leader will always act in any situation to instil confidence in his followers that he is with them in realising the future plans. All the concerned units in an organisation or institution should understand the plans in the same way. For example, a vision to achieve excellence and quality in higher education will not be successful if all the colleges and universities are not committed to the goal. The vision to develop an organisation into a market leader has to be understood not only by the marketing department. The production, finance, research and development and human resource departments should also have the same ideology of market leadership. Only then will the goals be achieved. For example, if the human resource department does not come up with proper training and development plans to increase the competency of the sales people, the entire proposal will fail. Thus a visionary leader has to ensure that all the units in the organisation work together.

From where does the leader get his vision? How is it transmitted to bring about organisational development? Michael Porter provided the answer to these questions. According to him the environment is a critical determinant of a leader's perception and priorities. Realising the environment causes leaders to adopt strategies to overcome ineptness, leading to organisational development.

LEADERSHIP FOR MILLENNIUM ORGANISATIONS

Organisational dynamics are changing at a very fast rate, much faster than in the past. This has led to a great deal of change. Competition, removal of barriers between countries, lifting protection given to national business, an open environment, liberalised policies, fast changing fashions and attitudes, rapid change in society, and being more open to adopting cultures, values and ethos are some of the reasons that distinguish millennium organisations. Today, political, economical, technological, legal, ecological, governmental and socio-ethical demographics are all subject to rapid change. Without energetic, visionary, trustworthy, ethical leadership and lemantorship (leader-manager-mentor used by the author) these organisations would not survive or withstand the millennium dynamics. Traditional leadership practices have become redundant for managing these organisations. The following discussion provides certain behavioural attitudes required for millennium organisations.

A. **Embal leadership:** Emotional balance (Embal) is one of the most recent behavioural attitudes needed for leadership, as leaders have to deal with different people and situations, which affect their emotions. Loss of emotional balance can lead to stress, anxiety, loss of memory and aggression in addition to physical ill effects, like blood pressure, heart attacks, strokes, ulcers etc. Within an organisation, emotional imbalance can destroy relationships, trust and confidence, and lead to poor judgement and disturbed functioning. Thus it is important that leaders maintain an emotional balance, especially in modern organisations where a number of internal and external environmental factors affect leaders' emotions. For example a customer relations manager will need emotional balance to retain customers and deal with their complaints.

The emotional balance of a leader depends on his emotional intelligence. For instance, suppose an employee left the office when the manager was away. On his return, the manager requires some information from the said employee, but finds he has left. The initial reaction of the manager will be anger, leading to tension and anxiety, as he cannot get the required information. However, after making enquiries the manager finds that the employee left because he received a call that his father has suddenly fallen sick. After this the emotions of the manager will change. With emotional intelligence the initial reaction will be avoided.

Emotional intelligence has five components. They are:

- **Self-awareness:** One should know one's inner self before dealing with people. Rational thinking about a situation with empathy relieves emotion. Self-confidence, realistic self-assessment and a sense of humour brings one's self-awareness. In the above example, instead of making assumptions, had the manager made enquiries first, he would not have experienced negative emotions. Self-awareness can be developed through yoga, attitude management, developing emotional intelligence and sidda samaja yoga.
- **Self-management:** Leaders should develop trust, personal integrity, and openness to change. These qualities allow him to control his emotions in tiresome situations. Impulsiveness causes emotions. It has active and dominance components. Dominance

leads to a feeling of ego. So one has to manage the ego to overcome dominance. Self-management is acquired by developing one's character, through education and learning.

- **Self-motivation:** Leaders must first develop a burning desire to achieve goals and always look at the positive side of a situation. They should have a high degree of personal commitment. All these characteristics enable the leader to understand his followers correctly, alleviating most unnecessary emotions.
- **Empathy:** Empathy is understanding and sympathising with others. A person who empathises with others will think rationally by placing himself in the other person's shoes and thus will be able to substantiate their actions. Empathy is not an easy trait. It requires a lot of visualisation. A leader shows empathy in building and retaining talent, cross cultural sensitivity and service to customers. In the area of customer relations, managers need empathy in order to avoid making emotional judgements of customers and provide them needed service. Leaders possessing the quality of empathy are emotionally balanced. In the earlier example, if the manager had placed himself in the subordinate's position, he would have avoided judging the employee, and also his own negative emotions.
- **Social skills:** In today's changing scenario, discrimination in education, gender, caste, nationality, language and racial aspects is disappearing. Thus a leader has to work with a variety of personalities. Being part of a team, and adapting to others is of great relevance to successful leaders, requiring him to handle the emotions of his subordinates, by maintaining his emotional balance. Social skills enable a leader to implement changes by overcoming any resistance effectively.

Leaders with high emotional intelligence quotient are likely to be more effective and successful in dealing with the followers, especially in millennium organisations. Thus organisations should develop 'embal leadership'.

B. Team leadership: Changing organisational dynamics demand that leaders work in cross-cultural teams rather than in traditional roles. The outcome of the Hawthorne movement was the formation of groups, however these are slowly disappearing from organisations, and being replaced by teams. In order to be effective in millennium organisations team leadership is needed. A team leader has to play a number of roles, which are described below. He has to:

- Represent teams
- Closely liaison with internal and external interventionists
- Facilitate the process of interaction among team members
- Gather information on a continuous basis
- Share information between team members and also with other teams
- Resolve problems faced by teams
- Encourage team members to ask questions and elicit more information
- Handle internal conflicts among team members
- Train and develop team members to ensure the optimum performance of the team

- See that every team member contributes according to their competencies rather than making every team member do every activity of the team

Team leadership is gaining popularity in modern organisations as it brings about more commitment in team members compared to members in a group.

C. **Trust leadership:** All interactions are based on some amount of trust and belief. Leadership based on trust and belief is gaining importance in modern organisations, in two ways. On one hand every leader is a trusted agent of the owners in managing the affairs of the business. On the other hand a leader has to trust his employees and subordinates. Thus he assigns activities to his subordinates believing that they are competent, motivated, sincere and interested in the tasks assigned to them. Trust is basically understood as a belief that others through their words, actions or decisions will not act opportunistically for their selfish benefit, rather they act for the benefit of all the concerned in a rational manner. Some of the propositions of trust are:

- Trust is built on information about others. This information enables a person to develop a belief in others. A person will not trust somebody else at the first meeting, because he has no information about him. So the expectations may be negative. Belief in another person is built up over time and with experience, leading to positive expectations and trust in others. Today leaders instil trust in their followers by being more open with them.
- Basically, an individual will always look to his or her own self-interest. Selfishness, greed, and possessiveness are some of the characteristics that drive a person to act selfishly rather than rationally. So, in the absence of trust, dealing with a person is basically risky. A good leader inculcates the significance of attaining organisational goals, rather than only looking for personal gain, in the minds of his subordinates. This makes them trustworthy, and they will not exploit any situation.
- Integrity is honesty and truthfulness. Personal integrity is very vital in leadership, otherwise followers will not believe in him and emulate him.
- Competence is possession of technical and non-technical knowledge and skills. Trust is developed when the inner ideas and outer actions of a person are the same. A leader assesses his followers' strength not only on the basis of his external presentation, but also on the basis of his own observations. When a leader develops trust in his followers he will have confidence that the assigned tasks will be performed in the way he expects them to be performed. Assessment based on factual information is thus very important. However, this may not always be the case.
- Consistency is reliability and predictability of individual actions over a period of time. It is based on past actions. If the actions of a person match his words, then consistency increases. Consistent actions strengthen trust. Leaders should take care to be consistent in their actions. Only then will their subordinates follow suit.
- Openness is the extent of truthfulness in projecting oneself. It is also related to transparency in actions. Concealing actions leads to poor belief and lack of trust. Followers prefer leaders who are open in their actions, as it enables them to gauge whether the leader's actions are in their interest.

- Loyalty is extending support in all situations. A leader should support his followers, especially in difficult situations, otherwise the subordinates will lose trust in the leader. Loyalty is a two-way process, the leader and followers should be loyal to each other.
- Honesty is the extent of sacrifice of self-interest for the common interest. The most missing link in the modern society is this. Dishonesty is more prevalent on the globe. Transparency of actions makes others feel about honesty. So openness is required to build trust and honesty in leaders.

Leadership is dealing with people. In millennium organisations trust leadership is required to understand organisational matters and use them to promote the welfare of the organisation. Organisational effectiveness through leadership effectiveness depends on the ability of a leader to gain the trust of his followers. Empowerment, transparent actions, sacrifice of personal interest as suggested by Fayol are some of the ways of increasing trust. Bartolome and Butler Jr. have suggested that the following be practised to build trust.

(i) Practice openness
(ii) Ensure fairness in dealings
(iii) Share feelings frankly
(iv) Always speak the truth
(v) Fulfil all promises
(vi) Maintain confidence
(vii) Show competence

D. Moral leadership: The words morals and ethics are used interchangeably. Moral behaviour is linked to ethics. Ethics is the expected conduct of behaviour in any social setting, and it may change from one society to another. What is ethical for an American may not be so, for an Indian. There are large number of examples of security scams, banking scams, taxation scams, and scams related to the poor quality of products. All these reflect the moral values of the leaders involved in these organisations. The moral dimensions of leadership in an enterprise are presented in the Figure 27.1.

Moral leadership is concerned with integrity, trust, confidence, fair and just behaviour, equal opportunities, constructive ideology, optimism, and honesty. Every style of leadership has certain moral and ethical values that make it effective. The democratic leadership style is characterised by the participation of subordinates in the decision making process. It recognises them as being equally important in implementing decisions. The path goal leadership shows the proper path on constructive ways to the followers. Embal leadership is concerned with exercising control over emotions, thus respecting the followers' intentions. Transformational leadership aims at modifying subordinates' attitudes to foster moral virtues. Moral charismatic leaders use their power over their followers to promote constructive ideology for the benefit of others.

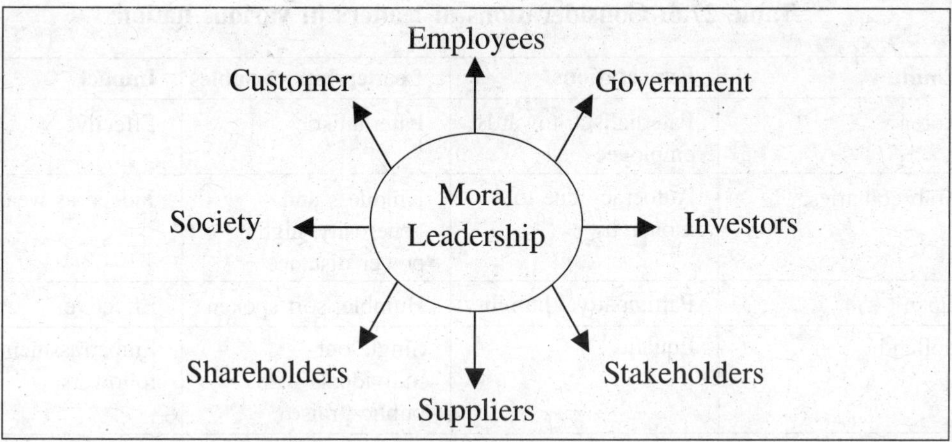

Figure 27.1: Ethical dimensions of leadership

Millennium leadership should thus be oriented towards developing values and ethics to craft itself into moral leadership. Survival of the organisation and effectiveness of leadership depend on the degree of moral values in leadership.

E. **Cross-cultural leadership:** With the increasing pace of globalisation, the world is becoming a 'global village'. Travel has become commonplace and information technology has connected people like never before. The number of multinational corporations has increased in all countries, and people are taking up jobs all over the world. Many multinational corporations bring in their own people to manage the concern, at least until they find a suitable person in the country itself. This has increased the importance of different cultures in an organisation. Both the leader and the subordinates need to understand the cross culture, to successfully manage such enterprises.

The culture of the native land, along with other personal and situational variables, has a profound influence on the specific style of leadership adopted. Cross cultures add to the list of determinants of leadership. Managers migrating to foreign countries bring in their styles of leadership to manage the enterprise. At the same time, the employees from the country influence the style of leadership so that it conforms to the culture of native country. The extent to which subordinates or others influence the style of leadership is not clear, but a certain degree of influence is obvious. Thus millennium leadership needs to be more adaptable to cross cultures in managing the employees. Training in cross cultures goes a long way in providing an adequate background for rapid adjustment. Moreover, management education should equip its students to deal with cross cultures. Some considerations of leadership in various nations are shown in Table 27.6.

Table 27.6: Considerations of leaders in various nations

Country	Expectations	Leadership variables	Impact
Korea	Paternalistic towards employees	Paternalistic	Effective
Arab countries	Autocracy due to monarchy	Kindness and generosity, high power distance	Judged as weak
Japan	Participative, humility	Humble, soft spoken	Effective
Holland	Equality	Single out individuals with public praise	Embarrassment to followers
United States	Followers' responsibility, hedonism, altruistic motivation	Centralisation, oriented towards democratic values, rationality	Effective
Norway, Finland, Denmark and Sweden	Low power distance	Participation	Effective
North America	Empowerment	Democratic	Effective
China	Obedience	Heartless management, rigorous military training	Learning from one's own mistakes

(*Source*: Taken from Robbins P. Stephen, (2000) Organizational Behavior. 9th ed. PHI, New Delhi.)

F. Lemantor leadership: Earlier literature on organisations emphasised managerial leadership. The Hawthorne movement emphasised leadership-oriented managers, whilst the latest is mentor-oriented management. Therefore, we have coined the term 'lemantor leadership' to mean leader-manager-mentor oriented leadership that is charismatic and leads the followers to develop sound attitudes.

The word mentoring originated from Greek mythology. A mentor provides emotional education and guidance to the younger generation. He nurtures and supports them to allow them to make full use of their talent, and is instrumental in shaping their careers. In the words of Cluter Buck a mentor is a person who helps to develop the individual's potential, capability, judgement and wisdom. It is personal involvement that aims to build competence and help with tasks and the acquisition of skills. Levinson described a mentor as a teacher, sponsor, counselor, developer of skills and intellect, host, guide exemplar, and most importantly supporter and facilitator in the realisation of the vision the young person has about self-actualisation. In adolescence, a suitable mentor can be of great help.

Millennium organisations emphasise organisational learning and organisational building.

This is especially important today with the prevalence of changing jobs. Retaining employees and ensuring psychological commitment to the job needs mentor-oriented leadership. Employees who are very ambitious, energetic, competent, and possess a great deal of potential, but fail to introspect and comprehend the reality, need such leaders. Only a manager with leadership qualities will become successful and effective. The current trend is that he should be a mentor too. The distinctions between a manager, leader and mentor are however, very thin. They are shown in Table 27.7.

Table 27.7: Distinctions between a manager, leader and mentor

The manager	The leader	The mentor
Sponsored by the organisation	Emerges from the group	Supported by his protégées
Uses authority	Influences through power	Brings emotional equality
Superior-subordinate relationship	Supportive relationship	Parent-child relationship
Status	Stature	Elder
Unilateral dependence	Bi-lateral dependence	Inter dependence
Organisational identification	Group identification	Personal identification
Aims to achieve organisational goals	Attainment of group goals is important	Attainment of psychological maturity and personal effectiveness

Leaders as mentors have to carry out the following tasks for managing millennium organisations.

1. Develop awareness of organisational culture.
2. Clarify perceptions to avoid misunderstandings.
3. Have model behaviour, which subordinates can emulate.
4. Listen effectively to work related issues and personal problems.
5. Help in taking decisions on complex problems.
6. Establish long lasting relationships and trust.
7. Share experiences.
8. Provide emotional support.
9. Create awareness of inner self.
10. Help the individual to realise all his talents.

Today managers need to become mentors. The process by which this is achieved is shown in Figure 27.2.

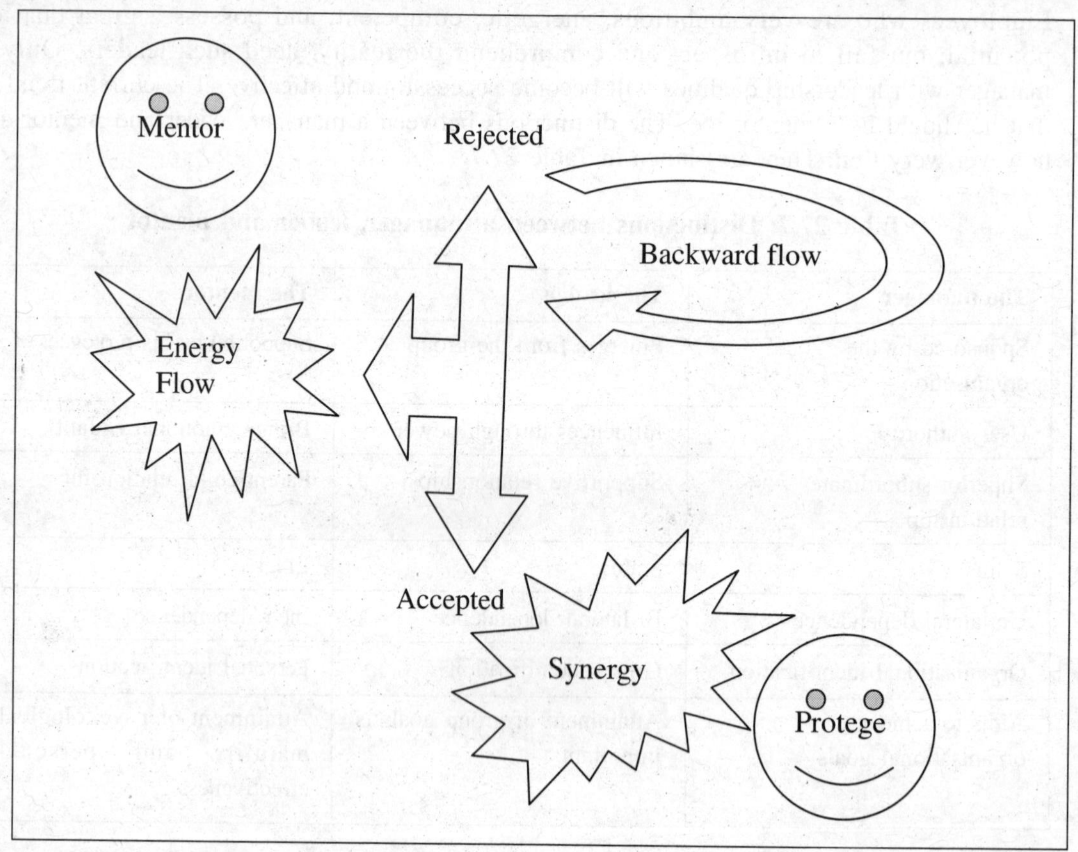

Figure 27.2: Leader mentoring process

A leader as a mentor should empower his followers. However, the protégé may or may not accept this empowerment. If it is accepted, its effect increases manifold.

Some aspects of leadership necessary for a lemantor are as follows:

Communication: Communication is a major function of a lemantor. He should be able to explain his ideas and listen. The latter is an art in itself. If a leader does not listen to the follower he cannot empower him. Thus the follower's acceptance of the leaders' communication is the essence of mentoring. The communication should be such that the cognitive message, feelings and ideas of the mentor should be clear to the protégé. In the words of Dr. Robert McHenry 'a good mentor knows how to listen and to ask probing questions'. Encouraging questions, giving patient replies, and developing inter-personal communication with empathy reinforces the confidence of the protégé. For this the mentor requires emotional balance. Emotion and anger are common in inter-personal communication, causing people to lose track of the subject and become irrational, which leads to poor expression of one's ideas, making communication difficult. Thus, both leaders and followers need to observe emotional balance.

Modelling: Modelling is projecting oneself as a model for emulation. Modelling is the process of imitating and learning from others, and is instrumental in learning. A mentor becomes a model for learning. In the process of developing himself into a model, he should observe the dimensions of modelling. Modelling involves two stages in the learning process.

Stage-I: Observation: The sensory organs of individuals collect information about actions of others. This is called observation. The protégé imitates his mentor by observation. The actions of the mentor and the consequences are stored in the cognitive structure of the brain with the help of various mental pictures. Thus, a mentor should remember that his actions are imitated by the protégé, and take care how he behaves. In an organisation, subordinates consider the managers' actions as parameters for emulation.

Stage-II: Learning: The behaviour of individuals is based on the mental pictures he has stored. If the consequences of an action are positive, a person will repeat it, otherwise he will not behave in that way again. Hence, learning occurs. A mentor should behave so as to produce positive consequences in the mind of the protégé. Modelling involves four sub-processes.

— *Attention process:* Individuals pay attention and recognise critical features of a model. Only attractive, important, reinforced and contrast characteristics receive attention. A mentor should develop critical features to attract the protégé.

— *Retention process:* A model's actions are likely to be remembered if they conform to the individual's requirements, and can be used in the future. A protégé remembers every action of the mentor, and will use them spontaneously in the future.

— *Motor reproduction process:* Individuals convert observed features of models into actions. This is imitating their behaviour. Therefore, the process of imitation produces certain actions. Swami Vivekananda cautions us by saying that '*each must assimilate the spirit of others and yet preserve his individuality and grow accordingly to his own law of growth*'. *(The Complete Works of Swami Vivekananda, Vol. I, page 24).* The essence of this message is that the mentor should become a model for imitation without depriving the protégé of his individuality.

— *Reinforcement process:* Individuals are likely to act according to the model as long as positive rewards are associated with the actions. Such repetitions result in learning from the model. A protégé imitates his mentor, whom he takes as his model. Employees try to identify themselves with the manager. Hence, a manager is expected to become a role model for his subordinates. Then he becomes a mentor in the organisation.

Empowering: Empowering is the flow of energy from the leader to his followers. Empowering is easy when the follower closely identifies himself with the leader. This identification process occurs when the former believes that the latter has an influence on him. This influence can be primary and secondary. The primary mode of influencing the followers aims at restricting their freedom. Here the leader uses criticism and punishment to bring about compliance. The secondary mode of influencing involves praise and recognition. This method increases the autonomy of the followers. Levinson identified several barriers to identification. Lack of time, repression of rivalry, intolerance of mistakes, complete rejection of dependency and unexamined relationships are a few examples. Here a manager as a leader-mentor in millennium organisations needs to introspect his behaviour and develop interaction with the subordinates. The power of influencing a follower's thoughts is a major force for empowering him. According to Swami Vivekananda '*the influence of thought on mind will vary according to distance and other causes, but the mind is always open to affection...and this power of mind upon mind is more or less according to the force of the tension is greater or less*'. *(The Complete Works of Swami Vivekananda, Vol. i, page 81).* The manager as a leader-mentor should be careful in laying a path for his followers.

Managers in organisations need to develop mentoring skills in order to direct the skills and mind of the subordinates to the ultimate organisational goals. This is not an easy task. Mentoring is time consuming. One may actually spend only a few hours with each protégé each month, but the preparation and aftermath adds up to almost a day, each month for each person mentoring. Attention has to be given first to training and developing commitment in the managerial team. Organisational learning and developing the overall personality of followers is possible by adopting a 'leader-manager-mentor' style of leadership.

LEADERSHIP FOR INDIAN ORGANISATIONS

Indian organisations are unique as far as styles of leadership are concerned. Indian organisations can be classified into three distinct kinds.

(i) *Family managed organisations:* Here leadership passes from one member of the family to another. Some examples are the Tata group of companies and the Reliance group. The style of leadership in these organisations is paternalistic, autocratic, task oriented and specific value oriented.

(ii) *Professionally managed organisations:* These organisations belong to the private sector. Most managers in these organisations are professionally qualified. The style of leadership in these organisations is democratic and a participatory climate is nurtured.

(iii) *Public sector organisations, financed by the government:* These organisations are managed for public interest, and therefore the management is bound by certain rules and regulations. The style of leadership is bureaucratic.

Some characteristic features of Indian organisations are high power distance, centralised decision making, orientation towards the management, dependency, motivation of money, poor educational background of subordinates, high degree of political involvement in organisations, heavy involvement of unions, frequently disturbed industrial relations, rigidity, and sentimentality. However, there is now a trend towards professionally managed organisations, with a democratic culture, adoptive orientation, increased educational levels of employees, higher aspirations, a larger number of female employees, dual career couples, less involvement of unions, privatisation, cross cultural orientation, and increased participation of all levels of employees in decision making. Some specific aspects of styles of leadership in Indian organisations are discussed below:

- **Adaptability:** Indian organisations are increasingly becoming proactive to change. So change is invited and planned. Human resources are developed to adopt the changes as quickly as possible. The leadership should therefore gear up to meet the challenges.
- **Integrity:** More openness, increasing emphasis on corporate governance, transparency, and living up to international standards are driving Indian organisations to be more oriented towards integrity. Therefore moral and ethical issues of leadership are widely discussed. Standard practices of moral leadership are emerging in India.
- **Cross functionality:** Globalisation has led to multinational organisations in the Indian business world. Divestment and lifting of protections are making Indian enterprises more competitive. Dynamic conditions in these enterprises require managers to develop cross-functional abilities rather than specialised skills. For instance, managers in marketing are required to not only manage sales figures; they should also manage salesmen so that they remain with the company.
- **Proactive:** Proactive leadership visualises changes and prepares strategies to adopt them, rather than waiting for resistance to develop and suggesting strategies. Indian managers are becoming highly proactive. Many public sector enterprises, that never used to care about their customers, are coming forward with customer relation management techniques. For instance, for the first time in India, BSNL has tried to inform the public about their facilities. It has also adopted the latest technology in order to be competitive and satisfy its customers.
- **Involvement:** Leaders today, are willing to share power with their subordinates, who in turn are ready to accept the responsibility. This is on account of the change in the leaders' vision regarding their employees, changing aspiration levels, better education, and a large female workforce.
- **Shared vision:** Indian leaders are not only visualising the future, but also sharing their vision with their followers. Earlier, leaders used to stay aloof from their followers and did not communicate their ideas to them. But learning organisations are increasingly emphasising on communication and interpersonal relationships. For instance, BHEL was recognised as a learning organisation, that promoted a culture of shared vision among employees in the organisation.
- **Self-competition:** For many years, Indian organisations looked to external competition. They judged their performance by external standards. Nowadays most organisations are developing their own standards. Inter divisional competition is becoming popular. MBO is adopted in most organisations. For example, the Andhra Pradesh State Electricity Board (APSEB) has been divided into two companies *viz.*, Andhra Pradesh Generation Company Limited (AP GENCO) and Andhra Pradesh Transmission Company Limited (AP TRANSCO). AP TRANSCO has again been divided into five distribution companies, which compete within themselves.
- **Carving an environmental niche:** Indian organisations are specialising in shaping an environment in which their success is guaranteed, rather than allowing the environment to control them. In this way these organisations are forecasting crises and managing them before they disturb the working of organisations.

Table 27.8: Certain other features of emerging Indian leadership

Leadership characteristics	Other supporting features and motivators	Activities	Some examples of personalities
1. Commitment	Drive, dedication, passion, obsession, zeal, energy, involvement, defining character, mission, prestige, power, enlightened interests, social cause, public benefit.	Farmers' Co-operatives, progressive farming, farmers' education, IPR movement, improving customer service process, information technology, chemicals, television, media entertainment.	Verghese Kurien, Bhavarlal Jain, Raghnath Mashelkar, Anu Aga, Pramod Chaudhari, Narayana Murthy, Manoj Tirodkar, Deepak Kanegaonkar, Ronnie Screwala.
2. Persistence	Doggedness, determination, hard work, insistence, tenacity, stretch power, learning experience.	Irrigation systems, Indian perfumes, television, sweets, enzymes.	Bhau Jain, Bhau Kelkar, Screwala, Rajabhau Chitale, Kiran Mazumdar.
3. Difference	Distinctiveness, differentiation, positive attitude, personality, innovativeness, talent.	Medical informatics, medical journalism, medico-legal issues, perfumes, electronics, ceramic magnets, ferrites, automotive castings, brewery plant.	Dhananjay Bakhle, Deepak Kanegaonkar, Sudheer Tillo, Narayana Murthy, Pramod Chaudhari.
4. Curiosity	Intelligence, creativity, clarity, kaleidoscopic thinking, originality, experimentation and drive, maverick.	Farmers' cooperatives, biotechnology.	Verghese Kurien, Manoj Tirodkar, Ronnie Screwvala, Kiran Muzumdar, Mashelkar.
5. Persuasiveness	Communication, negotiation, presentation skills, influencing, play acting, playing out ideas, sharing convictions, advocacy, use of appropriate words, empathise.	Patent literacy, insurance, information technology.	Ashok Soota, Ratnaparkhi, Anu Aga, Kiran Mazumdar, Deepak Parekh, Kurien, Mashelkar.

Leadership characteristics	Other supporting features and motivators	Activities	Some examples of personalities
6. Risk taking	Entrepreneurship, risk taking, responsibility, accountability, experimenting, learning from mistakes, using trial and error.	Medical and pharmaceuticals, brewery, jewellery, shipping.	Vikram Tannan, Pratap Pawar, Ravi Khanna, Manoj Tirodkar, Kanegaonkaar, Chaudhaari.
7. Focus	Centring, zeroing in, goal orientation, concentration.	Spark erosion machines, urban housing, financing, pharmaceuticals.	Prakash Ratnaparkhi, Deepak Parekh, Narayana Murthy, Dhanrajgir, Sudheer Tilloo, Bhau Jain.
8. Values	Honesty, integrity, honouring commitments, keeping one's word, truthfulness, independence, respecting culture, core beliefs, willingness to sacrifice, kindness, respect, hospitality, treating others well, courtesy.	Television.	Tilloo, Mazumdar, Narayana Murthy, Ronnie Screwala, Dhanrajgir, Ravi Khanna, Bhau Jain.
9. Energetic	Spiritedness, stamina, unbounded energy, intense involvement, loves action.		Manoj Tirodkar, Verghese Kurien, Pawar, Chitale, Jain, Dhanrajgir, Vikram Tannan, Screwala.
10. Continuous learning	Knowledge, acquisition of skills, modification, developing competency, passion to learn.	Drug information.	Bakhle, Anu Aga, Chitale, Tirodkar, Chaudhari, Ratnaparkhi, Parekh, R. Anand.

Leadership characteristics	Other supporting features and motivators	Activities	Some examples of personalities
11. Humility	Controlled ego, modesty, unpretentiousness, unassuming, shun flattery.		
12. Mentoring	Teaching, changing attitude, mindset management.		

Source: Prepared from Shrinivas Pandit, (2001) 'Thought Leaders: The Source Code of Exceptional Managers and Entrepreneurs', Tata McGraw Hill, New Delhi, pp. 395-409.

SUMMARY

Leadership is the fulcrum about which the effectiveness of the organisation revolves. At the same time it is an element that is widely discussed, but not well understood. The large number of different ideas about leadership in literature makes it difficult to understand. However it is a vital element in improving the performance of an organisation by ensuring the workers' psychological commitment. 21st century organisations are in no way different from earlier organisations, but the way they function has changed. This has led to new styles of leadership, associated with the charisma of the leader, transformation, vision, and emotional balance.

Charismatic leadership is powered by vision, risk orientation, sensitivity and the distinctive behaviour of the leader. The three types of charismatic leadership are envisioning, energising and enabling. A better understanding of charismatic leadership is possible by differentiating it from non-charismatic leadership. The points of distinctions are vision, power, follower base, behaviour, risk, emulation, articulation, sensitivity and expertise. For charismatic leadership to be effective the ethical dimension cannot be ignored. The distinction between ethical and unethical charismatic leadership depends on such factors as communication, followers' needs, learning, moral values, power, stimulation of thinking and vision.

Transactional leadership has been followed for many years to increase the effectiveness of an organisation. The modern trend is towards transformational leadership. It is driven by the ability of a leader to inspire his followers. The four pillars of transformational leadership are charisma, inspiration, intellectual stimulation and individual consideration. Charismatic and transformational leadership gave birth to visionary leadership. Certain distinctive skills of visionary leadership are visualisation of the future, a strong belief in translation of vision, clarifying and communicating vision, orientation towards action, reinforced vision and uniformity of vision in different situations.

Millennium organisations require certain unique skills and competencies in leadership. Some of the leadership competencies are embal (emotional balance), teaming, trust, morality, cross cultural adaptability and mentoring.

Adaptability, integrity, cross functionality, pro-activeness, involvement, shared vision, internal competition, carving an environmental niche, commitment, persistence, difference, curiosity, persuasiveness, risk taking, focus, values, energy, continuous learning, humility and mentoring are vital factors for the success of leadership in Indian organisations.

Key words:

- **Charisma:** The capability to exert an extraordinary influence on one's followers
- **Competence:** The possession of technical and non-technical knowledge and skill
- **Consistency:** Reliability and predictability of an individual's actions over a period of time
- **Cross cultural leadership:** The leader's ability to adapt to the native culture of a foreign corporate
- **Embal leadership:** Leader maintaining emotional balance even in turbulent times
- **Emotional intelligence:** Intelligence based on controlling emotions
- **Empathy:** The quality by which one can understand the other person's situation or views
- **Enabling leadership:** Psychologically helping people act or perform in the face of challenging goals
- **Energising leadership:** Directing the energy, and instilling the motivation to act, in the members of an organisation
- **Envisioning leadership:** Creating a picture of the future – or a desired future state – with which people can identify and which can generate excitement
- **Honesty:** The extent of sacrifice of self interest for the common interest
- **Integrity:** Honesty and truthfulness in the actions of individuals
- **Lemantor leadership:** Leader-manager-mentor oriented leadership that is charismatic and induces followers to develop sound attitudinal dimensions
- **Loyalty:** Giving support in all situations and at all times
- **Mentor:** A person who helps to develop an individual's potential, capability, judgement and wisdom
- **Mentoring:** The processes of providing moral support to followers to help them reach their full potential
- **Moral leadership:** Leadership based on moral values and ethical considerations
- **Sensitivity:** The perception of strengths, weaknesses, opportunities and threats

- **Team leadership:** Leadership competency to use each members' skill rather than directing every one to achieve specific objectives
- **Transactional leadership:** Behaviour associated with the attainment of goals by identifying the transactions, providing resources, rewards and directing the followers' effort to the objectives
- **Transformational leadership:** Behaviour that lays emphasis on the inspirational and developmental needs of followers
- **Trust leadership:** Leader, who operates based on his own beliefs and those of the followers
- **Vision:** The ability to foresee the future
- **Visionary leadership:** A leader who visualises the future to direct the followers towards the goals of the organisation

28. LEADERSHIP EFFECTIVENESS

This chapter enables you:

- *To explain the role of effectiveness as a dimension*
- *To understand leadership behaviour*
- *To analyse the change in leadership behaviour with environment*
- *To distinguish between attitudinal and environmental dimensions*
- *To understand the impact of maturity levels of subordinates*
- *To examine the factors that influence the selection of an effective style of leadership*
- *To appreciate the role played by the leader in building effective organisations*

The structure of the chapter is as follows:

- Introduction
- Reddin's tri-dimensional model
- Hersey and Blanchard's situational theory
- Drivers of leadership effectiveness
- Leadership to build an organisation
- Summary
- Key words

CHAPTER 28

Leadership Effectiveness

INTRODUCTION

The effectiveness of a style of leadership depends upon how appropriate it is in a situation. In modern organisations, leaders use a variety of styles appropriate to the demands of the situation. This chapter brings together styles of leadership and characteristics of a situation. The two dimensions of style of leadership discussed in this chapter are effectiveness and maturity levels of subordinates. Reddin conceptualised effectiveness, to distinguish between effective and ineffective styles of leadership. Hersey and Blanchard propounded the life cycle model of effective leadership. According to this model, the maturity level of subordinates is the main determinant of style of leadership. A leader plays a significant role in building a modern organisation by adopting a style appropriate to the demands of the situation.

REDDIN'S TRI-DIMENSIONAL MODEL

William J. Reddin was the first to introduce the 3-D theory. He used the managerial grid developed by Blake and Mouton to explain his 3-D theory. Concern for production and concern for people were the two dimensions in the managerial grid. To these he added effectiveness as the third dimension and therefore, the model became known as the tri-dimensional model.

Reddin used the four styles of leadership used in the managerial grid. He termed them separated, dedicated, integrated and related styles of leadership. The distinct characteristics of the various styles are as follows:

Separated style: Least concern for production and employees' welfare.

Dedicated style: High concern for production but less concern for employees' welfare.

Integrated style: Concern for both production and employees' welfare.

Related style: Maximum concern for employees' welfare, but minimum concern for production.

According to the model, if the style of leadership adopted is appropriate to the demands of the situation, it is regarded as effective, otherwise it is ineffective. The model identified four styles of leadership as effective, namely: Bureaucratic, benevolent autocrat, executive and developer, and four styles as ineffective, namely: Deserter, autocrat, compromiser and missionary. Figure 28.1 presents Reddin's 3-D model.

A cursory examination of the above reveals the following:

1. No single style is always effective. Each of the four basic styles could be effective or ineffective depending upon the situation.
2. The eight styles are not separate behavioural entities. They are only names given to the basic styles depending upon whether they are effective or otherwise.
3. There is a clear distinction between behaviour and effectiveness of behaviour.
4. The model uses eight behavioural dimensions to arrange them around basic styles using effectiveness.
5. According to this model, managerial effectiveness is the extent to which a manager achieves the requirements of the job.
6. There is flexibility in style (style flex). This means that leaders adopt a number of styles appropriate to situations.
7. An effective leader uses his skills in situational sensitivity, style flexibility and situational management. These skills are acquired by experience.
8. In a situation, five components determine effectiveness: organisational philosophy, technology, superiors' attitudes, co-workers' attitudes and subordinates' performance.

Reddin's 3-D theory is appreciated because it introduced the concept of effectiveness to explain styles of leadership integrated the behaviour of leaders with demands of the situation. Thus, the model is useful as it provides a variety of styles depending on the situation. It has become popular in training and development programs. Another merit of the model is that it emphasises style flexibility for effectiveness.

Critics of the model feel that it is complex. Moreover, it does not suggest strategies for managers to improve flexibility in their style of leadership.

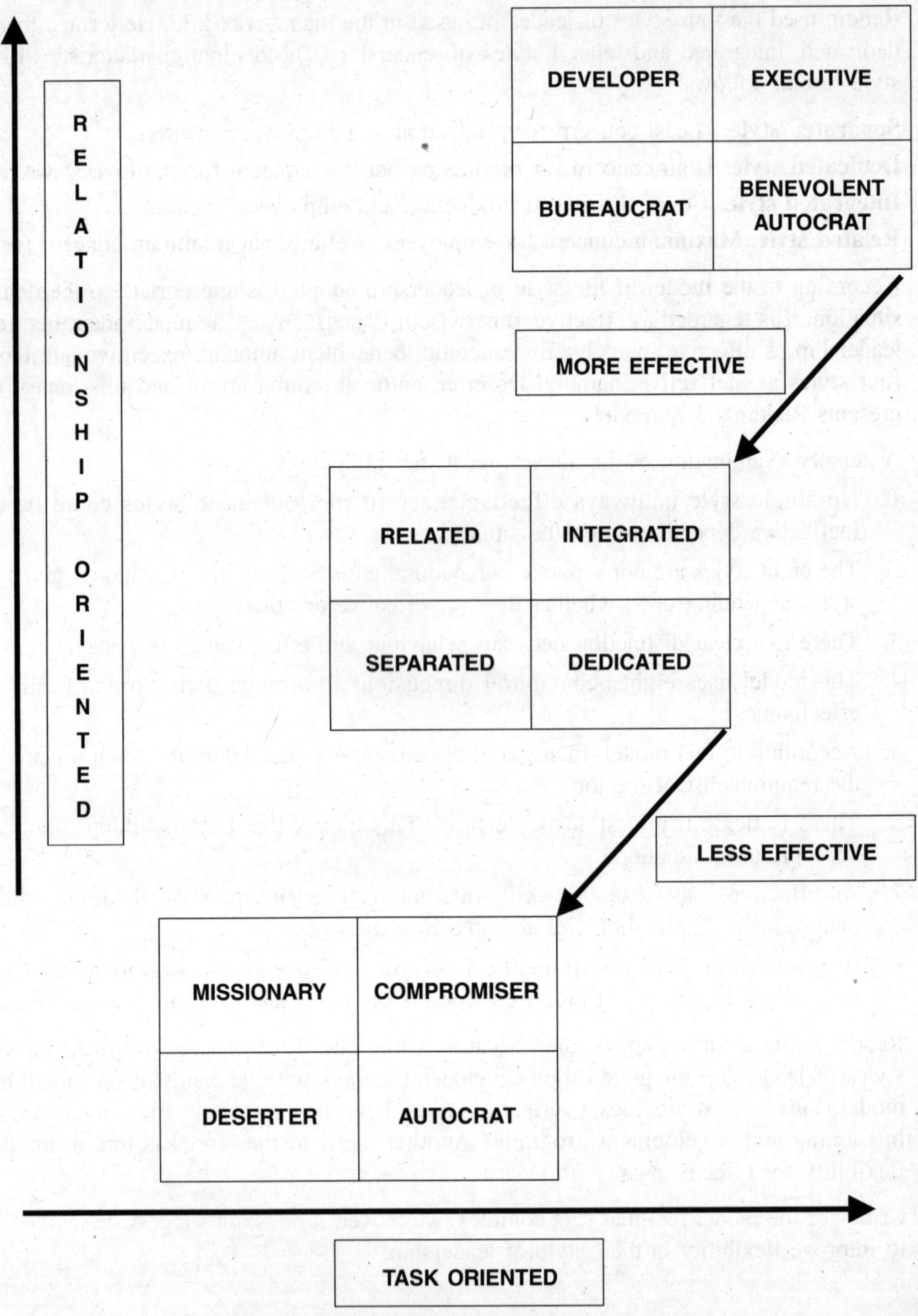

Figure 28.1: Reddin's 3D model

HERSEY AND BLANCHARD'S SITUATIONAL THEORY

Hersey and Blanchard have developed a model that adds environment of effectiveness as a third dimension to task behaviour and relationship behaviour, which were the two dimensions used in the studies at Ohio State University. Another name for this model is the life cycle theory.

The model differs from Reddins' 3-D model as it uses behavioural notions rather than attitudinal concepts, which were used by Reddin. According to this model, the most effective style of leadership depends on the maturity of the subordinates. The model uses the analogy of parent and child to explain the need to use high task and low relationship behaviour for immature subordinates, and low task and low relationship behaviour for mature subordinates.

The model defines maturity as the ability and willingness of people to take responsibility for their own behaviour. Job and psychological maturity are the two dimensions used to understand the maturity of subordinates. Job maturity is the use of knowledge, ability and experience to perform a task without direction from the leader, psychological maturity is the willingness and motivation to carry out the task. The model proposes that subordinates with high psychological maturity possess intrinsic motivation. Consequently, only a little external encouragement is sufficient to motivate them to attain the goals. Figure 28.2 shows the Hersey and Blanchard model.

The model uses the following styles of leadership to explain how effectiveness is related to the maturity levels of subordinates.

(i) **Telling style:** High emphasis on task and low emphasis on relationships characterise this style. In this style, a leader clearly defines the task and role of a subordinate. He gives them clear directions as to how to perform the job. Thus, the superior's behaviour is directive.

(ii) **Selling style**: This type of leader places high emphasis on both the task and relationships. While clearly directing subordinates, the leader provides the necessary support and warmth. Good interpersonal relationships are developed. The objective of supportive behaviour is to get the task accomplished.

(iii) **Participating style**: Under this style a leader places low emphasis on the task and high emphasis on relationships. The leader acts as a communicator and facilitator. He encourages followers to participate in the decision making process. Thus, enabling them to learn.

(iv) **Delegating style**: Such a leader has full faith in his subordinates. He delegates authority. Therefore, he uses low-task and low-relationship behaviour.

The model also clarifies four stages of maturity levels of subordinates, as given below.

(a) **M1 stage:** Subordinates are neither competent nor confident enough to perform the task. In this stage, they do not assume responsibility.

(b) **M2 stage:** Subordinates are willing to take responsibility, but they lack the necessary skills to do so.

(c) **M3 stage:** Subordinates possess the capacity to perform a task. However, due to lack of motivation, they are unwilling to do so and support their leader.

(d) **M4 stage:** Subordinates are ready to assume responsibility. They possess the adequate skill and capacity to carry out the task to the satisfaction of their leader.

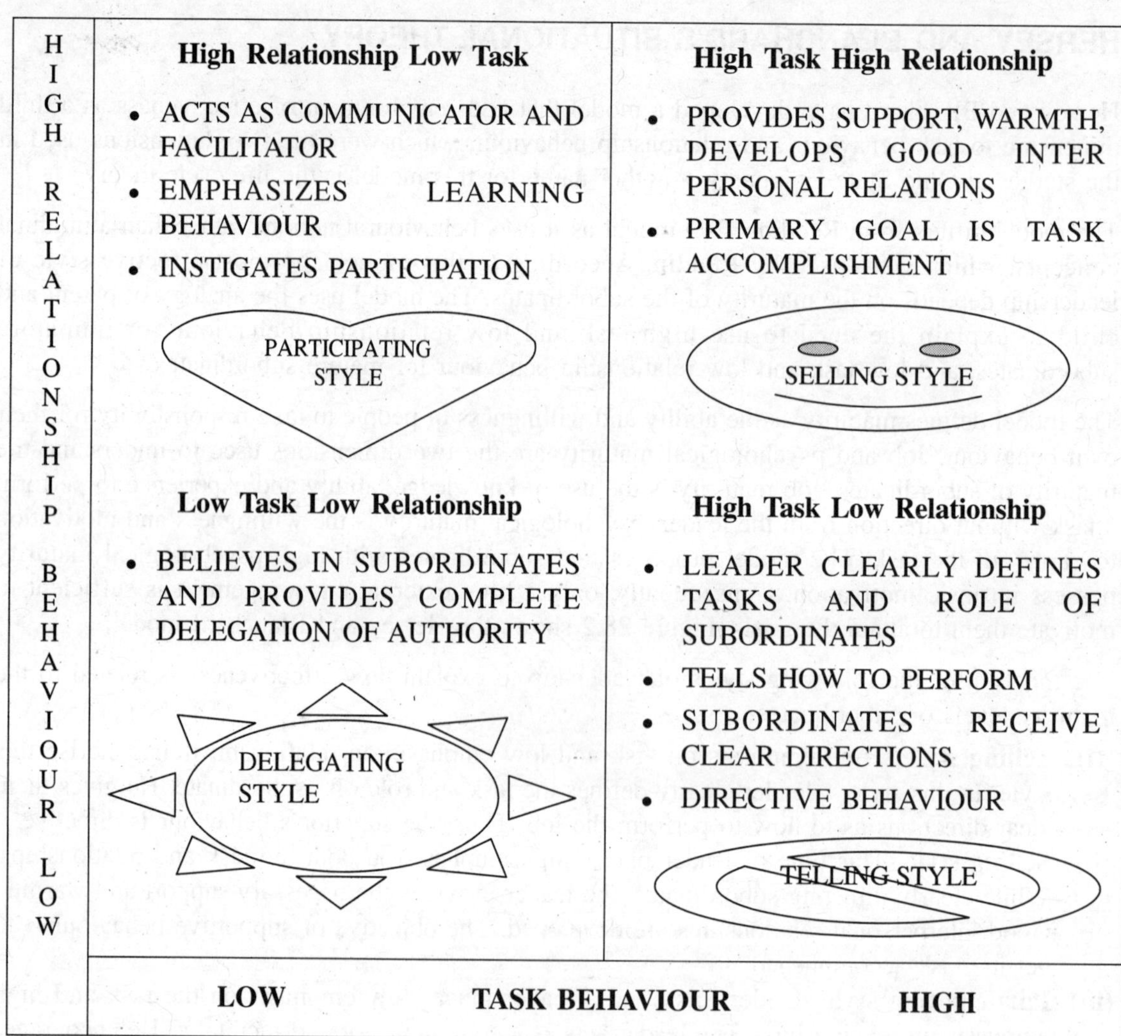

HIGH **MATURITY** **LOW**

M4	M3	M2	M1
• POSSESSES ADEQUATE SKILL AND CAPACITY • READY AND WILLING TO ASSUME RESPONSIBILITY	• POSSESSES CAPACITY • LACK OF MOTIVATION	• WILLING TO TAKE RESPONSIBILITY • LACK OF SKILLS	• NEITHER COMPETENT NOR CONFIDENT • DO NOT ASSUME RESPONSIBILITY

Figure 28. 2: Life cycle theory or Hersey and Blanchard model

A close examination of the above statements reveals the following propositions of the model:

1. Effective leaders use a combination of all four styles of leadership, depending on the maturity level of the subordinates.
2. New employees require the telling style, as they are immature and lack knowledge about the tasks and organisation.
3. Once employees have learnt the tasks, the leader should provide encouragement and emotional support. Hence, the selling style is appropriate.
4. After spending sufficient time in an organisation the employee learns the job completely, and takes initiative to complete the task. Hence, a leader avoids directive behaviour, but continues to provide support, using the participative style.
5. When subordinates grow further, they assume complete responsibility. Therefore, leader avoids close direction and support. He allows them to stand on their own. Thus, he practices the delegating style.

The situational model propounded by Hersey and Blanchard is reasonable and logical, due to consideration of maturity levels. In addition, this model states that leadership effectiveness is a function of environment and opportunities. A leader is required to manipulate opportunities to be effective.

The model was criticised due to the following:.

(i) The model is complex due to the introduction of the maturity dimension, which cannot be easily quantified.

(ii) It is difficult to understand the maturity levels of subordinates and to bring about a consensus as to what is meant by maturity level.

(iii) The leaders' flexibility in style, depending on maturity levels is an implicit assumption. Therefore, it becomes difficult for the leader to use a variety of styles to suit the different maturity levels of subordinates.

(iv) The model is not applicable to those organisations in which there is a high turnover of employees.

In spite of the criticism, the model has practical significance in understanding leadership effectiveness.

DRIVERS OF LEADERSHIP EFFECTIVENESS

Leadership is essential to accomplish organisational tasks, without affecting the morale of the employees. Hence, leaders should be effective, and at the same time achieve maximum performance, whilst preserving human values, sentiments and welfare, so that the organisation benefits in the long run. In today's complex environment, the effectiveness of leaders in an organisation depends on a host of factors, which are clarified below.

(a) Leader's Own Characteristics

The particular style of leadership adopted by a leader depends on the assumptions regarding subordinates, his own qualities, his inclination towards a particular style of leadership, and the demands of the situation. For example, a leader who assumes that his employees are motivated by economic factors will have a tendency to adopt an authoritarian or impoverished style. On the other hand, a leader who assumes his employees are socially inclined may adopt a democratic style. A leader who wants to project himself may practice an autocratic style, whereas a leader who has confidence in his subordinates' capacity, delegates authority and thus practices a democratic style.

(b) Characteristics of Subordinates

Subordinates who are not well trained, inadequately experienced, untrustworthy, unwilling to share responsibility and lack clear perception may force the superior to exercise close, detailed and strict supervision, i.e., an authoritarian. On the other hand, subordinates who are independent, willing to take responsibility, interested in solving problems and taking decisions, understand goals, are knowledgeable and experienced allow a leader to choose a participative or middle of the road style. In addition, age, sex, family background, informal relationships also determine whether a leader should be close to subordinates or maintain a distance.

(c) Characteristics of Superiors

A superior's predisposition towards a particular style of leadership has a profound influence on the style of leadership adopted by his subordinates. Subordinates, who want to meet the expectations of their superior, will adopt the same style of leadership. A subordinate may also knowingly or unknowingly adopt the superior's style of leadership, if he believes that the superior has a lot of power.

(d) Characteristics of Co-workers

Reinforcement of friendship, support, recognition and esteem come from co-workers, peers and associates who are working in similar positions. Frequent interaction with co-workers significantly affects the style of leadership, in terms of adapting group norms, behaviour and rules. A leader following an authoritarian style of leadership may change to a democratic style if the group he is associated with influences him towards a democratic style.

(e) Organisational Policies

Organisational policies, procedures, plans, expectations, goals, objectives, value systems, management controls and informal customs influence the style of a leader. These factors are developed over a period of time, through the process of institutionalization, and are referred to as the organisational climate. Organisations facing a climate of crisis of authority to enforce physical punishment naturally force the leaders to adopt authoritarian style. The bureaucratic climate in public sector enterprises in India, also leads to an authoritarian style of leadership. On the other hand, a supportive, friendly and warm climate, leads to a general feeling of well-being, and influences leaders to practice democratic and participative styles.

(f) Characteristics of the Job

The structure and definition of jobs, modules, amount of interaction required on the job, natural and environmental factors affect the style of leadership. A stable environment, with few changes, immediate adaptability, is conducive to a democratic style. A highly dynamic and volatile environment forces a leader to give clear instructions and make his own decisions. Therefore, his style will be closer to the authoritarian style.

The factors described above are not exhaustive. Many more variables, such as physical strength, stature, sex, past experience etc., may affect the style of leadership adopted by a manager.

LEADERSHIP TO BUILD AN ORGANISATION

The word leadership includes the leader, leadership and style. A leader has the power to influence an organisation and its resources, particularly human skills and potential. In India, the name *Gandhiji* is synonymous with the word 'leader'. The fact that he led the nation in its freedom struggle and that people voluntarily followed him, is testimony to his leadership. This is the best example of how a leader builds an organisation. The role of a leader in building an organisation is given below.

- **Leader – Empowerer**

A leader plays a vital role in empowering his team of subordinates to accomplish the goals of the organisation. The power of a leader is his personal capacity to influence others. Thus, organisational authority is not equal to power. A leader has to develop personal skills and competency, and have a comprehensive understanding of the environment to be able to empower his subordinates. There is a saying in Sanskrit about the importance of power, "*Athah shakthi prasarayat savam shivam bhavati, athah shakthi naprasarayat shivam savam bhavati*". This means that if empowered even a dead body can dance like the Lord Shiva, otherwise even a dancing body becomes a dead body.

- **Leader – Director**

In order to be a director, a leader should possess complete understanding of the tasks, confidence, energy and self-motivation. He should have a strong desire to accomplish the tasks. These traits distinguish him from others. He should work without fear or favour to accomplish the goals of the organisation, even if it means sacrificing personal gains.

- **Leader – Role model**

Subordinates will only follow a leader, if he is a role model to them, otherwise they will not be willing to emulate his actions. It is not easy to become a role model. A leader should not be afraid or aggressive, and may have to forego some personal traits and pleasures. For example, time management emphasises that a leader will only have the moral right to ask subordinates to adhere to time schedules scrupulously, when he maintains them himself. Similarly, he can order subordinates to follow his instructions only when he is an active worker. The failure of cooperative societies and banks, in recent years can be attributed to the failure of presidents and members of the managing committee, to repay debts, whereas they should have shown honesty and acted as role models for the other members. On the contrary, their behaviour led to non-payment of dues by other members.

- **Leader – Transformer**

As the saying goes, 'there is nothing permanent except change'. Today there is a need to transform the mindset of people along with their attitude and personality in order that organisation survives. The qualities necessary for a leader to be transformer are:

- Leader is supposed to possess intellectual capacity. His knowledge has to be transmitted to his subordinates. A leader should acquire the attitude and values, necessary to influence a subordinate to change his mindset.
- A leader should not only possess intelligence; he should be able to transmit his knowledge to his subordinates. This requires a good personal relationship and sound communication between a leader and the subordinates.
- A leader should be self-sacrificing, and interested in sharing his knowledge to transform subordinates.
- A leader should be a visionary and have confidence that he can influence subordinates to change their mindset, to accomplish the task on hand.

- **Leader – Visionary**

A leader has to think and plan ahead. He should be a role model for his subordinates and be able to visualise the future of the organisation. A leader should be a strategist and be capable of anticipating changes that may affect the environment of the organisation in the future. A leader is a manager and an achiever. He should be imaginative and determined. He should be able to envisage, plan, manage and implement a decision to build an effective organisation.

The facts mentioned above emphasise the role of a leader in building an effective organisation for the future.

Case study 28.1: Building an impeccable organisation – Thermax case

Thermax is an organisation with a number of divisions, involved in the design, manufacture and marketing of energy and environment systems. Included in its product portfolio are boilers, heaters, water heat systems, vapour absorption machines, boiler revamp, energy services, waste management systems, air, gaseous, pollution control systems etc.

Following the sudden death of her husband, Anu Aga took over the organisation. She was committed to complete the unfinished agenda of her husband – Rohinton Aga. She knew that Rohinton, who was educated at Cambridge, could have had a brilliant career with

Burma Shell. However, he felt he could do more for his country, rather than taking up a job, and so he started Thermax. A charismatic leader, with considerable entrepreneurial skills, Rohinton put together a team of committed professionals. The company achieved a breakthrough in the market. Its core ideology was to understand the market in depth, stretch it to the fullest potential, create new unfulfilled needs, and bring individual talent and that of the entire team in clear focus. The company was determined to emerge as a leader, and add value to society. The process was exciting, rewarding and continuous. Rohinton and his team did not look at success only in terms of monetary gains, but also in terms of values.

- At the time of the oil crisis the research and development wing of Thermax developed India's first packaged water tube boiler, Multitherm.
- The team of dedicated professionals developed water treatment plants for power stations, fertiliser and petrochemical plants.
- Thermax developed pre-treatment plants, ovens and turnkey painting systems.
- They developed the first fluidised bed boilers.
- Technical collaboration with a Japanese firm resulted in the development of steam fired vapour absorption chillers – a market leader for the company.

After the death of her husband, at the peak of his professional career, Anu had to face the personal tragedy of losing her son at the young age of 25. In addition, the company was not doing well. She believed that in spite of the slump in the economy, the company could have done well if it had improved the quality of their products. This was obvious from lost orders, and complaints received from customers. She found lack of accountability in the company, due to the simple reason that she was the major shareholder and the executive chairperson. This prevented other members of the board from raising questions about the poor performance. It was a challenge to her to build a successful organisation. An unusual lady, Anu Aga, strongly believed that the organisation should continue to be run by professionals. She took the bold step of handing over all the executive responsibilities to the professional manager of the company, entrusting him with autonomy, authority and responsibility for results. She remained as the chairperson, and by renouncing the executive responsibilities, she could have a perspective of the company at both a macro and micro level. Personal reasons also led her to withdraw from the executive responsibilities. She wanted to contribute to the well being of society, spend time with her grandchildren, read and meditate.

Anu Aga also realised that 'there is no permanent compatibility between a chair and the occupier'. She had to break out of her traditional way of thinking, to bring about the transition. Relinquishing her executive responsibilities, led to rumours that the company was being sold. However, she felt a strong attachment to the company and was actively involved in its growth and ideology, the main points of which, are given below.

- Thermax shall stand for a company that genuinely cares for its customers and shall be proud of its quality.

- The company will discover and invest in talented human resources to give direction to future growth.
- It will create an environment, where employees can openly share their views, ideas and fears. This will help them to realise their roles better.
- Anu Aga will involve herself in all issues relating to human resources and industrial relations.

Questions:

1. Describe how Anu Aga built an organisation with values.
2. How do you react to the traumatic experiences of the leader in the case?
3. What crises in leadership could have led Anu to take unusual decisions?
4. 'There is no permanent compatibility between a chair and the occupier.' Examine the leadership propositions in the statement.

SUMMARY

Every organisation needs effective leadership, therefore it is a widely discussed concept. William J. Reddin introduced the dimension of effectiveness in the model developed by him. His theory was popularised as the 3D theory. He used twelve styles of leadership, namely, developer, executive, bureaucrat, benevolent autocrat, related, integrated, separated, dedicated, missionary, compromiser, deserter and autocrat. A leader may adopt more than one style. Hersey and Blanchard's model is known as the life cycle theory. The theory introduced the dimension of maturity and explained how leadership styles differ according to the maturity levels of subordinates. The model used four styles of leadership, telling, selling, participating and delegating, relating to four levels of maturity of subordinates. In today's complex environment a number of factors influence a leader's effectiveness. They are a leader's own characteristics, characteristics of subordinates, characteristics of superiors, characteristics of co-workers, organisational policies and characteristics of the job. This list is not exhaustive. Leaders play a significant role in building modern organisations. To do this they need to be empowerers, directors, role modelers, transformers and great visionaries.

Key words:

- **Maturity:** The extent to which subordinates understand a situation, and act according to the requirements of the situation.
- **Style flex:** The possibility of a leader adopting a number of styles appropriate to different situations.

29. MOTIVATIONAL BEHAVIOUR

This chapter enables you:

- *To define the concept of motivation*
- *To understand the characteristics of human motivation*
- *To understand the process of motivation*
- *To explain the stimulants, which direct the human physiological and psychological process*
- *To examine the role of money as a motivator*
- *To distinguish between monetary and non monetary motivation*

The structure of the chapter is as follows:

- Introduction
- Definition of motivation
- Motivation process
- Financial motivators
- Non financial motivators
- Summary
- Key words

CHAPTER 29

Motivational Behaviour

Motivation stimulates potential

Human resources are valuable resources for any enterprise. Human beings are vital because they possess the required intelligence to make material, physical and financial resources productive and effective. Human potential is thus the crux of effectiveness in an organisation. Evaluating human potential in a scientific and systematic manner paves the way for enhanced corporate performance. The story of Arjuna in the Maha Bharata is well known. After seeing the two sides, with all his friends and relatives, arrayed in battle, knowing that they will be killed, Arjuna says 'Na kânkse vijayam Krisna, na cha râjyam sukhani cha, kim no râjyena Govinda, kim bhogair jivitena vâ'. This means 'I desire not victory, O Krishna, nor kingdom, nor pleasures. Of what use is the kingdom to us O Govinda? Of what use are pleasures or even life itself?' He then tells Krishna that he will not fight. He lost all motivation. Then Lord Krishna recited the Bhagvat Geeta. Arjuna understood His teaching and won the final battle.

The inner power is motivation. Arousing the inner potential is motivating. Motivating and assessing hidden strengths facilitates development of the organisation. Managers in an organisation should be able to motivate their subordinates and arouse their inner potential to direct them to realise the goals of the organisation.

INTRODUCTION

An individual's behaviour is directed towards goals. Motivation is also directed towards goals. It is the psychological energy of an individual, which enables him to carry out an activity using physical energy. Motivating employees in organisations is a challenge to the management, because different individuals require different motivation. For some the motivation may be financial gains and for others it may be prestige or recognition. Finding the correct motivation is difficult, but not impossible, for a skilled manager. Motivators can be financial or non-financial, and positive or negative. This chapter describes the basic concepts of motivation.

DEFINITION OF MOTIVATION

Motivation is a psychological concept. It is a qualitative description of the inner potential of a person inducing him to act in a predetermined way. The following definitions provide an understanding of the concept.

The Encyclopedia of Management has defined motivation as *"the degree of readiness of an organism to pursue some designated goal, and implies the determination of nature and locus of the forces including the degree of readiness."*

In the words of **Dalton E. Mc Farland,** *"Motivation refers to the way in which urges, drives, desires, aspirations, strivings, or needs, direct, control or explain the behaviour of human beings"*.

Michael J. Julius defined motivation *'as the act of stimulating someone or oneself to get the desired course of action'*.

Koontz and **O'Donnell** stated that *'motivation is a general term applying to the entire class of drives, desires, needs, wishes, and similar forces'*.

Dubin described motivation as *'the complex of forces starting and keeping a person at work in an organization. To put it generally, motivation starts and maintains an activity along a prescribed line. Motivation is something that moves the person to action and continues him in the course of action already initiated'*.

March and **Simon** have put motivation as *'the process or the reaction which takes place in the memory of individuals. It refers to the combination of forces or motives maintaining human activity'*.

Victor. H. Vroom defined the term motivation as *'a process governing choices made by persons or lower organisms among alternative forms of voluntary activity'*.

In the words of **Gray & Starke,** motivation is *'the result of processes, internal or external to the individual, that arouse enthusiasm and persistence to pursue a certain course of action'*.

Fred Luthans described motivation as *'a process that starts with a physiological or psychological deficiency or need that activates behaviour or a drive that is aimed at a goal or incentive'*.

According to **William G. Scott,** *'motivation is a process of stimulating people to action to accomplish desired goal'*.

The definitions of motivation provided above reveal the following characteristics of motivation:

(i) Motivation is an inner feeling and psychological aspect. However, its reaction is physical.
(ii) Motivation is a process. It is continuous and contains system orientation.
(iii) It stimulates a human being to release his energy and directs his behaviour to realise goals.
(iv) Motivation can be positive or negative.
(v) It is complex. A number of variables influence it.

MOTIVATION PROCESS

Figure 29.1 shows the process of motivation.

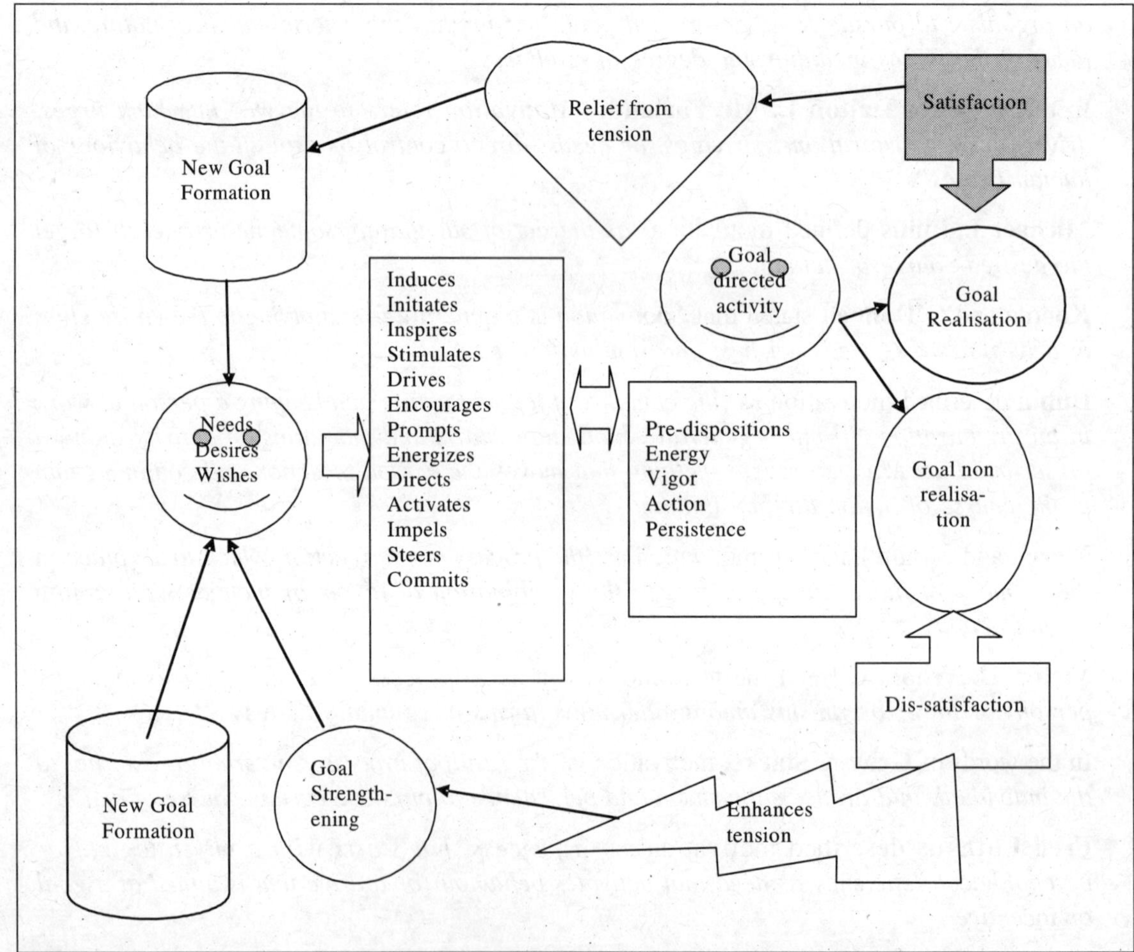

Figure 29.1: Motivation process

Motivation arises from the needs and desires of individuals. These induce a human being to expend energy in the pursuit of goals. Human energy is directed towards the realisation of goals. Realisation of goals produces satisfaction and relieves tension. This re-energises the individual and leads him to formulate new goals. New goals lead to new desires and wishes and the process continues. If the desired goal is not realised, an individual becomes dissatisfied. This causes tension but it can also re-energise an individual. In the latter case, goals are strengthened and the individual tries to realise the goal. If the goal is not realised, there are two possibilities. One is that the goal displacement occurs, which leads to formation of alternative goals, and the second is that entirely new goals are formulated. Thus, motive determines behaviour and behaviour leads to realisation of goal.

MANAGERIAL SIGNIFICANCE OF MOTIVATION

A manager uses motivation to realise the goals of an organisation. Managers use a variety of ways to ensure employees are committed to the job and perform better. Motivation is a challenge to managers as it is not a tangible element. However, in recent years motivation has been widely discussed in organisational circles. It was believed that motivation was linked to the wage and salary policy of the organisation. In the public sector managers often used to comment, that motivation was not in their hands. However, it has been shown that non-financial motivation is more important than financial motivation. Thus, motivation is well within the hands of managers. The following points will clarify the significance of motivation to managers.

- **Goal direction:** Motivation is the energy that directs an individual to realise goals. Without proper motivation an individual's actions may not be goal oriented. This is due to the fact that in most organisations individual goals and organisational goals are not congruent. By nature individuals lay more emphasis on individual goals over organisational goals. Thus, organisations have to think of ways of motivating employees, so that they give priority to organisational goals in spite of the fact that their individual goals are different from them. Henry Fayol refers to this in his principles as 'subordination of individual interest to common interest'. Therefore, motivation enables managers to direct employees toward organisational goals.
- **Productive orientation:** Evidence shows that motivation and productivity are positively related. Although productivity is influenced by a host of factors, motivation is found to be a significant factor. A motivated employee is likely to perform better than one who is not motivated. This is because his needs are recognised and satisfied by the organisation, which also provides more incentives to productive workers. Thus, the employee experiences a cause and effect relationship between performance and rewards. He will try to perform better with a view to earn more financial rewards. This is particularly true with blue collared workers. It is often seen that workers slow down productivity in demand of higher wages.
- **Quality consciousness:** Quality is a relative phenomenon. A highly motivated employee shows more concern towards the quality of a product or service, than a poorly motivated

employee. Even a manager will take the initiative to collect more information if he is motivated. This will lead him in taking more rational decisions.

- **Reduction of absenteeism and employee turnover:** One of the reasons for frequent absenteeism is dissatisfaction of employees, with the rewards offered for their performance. Employees frequently complain that their remuneration is not on par with that of others, who are performing the same or nearly similar jobs. Therefore, they simply avoid coming to work. This is particularly true with blue collared workers. One of the prime reasons for absenteeism in government offices, is the poor monetary rewards as compared to those of employees in the private sector. In electronic and software industry, employee turnover is high. Employees often leave a company, even if they are offered a small increase in salary and/or perquisites by another organisation. It is therefore a challenge to human resource managers to retain star employees. Hence, understanding what motivates an employee is important in order to reduce absenteeism and retain employees.

- **Neutralising friction and conflicts:** Personal friction in an organisation is the most common cause of poor inter-personal relations. Friction occurs due to comparison between employees with respect to rewards given for performance. Thus, carefully designed and upgraded plans to motivate employees reduce inter-personal conflict. Another area of conflict is industrial relations. The first reason for any strike is usually a demand for increased wages and other amenities. Appropriate motivation results in reducing employees' discontentment and improves employee-management relations.

- **Enhances satisfaction:** Most studies conducted on job satisfaction show that employees are most discontented about salaries and other criteria related to motivation. A properly motivated employee feels satisfied with his work and thus contributes more to the organisation. Moreover, employee satisfaction leads to a better corporate image of the organisation. Qamer and Junaibi conducted a study in Abu Dhabi. They gathered data on 360 employees in the manufacturing, trading and retailing, construction and service, and utility industries. The data is given in Table 29.1.

From Table 29.1 it can be seen that satisfaction of employees is closely related to factors such as pay, promotion, career prospects etc. Thus, it can be stated that understanding what motivates an employee helps in enhancing his satisfaction.

- **Perception and attitudes:** Motivation helps an employee to understand the culture and climate of an organisation. A poorly motivated employee develops errors in his perception of the organisation. This affects his performance negatively. Employees who are satisfied with their job and the rewards (both financial and non-financial) they receive, will develop a positive attitude and therefore their performance is likely to be better than that of others.

- **Overcoming resistance to change:** One of the reasons for resistance to change in an organisation is fear of losing monetary incentives and other opportunities. When the appropriate motivation is associated with the change, employees welcome it. They will

Table 29.1 Satisfaction from rewards, among the respondents

Satisfaction statement	%Yes	%No
My pay is satisfactory.	48.9	46.1
I am underpaid for what I do.	67.2	29.4
My income and the income of my subordinates differ significantly.	17.2	78.3
My income is as good as that of others.	45.8	46.7
My pay is poor.	35.0	60.0
I am highly paid.	60.3	36.1
My income is as good as the income of my friends.	33.1	61.4
The system of promotion in my organisation is very limited.	41.1	53.3
The prospects of promotion in my organisation are very limited.	56.1	2.8
It is easy to get a promotion in my organisation.	50.6	5.0
There is favouritism in promotion in my organisation.	56.7	4.7
There are good opportunities for promotion in my organisation.	50.3	46.1
The greater my experience, the greater the chances for promotion.	36.1	62.8
The job I do is a dead end job.	12.2	85.8
The good jobs are usually taken before you hear of them.	53.6	43.1

Source: Based on 'National Origin of Workers and its Implications on Satisfaction from Rewards in the Culturally Diverse Work Environment of the UAE.'

extend cooperation in bringing about the change. One of the major changes in modern organisations is introduction of new technology. The management can reduce resistance to this by explaining how this will benefit employees.

MOTIVATORS

Motivators are stimulants that drive an individual to pursue a certain action. They can be physical or psychological, and are classified as positive or negative and financial or non-financial. They are described below.

Financial Motivators

Financial motivators relate to money or any other benefit that can be converted or expressed into a monetary unit. Today, money is a means to satisfy physical needs. It is an instrument to obtain social position and power, and is thus a basic incentive for individuals. Wages, salaries, allowances, bonuses, financial incentives, commission etc., are financial motivators, which induce individuals to join an organisation. The financial package should motivate present and prospective employees.

However, it should be borne in mind that money is not an end but a means to an end. It can satisfy both physical and safety needs. Some people place little emphasis on money irrespective of how much they possess, whilst others are continuously driven by the desire to acquire more money even if they already have more than enough to meet their basic needs. They look for money to satisfy their desire for status, esteem and self-actualisation. Even research points to the use of money in satisfying the needs of esteem and recognition, as well as basic physiological needs.

Its role in motivation is unquestionable. However, behavioural theories place importance on non-monetary rewards and argue that if only money motivates, there would have been human machines and not human beings. The following points describe the importance of money as a motivator.

1. **Standard of living:** Money is a means of measuring and achieving one's standard of living. Economists view the prosperity of a nation by the standard of living of the people of the country. Therefore, to maintain a minimum standard of living, people have to earn money. If money was the only objective, motivation would not be a difficult task. However, some people look beyond money. For some, money remains important irrespective of their economic conditions, while for others, it is not important after a certain level.

2. **Performance-reward relationship:** There is a relationship, created in terms of money, between performance and rewards. Those who seek money are motivated if they see a link between higher performance and monetary rewards. For example at BHEL, in Tiruchirapalli, workers were given cash awards for suggesting solutions to certain production related problems. Awards were also given for zero defect performance and good house keeping. However, people are concerned not only with the amount of money they receive, but they are also concerned about the amount others would receive for similar efforts. Thus, they make comparisons. This suggests that people working at the same level should receive the same or nearly the same monetary rewards.

3. **Wealth accumulation:** Money is a strong motivation, for people who wish to accumulate wealth. In this context, Gellerman's statement that, 'People try to earn money by showing higher performance, if they feel that additional money earned by their efforts is significant', becomes important.

4. **Social status:** Social status is the relative worth attached to people in society. It is usually measured by wealth and monetary possessions. Thus, the social attitude towards wealth plays an important role in determining the relationship between money and satisfaction of human needs. In some societies, personal acquisition of wealth is viewed as evil, or beneath the dignity of man. For such cultural values, money cannot act as a motivator. However, in most

societies money is an indication of social status. Thus, most people are interested in acquiring money.

All these points clearly show that money plays a significant role in an organisation irrespective of the nature, class, and cadre of employees. Organisations are concerned with motivating employees by giving monetary rewards.

Non Financial Motivators

It is generally believed that financial incentives motivate employees to give a better performance. However, individuals have variety of needs that they want to satisfy while working in an organisation. People working at higher levels in the managerial hierarchy attach more importance to socio-psychological needs that cannot be satisfied by money alone. Thus the management, in addition to financial incentives, provides non-financial incentives to motivate people and satisfy their psychological and emotional needs. For example, a promotion gives psychological satisfaction, as it leads to better status, a more challenging job, greater authority etc. However, even to provide non-financial rewards, the organisation has to spend money. Some important non-financial incentives are described below.

1. **Status:** Status is the relative worth attached to employees in an organisation. It refers to the rank, rights and duties of an employee, in the formal structure of the organisation. Status brings with it more esteem, more authority and greater participation in decision-making. These are known as status symbols. Gaining higher status is an important motivator because it is extremely important for most people. Status should be related to the abilities and aspirations of people in the organisation.

2. **Promotion:** Promotion is moving to a higher position. Promotion brings with it greater responsibilities and gives prestige. Promotion depends on capabilities and good performance. It is an opportunity to develop one's career in an organisation. Due to the higher status it brings, a promotion also affects one's personal life. Therefore, promotion acts as a motivator to employees.

3. **Responsibility:** Most people prefer challenging and responsible jobs rather than monotonous and routine ones. A responsible job makes people feel they have contributed to the success of the organisation, and satisfies their natural and inherent desires. A person will usually put more effort into a responsible job.

4. **Recognition:** People have inherent desire for recognition. Recognition is acknowledgment of the work carried out and a show of appreciation. It motivates employees to perform better.

5. **Job security:** Employees want a job that is secure, and assures them of a stable income and work in the future. This relieves them of worry about their future. However, the negative aspect of job security, is that people can become complacent.

Case study 29.1: The dream of an individual is realised through motivation

Murali voluntarily retired from the Indian Air Force. He was a non-commissioned officer for a period of 20 years. Born in a small village, and educated in a nearby town, he completed his diploma in a Polytechnic and immediately joined the Air Force.

Unmistakable traits of the IAF are seen in his behaviour. He is punctual, sincere and hardworking, the embodiment of a perfect citizen. His life in the IAF was orderly and secure despite a strict code of discipline. Superior officers had unquestionable authority, and often overlooked the emotions of the junior officers, to enhance their authority. All these factors may have helped in shaping a good personality, but they also made him a poor communicator, presenter and leader. Despite this, he had a cherished dream of being a good speaker in front of a large audience.

After leaving the strictly disciplined life of the IAF, he found that values in society were altogether different. Punctuality and time management took a back seat and sincerity, values and ethics were not considered important. Even after so many years, there was no perceptible change in the mindset of students in his town. He decided to undertake personality development workshops, to help shape the younger generation into good citizens.

However, he was not sure whether he would be able to achieve his goal, despite the fact that he was seriously and sincerely searching for an opportunity. During this time, he happened to attend a seminar conducted for presenting a business proposal 'NW21', which is an international organisation started with the objectives of promoting leadership and relationship oriented growth, development of overall personality and social consciousness. To accomplish these objectives they chose a business model, in which networks of relationships are established for distribution of certain essential FMCGs. A weekly meeting takes place in which every member, in turn, is given an opportunity to interact. This develops communication skills, and removes complexes and inhibitions. Murali readily agreed to associate with the organisation. Today he is considered a good motivator, team player and manager. Above all, he helps many people earn an income. All this has given him a feeling of contentment and satisfaction.

One day, during a discussion regarding a business proposal with a friend, the friend suggested that he should join the Lions Club, as it would be an appropriate forum for him. He made enquiries and found that the club carries out social service activities. Its members are professionals, like doctors and lawyers, and well-placed businessmen. However, membership of the club is restricted and one has to be proposed by another member. He was able to find a member who would propose him, and became a member. He realised on the day of the induction ceremony itself, that he was a valuable member. He was given accreditation, as a personality development expert, and was introduced as business professional. The president of the club voiced the feelings of the members, when he said that Murali should organise programmes for the development of the club.

Around the same time, that he became a member of the Lions Club, he also had an opportunity to interact with a professor from the University. With his power of communication and expression, he made a very good first impression on the professor. Although he had intended to discuss a business proposal, the interaction turned out differently. The professor asked him if he would develop specific programmes on personality development, communication, and skills required to handle an interview, for the benefit of students at the University. The professor suggested that Murali team up with one or two other professionals in his field, so that continuous interactive sessions could be planned for the benefit of students. There was a commonality of interests, the professor wanted to develop the students and Murali wanted to become a good and purposeful presenter. Murali teamed up with another friend, a master practitioner of Neuro Linguistic Programming (NLP), who was interested in spreading the NLP technique. The professor named the association as CAMEL (Centre for Attitude Management by Education and Learning). The camel is an animal that always keeps its head up. The association would enable the students to keep their heads up, developing their attitude. Murali found this association absorbing and ambitious. It also fulfilled his self-actualising needs, and was indeed a 'dream come true.'

Assignment

- Carefully study the incidents in Murali's life and bring out the motivators in each case.

SUMMARY

Motivation is driving people to behave in a certain fashion. In the context of an organisation, motivation refers to encouraging employees to undertake the work and realise organisational goals. It is a process of converting the desires of individuals into a goal directed activity. Individuals formulate goals to realise their desires, wishes and needs; and they expend their energy towards this end. The energy induced is called motivation. Realisation of goals leads to satisfaction, which leads to formulating new goals. Motivators induce an individual to direct his energy in the right direction. They may be financial or non-financial, positive or negative. Positive financial motivators include: salary, incentives, bonus, increments, commission etc. Negative financial motivators refer to wage cuts, stoppage of increments, reducing bonus, moratorium on incentives etc. Praise, recognition, esteem, giving additional responsibility and/or status are examples of positive, non-financial motivators. Recriminations, demotions, withdrawing authority are examples of negative non-financial motivators. Since motivation is a complex process, it is difficult to understand.

Key words:

- **Job security:** To feel one's job is secure and permanent.
- **Motivation:** The process of stimulating one's desires to produce a response directed towards the goal.
- **Non-financial motivators:** Stimulants that appeal to an individual's psychological and emotional feelings.
- **Pre-potency:** The strength associated with needs.
- **Social status:** The relative worth attached to people in society.

30. MOTIVATION THEORIES

This chapter enables you:

- *To comprehend motivational concepts used in various theories*
- *To understand the various theories of motivation*
- *To assess the managerial implications of Maslow's theory*
- *To examine criticism of the hierarchy theory*
- *To identify two factors used in Herzberg's theory*
- *To distinguish between Maslow's and Herzberg's theories*
- *To understand the assumptions of theory X and theory Y*
- *To assess the managerial implications of McGregor's theories*
- *To understand the uniqueness of motivation in Japan*
- *To distinguish between American and Japanese management practices*

The structure of the chapter is as follows:

- Introduction
- Motivation theories
- Maslow's need hierarchy theory
- Herzberg's two factor theory
- Similarities and differences between Maslow's need hierarchy and Herzberg's two factor theories
- Theory X and theory Y
- Theory Z
- Summary
- Key words

CHAPTER 30

Motivation Theories

INTRODUCTION

Motivation is psychological energy that is realised by human actions towards realisation of goals. There are a number of theories that have identified various motivational propositions. Commencing from the early scientific management to the latest theories that relate to locus of control, motivational concepts have developed by leaps and bounds. How often have you heard a person say that he is not interested in something? Interest and disinterest are expressions of his inner motivation. Suppose you are standing at a bus stop, waiting for a bus. At that time you will only be thinking about the arrival of the bus, this is a basic need. Once the bus arrives you will try to get a place to sit. Once you have achieved this you will start to think of a safe journey. After travelling for some time, boredom will lead you to converse with other passengers. This is a need of belonging. If you find that your co-passenger is not as qualified or well-placed as you are, you may reveal your higher qualifications to get some kind of recognition or esteem. In this way, you unconsciously apply the need hierarchy concept during the journey. Thus, Maslow's need hierarchy theory is applicable to all acts of an individual.

Superiors, who complain that their subordinates are not interested in work, or that they are lazy and have to be coerced into carrying out their jobs are making the assumptions of theory X. Those who assume that their subordinates are mature and responsible are following the assumptions of theory Y. Some people are motivated to work only when there is a chance of achievement and promotion. In this case Herzberg's contention that there are two factors responsible for motivation becomes applicable. This chapter describes some of the important theories of motivation.

MOTIVATION THEORIES

Motivation has always been a challenge to managers and leaders, who are responsible for making workers committed to their jobs. Motivating requires understanding human nature and designing strategies to get work done. To this end, a number of motivation theories have been advanced. The various motivation theories and the motivation concepts are shown in Table 30.1.

Table 30.1 Motivation Theories

Early Motivation Theories

Proponent	Theory	Motivation Concepts
F.W. Taylor and his followers	Scientific management	Differential piece wage system, Halsey premium plan, Rowan premium plan, Bedaux point system, Scanlon plan
Elton Mayo and his associates	Human relations theory	Social motivation, recognition, social support
Douglas McGregor	Theory X and Theory Y	Coercion, threats, rewards, self-control
—	Fear and punishment theory	Punishments
—	Monastic theory	Monetary motivation
—	Carrot and stick theory	Money, penalties, fear, dismissals, demotions
—	Paternalistic theory	Kindness, generosity, interest, fairness, high wages, job security, good facilities, health, recreation, good work environment

Content Theories

Proponent	Theory	Motivation Concepts
Abraham Harold Maslow	Maslow's need hierarchy theory	Basic needs, safety needs, need of belonging, esteem needs, needs of self actualisation

Proponent	Theory	Motivation Concepts
Frederick Herzberg	Motivation – hygiene theory	Motivators: Company policy and administration, supervision, relationship with supervisor, work conditions, salary, relationship with peers, personal life, relationship with subordinates, status, security, hygiene factors: achievement, recognition, the work itself, responsibility, advancement, growth
Clayton Alderfer	ERG theory	Needs of existence, relatedness and growth
David C McClelland	Achievement motivation theory	Need for achievement, need for power, need for affiliation
H.A. Murray	Manifest needs theory	—
William Ouchi	Theory Z	Training and evaluation, job rotation, group participation, informal control

Process Theories

Proponent	Theory	Motivation Concepts
Kurt Lewin and Edward Tolman	Expectancy concerns theory	Cognitive motivation
Victor V. Vroom	Expectancy theory	Valence, instrumentality and expectancy
J. Stacey Adam	Equity theory	Inputs-outcomes ratio
B.F. Skinner	Reinforcement theory	Operant conditioning, Positive reinforcement and negative reinforcement
Edwin Locke	Goal setting theory	Goal, effort and success
Porter and Lawler	Performance-satisfaction model	—
Lawler	E-P and P-O expectancies theory	Effort, performance and outcomes

Psychological Approaches to Motivation

Proponent	Theory	Motivation Concepts
Leon Festinger	Cognitive dissonance theory	Dissonance
George Homans	Group exchange theory	Group support
Harold Kelly	Attribution theory	Casual structures of environment
De Charme	Cognitive evaluation theory	Cognitive elements
Fritz Heider Bem	Self-perception theory	Ability, effort, fatigue and environment
Rotter	Locus of control attributions theory	Internal locus of control and external locus of control

Maslow's Need Hierarchy Theory

Abraham Harold Maslow advocated the theory of motivation based on various needs. He has used clinical experience to propound his theory. Maslow identified five distinct categories of needs. He arranged these needs into a hierarchy, and stated that an individual tries to satisfy a particular need to a moderate extent, and then tries to satisfy the next need in the hierarchy. The theory makes the following assumptions.

(i) Human beings want to satisfy their needs

(ii) No single motive determines motivation and behaviour.

(iii) Not all needs are satisfied at once. Motives do not operate simultaneously.

(iv) Individuals attach importance to needs and try to satisfy the need, which they feel, is the most important. If this need is satisfied they move to the next one.

(v) People seek growth in their life, and have a goal or goals that they want to achieve before they die.

(vi) Human behaviour, which is multi-dimensional and multi-variable, is determined by motivation.

Basic Theory and Propositions

Maslow placed human needs into five distinct categories. They are arranged in the order of their importance forming a hierarchy, as shown in Figure 30.1

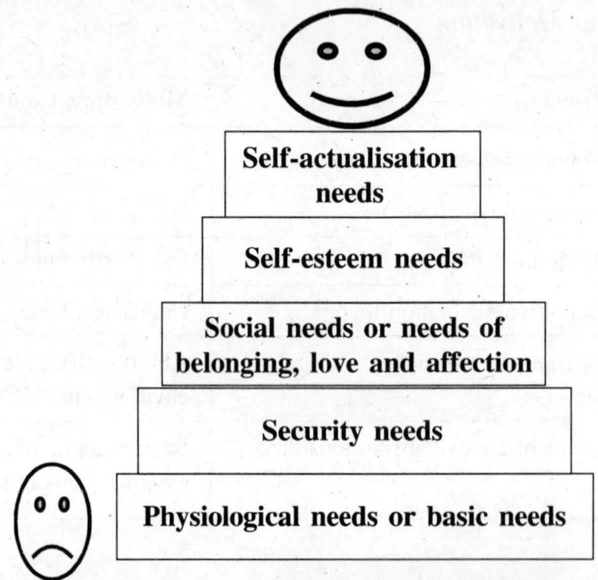

Figure 30.1: Maslow's need hierarchy

According to Maslow, certain concepts are relevant to understand needs. They are pre-potency, deprivation, domination, gratification and activation. Pre-potency is the strength associated with needs. Physiological needs have greater pre-potency. Deprivation is perception of an obstacle, which stands in the way of satisfying a need. Thus, a deprived need has high pre-potency. Domination means attaching importance to a need. A deprived need dominates an individual. In order to reduce dissonance associated with the deprivation, individuals try to gratify their needs by undertaking an action. Therefore, gratification is the satisfaction of a need. A gratified need does not dominate. At the end, activation of a need determines motivation. Need satisfaction at each level activates the need at the next higher level. Maslow believed that the process repeats itself until the highest level need is satisfied. Based on this concept Maslow identified five categories of needs and their role in motivating individuals. They are described below.

1. Physiological Needs

Physiological needs relate to the basic and primary needs required for human existence. They relate to biological processes and are required to preserve basic human life. These needs are identified with the human organs in the body. They are finite needs. They must be satisfied repeatedly until human beings die. They are not only financial needs, but relate to feelings and emotions. They are hunger, thirst, sleep, shelter, sex, and other bodily needs. The proposition relating to basic needs states that they are primary motivators to any individual and once they are satisfied to a reasonable level, they no longer motivate. The reasonable level depends on the individual. Thus, the next level of need becomes important for satisfaction, as long as the basic needs are dormant. Adequate monetary rewards to satisfy these needs motivate employees in organisations.

2. Safety Needs

Individuals seek protection from natural environment, biological danger, economic deprivation and emotional threats from other human beings and animals. For this purpose, they seek security, which may range from seeking shelter to forming primary groups to combat threats arising from the environment, animals and other human beings. The theory states that safety needs dominates as soon as physiological needs are satisfied. Once an individual's security needs are fulfilled to a certain extent, they fail to motivate him. In order to motivate employees, organisations provide security benefits such as fringe benefits, health and accident insurance, housing loans, medical benefits etc. In an organization for example, an employee works very sincerely when he is on probation. Once he is confirmed, and he feels secure, he will think of joining a union to combat what he thinks of as management oppression.

3. Social Needs

A human being is a social animal. He cannot live in isolation and silence. Thus, he intends to establish relationships with other human beings and animals. Social needs emerge from the basic urge of individuals to associate, belong with others, make friendships, seek companionship, be accepted by others and seek affection. These needs are secondary in nature. The propositions relating to social needs state that these needs are satisfied by symbolic behaviour and through mental contact with others in society. They are substantially infinite and exist until the end of human life. Amitai Etizoni states that individuals are born in organisations, live in organisations and die in organisations and when they die it is society that comes to the grave yard. This emphasises the importance of social needs to one's life. Organisations should provide scope for employees to form informal groups, encourage team work, and provide scope for interpersonal communication, interpersonal relationships and interpersonal understanding to motivate employees.

4. Esteem Needs

Maslow believes that people seek growth. They have a natural desire to be identified and respected by others. This instinct is called esteem. Esteem needs are associated with self-esteem and esteem from others. The need for power, self-respect, autonomy, self-confidence, achievement, recognition of competence, knowledge, desire for freedom, status, attention and appreciation from others, are some of the esteem needs an individual wishes to satisfy. Maslow identified them, as higher order needs. Esteem needs remain dormant until basic, security and social needs are satisfied. Satisfaction of esteem needs produces a feeling of self-confidence, strength, capability and adequacy in an individual.

5. Self-actualisation Needs

Self-actualisation is transforming an ambiguous idea, understanding, a dream or one's imagination, into reality. Individuals have the inner potential to be able to do some things differently from others. Realising one's inner potential, a person tries to become what he is capable of becoming. Fulfillment of self-actualisation needs is difficult, as individuals may not even be clear about their inner potential until an opportunity arises. Moreover, these needs change with time and in different situations. The intensity of self-actualisation changes during one's life time, and also varies with the environment and from person to person.

Based on Maslow's hierarchy of needs, the following propositions are made regarding the motivation of individuals.

(i) Five needs are classified into lower order needs and higher order needs. While physiological, safety and security needs are lower order needs; esteem and self-actualisation needs are higher order needs.

(ii) Lower order needs are satisfied externally and higher needs are satisfied internally.

(iii) Individuals start satisfying lower order needs first and proceed to satisfy higher order needs later.

(iv) No need is fully satisfied during the life of an individual. A need substantially satisfied no longer motivates.

(v) A need when substantially satisfied produces satisfaction and it becomes dormant. Immediately the next level need becomes active. Thus, an individual is continuously motivated to satisfy unsatisfied needs, and motivation is a continuous process.

(vi) Satisfaction of lower order needs does not produce contentment. In fact, it produces discontentment, as it awakens the desire to satisfy other needs.

(vii) Not all individuals have the same priority regarding which need to satisfy. Priorities differ from country to country and from situation to situation.

(viii) Individuals are aggressive in the satisfaction of basic needs and unconsciously demand their satisfaction. However, they use social consciousness in the satisfaction of other needs.

Maslow's need hierarchy theory of motivation was considered simple and logical to understand human motivation. The theory has received the attention of practising managers, as it is felt that identification of employees' needs provides an insight in designing and applying strategies to motivate them. This theory suggested that giving same reward in excess of individuals' desire results in diminishing marginal utility. This is relevant to the practising manager. The following criticism was levelled against the theory.

(i) **Theoretical:** Maslow's theory of motivation is only theoretical. It does not have adequate empirical evidence to support the propositions. Even the methodology of the theory was questioned on the ground that the data was obtained from small samples, which could not really justify the conclusions.

(ii) **Needs classification:** The classification of needs was criticised as being arbitrary and artificial. Needs cannot be classified into watertight compartments as is done in the theory. Moreover, the order of needs as identified by Maslow is not the same for all people. For instance, higher order needs are less important to a large section of the population in the under developed countries. Some countries consider esteem and prestige to be more important than monetary rewards.

(iii) **Degree of gratification:** Maslow suggested that a gratified need does not motivate. In fact, a need cannot be fully gratified during the lifetime of an individual, and critics stated that hundred percent gratification is only a myth. Certain needs can never be gratified. For example, a person will feel hungry (at certain times) throughout his life.

(iv) **Perception of self-actualisation:** Critics have pointed out that self-actualisation is only a psychological and ethical aspiration. Often, individuals are not able to specify their self-actualisation motives clearly. For example, the Managing Director of a company may still want a higher position or more power, even though he has reached the highest position in the company. Thus, it is difficult to define self-actualisation.

(v) **Needs are over simplified:** Maslow's identification of needs is over simplified. Human needs are much more complex than the needs identified in the theory. Human motivation is also complex and is determined by a variety of factors. Moreover, there is an internal conflict among the needs identified by Maslow. Some critics have pointed out that clear definition does not exist for each class of needs. For example, individuals are interested in forming groups to protect themselves from danger as well as to seek affiliation and belongingness. Thus, forming a group satisfies both security and social needs.

In spite of the criticism levelled against Maslow's theory, it is considered relevant even in the present context. It provides a basic understanding of human motivation and gives insights into their behaviour. It was pointed out that understanding needs is more important than how and why they are classified in a particular manner.

Herzberg's Two Factor Theory

Frederick Herzberg, a psychologist, proposed a theory of motivation. The theory was based on a study of 200 engineers and accountants working at Pittsburgh, USA. Others associated with the theory are Mausner, Peterson and Capwell. The methodology used was the 'critical incident method'. In this method, two interesting questions asked were

1. When did you feel exceptionally good about your job?
2. When did you feel exceptionally bad about your job?

They have identified two sets of distinct factors, known as intrinsic factors and extrinsic factors. Intrinsic factors are related to the job itself, they are concerned with the nature of the job, and occur during the time of performing the job. They relate to positive feelings about the job, and provide job satisfaction. Hence, they provide strong motivation. They are called motivational factors, and are needed to maintain a high level of job satisfaction and job performance.

Extrinsic factors are external to the job. They are hygiene factors or maintenance factors. They are related to the conditions under which the job is performed. Therefore, they are concerned with the environment. They relate to the job context. They occur after the work is complete. They are identified with job dissatisfaction and are associated with negative feeling of the employees.

They are not responsible for growth in productivity of the employees. Therefore, they provide no motivation.

This is the reason that the theory is also known as the two factor or dual factor theory. It is also called as the motivation-hygiene theory.

The factors identified by Herzberg are shown in Figure 30.2.

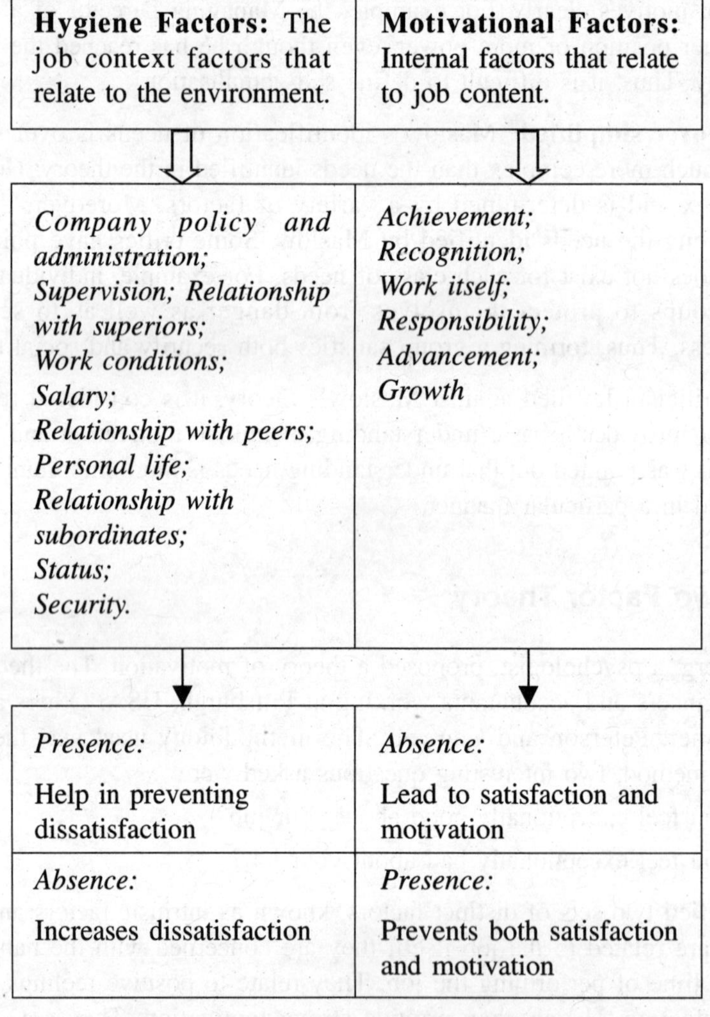

Figure 30.2: Two factors in Herzberg's theory

The central concept of the theory is that factors that contribute to job satisfaction are motivators and factors that contribute to job dissatisfaction are hygiene factors that do not provide any motivation. Existence of hygiene factors only prevents employees being dissatisfied. Thus, mangers improve these factors to prevent dissatisfaction, leading to the employees being satisfied with their job. Therefore, it is suggested that managers concentrate on the motivators rather than hygiene factors.

The Herzberg theory also received considerable attention because it identified the factors that motivate employees. It suggested that the environment is also an important factor in motivating the employees. The theory was appreciated for suggesting that the factors causing boredom and monotony in a job should be identified. It also suggested that mangers should eliminate these factors in order to motivate the employees. In addition, redesigning the job by providing an opportunity for growth and a sense of achievement, advancement, and personal development motivates them further. However, the theory was subject to certain criticisms, which are given below.

1. **Methodology:** The basic criticism levelled against the theory is that the methodology only identifies the factors of satisfaction and dissatisfaction, motivation is not taken into account. In addition, the sample was limited to a specific occupational group in an organisation. Thus, generalisations cannot be drawn.
2. **Environment:** The theory ignores the external environment and situational variables.
3. **Focus:** It is a theory based on satisfaction rather than motivation.
4. **Simplistic outlook:** The theory is too simplistic and it overlooks individual differences.
5. **Inconsistent relationships:** The theory originally assumed a relationship between productivity and satisfaction, but the final model did not present this relationship.

Despite the criticism, the theory is considered relevant in understanding the motivation of employees.

Similarities and Distinctions between Maslow's Need Hierarchy and Herzberg's Two Factor Theories

Maslow's theory of needs hierarchy and Herzberg two factor theory show certain similarities and dissimilarities. The similarities between needs in the two theories are depicted in Figure 30.3.

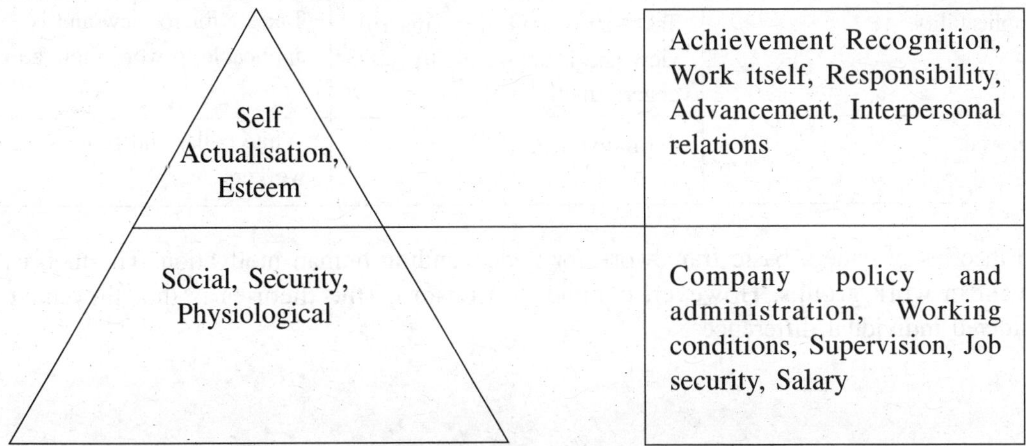

Figure 30.3: Similarities between the Maslow and Herzberg Theories of Motivation

Similarities: The following points of similarities are observed in the theories.

1. *Nature of motivation:* Both theories have identified that motivation is a process, which leads to performance.
2. *Human needs:* Both theories consider the totality of needs. Herzberg considered that certain needs act as motivators. Maslow considered these same needs as esteem and self-actualisation.
3. *Behaviour:* Both theories state that needs determine motivation, which in turn determines the behaviour of individuals.

Distinctions: The distinctions between the Maslow and Herzberg theories are shown below.

Differences	Maslow's Need Hierarchy Theory	Herzberg's Two Factor Theory
Nature	Descriptive	Prescriptive
Arrangement of needs	Sequential arrangement	Arranged into two categories
Classification	Higher order and lower order needs	Hygiene and motivators
Relationship	Unsatisfied needs are the reason for behaviour and behaviour is the reason for performance	Satisfied needs are the reason for performance
Motivation	A satisfied need is not a motivator	Higher order needs are motivators
Financial factors	Pay and financial benefits are motivators	Financial benefits are not motivators
Applicability	Takes an overall view (macro) view and is applicable to general motivation	Takes a micro view and is applicable to work motivation
Relevance	All individuals	White collar and professional workers

Both theories provide a basic framework for understanding human motivation. The theories are relevant in work groups. However, common criticism of the theories is that they have not considered individual differences.

THEORY X AND THEORY Y

Douglas McGregor is the pioneer of theory X and theory Y. Both the theories are in the form of assumptions about human nature. In these theories McGregor explained the pre-dispositions or attitudes toward people in organisations. These theories explain the nature of human beings and the relevant motivational style of the leader required so as to realise objectives of the organisation.

Theory X is a conventional approach to understand motivation. It is based on traditional assumptions about the nature of people.

Assumptions of Theory X

1. The average human being has an inherent dislike of work and will avoid it if possible.
2. Because of this human characteristic of dislike of work, most people must be coerced, controlled, directed and threatened with punishments to make them put forward adequate efforts towards achieving the objectives of the organisation.
3. The average human being prefers to be directed, wishes to avoid responsibility, has relatively little ambition and wants security above all.

In the theory, McGregor states that the management is responsible for providing facilities to members of the organisation, and directing employees so that the work is carried out with active intervention. This is because the average human being is indolent, avoids responsibility, resists changes and wants to be led by others. Hence, without the intervention of the management, people would be passive and indifferent towards organisational goals. The theory goes on to state that money and fringe benefits, and threats and punishments motivate people. Further, traditional division of work, specialisation, strict rules and regulations and multi-layered communication system are the chief characteristics of an organisation's structure. But this ultimately results in communication blocks, distortions and negative morale of employees.

This theory was criticised on the ground that it is based on faulty assumptions and misconceptions of human nature. Accepting the criticism McGregor developed theory 'Y' based on the human relation approach developed in the Hawthorne studies.

Assumptions of Theory Y

1. The expenditure of physical and mental effort in work is as natural as play or rest.
2. External controls and threat of punishment are not the only means of bringing about efforts toward organisational objectives. People will exercise self-direction and self control in the services of objectives to which they are committed.
3. Commitment to objectives is a function of the rewards associated with their achievement.

4. Under the proper conditions, the average human being learns not only to accept but also to seek responsibility.
5. The capacity to exercise a relatively high degree of imagination, ingenuity and creativity in the solution of organisational problems is widely distributed in the population.
6. Under the conditions of modern industrial life, the intellectual potentialities of the average human being are only partially utilised.

These assumptions were considered optimistic, dynamic and flexible. They emphasised self-direction and integration of individual needs and organisational demands. According to this theory people are self-directive and increase their competence if properly motivated. They have a sense of belongingness and exercise self control towards continued growth of the enterprise.

Motivational Implications of McGregor Theories

According to theory 'X' the superior sets objectives for subordinates. There is hardly any participation of subordinates in setting objectives and making plans, hence they are not very committed. The organisation is developed on traditional lines of hierarchical structure, communication channels, centralised decision making, specialisation etc. Leadership is autocratic and communication is one-way upwards. There will be little feedback. The superior decides what is to be done and judges the performance. The tendency of the superior is to find fault and award punishment. Therefore, motivation is through threats and punishments and is purely monetary.

According to theory 'Y', subordinates are allowed to participate and explore alternatives in developing plans and setting objectives. These joint decisions result in high motivation and commitment to objectives and plans. The organisation's structure is developed taking human relations into account and emphasises human needs. Leadership is democratic, participative and communication is two-way. Individuals are responsible, accountable and committed to performance due to positive motivation. Superiors trust their subordinates and appraise their performance accordingly. People try to learn from past experiences. The system of feed forward control lays emphasis on problem solving. Thus, the motivation is positive and mostly non-financial.

Criticism of the McGregor Theories

The following criticism has been levelled against the McGregor theories:

1. The assumptions of theory 'X' and theory 'Y' are not prescriptions or suggestions for designing and implementing managerial strategies.
2. Assumptions are only intuitive deductions. They are not based on research hence the approach lacks practicality.
3. Neither theory suggests the type of motivation required to direct subordinates' behaviour. In

practice, managers must recognise the dignity, capacity and limitations of people to be effective.

4. Theories should not be viewed as being on a continuous scale with theory 'X' and 'Y' at opposite extremes. They reflect completely different views of people in the organisation.
5. Theory 'Y' is not against authority, it suggested certain ways in which a manager can motivate subordinates.
6. Neither theory recognises the fact, that different tasks and situations require different styles of management.

Despite criticism, the theories have provided basic assumptions about the human nature.

THEORY Z

Theory Z has received considerable attention as a theory of motivation in recent years. It originated from the Japanese philosophy of management, which is characterised by the optimum use of human energy. Japanese organisations are successful on many fronts. Some notable features are increased productivity, lower rates of absenteeism and turnover and high degree of organisational commitment. These characteristics were of interest to scientists. Analysis of the Japanese styles of management led to the emergence of theory Z, put forward by William Ouchi and Alfred Jaeger.

Three important propositions were proposed regarding the success of Japanese organisations. They are given below.

1. **Technology:** Japanese organisations have installed new technology. However, it was found that the technology is not in any way different from that in the rest of the world, particularly American technology. Therefore, technology alone does not lead to effectiveness of an organisation. The increase in productivity of Japanese organisations goes beyond technology.
2. **Culture:** Japanese firms have inculcated a unique culture. An analysis of Japanese culture however, reveals that although there are certain unique aspects, it is not significantly different from the culture of other countries. Thus, success of Japanese organisations is not attributed to the culture. There must be certain other elements that determine the success.
3. **Styles of management:** Japanese management follows an integrated style. It is this that has led to the high productivity in their organisations.

William Ouchi integrated the characteristics of American organisations, which are called 'Type A' and Japanese organisations, which are known as 'Type J'. The integrated theory is known as theory Z.

The various characteristics are presented below:

Characteristics	Type A Organisations (American)	Type J Organisations (Japanese)	Theory Z
Decision making	Individual managers make decisions	Decisions are made by the group	Emphasis on participation by the group and consensus in decisions
Responsibility	Assigned on an individual basis	Shared collectively by the group	Assigned on an individual basis
Control	Explicit and formal controls are used	Implicit and informal controls are used. They are based on trust and good will	Attention is on informal controls and explicit measurements of performance are used
Performance evaluation and promotion of personnel	Very fast promotions. Job hopping is a common phenomenon	Very slow promotions.	Slower promotions. More emphasis on evaluation and training rather than promotion
Career paths	Very specialised careers. People stick to one area of specialisation.	Very general. Employees are allowed to learn all aspects of operations.	Very general. Job rotation is used as a training device and broad-based training is given to employees so that they feel that they are capable of working in any part of the organisation.
Concern for personnel	Concerned only with the employees' life at work	Concerned with an employees' life, both in the place of work and outside (social life)	Concern for workers' whole life

Some specific characteristics of theory Z are as follows:

(i) Selection, compensation and promotions: Employees are selected considering that they will stay with the organisation for a long time. The sources of selections are schools, institutions and other organisations. People of all ages are selected. Selections are based on job related formal education and specialised skills. Promotions are based on productivity of the employee.

(ii) Structure of the organisation: The organisation's structure is hierarchical. It lays emphasis on moderate job specialisation, decentralisation, job enlargement, quality circles and matrix form of organisation. Organisations are built around groups.

(iii) Decision-making: Decision-making is not highly centralised. Emphasis is on informal opinions and consensus. Verbal communication is encouraged. Written communication is used only to verify execution of decisions.

(iv) Management systems: The management tries to harmonise individual and organisational goals to achieve a high degree of goal congruence. Employees are considered as valuable assets. Employees have an inherent desire to work and supervision is not strict. Self-control is exercised.

(v) Employee relationships: Concern is shown for an employee and his welfare. Relationships are paternalistic (caring). Employment is for a lifetime. Problems are solved jointly by the employer and employee.

(vi) Human resources development: Potential skills are recognised. Job enlargement and career planning are given due emphasis. Socialising in the organisation, technical training, research and development are given priority.

Thus, theory Z advocated an organisational culture that motivated employees, laid special emphasis on development of employees, and encouraged employees to participate.

SUMMARY

Motivating people has always been a challenge to mankind and managers in particular. Significant research and development on the subject has resulted in certain theories of motivation. The concept of motivation dates back to early scientific management theory propounded by F.W. Taylor. Motivational theories are classified into three types. The early motivation theories consisted of scientific management, human relations theory, theory X and theory Y, fear and punishment theory, carrot and stick theory and paternalistic theory. Later, the content theories were developed. These are Maslow's need hierarchy theory, motivation hygiene theory, ERG theory, achievement motivation theory, manifest needs theory and theory Z. The process theories are expectancy concerns theory, expectancy theory, equity theory, reinforcement theory, goal setting theory, performance satisfaction model and E-P and P-O expectancies theory. Modern motivational theories are based on psychological concepts. They are the cognitive dissonance theory, group exchange theory, attribution theory, cognitive evaluation theory, self-perception theory and locus of control attribution theory. This chapter discussed Maslow's need hierarchy theory, Herzberg's two-factor theory, McGregor's 'X' and 'Y' theories and William Ouchi's 'Z' theory.

Maslow identified five categories of needs namely, physiological, security, social, esteem and self-actualisation needs. The theory is basic and significant even today for understanding motivation. However, it is criticised for its theoretical bias, classification of needs, degree of gratification, perception of self-actualisation and over simplification of needs. Based on a survey of engineers and accountants Herzberg identified motivational and hygiene factors. While hygiene factors prevent dissatisfaction, motivational factors are relevant to practising managers.

This theory was criticised on the grounds of methodological bias, ignoring the environment, focus on specialised groups, simplistic outlook and inconsistent relationships. The theories have certain similarities and dissimilarities. McGregor's theory of motivation is based on assumptions about human nature. Theory X made negative assumptions of motivation, while theory Y made positive assumptions. William Ouchi found that the technology and culture of Japanese organisations do not differ significantly from those of American organisations. Thus, the success of Japanese organisations can be attributed to the style of management. He named this style as theory Z. The characteristics of theory Z are selection, compensation and promotions, structure of the organisation, decision-making, employee relationships and human resources development.

Case study 30.1: How to handle the motivational predisposition of engineers.

Mr. Rama Krishna, who is a mechanical engineer, is a middle level manager in a large electronics company. He was recently appointed as a Project Manager. His superior told him that a number of engineers in the project had become lethargic and ineffective, however there were still many efficient and effective engineers.

During the first few months, Mr. Krishna laid great emphasis on targets, ignoring the personal feelings of his subordinates. He initiated a number of changes such as target-oriented incentives, additional perks for efficient employees, strict control and supervision of activities, cost control measures etc. However, several of his able and key subordinates became dissatisfied and showed signs of leaving. This caused concern in the top management.

Mr. Krishna seemed to be an efficient manager as the project engineers not only completed all the projects successfully, but the project team was also awarded new projects. However, the top management was apprehensive, as the project team tends to become ineffective in the long run. Mr. Krishna announced a package of benefits to his threatening subordinates.

Questions:

1. How would you classify the style of leadership, and motivational techniques followed by Mr. Krishna?
2. What are the problems of initiating changes in this case? How would you implement them successfully?
3. What could be the package of benefits Mr. Krishna wanted to announce to bear the threats?

Key words:

- **Deprivation:** Perception of an obstacle in the way of satisfying a need.
- **Domination:** Attaching importance to a need.
- **Hygiene factors:** The job context factors that are centred on the environment.
- **Intrinsic factors:** Positive feelings about the job at the time of performing the job.
- **Motivational factors:** Internal factors that relate to job content.
- **Physiological needs:** Basic and primary requirements for human existence that are required for preservation of human life.
- **Prepotency:** The strength associated with needs.
- **Self-actualisation:** Transforming one's imagination, an ambiguous idea, understanding or dream into reality.

31. BEHAVIOURAL THEORIES OF MOTIVATION

This chapter enables you:

- *To understand the role of growth needs in human motivation*
- *To examine the relevance of achievement motivation*
- *To distinguish between high and low achievers*
- *To understand the relationship between effort and performance*
- *To appraise the relationship between motivation and satisfaction of performance*
- *To understand various non economic approaches of motivating the employees*

The structure of the chapter is as follows:

- Introduction
- ERG theory
- McClelland's theory of need
- Expectancy theory
- Porter and Lawler's theory
- Managcrial strategies of motivating employees
- Summary
- Key words

CHAPTER 31

Behavioural Theories of Motivation

INTRODUCTION

Basic motivation theories have identified that individual performance is related to the feeling of being motivated. Thus, motivation is a psychological phenomenon and an individual's behaviour is related to their inner feelings of motivation. The important motivation theories developed are the ERG theory, McClelland's theory, the expectancy theory, and Porter and Lawler's model of motivation. It is true that monetary rewards often motivate our behaviour, however this is not always true, we undertake certain actions even if we do not get any financial incentives. Thus, more than money, we are motivated by psychological satisfaction. The theories discussed in this chapter purport this relationship. They try to explain the interrelationship between various needs and the relationship between needs-motivation-satisfaction. The degree of strength of association determines motivation. Greater the strength of association greater will be the motivation and vice versa. Most theories are oriented towards situations, and their assumptions relate to situational aspects. This relationship is of great relevance in understanding motivation. For instance, Victor Vroom identified a mathematical model of motivation, in which motivation depends on valence (i.e. the strength of an individual's preference for a particular outcome), instrumentality (the strength of belief about the certainty of the outcome), and expectations. By manipulating these variables, managers can motivate subordinates. Porter and Lawler have identified complex of relationship and presented the model using a diagrammatic approach. Understanding the relationship between variables, enables a manager to determine strategies to motivate employees. These variables are described in this chapter.

ERG THEORY

Clayton Alderfer propounded the ERG theory of motivation, which is basically an out growth of Maslow's and Herzberg's theories of motivation. The ERG theory is based on the concept of Existence needs, Related needs and Growth needs. The model has the following assumptions.

(i) Needs are classified into distinct categories.

(ii) There is a basic distinction between lower and higher order needs.

(iii) Needs proceed on a continuum rather than a hierarchy.

(iv) A need that is not properly satisfied is desired more.

(v) The desire to satisfy higher order needs arises after lower level needs are satisfied. However, the reverse may also occur and this is known as 'frustration regression'.

(vi) Motivation arises out of need frustration.

(vii) More than one need motivates an individual.

The ERG theory classifies needs into three categories. They are:

1. Existence needs
2. Relatedness needs
3. Growth needs

They are explained below:

1. ***E*xistence needs:** Existence needs relate to the basic survival of human beings. They are similar to the physiological and safety needs suggested by Maslow. Monetary rewards, working conditions, job security and incentives are some examples of existence needs.

2. ***R*elated needs:** An individual has a natural desire to develop social relationships. He wishes to belong with others and develop friendship and warm relationships. He wants his own identity, recognition and self-esteem. These are related needs, which are similar to the social and esteem needs enunciated by Maslow.

3. ***G*rowth needs:** An individual has an intrinsic desire to grow and develop in his career and personal life. He wants to realise his full potential and learn new skills and capabilities. These are growth needs, which are similar to the self-actualisation needs suggested by Maslow.

According to the ERG theory, all the three types of needs may operate simultaneously to provide motivation. The theory propounded a new dimension known as 'frustration regression'. According to this, a person tries to satisfy a lower order need, if he becomes frustrated trying to satisfy a higher order need. Unable to satisfy higher order needs, an individual looks back to a lower order need. The concept of need satisfaction arising out of frustration is the basic concept of the ERG theory. The theory makes the following propositions:

- An individual tries to satisfy a need, when he feels deprived of satisfying it. Therefore, deprivation is motivation.

- Needs are not satisfied in a particular order as suggested by Maslow. For example, a highly qualified employee may have a strong desire to occupy a higher position, even before he has satisfied his basic needs.
- Two relationships are important to understand motivation. One is the relationship between satisfaction and motivation and the second is the relationship between frustration and motivation. An example makes this clear. Suppose an employee feels he has been overlooked for a promotion, he will feel deprived. If he is then given a promotion it will motivate him. This is motivation from frustration. Having been promoted, the employee will be motivated to fulfill unsatisfied needs. He works hard to realise his potential to get the next promotion. This is satisfaction-related motivation.

The ERG theory is applicable to work motivation. The theory is considered workable and has realistic approach. This approach provides a clear understanding of human behaviour by recognising individual differences. However, the theory lacks adequate empirical support and critics feel that it is not universally applicable.

McCLELLAND'S THEORY OF ACHIEVEMENT MOTIVATION

David C. McClelland advocated the achievement motivation theory. It is also known as the three needs theory. He used the Thematic Apperception Test (TAT) to measure needs. In this test a series of ambiguous pictures are shown to individuals, and they are asked to write a story based on them. The experts interpret the stories, and draw conclusions about the need potential.

The following assumptions were made in the theory.

(i) Individuals have multiple needs. They try to satisfy many needs simultaneously.
(ii) There is a difference in the degree of motivation for various needs.
(iii) Motivation can be learnt. Individuals can be taught to achieve higher order needs. Individuals emulate model behaviour.
(iv) Attitudes can be identified, measured and changed.
(v) Measurable goals can be set for individuals.
(vi) A system giving feedback on performance is available.

McClelland has identified three needs that motivate an individual. They are described below:

1. Need for Achievement (NAch)
2. Need for Power (NPow)
3. Need for Affiliation (NAff)

Need for Achievement

It is the desire to excel, to achieve a certain set of standards, to strive to succeed, (Robbins).

According to the theory, certain people have the inner urge to succeed and do something different from others. This is the goal to achieve. Employees having an inner desire to achieve derive satisfaction from achieving goals. Therefore, challenging goals become motivators. People with a high need for achievement are high achievers, and possess the following characteristics.

(i) Monetary rewards do not motivate high achievers.

(ii) High achievers create situations in which they are personally responsible for finding solutions to problems.

(iii) They always set moderately challenging goals, in order to prevent dissatisfaction from not achieving higher goals. At the same time, they are not satisfied with easy tasks.

(iv) High achievers do not depend on chance. They assume responsibility.

(v) They are willing to work independently. They wish to establish relationship between their effort and success.

(vi) They always want to overcome difficulties by themselves.

According to McClelland, individuals are not necessarily born with the need to achieve. It can be developed and learnt. The need for achievement was demonstrated in India in 1970. A seaport in Kakinada, was selected for this experiment. Certain businesspersons operating in Kakinada port were selected, and asked to prepare plans that would help them realise their goals to become successful entrepreneurs. They were told what the goals were and how to realise them. The businesspersons started several industries, enlarged their business base and hired a large number of villagers to work in their industrial establishments. They became productive and successful. After 10 years, a re-assessment was conducted to test the achievement motivation levels of the businesspersons. The researchers found that these were exceptionally high and that the businesspersons were willing to carry out risk oriented projects.

The theory suggested certain techniques to enhance achievement motivation, which are described below.

- **Feedback:** Feedback is the process of providing information to employees about their performance. Regular feedback enables employees to assess their performance and learn from their mistakes. This helps them set challenging goals by understanding how to remove obstacles in the achievement of goals. For instance, most employees in private sector companies receive feedback on their performance at regular intervals. Review meetings are held to gauge their reactions on the feedback, and to suggest ways of improving their performance. No penalties are levied, but they are promised incentives to achieve the goals. This process is similar to the concept of Management By Objectives (MBO) enunciated by Peter F. Drucker.
- **Model building:** Employees who are high achievers and attained challenging goals are put forward as role models. This allows other employees to emulate their characteristics, and set high achievement goals for themselves. For instance, in APSRTC fleet drivers who achieve highest kmpl are identified. Their driving habits such as operation of clutch, changing gears, use of brake, speed at which they drive etc. are told to other drivers. This helped other drivers

to understand how to achieve the best kmpl. A study conducted in one of the bus depots revealed that a large number of drivers could achieve the best kmpl by observing the good driving habits.

- **Job redesign:** One way to develop achievement motivation is to redesign the tasks, adding additional responsibility and setting challenging goals. If tasks are very easy to achieve, employees do not feel motivated. On the other hand, if a task is very difficult it can lead to frustration and de-motivation. Therefore, jobs should be designed to provide moderately challenging goals, and should be designed so that they can be achieved independently. This will make employees feel self-sufficient in realisation of goals. The job should be redesigned in such a way that the outcome of the job is measurable and individual contribution is identifiable. This gives satisfaction to individuals as their contribution to the job, and thereby the organisation, is noted.
- **Attitude change management:** McClelland stated that achievement motivation could be taught, therefore an employee's attitude should be changed so that they think positively, are innovative and imaginative. This enhances their achievement motivation.
- **Measurable outcomes:** We know that high achievers believe in personal success. They want the outcome of their work to be measurable and identifiable, providing identity to the employee's skills relating to performance develops achievement motivation. In the absense of a measurable outcome an employee will not feel motivated to achieve. Here, the difficulty arises when the job requires team performance rather than individual performance or it has intangible results. Also in certain types of job the cause and effect relationship between performance and effort cannot be established. For example, consider a teacher, who teaches very well, but if the students are not mature enough to understand him, the results will be negative. This does not mean that teacher is a poor performer, but his achievement motivation will be adversely affected. Another example is of government and public sector enterprises, where employees work in a highly controlled environment that makes it difficult for them to identify the cause and effect of performance. Therefore, they will not set goals of achievement motivation.

Thus, the theory states that enhancing the achievement potential of employees motivates employees. At the same time, McClelland states that the need for power and affiliation influences motivation in individuals.

Need for Power

The need for power is defined as the need to make others behave in a way that they would not have behaved otherwise, (Robbins). According to the theory, certain people derive satisfaction by exercising control over others. They believe that they have ability to control others. They desire that the means to achieve goals should be related to exercise of power. The characteristics of individuals with high need for power is that they prefer situations which are competitive and status oriented. They believe that status and power are related to each other, and tend to be more concerned with prestige and influence than effective performance. Such individuals can be motivated by promoting them to positions of influence and power. The concept of need for power advocated by McClelland helps people to choose their career. It helps the management in an organisation to select individuals based on their need for power. Hence, the person best suited to the job can be selected thereby preventing dissatisfaction in employees.

Need for Affiliation

It is the desire for friendly and close interpersonal relationships. McClelland suggested that the need for affiliation is based on the concept of belonging as advocated by Maslow. Dale Carnegie also stated that individuals want to be liked and accepted by others. Affiliation oriented individuals exhibit high preferences towards inter-personal relationships, establish psychological contact with others and crave for social acceptance, strive for friendship and prefer cooperative situations. They look for a high degree of mutual understanding in relationships. Therefore, the theory states that a relationship oriented climate, inter personal understanding and inter personal communication develop motivation.

Some of the propositions of the theory, as a result of experimental research can be stated as follows:

- High achievers will be strongly motivated when they find that the job offers personal responsibility, feedback and a moderate risk of achieving goals.
- High achievement motivation leads to success for entrepreneurs, running their own business.
- Managers with high achievement needs are not successful managers in large organisations. They are best suited to perform the jobs independently. According to McClelland, the two essential ingredients of managerial success, especially at higher levels in an organisation are emotional maturity and a democratic style.
- Need for affiliation and need for power are closely related. Successful managers have a high need for power and low need for affiliation.
- High power motive is a requirement for managerial success.
- As individuals climb higher in the hierarchy, their need for power increases.
- Training can stimulate achievement need in employees.
- Individuals are motivated to succeed, and this motivation stems from achievement or power needs. Thus, it is important for an individual to believe that his efforts will result in a successful performance and, even more, that this successful performance will bring rewards.

The achievement motivation theory propounded by McClelland is considered a more practical theory than the theories of Maslow and Herzberg. The concept of overlapping needs suggested by the theory is of specific significance to organisations in designing motivational strategies. Similarly recognising that achievement needs could be created through training has brought a new dimension in managerial motivation. However, the theory has certain negative aspects, which are presented below:

(i) **Teaching and learning motivation:** McClelland suggested that attitudes and behaviour could be changed. Hence, motives can be taught through training. However, critics feel that motives are learnt in childhood and it is difficult to change them later on in life. Therefore, it is not possible to teach achievement motives to individuals, it is only a theoretical idea promoted by McClelland. However, it should be noted that McClelland has provided evidence that achievement needs can be learnt by individuals.

(ii) **Methodology:** As noted earlier, the methodology used by the theory is interpreting the results of TAT. However, critics have pointed out that the interpretation is subject to the bias of the interpreter. Thus, the results cannot be considered as unbiased and scientific.

(iii) **Acquisition of needs:** The theory suggested that employees could acquire achievement needs. In fact, achievement needs emerge out of a number of factors. Even if they are acquired, the change will be temporary. Therefore, one cannot motivate employees over a long period.

(iv) **Right placement:** According to McClelland, appropriate matching of jobs and needs motivate individuals. However, in practice, placing the right man in the right job is a difficult task due to limitations such as gender, caste, government policy, religion and regional feelings.

(v) **Creating a work environment:** An important proposition of the theory is that an appropriate work environment enhances the level of an employee's motivation. However, in practice what constitutes an appropriate work environment is yet to be established.

McClelland's theory suggests that providing feedback on performance and making a job more challenging, responsible, autonomous and result oriented motivates employees.

EXPECTANCY THEORY

Victor Vroom propounded the expectancy theory to explain motivation. It is a process theory, and states that motivation is a process which ultimately leads to satisfaction. The central concept of the theory is that an individual's motivation and actions depend on how closely his preferences are related to the actual outcome. Thus, the expected outcome determines motivation, hence the name expectancy theory. He stated that motivational force is the sum of valence and expectancy. This theory established the relationship between effort, performance and rewards. These relationships are explained below.

(i) Effort-performance relationship: The probability as perceived by an individual that exerting a given amount of effort leads to performance.

(ii) Performance-reward relationship: The degree to which an individual believes that performing at a particular level will lead to the desired outcome.

(iii) Rewards-personal goals relationship: The degree to which organisational rewards satisfy an individual's personal goals or needs and the attractiveness of those potential rewards for the individuals.

These three relationships are referred as valence, instrumentality and expectancy. Thus, the theory is also known as the VIE theory of motivation. The concepts used in the theory are explained below.

1. **Valence:** Valence is the strength of an individual's preference for a particular outcome. Every individual believes that his effort will lead to definite outcome. This is the expected utility or value. The greater the strength or the expectation of the outcome, the greater is the motivation to put forward effort. For example, if an employee believes that working hard and producing better quality goods will lead to payment of a bonus, he will work harder. However, if he is indifferent to the bonus, he will not be motivated. Thus, valence can be positive or negative. It is positive when an employee has a strong preference for a reward, zero if he is indifferent and negative if the employee prefers not to attain the outcome.
2. **Instrumentality:** Instrumentality refers to the strength of belief about the certainty of the outcome. Thus, it expresses the probability of the strength of association between performance and reward. This varies between ± 1. Therefore if the performance reward relationship is positive, there is positive instrumentality and *vice versa*. Employees try to estimate the probability about the reward associated with performance. For example, the management of a company announces a bonus if certain productivity is achieved. In the past, the company always paid the bonus, when the production crossed the management's target. Thus, employees are certain, the bonus will be paid and instrumentality is high. On the other hand, if the history of the company showed that the management tried to avoid paying the bonus, employees would be doubtful about receiving the bonus and instrumentality would be low.
3. **Expectancy:** Expectancy is a belief that efforts will lead to outcome and performance. Therefore, expectancy determines the strength of performance rather than the outcome. It is based on an employee's self-efficacy. Employees with a high level of self-efficacy are more likely to believe that exerting effort will result in a satisfactory performance. A high level of self-efficacy results in high expectations, while a low level of self-efficacy results in low expectations. Persons suffering from a low level of self-efficacy exhibit a phenomenon known as the '*imposter phenomenon*'. They feel inferior and incompetent, and are afraid that if they put in a lot of effort, their low capabilities will be revealed. Imposters have low expectancy. Expectancy is evaluated as a probability. It varies from 0 to 1, 0 being associated with complete uncertainty. As the employee becomes surer of his performance, expectancy rises and it will be high if the employee is certain of the outcome. Both the internal and external environment influence expectancy. Other factors influencing expectancy are personality, self-efficacy, experience, learning and perception. Thus, motivation is influenced by these factors.

According to the expectancy theory, motivation is the result of the sum of the products of valence, instrumentality and expectancy. It can be stated in the form of the following mathematical formula.

$$\text{Motivation} = \Sigma(\text{Valence} \times \text{Instrumentality} \times \text{Expectancy})$$

It should be observed here that all the variables are multiplicative in nature. They are not additive. Therefore, the following propositions can be made.

1. Motivation is positive only when all the variables are positive.
2. Motivation is negative when all or any one of the variables are negative.
3. Motivation is zero even when any one of the variables is zero.
4. Motivation is low if any one of the variables is low.

The relationship among various variables in the expectancy model and the impact on motivation is shown in the following table.

Valence	Instrumentality	Expectancy	Motivation
High	High	High	Strong motivation
Low	High	High	Moderate motivation
High	Low	High	Strong avoidance
Low	Low	High	Moderate avoidance
High	High	Low	Moderate motivation
Low	High	Low	Weak avoidance
High	Low	Low	Moderate avoidance
Low	Low	Low	Strong avoidance

The expectancy theory has brought new dimensions in understanding motivation. Managers can motivate employees by manipulating any one of the factors in a positive way and avoiding negative ways. However, the expectancy theory introduced complex and critical variables, hence it is difficult to understand.

PORTER AND LAWLER'S THEORY

Porter and Lawler have developed a more comprehensive model of motivation. This theory is also known as the performance-satisfaction theory of motivation. The model of motivation is based on the assumptions of the content theories of motivation. The content theories assume that satisfaction leads to performance and dissatisfaction limits the performance of individuals. Porter and Lawler's model is an outgrowth of Victor Vroom's model of motivation. The assumptions of their model are as follows.

(i) Motivation is not equal to satisfaction or performance.

(ii) Motivation, satisfaction and performance are independent variables but there exists some relationship.

(iii) The relationships between motivation and satisfaction can be expressed diagrammatically rather than mathematically.

(iv) More than valence and expectancy, some other variables and the cognitive process play a major role in determining motivation.

The motivation model of Porter and Lawler is shown in Figure 31.1.

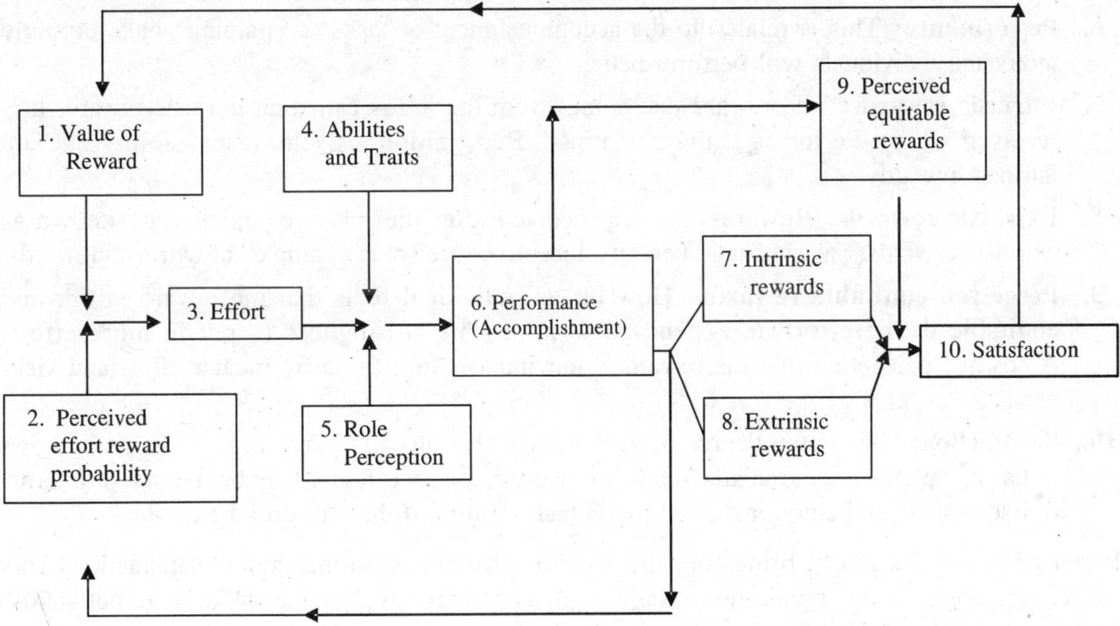

Figure 31.1: Porter and Lawler's motivation model

The motivation model suggested by Porter and Lawler is a multi-variable model. It explains the complex relationship between motivation, performance and satisfaction. According to the model, motivation is the result of effort when abilities, traits and role perceptions accompany it. Rewards and the perception of rewards determine the satisfaction of an individual. Thus, Porter and Lawler's model is concerned with the results of performance. It suggested that performance leads to satisfaction.

The concepts of the model are described below.

1. **Value of rewards:** An individual evaluates the reward that he is likely to receive after the performance of a task. The value can be expressed in monetary or non-monetary terms.
2. **Perceived effort reward probability:** An individual places a probability of receiving a reward for the effort put forward by him. The perception determines the effort. If the individual perceives a greater probability of a reward, his effort will be greater.
3. **Effort:** The effort an individual intends to expend, in relation to the rewards perceived by him.
4. **Abilities and traits:** The effort that an individual is willing to expend depends on his intrinsic ability and the characteristic traits possessed by him.

5. **Role perception:** A role is the expected way of behaviour of an individual. The way one perceives one's role in the organisation determines motivation. For instance, an employee who understands his role in the organisation clearly, discharges his responsibility. Ambiguous roles lead to employees being de-motivated.
6. **Performance:** This is related to the accomplishment of tasks or attaining goals. Properly motivated individuals will perform better.
7. **Intrinsic rewards:** The reward that comes from the job is called an intrinsic reward. It is received whilst the job is being performed. Recognition, esteem, responsibility etc. are intrinsic rewards.
8. **Extrinsic rewards:** Rewards that are received after the job is completed are known as extrinsic rewards. Salary, fringe benefits, incentives are some examples of extrinsic rewards.
9. **Perceived equitable rewards:** How far an individual feels that the reward is fair and equitable to the effort he expends determines his willingness to put in more effort. A positive perception that the reward is fair induces him to put in greater effort and vice-versa.
10. **Satisfaction:** This is the degree of contentment that an individual feels whilst he is doing or has completed a job. Satisfaction is an intangible aspect. It can only be measured in terms of expressions and emotions. If an individual is satisfied, he will do a better job.

Porter and Lawler's model brings out the relation between performance and satisfaction. This model suggested that an organisation should evaluate and redesign policies relating to motivation. It also suggested that the level of satisfaction and level of performance should be related to elicit greater performance on the job. Thus, the model helps in understanding the relationship between performance and satisfaction. The model suggested the following strategies to motivate employees.

(i) **Job placement:** An individual's abilities and personality traits should be matched with the requirements of the job. The best fit between perceived attitudes and the job provides the best motivation. Thus, the right person should be chosen for the right job. A misfit de-motivates employees. Understanding motivation from the perspective of the model avoids this.

(ii) **Job role specification:** Organisations should clearly communicate the roles of employees. It should be ensured that the employees have a clear understanding of the job, responsibilities, rewards and outcomes. The expectations of the organisation should be communicated to the employees in a clear and unambiguous manner.

(iii) **Job rewards:** Employees should be clear about the rewards they will receive after completing the job. They should also be persuaded to place greater significance on these rewards and realise that the rewards are beneficial to them.

Apart from the above, the following suggestions will also help a manager to motivate employees. These suggestions relate to the relationship between motivation and performance and performance and satisfaction.

Relationship between motivation and satisfaction	Relationship between performance and satisfaction
1. Clarify all doubts about ability, skill or knowledge. 2. Remove ambiguity in the job requirements. 3. Provide jobs that are interdependent, in terms of people or activities or both. 4. Clarify the physical or practical possibilities of the job.	1. Determine the rewards that each employee values. 2. Define the desired performance. 3. Make the desired performance attainable. 4. Link rewards which an employee values with their performance.

MOTIVATING EMPLOYEES: SOME APPROACHES

By this time, you must have realised that motivation is a complex process, which involves directing the psychological system of an individual. In an organisational setting, managers find it very difficult to motivate employees due to environmental factors and a number of other considerations. Employees in different organisations require different motivation. Even within an organisation, there are differences at different levels in the managerial hierarchy and between manager and non-manager categories. Though a number of theories have been advocated to explain motivation, a universal application of motivation is difficult. The theories lack practical application in all situations. The commonly used approaches to motivate employees may be economic or non-economic. They are briefly discussed below.

1. **Monetary motivation:** Money is a powerful motivator, especially in the modern era. It is believed that social status, position, power, prestige, recognition etc. are associated with money. Employees receiving a higher salary can lead a luxurious life and command respect from others. Organisations use various financial incentives to motivate employees, such as salaries, piece rate plans, performance-based incentives, profit sharing plans, gain sharing schemes, skill based incentive schemes, knowledge based financial incentive plans and flexible benefits. Though it is desirable to have differences in financial incentives for various jobs, the financial package should be adequate to the changing life styles and needs of employees. Otherwise, employees resort to unethical means of making money using their position and authority in the organisation. For instance, the salary of the average employee in a government office is insufficient to meet the mounting costs of their childrens' education and health. This leads to the employee accepting bribes. After certain time he becomes so habituated to this that he expects to be paid even for regular jobs he is supposed to perform. Consider the case of schoolteachers, who are paid very low salaries. They take up additional occupations to make extra money, treating the job as a source of livelihood. This is reflecting on primary education in our country, and the government should takes steps to rectify the situation.

2. **Job redesign:** Job redesign is thoroughly examining current job related matters such as authority, responsibility, accountability etc., and changing them to suit the situational demands.

Some job redesign strategies include job enlargement, job enrichment and job rotation. Job enlargement is adding more tasks and responsibilities, thus, providing an opportunity to employees to spend more time on the job but still feel comfortable with it. Job enlargement motivates employees as they are allowed to perform a variety of tasks. The work modules are made meaningful. Job redesign allows scope to utilise employees' abilities and provide feedback on performance. Job enrichment is making the job more meaningful by adding motivators such as challenging goals, scope for creativity and innovative processes, and incorporating growth opportunities. This motivates employees and gives them a feeling of satisfaction. Job rotation involves moving employees from one job to another. This provides an opportunity to avoid boredom and develop diversified skills. This motivates employees as they get an opportunity to learn a variety of skills that could be used in different situations.

3. **Employee involvement:** Employee involvement means providing an opportunity to participate in management decisions. This has been proved to be an effective way to motivate employees, as it allows employees to express their feelings regarding decisions. It gives scope for improved interpersonal communication between superiors and subordinates. Since employees feel that their suggestions are accepted, they will readily accept decisions. Some commonly used schemes to encourage participation are committees, task forces, employee representation, quality circles and employee ownership plans commonly known as Employee Stock Option Plan (ESOP).

4. **Quality of work life (QWL):** Quality of work life is a relatively new concept that has received attention of managers. It has a different meaning to different people. QWL includes provision of adequate and fair compensation, a safe and healthy work environment, continuous efforts for the growth and development of employees, provision of growth potential in the job, protecting self esteem, creating a sense of identity, maintaining self respect, and dignity of employees and integrating the job with family life.

5. **Management by objectives (MBO):** Management by objectives is a technique by which managers and subordinates are involved in setting goals at every level in the organisation. Peter F. Drucker advocated the technique, which allows employees to feel a personal responsibility and a sense of achievement. MBO was considered to have the potential to motivate as it protects the ego of the employees.

6. **Performance appraisal:** Performance appraisal is a technique of assessing employees' performance at regular intervals in order to appraise their abilities. It helps in assessing the merits and deficiencies of an employee's performance and develops employees' skills. Based on this appraisal, feedback is given to the employees, to enable them to understand and overcome their deficiencies. It makes employees feel that their capabilities are recognised and that they are suitably promoted.

7. **Potential appraisal:** Performance appraisal is in vogue in many organisations. It aims at analysing the performance with reference to set standards, both quantitative and qualitative. Obviously, the appraisal relates to activities and in some cases it is time bound. The data

generated from this appraisal is helpful in developing strategies for employees' growth. However, nothing can really be done about the past performance. Moreover, because of intricate problems of appraising human resources, employees rarely accept the performance appraisal. These limitations gave rise to a system of potential appraisal. Potential appraisal is appraising the skills, capabilities, and energy and motivation levels of employees before assigning job responsibilities. The results from this appraisal, if properly communicated to the employee, help in realisation of their true nature and potential. It appears logical to tell this to employees before the activity, rather than tell him the positive and negative aspects after he has completed the job. This kind of performance appraisal guides future performance. Since an organisation will have to bear the costs (both financial and non-financial) of inadequate performance, potential appraisal assumes significance. It is recognised as a strategy to motivate employees to develop their potential to undertake future responsibilities, and is popular as a technique for an employee's growth.

8. **Mentoring:** The word mentoring originates from Greek mythology. Mentor was the name of the friend to whom Odysseus assigned his son Telemachus. The model relationship between them protected the protégé from danger and was instrumental in shaping his career. Today mentoring means to provide emotional education and guidance to the young. In the words of Cluter Buck a mentor is someone who helps to develop an individual's potential, capability, judgement and wisdom. It involves personal involvement rather than coaching, and aims to build competence and acquisition of skills. Levinson described a mentor as a teacher, sponsor, counsellor, developer of skills and intellect, guide, example and most importantly a supporter and facilitator in realising the vision the young person has about self-actualisation. Having a suitable mentor at the adolescence stage is a great advantage. Bhagavad Gita purports that the undisciplined mind acts as our enemy, whereas a trained mind acts as our friend. This reinforces the importance of training the mind, under the guidance of a mentor. In the context of motivation in an organisation, mentoring has the following objectives:
   - Developing awareness of organisational culture.
   - Clarifying perceptions to avoid misunderstandings.
   - Setting model behaviour for emulation.
   - Listening effectively to work related issues and personal problems.
   - Helping to make decisions about complex problems.
   - Establishing long lasting relationships.
   - Sharing experiences.
   - Providing emotional support.
   - Creating inner awareness of the self.
   - Carving a 'complete man'.

All these activities make an employee feel cared for and nurtured, during the time they are with the organisation. They develop a sense of belonging and are committed to the organisation. This motivates them to use all their potential for the success of the organisation.

SUMMARY

Clayton Alderfer propounded the ERG theory of motivation based on the theories of Maslow and Herzberg. The basic assumption of the theory is that more than one need motivates individuals simultaneously. The theory identified the frustration regression relationship. While existence needs relate to the basic survival of individuals, related needs are concerned with associating with others, and growth needs are concerned with the desire for growth and development in life. McClelland's achievement motivation theory was a breakthrough in behavioural motivation theories. He recognised that individuals have a strong inner fire to achieve. By identifying this drive for achievement one can be strongly motivated. He used the Thematic Apperception Test to measure the degree of achievement motivation. Three needs are identified in the theory. They are need for achievement, need for power and need for affiliation. McClelland suggested certain techniques to induce achievement motivation. Some of the main techniques are feedback, model building, job redesign, attitude change management, and measurable outcomes. However, critics feel that teaching and learning motivation is not possible. They also pointed out other limitations of the theory such as methodological ambiguities, acquisition of needs, right placement and the necessity of creating a work environment. Victor Vroom suggested an entirely different approach using a mathematical relationship. It was suggested that motivation is the sum of the product of three variable *viz.*, valence, instrumentality and expectancy. The theory suggests that various levels of valence, instrumentality and expectancy result in strong, moderate and weak motivation. Porter and Lawler propounded a comprehensive model of motivation using a diagram. They assumed that motivation results from performance and satisfaction. The model used a number of variables to explain the complex process of motivation. They are the value of rewards, perceived effort reward probability, effort abilities and traits, role perception, performance, intrinsic and extrinsic rewards, perceived equitable rewards and satisfaction. Job placement, job role specification and job rewards are suggested as ways to motivate employees. Managers use a number of strategies to motivate employees. Some of the prominent techniques are monetary motivation, job redesign, employee involvement, QWL, MBO, performance appraisal, potential appraisal and mentoring.

Key words:

- **Existence needs:** Existence needs relate to the basic survival of human beings.
- **Expectancy:** The degree of belief that the effort put in will lead to the required outcome and performance.
- **Extrinsic rewards:** The rewards that are received after the job is completed.
- **Feedback:** The process of providing information to employees, to enable them to evaluate their performance.
- **Frustration regression:** The tendency to satisfy lower order needs, if one is frustrated trying to satisfy higher order needs.
- **Imposter:** A person suffering from low self-efficacy.

- **Intrinsic reward:** The reward that comes whilst one is performing the job.
- **Instrumentality:** The degree to which an individual believes that performing at a particular level will lead to the attainment of a desired outcome.
- **Job enlargement:** Adding more tasks and job responsibilities to the current job.
- **Job enrichment:** Adding motivators to the current job.
- **Job redesign:** Examining the current job components and changing them according to demands of the situation.
- **Job rotation:** Changing the jobs of employees at regular intervals to enable them to learn new tasks and responsibilities.
- **Mentoring:** Providing emotional education and guidance to the young.
- **Potential appraisal:** Appraising the skills, capabilities, energy and motivation levels of employees before assigning them job responsibilities.
- **QWL:** Providing monetary and non-monetary incentives to enable employees to have a reasonably fair standard of living.
- **Related needs:** The desire to establish social relationships for recognition and belonging.
- **Valence:** The strength of an individual's preference for a particular outcome.

32. JOB DESIGN

This chapter enables you:

- *To understand the meaning of job design*
- *To appraise the significance of job design in organisations*
- *To examine the factors influencing job design*
- *To appreciate significance of task characteristics in designing jobs*
- *To classify various models of job design*
- *To identify problems of modern organisations in employee development*
- *To understand the integrating elements in job design*

The structure of the chapter is:

- Introduction
- Meaning of Job Design
- Importance of Job Design
- Factors Influencing Job Design
- Task Characteristics Theory
- Job Characteristics Model
- Motivating Potential Score Model
- Social Information Processing Model
- Socio Technical Model
- Contingency Model
- Employee Development Model
- Integrative Job Design Model
- Summary
- Key Words

CHAPTER 32

Job Design

INTRODUCTION

Organisations are designed to attain common goals. In the process various activities are performed by various employees in the organisation. In order to integrate human effort various jobs are to be designed in a proper way. Improper job design kindles conflicts among employees and inhibits effectiveness in the attainment of jobs. Then what is job design? It is a statement of complete instructions relating to the goals, structure, and duties, responsibilities and timing of performance of job. Traditionally it was believed that technical and structural aspects are important for job design. Scientific management gave importance to the time and motion studies to determine the job elements. At the same time fatigue study seems to have taken care of human element. Human relations approach emphasized the importance of human satisfaction in designing jobs. Later contingency and situational approaches have stated that jobs are to be designed according to situational factors. Organisations should recognise that the ultimate aim of any job should be to obtain optimal performance with least cost and maximising human satisfaction. Thus jobs are to be designed by taking an integrated approach. This chapter describes the various approaches to job design.

MEANING OF JOB DESIGN

Organisations are created for attainment of goals. For this purpose, an organisation structure is created and jobs are designed to meet the goals. F.W. Taylor suggested that jobs should be designed to facilitate technology based on scientific principles to attain higher productivity.

However, Human Relations approach suggested that job design should provide human satisfaction. Even research has revealed that employees performing properly designed jobs showed greater performance, high quality, and high motivation and satisfaction levels. Conversely poor job design kindles boredom, monotony, ambiguity, conflicts and the result is poor quality, poor productivity and job dissatisfaction. Thus, it is suggested that job design help in directing human energy for an effective utilisation of employees for organisational effectiveness. In addition, job design has an influence on employee behaviour and organisational behaviour. Interestingly job design is not an easy task. Moreover, it is not a single time task. It changes with change in internal and external factors. Organisational objectives, environmental factors, social aspects, employee skills, training, status, job expectations, and individual goals and objectives are some of the factors considered in the process of job design. Job design is an outcome of job analysis. Some of the definitions provided hereunder will give you more clarity on the concept of job design.

> *Job design can be defined as 'a process of structuring job, deciding on job elements, duties and tasks in a manner that will help to achieve optimal performance and satisfaction.'* **Ivancevich, M. John.**
>
> *According to* **Taylor** *'job design is complete written instructions describing in detail the task to be accomplished. The task specifies not only what is to be done, but how it is done and exact time allowed for doing it.'*
>
> *Job design is making components and sub components of job clear, so that employee understands the goals of outcome of the job.*

The paradigm of job design has changed remarkably over the years. Traditionally job design was viewed as designing standard procedures, clarifying specific job descriptions for increasing productivity and efficiency. Nowadays job design is viewed from the perspective of total quality management. The jobs are designed to provide use of innovation, empowerment, autonomy and teamwork. The outcome of the job design is assuring total quality, customisation and customer satisfaction. Thus, job design as a quality of work life is concerned with the product, process, tools and techniques, design, plant layout, work measurement, standard operating procedures, human process, machine interaction and other activities related to job performance. The meaning of job design is:

(i) Job design is structuring of job tasks and responsibilities.
(ii) Job design and quality of work life are related.
(iii) It is concerned with written instructions about the job.
(iv) Job design is both technical and managerial.
(v) It is concerned with job, motivation and behaviour of individuals.
(vi) It is concerned with standardisation of job functions.
(vii) The goal of job design is to maximize human efficiency in jobs.
(viii) Job design is applicable to both blue and white collared employees.

IMPORTANCE OF JOB DESIGN

Though job design sounds technical it is essentially a strategy of human resource management. It has a number of potential benefits.

(a) Job design helps to improve productivity and quality of product.

(b) Job design clarifies the tasks and roles. Thus, it avoids ambiguities in the performance of jobs.

(c) Job design removes overlapping responsibilities. This leads to rationalisation of tasks. Conflicts among personnel are avoided.

(d) Job design allows proper placement of employees. Thus, an appropriate job fit will be achieved.

(e) It allows operational control over work performance and results.

(f) Job design allows incorporation of environmental changes in the job.

(g) It provides flexibility. Thus, employees are prepared to accept changes without much resistance.

(h) It inculcates work motivation. Job design allows managers to understand organisational behaviour by understanding the process of motivational behaviour.

(i) Proper job design leads to better quality of work life among employees.

(j) Job design relieves stress and improves performance and organisational effectiveness.

FACTORS INFLUENCING JOB DESIGN

Job design encompasses a number of factors. Understanding job design requires knowledge of these factors. They are goals, job content, job relationship, task, employees' response and job specialisation. These are described in terms of organisational context factors, task factors, job context and content factors, and employee factors. They are described below:

1. **Goals:** Job design aims at goal setting and communication to the employees. Goals provide direction and help in exercising control. They also influence human behaviour, motivation and satisfaction. Goals are means of performance measurement and also for achieving organisational performance. The internal and external environment of the organisation and jobs are considered for setting goals. For instance, Locke considered certain factors like values and value judgement, emotions, desires, intentions, or goals, responses, actions, performance, consequences, feedback and reinforcement in the process of setting goals. Even McClelland considered that goal achievement provides motivation and satisfaction. The following are the requirements of goal setting in the process of job design.

   (i) *Clarity:* Goals should be clear to understand. Clarity improves understanding of tasks. This improves performance.

   (ii) *Tangible:* Goals must be specific to the job. Specific goals are tangible.

   (iii) *Approachable:* Goals should not be too high or too simple. Too simple goals do not provide motivation. At the same time too high goals lead to feeling of difficulty for attainment. So they de-motivate when they are not achieved. The belief that goals are attainable provides right motivation.

(iv) *Challenging goals:* In order to provide right motivation goals must be challenging.

(v) *Participation:* Goals must be set by the participation of subordinates. This enables to bring psychological commitment. Otherwise, goals are not achieved.

(vi) *Satisfying:* The ultimate purpose of goals is to provide satisfaction. Then only subordinates will be motivated. Goals, which are not providing satisfaction, do not motivate the subordinates.

(vii) *Past experience:* Experience is a better guide in goal setting. This enables to set realisable goals. Otherwise, there is a possibility of setting too high or too low goals.

(viii) *Comments:* Comment is information provided to the subordinates on the performance. Goals must include a mechanism of feedback to appraise the performance.

Interestingly Peter F. Drucker has suggested Management by Objectives (MBO) approach for goal setting. According to this, goals are set in all key result areas with participation of functional managers. Performance is compared with goals by self-examination and managers are allowed to make self-appraisal and make correction in the performance or goals. Thus, the first step in job design is goal setting. Job design is prepared, described and allocations are made as per goals. At regular intervals, performance is evaluated with respect to goals. Goals are redesigned to improve organisational performance.

2. **Task accomplishment:** Task accomplishment is related to job design. Jobs are designed to accomplish tasks. Task accomplishment is viewed primarily in terms of productivity. Other outcomes of task accomplishment are economy in operations, efficiency and effectiveness. While efficiency is related to the attainment of more output with minimum input, effectiveness is related to the attainment of goals with utmost economy. Economy is related to the rational utilisation of physical, financial and human resources. Thus, job design should be done to economise resources, yet achieve maximum productivity.

3. **Employee Response:** The ultimate objective of job design is to maximize employee satisfaction. Job design should encourage employees to perform well. For the purpose of good job design and redesign employees' opinion about the job is important. This can be obtained by feedback. It enables management to clarify their expectations to employees. At the same time employees also report their performance and difficulties. This helps to redesign the jobs to provide greater job satisfaction.

4. **Task Variety:** Basically tasks are different though they are dependent. They require variety of skills. Repetitive tasks do not require variety of skills. Certain other tasks require a range of skills. These tasks are perceived as challenging. Repetitive tasks are considered monotonous and boring. Job design should provide an opportunity to demonstrate skills of employees.

5. **Task Identity:** Task identity is identification of individual contribution in the output.

Employees want that their contribution is recognised and rewarded. This is possible only when the tasks are identified. This gives them a sense of satisfaction. Independent jobs have measurable task identity. Hence individual contribution is appraised through performance appraisal. But the same is not the case with group tasks where the outcome is attributable to all members of the group. So, certain individuals feel less satisfied though their contribution is more. They feel that persons contributing less received more recognition than those contributing more. Even managers also find it difficult to appraise the performance and recognise the contributors. Sometimes the system comes in the way of appraising contributors in a group task. To avoid such feeling among employees, job design should provide task identity. It makes an employee satisfied with his achievement.

6. **Task Significance:** Employee feels that his role in the organisation is important if his task is considered significant by the organisation and others. For instance, line people feel that they are important than staff people, as they play a significant role in the attainment of major objectives of the organisation. Similarly, defence personnel feel that their job is significant as it involves protection of nation from invaders. Employees possessing a feeling of pride in the job get greater satisfaction. They are motivated to devote their energy, ability and skills to perform them. Employees should be given adequate significance of their tasks. Job design should provide adequate information to employees concerning the importance of their contribution to the organisational goals.
7. **Task Complexities:** Task complexity relates to perception of employees about the complexities involved in the job. Employee feeling that task is difficult, as it is beyond their capabilities makes them not to contribute their energy. This is on account of inhibitions. So they are de-motivated. At the same time easy jobs also do not provide adequate motivation. Feeling that jobs are challenging but not complex provides achievement motivation. McClelland found that moderate task complexity motivates high achievers. Therefore, jobs are to be designed to provide a feeling of equity of skills and tasks.
8. **Job Functions:** Job functions are designed as part of job design. This includes specification of authority, responsibility, work methods, co-ordination, control, feedback etc. Job design should include clarity about job functions to realise mutual expectations of employees and organisation.
9. **Job Relations:** Most of the organisational tasks require teamwork. This requires establishing relationship among various other organisational members. Relationships are required with superiors, subordinates and peers within organisation and outside public. Good interpersonal relationships create sound organisational climate and good employee relations. They help in organisational development. Obviously, nature and extent of job relations determine the job design. Moreover it was recognised that individuals have an innate desire to associate and establish relationships. Thus job design should provide an opportunity to employees to establish relations with peer, superiors and other internal and external members.
10. **Job Techniques:** Organisational jobs require continuous redesigning. Redesign of jobs relates to both breadth and depth of jobs. While job breadth means provision for inclusion

of different jobs, job depth relates to giving more power, responsibility and control. Job design should include various techniques for making job interesting and meaningful to the employees. This is achieved by redesign of jobs. Some of the techniques of redesign are job enrichment, job enlargement, job rotation and job reengineering.

MODELS OF JOB DESIGN

Job design is a continuous process. The aim of job design is to increase harmony between human effort, and technology and procedures of job. A number of factors influence the process of job design. A number of models were developed to explain the influence of these factors. Some important models are described here.

Task Characteristics Theory

Task Characteristics Theory was the outcome of the studies conducted by Turner and Lawrence. In these studies, an assessment was made about the effect of different kinds of jobs on employee satisfaction and absenteeism. The methodology was to identify the task characteristics and give scores. Higher score on the characteristics indicates that the job is more complex and vice versa. The major finding of the theory was that employees prefer complex and challenging tasks. The reason is that they provide more satisfaction. Even the achievement motivation theory also stated that the achievement and challenging jobs provide greater motivation. The result is lower absenteeism rate. In the process, the theory identified certain task characteristics. They are variety, autonomy, responsibility, knowledge and skill, required social interaction and optional social interaction. The propositions of the theory are as follows.

1. Employees performing high complex tasks showed more interest. Thus, their attendance was more.
2. There is an inverse correlation between task complexity and satisfaction in the employees coming from urban background. So more satisfaction with low complex jobs than highly complex jobs.
3. Positive correlation exists with respect to employees belonging to rural background. Thus high complexity leads to high satisfaction.
4. Poor motivation, low involvement and commitment have been observed in workers belonging to larger communities. This is because they had non-work interests.
5. Workers from smaller towns showed less non-work interests. They were more receptive to complex tasks.
6. Individual differences exist among job preferences.

The theory was considered as pioneering work on task design because of the following reasons.

(i) The theory suggested that employees response vary differently to different jobs.

(ii) Task attributes help in the assessment of jobs.

(iii) Individual differences are important to know the employee reaction to jobs.

Thus, the theory is the basic framework for formulation of various other theories of job design.

Job Characteristics Model

Based on the pioneering work of Turner and Lawrence, Hackman and Oldham propounded job characteristics model. The model identified certain job characteristics. It also identified the relationships between job characteristics and motivation, and performance and job satisfaction. The model showed that core dimensions viz skill variety, task identity, task significance and other dimensions viz autonomy and feedback, determine whether employees regard the work as meaningful. The presence of these characteristics lead to the understanding that the job is important, valuable and worthwhile. While autonomy provides a feeling of responsibility for the outcome, feedback provides employees an opportunity to evaluate their performance. According to the model internal rewards are obtained when employees learn that they personally have performed well on a task. The more these psychological states are present, the greater will be employee motivation, performance and satisfaction and the lower the absenteeism and turnover. It is also understood that employees' need for growth determines psychological states and corresponding motivation and satisfaction.

Motivating Potential Score Model

Motivating Potential Score (MPS) Model was developed based on job characteristics model. The model stated that three potential scores on the three core dimensions of job characteristics model possess additive property. The autonomy and feedback are multiplicative in nature. Thus, a Motivating Potential Score is calculated. The motivating potential score is equal to the product of the average scores of skill variety, task identity and task significance multiplied by the score of autonomy and feedback. This is expressed as follows.

$$\text{MPS} = \frac{\{\text{skill variety} + \text{task identity} + \text{task significance}\}}{3} \times \{\text{Autonomy} \times \text{Feedback}\}$$

MPS = Motivating Potential Score

The mathematical properties of motivating potential score are as follows.

1. Motivating potential score is high if all the variables are high.
2. The motivating potential score is zero if any one of the variables is zero.
3. Autonomy and feedback must always be positive if motivating potential score is to be positive.
4. Skill variety, task identity and task significance can be positive or negative.
5. Motivating potential score is negative if all variables or any one of the variables is negative.
6. All the variables cannot be zero. This indicates no MPS.

The propositions of motivating potential score model are shown below.

Core job dimensions	Motivation	Absenteeism and Turnover	MPS
High Skill variety	High	Low	High
Low Skill variety	Low	High	Low
High Task identity	High	Low	High
Low Task identity	Low	High	Low
High Task significance	High	Low	High
Low Task significance	Low	High	Low
High Autonomy	High	Low	High
Low Autonomy	Low	High	Low
High Feedback	High	Low	High
Low Feedback	Low	High	Low

Accordingly, the model proposes that people who work on jobs with high core job dimensions are generally more motivated, satisfied and productive than those who do not. Job dimensions operate through psychological states in influencing personal and work outcome variables rather than influencing them directly. The model received appreciation for its mathematical properties. However, the model was criticised on the following grounds.

1. **Core dimensions:** The core dimensions in the model were considered as not having absolute power to predict the motivational propensity. Skill variety was considered as a redundant variable as autonomy.

2. **Mathematical Properties:** The model uses both additive and multiplicative properties. However, critics have pointed out that instead of adding and multiplying, MPS becomes a better predictor if all variables are added.

3. **Growth Needs:** The role of growth needs in determining the motivation potential is not subject to evidence. They pointed that a number of other variables such as social cues, perceived equity of reward with other groups and propensity to assimilate work experience determine the motivating potential.

Despite the criticism the model is useful in designing the jobs to upkeep motivation of employees.

Contingency Model

A contingency model of job design was developed to explain the impact of job design on the performance and satisfaction. It considered quality of work life as a significant factor. The model suggested that techniques and knowledge be given more emphasis in job design. It identified that certain factors considered in the job design lead to satisfaction depending on the degree of presence or absence. They are:

1. Job scope perceived as simple or complex.
2. The high or low degrees of individual need strength.
3. The nature and type of overall organisational design. The two organisational designs are organic or mechanistic.

Thus according to this model a combination of perception of job scope, the degrees of individual need strength and the type of organisation structure determines the performance and satisfaction. Therefore, job design should be developed considering a number of permutations and combinations of these factors. The model has been used in developing social information processing model.

Social Information Processing Model

Individuals are part of the society. They have inherent desire to associate and belong to others. Obviously, they wish to work in groups rather than in isolation. Moreover, individuals have observational learning. They develop attitudes by social learning. They have capacity to learn work and work methods by the information provided by the group, with which they work and associate. This has given rise to formation of social information processing model. The following are the assumptions of the model.

Assumptions:

(i) People respond to the jobs based on the perception developed by them.
(ii) The objectives of the job are less important.
(iii) Social cues are important in the process of learning.
(iv) Work groups exert influence on how employees view and understand the jobs.
(v) Groups are the basic source of inspiration and information to the individuals.

The assumptions have led to the belief that information and attitudes are significant in designing the jobs. Thus according to the model employees adopt attitudes and behaviour in response to the social cues provided by work and other groups with which they associate. The groups are co-workers, superiors, subordinates, reference groups, friendship groups, family and customers. Therefore, understanding provided by the group on job aspects is more relevant than the basic job characteristics, employees' psychological states and outcomes of the jobs. The propositions of the model are as follows:

1. Three basic dimensions exist in social information processing. They are peer opinions, relative preferences and judgement dimensions.
2. Job design should therefore consider perceptions developed by social cues rather than performance dimensions.
3. Jobs can be made more interesting and challenging to the employees by telling them about the jobs than just providing job descriptions. Thus information provided and counseling helps in developing a positive perception about the jobs and this leads to greater performance.
4. Information processing and developing job attitude is more relevant to the new entrants and promoted employees rather than those already working for a long time.
5. Organism, attitude, behaviour, beliefs and reality are the determinants of job design.
6. Employees visualise the job using their cognitive evaluation, real task environment, past actions, reinforcement history and learning and immediate social context.
7. Social cues dominate the evaluation of job design than task environment and past actions.

Thus according to the model, the managerial strategy of job design is to consider information shared by the groups about the job. Managers can influence the employee attitude positively even to the poorly designed job by continuously counseling employees positively about the jobs. Though the model has received appreciation for its consideration of human element and informational element in the job design, it gave undue importance to the social cues ignoring the technical and other structural aspects of the job.

Socio Technical Model

The criticism levelled against certain earlier models gave rise to the development of socio-technical model. The model emphasised on the assumption that employees are important in organisations. They should be given a good quality of work life. Individual development is essential for organisational development. As such, they need continuous development. Thus, the model suggested that jobs should be designed and redesigned suitable to the needs of the employees. The central tenet of the model is that job design should be developed based on the technical as well as social factors. Technical factors relate to the factors in the input, processing and output mechanism. Social factors relate to the relationships prevailing among employees and management. An appropriate job design makes a best balance among employees, jobs, technology and environment. Further, the model assumes that these factors change continuously. Thus, job design should include three important elements. They are socio-technical impacts, work teams and flexible work schedules. They are explained below.

1. **Socio-technical impacts:** Organisations are social systems. The social aspects that influence the job design are organisational levels, status differences, self-control and self-regulation. Employees are encouraged to participate in the decision making process. They are provided with necessary information and are reinforced to discharge jobs effectively. At the same time, they are not allowed to misuse the system. Therefore, adequate care is taken to exercise

controls on the jobs. At the same time technological factors are suitably arranged to design a good job that helps in the employee development and organisational development.

2. **Work teams:** The model considers the significance of employees working in teams and the positive impact of teamwork. It suggested that job design is developed to provide autonomy and scope for team building. The work is designed to incorporate team spirit, rather than purely technical and structural aspects such as division of work and specialisation. The job module is developed to include task variety, task identity, task significance and feedback. Employees are counseled to develop team spirit. They are encouraged to learn working with teams. At the same time, the technical and structural aspects are not overlooked. For instance, all specialised jobs can be combined to form a team. Thus, a balance is achieved by both technical and social factors. The job design provides for continuous evaluation and reengineering of the jobs in order to integrate human needs. So job redesigns are made to suit employee development.
3. **Flexible work schedules:** The model recognised that jobs are not fixed systems. They change from place to place, time to time and person to person. Jobs are designed by giving due consideration to employees' preferences and desires. For instance, a teacher may be given preference of the time at which he intends to deliver a lecture to the class keeping in view the overall schedule of the school. Similarly, complex jobs are given to those employees preferring to work on complex jobs. However those who prefer to work on simple jobs are assigned simple jobs. These differentials are considered in designing the jobs. This allows development of a positive attitude on the job. Employees develop a unique culture of valuing the organisational goals. The entire job is autonomous, enriched, satisfying and provides motivation. This enables the employee to achieve greater performance.

Some examples of the organisations practicing the socio-technical model are Volvo car assembly plant, Kabuai, Toyota, General Motors, General Foods, Topeka, Kansas, Tennessee Valley Authority etc.

The model was considered as appropriate in developing job design as it considered technical and structural aspects along with human aspects. Employees have shown preference to work on the jobs designed by using this approach. Employees have reported satisfaction while working with the redesigned jobs. Organisations have reported an increase in productivity. It was also found that labour-management conflicts reduced and quality of the product improved. To sum up cost reduction, increased turnover, quality of work life, innovation and creativity, product quality and positive behavioural changes are some of the benefits found in the jobs designed using the model. However, the model was criticised for its belief that employees are mature enough to work as teams and adopt flexible work schedules.

Employee Development Model

Modern organisations considered that organisational development is possible with employee development. They considered employees as human assets. Thev have a need for career growth and development. Therefore, it is not just enough to consider technical and social issues in the job design. Accordingly, jobs are designed keeping in view the long run interest of the employees. The central tenet of the model is that employees should be developed into competent, responsible and satisfied employees in the end, in order that the organisation has a long run survival. This is possible only with the redesign of jobs. The model identified several aspects in the redesign of jobs. Some of them are scope for alcoholism treatment, non-discrimination, encouraging discipline, creating consciousness, responsibility and providing generic monitoring and direction. A brief discussion is presented here.

1. **Alcoholism and Drug Addiction:** Alcoholism and addiction to drug use are the common abuses found in employees of most organisations. These abuses have disastrous impact on the functioning of organisation. Some of the common problems of alcoholism and drug use are accidents, absenteeism, frequent quarrels, aggressiveness, lack of discipline, family conflicts, social recriminations etc. They have adverse impact on the productivity and employee behaviour. Certain organisations have adopted dope testing at regular intervals. For instance, in transport companies, drivers are examined regularly with an instrument to ensure that they are not in drunken position when they are on duty. Not all times such testing can be done ignoring the psychological aspects. Thus job design should include a scope for undertaking such programs as employee assistance programs, education and counseling to change the attitude. Further, rewarding non-addicted employees also helps in preventing alcoholism among employees. Thus job design should take care of preventing alcoholism.
2. **Discrimination:** Discrimination is another common problem in organisations. Discrimination against caste, creed, gender, colour, nationality, rural and urban demography, disease etc. has an adverse impact on the safety, security and behaviour of employees. For instance, harassment on women employees and discrimination against caste leads to a number of complaints and dissatisfaction among employees. A proper job design is to be developed to avoid discrimination against employees.
3. **Indiscipline:** Another common problem in organisations is lack of discipline. Poor discipline among employees causes problems in coordination and control. Discipline encourages proper work behaviour and motivation among employees. Though organisations use a variety of methods to inculcate discipline such as punishments, penalties, awards, rewards, praises etc., still lack of discipline exists in organisations. Thus, job design should include a scope for discipline. There can be self discipline, imposed discipline, corrective discipline, progressive discipline etc. Discipline is developed through enforcing a code of conduct and standing orders or organisational culture and climate.
4. **Callousness:** Still important problem in organisations is lack of responsibility on the part of the employees. Job design specifies employee tasks and responsibilities in a clear-cut manner. Still, the problem of not assuming proper responsibility exists in organisations. In this case, organisations adopt a number of techniques to improve consciousness in the employees about the responsibility. Some of them include assuming organisational citizenship, ethical leadership and whistle blowing. While organisational citizenship is encouraging the positive social acts in organisations, developing cooperation and coordination among employees,

sharing responsibility, encouraging harmony and resolving conflicts, ethical leadership promotes ethical behaviour among the subordinates. Whistle-blowing is a negative act of inculcating responsibility. It is cautioning the other employees against misconduct of a co-worker. Whenever an employee engages in non permitted act, the whistle-blower brings it to the notice of co-workers. This discourages the employee from repeating the wrong act. A positive way of improving the responsibility consciousness is provision of right direction. Counseling is another means of encouraging the responsibility by changing their attitude. Some of these can be included in designing the jobs.

5. **Poor Health:** Health hazards are very common in organisations. Most of the jobs lead to occupational diseases. Organisations also adopt generic monitoring relating to employee health. As the famous saying goes, 'Health is Wealth', a healthy employee is an asset to the organisation. Poor health leads to both personal problems and problems in the organisation. For instance, an employee suffering from ulcer will have aggressive behaviour. Similarly, employee suffering from contagious disease creates a scare among other employees. Some times employees health is adversely affected due to poor working conditions and presence of toxic or harmful substances. For example, employees working in chemical industries are subject to cancer. Thus, employee development is linked to protecting employee health. Organisations undertake a number of programs to promote health of the employees. Some of them are transferring suffering employees to some other place of convenience, medical facility, medical reimbursement, conducting health camps, health awareness, yoga and meditation, recreation facilities etc. For instance, police personnel suffer from high blood pressure due to stress, poor food habits, irregular timings of duty and tobacco chewing etc. So, regularly health camps are conducted to keep a close check on the employee health. Obviously, job design should include certain conditions of work for protecting the employee health, thus promoting a healthy atmosphere in the organisation.

The model suggested that employee development should invariably be included in the job design. This produces positive effect on productivity and satisfaction.

An examination of the above described models reveals that job design should be prepared taking into consideration a number of variables. This has given rise to a comprehensive model known as integrative job design model.

Integrative Job Design Model

Integrative job design model considered that job design is dynamic. The purpose of job design is to make the work interesting and employee-satisfying. Thus, the model developed an integration of all the factors such as cultural, social, technical and other situational factors in the process of job design. Some of the factors of the job design in the integrative job design model are presented below:

1. **Core design factors:** The model considered that the core design factors should be considered in the design of jobs. The factors are task identity, task variety, task autonomy,

task significance, feedback, job authority and responsibility, information flow, work methods, cooperation and coordination, interpersonal relationships, interpersonal interactions, team work and opportunities for growth and development. The core design factors influence productivity, effectiveness, efficiency, absenteeism, turnover and satisfaction. Therefore, the model suggested that job should be designed by using these factors.

2. **Individual factors:** Individual differences are important in the job design. The ultimate job performance is dependent on the individual differences. The factors of individual differences that influence job design are the needs, nature of man, personality, perceptions, values, attitudes, learning skills and physical factors. The model suggested that jobs designed based on these factors are considered motivating and satisfying to the employees.
3. **Organisational factors:** Organisations are designed to meet the individual needs and help achievement of common goals. An organisation structure is designed to facilitate the goal realisation. The structural factors determine the job design. Similarly, management competencies, economies of scale, administrative structure, bureaucracy, leadership styles, communication systems and motivation methods are some of the factors that should be considered in the process of job design.
4. **Situational factors:** Organisations are social systems. They are open and dynamic systems. Thus, a number of environmental factors influence the functioning of the organisation. So even these factors influence the job design. Environmental factors are Political, Economical, Technological, Legal, Government and Social and ethical factors. They are abbreviated as PETLEGS. For instance, economic factors such as the stage of economic growth, GNP, NNP, personal income, taxes, interest rates, money circulation and saving potential are some factors that determine the job design and satisfaction. If inflation is persisting the job design should enable the employee to earn more incentives. Similarly, technical factors like the rate of technological change and scope for new technological developments are to be considered in the process of job design. Introduction of computer assisted accounting packages for organising and reporting accounting data should be introduced to make the accountant's job easy and effective. In the same way, the political factors, unionism, legal framework, government policies such as fiscal and financial policy, pricing policy etc., and social, cultural and ethical factors are to be considered in the job design. Take the example of providing enough holidays to attend cultural functions makes employees contended about the job. In India a number of festivals and worshipping deity exist. So job design should include a provision for attending the same.

Overall, the model suggested that job design is developed based on the contingency of a situation. Jobs designed ignoring situational factors do not produce effectiveness and satisfaction.

SUMMARY

Job design is developing complete written instructions, task characteristics and job components. Developing proper job design is important for every organisation. It enables effective performance by clarifying roles and responsibilities, removing overlapping responsibilities, rationalising tasks, designing operational control over performance and providing flexibility for adoption of environmental changes. Internal and external factors influence job design. Goals, task accomplishment, employee response, task variety, task identity, task significance, task complexities, job functions, job relations and job techniques are the factors that influence the job design. Studies conducted by Turner and Lawrence led to the formulation of Task Characteristics theory that suggested that job design should be done with the help of certain task characteristics. Hackman and Oldham developed Job Characteristics model. Motivating Potential Score model suggested that skill variety, task identity, task significance, autonomy and feedback determine motivating potential. Social Information Processing model advocated that information and attitudes should be taken into consideration in designing the jobs. Socio Technical model suggested socio-technical impacts, work teams and flexible work schedules are important in designing the jobs. According to Contingency model a number of contingency factors of the environment determine job design. Employee Development model suggested that job design should address such common problems as alcoholism, discrimination, and lack of discipline and lack of responsibility. Integrative Job Design model considered core design factors, individual factors, organisational factors and situational factors.

Key words:

- **Job design:** The process of structuring the job elements, duties and tasks.
- **MBO:** Functional manager setting goals in all the essential areas with participation of subordinates.
- **MPS:** The motivating potential score, which is equal to the product of average scores of skill variety, task identity and task significance and autonomy and feedback.
- **Task identity:** Identifying individual contribution in the output.
- **Task significance:** Recognising the importance of task performed by the employee.

33. JOB REDESIGN

This chapter enables you:

- *To understand the meaning of job redesign*
- *To define the term job enrichment*
- *To identify the process of job enrichment*
- *To understand the process of incorporating a variety of tasks*
- *To distinguish between job enrichment and job enlargement*
- *To understand the concept of job reengineering*
- *To examine the factors that influence the process of job reengineering*
- *To distinguish between job reengineering and job restructuring*

The structure of the chapter is as follows:

- Introduction
- Job redesign
- Job enrichment
- Job enlargement
- Differences between job enrichment and job enlargement
- Job rotation
- Job reengineering
- Factors influencing job reengineering
- Summary
- Key words

CHAPTER 33

Job Redesign

INTRODUCTION

Today, organisations are functioning in a dynamic and vibrant environment. Various jobs performed are also becoming vibrant. So organisations are seriously thinking of restructuring of jobs in order to meet the challenges of environment. This process is called job redesign. Job redesign is also becoming popular with the concept of learning organisations. Organisations use a number of techniques in the process. Some of the techniques are popular for motivating employees. For instance, Herzberg suggested job enrichment as a technique of motivating employees. This is because employees performing routine and redundant jobs feel dissatisfied with the jobs. Thus to reenergize them jobs are to be redesigned. Job redesign is undertaken with the help of certain tools like job enrichment, job enlargement, job rotation and job reengineering. This chapter explains all these concepts.

JOB REDESIGN

Job redesign is an emerging approach in most of the organisations. It has become a popular tool for creating an interest on the job amongst employees in organisations. It is also used as a technique of motivating employees. Today learning organisations are increasingly adopting this for making their employees meet the ever-changing environmental demands. Job redesign attempts to restructure various aspects of the jobs, taking into consideration the characteristics, skills and personality of employees and organisational demands. It indicates the rotation of employees to a number of related jobs. This makes employees acquire the necessary skills required to perform all related jobs. In modern organisations, there is a tendency of fundamental rethinking and radical redesign of the business process in accordance with the challenges posed by the environment. Thus job redesign is creating an atmosphere of learning organisations. The following are some of the means of redesigning jobs in organisations.

JOB ENRICHMENT

Job enrichment was suggested by Herzberg. It is a vertical expansion of jobs. According to Hackman and Oldham, job enrichment organises tasks so that the employee carries out the complete activity. It increases the employees' freedom, independence and responsibility and provides feedback, so that an individual can assess and correct his or her own performance.

> *Fred Luthans stated that job enrichment is 'concerned with designing jobs that include a greater variety of work content; require a higher level of knowledge and skill; give workers more autonomy and responsibility in terms of planning, directing and controlling their own performance; and provide the opportunity for personal growth and a meaningful work experience'.*

Job enrichment assumes that in order to motivate employees, jobs in organisations are to be designed to provide an opportunity for achievement, recognition, responsibility, advancement and growth. The following are the characteristics of an enriched job.

- Enhanced decision making power
- Flexibility to establish relationships
- Opportunity for learning
- Enjoying greater freedom
- Finding uniqueness
- Exercising control over resources
- Clear communication
- Provision of achievement orientation
- Giving greater responsibility
- Shouldering reasonable accountability
- Opportunity for personal growth and development
- Continuous feedback

Job enrichment is not a one-time activity. It is a process which involves certain activities. They are:

- Combining tasks
- Creating natural work units
- Establishing relationships among personnel
- Expanding the job vertically, and
- Providing feedback channels

All these activities are performed for making the job more interesting and challenging. Thus the job becomes more promising to employees. Job enrichment has certain advantages. They are mentioned below:

(i) Increased quality and productivity. Enhanced quality benefits the organisation and the consumer and at the same time employees are likely to get higher wages for increased productivity.

(ii) Enhanced motivation and job satisfaction. These provide benefits to the organisation, employees and the society at large.

(iii) Development of additional skills. Learning of skills makes the employee development in the long run.

(iv) Less work load on employees. This makes employees happier.

(v) Enhanced creativity in employees. Employee creativity becomes a boon to the organisation.

(vi) Increase in pay and perquisites. These makes employees satisfied and commit themselves to the organisation.

(vii) Decreased absenteeism and turnover.

(viii) Less number of grievances. This leads to more cordial work environment and better industrial relations.

(ix) Optimum use of human energy.

(x) Increased social benefits due to increase in quality and productivity.

The limitations of job enrichment are:

- Increased training costs.
- Problems of provision of resources.
- Inability to identify failures of employees.
- Feeling of more responsibility leading to de-motivation.
- Resistance to change.

In spite of the limitations, job enrichment became popular and many organisations adopted it. Some organisations reaping benefits of job enrichment are AT & T, Chicago Corporation, Texas Instruments, Bell Telephones, Tata Steels, Mitshubishi and L&T.

JOB ENLARGEMENT

Job enlargement is the horizontal expansion of a job to increase the variety of tasks within a job. Recently, there has been an increase in the number and variety of jobs performed by an employee in an organisation. This is due to an increase in the complexity of the environment and challenges in a job. If an employee feels that his job is not very challenging, oversimplified, lacks diversity and is not very meaningful, the answer is perhaps job enlargement. For instance, suppose a worker is assigned the job of counting finished products, and finds it boring and repetitive. The job can be enlarged by including certain tasks connected to the job, such as checking the products before counting them, packing and delivering the products to the warehouse where the finished goods are stored.

The potential benefits of job enlargement are given below.

- **Reduction in the level of boredom:** Job enlargement provides scope to increase the number of tasks performed by an employee. It reduces an employee's monotony and boredom.
- **Utilisation of skills:** Job enlargement enhances the scope for an employee to use his skills and abilities. This provides greater satisfaction and consequent motivation in employees.
- **Quality and efficiency:** Job enlargement leads to increased efficiency of employees as they receive training to carry out all the newly added jobs. This results in an increase in the quality of production and overall effectiveness of the system.
- **Job enjoyment:** In an enlarged job, an employee feels less fatigued. Employees enjoy the enlarged work because of the greater variety of tasks.
- **Feedback:** Job enlargement includes providing feedback to an employee. Thus, he knows where he stands as regards his performance. This enables him to develop his career and provides the right motivation.

However, job enlargement has the following drawbacks.

- Job enlargement enhances training costs
- Job enlargement means introduction of new systems. This may considerably reduce the productivity of employees.
- It creates a feeling of overburdening in employees.
- Job enlargement requires retrenchment of redundant employees. Moreover, employees may demand increased pay for the additional tasks added to the job. This may lead to labour relation problems.

In spite of certain drawbacks, job enlargement is one of the best techniques of job design. It continues to be a good method of motivation.

DIFFERENCES BETWEEN JOB ENRICHMENT AND JOB ENLARGEMENT

The distinctions between job enrichment and job enlargement are described below:

Distinctions	Job enrichment	Job enlargement
Definition	Job enrichment is concerned with designing jobs that include more work content; require a higher level of knowledge and skill; give workers more autonomy and responsibility in terms of planning, directing and controlling their own performance; and provide an opportunity for personal growth and a meaningful work experience.	Job enlargement is including a variety of tasks in the job. Job enlargement is horizontal expansion of the jobs to include a variety of tasks within the scope of the job.
Nature	Vertical expansion of the job	Horizontal expansion of the job
Aim	Specialisation of the jobs	Diversification in the job
Scope	Its objective is to motivate	Its object is to give job satisfaction
Tasks	Not necessarily more tasks, but more responsibilities and accountability	Adds more tasks. It is increases the diversity of tasks
Cause and effect	Job enrichment is an extension of job enlargement	Job enlargement leads to job enrichment
Job	The job is enriched to give psychological satisfaction. The scope is to make the job challenging and meaningful, and oriented towards achievement.	The job is enlarged to increase physical work. Thus, it results in addition of tasks rather than additional responsibilities.
Focus	Job enrichment focuses on satisfaction of higher order needs.	Job enlargement focuses on satisfaction of lower order needs
Effect	Workers are given more responsibility and accountability	Redundant workers are retrenched

JOB ROTATION

Job rotation is periodically shifting an employee from one job to another at the same level of skill requirements. It is also known as cross training. The need for job rotation arises if the job is routine, boring, non-challenging and is not achievement-oriented. Job rotation helps an employee perform all the different tasks in a job. Job rotation has certain benefits and drawbacks, which are given below.

Some of the benefits are:

(i) Reduction of boredom and employee turnover.
(ii) Better diversification and development of a wide range of skills that helps to develop competent employees.
(iii) Greater challenges in the job leading to a better variety of tasks.
(iv) Increased flexibility of jobs providing scope for better job scheduling.
(v) Greater adaptability to changes.
(vi) Increased motivation and job satisfaction.

Some of the drawbacks of job rotation are:

(i) Increase in the costs of training an employee in the related tasks.
(ii) Increase in the cost of time overruns in performing the job.
(iii) Decrease in productivity because an employee may take some time to reach the optimum performance.
(iv) Greater disruption in social contacts as frequent rotation requires adjustment to social groups.
(v) Increased monitoring and controlling of employees requires additional costs of supervision.

Robbins pointed out that job rotation could demotivate intelligent and ambitious employees who seek specific responsibilities in their chosen specialty. In spite of certain drawbacks, job rotation is considered to motivate employees. It is also considered to be a useful technique for development of human resources.

JOB REENGINEERING

Job reengineering is another technique of job redesign. It is redesigning jobs based on feedback. A job is an ongoing process. Similarly, evaluation of reactions, level of satisfaction and contribution to goals is also an ongoing process. There may be discrepancies in the objectives of an organisation, and goals and final outcome of the job. Jobs should be reengineered to make them suitable to achieve objectives and at the same time enhance employee satisfaction. Job reengineering is defined as reallocation of jobs to achieve congruence of goals of an individual and the organisation.

> *Michel Hammer defined job reengineering as "the fundamental rethinking and radical redesign of business processes by application of variety of tools and techniques focussing on related customer oriented core business process to achieve dramatic improvements in critical and contemporary measures of performance such as cost, quality, service and speed."*

He considered that even though job reengineering can be applied to any level of management, customer oriented designing and reengineering is more important for the survival and growth of the company. Job reengineering involves use of new technology and changes in the process of working. The basic objective of job reengineering is attaining corporate objectives and goals through increased employee satisfaction. Some of the corporate goals achieved through job reengineering are customer satisfaction, profit maximisation, growth and enhanced corporate image.

The nature of the job, personality and experience of the employees, job performance and satisfaction are some of the factors considered in reengineering of jobs. It varies from person to person, job to job and company to company. Thus, it depends on different levels and nature of jobs. It is carried out to suit the requirements of employees. In this context, Edward E Lawler noted that organisations must recognise the importance of treating people differently and placing them in environments and work situations that fit their unique needs, skills and abilities. Job reengineering leads to job enrichment.

The principles of job reengineering are given below.

(i) Allocation of jobs according to employees' interest.
(ii) Employees preferring routine jobs are allowed to perform routine jobs.
(iii) Low skilled employees are given jobs requiring low skills.
(iv) Achievement oriented employees are given challenging jobs.

FACTORS INFLUENCING JOB REENGINEERING

Several factors are considered in the process of job reengineering. They are: Information system, Government policies, Organisational policies, Technology, Competition, Appraisal of costs and benefits, Prospective challenges. They are abbreviated as 'I GOT CAP' and are explained below.

1. **Information system:** Information is an important element in job reengineering. In fact, the success of reengineering depends on the volume and value of information available. Inadequate information leads to improper job reengineering. In this context, it should be noted that information on price policies, marketing techniques, production functions etc., is considered as the most important and valuable information.
2. **Government policies:** Government policies have a significant bearing on the reengineering of jobs. Rationalisation of tax structure, tariffs and bounties, encouragement of FDI, liberalisation of investment policies and restructuring interest rates are some of the government policy considerations that have a bearing on the job reengineering process. For instance, many banks have reengineered their jobs to serve customers better. This was done to suit the government policy of a 'golden handshake.'
3. **Organisational policies:** Job reengineering is carried out according to the existing policies of the organisation. Sometimes, organisational policies are modified to suit to the requirements of the job reengineering process. Some of the organisational policies that have an impact on job reengineering are production policies, human resources recruitment and selection policies, training policies and research and development policies. For example in

software companies the organisation adopts a policy of allocating more funds to training and development of employees. They send their employees for a periodical training even to foreign countries at heavy costs. So in those companies job reengineering is done at regular intervals.

4. **Technology:** Technology is the basic thrust of job reengineering. Innovations and advancements are fast emerging in the globalised world. Survival of a business relates to the adoption of the latest technology. Some functions of organisations that are reengineered based on the technology are production functions, marketing, human resources development and information systems. Thus, technology based job reengineering has become essential for organisations today. CRM is an outcome of technology that supported to focus on serving customers in a more effective manner. Organisations are banking on technology to implement CRM function. In fact CRM has become the life saving pharmacy for most of the companies.

5. **Competition:** Competition grew out of globalisation. Only organisations that can face competition effectively will survive and grow in face of the global competition. In a competitive environment, effectiveness is ensured when scarce resources are effectively and efficiently utilised. Therefore, to face competition effectively, job reengineering is essential. For instance, many Indian firms overlooked Japanese philosophy of quality on the pretext that Indians are not quality-conscious. But when some of the Japanese firms entered India (Suzuki tied up with Maruti and Honda aligned with Hero motors) and demonstrated quality, they started feeling that Total Quality Management (TQM) is needed for effectiveness. TQM is based on job reengineering.

6. **Appraisal of costs and benefits:** Cost-benefit analysis is critical for job reengineering. There are two implications relating to cost benefit analysis. One is that the basic objective of job reengineering is cost reduction. The second is that the cost of reengineering the job should not overrun the benefits that accrue from it. It is a paradoxical situation. Thus, an appropriate analysis of cost and benefit is essential before an attempt is made to reengineer the jobs. In soft drinks manufacturing process, bottles are filled with soft drink by hand, gas is filled by manual technology and caps are fitted. It was decided to reengineer the job by using technology so that the human resources can be used in an alternative productive employment. When it was budgeted, it was found that the cost of establishing fully automated bottling machine exceeds the costs of manual operations and benefits that accrue from the alternative use of surplus labour. So appraisal of costs and benefits in the process of job reengineering is necessary.

7. **Prospective challenges:** Future challenges are also important for job reengineering. Reengineering makes the jobs interesting, challenging, motivating and achievement-oriented. All of which are required to meet future challenges.

Job reengineering should not be confused with job restructuring. Job reengineering aims at redesigning the process and finding radically different ways of carrying out the existing process. Restructuring aims to redesign the organisation's structure. Reengineering is an ongoing process, whereas restructuring is reforming the structure only when needed.

Job reengineering is an important technique of job redesign in modern organisations. It has a number of potential benefits, such as improved customer service, increased growth opportunities, rapid decision-making, improved learning skills, easy and comfortable attainment of tasks, effective inter personal interactions and inter personal communication, and improved inter personal relationships.

Finally, it should be noted that changes brought about by globalisation, liberalisation and privatisation have forced organisation to go in for job reengineering. This is due to the fact that, successful redesigning of managerial practices and organisation structure adds value to the product and service of the organisation. Moreover reengineering dispenses with traditional methods of work process.

SUMMARY

As organisations are open dynamic systems, changes in environmental factors influence their structure, managerial practices and functions. Organisations should redesign jobs continuously to adapt to environmental challenges. Job redesign attempts to restructure jobs so that they are suitable to the employees' and organisation's demands. Job enrichment, job enlargement, job rotation and job reengineering are some of the job redesign techniques. While job enrichment is a vertical expansion, job enlargement is the horizontal expansion of a job. Job rotation aims at moving employees from one job to another. Job reengineering is reallocation of jobs to achieve objectives and at the same time enhance employee satisfaction. A number of factors are considered in the process of job reengineering. They are information systems, government policies, organisational policies, technology, and competition, appraisal of costs and benefits and prospective challenges.

Key words:

- **Job enlargement:** Horizontal expansion of a job to include a variety of tasks
- **Job enrichment:** Vertical expansion of a job to include a greater variety of tasks.
- **Job redesign:** Restructuring of various aspects of jobs to suit the characteristics, skills, and personality of employees and organisational demands.
- **Job reengineering:** Fundamental rethinking and radical redesign of the business process.
- **Job rotation:** Periodically shifting employees from the existing job to a new job at the same level of skill requirements.
- **Job satisfaction:** A psychological expression of contentment on the job.
- **Rating scales:** A measurement scale containing certain statements with specific answers.

34. JOB SATISFACTION

This chapter enables you:

- *To define the concept of job satisfaction*
- *To understand how organisations can increase job satisfaction*
- *To identify personal determinants of job satisfaction*
- *To understand the measurement of job satisfaction*
- *To identify the relationship between job satisfaction and productivity*
- *To appraise the relationship between job satisfaction and turnover*

The structure of the chapter is as follows:

- Introduction
- Determination of job satisfaction
- Characteristics of job satisfaction
- Organisational determinants
- Personal determinants
- Measurement of job satisfaction
- Job satisfaction and productivity
- Job satisfaction and absenteeism
- Job satisfaction and turnover
- Summary
- Key words

CHAPTER 34

Job Satisfaction

INTRODUCTION

Job satisfaction has been an interesting variable for managers and academics for many years. Job satisfaction influences the efficiency of employees and thus determines organisational effectiveness. Interestingly it is an intangible and qualitative variable. It relates to feelings, emotions and expressions. So unless it is expressed it cannot be known. However, over a period of time researchers were able to find certain quantitative measurement of this variable in order to help managers understand it and direct the energy of subordinates in a proper manner. It is interesting to note that more than a half million reported works exist on this variable. Job satisfaction has a positive influence on the functioning of organisation as well as personnel. Similarly it is influenced by number of variables. They were identified as organisational and personal. You must have noticed an expression of your employed parents that their job became disgusting and not interesting. This expression simply represents feeling of job satisfaction. Even persons engaged in profession and business too must have expressed that they are not satisfied with the work they are doing. So they want a change. Such expressions are very commonly observed. They are feelings of job satisfaction. It includes expression of satisfaction or dissatisfaction on nature of job itself, monetary rewards, persons they work with, work environment, organisational culture and climate and certain aspects of personal life also. Understanding this becomes imperative as it has certain influence on productivity, absenteeism and employee turnover, interpersonal relations, organisational climate and culture, employee psychological commitment and above all on the society at large. This chapter explains certain basic concepts of job satisfaction to provide an understanding at this level. It is suggested that one should carefully listen to employees talking about their dissatisfaction to understand it better and examine the impact on behaviour of employees.

DEFINITION OF JOB SATISFACTION

Job satisfaction is an expression of feeling about the job. Thus it is a psychological aspect of expression of an attitude. Attitude is a permanent impression formed about the job. Employees interact with people and other resources while on the job. In the process, they experience positive or negative feelings on various aspects of structure and environment of the job. This feeling is called job satisfaction. The concept of job satisfaction has gained importance ever since the Human Relations approach became popular. When a person is considered as important in the organisation, his satisfaction on the job is all the more important to direct the energy for the realisation of goals. It is evident from the number of research articles published that the concept is important. For instance more than 5000 research articles have been published on job satisfaction.

Job satisfaction is an intangible variable. It consists of a complex number of variables, conditions, feelings and behavioural tendencies.

Roberts Dictionary of Industrial Relations defined job satisfaction *'as those outward or inner manifestations which give the individual a sense of enjoyment or accomplishment in the performance of his work'*.

According to **Locke**, *'job satisfaction is a pleasurable or positive emotional state resulting from the appraisal of one's job or job experience'*.

P.C. Smith defined job satisfaction as *'the persistent feeling towards discriminating aspects of the job situation'*.

Andrew Brin stated that job satisfaction *'is the amount of pleasure or contentment associated with a job'*. Further, he stated that if one likes a job intensely he will experience high job satisfaction and if he dislikes the job intensely he will experience job dissatisfaction.

Keith Davis and **Newstrom** define job satisfaction as *'a set of favourable or unfavorable feelings with which employees view their work'*.

Stephen Robbins viewed job satisfaction in a narrow sense as *'a general attitude toward one's job; the differences between the amount of reward workers receive and the amount of reward that they believe they should receive'*.

CHARACTERISTICS OF JOB SATISFACTION

The definitions of job satisfaction reveal the following characteristics.

1. Job satisfaction is an inner feeling. It can only be inferred through the expression of behaviour. Interestingly it cannot be seen. It is thus intangible.
2. Job satisfaction is an attitude. It is a sub set of attitude.
3. Job satisfaction influences the skill and energy of an individual.
4. It can be positive or negative. It is expressed in a high or low degree.
5. Job satisfaction is associated with the emotional state of human mind.

Determinants of Job Satisfaction

Job satisfaction is both intangible and it is multi-variable. A number of factors influence job satisfaction of employees. They can be classified into two categories. They are organisational and personal variables. They are discussed below:

Organisational Determinants

A number of factors in the organisation determine job satisfaction of the employee. Organisations can increase job satisfaction by suitably organising and managing certain factors, which are described below.

1. **Wages:** Wages are the monetary benefits a worker earns from the job. They fulfill an employee's needs. Everyone expects a commensurate reward. The wage should be fair, reasonable and equitable. If an employee feels that the reward is fair and equitable, it produces job satisfaction. Often the definition of fair and equitable wage does not exist. So wages are not perceived as equal to the labour exerted by employee. This leads to dissatisfaction and poor performance on the job.
2. **Nature of work:** The nature of one's work has a significant impact on job satisfaction. Jobs involving use of intelligence, skills and abilities, and which are challenging and have scope for greater freedom, lead to job satisfaction. Feelings of boredom, frustration and failure, and a poor variety of tasks, leads to job dissatisfaction.
3. **Working conditions:** Good working conditions are needed to motivate an employee to spend the required time at the work place. Safety and comfort motivate an employee to work. Poor working conditions may lead to a feeling that one's health is in danger. Thus, working conditions determine the level of an employee's job satisfaction. For instance, employees working in a software company express job satisfaction on this variable as they work in very neat and comfortable air-conditioned rooms. But, a mineworker is likely to express dissatisfaction with respect to working conditions in the mine. There are a number of possible dangers to life like paucity of oxygen, falling of roof, untidy and slippery floor and poor lighting and ventilation. So expression of feeling of satisfaction depends on the work environment of organisations.
4. **Job content:** Job content refers to factors that are inherent in the job such as recognition, responsibility, advancement, achievement etc. Jobs involving a variety of tasks and which are less repetitive result in greater job satisfaction. A job, whose content is poor, produces job dissatisfaction. Herzberg, Mausner and Snyderman found that job content factors like achievement, responsibility etc., lead to greater job satisfaction. In a study conducted by Walker and Guest, it was found that repetitive work was the most dissatisfying factor, whereas pay and security were satisfying factors.
5. **Organisational level:** The level at which an employee is working determines job satisfaction. Jobs at a higher level are viewed as prestigious. Employees working in such jobs express a greater degree of job satisfaction than those working in jobs at a lower level.

Glimer found that professional people have greater job satisfaction than salaried workers, and factory workers are least satisfied with their jobs. Porter's results were similar, he found that at each successive lower level the managers were less satisfied.

6. **Opportunities for promotion:** Promotion is an achievement in life, it leads to a higher salary and perks, and greater responsibility, authority, independence and status. It provides both monetary and non-monetary incentives. Therefore, opportunities for promotion determine the degree of satisfaction of employees.
7. **Work group:** Existence of groups in organisations is a common phenomenon. It is natural for human beings to associate with others. This characteristic results in the formation of work groups at the work place. Isolated workers dislike their jobs. The work group exerts a tremendous influence on the satisfaction of employees at the place of work. The satisfaction an individual derives from his association with the group depends largely on his relationship with other group members, group dynamics, group cohesiveness and his own need for affiliation. Sales persons working in different areas and meet once in a fortnight expressed greater dissatisfaction on the aspect of group process. Similarly, persons working in an office expressed greater satisfaction as they were allowed to interact frequently. Employees working in cabin culture offices expressed greater dissatisfaction than employees working in a front-end office as a team.
8. **Styles of leadership:** The style of leadership of the superior also determines the level of satisfaction of an employee. A democratic leader, who promotes friendship, respect and warm relationships among employees, enhances job satisfaction. On the other hand, employees working under authoritarian leaders express a low level of job satisfaction. Trow and Sanford have found that subordinates under an authoritarian leader are likely to be more satisfied under supervision of high status, and strong, hard-nosed leaders. Transactional and transformational leaders are found to have promoted job satisfaction among their subordinates. Similarly charismatic leaders also promoted job satisfaction among their subordinates. For example, police personnel express dissatisfaction on the supervisory style of their superior officers. This is common at all levels of hierarchy. Employees working under bureaucratic supervisors also expressed job dissatisfaction.

Personal Determinants

A number of personal factors determine job satisfaction of an employee. They are mentioned below.

1. **Personality:** Factors such as perception, attitudes and learning determine psychological conditions, which in turn determine the personality of an individual. Therefore, these factors determine the satisfaction of individuals. An employee possessing a negative attitude about his job becomes disinterested in it. He is likely to express job dissatisfaction. An employee possessing limited knowledge of the job, or poor learning capability is not likely to perceive his job as interesting. Thus, one's personality determines whether a person is satisfied or dissatisfied with his job.

2. **Age:** Age is a significant determinant of job satisfaction. Younger employees possessing higher energy levels are likely to feel more satisfied. As employees grow older, aspiration levels increase. Unable to fulfill these aspirations, he feels dissatisfied. The relationship between age of the employees and job satisfaction is complex and fascinating. According to Hammer and Organ, people start a job with unrealistic assumptions about what they are going to derive from it. Over time, they realise that reality falls far short of their perceived expectations, and become disillusioned. They start to develop more realistic expectations about their job, and evaluate it in a more positive perspective. This positive evaluation produces higher job satisfaction. Thus, older workers can also be more satisfied workers.
3. **Education:** Education provides an opportunity to develop one's personality. It enhances individual wisdom, visualisation, judgement, understanding and common sense. Highly educated employees possess persistence, rationality and thinking power. They can understand a situation and appraise it positively. Thus, they are likely to express satisfaction with their jobs. However, employees with a higher level of education have higher expectations from their jobs. Dissatisfaction will be greater when educated persons are employed in lower level jobs. A poorly educated employee, who cannot appraise the situation positively is likely to express job dissatisfaction. In practice, many people with good educational qualifications hold higher positions, thus the conflict resolves itself.
4. **Gender differences:** The gender and race of an employee also influence job satisfaction. Women are more likely to be satisfied than their male counterparts even if they have small jobs. This is because women have lower levels of aspirations. Job satisfaction among blacks and other minority groups has been consistently lower than that of whites in America. Similarly, investigating the sex difference in job satisfaction Charies N. Weanch, found that there is no significant difference in job satisfaction when males and females were equally affected by such determinants of job satisfaction as wages, prestige, and supervisory positions. For instance, a woman placed in a prestigious position derives the same satisfaction, as does a man in a comparable position. Barrick stated that generally females are dissatisfied than males because they have less job and pay opportunities than males.

Certain other factors that determine job satisfaction are learning, variety of skills, autonomy, job characteristics, unbiased attitude of the management, social status etc. Managers should consider all these factors in assessing the satisfaction of employees and increasing their level of job satisfaction.

MEASUREMENT OF JOB SATISFACTION

Job satisfaction is a qualitative aspect. It cannot be understood strictly in quantitative terms. Therefore, job satisfaction should be measured by a survey of employees' attitudes. In most organisations, employee surveys are carried out regularly. Some techniques employed to measure job satisfaction are discussed below.

(i) **Rating scales:** Rating scales are the most commonly used method of measuring job satisfaction. A rating scale consists of statements describing the attitude of employees with respect to their job, organisation and personal factors. The employee then rates each statement. For example, a scale may consist of the five expressions given below.

Strongly agree	Agree	Do not know	Disagree	Strongly disagree
1	2	3	4	5

These scales could be standard scales or tailor-made ones specially prepared for a specific situation. Some well known standard scales are the job description index and the Minnesota satisfaction questionnaire.

(ii) **Personal interviews:** Another important method of measuring job satisfaction is conducting personal interviews with the employees, in which they are asked questions related to job satisfaction. Their responses are analysed to determine their level of job satisfaction. However, this method may reflect the personal bias of the interviewer.

(iii) **Tendencies:** Employees are asked to describe their tendency or inclination on various aspects. Their tendency reveals their satisfaction or dissatisfaction. For instance, if a question 'Do you often feel like going to lunch sooner than you would?' is asked, a positive response indicates the employee dissatisfaction.

(iv) **Critical incidents:** Herzberg developed this approach to measure job satisfaction. In this method, employees are asked to describe incidents on the job when they were particularly satisfied or dissatisfied. These incidents were analysed to determine the positive and negative attitudes of employees.

Job Satisfaction and Performance

Job satisfaction is an important indicator of organisational performance. A satisfied worker contributes to productivity and organisational effectiveness, and is an asset to the organisation. A dissatisfied worker inhibits performance, and is a liability to the organisation and society. Therefore, managers should be concerned about the expression of dissatisfaction and understand the impact of job satisfaction on employees' performance. The various aspects are discussed below.

JOB SATISFACTION AND PRODUCTIVITY

A famous saying goes that, 'A satisfied worker is a productive employee'. Managers and administrative personnel are concerned with questions such as 'Does job dissatisfaction lead to lower output? Does increased job satisfaction lead to higher output?' The results of various studies were contradictory. A number of studies found that job satisfaction has a positive influence on the productivity of employees. A number of empirical studies were carried out to identify the relationship between productivity and satisfaction. The study conducted at the University of Michigan revealed that productive groups did not show greater satisfaction than less productive work groups. Two other studies substantiated this finding. Victor Vroom showed that there is no evidence supporting a direct link between satisfaction and productivity. While the attitude of an employee towards his job is related to absenteeism and labour turnover, available evidence suggests that there is no positive relationship with productivity. In fact, the relationship between satisfaction and productivity cannot be proved due to various difficulties associated with the measurement. However, it appears logical that an efficient worker will be satisfied and is likely to produce more.

(i) **Difficulty in measuring satisfaction:** In many jobs, concrete and objective measurement is not possible. In such cases, managers depend on subjective evaluation by the immediate superior, however this may be biased. In the absence of objective criterion, subjective evaluation is unreliable. Thus, the evaluation is distorted.

(ii) **Variation in the performance:** In reality an individual's level of performance cannot vary significantly. A worker, under normal operating conditions and under certain technological constraints, does not produce beyond a particular level. In some cases, the superior even discourages increased performance as it interferes with the overall production. So, a linear relationship between productivity and satisfaction cannot be proved always.

(iii) **Rewards:** If a job holds little potential for intrinsic rewards and if extrinsic rewards bear hardly any relationship to the performance level of the individual the relationship between satisfaction and performance tends to be weak and tenuous. Under such circumstances, the immediate duty of the top management is to strengthen this relationship, as satisfied employees tend to stay in the organisation.

JOB SATISFACTION AND ABSENTEEISM

There exists a relationship between job satisfaction and the frequency of absence of employees, both absence due to minor ailments (casual leave) or long absence (paid leave). Absenteeism and the level of job satisfaction are inversely related. Job dissatisfaction leads to a 'lack of will to work', which alienates employees from their work. For instance, a survey conducted in a colliery company revealed that coal miners stay off work due to a feeling of poor job satisfaction. Similarly, in postal department also survey revealed that postmen who have expressed poor job satisfaction were found to be frequently absent from duty.

JOB SATISFACTION AND TURNOVER

Satisfaction and turnover are inversely related. A satisfied worker tends to continue with an organisation, while a dissatisfied worker will leave and seek satisfaction elsewhere. It is reasonable to expect that workers derive different levels of satisfaction from their work roles. The cost of turnover and absenteeism is substantial. With high labour turnover rate, the cost of recruitment and training new employees goes up. However, satisfaction is not the only factor, an employee may remain with the organisation because of recognition, loyalty to the organisation, conditions of the employment market, praise and other rewards, or because he is not confident of getting employment elsewhere. The relationship between job satisfaction and turnover has been reported in studies conducted by Porter and Steers, Muchinsky and Tuttle, Mobley and others, and Arnold and Feldman.

Some other relationships between performance and job satisfaction are mentioned below.

1. **Negative publicity:** A common consequence of job dissatisfaction is 'bad mouthing' the organisation. The disgruntled employee expresses his discontent with negative comments. This sometimes acts as negative publicity and makes the organisation unpopular. Such negative publicity leads to difficulty in recruiting new employees, poor corporate image, loss of goodwill and brand name, misapprehensions in the public, poor organisational climate and culture, loss of confidence, and loss of business.

2. **Poor safety:** A dissatisfied employee is more prone to accidents, due to lack of attention to his work. Poor coordination with tools and equipment, lack of confidence on safety instructions, dislocation in positive moods leads to increased rate of accidents. A study in coal mines revealed that dissatisfied employees resist wearing protective caps and specially designed shoes issued to them for protection against dangerous conditions in the mines. The result of all these violations is increased number of accidents sometimes leading to loss of life and at other times serious injury resulting in total and permanent loss of earning power. This is not only a loss to the family but also to the organisation as it loses an employee.

3. **Work stress:** Job contentment is a tonic for good health. A satisfied employee has a lesser chance of feeling bored or tired. Consistent job dissatisfaction produces work aversion, communication hurdles, and poor relationships with colleagues, superiors, peers, subordinates, and negative attitude which leads to work stress. An employee experiencing prolonged dissatisfaction may even become addicted to alcohol or drugs. This has a negative effect on performance.

4. **Unionisation:** Employees, who are dissatisfied with their salary, job security, lack of fringe benefits, lack of promotion opportunities and relationship with superiors, turn to unions to solve their grievances. This may lead to 'go slow' tactics and strikes. In public enterprises one of the prime reasons for frequent disruption of industrial relations is dissatisfaction of employees on certain job-related factors.

5. **Mental health:** Job dissatisfaction can lead to disturbed mental health. Many unresolved personality problems and maladjustments arise out of a person's inability to find satisfaction in his work. This can affect his personal and family life. Job satisfaction is important for the psychological adjustment and happiness of an individual. A study by Arthur Kornhausen showed a positive relationship between job satisfaction and mental health. In fact, job satisfaction is inextricably related to a person's overall satisfaction. Nowadays, many

companies conduct courses on the 'art of living' to articulate a desire of living in employees who experience poor satisfaction.

6. **Physical health:** Job satisfaction has a positive correlation with the physical health of employees. Palmore observed that people who like to work are likely to live longer. The logic behind this is that people with greater satisfaction tend to have higher incomes and more education and thus enjoy greater benefits, which promote longevity. Chronic dissatisfaction with work leads to stress, which in turn takes its toll on the individual and the organisation. It is a known medical fact that emotional stress acts as a contributory factor in hypertension, coronary artery disease, digestive ailments, and even cancer. Therefore, job satisfaction is essential to maintain physical health.

People who are satisfied with their working life develop 'favourable sentiments' about the organisation. A happy and satisfied individual finds it easy to function inside the organisation as well as outside of it. On the other hand an individual who is unhappy can make life miserable for others with whom he interacts both in his place of work and elsewhere.

SUMMARY

In organisations employees develop certain impressions about the nature of job, working conditions, peer, superiors and subordinates, climate and culture of organisation and their willingness to work in the organisation. Attitude is developed with continuous feeling relating these variables. Interestingly attitudes are expressed in the name of satisfaction or dissatisfaction. There is quite a large list of definitions. Perhaps each of these definitions has identified variables that influence it. These variables are classified as organisational and personal. Some of the organisational variable are wages, nature of work, working conditions, job content, organisational level, opportunities for promotion, work group and leadership styles. Personality, age, education and gender differences are certain variables that influence job satisfaction. It is relevant to note that job satisfaction is an intangible, qualitative and psychological variable. Its direct measurement is not possible. It is measured indirectly. Certain popularly used methods are rating scale method, personal interviews, observation of tendencies and critical incident method. Job Description Index and Minnesota Satisfaction Questionnaire are popularly used scales of measurement. Job satisfaction has a positively influence on productivity and performance, reduces absenteeism and turnover. It has negative impact on personal and societal health. Dissatisfied employees often involve in negative publicity, ignorance of safety, experience work stresses, develop unionization and adverse mental and physical health.

Key words:

- **Absenteeism:** Intentional or unintentional cessation of work by staying off form work place
- **Bad mouthing:** Employees engaging in negative publicity by unpopular and negative comments

- **Critical incidents:** Situations in which unique feelings and emotions are experienced
- **Job content:** Factors inherent in job such as recognition, responsibility, advancement, achievement etc.
- **Rating scale:** A tool to measure qualitative aspects that consists of certain statements describing the attitude, behaviour, personality, emotions etc.
- **Turnover:** Employees leaving employment

35. STRESS BEHAVIOUR

This chapter enables you:

- *To define the term stress and understand its meaning*
- *To identify the components of stress*
- *To distinguish between stress and anxiety*
- *To distinguish between stress and burnout*
- *To examine various intra organisational factors influencing stress*
- *To understand the role of external factors that determine stress*
- *To understand the physiological feelings of stress*
- *To understand the behavioural dimensions of stress*
- *To explore organisational effects of stress*

The structure of the chapter is as follows:

- Introduction
- Definition of stress
- Components of stress
- Individual factors
- Organisational factors
- Environmental factors
- Managerial implications of stress
- Summary
- Key words

CHAPTER 35

Stress Behaviour

INTRODUCTION

Stress is a very common phenomenon in modern organisations. It is both physical and psychological. It is understood through biological disorders leading to a psychological illness. Stress does not result from a single experience, but occurs when the realisation of desires and wishes are constrained by certain internal and external factors. People often confuse stress, anxiety and burnout, but they are not the same concepts, although stress is accompanied by anxiety, whereas anxiety need not result into stress and burnout is a state of mind, resulting from emotional stress. A person might feel strained when over worked on a particular day. If this strain continues, it may result in burnout. The factors that convert potential stress into actual stress are called stressors. These can be intra organisational or extra organisational. Intra organisational factors are again divided into individual factors and organisational factors. Individual factors responsible for stress relate to purely personal dispositions, whereas organisational factors are related to the conditions in which individuals work in organisations. Environmental factors responsible for stress are outside the control of both managerial and individual actions, and hence are uncontrollable. Stress need not always be negative, but can have also have positive consequences. The positive form of stress is known as "eustress." However, negative consequences of stress are of greater concern as they have a negative impact on organisational performance. They have an impact on individual psychology and behaviour on one hand and affect the organisation on the other hand. This chapter provides a detailed discussion of stress that enables one to understand the phenomenon, and hence design strategies to combat it effectively.

DEFINITION OF STRESS

Stress is a very common phenomenon, in which individuals experience an emotional state in which both physical and mental discomfort are present. It leads to loss of emotional stability, which is one of the most common forms of expression of stress. It has a positive association with one's age, life style, food habits and personality on one hand and time constraints, job demands, organisational structure, and the nature of occupation on the other. Certain occupations are more prone to stress than others. For example, doctors, lawyers, consultants, and managerial personnel at decision-making levels are more likely to experience stress than people like teachers, bankers, and operating personnel. Frustration is one of the most important drivers of stress. Individuals feel stress when their needs or desires are not fulfilled in the normal expected ways. The more the intensity of the desire and the greater the uncertainty associated with achieving the goals, the greater is the degree of stress. Employees are working longer hours, taking on more work, meeting tighter deadlines and cutting back on expenses. These are some of the causes of stress. Combined with the double-income family demands of monthly mortgages, childcare issues and aging parents, the result for many is anxiety, sleeplessness, irritability, and physical and mental deterioration. These are potential reasons for stress in employees. Though stress is a psychological phenomenon, certain definitions, given below can make the term clearer.

In the words of **Fred Luthans,** stress is defined as *'an adaptive response to an external situation that results in physical, psychological, and/or behavioral deviations for organizational participants.'*

Ivancevich and **Matteson** define stress as *'the interaction of the individual with the environment. It is an adaptive response, mediated by individual characteristics and/or psychological processes, that is consequence of any external action, situation or event that places special physical and/or psychological demands upon a person.'*

Beehr and **Newman** defined job stress as *'a condition arising from the interaction of people and their jobs and characterized by changes within people that force them to deviate from their normal functioning.'*

'Stress is a dynamic condition in which an individual is confronted with an opportunity, constraint, or demand related to what he or she desires and for which the outcome is perceived to be both uncertain and important'. **Schuler.**

In the words of **Szilagyi** and **Wallace**, stress is *'an internal experience that creates a psychological or physiological imbalance within an individual and results from factors in the external environment, the organization, or the individual'*.

Definitions of stress enable us to understand the following characteristic features of stress.

1. Stress is both a psychological and physical aspect.
2. It is common to both genders.

3. It results from the deviation of expectations from the actual situation.
4. It is symptomatic. Potential stress appears with the symptoms. If the potential stress is ignored it leads to actual stress, thus causing damage to the biological system of the human being.
5. Stress is treated to be negative. Nevertheless, it can have positive consequences, called 'eustress'.
6. Stress is an interactive concept. It does not simply arise from the internal organs of an individual, but comes from the interaction of a human being with the environment. Thus, environment has a profound influence on the stress.
7. Stress is a generic term that applies to all individuals. If it is applied to the context of organisation, it is known as work stress or job stress.
8. Stress occurs only when a person feels the internal or external factors.
9. Stress is related to the attitude of the person. Stress does not occur when the person has an indifferent attitude to a person or situation.
10. Stress is associated with certain common biological disorders such as heart attacks, strokes, diabetes, blood pressure, neurological disorders etc.

COMPONENTS OF STRESS

Figure 35.1 shows the components of stress.

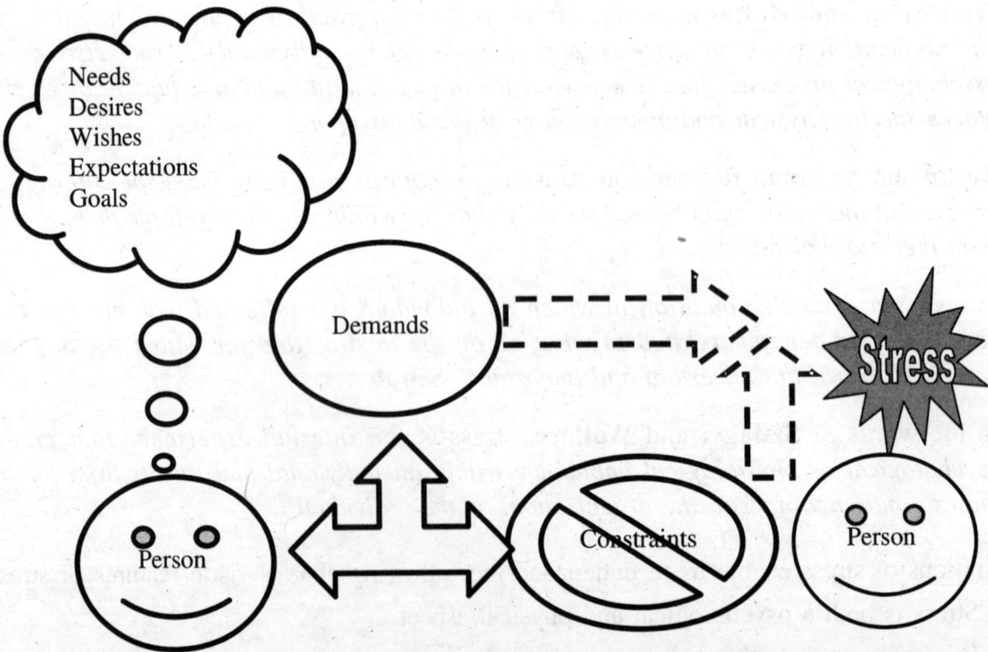

Figure 35.1: The components of stress

Stress is multidimensional. It is composed of a number of elements. Thus, understanding stress and evolving a strategy to overcome it requires understanding these elements. Stress is caused when a person has needs, desires, wishes, and expectations from a person or situation. He experiences a demand to realise the goals both physically and psychologically. When the forces that demand gratification are more powerful than the means available, a person experiences stress. Certain forces can prevent a person from satisfying his or her needs and desires thus not realising the goal. These forces are known as 'constraints', and they cause stress. Similarly, loss of something that is strongly desired leads to stress. Thus, two conditions are important in leading to stress.

i. Uncertainty of the desired or expected outcome, and
ii. A satisfactory outcome for the gratification of desires.

Stress and anxiety are often used synonymously but they are not similar concepts. Anxiety occurs as a result of emotions that are caused by the interactions of environmental stimuli. Thus, it is confined to a psychological disturbance. Stress on the other hand, originates in psychological tensions and slowly leads to a physical or biological breakdown. While stress is accompanied by anxiety, the latter need not always lead to stress. These two concepts are distinguished based on certain factors. They are shown in Table 35.1.

Table 35.1 Distinction between stress and anxiety

Nature	Stress	Anxiety
1. Cause	Stress is not tension or anxiety. Stress causes an imbalanced mental state. Anxiety causes stress.	Anxiety is not always the cause of stress.
2. Occurrence	Stress does not occur regularly.	Anxiety can occur frequently in a person.
3. Visibility	It is visible in the form of a physical breakdown.	It is not visible, as it is psychological. Often it may not cause any physical breakdown.
4. Nature	Stress originates from psychological tensions and leads to physical consequences.	Anxiety remains purely a psychological and emotional aspect.
5. Time	Stress is long lasting.	Anxiety is a shorter phenomenon.
6. Impact	It has a physical impact on the person and may negatively influence a person's job performance.	It does not cause any physical impact and may not impair working capacities of employees.

Similarly, stress and burnout are different concepts. Burnout is a state of mind. It results from a continuous feeling of emotional stress. When an individual feels physical, mental and emotional exhaustion, job burnout is characterised by emotional exhaustion, depersonalisation, and diminished personal accomplishment. Burnout is closely associated with professions such as nursing, education, and social work, which involve an emotional input in carrying out the work. The distinctions between stress and burnout are shown in Table 35.2.

Table 35.2 Distinction between stress and burnout

Nature	Stress	Burnout
1. Nature	Stress results in fatigue and anxiety.	Burnout leads to hypertension and a feeling of chronic exhaustion.
2. Expressions	An individual feels guilty and moody and expresses his or her feelings through facial gestures.	An individual feels mentally depressed, and as a result feels impatient, irritable and unwilling to talk to others.
3. Mental attention	An individual loses his or her mental attention. Forgetfulness increases	An individual becomes forgetful.
4. Satisfaction	An individual feels dissatisfied with his job.	An individual feels boredom and becomes cynical.
5. Psychological commitment	An individual's psychological commitment decreases.	A person loses psychological commitment and becomes mentally detached.
6. Physical impact	An individual experiences increased blood pressures and the heart beat escalates.	An individual experiences psychosomatic situations and complains of exhaustion.

FACTORS INFLUENCING STRESS

When an individual experiences any deviation in his or her biological system, it is potential stress. Individual, organisational and environmental variables (stressors) affect potential stress, which ultimately leads to actual stress. Intra-organisational stress arises from individual, group, and organisational factors. Extra organisational factors relate to environment of the organisation. Intra organisational factors causing stress are divided into individual factors and organisational factors.

Intra-organisational Factors

Intra organisational factors of stress are individual and organisational factors. They are discussed below.

INDIVIDUAL FACTORS

Personality and individual differences, family problems, economic problems, life styles and demands of one's role are some of the individual factors, which cause stress. They are discussed below.

1. **Personality and individual differences:** An individual's basic disposition is the main reason for potential stress. Introversion, extroversion, masculinity, rigidity and locus of control, are some of the personality factors that lead to stress in individuals. Personal life, demographic differences such as age, health, education, and occupation are some of the individual differences that cause stress in individuals. It is found that a type A personality is more prone to stress than a type B personality. The type A personality is characterised by emotion and sensitivity to organisation goals, a competitive spirit and strong achievement oriented behaviour. This leads to frustration even if there are small deviations from expectations, and more stress. A type B personality is typically relaxed, carefree, patient, and less serious in achieving objectives. Thus, they feel less stress. Some propositions relating to stress associated with personality and individual differences are mentioned below:
   - Age is positively related to stress. When a person grows older, expectations increase; he becomes less patient and more anxious to realise his expectations. If he is unable to find avenues for realising these expectations, he experiences stress.
   - Sound health enables a person to cope with stress more easily than unsound health. Thus, health and stress are inversely associated.
   - Education and stress are related positively. Better education provides an opportunity to understand things in a better manner. Even the level of maturity increases with better education. So better educated persons are less prone to stress. Poorly educated people are likely to feel more stress due to poor adaptability on a job.
   - The nature of the occupation and stress are related. Certain occupations, such as doctors, lawyers, politicians, are inherently more stressful than others. However, the same occupation also gives stress tolerance ability. Politicians are found to possess more stress tolerance ability. Nowadays it is found that corporate responsibilities and project demands are causing a lot of stress. Software personnel are found to be prone to stress.
   - A strong urge to satisfy their needs compels people to over work, leading to stress. Thus, strength of the need has a positive association with stress.
   - A greater degree of locus of control leads to stress. Persons with an internal locus of control feel that internal factors are responsible for their success or failure. They are likely to experience more stress. A person is less likely to feel stress if he believes that he

can exercise control over external factors that influence his success.

- Self-efficacy and stress are negatively related. A higher degree of self-efficacy elevates motivation levels. Therefore people with greater self-efficacy remain calm and can effectively face stressful situations. The capacity to bring changes provides greater ability to withstand stress.
- Achievement motivation and stress are negatively related. People with strong achievement motivation are less likely to feel stress. They believe that achievement is possible with increasing failures. So every failure is a stepping stone to success.
- Another personal disposition related to stress is psychological hardiness. Hardiness is the ability to withstand provocation from others. People with greater psychological hardiness are able to survive and withstand a stressful environment.
- Perception is understanding of the worldly environment. A person possessing a positive perception understands reality and appraises events objectively. Thus, he feels less stress.
- Job experience and stress are negatively related. As one gains experience he develops adaptability to various jobs and organisational demands. He realises the job expectations, and develops a mechanism to deal with stressful situations. Therefore more experienced people remain cool, calm, and ignore stressors than young and inexperienced employees.
- Hostility and aggressive behaviour is positively related to stress. Aggressive persons become angrier faster, become more cynical and do not trust others. They feel more stress than other people, who are cool and docile.

  This suggests that managers should understand the personality and appraise individual differences to deal effectively with the self-stress and advocate stress relaxation to their subordinates.

2. **Family problems:** Family issues influence the personal life of individuals. Sound marital relationships, marital discipline and healthy children lead to a happy personal life of individuals. They enjoy the life and become positive in their attitudes, so they are less stressed. Poor marital relationships, family separations, problematic children, aging parents, early death of spouse or other close family members are some of the reasons for greater stress in an individual. Although some of the personal reasons are out of one's individual control, one has to develop a strong will power to overcome the problems to reduce stress.

3. **Economic problems:** Economic difficulties are the main cause of stress. Poor management of personal finances, heavy family expenditure, constant demand for money, poor income earning capacity and slow financial growth in one's job are some of the economic reasons responsible for greater stress. For instance, increased family expenditure due to increased cost of living and increased expenditure on children's education and health create heavy demands on an individual, creating greater stress. These are external factors beyond an individual's control. Thus, carefully planning one's life style and developing contentment can really help a person to feel less stressed.

4. **Life styles:** In the modern world, the life style of an individual is one of the main reasons for stress. Ever-increasing ambitions, changing fashions, etc., can cause envy and a feeling of

discontentment. Some situations that cause stress are given below.

- A sudden change in life style.
- Trauma, wherein an individual experiences situations that compel them to alter their attitude, emotions and behaviour.
- Rapid changes in career, bringing more responsibilities to the individual. Persons occupying higher positions at a younger age are prone to heart attacks due to greater stress. This is because of their inability to adapt to the new career responsibilities.

5. **Role demands:** Individuals play multiple roles in their personal, social, and organisation life. In their personal life, they play the roles of, husband or wife, father or mother, brother or sister and so on. In their social life they play the roles of members of a club, informal community groups, recreation groups, religious groups, etc. Similarly in organisations, employees play the role of superior, subordinate, co-workers, members of various formal committees, union leaders, informal group leaders etc. All these roles are performed simultaneously. Balancing the demands in these roles is like walking a tight rope. They cause tension, anxiety, and emotion, due to conflicting demands. For instance, an employee may be required to attend a function for their child and have an important board meeting at work. Another example is the case of an employee, who follows a strict moral code, but is forced into a situation at work, which goes totally against his principles. Another potential reason is role conflict. This arises due to poor role perception, role ambiguity, role overload, and role overlapping. Role perception is the understanding of the demands of the role. Role ambiguity arises out of poor communication and frequent changes in role demands. Role ambiguity and stress are positively related. Role overload is confronting a situation, which has greater demands than the capacity of the individual occupying the position. Role overlap arises out of simultaneous discharge of responsibility. An employee, who is both a superior and subordinate, is in a situation of overlap. All these role related complexities create stress in individuals. The greater the role conflict, the higher is the degree of stress.

ORGANISATIONAL FACTORS

An organisation is a combination of resources, goals, strategies, and policies. In order to make people work, organisations create a structure, process and working conditions. In modern organisations, a number of factors create a situation of stress. Changing environmental dynamics, globalisation, organisational adjustments like mergers and acquisitions, downsizing, resizing, collaborations etc., lead to stress among employees. In addition, a number of internal organisational factors cause employee stress. Some of them are poor working conditions, strained employee management relations, disputed resource allocations, behaviour of colleagues, organisational design and policies and unpleasant styles of leadership of superiors. Moreover, misunderstandings in organisational communication, bureaucratic controls, improper motivation, job dissatisfaction, and less attention to merit and seniority also become reasons for stress. Organisational stressors are described below.

1. **Working conditions:** Working conditions and stress are inversely related. Employees in poor

working environment are subject to greater stress. Some of the working conditions that lead to more stress are crowded work areas, dust, heat, noise, polluted air, strong odour due to toxic chemicals etc., radiation, poor ventilation, unsafe and dangerous conditions, lack of privacy etc. Even traditional organisation theories demonstrated that working conditions jeopardise the efficiency of productivity. For example, miners working in a coal mine are found to experience more stress than an employee working in a management information systems department who works in an air-conditioned environment. Pharmacists and chemical analysts are prone to more stress due to continuous exposure to chemicals.

2. **Organisational tasks:** Organisational tasks are designed to meet objectives and goals. Poorly designed tasks lead to greater stress. Task autonomy, task inter-dependency, task demands, and task overload are some of the factors of organisational tasks that become potential reasons for stress if not properly designed. For instance the greater the task interdependence, the greater is the coordination required. This requires employees to adjust themselves to co-workers, superiors, and subordinates, irrespective of their willingness. They are expected to communicate, coordinate, exchange views with other people irrespective of caste, creed, gender, religion, and political differences. So they require a greater degree of emotional tolerance. Inability to adjust and poor tolerance of others leads to a greater degree of stress.
3. **Administrative policies and strategies:** Administrative strategies followed by an organisation and employee stress are positively related. Downsizing, competitive pressure, unfair and discriminating pay structures, rigidity in rules, frequent transfers, job rotation and ambiguous policies are some of the reasons for stress in organisations. In recent years, employees working in banks have expressed strong concern over privatisation and consequent loss of employment. They have expressed anxiety due to the decision of the management to implement a 'golden handshake'. In many private organisations a discriminative pay structure is followed with specific instructions to employees not to disclose their pay and perquisites with colleagues. This leads to covert stress.
4. **Organisational structure and design:** As pointed out earlier, organisational structure is designed to facilitate individuals' interaction in the realisation of organisational goals. Certain aspects of design like specialisation, centralisation, line and staff relationships, span of control and organisational communication can together create stress in organisations. For example, wider span of management compels the executive to manage a large number of subordinates and consequent relationships. This may place greater stress on the executive. Similarly, frequent line and staff conflicts lead to obstacles in performance of the work. Inability to resolve the conflicts leads to great stress in the managers.
5. **Organisation process and styles:** A number of organisational processes are designed to meet organisational goals. The communication process, control process, decision making process, promotion process, performance appraisal process, etc. are designed for smooth working in the realisation of organisational objectives. These processes limit the scope of employees' functions. Improper design of various organisational processes leads to strained relationships among the employees. They may also cause de-motivation and job dissatisfaction. Consequently, employees feel stress in adapting to the processes. The

performance appraisal process is designed to control as well as motivate employees. Often the parameters of appraisal are kept confidential. This makes employees anxious regarding their performance, leading to stress.

6. **Organisational leadership:** The top management is responsible for creating a sound organisational climate and culture by an appropriate managerial style. The climate provided should be free of tension, fear and anxiety. The authoritarian leadership style creates an environment in which employees are pressurised to attain targets. They work under impersonal relationships and tight control. This creates greater work stress in employees. On the other hand, a climate of warmth and friendliness, scope for participation in decision making, non financial motivation and flexibility is encouraged under a democratic leadership style. This relieves stress in employees. Therefore, employees working under an authoritarian leadership style experience a greater degree of stress than employees working under a democratic leadership style.

7. **Organisational life cycle:** Every organisation moves through four phases of an organisational life cycle, namely, birth, growth, maturity and decline. In each of these stages the structure and design of an organisation undergoes frequent changes, to which the employees must adjust, subjecting them to job stress. For instance in the initial stages of organisational birth, stress is caused because of ambiguous policies and designs. In the growth stage, employees experience stress due to failure to meet conflicting demands. In the maturity stage, employees are pressurised to achieve higher targets to meet the demands of the market. At the time of decline, stress is caused due to downsizing, retrenchment, and loss of financial rewards and changing organisational systems.

8. **Group dynamics:** Groups always exist in organisations. They arise from the inherent desire of human beings and spontaneous reactions of people. Both formal groups, such as committees and informal groups exist in organisations. Groups have a number of functional and dysfunctional consequences. They provide social support and satisfaction, which are helpful in relieving stress, but at the same time, they can also be a source of stress. Lack of cohesiveness, social support and recognition in the group and incompatible goals cause stress. These factors are described below.

   i. **Lack of group cohesiveness:** Group cohesiveness is a feeling that members support each other in all situations. Group cohesiveness involves members' appreciation of each other, provides an opportunity for leadership, esteem, self-actualisation, support, communication and satisfaction. These are stress relievers to the members of the group. However, management restrictions to forming groups and their apprehensions regarding groups results in poor cohesiveness, causing employees to develop tension and anxiety, which lead to stress.

   ii. **Lack of social support:** Groups provide strong support to members, not only in the realisation of goals but also by providing an opportunity to share information. Employees are likely to share their unpleasant experiences with other members of the group and seek support and consolation. In the process, their mental tension is relieved. Therefore, members who do not enjoy support from the group develop tension leading to stress. Sometimes it happens that an employee is berated by his or her superior, sharing the experience with others who have been meted out the same treatment, relieves anxiety and tension.

iii. **Group conflicts:** Conflicts are common in all situations and groups are not an exception to this. Intra and inter group conflicts arise in organisations because of incompatible goals, poor leadership, incompatible communication, misunderstandings and inter group competition. All these lead to stress in individuals.

From the above discussion, it can be understood that a number of organisational factors cause stress in the individuals.

Extra-organisational Factors

Extra-organisational factors are related to environment of the organisation. They are outside the scope of the organisation, managerial and individual control.

ENVIRONMENTAL FACTORS

Environmental factors create job stress in individuals; they may be internal or external. Most of the internal environmental factors relate to organisational goals, management systems, organisational structure, processes, and design of organisations, and have been discussed in the preceding section. External environmental factors relate to the general environment of the organisation. They are political, economical, technological, legal, ecological, governmental, social, cultural, and ethical (PETLEGS). Certain propositions describing the impact of environment on stress are presented below:

Political: The political party in power enacts legislation in Parliament, which reflects their ideology. Every political party that forms the government wishes to either enact new laws and regulations or bring changes in the existing ones. Thus, political changes cause uncertainty in the environment. Employees are compelled to adapt to the new legal order, which can create stress.

Economic: This encompasses income levels, demand and supply, inflation etc. Changes in these factors make new demands on both the organisation and employees. This creates stress if the employees are unable to adjust to the new situations. For instance, increased inflation levels create pressures on employees' income levels, leading to stress.

Technological: Changes in technology bring in new methods of production and new ways of handling organisational tasks. Employees are required to learn new skills in order to discharge their jobs effectively. Inability to cope with the new technology creates stress in employees. For example, bank employees initially resisted the move to introduce computers as they felt it would lead to retrenchment, which caused them stress.

Legal: Organisations have to follow the legal provisions, but often, practical difficulties arise in the implementation of the complex laws and regulations intended to control operations. Unable to respond properly to the laws and regulations, employees find themselves in stressful situations.

For example, in a particular company, the personnel officer is responsible for sending the occupier notice required by the Factories Act. As he was busy executing instructions given by the managing director, he was unable to furnish the notice in time. Later, when the Inspector of Factories served a notice on the organisation, the managing director held the personnel officer responsible and imposed a fine. This created anxiety and stress in the personnel officer.

Ecological: This environment is of great concern to organisations, as the government is enacting legislation to protect the ecological environment and organisations are compelled to adapt to it. Protecting the ecological balance can be a cause for potential stress. For instance, disposal of industrial waste or toxic substances creates cost pressures on the organisation.

Government: The government is composed of the administrative machinery and institutions that enforce laws, regulations, policies and other government instructions. The bureaucratic practices of the administrative machinery can create stress in executives. For instance, an organisation intending to expand its capacity needs to take permission from the concerned officer. For example, in a particular organisation, the management decided to install a new boiler to increase the capacity of power generation. In spite of the fact that the boiler was imported from Germany complying with all the international standards of safety, the inspector of boilers refused to give permission without satisfying certain formalities. However, the top management started pressurising the general manager to install the boiler immediately, which he was unable to do and neither could he convince them that the inspector was causing unnecessary delays. This led to considerable stress for him.

Social, cultural and ethical environment: Social factors influence the life styles of employees. Certain social measures such as health protection, civic facilities, and social groups reduce stress in the employees. Certain sociological variables such as race, sex, social class, gender etc. and cultural factors such as beliefs, customs, and traditions are potential stress factors.

Certain other environmental factors that can lead to stress are stock market crashes, frequent elections, downsizing, and information technology and the related changes in the business, dual career couples, racial and gender discriminations, health hazards due to pollution and imbalance in the natural environment.

MANAGERIAL IMPLICATIONS OF STRESS

At first, an individual experiences stress through imbalanced psychological emotions. A physiological breakdown or biological changes disseminate this stress. However, mild stress elevates the body's metabolic and biological rates, leading to secretion of juices from the glands that increase the inner drive for achievement. Such stress, or eustress is a positive form of stress, as the word itself, taken from the Greek language meaning good stress, implies. In its mild form it enhances job performance, leads to excellence, and provides the impetus to work hard and perform better. Individuals involved in the discharge of professionally oriented jobs, jobs involving creativity, challenge, interpersonal communications and certain managerial jobs, will be benefited by eustress, which leads to positive performances. Thus, individuals perform tasks better and faster. The inverted-U relationship illustrates this phenomenon. The inverted-U relationship states that as stress increases some of the positive consequences also increase. Some positive consequences are increased productivity, positive response to targets, development of proper perception in decision making, increased motivation and performance, increased adaptability to change and increased quality of job performance. For instance, an employee experiencing moderate stress of repetitiveness of work finds new ways of discharging the job. Thus, stress promotes creativity in employees. However, jobs involving physical effort are not benefited from stress.

The inverted-U relationship can be illustrated with the help of Figure 35.1.

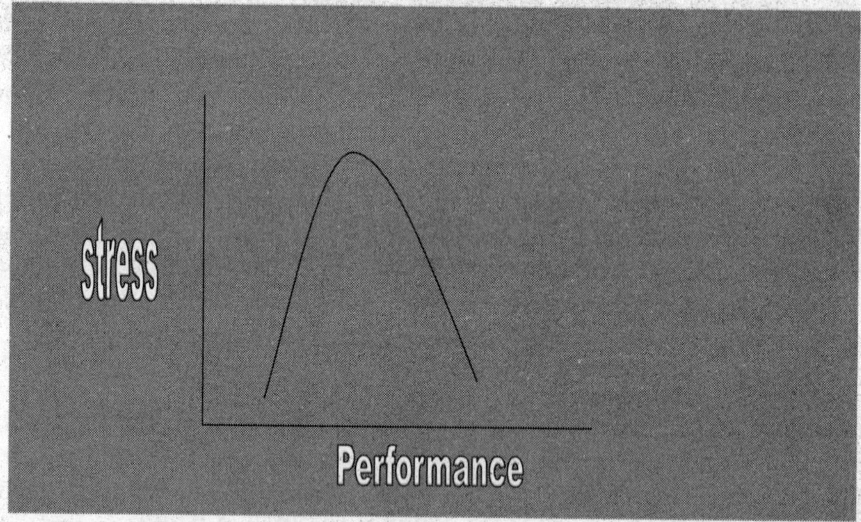

Figure 35.1: Relationship between stress and performance

However, in the modern organisations the negative consequences of stress are more cause for concern to the management and employees. As pointed out by Schuler, Khan, and Byosiyere, stress leads to high blood pressure, ulcers, cancer, accidents, and irritation. Though there is no perfect association between stress and its consequences, stress itself results in physiological, psychological, behavioural, job and organisational consequences. The positive and negative consequences are discussed below.

Physiological consequences

Stress influences the biological system of a human being. Certain visible forms of stress are increased blood pressure, tendency towards heart disease, cancer, sweating, dry mouth, hot and cold flashes, frustration, anxiety, depression, increased level of cholesterol, ulcer, arthritis etc. Physical stress increases the body metabolic rate. This results in malfunctioning of the internal glands and consequent body disorder, which manifests as increased heart beats and breathing, and headaches. Physical stress can also create psychological problems as the two are interrelated.

Psychological consequences

By themselves, psychological consequences are not visible, but they have a considerable effect on the employees' performance. Psychological stress creates pressure in the mind, which is expressed in terms of psychological symptoms such as anger, anxiety, depression, nervousness, irritation, tension, boredom, aggressiveness, moodiness, hostility and poor concentration. Tensions, anxiety and emotions lead to procrastination. Psychological stress produces interpersonal aggressions, misunderstanding in communication, poor interpersonal communication, and low interpersonal attraction. This shows in aggressive attitudes, increased interpersonal complaints, poor job performance, low self-esteem, increased resentment, low concentration and increased dissatisfaction. Psychological stress leads to harsh behaviour and may lead to assumption of an authoritarian style of leadership.

Behavioural consequences

Stress impacts employees' behaviour. Abnormal behaviour is observed in individuals who are prone to stress. A change in eating habits, sleep disorders, increased smoking, alcoholism, fidgeting and aloofness are some of the behavioural changes observed in stressful employees. It can also lead to anxiety, apathy, depression, and emotional disorder. This leads to impulsive and aggressive behaviour and frequent interpersonal conflicts. Under-eating, overeating, drug abuse and sleeplessness are some of the behaviour consequences. The following are some of the propositions relating to stress and behaviour.

Perception: Individuals who are stressed develop tension and anxiety, with the result that their level of understanding considerably decreases and perceptual distortions increase. When perceptual distortions occur in employees, it may adversely affect the decision making process, interpersonal understanding, interpersonal communication, and capacity to work with teams. They become stress intolerant. All these lead to increased levels of interpersonal conflicts.

Attitudes: Continued stressful environment creates certain permanent negative impressions (negative attitudes) in the mind of employees, which adversely influence their work performance. Workers also become demoralised and their satisfaction levels decrease.

Compulsion in learning: Employees in organisations continuously learn new skills and techniques. Learning new methods and techniques in order to adapt themselves to change and discharge their jobs effectively is inevitable for employees. Employees who are stressed cannot learn things quickly, as they are behaviorally unstable and their learning levels are inadequate for the organisational requirements.

Organisational Consequences

Organisations severally face problems of poor performance and other negative consequences due to excessive stress of employees. Some of them are described below:

Absenteeism: Employees subject to stress were found to be addicted to drugs and alcohol. Thus, they are frequently absent from work, which creates discontinuity in their work and adversely affects the performance of other employees.

Turnover: Employees under continuous stress become disgruntled and frustrated, therefore, they are likely to leave. This increases employee turnover.

Decision-making: Excessive stress distorts the perception of managers. This adversely affects analysis and development and selection of alternative courses of action. Thus, stressful executives make irrational decisions, leading to loss of organisational resources and reputation.

Disturbed customer relationships: Employees experiencing excessive stress become irritable, and lose emotional stability and emotional tolerance. Intolerance impels them to enter into conflicts due to misunderstandings. This is particularly relevant in the case of employees dealing with customers. These employees have to be extremely careful in their behaviour with the general public. Thus sales persons, bank employees, public relation executives must be emotionally stable, otherwise, customers dealing with them will have trouble in dealing with the company. The corporate image of the organisation is reflected in their behaviour.

The consequences of stress are multifaceted. Stress is a vicious circle, with most consequences of stress being interdependent. For instance, psychological consequences result in physiological disorders, the latter produce behavioural consequences, and ultimately the organisation suffers from adverse effects. The ill effects of stress are more dangerous. Addiction to smoking, drinking taking narcotic drugs, perverted sex, atrocities on women and children, criminal attitude; terrorism and indecent behaviour are some of the social consequences of stress. It is in this context that stress has received greater attention from the management of organisations, psychologists, and medical practitioners in recent times. A number of strategies exist to overcome stress. Most of them suggest leading a peaceful, calm and regulated life. Since this may be easier said than done, a number of strategies to manage stress in organisations exist, and these are presented in the following chapter.

SUMMARY

Stress is a psychological concept and is symptomatic. Stress and anxiety are different concepts. Anxiety is a cause of stress, but stress need not result into anxiety. Prolonged stress leads to burnout. A host of factors cause stress. Stressors are factors that cause stress in individuals. They can be intra or extra organisational. While individual stressors are intra organisational, environmental stressors are extra organisational. Individual stressors are the personality of a person, individual differences, family problems, economic problems, life styles, and role demands. A number of organisational factors that cause stress in individuals are poor working conditions, poor task design, unfair administrative policies and strategies, improper organisational structure and design, organisational process and design, organisational leadership, organisational life cycle, and group dynamics. Environmental factors comprise political, economical, technological, legal, ecological, governmental, social and ethical factors.

Nevertheless, stress and personality, occupation, age, life styles and time demands are related to each other. Excessive stress leads to both biological and behavioural disorders. Although, stress is usually considered as a negative factor, there is also positive stress called eustress, which is mild stress and enhances performance. However, the negative consequences of stress are greater than the positive consequences. Physiological consequences are increased blood pressure, heart attacks, cancer, sweating, frustration, anxiety, and depression. Psychological consequences are anger, aggressiveness, moodiness, hostility, poor concentration, tension and anxiety. Abnormal behaviour is observed in stressful situations. Poor perception, inconsistent attitudes, and poor learning are some of the behavioural consequences. The outcomes of stress are absenteeism, employee turnover, irrational decision-making, and disturbed customer relationships that lead to a negative corporate image.

Key words:

- **Anxiety:** A state of psychological disturbance
- **Burnout:** A feeling of emotional exhaustion
- **Eustress:** The good form of stress
- **Organisational life cycle:** The stages of birth, growth, maturity and decline in the existence of an organisation
- **Potential stress:** Deviation in the biological system of individuals
- **Psychological hardiness:** The ability to withstand provocation from others
- **Self-efficacy:** The perception of one's capacity to bring about changes
- **Stress:** Stress is an internal experience, which creates physiological and psychological disorders
- **Stressors:** Factors that convert the potential stress into actual stress

36. STRESS MANAGEMENT

This chapter enables you:

- *To understand stress management*
- *To distinguish between self management and organisational management*
- *To comprehend the various individual management strategies*
- *To determine organisational strategies of stress management*
- *To determine whether it is possible to create a stress-free working environment for employees*
- *To distinguish between individual and organisational stressors*

The structure of the chapter is as follows:

- Introduction
- Stress management techniques
- Self management
- Organisational management
- Stress-free working
- Summary
- Key words

CHAPTER 36

Stress Management

INTRODUCTION

Contrary to popular belief, stress is not difficult to combat. If a person is concerned about his or her own health, they will make an effort to fight the stress themselves. Today, morning walks, exercise, meditation and relaxation are becoming very common, and the number of clinics offering stress relief is growing rapidly in metropolitan areas. Their objective is to prevent potential stress being converted into actual stress. Organisations are also interested in offering a number of programs to reduce stress in employees. Towards this end they are adopting structural redesigns, career planning, and employees' development and counseling methods. However, it should be remembered that stress relief is more about an individual being prepared to adopt strategies to prevent stress, rather than enforcing them upon a person.

STRESS MANAGEMENT TECHNIQUES

The causes and consequences of stress have been explained in Chapter 35. Employee stress has more negative than positive consequences, and thwarts organisational effectiveness. In the light of this, stress management has assumed considerable importance in modern organisations. Prevention of stress is better than attempting to cure it, as experiencing stress even for a short period has negative consequences. However, there is a vast difference between the theoretical techniques and actual practices of prevention of stress. Although, there is negative perception of stress, there is a need to create moderate levels of stress to induce better performance. The difficulty arises in determining the acceptable levels. In addition, many people prefer sleep to a morning walk and only when a problem occurs do they make an effort to exercise and control their diet, which is a very ineffective way of fighting stress. To lead a stress-free and balanced life, one has to recognise the significance of things before they become urgent. Stress management techniques fall under this category, as is explained in Figure 36.1.

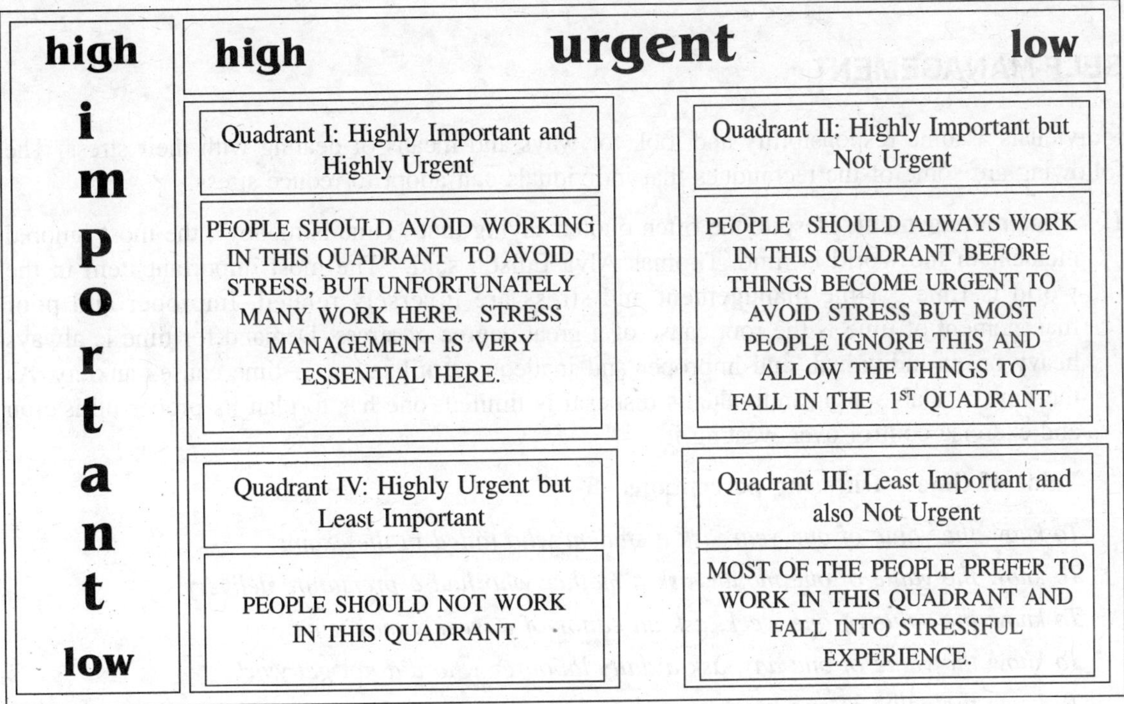

Figure 36.1: Matrix of urgent and important quadrants

Also observe the matrix shown in Figure 36.2, which shows the different quadrants in which some effects occur.

	Urgent	**Not urgent**
Important	• Deadlines • Crises • Pressing • Interruptions	• Prevention • Relationship building • Recognise opportunity • Planning
Not Important	• Some phone calls • Some meetings • Popular activities • Pressing matters	• Time wasters • TV • Some phone calls • Time pass • Pleasant activities

Figure 36.2: The different quadrants in which some effects occur

Stress has to be managed by both individual and organisational strategies. Individual management techniques are more popular and effective than organisational management techniques. The strategies of stress management are described below.

SELF-MANAGEMENT

Individuals assume responsibility and look for ways and means of dealing with their stress. The following are some of the techniques that individuals can adopt to reduce stress.

1. **Time management**: Despite the often quoted saying that "Time is money", the most ignored element in the world is time. Thomas Alva Edison said, "The most important item in the world is time". Time management and stress are inversely related. Improper and poor management of time is the root cause of a great degree of stress. Demand for time is always heavy on an individual, and improper and inadequate utilisation of time causes anxiety. As the time available at an individual's disposal is limited, one has to plan its proper utilisation and exercise control over wasting it.

   Value of time – Differing perceptions

   To know the value of one year, ask a student who failed in the exams.

   To know the value of one month, ask a mother who had a premature delivery.

   To know the value of one week, ask an editor of a weekly magazine.

   To know the value of one day, ask a daily labourer who did not get work.

   To know the value of one hour, ask a lover who is waiting for his/her mate.

   To know the value of one minute, ask a traveler who missed the train.

   To know the value of one second, ask a person who has just missed an accident.

   To know the value of one millisecond, ask an athlete who missed a gold medal.

   The following principles of time management can help in combating stress.

   Identifying and listing daily activities in a logical order.

   Arranging the activities of the day based on importance and urgency.

   Preparing a logical schedule of activities.

   Knowing the daily cycle and nature of the job.

   Allocating time properly to the various activities based on time demands.

   Delegating minor tasks to subordinates in order to make a better use of time.

   Discouraging unwanted visitors.

   Setting unfinished tasks on the top of tomorrow's list.

2. **Physical management:** Management of stress relates to understanding one's own biological

and body conditions. Knowing heredity ailments, considering habits like smoking and drinking, understanding life styles and body conditions help in understanding one's physiological conditions. Overcoming stress is possible by physiological relaxation. Physical exercise is a great help in relieving tension and stress. When the body is conditioned by physical exercise, oxygen is inhaled properly and blood circulation increases. This promotes healthy secretions from glands and ensures the supply of blood to all the parts of the body, with the result that all the organs are active. Consequently, immunity to withstand stress increases. Physical exercises could be reactive or proactive. Non competitive physical exercises like walking, jogging, swimming, riding, aerobics and playing games provides mental diversion from work pressures and increases the capacity of the heart to withstand stressful situations. The chances of heart attacks, high blood pressure and diabetes are reduced.

Health is wealth. Every one agrees with this saying, but unfortunately do very little to protect their health and everything to protect their wealth. Remember the saying that "if wealth is lost nothing is lost, if health is lost something is lost and if character is lost everything is lost." However, in today's competitive environment and fast paced lives, we tend to neglect our health and ill-treat our minds and bodies in the name of life style and comfort, by lack of exercise, pollution, toxins and improper diet leading to stress. If you remember Exercise, Attitude and Rest (EAR), it will give you optimum health and a stress-free life:

(a) **Exercise**: Regular exercise is a must to keep us in good condition, a strict regime of 30 minutes of brisk walking, 5 days a week is very beneficial.

(b) **Attitude**: The more positive one's outlook on life, the better is one's health.

(c) **Rest**: Researchers have found that more than the body the brain needs rest every day to rejuvenate itself. Six to eight hours of sleep daily is mandatory for good health.

3. **Psychological management**: Most stress arises due to psychological tensions. Therefore, it is suggested that managing psychological aspects leads to effective management of stress. The following methods are some of the psychological management techniques.

(a) **Relaxation:** Relaxation of mind through meditation, hypnosis and biofeedback can effectively reduce mental tension. Meditation takes the mind into deep relaxation. This technique relaxes both body and mind. It can also bring about significant changes in the heart rate, blood pressure, lung capacity and other body organs. Transcendental meditation, Sidda Samaj Yoga, Soul management, Atma yoga, Anthahakarana, and prayer are some of the relaxation techniques available, which if practiced can significantly reduce stress.

(b) **Self-control:** Stress also results from behavioural disorders. Exercising proper control over behaviour when dealing with others can bring down the levels of stress of both parties. Self-introspection brings self-awareness and promotes proper behaviour. Similarly knowing the antecedents and consequences of one's own behaviour enables behavioural self-control. Stress can be reduced by developing proper perception, practicing good listening skills, maintaining a calm and tension-free mind when listening to others, empathy and a positive attitude.

(c) **Cognitive therapy:** This is a technique of clinical psychology. Cognitive therapy involves knowing one's own emotions, thereby releasing anxiety and tension. In this technique, people are made to understand the reasons causing stress in them by the process of self-observation. For example, if an employee develops a feeling that he is incompetent to handle a new job, he can be positively counseled to develop a confidence to handle any new job. Thus, with the help of cognitive therapy, a positive impact is created on the mind, enabling people to exercise self-control to reduce stress.

4. **Yogic management:** Yoga is an effective technique of relieving stress. Yogic practices involve *asanas, pranayama, mudras* and *kriya*. Practicing a number of *yogasanas* relaxes muscles, reduces blood pressure, controls asthma, relieves neurological problems, improves lung capacity, enhances proper flow of blood and helps relax tensions and strains.

5. **Social management:** Developing good social networks involves grouping of people who are good listeners and confidence builders. This increases social support. Encouraging informal groups to share information without inhibitions, having a free exchange of ideas, views and experiences, promoting confidence through social support decreases tensions and stress. Social clubs, recreation clubs, friendship clubs, informal gatherings, parties, and family are some of the social networks that increase social support and reduce stress.

On their deathbed, nobody has ever repented the fact that he or she spent less time in the office or did not earn enough money, but many have regretted the fact that they did not spend enough time with their loved ones, or for not maintaining a better relationship with them. We play different roles in our life like son/daughter, brother/sister, grandson/granddaughter, husband/wife, father/mother, etc. One should ask how one performs these roles, whether one is satisfied, and whether one can improve in any area.

Having better relationships makes one feel happy and satisfied in life, and building relationships takes time rather than money. Good relationships are one of the few things which money cannot buy. One successful businesswoman says that she works everyday to improve her marriage. Yes! It takes work to build good relationships. Not only do we have to spend enough time but also we have to spend the right time.

6. **Self-awareness management:** Self-awareness is similar to self-audit or personal audit. In this, managers should try to understand themselves in a free and fair manner. They should encourage open communication and be willing to listen to others, especially on their deficiencies. Being aware of oneself is a difficult task, as individuals are unprepared to accept their defects when pointed out by others. Self-awareness management involves three stages.
   - **Stage I:** Identify, understand and analyse one's own skills, capacities, limitations and defects.
   - **Stage II:** Encourage feedback from others *viz.*, subordinates, peers, superiors, friends, family members and other social associations. This requires patient hearing without inhibitions.
   - **Stage III:** Develop a program to improve one's skills and capacity to overcome limitations in a scientific way. Attend self-management training programs to develop an all-round personality.
7. **Interpersonal management:** One of the most successful techniques of stress management is developing interpersonal understanding. Interpersonal communication, interpersonal attraction and interpersonal knowledge improves one's understanding of others. Most stress in an organisation is created due to misunderstandings, organisational politics, keeping aloof from others and encouraging emotional and baseless comments. Thus, maintaining open communication and giving proper value to people's comments enable development of inter personal understanding. Transactional analysis, the Johari window and grid techniques help in the development of inter personal understanding and consequent relief from stress.

ORGANISATIONAL MANAGEMENT

In modern organisations, human resources are vital, thus their well being is important to the management. Most stress in organisations is caused by the structure and design of the organisation, its policies, programs and procedures of administration and managerial styles and strategies. Thus organisations are interested in determining the organisational stressors and removing them as far as possible. Organisations adopt the following techniques of stress management.

- **Selection and placement policy:** Stress and the personality characteristics of employees are closely related. Thus selecting employees with the appropriate personality to fit a job minimizes the chance of stress in individuals. For instance a salesperson's job requires extensive travelling rather than experience. If a person who does not like travelling is selected, he is likely to experience more stress in performing the job. Therefore, a proper recruitment and selection policy should be followed by the organisation to help reduce stress.
- **Goal setting:** Ambiguity in goals, lack of proper perception of goals, and challenging and unattainable goals cause stress in individuals. Therefore, organisations should follow a strategy of participation in goal setting to provide motivation, reduce frustration and ambiguity of goals. Management by Objectives (MBO) is an appropriate technique of goal setting that reduces stress.

- **Job enrichment and job design:** Job enrichment provides motivation to employees. It enriches job factors such as responsibility, recognition, and opportunity for advancement, growth and self-esteem. Routine, unstructured and poorly designed jobs cause greater stress in individuals. Job redesign provides greater responsibility, more meaningful work, more autonomy and increased feedback. This leads to greater control over work activities and reduces dependence on others. Therefore, job enrichment and job redesign provide an effective way of reducing stress.
- **Role clarity:** Organisational stress is associated with role ambiguity, role overlap, lack of role clarity and role conflict. Proper role definition helps employees understand their role in the organisation and appraise interpersonal roles. This reduces the chance of role conflict and increases role compatibility, thereby eliminating stress in individuals. Wherever role conflict arises, counseling and negotiation can be used to resolve inter-personal role conflicts thus avoiding stressful situations.
- **Communication and counseling:** Barriers in communication are potential moderators of organisational stress. In organisations, formal communication can create misunderstandings between personnel. Thus redesigning formal communication channels can improve communication and consequently reduce stress. For instance, a scalar chain intended to improve the speed of formal communication can be misunderstood as overlooking the immediate superior, leading to ego defensive stress in the superior. Counseling is the exchange of ideas and views in a free and fair manner. It allows employees to share problems, which helps them cope with the stressful situations. Counseling has six functions, namely advice, reassurance, communication, release of emotional tensions, clarity in thinking and reorientation. The techniques of counseling used to reduce the stress are non-directive, participative and directive counseling.
- **Career planning and development:** Employees in general are free to plan their careers. However, organisations also aim at employee development. The intention of employee development is to enrich the skills of the employee, develop their all-round personality and prepare them to undertake managerial jobs. Stress is caused when employees' expectations of their career in an organisation are not fulfilled and when they are promoted without having the necessary skills. Not many organisations take an interest in career planning of employees, but designing appropriate career plans, education programs, development programs and organisation development considerably reduce employee stress.
- **Democratic leadership:** Democratic leaders create confidence in subordinates and allow participation in the decision making process. They create an atmosphere of warmth, friendship, and are supportive. Under such circumstances employees feel satisfied, motivated and psychologically committed to the achievement of objectives. In addition, open communication leads to avoiding conflicts and improving coordination. This enables employees to relieve stress and promotes a healthy working atmosphere.
- **Organisation climate:** The design of the organisation is the basic reason for job stress. Bureaucratic, directive and ambiguous administration and poor organisational climate

characterised by unhygienic, dangerous and untidy working conditions, poor relationships among employees, frequent and baseless conflicts, all lead to greater stress. A sound organisation climate and culture characterised by sound administrative policy, good organisational communication, participative culture and supportive climate ensures reduction of stress.

- **Wellness programs:** Programs organised by the management that focus on employees' physical and mental conditions are known as wellness programs. As part of these programs, workshops, seminars and counseling sessions are conducted to help the employees understand the dangers of smoking, alcoholism and drug abuse. They promote better nutrition, regular physical exercise and developing a positive personality. However, these programs are successful only when the employees themselves take a personal interest in their physical and mental health. Organisations can only act as a catalyst by promoting programs that facilitate stress reduction. An example is the Singereni Collieries Company, which undertook a program to educate the wives of the miners on the importance of eating after consumption of alcohol. This program prevented ill health in the miners. Later, the company organised a program to educate the miners on the dangers of consuming alcohol. Although these programs were initially misunderstood, they later proved to be very effective.
- **Quality of work life:** This concept has been increasingly recognised in recent years. It involves improving the working conditions and other internal and external aspects of work life. Providing good housing facilities and living conditions, social and recreational facilities, training and development of employees for overall development of human resources in the organisation and the country will also promote the quality of work life.

Stress is a multi faceted phenomenon. The cause and effect relationship in stress is not a direct one, as it is a qualitative psychological concept. Moreover, individuals overlook the symptoms of stress until they experience a physiological breakdown. They often have unhealthy habits and lifestyles, which are difficult, but not impossible to change. Moreover, in large organisations functioning in a competitive and dynamic environment, organisational redesign, job redesign and administrative reorientation are more theoretical than practical. Personal strategies sound good theoretically, but often lack implementation. Hence, stress management needs to be taken very seriously by both the individual and the organisation.

STRESS-FREE WORKING

It has been pointed out earlier that mild to moderate levels of stress can lead to a positive performance and is in fact good for an organisation. However, the negative consequences of stress always outweigh the positive ones. Thus, it is generally agreed that both the management and the individual should take stress reduction seriously. The individual's responsibility is always greater than the organisation's responsibility, as 'protecting one's health is really an individual's responsibility'. Organisations can help by developing certain programs for stress reduction, but theoretical management of stress and practical management are really two different things. Most individual techniques relate to the personality of individuals, and require them to sacrifice the concept of 'self' and come out of their comfort zones. Thus, it is not easy to persuade individuals to adopt strategies of stress reduction. Creating a stress free environment requires a thorough investigation of the stressors, understanding, analysing the implications, appraising the costs and benefits and above all eliciting commitment to the programs through changing attitudes. The stressors and the related techniques that help us in understanding the creation of a stress-free environment are given below.

Individual stressors	**Stress management**	**Organisational stressors**	**Stress management**
Family problems	Family counseling	Demands of the task and role	Job redesign and role clarification
Economic problems	Increased earning potential	Inconsistent structure of the organisation, process and functions	Redesign of organisational structure
Personality characteristics	Personality development	Square peg in a round hole	Redesign recruitment and selection policy
Inability to cope with the demands on one's time	Time management	Goal ambiguity	Goal feedback
Suffering from lowered self-esteem and lack of recognition	Democratic and participative management	Role ambiguity	Role redesign
Aloofness and lack of social support	Promotion of informal groups	Corporate policies	Development of sound organisational culture
Conflict among employees	Development of interpersonal communication	Physical conditions	Redesigning the organisational climate
Physical disorders	Counselling on dietary habits	Economic problems	Restructuring pay and promotion policies
Inability to communicate and aggression	Self-awareness, behavioural self-control, and cognitive therapy.	Communication	Transactional analysis
Problems of concentration	Relaxation, Neuro Linguistic Programming (NLP).	Career ambiguity	Career planning

SUMMARY

Stress management is of paramount importance in modern organisational settings. It requires input from both the individual and the management of the organisation. Individual management techniques are superior to organisational management techniques. Certain individual management techniques are time management, physical management, psychological management, yogic management, social management, and self-awareness management and interpersonal management. Although management of stress is mainly the responsibility of the individual, the role of organisations cannot be undermined. Organisations follow techniques such as proper selection and placement policies, goal setting, job enrichment and job design, role clarity, communication and counseling, career planning and development, democratic leadership, organisational climate and wellness programs. Creating a stress-free environment requires diagnosis and analysis of the stressors. It aims at changing the attitude of the employees. However, it should be remembered that theoretical and practical stress management are two different things, because most techniques require one to sacrifice their personal comfort. However, stress management is not impossible.

Key words

- **Behavioural self control:** Self-introspection to bring about self-awareness in an individual, to promote proper behaviour.
- **Cognitive therapy:** Knowing one's own emotions and releasing anxiety and tension by developing an understanding of the reasons causing stress by the process of self-observation.
- **Counseling:** The exchange of ideas and views in a free and fair manner.
- **Goal feedback:** Continuously eliciting a response from employees regarding the understanding of organisational goals.
- **Meditation:** Sitting silently and watching one's thoughts.
- **Quality of working life:** Improving working conditions and other internal and external aspects of one's working environment.
- **Relaxation:** Keeping the mind in a state of tranquility through meditation, hypnosis and biofeedback.
- **Self awareness management:** Identification, understanding and analysis of one's own skills, capacities, limitations and defects.
- **Time management:** Planning and making optimum use of the available time.
- **Yogic management:** Practicing various *yogasanas* under the supervision of a guru.

Exercise on time management:

(Please write here how your day is spent time-wise)

05.00am-053.0am :..

05.30am-06.00am :..

06.00am-06.30am :..

06.30am-07.00am :..

07.00am-07.30am :..

07.30am-08.00am :..

08.00am-08.30am :..

08.30am-09.00am :..

09.00am-09.30am :..

09.30am-10.00am :..

10.00am-10.30am :..

10.30am-11.00am :..

11.00am-11.30am :..

11.30am-12.00pm :..

12.00pm-12.30pm :..

12.30pm-01.00pm :..

01.00pm-01.30pm :..

01.30pm-02.00pm :..

02.00pm-02.30pm :..

02.30pm-03.00pm :..

03.00pm-03.30pm :..

03.30pm-04.00pm :..

04.00pm-04.30pm :..

04.30pm-05.00pm :..

05.00pm-05.30pm :..

05.30pm-06.00pm :..

06.00pm-06.30pm :...

06.30pm-07.00pm :...

07.00pm-07.30pm :...

07.30pm-08.00pm :...

08.00pm-08.30pm :...

08.30pm-09.00pm :...

09.00pm-09.30pm :...

09.30pm-10.00pm :...

10.00pm-10.30pm :...

10.30pm-11.00pm :...

Real time exercise for managing your time effectively:

There are a number of tools for managing your time properly. A simple but very effective one is to write a list of activities to be done on any day and prioritise them based on the importance and realisation of goals. All urgent things need not be important things, and even after putting in a full day's hard work, one may not be happy, as the most important task is still pending. The following exercise will help you not only to organise your day-to-day work but also help you to focus on important things over urgent and not important things.

Please write down 10 things you are required to do in the coming 24-48hours, write all the things whether they are important or not so important.

In a particular day you may have less than 10 or more than 10 things to do, but spend about 15 minutes either at the end of the day or in the morning before you go to work to write them down. Now label them from A to F based on their priority:

A. The most important thing. If not done you have to face serious consequences, now or in the future. Should be done immediately.

B. Important, but not as important as 'A'. If not done you have to face minor consequences. Should not be done if 'A' is pending.

C. There are no consequences, these things have to be done and are part of routine day-to-day work.

D. These are the things that can be delegated to others. You have to assign this work to somebody else so that you will have enough time to do 'A's & 'B's.

E. These are things, which can be eliminated all together. You wrote them out of habit or they are no longer relevant.

F. At the end of assigning the priorities, you are left with As, Bs and Cs to do. You may have more than one in each or one category. Just assign a numeral based on the priority within As, Bs and Cs, e.g., A_1, A_2, A_3, B_1, B_2, etc....

Now you have come to the end of this exercise, and should get down to the actual execution of the tasks. Start with the activity A_1, and do not jump to the next activity until that is finished. If you follow this scheme, you will arrive at the Cs.

37. ORGANISATIONAL CHANGE

This chapter enables you:

- *To define and understand the nature of organisational change*
- *To analyse the factors that drive organisational changes*
- *To distinguish between the various types of changes that occur in organisations*
- *To explain the behaviour of employees towards change in an organisation*
- *To suggest management strategies to overcome employees' resistance to change*
- *To understand the process of introducing change in a large organisation*

The structure of the chapter is as follows:

- Introduction
- Definition of organisational change
- Drivers of organisational change
  - External drivers
  - Internal drivers
- Types of changes
- Behavioural management of organisational changes: Resistance to change
- Strategies of change management
- Introducing change in organisational settings
- Summary
- Key words

CHAPTER 37

Organisational Change

INTRODUCTION

Change is the order of the day. It is often said that only change is permanent. Change is natural to a human being, and changes are very common in nature. Organisations are no exception to this. Organisations change according to the environment. Organisations should welcome the phenomenon and adapt to changes occurring in its internal and external environment.

DEFINITION OF ORGANISATIONAL CHANGE

Change is dis-equilibrium in the current status. As change is an abstract concept, the following definitions clarify the concept.

According to **Glueck,** *'Change is to make the enterprise different in some way in order to achieve its objectives'.*

Darwin Cartwright defined change as *'A dynamic process. It is an attempt to distinguish sharply as possible the actions and reactions of a force'.*

According to **Fleishman, Harris** and **Bunt**, *'Change is remolding the whole system of relationships in an organization in an attempt to bring effective goal realisation'.*

Thomas and **Bennis** defined change as, *'The deliberate design and implementation of a structural innovation, a new policy, or goal, or a change in operating philosophy, climate, and style'.*

Change in an organisation is alteration of the existing roles, authority, responsibility and accountability of individuals to bring about more order and environmental accountability. Changes in an organisation bring about a change in the employees working in the organisation. It may also refer to a change in the physical structure of the organisation.

The nature of organisational change is explained below:

(1) Change is the result of some forces from both outside or inside the organisation.

(2) It is inevitable and occurs in all parts of the organisation, at all times during the life cycle of an organisation, which is continuous.

(3) Change is interdependent. Change in one part of an organisation brings about changes in other parts.

(4) It differs in its intensity and degree.

(5) Organisations have to accept change.

Since an organisation has no option but to change, it has to formulate strategies and long term plans to bring changes into the enterprise. Therefore managers have to analyse the causes and consequences of change, to be able to implement them effectively.

DRIVERS OF ORGANISATIONAL CHANGE

The drivers influencing change in an organisation can be external or internal. They are described below.

External drivers

External factors of change are those factors that are outside the control of an organisation. It is seldom possible to modify these factors. These external forces to a large extent influence the ability of an organisation to procure and provide resources. These factors include technology, markets, competition, economic growth and development, availability of labour, managers, finance, the government, five year plans, government policies, financial and fiscal policies, laws and regulations, social factors such as fashions, attitudes, assumptions, prescriptions and behaviour of people, value system, culture, ethical code of conduct, political changes etc. Some of the important forces are given below.

(a) **Technology:** Technology is the essence of any organisation. Ever since the industrial revolution technology has become a dynamic variable due to continued research, faster communication, improved methods and processes of production, material handling, methods of cost reduction and control etc. These improvements have resulted in significant changes in technology. A change in technology, followed by a change in an organisation's processes, goals, plans, policies, strategies and structure is very common today. For instance the introduction of computers has totally modified the structures of many large enterprises besides leading to a change in decision making, delegation, communication and control systems. They have created the need for training in computer skills. Changes in technology are the most important source of organisational change.

(b) **Economic factors:** Economic factors include prices, demand and supply, competition, market segments, distribution systems, availability of finance and rates of interest. They also include certain other macro factors like general increase in costs, scarcity of resources, growth of national income, per capita income, GNP, NNP, industrial production, government spending, labour supply, productivity etc.

A change in any one of these aspects significantly affects the general planning, cost structure, production planning and control, marketing methods, price determination, advertisement policies, physical distribution policies, capital structure, cost of capital and financial policies such as divided policy, mergers and consolidations etc. For example, a general rise in inflation brings about an upward change in the prices of all inputs, so without an upward revision in the price, it would become unprofitable to run the organisation.

(c) **Social and ethical factors:** Social factors contributing to change include aspirations, beliefs, attitudes, expectations of people, tastes and ability to consume, educational levels and degree of intelligence. The other factors are customs, traditions, culture, history of society, group norms and behaviour, levels of satisfaction, safety and security needs of people, need for love and affection, self-actualisation needs, and growth of population and division of labour in the society. Religion, community, caste system, age distribution, sex, income levels and consumption habits, language etc., are some of the other factors to be taken into consideration.

These social and ethical changes lead to changes in organisations. For instance, changes in managerial styles, upsurge of trade unions and informal groups bring about changes in managerial structure and levels, quality and quantity of production, techniques of decision-making, and degree of centralisation. Concern for workers safety, welfare, assumption of social responsibility and its effects, marketing practices, personnel practices are some of the changes that take place in organisations due to changes in social and ethical factors.

(d) **Political and legal factors:** Political factors represent the political behaviour of the society. Legal factors relate to the general framework of legislation that guides the actions and behaviour of people in society. The strength of the political party in power determines the legal framework in any nation. Political factors include administrative systems of the government, individual ministries, representation of political parties in the government, capacity to frame policies reflecting the government's fiscal, financial, foreign policies, and licensing policies. Legal forces include legislation passed by the central and state government such as financial and taxation laws, general laws, labour laws, trade laws, foreign laws and other legislation and general legislative framework. These factors have an enormous impact right from the determination of corporate objectives, goals, plans, policies and strategies of the enterprise, price fixations, import and export of goods, procurement of capital, depreciation policies, dividend policies, to general trade pacts and agreement etc. For instance, in the 1990s' the Congress party in power brought about liberalisation, privatisation and globalisation policies. Most of the organisations have had to change their structures by down-sizing the organisation, resulting in enforced voluntary retirement schemes in many organisations.

Hence, unless managers take care of these factors, they tend to retard the progress of an organisation.

Internal drivers

Internal forces consist of factors within control of the management. These factors can be effectively modified through executive actions.

(a) **Organisational structure:** Organisational structure clearly defines the role of every individual member. While clarity in the definition results in improved functioning, deficiencies considerably increase chances of change due to frequent redefining and redesigning of roles.

(b) **Personnel:** Continued inflow and outflow of managerial and non-managerial personnel often causes change. These changes results in a change in attitude and behaviour of employees, authority, status relationships, informal group relationships and adaptation of different styles of leadership etc. Therefore, changes in personnel also bring about organisational changes. For example in one particular organisation, a new recruitment policy totally changed the structure of the union, making it stronger and counter management.

(c) **Adoption of new objectives and strategies:** As a result of the dynamic environment around an organisation, every organisation is compelled to modify its objectives, goals and strategies. Either external or internal forces may act as the impetus for modification.

(d) **Psychological factors:** Psychological factors are a combination of attitudes and behaviour of employees, their values, thinking, level of satisfaction and other factors relating to society. All these factors collectively reflect in the group dynamic process, which is critical in enhancing or detracting organisational performance. Changes in these variables result in a total change in an organisation. For instance, a persistent feeling of dissatisfaction makes employees develop a poor attitude towards the organisation's climate and culture, leadership, communication and the general management of organisation, leading to demands for changes.

(e) **Training and development:** Another strong internal impetus is executive training and development activities. A natural desire to try new methods and techniques learnt during training period necessitate a change in existing methods, procedures, authority, responsibility, status, etc. This automatically accelerates the process of change. Suppose, for example that the managers are sent for an executive development program on democratisation of decision making. After the program it is natural that they will encourage the participation of their subordinates. This will make their subordinates learn the skills necessary for assisting and participating in the decision making process.

TYPES OF CHANGES

Changes are a natural, continuous and inevitable phenomenon. They have a tremendous impact on the behaviour of people in an organisation. Hence, a successful strategy to manage change requires an understanding of the types of changes. The following discussion provides an explanation of these changes.

(i) **Evolutionary or revolutionary changes**: Evolutionary changes are also known as gradual changes. They occur gradually and slowly over a period of time in the life of an organisation, and automatically become a part of the organisation's process without the employees realising the changes are being implemented, so by the time employee understands that a change has taken place, it has been adopted by them. Hence such changes are seldom resisted. Instances of changes in production, marketing and finance strategies are very common in organisations. They are accepted as part of the job responsibilities.

Revolutionary changes are radical or emotional changes. They are implemented rapidly and suddenly. It is not possible to forecast such changes and prepare plans or strategies to implement them. These changes are brought in immediately due to abrupt changes in the environment. For instance changes in demand, supply, price, competition, consumer tastes, fashions are sudden in nature and often difficult to forecast beforehand.

(ii) **Planned or unplanned changes:** Planned changes are strategic changes. They are the result of deliberate actions of the management to make the enterprise different by introducing new technologies, personnel, materials, strategies etc. These changes are made in a phased manner. Increasing the plant capacity, automation of the production process, expansion into new markets etc., are some examples of planned changes. On the other hand, unplanned changes are brought in without any prior planning. They are introduced for a short period. Sometimes these changes are made to test reactions to a long-term change. In a planned change the goals and objectives are determined, alternative strategies are investigated to find the best course of action. After careful analysis and thinking the path of action is developed and implemented systematically. Hence, changes, which occur scientifically, are not resisted. However, unplanned changes are often resisted.

(iii) **Pro-active or reactive changes:** These are psychological notions of change. Pro-active changes are seen as favorable changes that are necessary and desirable for the growth and development of the organisation. These changes are brought in before the actual demand for change. Hence they will be more scientifically thought out. Reactive changes are viewed as unfavorable and unnecessary changes, thus they are treated as negative, undesirable elements and are frequently resisted. Consider the example of changes initiated due to liberalisation, privatisation and globalisation. They were reactive in the initial stages, and hence there was large-scale resistance to them at the time of implementation. Nowadays most Indian organisations have adopted a proactive approach to these changes and thus resistance to them is low.

(iv) **Directive or participative changes:** Directive changes are coercive and imposed by an authoritarian management. On the other hand participative changes are widely discussed and brought to the notice of subordinates well in advance. They are developed through effective involvement and participation of all the concerned personnel. While directive changes are often resisted, employees have a positive attitude and commitment towards participative changes.

(v) **Minor and major changes:** The former is an attempt to change a sub system of the organisation, while the latter is intended to change all the systems of the organisation.

MANAGEMENT OF ORGANISATIONAL CHANGES

People have a natural tendency to resist change. Most changes are resisted due to poor understanding of the implications of the change. Unfortunately, neither the management nor the personnel have the patience to share their knowledge adequately to develop a strong psychological cognitive base. So managing changes is not to be considered as a physical process but rather management of behaviour. Any management strategy of change has to determine the reasons for the resistance. Management of organisational changes is presented hereunder. It is divided into two sections *viz.*, resistance to change and change management strategies.

RESISTANCE TO CHANGE

Any organism not responding to the changing environment faces negative issues due to ill effects on its survival and growth. In spite of this, resistance to change is not uncommon. Resistance to change comes from three groups, namely, (a) individuals, (b) groups and (c) the organisation as a whole.

Individual resistance to change: Personnel in an organisation often resist change due to certain reasons, which affect them individually. They are:

1. **Economic reasons**: Economic reasons are closely related to monetary remuneration. People perceive change as painful and threatening if it brings even a nominal reduction in their salary. The reasons include loss of monetary remuneration due to reduction of work, displacement of labour by technology resulting in loss of employment, demotions, loss of other incentives etc. Even today, in India, loss of monetary emoluments and loss of employment are the major reasons behind certain political parties who organise demonstrations to resist the moves of the governments to introduce changes in public sector enterprises.

2. **Displacement of skills:** A common resistance to change stems from anxiety that the skills possessed by a person are obsolete. This is more pertinent in the case of technological changes. A technological change normally calls for a certain amount of new operating and technical skills. The perceived effect is two-fold. A possible displacement of employees by technically competent persons resulting in loss of employment, or compelling the employee to acquire the required skills through education and training. While the former is a threat to

the primary need, the latter upsets the existing status of activities. Therefore, changes are resisted. One of the major reasons the employees' unions advanced when technology was introduced in the banking and insurance sectors in India, was substitution of human beings by technology, resulting in loss of livelihood.

3. **Personal reasons:** Personal reasons for resistance to change are mostly due to fears of how the change will affect them. Some of the well advanced reasons are:
   (a) **Egoistic:** A change disturbing the equilibrium of the relationship existing between authority, responsibility and accountability may result in loss of authority and shifting of responsibility. This can have a major impact on the ego of an individual causing a tendency to deny these changes.
   (b) **Ignorance of the effect of the changes:** This is related to the feeling that inadequate or no information has been provided to the employees, who will be affected by the changes. A properly conceived and clearly manifested change is communicated to each and every member of the organisation, which opens a way for anticipating the possible effects of the change and preparing for it. However, poorly communicated, untimely changes and changes for which little time is allowed for adjustment leads to the possibility of speculation about future effects. This obviously results in ignorance and possible resistance to the change.
   (c) **Desire for status quo:** Certain individuals fear disturbance in status-quo due to lack of understanding, fear of adjustment, lack of knowledge to adapt, inadequate time to shift to a new situation, and inability to accept the consequences of change. Hence, they are distrustful of changes and strongly object to them.

Group resistance to change: Groups in organisations develop certain norms of behaviour and a code of conduct, which are strictly adhered to by all members of the group. Besides groups also participate in protecting individuals against unfavorable changes. Thus groups resist changes that are a potential threat to these social relationships.

Organisational resistance: Organisations are open dynamic systems, which continuously interact with the outside environment. Any change in this environment is seen as a potential threat to the survival and growth of the organisation, and hence, may be resisted by the organisation. Reasons for organisational resistance are as follows:

1. **Financial implications:** Financial implications include limitations on resources and sunk costs. Any change requires modification in either the physical structure of the organisation or human resources. These modifications require finances. Scarcity of finances places a limitation on the adoption of changes resulting into resistance. Sunk costs represent the costs incurred by the various production facilities, physical structure, wages and salaries etc. They consist of time, labour and money spent over the years to bring about the present status of the organisation. Sunk costs are very difficult to avoid and seldom easy to recover immediately. Organisations with relatively higher sunk costs resist changes more than other organisations.

2. **Difficulty in designing new structures:** Structuring involves the process of defining

authority, responsibility, delegation, design of communication and control systems etc. Revamping the existing structure requires time and energy. In addition, there may be resistance from all sides resulting in complicated problem of industrial relations. Therefore, changes are normally resisted by organisations.

3. **Value system in an organisation:** The value system in an organisation comprises established internal precedents, procedures developed over a long period etc. These values are normally adhered to by an organisation in all its important decisions. For instance, reservation for internal personnel, in internal promotions. Changes that counter the existing value system are strongly resisted by an organisation.

MANAGEMENT STRATEGIES TO MANAGE CHANGE

Most reasons for resistance to change are not difficult to manage and can be overcome. The various strategies adopted to overcome resistance are discussed below.

1. **Implicit or explicit coercion:** This is the traditional and negative method of dealing with resistance to change. Changes can be brought in by forcing the people to accept them by threatening them, either explicitly or implicitly. Although this method is useful to overcome resistance to immediate changes, it has a negative impact on the psychology of employees. If it is applied unnecessarily, it results in a greater resistance.
2. **Support by top management:** This includes technical, facilitative and emotional support. Technical support is an attempt to remove barriers relating to a technical change, for instance providing the appropriate tools and materials, giving technical advice, imparting technical training etc. Facilitative support deals with removing organisational and structural blocks, which come in the way of implementing plans, policies and strategies of change. It includes creating an environment for defining and redefining goals, communication, mutual coordination, appropriate delegation and participation, education and training to support personal growth etc. Lastly, emotional support is concerned with psychological help to subordinates. Top management and the full managerial team should try to inculcate a feeling in the employees that the changes have been brought in for their benefit. They have to make efforts to reduce employees' anxiety, stress and work tensions besides developing a compassionate view towards them. This can be achieved through attentive listening, rendering help in solving certain problems, mutual understanding etc.
3. **Communication:** Dissemination of information relating to change beforehand can be of great help in reducing resistance to change. Establishing effective communication channels across the organisation removes barriers due to inadequate or distorted information, misapprehensions, rumours, false news about change etc. In addition, the communication gap can be reduced by arranging workshops and seminars to provide information, ascertain the employees' opinions, ideas and any other valuable information that facilitates accommodation of change. In this regard, communication through the grapevine can be used to reduce resistance to change.

4. **Participation:** Participation of the concerned personnel in decisions relating to change and involving the employees in the process of implementing change makes them feel that their involvement is essential and the changes have been brought in for their benefit.

   Another frequently used method of participation is negotiation. Negotiating the decisions on change with trade union representatives and other informal groups is a relatively easy method to avoid resistance to change.

5. **Training:** Training the employees is an effective method of reducing resistance. In this method a group of people, drawn from various levels and departments of the organisation, are allowed to discuss any problem relating to the change. This sort of training enables managers to gain greater insight into the problems associated with the change. Hence, they can develop plans and strategies to deal with its resistance.

ORGANISATIONAL DEVELOPMENT

According to Bennis, organisational development is a response to a complex educational strategy intended to change the beliefs, attitudes values and structure of the organisation, so that it can better adapt to new technologies, markets and challenges and the rapid rate of the change itself. A systematic effort of organisational development is a long reaching approach to reducing resistance to change. This involves familiarising employees with the change and attempting to implement the proposed changes.

Although organisational development programs are time consuming and costly, according to Breton and Scott they help in solving problems, improve communication, enhance skills in interpersonal and group relations, clarify management goals and lead to greater decentralisation of authority. Therefore, the use of this technique needs care and diligence. Moreover selective use goes a long way in introducing changes successfully.

SUMMARY

Change is a disturbance in the existing status. It is natural, inevitable and always present. Every organisation experiences change during its lifetime to some degree. Thus organisations have to adapt themselves to the dynamics of change, otherwise they will face problems. Change in organisations is forced from both inside and outside the organisation. The forces that force organisational change are known as drivers. External drivers are technology, economic factors, social and ethical factors and political and legal factors, and they are outside the control of the management. Internal drivers are within the control of the management, they comprise the structure of the organisation, personnel, and adoption of new objectives and strategies, psychological factors and training and development of employees.

Organisations experience slow and gradual changes called evolutionary changes. However certain changes occur suddenly and arise out of emotional elements. While the former are seldom resisted, the latter are usually vehemently resisted. In order to improve human acceptance, organisations should plan ahead strategically, yet unplanned changes are not uncommon, and these are usually resisted. Every organisation reacts to change in some way or the other. However today Indian organisations are reacting proactively to the changes.

Just as change is inevitable, human resistance is also inescapable. Probably there is not a single change that has been adopted without resistance. However, ultimately human beings accept change as the nature of things. Thus, organisations have to understand human nature to effectively deal with change. The reasons for resistance to change fall into three categories, namely individual, group and organisational. Economic reasons, displacement skills, ego, and ignorance of the effect and desire for status quo are personal reasons. Group resistance comes from the structure and status of the group, leadership, norms, and group cohesion. Organisational resistance is due to financial implications, difficulty in designing a new structure and an inconsistent organisational value system. In spite of these reasons, organisations cannot overlook changes. At the same time the organisation cannot overlook human resistance. An organisation follows a number of strategies to overcome resistance to change. No single strategy is sufficient to deal with resistance, so organisations use a number of strategies simultaneously to introduce changes effectively. Some of the important strategies are implicit or explicit coercion, support by top management, communication, participation, and training and organisational development. Each of these techniques needs careful understanding of the human element before their use. Properly adopted changes help an organisation to grow and enhance organisational effectiveness.

Key words

- **Evolutionary changes:** Gradual changes occurring over a period of time.
- **Planned changes:** Changes that are introduced in a planned manner through deliberate actions of the management.
- **Proactive changes:** Changes brought in before the demand for change.
- **Reactive changes:** Changes brought in as a reaction of a force for change.
- **Revolutionary changes:** Changes that occur suddenly and cannot be forecast.
- **Unplanned changes:** Sudden changes introduced for a short period of time.

38. ORGANISATIONAL CULTURE

This chapter enables you:

- *To define and understand the meaning of organisational culture*
- *To understand the importance of understanding culture*
- *To understand organisational climate and distinguish it from organisational culture*
- *To classify the various dimensions used in describing organisational culture*
- *To distinguish between strong and weak organisational culture*
- *To understand certain indicators of organisational culture*
- *To appreciate the factors that influence the development of organisational culture*
- *To examine the methods for managing the changing cultures in a global context*
- *To explain the approaches used for building a new organisational culture*
- *To know the process of socialisation*

The structure of the chapter is as follows:

- Introduction
- Definition of organisational culture
- Significance of organisational culture
- Organisational climate and organisational culture
- Dimensions of organisational culture
- Drivers of organisational culture
- Managing global cultural dimensions
- Building an organisation
- Socialisation
- Summary
- Key words

CHAPTER 38

Organisational Culture

INTRODUCTION

Humans are social beings. Society plays a major role in shaping the culture of human beings. As they enter an organisation they are bound by the culture of the organisation, but the actual behaviour required in organisations will be learnt only after becoming an employee of the organisation. Organisational culture is the practice of shaping human behaviour in order to facilitate smooth interaction between employees, which enhances the effectiveness of the organisation. The culture of an organisation is influenced by the nation's culture. Multinational companies that establish branches in various foreign locations have to adhere to the native cultures in order to utilise local human resources. At the same time they can also influence people to work according to their own organisational culture. Thus building organisational culture is both proactive and reactive. Socialisation is critical to shape human beings to the culture of the organisation. It changes an individual's attitude so that he or she will accept and follow the culture of the organisation. In the context of globalisation, organisational culture is extremely important.

DEFINITION OF ORGANISATIONAL CULTURE

Culture as generally understood implies a set of code of conduct, which regulates human life. It is a combination of factors learnt through interaction with the environment during the development and growth stages in an individual's life. Thus, the terms used in the description of culture are values, beliefs, ideas, perceptions, preferences, and concept of morality, code of conduct and expected ways of behaviour of people of the society. The culture of an organisation emerges from the culture of the country in which the organisation exists. It will also be influenced by the culture of the country to which a majority of the employees belong. It is possible to group countries together based on certain culture attributes such as differentiation, value orientation, assertiveness etc. For instance certain countries like Great Britain, Australia, Canada, Netherlands and New Zealand value individualism and give importance to material possessions, whilst countries like Japan, Colombia, Pakistan, Singapore, Venezuela, and the Philippines lay emphasis on the value of collectivism and relationships. The following definitions help in providing an understanding of the term organisational culture.

Edgar Schein defined organisational culture as *'the pattern of basic assumptions invented, discovered or developed by a given group as it learns to cope with its problems of external adaptation and internal integration – that has worked well enough to be considered valuable and, therefore, to be taught to new members as the correct way to perceive, think and feel in relation to those problems'*.

Organisational culture refers to *'the system of shared meaning held by the organization's members that distinguishes the organization from other organizations'*. **Robbins.**

Killmann defined organisational culture as *'the philosophies, ideologies, values, assumptions, beliefs, expectations, attitudes and norms that knit an organisation together and are shared by its employees'*.

Certain other definitions are also worth mentioning here.

Corporate culture consists of *'the normal values and unwritten rules of conduct of an organisation as well as management styles, priorities, beliefs and inter personal behavior that prevail. Together they create a climate that influences how people will communicate, plan and make decisions.'*

Examination of the above definitions reveals the following characteristics of organisational climate:

1. Organisational culture is a common ideology of employees in an organisation.
2. Organisations are distinguished based on the organisational culture.
3. Organisational culture is a set of unwritten rules of conduct that guide the actions of the employees.
4. It influences the effectiveness of the organisation and the employees' efficiency.
5. New employees learn the culture of the organisation as the work in the organisation.

According to Reilly and others (Robbins, p. 580) the following are the primary characteristics of organisational culture. They can be abbreviated as STOP AT A INN.

1. **Stability:** The degree to which organisational activities maintain a status quo with respect to growth.

2. **Team orientation:** The degree to which work activities are organised around teams rather than individuals.
3. **Outcome orientation:** The degree to which the management focuses on results or outcomes rather than on the techniques and processes used to achieve these outcomes.
4. **People orientation:** The degree to which management decisions take into consideration the effect of outcomes on people within the organisation.
5. **Attention to detail:** The degree to which employees are expected to exhibit precision, analysis, and attention to detail.
6. **Aggressiveness:** The degree to which people are aggressive and competitive rather than easygoing.
7. **Innovation and risk taking:** The degree to which employees are encouraged to be innovative and take risks.

There are a number of factors in the organisational culture of an enterprise. Some aspects are: performance standards, performance evaluations, expectations of various people, communication among employees, interpersonal relations, interpersonal trust, mutually shared purpose, leadership support, participation, socialisation, quality of work environment, customer support, Customer Relationship Management (CRM), and social responsibility.

Case study 38.1: Which matters most, individual or organisational culture?

This typical experience of two organisations and the people involved, show how individual culture differs from that of the organisation. A customer approached the branch manager of a bank, with a request to clarify whether a certain cheque had been encashed by him. He explained that the said cheque had been received by one of his employees and handed over to him, but that he could not remember the incident. It was a simple request but the manager instead of attending to the customer immediately made him wait while processing certain routine transactions. Finally the vouchers were called for and it was verified that the cheque had been encashed, but everything was done with ill humour. In fact, giving information when a customer approaches is the responsibility of any organisation. When the same customer approached the branch manager of his Life Insurance Company, for a copy of the charter of the company, the branch manager went out of his way to help him. Organisations have to inculcate customer responsive cultures in their employees, as they reflect the culture of the organisation.

SIGNIFICANCE OF ORGANISATIONAL CULTURE

Organisational culture determines the way employees in the organisation perform various roles. While a strong and positive organisational culture does not necessarily ensure an organisation's success, a weak organisational culture will surely kill it. If properly nurtured, however a strong organisational culture promotes a positive performance in the employees. The significance of organisational culture can be understood from the following.

1. **Bonding:** Organisational culture creates a strong sense of bonding between the organisation and its employees. An employee's willingness to perform in an organisation depends on the internal environment and good interpersonal relationships, which are determined by the organisational culture.
2. **Sense of identity:** Employees identify with the organisation based on the culture. For example, employees working in organisations like Tata, Infosys and Wipro express pride in their organisations. Such identification makes them committed to the success of the enterprise, and willing to sacrifice their individual interests for the sake of organisational interests.
3. **Attitude development:** Employees joining an organisation have different various backgrounds, interests, education, etc. Although the HR departments take care to select the appropriate candidates, perfect selection is a myth. Once they join the organisation employees develop a positive work attitude towards the organisation, if the culture of the organisation is such that it has a positive attitude towards its employees.

In fact organisational culture performs a number of functions, the list provided above is not exhaustive. It develops a positive personality, motivates employees, provides satisfaction, enhances morale, develops good interpersonal relations among the employees, provides a congenial environment, enthusiasm to work, and positive thinking, which are all qualities of a good citizen. Thus sound organisational culture not only benefits a single organisation but helps to build a better nation.

ORGANISATIONAL CULTURE AND ORGANISATIONAL CLIMATE

The terms organisational culture and organisational climate are used synonymously and interchangeably. Sometimes, organisational climate is used to refer to the physical climate at the work place, but even the physical work climate can be enriched with the help of the psychological climate. For example even in a hot climate, if the interpersonal relations are positive, leadership style is supportive, ego is recognised, the climate becomes cool and healthy to work. So organisational climate refers to the psychological climate created in the minds of employees rather than the physical climate experienced by them. Bowditch and Buono stated that '*organisational climate is an indicator of whether beliefs and expectations are being fulfilled.*' He states that '*organisational culture is concerned with the nature of beliefs and expectation about the organisational life created in the minds of employees.*' According to Campbell, '*organisational climate is a set of attributes specific to a particular organization that may be induced from the way that organization deals with its members and its environment. For the individual members within the organization, climate takes the form of a set of attitudes and experiences, which describe the organization in terms of both static characteristics and behavior outcome and outcome-outcome contingencies*'. Forehand and Gilmer defined organisational climate as '*a set of characteristics that describe an organization, distinguish it from other organizations, are relatively enduring over time and influence the behavior of people in it*'. Some of the indicators of organisational climate are job specifications, role analysis and description, organisational structure, communication chain, leadership style, performance evaluation, innovations etc. Likert developed a profile of the organisational climate with the help of six variables, namely decision making, leadership styles, motivation, communication, goal setting and controls.

Distinctions between organisational culture and organisational climate are shown in Table 38.1.

Table 38.1: Distinction between organisational culture & organisational climate

Variable	**Organisational climate**	**Organisational culture**
Concept	Employees' perception of the organisation	The unwritten code of conduct that guides the actions of most of the employees
Measurement	The employees' perception of the organisation at a certain point of time	The employees' perception of the organisation over a longer period of time
Indicators	Job specifications, role analysis and descriptions, organisational structure, communication chain, leadership style, performance evaluation, and innovations	Philosophies, ideologies, values, assumptions, beliefs, expectations, attitudes and norms
Creation	Created in a short span of time by changing the factors that influence it	Created by changing the attitudes of employee. It requires a long time

Organisational climate and culture also have comparable characteristics. Both the concepts are abstract and intangible. Their existence or otherwise are understood by the general perception of the employees and others who deal with the organisation. Both distinguish a particular organisation from other organisations. They represent the long lasting quality of internal processes, but at the same time both organisational climate and culture are multi-dimensional. They can both have a positive and negative impact. Various physical, material and psychological symbols indicate organisational climate and culture.

According to Hodgetts organisational climate can be understood as an iceberg where the tip of the iceberg appears outside in a smaller plane, and the root is fathomless. Overt and covert factors indicate and influence organisational climate. They are shown in Figure 38.1.

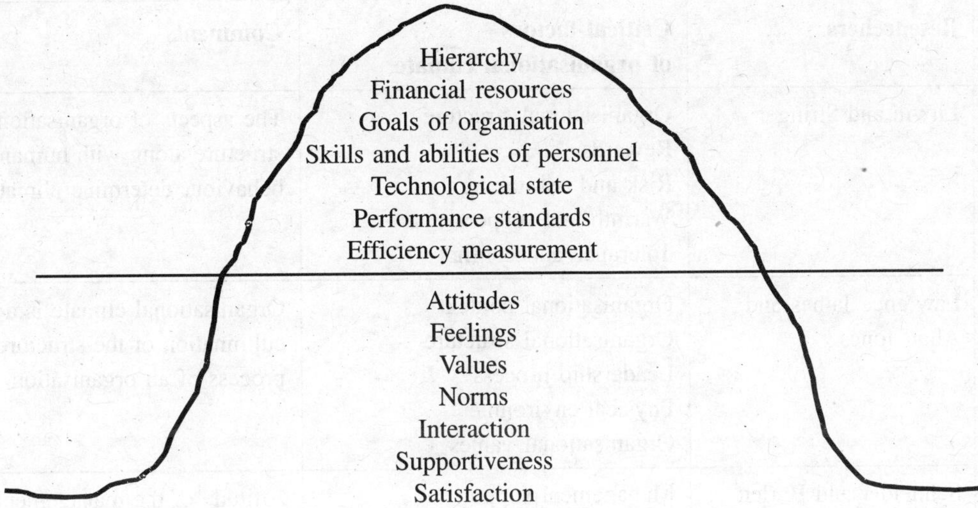

Figure 38.1: Overt and covert factors of organisational climate

Figure 38.1 indicates that the overt factors appear outside, in the tip of the iceberg and employees show their feelings relating to these factors. They are related to the structure and process of the organisation. They are tangible and measurable. Covert factors relate to human feelings and behaviour. They are qualitative and indirectly measurable. They are known only when expressed by the employee. They reside in the minds of employees yet influence the climate and functioning of the organisation. So they are fathomless. Table 38.2 summarises the various factors of organisational climate. By understanding these factors managers can identify lapses in their organisational climate and create a congenial climate in their organisations.

Table 38.2: The various factors of organisational climate

No.	Researchers	Critical factors of organisational climate	Comments
1.	Tagiuri	Sense of direction Opportunities for initiative Leadership qualities Interpersonal co-operation Corporate image	Organisational climate reflects in the factors of human psychology and evaluation by others
2.	Katz	Rule orientation Subordinates' characteristics Closeness of supervision Universalism Promotion-achievement orientation	Internal factors of structure and human beings determine organisational climate

No.	Researchers	Critical factors of organisational climate	Comments
3.	Litwin and Stringer	Organisational structure Rewards Risk and risk-taking Warmth and support Tolerance and conflict	The aspects of organisational structure along with human behaviour determine climate
4.	Lawrence James and Allan Jones	Organisational context Organisational structure Leadership process Physical environment Organisational values	Organisational climate is a culmination of the structure and process of an organisation
5.	Schneider and Barlett	Management support Management structure Concern for new recruits Inter agency conflict Agent dependence General satisfaction	Attitude of the management has a profound influence on the climate of the organisation. A positive climate results from positive assumptions regarding people (Theory Y)
6.	Richard M. Hodgetts	Hierarchy Financial resources Goals of organisation Skills and abilities of personnel Technological state Performance standards Measurement of efficiency Attitudes, Feelings, Values, Norms, Interaction, Supportiveness, Satisfaction	Organisational climate is influenced by both overt and covert factors. Covert factors have a greater influence on the climate. Overt factors are influenced by external factors. Covert factors are only influenced by changing the attitude and behaviour of people in the organisation

DIMENSIONS OF ORGANISATIONAL CULTURE

The dimensions that identify organisational culture developed over a period of time. They describe the orientation of employees and management in organisations. Some important dimensions are given below.

1. **Dominant culture:** Robbins described dominant culture as '*the expression of the core values shared by a majority of the organisation's members.*' According to him, core values are the primary or dominant values accepted throughout the organisation. Thus, core values emerge as culture over time. All organisations have a dominant culture, which is followed by a

majority of the employees, and therefore it also influences the other members. For example, it is often observed that although office timings are specified, a majority of the employees arrive a little late and then stay late to complete the work. This is a dominant culture. Even a new employee who joins the organisation and desires to adhere to office timings, tends to ultimately fall into the same pattern.

2. **Sub culture:** The sub units of an organisation form its sub culture. They represent the unique values, beliefs and practices that the sub unit desires to follow. However, sub culture does not override the dominant culture. Various departments and managerial levels define a certain code of conduct that is uniquely applicable to them. This becomes their sub culture. For instance, in banks, even if the other employees leave the office at the specified time, the cashier, accountant and manager remain in office until the cash register is tallied and the cash chest closed. This is a sub culture. It is important to observe here that in some organisations, sub culture develops initially and over a period, it transforms into the dominant culture.
3. **Strong and weak culture:** Strong and weak culture represent the degree of acceptance by the majority of employees. A culture that most agree on and which is widely shared by the organisation's members becomes a strong culture. Strong cultures have greater influence in regulating the behaviour of a larger number of employees, whereas a weak culture does not wield so much influence. Table 38.3 describes the difference between the strong and weak cultures.

Table 38.3: The difference between the strong and weak cultures

	Strong culture	**Weak culture**
1. Meaning	The core values accepted and followed by a large majority of members.	The values that are developed and accepted by a minority of opposition groups.
2. Behavioural impact	Because of its wider acceptability, it significantly influences the behaviour of members	It influences the behaviour of those members who have accepted it. However, it exerts minimal influence but not as much as a strong culture.
3. Turnover	Employees' feeling that the organisation has a strong culture consistent with his values. So employee turnover is less	Employees working in an organisation with a weak culture find inconsistencies due to adoption of different practices by different members. He finds it difficult to adjust and with the result that he prefers to leave the organisation.

	Strong culture	Weak culture
4. Employee commitment	Employees influenced by a strong culture derive satisfaction and develop an identity with the organisation. This leads to high psychological commitment.	A weak culture cannot produce employee identity. Employees are not willing to identify with the organisation. Hence, his commitment is low.
5. Group dynamics	Existence of a strong culture leads to strengthening of highly cohesive groups.	A weak culture cannot keep the members together. So group dissonance develops.
6. Development	A strong culture, resisted by the majority of employees vanishes.	Initially, a weak culture develops slowly within minority groups. When the majority accepts it, it grows and develops into a strong culture.
7. New culture	A strong culture does not often lead to the development of a new culture.	Sometimes the adverse impact of a strong culture reinforces a weak culture. This in turn leads to the formation of a new culture.
8. Adverse impact	A strong culture is not always safe for an organisation. It promotes group thinking and forces the members to resist change and innovations.	A weak culture does not harm the organisation as only a minority follows it. Moreover, it always tries to become a strong culture and hence its adverse impact is less.

4. **Culture and formalisation in organisations:** A strong culture leads to behavioural consistency, which brings predictability and orderliness into the organisation. Thus, a strong culture acts as a set of unwritten rules to regulate employees' behaviour. The management need not worry about the development and implementation of rules. In fact, formalisation is the essence of formal organisations and it aims at controlling and regulating the activities of the employees in an organisation. If a strong culture is against the written rules, a redefinition of the rules takes place, so a strong culture influences and brings new formalisation in organisations.

Although an organisation is a social system that exists in society of a nation, human resources determine the organisational culture. This implies that organisations adapt the national culture. A change in the practices of an organisation takes place according to the cultural practices of the nation. It has been shown that national culture overrides organisational culture.

DRIVERS OF ORGANISATIONAL CULTURE

Organisational culture does not develop spontaneously. It grows over a long period of time. Employees need to develop an understanding of the culture by empathy and introspection. Figure 38.2 shows the factors that lead to the development of organisational culture.

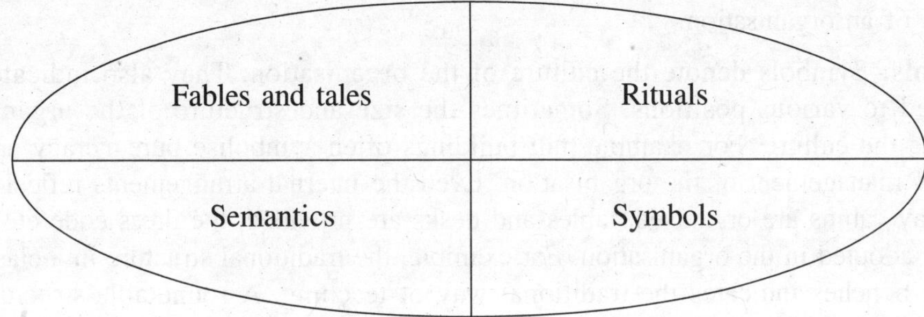

Figure 38.2: Drivers of organisational culture

1. **Fables and tales:** As a child your parents must have told you a number of moral and heroic stories. Many stories are a way to teach values to children. For example, the famous *Panchatantra* tales inculcate moral values. Similarly, a number of stories of the success and failure of an organisation usually exist. These stories relate to a number of organisational practices such as recruitment, selection, criteria for training, transfers, promotions, firing, quality management, decision making process, leadership behaviour, customer relations management, grant of leave, festival advances, facilities, status and are a basis for both old and new employees to understand what kind of behaviour is acceptable or unacceptable in the organisation. For example there are a number of stories about American companies that emphasise the importance of the customer, however most Indian companies do not adhere to this dictum. They have still not placed much emphasis on customer relations and after sales service.
2. **Rituals:** A ritual is a repetitive activity undertaken to remember certain unique events. For example people celebrate wedding anniversaries, birthdays etc., to remember these events, usually by hosting a special party. In the same way organisations also create rituals to reinforce their goals, values, and activities. For example, companies celebrate productivity day, foundation day, awards functions, and annual day. On these days productive employees are rewarded in cash or kind. Foundation day is celebrated to honour the best managers and a party will be thrown when there is a new managing director. Banks have introduced the practice of giving gold coins to employees who have achieved their goals, whereas pharmaceutical companies reward employees who attain their targets with trips abroad. These rituals really emphasise the organisation's performance and reflect organisational culture.
3. **Semantics:** In an organisation a number of terms that reflect the work environment are developed over a period of time. Such terms may relate to the physical facilities, machines, superiors, suppliers, customers, and procedures of recognising other employees and products.

Terms such as 'value oriented organisation', 'high-ended company etc., signify the culture of the organisation. For example, Hindustan Lever labelled shops that sold their products as 'super value stores'. HMT once labelled their watches as 'time keepers of the nation'. HCL branded one of its computers 'busy bee' to denote that it could work continuously without any breakdown. HR personnel often use the term 'no issues' to denote no problem, 'Com skills' to denote communication skills. Such semantics becomes official language in the culture of an organisation.

4. **Symbols:** Symbols denote the culture of the organisation. They also indicate the status attached to various positions. Sometimes the size and structure of the organisation also indicate the culture. For example, tall buildings often symbolise bureaucracy and a narrow span of management of the organisation. Even the internal arrangements reflect the culture. The way cabins are organised, tables and desks are provided, the dress code etc., reflect the culture adopted in the organisation. For example, the traditional structure in a classroom, of a line of benches indicates the traditional way of teaching. A roundtable structure indicates more discussions in the classroom. In some organisations the best sales persons are given laptops, other organisations give employees T-shirts to wear that bear the symbol and name of the organisation. Such things reveal a great deal about the organisation's culture.

Citizens' Charter of Life Insurance Corporation of India Reflecting the Organisation's Culture (as revised 2003)

Vision: To transform ourselves into a competitive financial conglomerate of significance to societies and the Pride of India.

Mission: To ensure and enhance the quality of life of people through financial security by providing products and services of aspired attributes with competitive returns and by rendering resources for economic development..

Values	Culture
• Caring and Courtesy	• Agility
• Initiatives and Innovation	• Adaptability
• Integrity and Transparency	• Collaboration
• Quality and Returns	• Commitment
• Participation and Relationship	• Discipline
• Trustworthiness and Reliability	• Empowerment
	• Sensitivity
	• Excellence

Commitment Statements that Symbolise LIC's Culture

To the Community: We will

- Provide insurance cover and financial security to every insurable segment including socially and economically weaker sections of the society
- Meet its insurance needs in consonance with the changing social and economical environment
- Conduct all aspects of our business keeping in view the interest of the community and the national priorities

To our Customers: We will

- Provide them prompt, efficient and courteous service
- Act as trustees of their funds and invest them to their best advantage
- Conduct our business with utmost economy and on sound business principles
- Build and maintain enduring relationship
- Keep them informed about our products and services etc.

To our Workforce: We will

- Promote a sense of participation and make them partners in progress
- Work towards ensuring their job satisfaction and sense of pride
- Provide an environment and the opportunities for growth to enable them to realize their full potential
- Take steps to develop professional skills to enable them to handle their assignments more efficiently

Standards reflecting LIC Customer Responsive Culture

Fairness in dealing with Customers: We will

- Strive to deal with our customers in an open and transparent manner
- Explain the rationale behind our decisions, consistent with requirements relating to business principles
- Continuously expand our product line and services to afford wider choice
- Waive/allow payment of interest as a measure of compensation wherever service deficiency occurs which is attributable to us

Easy Access to Information for Customers: We will

- Educate the customers and the public of the various options available in the area of products and services
- Make available to the customers the literature and brochures relating to our products and services in the regional languages and in "easy to understand" style
- Enlarge the access of the customers to reach out to the organisation through different channels like Help Lines, Call Centres, Internet etc.
- Make available various information on products and services through our Web page on the Internet, Interactive Voice Response System, Information Kiosks etc.
- Enhance the content, frequency and quality of our communication with the customers, especially through the mass media like Press, Television, Radio etc.

Policy Servicing: We will

- Strive to achieve and excel the benchmarks set forth in the charter as displayed in our Branch Offices and those prescribed by the Regulatory Authority in respect of various aspects of policy servicing
- Review the standards of servicing annually with a view to improving the benchmarks, wherever necessary
- Respond to all customer enquiries promptly
- Afford the customers, opportunities to provide the organisation with feedback about their perception of our services and to suggest improvements through customer surveys and customer meets
- Enhance customer conveniences through adoption of higher technologies in the areas of information and communication, simplification of processes, review and revamp of the systems and methods
- Improve our communication with the customers under SSS policies in order to keep them informed periodically of the gaps and defaults, if any, and the policy status
- Enhance the frequency of our liaison with the employers to render high quality of services free from errors and omissions

Claim Settlement: We will

- Strive to settle all maturity claims well in time preferably on or before the due date, on receipt of all requirements from the policyholders
- Strive to settle all death claims, which do not require investigation, within 30 days of submission of all requirements by the claimants. If there is a delay on our part beyond the stipulated days, we will pay interest for the delayed period as prescribed by the IRDA

Redressal of Customer Grievances: We will

- Provide opportunity to our customers to meet the designated Grievance Redressal Officer in all offices of the organisation without prior appointment during the second half of the working hours on all Mondays and with prior appointment on other working days
- Register all grievances received and strive to dispose of the same within seven days of their receipt. In case of delay beyond this period, we will explain the reasons for delay on request
- Enable a claimant whose claim has been repudiated by the Divisional Office, the opportunity of appealing for a review by the Claims Review Committees functional at the Zonal and Central levels
- Provide information to the aggrieved customers about the availability of the external grievance redressal machinery in the form of Ombudsman

Source: Citizens' Charter (revised 2003), Life Insurance Corporation of India.

MANAGING GLOBAL CULTURAL DIMENSIONS

Today organisations are going global. Internationalisation of corporates, preferring low cost destinations, global marketing opportunities and changing attitudes of people on mobility is leading to workforce diversity. Thus organisations are filled with manpower from different countries. This naturally leads to cultural diversity. Either personnel drawn from foreign cultures have to adjust to the native culture or bring a change in the culture of the organisation to suit their working styles. Thus managing global cultural dimensions is of paramount importance. There are a number of strategies to manage this cultural combat. Organisations may quickly adopt the new culture. This normally happens when the existing culture is weak, then the new culture is assimilated without much resistance from the employees. Integrating the existing culture with the new culture to give birth to entirely different culture is another way to manage global cultural dimensions. This is not an easy task as there will be strong supporters of the existing culture, therefore the process will be slow. In such situations, deculturation is the best process, however it is time consuming and risky. Deculturation involves changing the mindset of the employees regarding the existing culture by totally changing their attitudes. Since old habits die hard, it is a challenging task. Another method is to maintain two cultures simultaneously, but this can lead to a lot of confusion in the organisation. Thus many organisations find it difficult to adapt a new culture easily. Change agents can play a vital role in the process.

According to Rhinesmith the following guidelines help in creating global organisational culture.

Create:

1. A clear and simple mission to be shared among individuals to unite diverse cultures.
2. Systems of effective flow of communication and information. Co-ordination councils and

global task forces can be effective for a consistent flow of information throughout organisation.

3. Matrix minds among managerial personnel in order to make managers think globally not locally. Deputation of managerial personnel to foreign assignments can help in this.
4. Global career paths by allowing human resources to go global.
5. Cultural difference as a major asset wherein the global cultural practices flow to native organisations.
6. World-wide education and team development programs in order to establish shared identity among employees.

BUILDING AN ORGANISATION

Building an organisation with sound organisational culture is a stupendous task. It requires working hard, learning for unlearning, encountering difficulties etc. Organisational building and socialisation should take place hand in hand. The following phases indicate building an organisation with a positive culture.

1. Formulate
2. Educate
3. Reinforce
4. Sustain
5. Adopt

1. **Formulate:** As noted earlier culture is a long-term process. Every organisation must have a number of strategies for building a new culture. It might start with building physical facilities like the building itself, work place, arrangement of machines, tables, desks, dress, intercoms etc. Good values, ethics and processes have to be formulated carefully. This requires the commitment of the top management.
2. **Educate:** Formulation of culture alone does not help an organisation. Every employee should be educated regarding the culture. In fact employees learn certain aspects of culture from educational institutions, family and society before they join an organisation. If these values are inconsistent with the culture of the organisation, they have to unlearn them and relearn the new culture or reinforce their own culture. Training imparted during the induction period and socialising within the organisation will help them learn the new culture. Thereafter, their immediate supervisors, peers, and subordinates can help them. For example most organisations are teaching Customer Relationship Management (CRM) to newly recruited employees as well as existing employees. Banks have appointed customer relationship executives. In ICICI bank, front line executives are appointed to receive customers and process their queries. Some organisations impart training on various sophisticated methods of body language. Therefore employees learn and adopt the culture only when there is an environment created for them to do so. It is the responsibility of the top management to inculcate the culture of the organisation in the newly recruited employees.

3. **Reinforce:** More than educating the employees regarding the culture of the organisation, getting their commitment to follow it is a more difficult task. This is because of the dynamic nature of human behaviour. If the learnt culture is to be followed in transactions, it must be reinforced by adequate rewards. Only then will employees sustain it for a longer time. For example if an employee was extremely polite and patient with a trying customer, but his patience was never acknowledged and reinforced by his superior, he may feel that his behaviour is not going to help him in any way in his job. Thus, every employee should learn to reinforce the behaviour of other employees with appropriate financial or non-financial rewards.
4. **Sustain:** Sustenance of organisational culture is a challenging task. An organisation making an effort to create a sound organisational culture should also design strategies to sustain it for a long time. Continuous training in the new culture and reinforcement of existing cultures, building role models, creating a structure of rewards and awards, and minimising employee turnover are some of the strategies followed.
5. **Adopt:** Organisations are dynamic entities, so changes are always going to come about, particularly changes due to the recruitment of new employees. In spite of the fact that an organisation may have its own culture, a culture will have to be adopted for the organisation to survive in a dynamic environment. For instance, most Indian organisations were not customer oriented; however, with globalisation and the entry of foreign players, they are learning and adopting this culture. Moreover, retaining customers has become a challenge in the light of competition. Changes in the top management of an organisation can also bring in a new culture. There may however be some difficulty in changing the attitude of the employees, but this can be overcome, by formulating a clear statement of the culture, building role models, training, counselling, cultural modification and above all commitment of the top management in changing and adopting the new culture.

"Smile, it costs nothing."

Mahatma Gandhi once stated that people adorn themselves with all manner of clothes and jewellery, but they fail to wear the ornament that is really worth wearing – that is a smile. In our ancient works, a smile is considered to be one of the 64 arts, because there are so many different types, inviting, happy, sorrowful, parting, thanking, questioning smile, to name but a few. A smile is so important that some organisations are training their employees on how to smile.

Socialisation

Socialisation is one of the most important methods of building an organisation with a sound organisational culture. It is the process of making new employees learn the culture of the organisation. The characteristics of socialisation are given below.

1. Socialisation is a process of learning.
2. It is a continuous process.
3. Socialisation is a process of understanding acceptable and unacceptable behaviour, which begins in childhood.

4. New employees are subject to socialisation.
5. Socialisation is not spontaneous, it takes place over a period of time.

Schein identified three stages of socialisation *viz.*, prearrival, encounter and metamorphosis, which are discussed below. There are three types of socialisation:

1. Academic socialisation
2. Personalisation
3. Internalisation

Academic socialisation: Socialisation starts from the moment a child learns to understand the cues in a worldly environment. Initially socialisation is done in the family, and later in school, college and various social groups. All these contribute to the development of certain values, ethics and culture in individuals. For example a child is taught to speak the truth in school, but often observes that his parents lie sometimes, and hence learns to do likewise. Although, academic institutions make commendable efforts to mould the academic talent and technical skills of an individual, organisational practices are not effectively taught in these institutions. An individual, due to his or her previous academic background has a certain set of values, before taking up employment. While sharing his views at an informal discussion with the author, the vice president of Danlaw Technologies stated that most information technology students come with the specific idea of showing excellency as individuals, but when they are asked to work with teams, they are failures. Nowadays, however most business schools are introducing academic courses on values and ethics, business practices and are trying to work closely with industries. The selection process is intended to identify the right candidate with cultural values close to the organisational culture. In spite of the efforts of HR recruiters, employees come to the organisation with pre-conceived attitudes that are contrary to those of the organisation. Thus, organisations have to make an effort to integrate them with their own training and socialisation process.

Personalisation: As stated earlier individuals enter an organisation with certain notions, expectations, values and culture learnt during the course of academic interaction. Their expectations are related to the job, work environment, superior's behaviour and style, co-workers, organisation process and the organisation in general. However they find that these expectations often differ with reality. Louis calls this phenomenon 'reality shock'. The difference in expectations and reality leads to conflict. Here the role of organisation is critical in making their culture compatible with that of the organisation. The organisation's socialisation should be strong enough to change their earlier expectations and allow them develop a new set of expectations and culture compatible with that of the organisation. Some employees adapt easily, while others resist. Adapters remain in the organisation and resisters either leave the organisation or have to make more efforts to change. Sometimes it is the individuals, who build the organisation's culture. For instance, Infosys is known for its unique culture that originated from its chief mentor Narayana Murthy.

Internalisation: Only change is permanent in individuals. The unique nature of individuals makes it possible for them to adapt to any type of situation. Though attitudes and culture are learnt permanently, human beings can change their attitudes with the proper stimuli. It is said that the most important discovery after 'fire' is the discovery that an individual can change their life by changing their attitude. Thus organisations should enable the internalisation of organisational culture and change themselves accordingly. As noted earlier, conformists internalise culture, while creative people try to change it. The internalisation of culture is complete when employees overcome inconsistency and internal conflict, start accepting organisational practices, procedures, norms, values, ethics. At the same time existing employees should also accept new employees as their equals.

The outcome of effective socialisation is rapid adjustment to the working environment that makes employees productive, committed and satisfied. If employees find the organisational culture comfortable, they are less likely to leave, so the turnover of employees will be less.

How does an organisation integrate new employees? Many organisations adopt formal socialisation through induction programmes. An initial training session helps them to know the various aspects of the organisational culture. This is called formal socialisation. Another way is to provide on the job training during a probationary period, or to employ them as project trainees. In all these cases a number of people help the new employees to learn various aspects of both the technical and social environment of the organisation. They are called internal informal socialisation agents. Superiors and co-workers are informal socialisation agents. They not only provide technical support, but also emotional support. They provide information on critical aspects such as major and minor job roles, performance evaluation, overall leadership of the organisation, promotion practices, hiring and firing policy, transfer practices, behavioural practices towards seniors, decision making practices, confidential reports etc. The fact is that in many organisations most socialisation is done informally. Formal training lasts only for a few days to a few weeks. Employees will obviously develop closer bonds with co-workers than with their superiors due to their easy accessibility, freedom in communication, and easy sharing of opinions. Thus co-workers act as vital socialisation agents. They provide invaluable information to new employees on how to behave towards superiors, co-workers and customers, and on organisational practices, work evaluations etc. For example in your college days, the professors in their initial classes must have explained the manner of study, seminars, debates, respecting professors, attendance, examinations, extra and co-curricular activities and expected behaviour. However, it was natural for you to rely on your seniors, to learn the ropes. The author proposes a new concept of 'finishing schools,' whereby graduate students will be trained in the process of socialisation by experts from various industries, who will share the culture of their organisations. At the same time they can also recruit suitable candidates who they believe will quickly adapt to their organisation's culture. This concept is known as external socialisation agents. A finishing school can work as an external socialisation agent. Organisations will save a lot of time in socialising their employees, improve the selection of candidates, overcome initial losses, develop easy and harmonious relations and above all will retain most of the employees.

Case example 38.2: Religious spirituality – Brand India organisation culture

India is a land of religion and spirituality. Belief in God is predominant amongst the Indian masses. India is known for unity in diversity. There are a number of religions within the country. The largest democratic country in the world allows all religions to prosper and grow. In western cultures the concept of materialism is deep rooted. In India the joint family that gives a great learning experience and is a source of protection is still very common. Many Indians who have emigrated to western countries are often known to comment that there is no scarcity of earning, but practically no social and ethical life. Thus overall growth is not found in the western organisations. The recent construction of happiness index shows some facts about this. Even in India, happiness is becoming a scarce commodity due to invasion of western culture. The country is ranked in the 124th position on the happiness index. This is only a signal to Indian organisations to introspect and re-look at developing congenial organisational cultures to prevent any brain drain. India, accredited with producing world class brains, has over the years shown poor development in all spheres of life. The day has come for India to regain its past glory and incredible spirituality.

SUMMARY

The culture in an organisation is an enduring pattern of behaviour shaped over a period of time. It is shaped, reshaped and finally internalised by the employees in an organisation. The characteristics of an organisation's culture are stability, team orientation, outcome orientation, people orientation, attention to detail, aggressiveness, and innovation and risk taking. Developing a sound organisational culture can ameliorate organisational performance by creating a sense of identity and helping in development of the correct attitude. It is not an easy task to create and maintain a sound organisational culture, as it is a dynamic and intangible concept. The expression of core values shared by a majority of people in an organisation becomes the dominant culture. The sub culture consists of the values and beliefs that a sub unit desires to follow. A strong culture is accepted and widely shared in the organisation as against a weak culture, which is shared by a minority of employees in an organisation. An organisation is developed over a period of time with the help of fables and tales, rituals, semantics, and symbols. In the context of organisation culture, building an organisation that is culturally sound is of paramount importance. This is a five-stage process. The steps in organisational building are formulation, education, reinforcement, sustaining and adoption. Socialisation is very critical in carving the organisational culture. It is a process of learning, carried out through academic socialisation, personalisation and internalisation. Every organisation tries to develop its own unique culture to reap the full potential of its human resources.

Key words

- **Attention to detail:** The degree to which employees are expected to exhibit precision, analysis, and attention to detail.
- **Corporate culture:** The values and unwritten rules of conduct of an organisation as well as management styles, priorities, beliefs and interpersonal behaviour that prevail
- **Culture:** The code of conduct, which regulates human life
- **Dominant culture:** Expression of the core values shared by a majority of the organisation's members
- **Finishing school:** A school that trains graduates regarding organisations' culture with the help of experts drawn from the industry
- **Internal socialisation agents:** Superiors and co-workers who teach various aspects of the organisation to newly recruited employees
- **Internalisation:** The process of identifying with organisational culture by changing oneself
- **Personalisation:** Identifying oneself in the culture of an organisation with internal conflict
- **Reality shock:** Mismatch between learnt culture and the actual culture in an organisation
- **Rituals:** Repetitive activities undertaken to mark certain unique events
- **Socialisation:** The process of teaching new employees the organisational culture
- **Socialisation agents:** Persons within or outside the organisation who are responsible for teaching organisational culture to new employees
- **Strong culture:** Core values accepted and followed by a majority of the employees
- **Sub culture:** Unique values, beliefs and practices that a sub unit desires to follow
- **Weak culture:** Values that are developed and accepted by certain minority opposition groups

39. ORGANISATIONAL EFFECTIVENESS

This chapter enables you:

- *To define and understand the meaning of organisational effectiveness*
- *To distinguish between organisational effectiveness and managerial effectiveness*
- *To distinguish between efficiency and effectiveness*
- *To comprehend the various approaches developed to understand organisational effectiveness*
- *To understand the factors that indicate the effectiveness of organisations*
- *To explain the various factors influencing organisational effectiveness*
- *To explain the strategies used to develop organisational effectiveness*
- *To understand empirical models of organisational effectiveness*

The structure of the chapter is as follows:

- Introduction
- Definition of organisational effectiveness
- Distinction between efficiency and effectiveness
- Models of organisational effectiveness
- Indicators of organisational effectiveness
- Summary
- Key words

CHAPTER 39

Organisational Effectiveness

INTRODUCTION

Organisational effectiveness has become a catchword in the recent times. The concept has been studied and explored extensively in the recent past because of the intensive competition, which now exists. However, despite the amount of research carried out, a lot of ambiguity still exists. Conflicting views and opinions prevailing in the literature have made the concept more confusing and very difficult to document. For example how would you gauge the effectiveness of your own academic institution? What parameters would you use? The number of students who obtain a first class, the effectiveness of the teachers, the classroom, new pedagogical tools used in teaching, new and improved technological gadgets used, extracurricular activities, placement opportunities and so on, would be some of the factors used. However, one could add many more and subtract a few, so that different institutions can use different parameters, there are no standard parameters. The same holds good for any business organisation. However, it has become imperative to understand and assess organisational effectiveness, in order to prevent business losses.

DEFINITION OF ORGANISATIONAL EFFECTIVENESS

The concept of organisational effectiveness is easy to understand but the various interpretations make common agreement difficult. There is no single and concise definition of the concept, and the meaning of organisational effectiveness can differ from organisation to organisation. Different criteria may also be used to measure organisational effectiveness depending on the stage in the life cycle of the organisation and even within an organisation effectiveness differs from unit to unit and person to person. It also varies among different sub systems of an organisation. The concept of organisational effectiveness can be understood with reference to the criteria used to measure the effectiveness. The common definition used to understand organisational effectiveness is *'the degree of realisation of goals'*. Other popular terms used to describe organisational effectiveness are organisational success, growth, efficiency, productivity and profitability. The following definitions enable us to understand the concept of organisational effectiveness.

The general definition of organisational effectiveness *'is the extent to which organisation achieves its goals in an environment and with a given value of resources'*.

A comprehensive definition of organisational effectiveness states that *'the growth, development, morale, motivation and satisfaction of the employees in the system combined with the good image projection of the organisation in the eyes of the general public. This in turn, account for continued organisational health, vitality and growth which account for the organisational effectiveness.*

According to **Georgopolus** and **Tannenbaum** organisational effectiveness can be defined as *'the degree of realization of goals. It is the extent to which an organisation gives certain resources and means, to achieve its objectives without placing undue strain on its members'*.

Miles defined organisational effectiveness as the *'extent to which an organisation is able to satisfy the claims of its owners, suppliers, customers and the Government'*.

Mott defined organisational effectiveness as *'the ability of an organization to mobilise its centres of power for action, production and adaptation'*.

The above definitions reveal the following characteristics of organisational effectiveness.

1. The degree of realisation of goals.
2. Utilisation of various resources in relation to the environment.
3. The corporate image developed by the organisation.
4. The ability to satisfy the claims of various stakeholders.
5. The successful creation of a sound and positive culture.

Organisational *vs* Managerial Effectiveness

Sometimes, organisational effectiveness and managerial effectiveness are used synonymously to describe the same phenomenon. Organisational effectiveness is related to the realisation of objectives by the efficient use of physical, financial and human resources. Managerial effectiveness is concerned with the efficiency of managerial personnel in achieving desired outcomes in the realisation of the objectives. Hence, it is related to the human beings rather than the structure, technology and environment of the organisation. Essentially, it relates to managerial behaviour in directing the efforts of the employees in the pursuit of organisational objectives. Thus when a manager adopts an appropriate style and behaviour to influence the subordinates to achieve the goals, it is managerial effectiveness.

DISTINCTION BETWEEN EFFICIENCY AND EFFECTIVENESS

Effectiveness and efficiency are often used as inter changeable terms. However, in practice these terms have different meanings and interpretations. While efficiency is related to the capacity to be effective, measured by the extent of usage of inputs to produce a given output, effectiveness is measured by the extent of goal realisation. It is to be remembered that efficiency leads to effectiveness. At the same time an effective organisation need not be efficient and *vice versa*. Efficiency is only part of organisational effectiveness. While efficiency helps in utilisation of all available resources in the optimum manner, for long term success, effectiveness is the ultimate solution. The distinction between these terms is presented in Table 39.1.

Table 39.1: The distinction between efficiency and effectiveness

	Efficiency	**Effectiveness**
Meaning	Efficiency is the attainment of a certain output with a given input. It is related to the input output ratio.	Effectiveness is the degree of goal realisation.
Measurement	It is measured by the input output ratio. The measurement is thus easy and is not affected by many factors.	It is a multidimensional concept. The measurement is not easy, as no single criterion exists to describe effectiveness.
Scope	It is related to the internal capacity of the organisation. Economic and technical capacities fall within the scope of efficiency.	It is related to the external environment of the organisation. It is a broader concept than efficiency. It denotes the survival and growth aspects of an organisation.
Interface	Efficiency has an interface with the technical aspects of the organisation. It is largely affected by the structure and technology.	Effectiveness has an interface with the environment and human beings in an organisation. It is affected by the total organisational life.

An organisation should be both effective and efficient, which will enable them to realise organisational effectiveness.

MODELS OF ORGANISATIONAL EFFECTIVENESS

The concept of organisational effectiveness has been continuously studied and explored over the past decade. However, certain practical difficulties still prevail in its understanding. For instance, Campbell mentioned 32 variables to judge organisational effectiveness, whereas Steers reviewed 17 difference approaches. Thus, a number of models exist that explain the concept of organisational effectiveness, some of the important models are described below.

1. Goal model
2. Derived goal model
3. Systems resource model
4. Adaptive coping cycle model
5. Strategic constituencies model
6. Behaviour model

Goal Model

A goal is the desired state of an organisation's existence. According to Talcott Parson a goal is primacy of orientation to the attainment of specific goal defining characteristic of an organisation that distinguishes it from other type of social systems. Goals are also understood as the objectives, aims, purposes, targets, standards, missions etc. Peter F. Drucker noted that goals are important in every field, more specifically where performance and results are directly related to the survival and growth of the organisation. The following are the functions of goals.

(i) Goals organise and explain the whole range of business phenomenon in a few general statements.

(ii) They enable us to test these statements in actual practice.

(iii) Goals allow one to predict the behaviour of employees in an organisation.

(iv) They appraise the soundness of decisions when they are still being made.

Thus the goal model was developed to explain organisational effectiveness, based on the importance of the goals in an organisation.

Assumptions of the model

The model is developed on the following assumptions:

(a) Organisations primarily exist for realisation of goals.

(b) Organisational goals are tangible and measurable.

(c) Every organisation has multiple goals.

(d) Organisations try to maximise realisation of goals.

(e) There is a possibility of arriving at a consensus among the employees of an organisation.

The basic proposition of the goal model is that 'organisational effectiveness is the attainment of stated goals by the organisation'. Therefore, the goal becomes the central theme in the model. A goal is a concept. Thus according to the model a goal must be specified in a clear manner. Every member of the organisation should be able to understand and follow the theme of the goal. Only then will the goal be attainable. Many conceptualisations and descriptions of goals exist in reality. Some of the well-known criteria of goals are listed below:

Different criteria of goals

Goal identification	Goal specification
Steers	Productivity measured by actual output Rate of return Self-assessment of employee satisfaction Absenteeism and employee turnover Supervisory assessment of overall performance
Mahoney and Weitzel	Productivity Utilization of resources Planning Reliability Imitation Cooperation and development
Campbell	Quality Productivity Readiness Efficiencies Profit or rate of return Utilisation of the environment Stability Turnover or retention Accidents Morale Motivation Satisfaction Internalisation of organisational goals Conflict-cohesion Flexibility Adaptation Evaluation by external entities

Goal identification	Goal specification
R.M. Gross	Procurement of resources Making efficient use of inputs relative to outputs Producing services or goods Performing technical and administrative tasks rationally Investing in the organisation Conforming to ethical codes of behaviour Satisfying the varying interests of different groups with whom the organisation has interaction
R.L. Thorndike	Organisational productivity Net profits Accomplishment of missions Organisational expansion
Bernard Bass	Productive Profitable Self maintaining Value creation to members Value creation to the society

It can thus be seen from the above that a number of goal propositions exist, however, none of them can provide a single goal to an organisation. According to Steers the model is goal optimisation rather than goal maximisation. This is because goals pursued by the organisation change as the constraints associated with them change. Every time a new optimal solution emerges, which could represent the new criteria for evaluation. Thus every time an organisation seeks to optimise the goal rather than maximise it. The goal model is a universally acceptable model, which can be used to understand organisational effectiveness. However, there are certain difficulties in using the model, which are listed below.

(i) Tangibility: Determination of single tangible goal is a difficult task.

(ii) Goal congruence: Although organisational goals are derived from individual goals, they do not represent individual goals in a full-fledged manner. In an organisation different employees have different goals, and the various sub units also have varied goals. Thus consensus on an unambiguous goal becomes difficult.

(iii) Multiplicity of goals: Organisations often pursue multiple goals in order to survive in the environment. Moreover pursuing multiple goals become necessary to satisfy the different employees in an organisation. Therefore, difficulties arise in measuring organisational effectiveness.

(iv) Measurement: The model assumes that goals are measurable. In practice, many goals are specified in ambiguous and intangible terms. For example, the quality of work life as a goal is intangible and not measurable in specific terms. This is more relevant in the case of service organisations such as universities, hospitals, educational institutions, public service organisations, transport entities etc.

In spite of the limitations of the goal model, it is used as a basic model for understanding organisational effectiveness.

Derived Goal Model

Evan has proposed this model. According to the model, organisational effectiveness can be measured from tangible measurements derived from the goals. Therefore, goals themselves do not serve as measurements for organisational effectiveness. According to him, the following ratios should be used for measuring organisational effectiveness.

(a) Return on Investment (ROI)

(b) Inventory turnover

(c) Change in inventory turnover

(d) Change in working capital

(e) Change in volume of sales to quantity of product

(f) Research and development to volume of sales

(g) Change in administrative personnel to total personnel/change in labour cost

Systems Resource Model

Yachtsman and Seashore developed the systems resource model. According to this model, the highest level of organisational effectiveness is reached when the organisation maximises its resources procurement. Organisational productivity, flexibility and absence of intra organisational strains are the basic requirements for effective organisations. The assumptions of the model are as follows:

(i) Organisations are social systems

(ii) Organisations are open and dynamic systems

(iii) The environment is a supra system for all organisations

(iv) Organisations depend on the environment for their input and output

(v) Organisations process the inputs

(vi) An organisation uses feedback to adapt itself to changes in the environment

The systems resource model is an outgrowth of the systems approach to understanding an organisation. According to the systems approach, organisations are composed of inter related and interacting elements. Further, the open dynamic system concept emphasised the inter relationship and inter dependency of an organisation with the environment for inputs and outputs. Therefore, this model states that an organisation is efficient if it acquires its resources from the environment and contributes its products to the environment. Therefore, organisations are systems that receive physical, technological, financial and material inputs and transforms them with the help of technical and managerial process and functions. Finally, the output is exported to the environment for consumers' use. Thus, the process of transformation of the input, and the output are the basic aspects of any system.

Using the systems resources approach, Bennis developed the following criteria for measuring organsiational effectiveness.

(i) **Adaptability:** This is the capacity of an organisation to change itself according to changes in its environment. Flexibility to change determines the effectiveness of the organisation.

(ii) **Sense of identity:** In an effective organisation, employees develop a sense of identity. This makes them feel that they are important in the organisation. A sense of identity is developed when the employees know the goals and understand the structure of the organisation.

(iii) **Integration:** Effective organisations are capable of integrating the goals, activities and structure of the sub units and the organisation as a whole. This eliminates the possibility of various sub units working in contradiction with each other.

Thus according to this approach an effective organisation has the following characteristics.

- Continuous availability of inputs
- Environment friendly
- Flexibility and adaptability
- High degree of employee job satisfaction
- Clarity in communication
- Setting realistic goals
- Clarity of environment
- Structural facilitation

The systems resource model is useful in understanding the organisational effectiveness in modern organisations. Nevertheless, the model is subject to certain limitations. If goals are not clear, the acquisition of resources will not be efficient. Thus, goal conflict vitiates the process of utilisation of resources. Moreover, acquisition of resources is subject to the natural environment that is difficult to influence. Thus, effectiveness in terms of natural resources is not really significant.

Adaptive Coping Cycle Model

Edgar Schien developed a slightly different approach based on the systems model. It is known as the adaptive coping cycle approach. The essential theme of the approach is that the sequence of activities responsible for some changes in the internal or external environment should bring about a more adaptive and dynamic equilibrium in the organisation for its effectiveness. This approach considers productivity, adaptability and flexibility as criteria for organisational effectiveness. The approach has identified six stages in the adaptive process in any organisation, namely:

1. Identifying changes
2. Designing relevant information
3. Changing conversion process
4. Stabilising the internal environment
5. Exporting new outputs
6. Feedback

Thus an organisation will be effective or otherwise based on how it adapts to the dynamics of the environment.

Strategic Constituencies Model

Strategic constituencies refer to individuals or groups who have a substantial interest in the organisation. They consist of users of the organisation's products or services, producers of the output and groups whose cooperation is essential to the organisation's survival. The model is an integration of the goal model and systems resources models. According to the model, an effective organisation is one that satisfies the demands of those constituencies in its environment from which it requires support for its continued existence. Realising the goals of these constituencies is the indicator of effectiveness. The constituencies are shown in Figure 39.1.

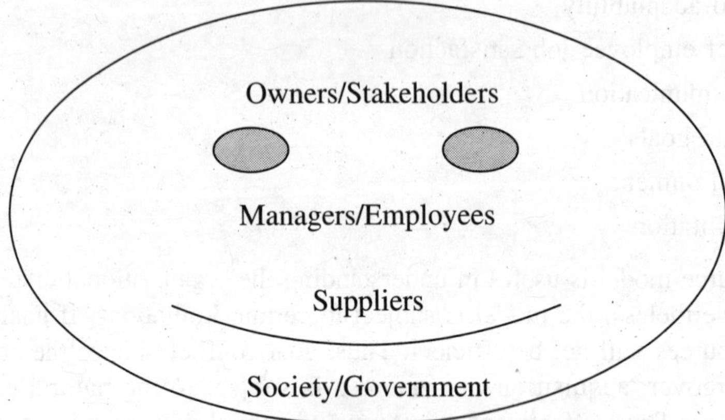

Figure 39.1: Constituencies used to realising goals

The approach is relevant as it recognises all parties interested in the organisation. All of them have their own expectations regarding the organisation. So an organisation should satisfy them in order to be effective. However, there are a number of limitations to this approach, which are given below.

1. Identifying the constituencies and mapping their goals and expectations is difficult.
2. The principle of maximisation of self-interest makes it difficult to satisfy all the constituencies.

3. It is not easy to keep them constant. The changing environment makes them change. So problems arise in identifying them afresh.

In spite of the limitations this approach is popular in managerial circles in assessing the effectiveness of an organisation. The basic concept of corporate social responsibility is developed based on the model.

Behaviour Model

Organisations are basically social units that aim at realising their goals. Organisations develop their goals from the goals of individuals. However it is not always possible to reflect all individual goals in organisational goals. Thus goal incongruent situations arise. This approach considers goal congruence as the indicator of effectiveness. The behaviour of the employees determines the success or failure of the organisation. An organisation with high integration of goals is considered to be an effective organisation. Integration of goals is said to exist when organisational goals are identical and compatible with the goals of individual members in the organisation. According to McGregor there could be three situations of integration of goals. Figure 39.2 shows three situations of integration and effectiveness organisation.

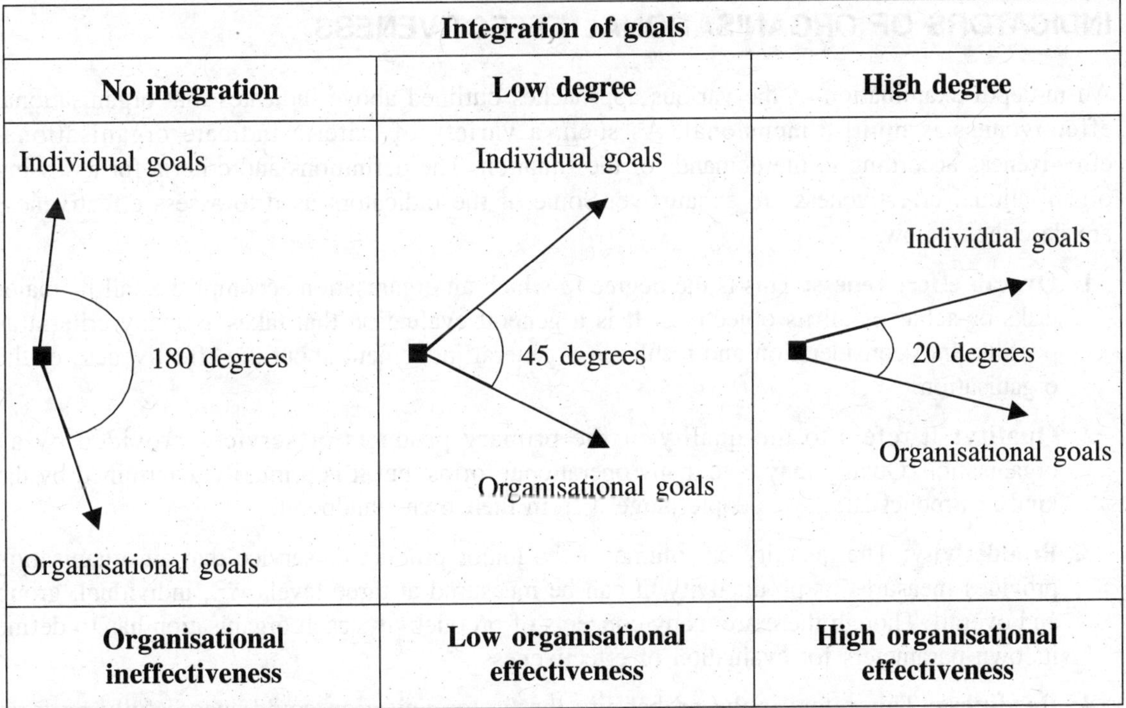

Figure 39.2: Integration of organisational and individual goals

As can be observed from the first situation the individual and organisational goals run parallel to each other. Thus no integration is observed. The angle of integration is almost 180 degrees. There is conflict in the behaviour of the organisation and employees and hence ineffectiveness. In the second situation the angle of integration is about 45 degrees. This shows that there is integration but it is low. These organisations have low effectiveness. Some of the goals of the organisation and the individuals are compatible. In the third situation, the degree of integration of goals is very high as can be seen from the angle of integration. The angle is about 20 degrees. Thus as the angle of integration decreases, the degree of integration increases. In the case of these organisations the effectiveness is high, as individuals recognise that their goals are realised by working in the organisation. Thus a greater degree of effectiveness is seen in these organisations. According to this approach, commitment of the employees is essential to the effectiveness of the organisation. A number of factors within and outside the organisation influence integration of goals.

This model is appropriate due to the emphasis on the behaviour of employees; the more consistent their behaviour, the greater the effectiveness. The limitations of the model are that defining the goals of an organisation and individuals is not easy and integration will never result in actual practice.

INDICATORS OF ORGANISATIONAL EFFECTIVENESS

An in-depth examination of the various approaches outlined above indicates that organisational effectiveness is multi-dimensional. As such, a variety of criteria indicate organisational effectiveness according to the demands of the situation. The definitions and criteria for assessing organisational effectiveness are exhaustive. Some of the indicators used to assess effectiveness are described below.

1. **Overall effectiveness:** This is the degree to which an organisation accomplishes all its major tasks or achieves all its objectives. It is a general evaluation that takes as many criteria as possible into consideration and results in a general judgement about the effectiveness of the organisation.
2. **Quality:** It refers to the quality of the primary products or services provided by an organisation. Quality may take many operational forms, but it is primarily determined by the kind of product and how people judge it from their own standpoint.
3. **Productivity:** The quantity or volume of the major product or service that an organisation provides measures its productivity. It can be measured at three levels *viz.*, individual, group and overall. Though there are many concepts of productivity, each organisation has to define its own parameters for evaluation of effectiveness.
4. **Readiness:** This refers is the probability that an organisation could successfully perform some specified tasks, if asked to do so in the case of emergencies.
5. **Efficiency:** It is the ratio of some aspects of performance of the unit to the costs incurred for

the performance. Briefly, it is the input to output ratio. It indicates the usage of the various resources of the organisation. Some examples are rupees per single unit of production, amount of down time, and the total amount of costs a unit has incurred over some period of time.

6. **Profit or return:** The Return on Investment (ROI) is used to measure the profit. It is the percentage of profit obtained for every rupee invested in the business. Profit is the amount of resources left after meeting all costs and obligations.
7. **Growth:** This is understood by the increase in manpower, physical facilities, assets, sales, profits, market and innovations. It is a comparison of an organisation's present state with its past state.
8. **Utilisation of environment:** The extent to which an organisation successfully interacts with its environment by acquiring scarce and valued resources necessary for its effective operation. This is viewed in a long term optimising framework and not in a short term maximising framework. An example is the degree to which it acquires a steady supply of manpower and financial resources.
9. **Stability:** The maintenance of structure, function and resources over time and more particularly through periods of stress.
10. **Turnover and retention:** The major problem confronting the industry today is retention of talented employees. Thus the degree of retention or the frequency of voluntary terminations could become an appropriate measure of organisational effectiveness.
11. **Absenteeism:** It is the number of times personnel are absent from work. It is a major concern in public sector industries.
12. **Accidents:** The frequency of accidents in the work place shows the effectiveness of maintenance and skills imparted to the workforce. The greater the number of accidents, the greater is the possibility of down time or recovery time. Effectiveness lies in reducing the rate of accidents to the minimum.
13. **Morale:** Morale is the predisposition of the employees to put in extra effort to achieve organisational goals and objectives. It includes commitment. A higher morale leads to higher productivity, which is associated with a greater degree of job satisfaction and *vice versa*.
14. **Motivation:** It is the strength of the predisposition of an individual to engage in goal directed action or activity on the job. It is synonymous to readiness or willingness to work to accomplish the goals of the organisation.
15. **Satisfaction:** It is measured by the degree of commitment felt by a person towards his or her roles or jobs in the organisation. It is the degree to which individuals perceive that they are suitably rewarded with various financial and non-financial incentives.
16. **Internalisation of goals:** This is the acceptance of organisational goals by individuals and units within the organisation. When goals are perceived as congruent they are internalised. It also includes the belief that organisational goals are just and proper.

17. **Innovation:** It is the extent of new processes and methods adopted by the employees in an organisation. Innovations relate to the performance of jobs in new and improved ways so as to save the costs and reap the benefits of economy of operations.

18. **Conflict – Cohesion:** Conflict is the extent of disagreement among employees on organisational related matters. Cohesion is the extent to which employees like one another, work well together, communicate fully and openly and coordinate their work efforts.

19. **Flexibility and adaptability:** This is the feasibility of an organisation to change its standard operating procedures in response to environmental changes and to resist becoming rigid in response to environmental stimulus.

20. **Evaluation by external entities:** This relates to the evaluation of an organisation by individuals and organisations with which it interacts. It relates to the effectiveness of the organisation or organisational units. Loyalty expressed, confidence reposed, and support given to an organisation by suppliers, customers, stockholders, enforcement agencies and the general public are criteria for this evaluation.

21. **Organisational climate and culture:** It is the extent to which the internal physical and psychological conditions are understood as being supportive and encouraging.

22. **Quality of working life:** It is related to the quality of the employees' relationships to the internal work environment.

23. **Corporate social responsibility:** Organisations are social entities. They must share a part of their earnings with society. The new trend is to judge organisations based on their involvement in social activities.

24. **Creativity:** Creativity is the extent to which employees take the initiative to think in different ways to improve the performance of the organisation.

25. **Ethics and values:** The values and ethics followed by the organisation in dealing with various constituencies.

26. **Customer relation management:** This is related to the efforts of the organisation to keep customers loyal to it.

In the Indian context, Khandwalla, did a literature survey and reported that an organisation needs to be assessed not only in terms of its performance *vis-a-vis* its specific goals, satisfaction of its various stakeholders or its viability as a system, but also in terms of such criteria, as the extent to which it has upgraded technology or pioneered new technology, penetrated into foreign markets, pioneered products previously imported, innovated strategically important products and contributed to the community and human resource development.

In addition to the above, a list of indicators, suggested by various researchers to measure the effectiveness of organisations in the Indian context, is provided below.

Author	Indicators
Bidani and Mitra	Financial solvency
George, Khandwalla, Maheswari	Scope, Profitability, growth
Khandwalla, Minocha, Pestonjee, Sinha	Productivity
Khandwalla & Jain, Sayeed & Mehta, Sharma	Organisational health, job satisfaction
Ganesh	Capability of development
De Souza	Quality of working life, an organisation's ability to change society
Chaganti, Khandwalla, Mascarenhas, Morehouse, Pengasa, Natarajan	Creativity, innovation
Zahir	Organisation's contribution to national objectives
Agarwal, Beri, Goyal, Pandey, Suri, Tommappaya, Chaattopadhyaya & Agarwal	Productivity, output, profitability, innovation, organisational health, work satisfaction, work motivation
Singh	Acquisition of inputs, the process of transformation, disposition of outputs, an organisation's ability to respond to feedback

In the Life Insurance Corporation of India the indicators of organisational effectiveness are chartered in the name of values, culture, commitment, and standards. They have been given in the previous chapter.

Factors Influencing Organisational Effectiveness

Organisational effectiveness is multidimensional. There are several factors that influence an organisation's ability to become effective or otherwise. Some factors are quantitative, while others are purely qualitative in nature. These factors can be classified as internal or external based on the degree of control an organisation can exercise on them. Internal factors can be well modified by the actions of the management. Most external factors are not within the control of the management. Thus organisations have to continuously study the impact of internal factors in order to change them appropriately to increase organisational effectiveness. External factors are nothing but environmental factors. They can be remembered by the word PETLEGS. Internal factors include human resources, management and organisation. Figure 39.3 shows the factors influencing organisational effectiveness. They are discussed here.

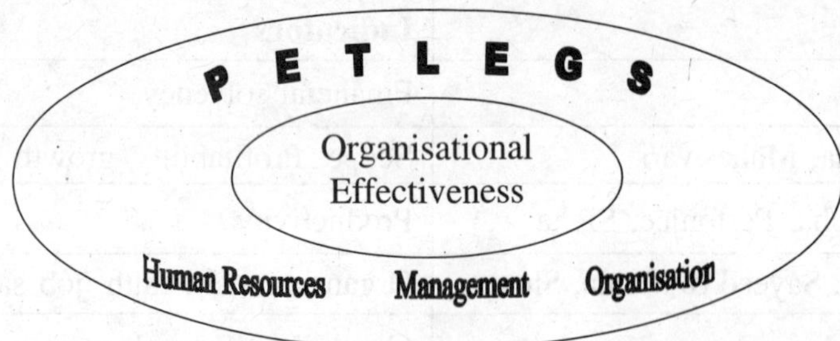

Figure 39.3: Factors influencing organisational effectiveness

Political, economical, technological, legal, ecological, government and social and cultural (PETLEGS) factors are external environmental factors. All these factors are dynamic. They are outside the scope of the organisation, yet they influence effectiveness. For example economic environmental factors such as demand, supply, type of market and stage of growth of market, GDP etc., have a direct bearing on the productivity, profitability, survival, and growth of organisations. Organisations have to develop appropriate environmental information systems to forecast the likely changes in these environmental factors, so that they can change and adapt their internal systems to gear up to the environment before it unduly influences its effectiveness.

Internal factors that influence organisational effectiveness can be controlled by the organisation itself in order to prevent a negative influence on the effectiveness.

Human resources are vital for any organisation. Their effectiveness is influenced by such factors as goal congruence, role clarity, interpersonal conflicts, interpersonal relationships, psychological commitment, motivation, satisfaction, knowledge management etc. If there are poor interpersonal relations amongst employees, there will be a breakdown of communication and interpersonal trust and confidence. This can lead to emotional outbursts amongst the employees. Loss of emotional intelligence may ultimately spoil the internal working conditions and this will negatively influence organisational effectiveness.

Management policies and practices have a profound influence on effectiveness. Some of the important variables are goal setting, strategy formulation, human resource policies on recruitment, training, transfer, promotion, performance evaluation, decision making policies, leadership styles of managers, acquisition and utilisation of resources, customer relations, corporate social responsibility and statement of vision and mission. For example, in the case of organisations with a bureaucratic style of management and leadership *viz.*, public sector organisations, the effectiveness is impaired by delays in decision making, flouting of rules for personal benefits, and undue influence of politics in the day-to-day administration of the organisation. The recent controversy between the Director of AIIMS, Delhi, and the Central Minister for Health is an example of the influence of politics and the effect on the effectiveness of institutions.

Case example 39.1: Acquisition brings organisational effectiveness

Ballarpur Industries (Bilt), India's largest paper manufacturer will incur substantial cost savings. This is an example of organisational effectiveness. According to The Group Director (Finance), 'We are a fibre driven paper manufacturer. So we are expanding where pulp is available'. The acquisition of Malaysia's Sabah Forest Industries (SFI) proved to be a boon to Bilt as far as conservation is concerned. SFI operates the largest pulp and paper mill in Malaysia with a paper capacity of 144000 tpa and pulp capacity of 120000 tpa. Its capacity can be expanded to 4 times the present capacity, as it holds a concession for approximately 289000 hectares of forestland from the state government of Subah for 99 years from 1996. Imported pulp from the Malaysian company, which Bilt bought in a $261 million deal, will cost half as much as it does in India. The acquisition of SFI is viewed as a strategic fit into Bilt's growth plan in terms of retaining leadership in the Indian paper market and increasing its presence in the region. SFI had a turnover of $107 million with a net profit of $9.62 million for the year ended June 2005. Bilt has acquired a 75 per cent stake in SFI. The stock of Bilt closed at Rs. 120.15, gaining 1.48 per cent on the BSE in June 2005.

This case explains how the policy of an organisation relating to mergers and acquisitions can bring about effectiveness. The effectiveness is seen in terms of such indicators as cost saving, expansion, growth, market leadership, increase in stock price, stability and long run survival.

Source: Based on Rohit Viswanath, Bilt goes to Malaysia, Business World, 19 June, 2006, p.16.

Organisational characteristics affect organisational effectiveness in different ways. The structure and process of the organisation and the technology influence its effectiveness. Most organisations are revamping their organisational structure in the name of down-sizing, right-sizing and re-sizing in order to meet the challenges posed by technology as well as competition. Organisational structure that facilitates decision making in an organisation affects the way it functions. For example in most public enterprises, the delay in decision making is due to centralisation of the organisational structure. Both changes in an organisation's structure and technology influence its effectiveness. It can bring change in the operations, costs, span, capital investment, retrenchment etc. Thus both technology and structure significantly influence organisational effectiveness.

Case example 39.2: Structural composition can adversely affect organisational effectiveness

The sudden resignation of Mr. Pratip Kar, who was a member of the initial team that worked to set up the Securities Exchange Board of India (SEBI) in 1989, gave rise to a number of questions. He joined the SEBI as division chief and climbed rapidly through the ranks to become a Chief General Manager and consequently the Executive Director. He was instrumental in formulating mutual fund and investment banking regulations. The resignation of the ED was an outcome of several changes within SEBI's organisational structure, the most important being the diminished powers of the ED with the introduction of full time members. The changes created a bench of three full time members who had more powers than the ED. The full time members mapped out the policy, while the CGMs' executed it. In view of this, Mr. Kar felt that he was sidelined in the new regime. This case explains how changes in the structure of an organisation can bring about a change in a member's attitude. Sometimes there will be an outflow of efficient human resources that may adversely affect organisational effectiveness.

Source: Based on Rachna Monga & Gargi Banerjee, Pratip Kar Quits, Business World, 7 August, 2006, p. 9.

In India, organisational effectiveness in influenced by diverse factors. Scarcity of resources, underdeveloped transport and communication systems, shortage of electric power and other inputs are some of the factors that largely limit organisational effectiveness. Differences in social responsibilities, differences in the integration of needs of employees, and corrupt management practices leading to misuse of funds also influence organisational effectiveness.

Developing Organisational Effectiveness

Organisations continuously strive for effectiveness in spite of a host of factors that adversely influence it. Managers in an organisation face a number of challenges every day in developing strategies to make it more resilient and effective. It is a continuous process. Thus managers should continuously learn and understand various indicators and factors of organisational effectiveness in order to develop effective organisations. There is no single method to develop effectiveness. Managers have to make use of their own knowledge to develop appropriate solutions for each situation as it arises.

Models of Organisational Effectiveness

Two models of organisational effectiveness are discussed here. One is based on Rensis Likert's Management Systems. According to this model there are three variables that are relevant in understanding organisational effectiveness, namely causal, intervening and end result variables. They are presented in the Figure 39.4.

Likert assumes that there is a relationship between all the variable shown in Figure 39.4. The causal variables relate to the character of the organisational structure, the leadership principles employed and the major assumptions concerning motivation. The intervening variables are divided into two broad sub categories; the intervening attitudinal, motivation and perceptual cluster, and the intervening behavioral cluster. He believes that causal variables are the key to improving an organisation. The propositions of the model are given below.

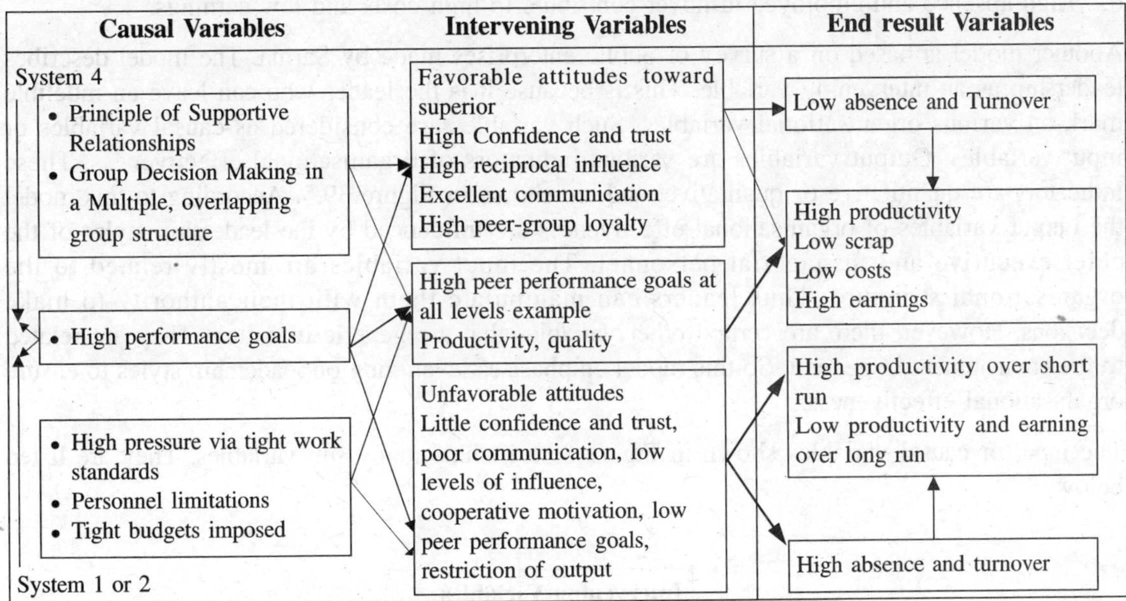

Figure 39.4: Likert's model of organisational effectiveness. (The model and propositions are based on Rensis Likert, The Human Organization, McGraw Hill Kogakusha Ltd. Tokyo, 1967.)

1. The principle of supportive relationships is applied and group methods of decision making are used in a multiple, overlapping group structure. These two key variables lead to intervening variables such as favourable attitudes toward superiors, high confidence and trust, high reciprocal influence, excellent communication and high peer group loyalty. These and similar intervening variables, in turn, lead to absence of employee turnover.
2. To achieve high productivity, low costs and high earnings, superiors must also have high performance goals.
3. When a manager's behaviour reflects the principle of supportive relationships and high performance goals, and when he uses the group as the decision-making unit, the employees will display the intervening variables shown, *viz.*, favourable attitudes toward superiors etc., and high performance goals for themselves and the organisation. In turn these intervening variables result in low turnover and costs and high productivity and earnings.
4. Absence and employee turnover should be thought of as intervening behavioural variables, which influence productivity, costs and earnings.
5. High performance goals by superiors, coupled with high-pressure supervision using tight budgets and controls, yield high productivity initially because of compliance based on fear. In the long run however, these variables will yield unfavourable attitudes, distrust, poor communication, low levels of both influence and cooperative motivation, low peer

performance goals, and restriction of output. These in turn result in high absence and employee turnover and low productivity.

6. High absence and employee turnover contribute to high costs and low earnings.

Another model is based on a survey of public enterprises made by Sarma. The model describes leadership as an intervening variable. This is because it is the leader who can leave an indelible mark on various organisational variables. Such variables are considered as causal variables or input variables. Output variables are various indicators of organisational effectiveness. These indicators are quantitative or qualitative, and are shown in Figure 39.5. According to this model the output variables of organisational effectiveness are influenced by the leadership styles of the chief executive and managerial personnel. The input variables are mostly related to the organisational structure. Thus leaders can manipulate them with their authority to make decisions. However, there are certain other variables that are generic in nature. They are related to the environment in general. So this model emphasises leveraging on leadership styles to ensure organisational effectiveness.

The input or causal variables shown in Figure 39.5 include many sub variables. They are listed below.

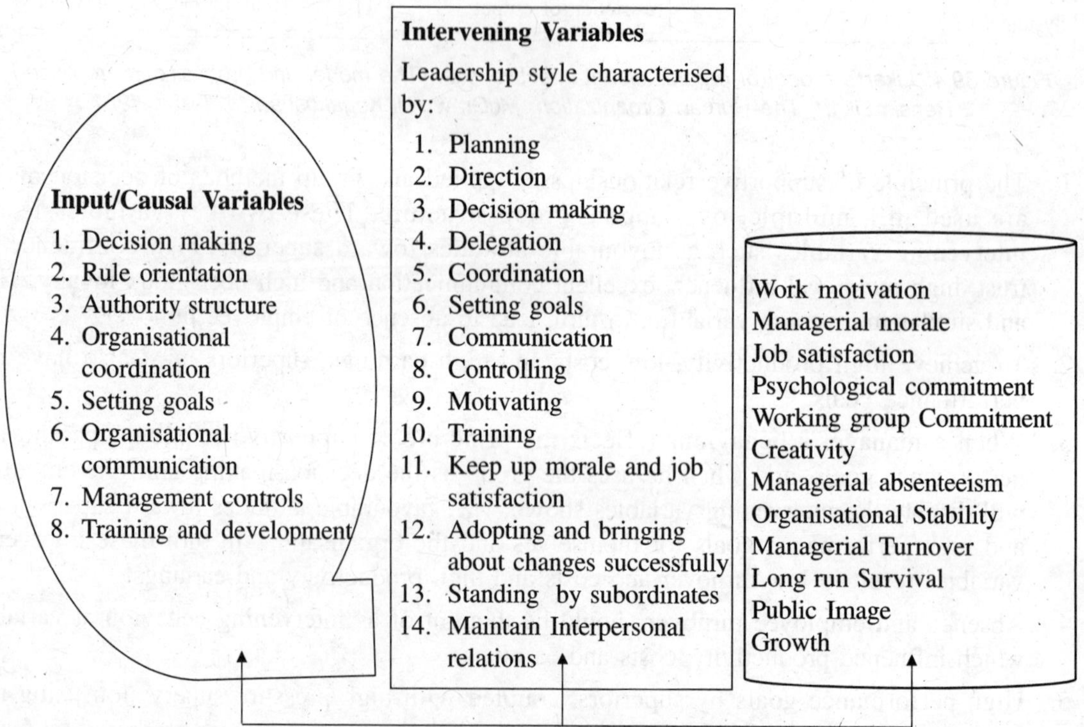

Figure 39.5: Model of organisational effectiveness

- **Decision-making:** These variables relate to the characteristics of decision making. They are quality, effectiveness, promptness, participation, acceptance, fairness, adequacy, and contribution to increased motivation and top management adherence to decisions.
- **Rule orientation:** The factors that influence organisational effectiveness relating to rule orientation are existence of clear rules, self-awareness of organisational rules, self-awareness of department rules, superiors' awareness of organisational rules, superiors' awareness of departmental rules, colleagues' awareness of rules. Communication, interpretation, implementation and acceptance of rules, reliance on rules and precedents, conflict in rules and precedents and frequency of changes in rules.
- **Authority structure:** The characteristics of the authority structure that influence organisational effectiveness include clarity of authority, frequency of detailed instructions on policy matters and routine matters, encroachment of authority on policy and routine matters, compulsion in consultations on policy and routine matters, extent and adequacy of delegation, centralisation index and delegation index.
- **Organisational coordination:** The various factors that influence effectiveness are logical organisation of activities, integration, definiteness, and predictability, intra and inter departmental planning of task structure, sharing of information, strained relations with superiors, and colleagues, frequent intra and inter departmental consultations, understanding problems of the top management and lower levels by the top management.
- **Setting goals:** The various sub variables that are part of goal setting are communication, awareness, clarity, fairness, conflict of goals, extent of goal realisation, effectiveness of goal setting and attitude towards goals, acceptance of goals by top management, middle level management and lower levels, responsibility to realise goals by top management, managerial personnel and lower levels and open resistance and internal resistance towards goals.
- **Organisational communication:** The variables affecting communication are direction, quantum, frequency, timeliness, willingness, initiation, responsibility, distortions, clarity, acceptance, adequacy and accuracy of communication.
- **Management controls:** The variables that are part of management controls are accuracy, support, resistance, effectiveness, changes, nature, kind and usage of controls and overall effectiveness of controls.
- **Training and development:** The variables that influence training and development are availability of clear training goals, regularity of training, responsibility for training, adequacy of resources for training, effectiveness of training, cost effectiveness of training, review and evaluation of training and executive development index.

The model presented here is useful in understanding organisational effectiveness in a more detailed manner. But it is complex due to the existence of a number of variables.

The study that was conducted using the model of organisational effectiveness showed that it is adversely influenced by delay in decisions, frequent changes in top management structures and non-adherence to their own policies by the top management. In addition, lack of clarity in interpretation of rules, consistent resistance towards rules and precedents and personalisation of rules also affected the performance negatively. Lack of harmonious relationship between superiors and subordinates and a lesser degree of coordination resulted in organisational conflicts. If the quantitative goals set in areas of production and sales are over ambitious and unrealistic and there is a lack of unified perception regarding fairness and reasonableness of goals, then it resulted in low participation, motivation and commitment. Inadequate, rigid, tardy and repressive controls are shadows of bureaucracy. Thus the model has effectively displayed the reality in the organisations under study.

SUMMARY

The concept of organisational effectiveness has existed for some time, but its conceptualisation is of recent origin. It is subject to various interpretations. It is different from managerial effectiveness. Managerial effectiveness is concerned with the realisation of desired outcomes with given resources. Organisational effectiveness is realisation of the overall goals of the organisation. Efficiency and effectiveness are also two different, but closely related concepts. Efficiency is related to the capacity of obtaining a certain output with a given input, thus it is the ratio of input to output; effectiveness is the extent of realisation of objectives. Due to the various interpretations of organisational effectiveness, many models have been developed to understand it, namely the goal model, derived goal model, systems resource model, adaptive coping cycle model, strategic constituencies model and behaviour model. The goal model uses different conceptualisation of organisational goals to measure effectiveness. The derived goal model relies on tangible measurements derived from goals to measure effectiveness. Yachtsman and Seashore developed the systems resource model that states that resource procurement is the indicator of organisational effectiveness. Edgar Schien developed the adaptive coping cycle approach. According to this approach effective organisations adapt themselves to changes in the environment. The essence of the strategic constituencies model is that organisational effectiveness results from satisfying the demands of various internal and external parties on whom the organisation relies for its survival. Integration of individual and organisational goals leads to commitment of employees. This is the central theme of the behaviour approach. As the concept of organisational effectiveness is multidimensional, various researchers have developed a number of indicators.

Both internal and external factors influence organisational effectiveness. External factors are beyond the scope of managerial control. They comprise political, economical, technological, legal, ecological, government and social and ethical factors. Internal elements are related to human resources, management and the organisation. Developing organisational effectiveness is a difficult task due to the existence of varied interpretations on one hand and the influence of multidimensional factors on the other. Two models help managers to understand causal, intervening and output variables for developing organisational effectiveness.

Key words

- **Adaptive coping cycle:** Adaptation of an organisation to the dynamic environment
- **Derived goals:** Tangible measurement derived from the primary goals
- **Efficiency:** The capacity to achieve maximum output with a given input
- **Effectiveness:** The realisation of goals
- **Managerial effectiveness:** The efficiency of managerial personnel in achieving desired outcomes
- **Organisational effectiveness:** The degree of realisation of goals and purpose of the organisation
- **Strategic constituencies:** All persons and institutions on whom an organisation depends upon for its existence

Index

F

S

T